Reputation Analytics

Reputation Analytics

Public Opinion for Companies

DANIEL DIERMEIER

THE UNIVERSITY OF CHICAGO PRESS   CHICAGO AND LONDON

The University of Chicago Press, Chicago 60637
The University of Chicago Press, Ltd., London
© 2023 by The University of Chicago

Published 2023
Printed in the United States of America
32 31 30 29 28 27 26 25 24 23   1 2 3 4 5

ISBN-13: 978-0-226-02962-7 (cloth)
ISBN-13: 978-0-226-02976-4 (e-book)

DOI: https://doi.org/10.7208/chicago/9780226029764.001.0001

Library of Congress Cataloging-in-Publication Data

Names: Diermeier, Daniel, author.
Title: Reputation analytics : public opinion for companies / Daniel Diermeier.
Description: Chicago : The University of Chicago Press, 2023. | Includes
    bibliographical references and index.
Identifiers: LCCN 2022042470 | ISBN 9780226029627 (cloth) |
    ISBN 9780226029764 (ebook)
Subjects: LCSH: Corporate image. | Public relations firms. | Institutional
    advertising.
Classification: LCC HD59.2 .D53 2023 | DDC 659.2—dc23/eng/20221011
LC record available at https://lccn.loc.gov/2022042470

♾ This paper meets the requirements of ANSI/NISO z39.48-1992
(Permanence of Paper).

TO TIM

In order that everything should be reduced to the same level, it is at first necessary to procure a phantom, its spirit, a monstrous abstraction, an all-embracing something which is nothing, a mirage—and that phantom is *the public.*—Søren Kierkegaard, *The Present Age*, p. 33

To speak with precision of public opinion is a task not unlike coming to grips with the Holy Ghost.—V. O. Key, *Public Opinion and American Democracy*, p. 8

Contents

Preface

James E. Burke, the former CEO of Johnson & Johnson, passed away on September 28, 2012, at the age of 87. He had led the company as chairman and chief executive from 1976 to 1989, overseeing a vast growth of products, international expansion, and a tripling of total sales.

Yet these accomplishments are not what Jim Burke is remembered for. His *New York Times* obituary dedicated no more than two sentences to these career achievements. The remainder focused on a few days in December 1982, when Jim Burke's legacy was forged. The event was his handling of the Tylenol recall. And it has stood as a paradigm of crisis leadership ever since.[1]

The crisis started when seven people died in Chicago after being poisoned by Tylenol capsules that had been laced with cyanide by an unknown serial killer. Johnson & Johnson spent more than $100 million pulling more than 32 million Tylenol bottles from the shelves, followed by their introduction of tamper-proof packaging. During the crisis, Burke never became sidetracked by the question of guilt, but focused on the most important issue: protecting customers' safety and maintaining their trust. His forceful, candid, and empathetic approach set the standard for modern corporations.

In the world of corporate crisis management, a reference to the Tylenol crisis has almost become a cliché. No crisis management or business ethics textbook would be complete without it. Indeed, it has become so prevalent that some authors define themselves in opposition to Burke's handling of the Tylenol crisis (e.g., Dezenhall and Weber 2007). But it is exactly its long-lasting impact and its iconic status that concerns us here. Almost 40 years later, it is still viewed as the paradigm of how to lead when times are tough.

Jim Burke later stated that the Tylenol recall was one of the easiest decisions of his life. All he had to do was to apply the company's value statement, the renowned Johnson & Johnson credo. Its first line reads as follows:[2]

> We believe our first responsibility is to the patients, doctors and nurses, to mothers and fathers and all others who use our products and services.

This may suggest that safeguarding a company's reputation consists in simply "doing the right thing." If this were true, reputation stewardship would simply be an exercise in business ethics.[3] But things are not quite as straightforward. For every Tylenol, there are companies that never recovered from a reputational crisis, even though the issue that triggered the incident later proved to be far less serious than originally believed. Companies continue to struggle with adapting to a world of 24-hour global news coverage fueled by competing cable news channels and the widespread use of social media. Expectations about proper corporate conduct are ever increasing, and if companies do not live up to these expectations, they are confronted with public outrage, often fueled by attacks from NGOs, activists, politicians, regulators, or attorneys general. Losing the battle for its reputation can hurt a company in many ways. The first important dimension is the company's perception in the marketplace among customers, investors, and business partners. Any business model that is based on maintaining a strong brand depends on maintaining customer trust. This is not only true for well-known consumer brands, but increasingly for business-to-business companies, especially in the service sector.

But customers are not the only relevant constituency. Investors will lose trust in a stock after a string of earnings restatements or doubts about accounting practices. They also may not believe a company's investment story or may have doubts about its corporate governance practices. Successful interactions with dealers, suppliers, and other business partners often depend on ongoing relationships of trust. Finally, ongoing competition for talent requires an excellent reputation among potential employees and the people they listen to. A professional service firm or hospital needs to be viewed as an attractive, prestigious destination to attract and maintain top talent. Potential employees may consult websites such as Glassdoor or ask a relative, friend, or teacher for advice.

Often reputation is influenced by third parties. That is, a company's reputation is no longer simply a consequence of customers or business partners having a good experience with the firm, but is also shaped by what others are saying about the company. Perceptions and attitudes are influenced by peers, third-party experts, and the media, both traditional and user-generated. In this environment, building and maintaining a successful reputation in the marketplace requires a deep understanding of such channels of influence.

But perception in the marketplace is not the only important domain to consider. Losing the battle for public perception often leads to political pressure, resulting in new laws and regulations that can fundamentally change industries and alter the respective competitive positions of firms. How an issue is perceived will influence which policy solutions will be supported by the public. In the case of childhood obesity, for instance, if marketing of sugary drinks to children is believed to be the main source of childhood obesity, public support for banning vending machines in schools will grow. If, on the other hand, lack of exercise is believed to be the cause, subsidies for physical education in schools will be favored. While shifts in public opinion may be fickle and do not inevitably lead to regulatory change, such shifts can create policy windows that can significantly improve the odds that a proposed legislation will pass, an agency will issue a ruling, or a firm will get convicted by a jury (Jones and Baumgartner 2005; Kingdon 1984).

Companies have not been able to handle these challenges effectively. Over the last few years, we have seen a dramatic increase in the frequency and severity of corporate crises, with leaders caught unprepared to respond effectively. In contrast to an earlier cluster of crises (e.g., Enron, Arthur Andersen, WorldCom), these crises are not concentrated on a particular business issue (e.g., accounting), but include issues such as safety concerns (e.g., Toyota), disclosure and compliance (e.g., Goldman Sachs), risk management (e.g., J. P. Morgan Chase), money laundering (e.g., Standard Chartered), hacking (e.g., News Corp.), accidents (e.g., BP, *Costa Concordia*), bribery (e.g., Wal-Mart), privacy and politics (e.g., Facebook), supply chain safety (e.g., Mattel), racism (e.g., Paula Deen, Texaco), gay marriage (e.g., Chick-fil-A, Barilla), abortion (e.g., Susan G. Komen Foundation), a disgraced founder (e.g., Livestrong Foundation), executive compensation (e.g., AIG), pricing (e.g., Netflix), employee incentives (e.g., Ergo), oil spills (e.g., BP), global labor standards (e.g., Apple, H&M), corruption (e.g., FIFA), customer relations (e.g., United Airlines), manipulation of environmental standards (e.g., VW), and many more. In some cases, the company was clearly at fault (e.g., News Corp, VW), in others an executive made an ill-considered remark (e.g., Barilla), and in yet other cases the issue originated outside the legal boundaries of the company with a supplier but quickly reached the well-known consumer brand (e.g., Apple and FoxConn).[4]

This plethora of crises is not simply a coincidence, but the manifestation of an increasingly glaring mismatch between the reputation management capabilities of firms—even leading ones—and the risk profiles that most companies face. In Diermeier (2011), I argue that the increase in reputational risk is due to three broad trends that have significantly raised the stakes for global corporations.

First, media coverage, whether traditional or user-generated via social media, has dramatically increased across the globe. This increased public scrutiny has made it virtually impossible for companies to hide. Transparency is expected, while companies have less control over their messages. The rapid growth of social media has further accelerated this trend. Indeed, it is often a concern over social media that leads companies to think more carefully about reputational risk. In addition to the increased scope of coverage, companies also struggle to adjust to the increased speed (e.g., Boydstun, Hardy, and Walgrave 2014; Kwak et al. 2010; Leskovec, Backstrom, and Kleinberg 2009).

The second, less appreciated, trend is the increasing reliance of many businesses on complex supply chains. Specifically, there are two mutually reinforcing factors. The first is the globalization of value chains. The second is the tendency for modern companies to focus on core competencies and outsource all other functions. Apple, for example, excels at innovation and design, as well as at marketing and retail, but has no such competitive advantage in manufacturing. Hence, manufacturing is outsourced to contract manufacturers such as FoxConn. These developments have created a tremendous amount of value, but also new risks. Complex supply chains are more likely to have problems, especially if they are designed for "leanness" rather then resilience. Such problems can be caused by external factors (e.g., earthquakes or a global pandemic such as COVID-19),[5] can be a result of sloppy business practices (e.g., quality and safety), or may be triggered by nongovernmental organizations (NGOs) (e.g., a boycott threat over labor practices at a foreign supplier).

In addition, companies are unlikely to spot supply chain problems early. This is in part due to the complexity of modern supply chains and in part due to the fact that monitoring is more limited in arm's-length contractor relationships than if the company is fully vertically integrated. Furthermore, even when a problem is identified, complex supply chains make managing it more challenging. A vertically integrated company that manufactures in its own plant can quickly address an emerging problem, for example, by replacing the plant manager or by adopting stricter manufacturing standards. With a contract manufacturer, such actions require the consent of the supplier, which may or may not be forthcoming depending on the state of the business relationship, contracting arrangements, legal issues, and so on. If collaborative relationships break down, suppliers and their customers may engage in mutual recriminations and finger pointing. Well-known examples of these difficulties are the Ford-Firestone crisis from 1996 to 2001 (e.g., Pinedo, Seshadri, and Zemel 2000) or Baxter's Heparin crisis in 2008 (e.g., Diermeier and Dickinson 2012).

Exacerbating the difficulties brought about by global supply chains is the increasing importance of NGOs. In response to the globalization of commerce, activist organizations have globalized as well, and they have developed strategies that match the global nature of supply chains. For example, an environmental activist group that wants to change logging practices in Malaysia usually will not attack the, typically unknown, Malaysian company directly, but rather its Western customers, especially if they are well-known consumer brands. If such activities trigger sufficient media outrage, companies are forced to abandon or modify controversial business practices. Using this approach, NGOs have increasingly succeeded in forcing private regulation, the "voluntary" adoption of rules and standards that constrain certain forms of company conduct without the involvement of public institutions, such as legislatures, courts, or executive agencies. In many cases, the mechanism driving change is the creation of reputational crises for globally operating companies that, when effective, leave the companies with no choice but to change their business practices (Abito, Besanko, and Diermeier 2019; Baron and Diermeier 2007).

The third trend is a shift in expectations about corporate conduct. Such expectations are not limited to core brand attributes, but extend to more generic business capabilities. Among the clearest examples are data security and privacy concerns. When a business is hacked and customer data is compromised, the typical public response is not to feel sorry for the business, despite the fact that the company may have been the victim of organized crime, but to blame its managers for not having invested more in IT security.[6] This is a lesson Target experienced firsthand in 2013 when it was hacked during the height of the holiday season. These expectations are not brand-specific, but apply to companies in general. Target's brand does not include claims of superior data security. Indeed, for retailers like Target, there is little to be gained from being known as a leader in IT security, as few customers decide where to shop based on data security.[7] Yet the loss of 70 million customers' data led to a dramatic sales drop and cost the CEO his job. In other words, while there was little upside for Target on the issue of data security, the downside was substantial.

In general, customer expectations go far beyond the explicit promise made by a company in defining its brand, value proposition, or market positioning, and often include general operational issues such as data security or working conditions. In other words, customers expect high levels of performance not only on explicit brand promises, but also on back-office functions or manufacturing processes. Exceeding such standards often yields few benefits, but failing to meet them carries significant reputational risks.

Increased expectations about corporate conduct often go beyond business performance issues and include social, political, and moral concerns. This is especially true for the expectations of younger customer segments. Evidence for these trends can be found in the growth of areas such as corporate social responsibility (CSR), sustainability, and socially responsible investing. Recent examples include the 2019 Business Roundtable statement on the importance of stakeholders or the rise of the Environmental, Social, and Governance (ESG) investor movement. While some critics have dismissed these trends as passing fads that lack impact, it is clear that reputational crises are increasingly being driven by moral outrage, whether over environmental concerns or executive perks (e.g., Diermeier 2011; Lindenmeier, Schleer, and Pricl 2012).

The impact of these trends is further enhanced by the rise of business models based on trust. To develop compelling customer experiences and solutions, companies need to get closer to customers' unarticulated—perhaps even subconscious—desires and needs. This requires trust. While this shift has undoubtedly created new opportunities for value creation, even the mere perception of broken trust during a reputational crisis will lead to a feeling of betrayal, a powerful emotion that often triggers a hostile response.

How have companies responded to these trends? Poorly. Most companies still view stewardship of the company's reputation as a narrowly defined task best left to the PR department. For the most part, the response is an underfunded initiative accompanied by nervous questions from the board. Yet underdeveloped capabilities in the presence of growing reputational risks will lead to an increase in the number and severity of reputational crises. This mismatch between risk and capabilities is untenable.

Most companies still believe that building a strong reputation is easy and requires only common sense; it is merely a natural consequence of doing right by customers, employees, and business partners. This approach is flawed. Good business practices are important, even necessary, but they are not sufficient for successfully safeguarding a company's reputation. A company's reputation needs to be actively managed by the business leaders, led by the CEO as the steward of the company's reputation, incorporated into daily management practices by the senior team, and supported by an engaged board. While experts such as public relations specialists may play an important role, they should not own the process. Challenges to a company's reputation typically arise out of a specific business decision, but reputational risk awareness is often not part of the decision process that led to the problem in the first place.

Simply including reputational concerns among a long list of risks in an enterprise risk management (ERM) process is similarly inadequate. Reputational risk is not simply one of many other risks that can be added to an ever-growing list, such as supply-chain disruption or currency exposure. Rather, reputational crises tend to emerge *in conjunction* with specific events or decisions that serve as triggers. A safety issue constitutes a risk in and of itself but, if poorly managed, it can also trigger a reputational crisis where the company and its management as a whole are evaluated for their performance, competence, and trustworthiness. Often the reputational impact far exceeds the direct financial cost associated with the triggering event. In this sense, reputational risk is a *multiplier* that can amplify any given operational, legal, or financial risk. Therefore, it should not be treated in isolation from the underlying business issues.

Successful reputation management is difficult. It requires a high level of strategic sophistication and mental agility that sometimes runs counter to day-to-day business decisions and common intuitions. A company's reputation is shaped not just by its direct business partners, customers, and suppliers but also by external constituencies, especially the media. Constituencies that have lain dormant for many years can suddenly spring into action, particularly in the case of reputational crises. Companies need to have processes to identify such risks and manage them.

A company's reputation consists in what others are saying about the company, and not just its business partners and customers. It is essentially public.[8] This necessitates the ability to assume external actors' perspectives and viewpoints, especially when they are critical or even hostile toward the company. It requires a strategic rather than defensive approach.

A strategic approach requires the emotional fortitude to treat reputational difficulties as understandable—and even predictable—challenges that one should expect in today's business environment. As a result, companies should handle reputational crises like any other major business challenge: based on principled leadership and supported by sophisticated processes and capabilities that are integrated with the company's business strategy and culture. Anger or self-pity is not helpful.

Luckily, the old perceptions are starting to change. Recent work has begun to define reputation management as a capability tightly connected to a company's strategy (e.g., Diermeier 2011, Leinwand and Mainardi 2011). Various authors have pointed to different channels that may engender sustained competitive advantage and increased profitability (e.g., Roberts and Dowling 2002). Among the listed strategic benefits are charging premium prices (e.g., Deephouse 2000; Fombrun 1996; Rindova et al. 2005), building barriers to competitors (e.g., Deephouse 2000), and attracting employees (e.g., Deephouse 2000; Fombrun 1996; Turban and Greening 1997), investors (e.g., Srivastava et al. 1997), and customers (e.g., Fombrun 1996).

In parallel, managing corporate reputations has moved to the top of the agenda for many CEOs and board members. A 2014 survey of board members by accounting firm EisnerAmper ranked reputational risk as the highest nonfinancial risk, ahead of cybersecurity/IT and compliance. Of those surveyed, 72 percent listed reputational risk as their top concern.[9]

However, while awareness of reputational risks is increasing in the board room, business leaders and corporate boards are unsure what to do about it. The increasing prominence of reputational concerns is not matched by a coherent set of principles and processes. This mismatch is exacerbated by the fact that, despite its recognized importance, the study of corporate reputation does not yet exist as a coherent academic field. What little research does exist is scattered among various disciplines that do not communicate with each other and largely proceed in isolation. The knowledge base that could guide the development of a well-functioning reputation management capability is slim; a conceptual or empirical foundation is lacking. As a consequence, "corporate reputation" has remained an elusive concept, difficult to analyze, measure, and manage.

The goal of this book is to take a first step in filling this gap. There are many books that provide advice for managers on how to manage reputations and handle reputational crises, but much of the practice of reputation management is based on case studies or the experience of practitioners.[10] While these perspectives are valuable, the time, it seems, is ripe for a more rigorous approach. Specifically, we will apply the perspectives and methods of modern social sciences to corporate reputation. Our goal is to show that a rigorous approach can be fruitfully applied to this most elusive of phenomena. While this approach, we hope, will yield useful and important insights, it will also point to the limits of our knowledge of corporate reputation. Indeed, if this book succeeds, it will point out how little we know and how big the opportunities for future research are.

The approach is based on a simple premise: A company's reputation consists in what others are saying and believing about it; it is essentially public. Personal experiences of people such as customers or business partners comprise only one of the factors that shape corporate reputations. The Mayo Clinic, for example, has a stellar reputation, but most Americans have never experienced its services firsthand.

Therefore, corporate reputation should be conceptualized as *public opinion for companies*. However, in contrast to areas such as political domains, where public opinion is concentrated on a single constituency—for example, the electorate in campaigns for public office—corporations have multiple "publics" or constituencies. These groups include customers, employees, investors, local communities, regulators, and so forth. This necessitates the ability to understand the perspectives and viewpoints of numerous relevant external actors, especially when they are critical of the company or even hostile toward it.

The concept of "public opinion" may immediately trigger associations with its dominant research methodology: mass sample surveys. And indeed, the (small) empirical literature on reputation management has essentially followed this approach and relied largely on survey methodology borrowed from public opinion research in political science and marketing. One of the goals of this book is to move beyond the exclusive reliance on survey methods by providing complementary methodological approaches.

A deeper understanding of what drives a company's reputation must include the psychological mechanisms of how opinions are formed, how they are changed and disseminated through social interaction, the role of the media (including social media), and the strategic interactions between firms and external constituencies trying to shape public opinion. An analytical approach to reputation management consists in identifying these components and understanding how they interact using the methodologies of modern social science.

The complex nature of corporate reputations necessitates a multidisciplinary approach developed in an integrated fashion. Specifically, I discuss the use of laboratory experiments (as used in marketing research as well as social and political psychology), models of public opinion dynamics (as used in behavioral economics and the study of social networks), game theory (as used in political economy and analytical political science), and computational linguistics (as used in communication studies and finance research). Such a multidisciplinary perspective is quite common in other areas of management research, such as marketing or finance, but not (yet) in the study of corporate reputations. Indeed, this methodological pluralism is driven by the complexity of the phenomenon, not methodological convenience. To develop such an integrated approach is the main goal of the book.

This requires introducing various methodologies in some detail. Specifically, we discuss controlled experiments, statistical methods, formal models (both behavioral and game-theoretic), and text-analytic approaches. Each one of these methodologies deserves a separate textbook-length treatment. This book is not the appropriate venue for such a purpose. However, it is important to appreciate why such advanced methods are necessary. Therefore, we introduce the basic ideas underlying each method in the context of a specific problem and show how each method can help us make progress in resolving it.

One final comment to any reader with a noncorporate background or interest. We mostly talk about companies and their reputations as the object of study, but the same issues apply to nonprofits (both Greenpeace and Harvard have clearly defined reputations), public agencies (compare the reputation of the FBI and FEMA), and even individuals (Lance Armstrong versus Warren Buffett). Similarly, while our focus is on organizational reputation, many of our insights apply to other entities, such as products (e.g., a Porsche 911), services (e.g., customer service at Zappos), or ingredients (e.g., sugar). Much of what we have to say about companies will apply to other organizational forms and entities. When there are significant differences, we point them out.

CHAPTER ONE

Overview

The book is divided into six parts. In the first part, we introduce the approach that governs this book: *corporate reputation is public opinion for companies*. We briefly review the development of public opinion research since its origins. Much of this development occurred in political science, where the dominant methodology of public opinion research, the mass sample survey, was introduced and refined (e.g., Berelson, Lazarsfeld, and McPhee 1954; Campbell et al. 1960). While there are many similarities between the political and the corporate domains, there are some differences. First, in contrast to public opinion research in political science, which focuses on the electorate, companies have multiple "publics" or constituencies, such as customers, employees, investors, suppliers, regulators, and so forth.[1]

Second, the fundamental concept of public opinion research of voters, at least in the US context, is "party identification" (Campbell et al. 1960). Party identification is conceptualized as a long-term, consistent disposition developed early in life to vote for a particular political party. In any given election, short-term factors such as the personal appeal of a given candidate or a salient political issue may influence vote choices, but voting decisions are best explained by party identification when examined over time (Bartels 2010).[2] There is no direct counterpart to party identification in the study of corporate reputation. For customers, the concept of "brand identity" may have some similarities. Brand identities, however, are highly company- and product-specific, with few generalizable attributes (e.g., Aaker 1991, 1996).[3]

Third, in political competition, often all that matters is winning. Electoral campaigns are usually zero-sum games: one side wins, the other loses. Negative advertising, for example, may be an attractive strategy if it lowers support for the other side. Strategies to depress turnout can be effective even if overall turnout goes down, provided that the other side's turnout is reduced even more. In electoral competition the goal is to get more votes than the other side; the absolute number of votes cast matters little. The zero-sum nature of electoral campaigns leaves a candidate or party no choice but to engage in an arms race to raise and spend prodigious amounts of money lest it be outgunned by the other side.

Business competition, however, is rarely zero-sum. A bruising battle between two companies may damage the reputation of the entire industry. A conflict between an NGO and a company may be resolved by developing a business approach that benefits both sides, for example, by redesigning a business process that reduces harmful emissions but also lowers the cost of production (e.g., Heal 2005). Hence, there is much less rationale for negative advertising, even against competitors, especially if it damages the reputation of the industry. Moreover, companies need to weigh spending resources in a reputation management campaign with other business objectives, such as improving quality or manufacturing efficiency. Thus, companies rarely have the same single-minded objective of winning the battle for public opinion that is so characteristic of elections. That said, some battles, such as a proxy fight or a hostile takeover bid, tend to resemble zero-sum games dominated by short-term objectives. In such cases, well-funded communication strategies that closely resemble political campaigns are more common.

Finally, public opinion research has been fueled by the existence of mass surveys that are repeated at regular intervals, leading to rich datasets. Such datasets are usually not available in the context of corporate reputation research or are proprietary (e.g., Walker 2010). In addition, there are many factors that shape the dynamics of a company's reputation, most of which are not easily captured through survey research. These include the psychological mechanisms of how individuals form opinions, how opinions are changed and disseminated through social interaction, the role of the media (including social media), and the strategic interactions between firms and external constituencies such as NGOs and activists. These dimensions necessitate the development of new methods that go beyond the exclusive reliance on sample surveys and instead require the use of diverse tools from fields ranging from social and cognitive psychology to complex systems and game theory.

This approach is then developed in the rest of the book. We first show that a naïve view of opinion formation, the "mental database model" where respondents are retrieving well-formed opinions from a mental file cabinet, is flawed. Decades of research on opinion formation has shown that opinions are not retrieved from a preexisting dataset but are constructed on the spot and involve complex cognitive processes that crucially involve the coding, storage, and retrieval of impressions governed by a network of associations stored in long-term memory. These associative networks change over time due to external factors such as personal experience, media coverage, and peer influence. We then discuss the extensive research on attitude formation and distill its main insights into six major principles.

In part 2, we investigate three domains that impact corporate reputation and are major sources of reputational risk: moral evaluations, risk perception, and trust. We review the psychological and cultural processes that shape evaluations of corporate conduct, including value orientations, person-centered morality, and social relations theory. We show the crucial role of affect and emotions and establish how belief formation, such as risk perception and trust, is often influenced by the same principles. Having discussed these processes in detail, we derive implications for corporate strategies with an emphasis on the assessment and measurement of reputational risk.

In part 3 we discuss the roles of attention and perspective in opinion formation: Which issues do people pay attention to, and how do they view an issue? We show the importance of framing in shaping perception and public debate. We next discuss the importance of the media, both traditional and social, in determining dominant frames and public attention. In this context we pay particular attention to some of the severe methodological challenges in properly assessing media influence and show how they can be overcome.

In part 4, we discuss the role of stakeholders in shaping corporate reputations, with an emphasis on NGOs and social activists. Social activism has grown significantly in recent years and now operates globally. Activist campaigns are typically designed to put pressure on companies over specific business practices—often through the threat of inflicting reputational damage on companies. We introduce various models to better understand the strategic complexities of activist campaigns. This approach allows us to develop a new perspective on corporate social responsibility as a form of reputational risk management.

Our penultimate part, part 5, focuses on measurement and metrics. We discuss the promise and limitations of using mass opinion surveys as the main instruments for measuring public opinion. Next, we discuss alternative approaches to measuring corporate reputation. Our focus will be on text-analytic methods, which offer the possibility of using large-scale data analytics in the study of corporate reputations. We review various methodologies and approaches, ranging from sentiment analysis and topic identification to the measurement of emotions, values, ideologies, agendas, and frames, and discuss their scopes and limitations.

The last part summarizes our main findings and shows how they can be used to build a reputation management capability consisting of the proper mindset and processes based on the company's business model and core values. We conclude with a brief discussion of governance structures and the role of culture.

This book has twin purposes. On the one hand, it aims to develop a coherent view of corporate reputation that can inform practice. On the other hand, its goal is to demonstrate a list of methodologies and show how they can be useful, even essential, in gaining a deeper understanding of corporate reputation. That is the "analytics" part of the book's title. These methodologies draw from different fields but aim to represent the most advanced work in these areas that can now be applied to corporate reputation. In part 2 the focus is on methods from psychology and cultural anthropology, ranging from laboratory experiments to qualitative, interpretive approaches. Part 3 draws on a variety of methods from political science and economics, ranging from controlled experiments to econometrics. In this part we also develop our first mathematical model. Formal models, now from game theory, are the focus of part 4, where we discuss the interaction between firms and activists. Part 5 discusses surveys known from sociology, political science, and marketing, as well as text-analytic methods developed in computational linguistics, computer science, and data science.

The broad range of methods, we believe, is necessary to fully capture this most elusive phenomenon. In that sense the study of corporate reputation is not different from other areas of management research such as marketing, finance, strategy, leadership, and organizational behavior. Their coherence is not based on a shared methodological commitment but on a common interest in an important area of management. Understanding any such area requires multiple perspectives and methodologies.

PART I

Reputation and Public Opinion

CHAPTER TWO

Principles of Public Opinion

The conceptualization that governs this book is simple: corporate reputation is public opinion for companies. This approach has important implications.[1]

First, corporate reputation is based on perceptions of various "publics" or "constituencies." Reputation is not limited to customers, but may also involve potential customers, investors, employees, suppliers, and other business partners, as well as external constituencies such as regulators, politicians, NGOs, the media, and the general public, whether or not their views are invited by the company.

We prefer the term "constituency" to the more familiar "stakeholder" as the latter carries the connotation of bestowing a sense of legitimacy on any group that forms or expresses an opinion about the company. Within the context of reputation management, such normative questions are best set aside, at least for now. The focus here is on understanding the processes that shape opinions and their impact on companies, not on whether such attitudes are deemed legitimate by companies or society.

Second, corporate reputation is about actual — not desired — perceptions and attitudes. This is one of the important distinctions from more aspirational concepts, such as "corporate identity" or "image," that are designed to shape and align attitudes, especially among internal constituencies such as employees or business partners. The fundamental question in reputation management is how others see a company, not how the company sees itself or wants to be seen.

Third, reputation does not need to be based on experience or direct interaction. A traveler may avoid a certain hotel because of an unfavorable online review rather than because of an unpleasant experience during her last visit. Corporate reputation crucially involves what others are thinking and saying about the company; it is irreducibly public.

Fourth, corporate reputations may differ across markets, products, constituencies, and issue dimensions. The reputation of McDonald's in China may be quite different from its reputation in France. Wal-Mart may have an excellent reputation among its customers for low prices but a poor one with labor activists over its stance on unionization. These specific dimensions may depend on market and brand positioning as well as cultural, social, and political factors.

The interpretation of reputation as public opinion for companies, however, faces an immediate obstacle. According to one overview (Walker 2010), almost all empirical studies of corporate reputation use some form of ranking of companies as their measure of reputation (Fombrun 1998, 2007; Schultz, Mouritsen, and Gabrielsen 2001). Indeed, 39 percent use the annual list of Fortune's most admired companies. But using rankings limits the scope of research questions significantly. First, the available time series is very limited; most rankings, such as the Fortune rankings, are collected only annually. Second, such rankings typically are not differentiated by constituency, market, or issue.

Mass surveys provide an alternative. Such survey methods have been extensively used in other areas of pubic opinion research, such as elections (e.g., the American National Election Surveys) or value orientations (e.g., the World Values Survey). The availability of such mass surveys has been extremely important for the development of public opinion research. In her history of survey research, Converse (1987) concludes that the sample survey has become the social scientists' "telescope," an indispensable and irreplaceable tool to measure the flows of public opinion. While some consulting firms have started to collect them, such surveys are conducted infrequently and the resulting data are proprietary. Similarly, very few individual companies maintain regular corporate opinion surveys over extended time periods, and if they do, they are not commonly available to researchers.

2.1 The Mental Database and Its Problems

These are the practical problems, but there are also more important methodological issues. In existing corporate reputation surveys, respondents are presented with a stimulus by the researcher, such as a survey question, and then express some behavior, for example, they check a box or answer a question. Often such answers are interpreted as revealing a person's attitude on a particular issue, such as whether they trust a company or its CEO. Such survey design presumes that respondents are well informed about companies and industries and have well-formed opinions that simply need to be collected and aggregated. According to this view, once queried, respondents simply retrieve their well-formed attitudes about the target corporation from a mental database. Modern public opinion research, however, has shown that survey responses bear little resemblance to such a naive mental file drawer model. Opinion is not simply "expressed" and cannot simply be "retrieved" by asking questions.

The problems with the mental database model of public opinion were already appreciated at the very beginning of modern public opinion research, starting with the Columbia school (e.g., Berelson et al. 1954) and the Michigan school (Campbell et al. 1960). In their assessment of voter attitudes, these classic studies found that respondents typically lacked information about even basic political facts, failed to exhibit attitudes that were persistent and consistent, and were uninterested in most policy debates.[2] Structured or coherent opinions were nowhere to be found. Subsequent research identified a growing list of problems:[3]

1. Ignorance: many respondents lacked even elementary knowledge of politics and issues (e.g., Althaus 2003; Barabas and Jerit 2009; Delli Carpini and Keeter 1996; Fowler and Margolis 2014; Gilens 2001; Nyhan and Reifler 2010).
2. Question wording and sequencing effects: respondents' attitudes would change dramatically due to minor changes in question wording and the order of questions (e.g., Druckman 2001b; Krosnick, Malhotra, and Mittal 2014; Schuldt, Konrath, and Schwarz 2011; Schuman and Presser 1981).
3. Willingness to answer opinions on fictitious issues: respondents would offer opinions on entities and attitudes that did not exist (e.g., Bishop, Tuchfarber, and Oldendick 1986; Graeff 2002).
4. Instability and incoherence: the same respondents would not only hold apparently contradictory attitudes but dramatically change attitudes over time. Correlations of attitudes over time were barely better than coin flips (e.g., Converse 1964).[4]

In a classic article, Converse (1964) concluded that substantial portions of the mass public had no identifiable attitudes at all.

Large portions of an electorate do not have meaningful beliefs, even on issues
that have formed the basis for intense political controversy among elites for
substantial periods of time. (Converse 1964, p. 245)

Instead of providing reliable and consistent responses that reflect stable
underlying beliefs, many respondents seemed to simply make up responses
during the interview. These phenomena are not limited to political contexts. Kahan et al. (2009) report that more than 80 percent of Americans
stated that they know either "just a little" or "nothing" about nanotechnology. Yet they still expressed an opinion: around 90 percent of the
participants polled had an opinion about the technology. About 61 percent
saw the benefits as outweighing the risks.[5]

Evidently, the lack of familiarity does not prevent respondents from
expressing opinions; they are quite willing to report attitudes in surveys
on a variety of topics. One possible explanation for this behavior is that,
during a survey, respondents feel social pressure to answer the questions,
either because they do not want to embarrass themselves in front of the
interviewer or because they want to conclude the interview quickly. They
may be unfamiliar with an interview setting, flattered by the attention,
or, if they are compensated, feel the need to earn the money offered. In
sum, respondents may feel the need to respond "truthfully" to the question
even if they have no idea what the question is about (Bishop, Tuchfarber,
and Oldendick 1986; Duffy et al. 2005; Paulhus 1984; Phillips and Clancy
1972).[6]

Related phenomena can be found in the context of consumer attitudes. In a famous experiment, participants were presented with four pairs
of stockings arranged left to right and asked to choose which one was
the highest quality. What they did not know was that the stockings were
identical. When prompted, participants were not only willing to make a
choice, they were also willing to provide reasons for their choice. Indeed,
most participants chose the rightmost stocking, but none suggested that
the stocking's position may have guided their choice (Nisbett and Wilson
1977).

These deviations from a model where respondents report well-formed
attitudes or preferences pose a number of special difficulties for companies seeking to gauge measures like consumer satisfaction through survey
research. First, consumers usually express very high rates of consumer
satisfaction, even in cases where they switch to other products (Reichheld 1996). This suggests that participants are reticent to report low levels
of customer satisfaction even for products that are highly dissatisfying.

Second, companies typically ask consumers to assess them only on criteria according to which there is variance among their competitors rather than on criteria that are homogeneous across competitors. As a result, these surveys may fail to capture latent dissatisfaction, leaving companies vulnerable to disruption. For example, in the late 1990s, record companies asked consumers to assess them based on the quality of their artists and the breadth of their selections, as these were the criteria according to which they competed. They did not ask consumers about their attitudes toward storing music on CDs rather than digitally, bundling songs into albums rather than selling them individually, or requiring consumers to purchase music in physical stores rather than online, as these were not criteria that varied among the major record companies and, indeed, were not imagined by consumers or record executives at the time. As a result, record companies were ill-prepared to deal with the advent of Napster, iTunes, and other digital music-sharing services (Moon 2005). This insight was well expressed by Steve Jobs, who once famously said that he did not like to use consumer research because "a lot of times, people don't know what they want until you show it to them" (Reinhardt 1998).

Converse's "nonattitude" thesis triggered an extensive research effort to address these difficulties. Some approaches, focused on measurement error (e.g., Achen 1975; Feldman 1989), effectively interpreted public opinion as a latent variable that is imperfectly measured in any given survey. This led to improvements in survey design as well as the practice of pooling opinion polls. The measurement error approach, however, had difficulties in accounting for systematic biases, like the willingness to offer answers to fictitious questions, or predictable context effects, such as the case where an interviewer or questionnaire providing a possible reason or permission to express a particular attitude increases its frequency (Krosnick, Malhotra, and Mittal 2014).

One well-known example is the attitude of the US public toward the presence of Soviet journalists from surveys conducted in the 1970s. When simply asked whether Soviet journalists should be allowed in the US, only 37 percent agreed. When the same question was prefaced by another question on whether US journalists should be allowed into the Soviet Union, support increased to 73 percent. Rather than being the result of random measurement error, examples such as these suggest that the question about US journalists in the Soviet Union triggers a reciprocity norm which resonates with most respondents. With such a norm fresh in their mind, approval increases, since allowing Soviet journalists into the country is consistent with that norm (Schuman and Presser 1981).[7] Such "response effects" and other biases suggest that a richer process of opinion formation is needed.[8]

The persistent difficulty in accounting for such anomalies eventually led to a reconceptualization of public opinion research based on cognitive and social psychology. This "cognitive revolution" radically departs from the traditional model of opinion research, where respondents simply retrieve their opinion from a mental file (Wilson and Hodges 1992). Rather, when queried, for example, in a survey or by an acquaintance during a conversation, respondents are now thought to "construct" an opinion on the spot (Lodge 1995; Lodge, Steenbergen, and Brau 1995; Lodge and Taber 2013; Zaller 1992; Zaller and Feldman 1992). This process of "opinion construction," while driven by well-established psychological principles, has profound consequences for our understanding of public opinion and corporate reputation.

2.2 The Role of Memory

At the basis of this approach is an appreciation of the role of memory. The capacity of working or short-term memory is extremely limited. It can hold roughly 7 ± 2 bits of information (Miller 1956), must process information serially, and requires mental energy, among other characteristics. In contrast, a person's beliefs, values, feelings, and experiences acquired over a lifetime are stored in long-term memory. The storage capacity of long-term memory is vast, processing is more efficient through parallel processing, and long-term storage requires little energy.

Cognitive scientists conceptualize long-term memory as a network of associations (Anderson 1983, 1996). Such associations may include entities, attributes, images, attitudes, beliefs, and feelings. For example, a concept such as *Google* may be connected with *search*, *street-view*, *computer*, *company*, the Google logo, *Silicon Valley*, and *California*. In addition, there may be associations with less direct entities or events, such as the Super Bowl commercial about the American exchange student who falls in love with a French girl, the movie *The Internship*, privacy concerns, self-driving cars, and so forth. These networks are dynamic, where new impressions are integrated into an existing associative network, and the network itself changes in response to new impressions. In particular, components that have been coactivated repeatedly tend to be coactivated in the future; their associative bond increases. This is an instance of the general cognitive principle known as Hebb's Law: "Neurons that fire together, wire together" (Hebb 1949). That is, mental entities (such as thoughts, feelings, and attitudes) that tend to be activated together tend to build stronger associative connections, which makes it more likely that they will be coactivated in the future.

In general, the activation of stored components depends on the network structure. Components that are linked tend to be activated together and are more likely to move into working memory. The closer the connection is between an object and an attribute, the more readily the attribute comes to mind when the concept of the object is triggered by seeing it or reading it. In contrast, a disassociated attribute will take longer. For example, if a word such as *internet* is read immediately before reading the word *Google*, other associations related to *internet*, such as *search*, come to mind more quickly than if *Google* is preceded by *California*.

This implies that attitudes are constructed in real time from whatever associative components are currently activated; attitudes are not well-defined, isolated elements in a database that are simply retrieved. Instead, they are formed through the spreading of activations in a network of associations between beliefs, images, feelings, and so forth. In practice, this means that respondents report those attitudes that are "top of mind" for them, but what is top of mind depends on context and changes over time.

These ideas provide possible explanations for some of the puzzling phenomena discussed earlier. For example, according to the cognitive perspective, response or question ordering effects occur because different contexts activate different parts of memory, which makes different considerations accessible. In the example of Soviet journalists in the US, the direct question may activate "Cold War" considerations where *Soviet Union* is associated with *enemy* or *hostile*, which lowers approval for allowing Soviet journalists in the US. On the other hand, a context that talks about US journalists in the Soviet Union makes a reciprocity norm salient, triggering associations with ideas such as *fair* or *tit-for-tat*, resulting in higher approval rates (Zaller 1992; Zaller and Feldman 1992).

This approach also provides an elegant explanation for inconsistent responses over time: at different times, different associations are triggered, which lead to differences in the reported attitudes. More specifically, at different points in time, attitudes are constructed by accessing the dynamic network of a respondent's long-term memory. While the resulting survey responses may accurately reflect the constructed attitudes at that time, the dynamic associative structure of long-term memory means that what is top of mind at time *t* may be very different from what is top of mind at *t* + 1, as the associative network changes over time in response to personal experience, media exposure, or specific features of the survey context. As a result, survey responses can vary significantly over time with only minimal changes in survey context.

The cognitive approach to attitude formation also raises some important methodological questions about the use and interpretation of survey results (Lodge and Taber 2013). If survey responses are not retrieved from a mental database but are constructed in real time from long-term memory, then the attitude is not, strictly speaking, fully independent of the act of surveying. That is, the presence of an interviewer or questionnaire constitutes another stimulus that activates associations from long-term memory and moves them into short-term memory, where they form the basis of the survey response. Note, first, that the context of the survey may trigger peculiar associations or affect. For example, a sympathetic interviewer may influence the retrieval process. Moreover, the very act of asking for an answer may trigger an intellectualization and distancing process that separates the reported from the immediately felt response (Epstein 1994; Lodge and Taber 2013; Wittenbrink, Judd, and Park 1997).

As a consequence of these problems, survey tools need to be complemented by experimental methods that can map out a person's associative network more directly. This is the domain of implicit attitude measurements (e.g., De Houwer et al. 2009; Fazio and Olson 2003; Gawronski and Bodenhausen 2007; Greenwald and Banaji 1995; Greenwald, McGhee, and Schwartz 1998; Nosek, Hawkins, and Frazier 2011; Uhlmann et al. 2012). One commonly used approach is the analysis of reaction times in cognitive tasks. A typical experiment works as follows (e.g., Collins and Loftus 1975; Collins and Quillian 1969; Verhulst and Lodge 2013): A subject is placed in front of a computer screen where she has to push a button in response to a question. The goal is to push the button correctly in as short a time as possible. After some practice with the setup, subjects are shown an initial word, the so-called *prime*, such as the word *Google*, followed by a blank screen, followed by another stimulus, the so-called *target*, such as the word *company*. In the *lexical decision task* subjects need to decide whether the target is a word. That is, respondents are sometimes given a word, such as *company*, and sometimes a nonsense term, such as *ponacym*, and need to decide whether the term is a word. A variant is a *sentence verification task*, where subjects are asked to decide whether the target sentence is true when applied to the prime, here whether Google is a company. The idea is that the closer the association is between the prime and the target, the shorter the respondent's reaction time. For example, subjects should be able to identify that *company* is a word more quickly when primed with *Google* rather than, say, *ocean*. This effect has been demonstrated in hundreds of experiments (Lodge and Taber 2013).[9]

Primes can have an effect even if the exposure time is too short for the subject to consciously recognize that she has been exposed to a prime. In the *lexical decision task* even exposure of less than 100 milliseconds can have an effect on how quickly a target can be correctly recognized as a word. This suggests that primes trigger preconscious expectations shaped by long-term memory. If such expectations are fulfilled (through a strong association between the prime and the target), reaction time is shortened; if they are frustrated, reaction time is extended.

These phenomena are well known in the context of branding. In one experiment, participants were asked to memorize word pairs and were then asked to name products in various categories. It was found that when participants were asked to memorize word pairs such as "ocean-moon," they were more likely to name associated products in a given product category, such as "Tide" when asked to name a detergent (Nisbett and Wilson 1977). In real-life settings, people are often exposed to associations and cues, some of which are only very tangentially related to the product. For example, when asked to spontaneously generate products in different product categories, participants are more likely to generate products associated with the color orange, such as Orange Crush or Sunkist in the soda category, when writing with an orange pen or when tested on the day before Halloween (Berger and Fitzsimons 2008). In a famous case, sales of Mars candy bars increased in the months following NASA's landing of the Pathfinder rover on the surface of Mars (White 1997). Brendl et al. (2005) and Pelham, Mirenberg, and Jones (2002) have provided evidence that respondents choose brands, locations, occupations, or objects that are similar to their name, for example, starting with the same letter.[10]

In general, such associations are of great practical consequence for the reputation of companies and industries. For example, the word *plastics* may trigger associations of trash heaps and polluted oceans, or it may trigger associations with useful products, such as bicycle helmets or medical devices. Once recognized, companies may try to use advertising and other approaches to shift such patterns of association.

Tybout, Calder, and Sternthal (1981) show how strategies that influence memory directly can affect attitudes toward companies. Tybout and colleagues study the case of bizarre rumors, such as whether McDonald's used red worm meat in its hamburgers to save money, a persistent rumor that depressed sales in the late 1970s by as much as 30 percent. To combat the rumor, McDonald's employed various strategies. It used advertising, emphasizing its "100% pure beef" promise as well as independent third-party sources, such as a letter from the US secretary of agriculture stating that McDonald's food is "wholesome, properly identified, and in compliance with standards prescribed by Food Safety and Quality Service regulations" (Tybout, Calder, and Sternthal 1981, p. 73). McDonald's also pointed out that using worm meat would not even make financial sense, as worm meat is five to eight times more expensive than beef, undercutting the cost savings argument. But these appeals to reason had little to no effect.

In their experiments, Tybout, Calder, and Sternthal explore a different approach that directly operates on memory formation. The problem with McDonald's strategy is that the audience's evaluation and processing of the company's messages also triggers retrieval of memories associated with the worm meat rumor, including unpleasant feelings of disgust, fear, and anger. Consumers are affected by the rumor because they process it, not because they necessarily believe it (Tybout, Calder, and Sternthal 1981, p. 74). Tybout explore the effectiveness of two strategies, one focused on storage, the other on retrieval. In both cases, subjects in a laboratory setting were exposed to the rumor. In the storage strategy, subjects were told about a different context in which worms appear in food after hearing the McDonald's rumor in order to store the worm concept with a different object than McDonald's. In the retrieval strategies, subjects were also asked questions intended to trigger positive or neutral memories associated with McDonald's, such as the location of the McDonald's they frequent, the number of meals eaten there, and characteristics of the restaurant.[11] The strategies were compared to a straightforward refutation strategy that was designed to replicate the strategy of McDonald's by providing factual information. Finally, a base case was considered where only the rumor was provided.

As expected, evaluations of McDonald's were lower when the rumor was provided. Adding the refutation strategy had no effect. However, both retrieval and storage strategies improved evaluations of the company. The results suggest an explanation for why even bizarre or implausible rumors can have an effect on evaluation and why refutation strategies may be ineffective: the rumors are stored in memory accompanied by negative emotions, and refutation strategies remind audiences of the rumor and reinforce stored associations.[12]

2.3 Principles of Opinion Formation

The research literature in psychology has identified a few core processes that have shaped the dynamics of memory formation, activation, and attitude formation. The first and most easily appreciated factor is *repetition*. Pioneers in public relations and political demagogues have both long been aware of the power of repetition in political competition and advertising (e.g., Le Bon 1895). The effectiveness of repetition is rooted in basic processes of memory formation (e.g., Baddeley 1999; Howard 1995; Loftus and Loftus 1976) and has been understood since the inception of the scientific study of memory in the work of Ebbinghaus ([1885] 2016). For example, rote learning of facts, such as foreign vocabulary, consists of repetitive exposure to stimuli. Once subjects are repeatedly exposed to similar stimuli, the content of the stimulus becomes part of semantic memory. That is, the specific context of the stimulus is forgotten and its content is remembered as a general fact.[13] This is a desirable feature for demagogues and marketers alike. Entities are better encoded in semantic memory due to repetition, the defining characteristic of rote learning.[14]

We can summarize this in our first principle.

Repetition

Repeated exposure to entities makes it more likely that such entities are encoded in memory.

Ebbinghaus ([1885] 2016) was also the first to identify the forgetting curve, that is, the empirical regularity that memory decays exponentially.[15] This leads to our second principle: *recency*. The more recently a stimulus has been activated, the less time it takes to retrieve the stimulus, or related considerations, from memory (e.g., Higgins and King 1981; Wyer and Srull 1989). Recency effects are a direct consequence of memory decay and can be identified in various areas of public opinion formation (e.g., Bartels 2008; Chong and Druckman 2010; Druckman and Nelson 2003; Gerber et al. 2011; Hill et al. 2013; Huber, Hill, and Lenz 2012; Zaller 1992). We can summarize recency effects in the following principle.

Recency

More recent impressions are more likely to be activated and retrieved from memory.

Much of the evidence for recency effects comes from the study of electoral campaigns. Politicians time and target their advertising messages and campaign events for maximal impact on election day. There is also evidence that incumbent politicians tend to time macroeconomic policy and pork-barrel spending before they face the voters, leading to "political business cycles" (e.g., Hibbs 1977; Nordhaus 1975). Recency effects are particularly relevant where there is a fixed, known, important decision point such as an election in the future, allowing competing parties or interests to time their messaging. Examples in the corporate domain include important product launches and proxy battles, as well as regulatory or political decisions. In such cases, companies may engage in campaigns not too dissimilar from electoral campaigns where recency effects matter most. However, in most other contexts, companies need to protect their reputation on an ongoing basis. Moreover, particularly important times where more effort is required, such as corporate crises, tend to occur unexpectedly. Hence, timing efforts is usually not a feasible strategy.

Our third principle of attitude formation is *attention*.

Attention

The greater a person's level of attention, the more likely he or she is to be aware of an impression, to memorize it, and to recall it.

The attention principle is of crucial importance for successful reputation management.[16] In many industries, the public rarely pays attention to a company except in special situations.[17] This is an important difference from electoral campaigns, which are characterized by sustained public and media interest. Companies often try to overcome this lack of interest through product advertising and other marketing activities. But such activity is mostly focused on promoting products and services, while companies tend to find it challenging to increase public interest in themselves and their general activities. Increased interest by the public can be desirable, for example, during a corporate branding campaign or when a company promotes its corporate social responsibility activities. Earned media coverage in such cases, however, tends to be limited. But there are special moments when the customers and other constituencies do pay attention. Most customers pay attention to service providers, such as their public utilities, their cell phone carrier, their insurance provider, or their bank only when there is a problem or when they receive a bill. Every good hotel manager knows that the moment there is a problem with a reservation or the service is when lasting impressions are formed, either positive or negative, especially when the guest is visiting for a special occasion; a mixed-up reservation on a routine business trip is one thing, at a daughter's wedding quite another.

It is during these special times that customers and the public pay attention, and when they pay attention, they remember, often for a long time. Episodes that an audience pays attention to are then more easily memorized and recalled (e.g., Craik et al. 1996). As we discussed in the preface, US audiences associate Johnson & Johnson with a principled response to the Tylenol crisis. Four decades later, the Tylenol recall remains the textbook example of how to manage a corporate crisis. Similarly, the *Exxon Valdez* accident is still top of mind for US audiences when they think of Exxon Mobil, even though the oil spill occurred over 30 years ago in March 1989.[18]

Intuitively, we can think of the network of attitudes toward a company as being rather fixed. But during periods of engagement, they become more fluid. New impressions and associations are added, old ones change, and the weights among associations are rebalanced (Taylor and Fiske 1978). Such periods of engagements are often brief, and once they end, considerations become frozen again. When it comes to shaping reputations, such moments of engagements thus are decisive, turning points for better or worse, and companies are well advised to seize them.

This process is particularly important in the context of a reputational crisis that emotionally engages the public and captures its attention. The attention principle implies that, during such times, short as they may be, an audience is particularly receptive to messages. Once this crisis phase ends, engagement and receptivity decline. Thus, associations remain fairly unchanged unless a new period of engagement, perhaps triggered by a new crisis, commences. At a practical level, this means that corporate reputations tend to be disproportionately shaped during periods of crisis. While these crises are often triggered by a negative event, such as an accident, a scandal, or some grave concern over business practices, the attention principle implies that they also present opportunities for improving a company's reputation, since it is during such times of high emotional engagement and attention that attitudes are most fluid. Thus, leaving a positive impression during these periods may pay long-term benefits.

Such moments of high attention may not always be triggered by the company's action. Natural disasters, terrorist attacks, or public health crises also engage the public profoundly. For example, the conduct of companies during the COVID-19 crisis, such as how they handle layoffs and furloughs or how they support their community, can leave lasting impressions.

We can illustrate these dynamics by considering the Toyota unintended acceleration crisis.[19] On August 28, 2009, Mark Saylor, an off-duty police officer, was driving a 2009 Lexus ES350 sedan on loan from his Toyota dealer near San Diego, California, when the car suddenly accelerated to more than 120 miles per hour. Saylor's brother-in-law, Chris Lastrella, desperately called an emergency 911 operator for help, a chilling recording of which was later released on the internet and quickly went viral.[20]

> We're in a Lexus . . . and our accelerator is stuck . . . we're in trouble . . . there's no brakes . . . we're approaching the intersection . . . hold on . . . hold on and pray . . . pray.

Unable to stop, Saylor's vehicle sped into the intersection, struck a vehicle, went through a fence, over an embankment, and into the bed of the San Diego River. Lastrella, Saylor, and his wife, as well as their 13-year-old daughter, died instantly. Thus began the biggest crisis in the history of Toyota. On September 29, 2009, Toyota announced it would soon launch a voluntary recall of 3.8 million vehicles, followed by additional recalls in 2010, and urged customers to remove their floor mats immediately, regardless of make and model, while possible design changes were evaluated. Unsecured rubber floor mats that became tangled up in gas and brake pedals were among the suspected causes for unintended acceleration. The US safety regulator, the National Highway Traffic Safety Administration (NHTSA), simultaneously issued a safety alert that also pointed to the use of unsecured mats, as well as the configuration of pedals in the affected vehicles, and the processes necessary to turn off the engines in vehicles.[21]

Within a month, Toyota lost about $35 billion in shareholder value, a drop of about 21 percent, more than the market cap of, for example, Time Warner at the time. Resale values of Toyota vehicles dropped by about 3 percent.[22] In 2010, Toyota was the only major car company to lose sales in the US market, while the industry grew by over 13 percent. Perhaps even more troubling for Toyota, surveys by *Consumer Report* and others indicated that Toyota had lost its leadership position on quality among US consumers (Diermeier, Austen-Smith, and Zemel 2011; Liker and Ogden 2011).

This may seem to be simply another example of a product flaw leading to a crisis for the company, but things are more nuanced. From the very beginning, Toyota had stated it had no evidence that any of the vehicles contained a safety-related defect.[23] Ten months later a NASA-led study into Toyota's electronic system, a possible hidden cause of unintended acceleration, "found no evidence that a malfunction in electronics caused large unintended accelerations." Ray LaHood, the US transportation secretary, summarized the findings as follows: "The jury is back. The verdict is in. There is no electronic-based cause for unintended high-speed acceleration in Toyotas. Period."[24]

Unfortunately, even this very positive report yielded few benefits for Toyota. The reason is that its release did not capture the public's attention and failed to counteract the vivid memories of the Saylor accident. Thus, while it strongly supported Toyota's original position, the report did not sufficiently change public attitudes toward the company or protect Toyota from lawsuits.[25]

Of course, positive stories, such as the NASA report, tend to generate less news coverage than negative ones, especially if they are of a somewhat technical nature. But the lack of public attention is not a given, and companies can try to increase high receptivity during periods of good news. A textbook example of this strategy is Mercedes Benz's handling of the so-called Moose Test.[26] In 1997, Daimler-Benz's Mercedes division found itself in the spotlight when its newly introduced compact car, the A-class, rolled over during an avoidance maneuver (known as the Moose Test) conducted by Swedish journalists. The failed Moose Test created extensive negative media coverage in Germany and other European countries, threatening the success of the A-class launch. Mercedes originally mishandled the crisis by focusing too much on the purely technical aspects of the crisis and was perceived as arrogant and stonewalling. As part of its recovery strategy, Mercedes recalled and modified the vehicle (while publicly maintaining that there were no safety issues) and then relaunched it with an aggressive public relations campaign that included a widely publicized A-class test drive with journalists and celebrities as test-car drivers, an extensive advertising campaign featuring German tennis idol Boris Becker, and a two-minute commercial on German television.[27]

Such recovery strategies exemplify the attention principle. Going back to "business as usual" and hoping that audiences will forget the event rarely works, as audiences' current attitudes have been shaped during the reputational crisis. If primed, images of a flipped over A-class (in the case of Mercedes) or oil-covered birds (in the case of Exxon Mobil) are most likely to be accessed from memory. Even if companies find a solution to the original problem or can show that it was far less serious than originally feared (as with the NASA report in the case of Toyota), this will not significantly change association networks (and thus attitudes) unless companies are able to change associations by taking advantage of periods of high receptivity or by creating their own.

Periods of high attention may occur for arbitrary or unrelated reasons. The reason Toyota faced its unintended acceleration crisis is not that it had experienced more cases than other companies (it had not), or that there was a dramatic increase in reports of unintended acceleration (there was not), but because of the dramatic circumstances of the Saylor accident, most importantly the 911 cell phone call. Other attention triggers include the presence of celebrities, vivid visuals, or well-known brands (Diermeier 2011). For example, in 2013, sports car maker Porsche faced serious concerns over the safety of its vehicles after actor Paul Walker—star of the movie franchise *Fast and Furious*, in which he played an expert driver in illegal street races—died in a car crash inside a Porsche Carrera GT. Such attention-triggering events are difficult to anticipate or control, but they significantly raise the stakes of any crisis response.

Natural disasters, such as hurricanes, tornadoes, or earthquakes, have a similar effect. They generate disproportionately high media coverage (Eisensee and Strömberg 2007) as well as substantial audience interest. Companies that provide assistance to affected areas are more likely to shift attitudes in a favorable direction than during regular times. One such example was Wal-Mart's response to Hurricane Katrina in 2005. Despite facing numerous reputational challenges, Wal-Mart was widely praised for its effective and fast relief efforts.[28] It was able to deliver bottled water and other essential supplies well before federal relief agencies reached the victims. The company also allowed store managers and truck drivers to talk directly to the media. The emotional impact of their personal stories of neighbors helping neighbors played an important role in boosting positive perceptions of Wal-Mart and energizing the business's employees. The company was perceived as both competent and caring without being seen as blowing its own horn. If done correctly, effective disaster assistance can serve as a paradigm for doing the right thing and getting credit for it. In general, periods of high receptivity are largely driven by the media cycle, a topic we return to in chapter 8.[29]

The fourth major principle in attitude formation pertains to the role of *affect*, small flashes of negative or positive feeling associated with an impression. Affects are not fully developed emotions—they are too fleeting and undifferentiated—but they can give rise to emotions such as anger, fear, or disgust. Affect is a basic mental process rooted in the evolutionary need to quickly distinguish whether an object or situation is safe and can be approached or whether it should be avoided (e.g., LeDoux 1998; Zajonc 1980, 2000). Affective reactions are binary (positive versus negative), happen rapidly and automatically, and are unintentional and difficult to suppress (Bargh et al. 1992).[30] Affective stimuli require few mental resources and can operate at low levels of awareness (e.g., Bargh 1997). A stimulus, for example, may trigger affect before the subject is aware that she has been exposed to a stimulus (so-called consciously unnoticed events). In other cases, a subject may be conscious of the existence of a stimulus, such as upbeat music during a commercial, but may be unaware of the stimulus's affective impact (so-called consciously unappreciated events).[31]

Research about the impact of affect and emotions on cognition (e.g., Damasio 2000; LeDoux 1998, 2000; Phelps 2006) has shown that emotions may directly trigger actions and reactions without involving higher cognitive reasoning. Rather, associated with older regions of the brain, they require shorter response times and are quasi-automatic, especially when confronting threats. This increased response speed is highly functional and evolutionary beneficial, but it relies on (imprecise) similarity matching rather than a conscious detailed assessment of risks and benefits.

The impact of affect can be demonstrated by priming experiments (e.g., Bargh et al. 1992; Fazio et al. 1986). The design of the experiments is similar to the lexical decision and sentence verification tasks discussed above, but focuses on affect. In a typical experiment, a subject is presented with an affectively charged prime, such as *cockroach*. Subjects are then given a target word, for example, *cancer*. Subjects are then asked to correctly classify the target word as positive or negative as quickly as possible. The general finding, replicated hundreds of times in various contexts, is that subjects are able to classify prime-target pairs that are affectively congruent (both positive or both negative) more quickly than incongruent pairs. Lodge and Taber (2000, 2013) show that similar effects also apply to political candidates, issues, and groups.

Affect influences memorization and attitude formation at various levels. In general, affect and emotions positively impact the encoding, consolidation, and retention of associated memories (e.g., Phelps 2006), an idea already expressed by William James in *The Principles of Psychology* ([1890] 2013, p. 670):

> An impression may be so exciting emotionally as almost to leave a scar upon the cerebral tissues.

Lodge and Taber (2013) show that affect influences memory encoding, activation, and retrieval at various stages of attitude formation.[32] At the perception and encoding stage, impressions are affectively charged, and that affective charge (positive or negative) becomes associated with the object in long-term memory. This effect can be triggered even by affectively charged but otherwise irrelevant primes, such as unrelated words (e.g., *sunshine* or *cancer*) or emoticons such as "smiley faces" (Lodge and Taber 2013). For example, if a viewer felt negative affect when seeing the Exxon Mobil oil spill on television, perhaps even rising to emotional responses such as anger and outrage, that affect will be stored in long-term memory and will tend to be activated when the person sees Exxon Mobil's logo or reads a story about Exxon Mobil. The subject may experience negative feelings about Exxon Mobil, often without any discernible reason. When prompted and given time to reflect, subjects can provide reasons, but often these "reasons" are mere rationalizations of the immediate affect. These effects are not limited to uninformed audiences. Indeed, the effects are *stronger* for well-informed and politically engaged audiences, especially on attitudes on policy issues (Lodge and Taber 2013). As we discuss below, affect also plays a major role in moral judgment and risk perception. We can summarize these insights in our fourth principle.

Affect

Affect influences the coding, formation, storage, and retrieval of memories and attitudes.

These effects apply not only to "snap judgment," that is, quick evaluations, but also to reasoning processes. When primed with affect, subjects tend to more easily recall arguments and reasons that are congruent with their initial affect, even if the affective prime is completely unrelated. When being primed with negative affect, subjects will more easily retrieve and formulate considerations that are congruent, that is, negative, and will be less likely to recall incongruent, that is, positive, arguments. Moreover, these considerations will effectively mediate the evaluation of an issue: positive affect facilitates positive thoughts and inhibits negative thoughts; negative affect facilitates negative thoughts and inhibits positive thoughts (Lodge and Taber 2013). We can see how these processes can lead to a snowball effect. Initial negative feelings about a company, perhaps caused by negative media coverage, trigger negative snap judgments. Moreover, affectively charged events are better remembered, and when they are recalled, the events are associated with the original affect. Future deliberation and consideration, then, will tend to be biased in the direction of the original affect, with new information interpreted in a nonneutral fashion that reflects affective coloring and prior attitudes. Subjects will tend to seek out new information and interpret information in the direction of their initial bias. Congruent information will tend to be less scrutinized and interpreted more favorably, while challenging information will be avoided and more critically scrutinized.

The selection, evaluation, and storage of new information is also influenced by the ideological orientation of the audience. The evidence for this effect is not limited to anecdotes (e.g., political liberals watch MSNBC and find its messages more credible; conservatives watch Fox News, etc.) but can be induced in the laboratory. Information boards—tables on a computer screen, whose cells contain hidden arguments for or against an issue—are particularly useful to demonstrate these effects. On an information board, each cell is labeled by the source of its argument. For example, a pro-gun argument may be labeled "NRA statement." Subjects can click on the cells and read the arguments. By measuring initial attitudes and comparing them with clicking patterns, one can assess whether subjects tend to seek information consistent with their value orientation; they do, at a proportion of 3 to 1. To measure their reactions to new information, subjects can then be asked to record responses to the read arguments in an open ended format, or reactions can be observed by providing subjects with a fixed list of arguments and then recording their responses. Again we find a clear bias. Political conservatives evaluate a liberal argument far more negatively than political liberals, and vice versa for a conservative argument; the opposite pattern holds for liberals. Thus, political ideology shapes the evaluation of political arguments in the direction of the subject's ideological orientation. Many of the responses are merely an expression of affect ("this is a stupid statement") rather than detailed counterarguments. And, as above, the effects are strongest for political sophisticates and subjects who have the strongest initial bias (Lodge and Taber 2013).[33]

According to this approach, information is not evaluated neutrally, but in light of existing beliefs and values. Messages are not received and evaluated in isolation, but are accepted or rejected based on their fit with existing attitudes. Attitudes are not adjusted toward new information, but new information is processed in the direction of preexisting attitudes. These effects can be identified for both the direction and the strength of attitudes (Lodge and Taber 2013) and are *stronger* for sophisticated audiences, as they have a larger repertoire of potential counterarguments that can be marshaled against new information that challenges existing beliefs.

This is expressed in the next principle.

Consonance

Messages that are consonant with a person's current beliefs or attitudes are more likely to be sought out, received, accepted, and stored in memory. Messages that are inconsistent with a person's current beliefs or attitudes are less likely to be sought out, received, accepted, and stored in memory. Messages that are neutral will tend to be interpreted in line with a person's current beliefs and attitudes.

On closer examination, the Consonance Principle has two subcomponents.[34] First, there is a general conservatism. Audiences tend to maintain their considerations and are unlikely to radically alter them, even if confronted with new information that challenges previous beliefs and attitudes. Such new information may be incongruent due to its content or its source. The cognitive dissonance created by a new, inconsistent message is likely to be resolved toward the established set of considerations. Specifically, people who feel strongly about an issue will evaluate supportive arguments more strongly than opposing arguments and will tend to seek out information that confirms their prior attitude (Lodge and Taber 2013; Redlawsk 2002). This means that opinion formation exhibits positive autocorrelation; current opinions shape future attitudes. This has important consequences for the identification and management of emerging issues (Diermeier 2011). If opinion formation is shaped by early impressions, then companies need to engage early to shape the emerging public perception of an issue. However, such interventions, though valuable, face both practical and systematic difficulties. On the one hand, companies are potentially affected by many emerging issues, most of which never gain any momentum and can safely be ignored. On the other hand, investing in issue management is costly, and companies may be reluctant to incur such expenses in the absence of any clear evidence that a given issue warrants such engagement. These problems cannot be solved in principle, but they can be alleviated by developing models of intrinsic reputational risk and media coverage, tasks we turn to below.

Second, the deeper attitudes are embedded in a person's belief system, the more difficult they are to dislodge. General evaluative principles like values and other firmly held convictions, such as religious or ideological beliefs, will thus influence how new information is interpreted and retained. In political domains, public opinion researchers have found that party identification shapes an individual's positioning on many issues while staying fairly constant over a person's life (Campbell et al. 1960). Similarly, cross-national research has pointed to fairly constant value orientations (e.g., Inglehart 1990).

The Consonance Principle also operates on neutral information or in issue areas where respondents may not yet have formed specific attitudes. Here, fundamental beliefs and attitudes shaped by value orientations come into play. As an example, consider attitudes toward new technologies in the context of nanotechnology discussed earlier (Kahan 2009). Kahan and colleagues (Kahan, Braman, et al. 2008, 2009; Kahan, Slovic, et al. 2008) conducted a series of surveys on public attitudes towards nanotechnology. The overwhelming majority of respondents knew little or nothing about the technology, yet still reported an opinion. One subset of respondents also received additional information about nanotechnology. The information was designed to be neutral in tone, but it led to a significant shift in respondents' attitudes toward the new technology. That shift was neither uniform nor random. Rather, the belief shift was heavily influenced by each respondent's overall value orientation as measured in surveys. Specifically, two value dimensions—individualistic versus communitarian and hierarchical versus egalitarian—had substantial impacts on attitudes. The dimensions were highly correlated; individuals who scored high on a individualistic value scale also tended to score high on a hierarchical value scale. They can thus be combined into one scale, defined as individualist-hierarchical versus communitarian-egalitarian value orientations.

Having received information on nanotechnology, respondents who scored moderate to high on the individualist-hierarchical dimension reported higher benefits and lower risks associated with nanotechnology, while respondents with moderate to high communitarian-egalitarian value orientations recorded lower benefits and higher risks. Indeed, the effect was substantial. Compared to the no-information condition, where 61 percent of both the individualist-hierarchical participants and the communitarian-egalitarian participants believed the benefits outweighed the risks, the likelihood that hierarchical individualists perceived the benefits as outweighing the risks of nanotechnology grew by 25 percent, while for communitarian-egalitarians it decreased by 38 percent, opening a 63 percentage point gap after the information was received (Kahan, Braman, et al. 2009). Similar dynamics can be found in the context of stem cell research (Nisbet 2005) and biotech (Druckman and Bolsen 2011).[35] Nisbet (2005), for example, demonstrates the impact of religious and ideological orientations on attitudes toward stem cells.[36]

According to the Consonance Principle, the additional content and terms used in the neutral information about nanotechnology triggered a retrieval process over considerations in the person's long-term memory, favoring those that were more accessible in the respondent's mind. The networks of associations in the respondent's long-term memory will likely be different for individuals with different value orientations, leading to differences in expressed attitudes toward nanotechnology. Neutral subject-matter information is not necessarily interpreted in a neutral way, but in ways consistent with the subject's underlying value orientation. Note that it took a trigger, here providing new information about nanotechnology, to activate the retrieval process. The control condition, where no information was provided, did not show similarly polarized attitudes toward nanotechnology. Beliefs, associations, and feelings needed to be retrieved from memory before they could influence attitude formation.[37]

When messages are received over time, these dynamics engender a *polarization effect* along value orientations or ideologies. As subjects become more attentive to an issue, they will tend to retrieve considerations with higher frequency. For hierarchical individualists, for example, these will tend to be considerations that further favor the position that seems to be most aligned with a hierarchical-individualist value orientation. Thus, for an approximately even flow of incoming messages, increasing awareness will lead to increased polarization.[38] This effect has been well documented in the context of political issues (Bolsen and Palm 2021). Zaller (1992, pp. 101–102) states this as follows:

Thus, in the case of an evenly divided partisan elite and a balanced flow of partisan communications, the effect of political awareness is to promote the *polarization* of attitude reports as more aware liberals gravitate more reliably to the liberal position and more aware conservatives gravitate more reliably to the conservative position (Emphasis in original).

Note that increased awareness will lead to increased polarization only on issues where there is a value conflict in public discourse, such as climate change, controversial new technologies, or the legal status of same-sex couples.[39] On other issues where there is widespread value consensus, such as product safety or corruption, increased awareness will not lead to polarization. Rather, aggregate opinion will tend to become more uniform, less noisy, and less volatile. Polarization along value orientations also occurs if subjects are exposed to arguments by unidentified experts (Kahan, Slovic, et al. 2008). Importantly, subject-matter expertise is not interpreted in a value-neutral way either. Domain-specific expertise did not sway subjects. What mattered more to subjects was not subject-matter credibility, but *cultural* credibility.[40] That is, subjects who were exposed to an expert who shared their value orientation adjusted their attitudes in the direction of the expert, even if the expert's position was, taken at face value, at odds with their value orientation.[41] That is, egalitarians who were matched with an egalitarian expert who defended continued nanotechnology development were *more supportive* of nanotechnology than subjects with a hierarchical orientation. The same held for the mirror condition where subjects with a hierarchical value orientation reduced their support if exposed to an expert with hierarchical values who had argued for a moratorium on nanotechnology.[42]

Heinze, Uhlmann, and Diermeier (2014) show that the mere intention of involving a third party with similar values can shift perception. In their experiments, subjects were exposed to a fictitious news story about a company that was accused of using an unhealthy food additive. In one of the conditions, participants further read that the corporation had invited a (fictitious) consumer advocacy group to test its products. Subjects improved their assessment of the company after the announcement of the independent investigation compared to the condition of noinvestigation. An internal investigation conducted by the company had no such effect. After reading about the investigation by a consumer advocacy group, however, more liberal participants (a group usually associated with a more liberal "pro-consumer" agenda critical of business) rated the company higher compared to conservative participants. That is, the political orientation of the respondents had a significant effect on the shift in attitudes. There was no effect of political orientation on the impact of the internal investigation conducted by the company. That is, merely announcing the involvement of a third party with shared values shifted audience perception even if no new information was received.

The same effect can also be generated through direct priming (Heinze, Uhlmann, and Diermeier 2014). In an ostensibly unrelated "memory" study, participants read a paragraph about a college student who planned to volunteer over the summer in support of a political candidate who backed gun control, a typical liberal policy position. They were then exposed to the same fictitious news story about the company's use of a food additive. For participants in the liberal prime condition, an independent investigation by a consumer advocacy group led to more positive company evaluations than no investigation.[43]

Being aware of these distinctions is of significant practical importance. The use of third-party experts is a very common strategy when companies are confronted with a skeptical public. For example, in the "worm meat" crisis, McDonald's used the US Department of Agriculture for this purpose. Such strategies are also known as "credibility transfer" (Diermeier 2011). According to the Consonance Principle, however, what matters most is not general domain expertise, but cultural credibility that is based on a tight value-based match between the expert and the audience. If such a match is present, the effect can be quite strong. Subjects even reverse attitudes on policy issues that they would otherwise hold. Indeed, even the mere announcement of the involvement of a third party with matched values can significantly shift beliefs and attitudes.

The fifth and final principle relates to the dynamics of attitude change. Customers and other members of the public rarely take the time to evaluate the pros and cons associated with a given issue. Rather, they rely on general evaluations of a company or industry. It is such tallies that are first activated in response to a new impression. If the impression is sufficiently strong, for example, due to attention, affect, or congruence, the running tally is adjusted accordingly and stored in long-term memory, while the specific details of the event are quickly forgotten. This approach is known as the *online processing model* (Anderson 1965; Hastie and Park 1986; Lodge 1995; Lodge, Steenbergen, and Brau 1995; Lodge and Taber 2013) and has strong empirical support in public opinion research.[44] Lodge and Taber (2013, p. 51) summarize this approach as follows:

When people form or revise their overall impressions of persons, places, events, or issues, they are found to spontaneously extract the affective value of the message, and then within milliseconds integrate their appraisal of the object into their prior evaluation, all without any conscious query of memory for a set of considerations on which to compute an updated evaluation.... The "running" OL tally, representing an automatic integration of all prior evaluations of the object, is then restored to long-term memory where it is readily available for subsequent evaluations.

We can capture this in the following principle.

Online Processing

Evaluations of entities are based on an online tally that, over time, aggregates experienced affect and considerations associated with an entity, while the specific details that originally gave rise to the evaluation are forgotten.

The online processing model has important consequences. At any point in time, an attitude is not based on a detailed evaluation of recalled or current considerations, but on the online tally, and thus on the history of affect-laden events. Online tallies effectively serve as impression and affect aggregators. If initial tallies are persistent, early impressions will dominate online tallies and thus attitudes, in line with the principles of attention, affect, and congruence. In contrast, the recall of *specific* considerations is aided by recency. Thus, subjects may have forgotten the details that shaped their evaluation of a company but retain a basic, global attitude. When asked to state their preference, for example, in a survey, they may search their memory for supporting evidence. Now more recent impressions will come to mind more easily. By the Consonance Principle, impressions that are consistent with the general assessment will be retrieved more readily. Thus, such considerations may well be coherent with their current evaluations, but may have little to do with the *original* considerations that influenced a particular evaluation in the first place. Rather, they constitute post hoc rationalizations of an existing general attitude shaped by a general evaluative tally.

From a practical point of view, this means that great care should be utilized when interpreting survey responses related to the public perception of a corporation. Consider the following example. Suppose that in a survey a significant segment of the public states that it dislikes McDonald's because the company pays its workers low wages. Moreover, suppose that in an open-ended questionnaire respondents overwhelmingly state strong support for paying a "living wage." Finally, suppose that rigorous statistical analysis reveals that attitudes on living wage pay issues correlate most highly with the dislike of McDonald's. It is thus natural to conclude that the best reputation management strategy for McDonald's is to pay higher wages. Let us assume that the company decides to do so. A few months later a new survey is conducted and trust likability scores are as low as they were before; McDonald's has been unable to improve its reputation but its labor costs have increased.

Online processing can account for such puzzling phenomena. For example, suppose our respondents formed a negative impression of McDonald's a long time ago, for example, by watching the movie *Supersize Me*. The focus of that movie was concern over nutrition, not wage levels, but these details tend to be quickly forgotten by the public. What matters is that the movie created an initial negative affect that, via confirmation bias, led to biased selection of information sources about McDonald's, such as reading the book *Fast Food Nation* (Schlosser 2002), which is highly critical of McDonald's and its business practices. Over time, this process will lead to a negative online tally toward McDonald's, while the underlying reasons and concerns are largely forgotten or are no longer salient. For example, the graphic depiction of labor and hygiene standards in *Fast Food Nation* may have created significant negative affect, while the details of the book, even the companies mentioned, may have been forgotten.[45] When now queried about McDonald's in a phone survey, subjects report their negative online tally. When prompted for a reason, due to the recency principle they are most likely to recall some current controversy related to McDonald's, say over the issue of a living wage. Subjects may then report that reason because it is at the top of their mind, even though it never played an important role in their initial assessment of McDonald's. The stated reason is influenced by recency, while the overall evaluation is shaped by attention, affect, and congruence as summarized in an online tally.

2.4 Methodological Implications

The turn toward a cognitivist model of opinion formation has important methodological consequences. Importantly, approaches that focus on the the dominant use of mass surveys need to be complemented by in-depth experimental and other approaches that focus on identifying and mapping implicit and preconscious attitudes. Such methodologies will generate additional insights and improve the design and interpretation of opinion surveys.

These methods employ implicit measurement techniques that directly evaluate underlying attitudes without reference to explicit responses. A large number of these techniques exist and have been utilized in a variety of fields. Uhlmann et al. (2012) provide an excellent introduction to these techniques and classify them into three categories depending on whether they focus on accessibility, association, or interpretation.

The first group of implicit measurement techniques are accessibility-based measures used to assess whether a concept is easily accessible in a respondent's memory. Classic examples of this type include the lexical decision task and the Stroop task (Collins and Loftus 1975; Stroop 1935). For the lexical decision task, respondents are asked to verify that a string of letters is a proper word, while the Stroop task asks respondents to describe a word or object in the face of an irrelevant but influential stimulus.[46] In both cases, researchers use a subject's response times as an indicator of a concept's accessibility, with longer response times indicating less accessible concepts. These tasks provide insight into an individual's evaluations of singular concepts and are standards for assessing familiarity and the function of memory. However, these tasks are less useful for examining affective dispositions toward a concept and the relationships between multiple concepts.

In contrast to accessibility-based measures, association-based measures seek to determine whether a set of concepts is linked in an individual's memory. The implicit association task (IAT) and various priming measures are the canonical examples of this category of measure (Fazio et al. 1995; Greenwald, McGhee, and Schwartz 1998; Greenwald et al. 2009). In both of these techniques, respondents are tasked with evaluating a target concept in light of a simultaneously or previously presented stimulus. These additional stimuli are designed to influence the subject's evaluation of the target in expected ways, and responses are recorded either in the form of reaction times to a classification task or via self-reported evaluations. Taken together, these two techniques have formed the core of a large body of research on underlying attitudes and beliefs.

In an IAT, subjects are presented with two opposing concepts and a host of related synonyms and related objects. For instance, subjects may encounter a test involving the concepts "like" and "don't like" as well as the concepts "fruit" and "not fruit." In the core components of the test, subjects are asked to categorize examples from these two groups according to some rule. For instance, during one round of the test, subjects might be asked to determine whether the presented pair is either a fruit or a synonym for "like." However, in another round this categorization rule will change and subjects might be asked to determine whether the pairing either is *not* a fruit or is a synonym for "like."

The logic behind this iterative procedure is that, by comparing response times to this categorization task, researchers can determine how strongly the two overarching categories are associated. For instance, quick response times under the fruit/like condition compared to the not-fruit/like condition are taken as evidence that the subject prefers fruit over nonfruit items. This interpretation is based on the idea that subjects are slower to classify pairings that are incompatible to them. Further, by iterating through all combinations of these pairings and rules, average response times can be determined and a full picture of the relationships between the concepts can be established.

While an individual's views toward fruit are hardly a complex issue, IATs have been developed to assess a variety of complex and sensitive social issues. For instance, in an IAT assessing racial bias, researchers might compare a subject's response time when simultaneously shown the words "black" and "angry" with their response time when shown the words "white" and "angry." In this case, for individuals with relatively negative attitudes toward blacks, researchers expect to see faster reaction times in the black-angry condition than in the white-angry condition due to a stronger association between blacks and anger (Banaji and Greenwald 2013; Sabin et al. 2009).[47]

In contrast to the complexity of IATs, many priming studies rely on a much simpler framework to assess the connections between a target and a stimulus. For example, in a priming study designed to assess racial bias, individuals might be asked to classify words as positive or negative (e.g., happy, sad, angry, joyous, depressive) after having been primed by briefly viewing a picture of a white or Black individual (Fazio et al. 1995).[48] For subjects with a negative view of Blacks, response times to the negative/Black conditions are expected to be faster than response times to the positive/Black conditions. Once again, the logic behind this disparity in response times is that the incompatibility of the two ideas (i.e., "Black" and "positive") leads to respondents taking more time to provide the correct answer.[49]

While these two techniques use different types of measurements, they both aim to illuminate the connection between a target concept and a stimulus. Such connections are especially informative when the prime has a clear negatively valence and the goal is to assess whether the target is also viewed negatively. The ability to assess these connections has caused the IAT and priming tasks to become the most widely used tools to assess implicit attitudes.

Interpretation-based approaches seek to evaluate attitudes and beliefs based on individuals' interpreted responses to intentionally vague queries. The basic premise of these techniques is that individuals with specific underlying attitudes will respond to vague stimuli differently. In theory, clear patterns in responses to ambiguous prompts indicate a well-defined and powerful underlying attitude that shapes interpretations in a particular way.

The Rorschach inkblot test is perhaps the best-known of this type (Rorschach 1927). In a Rorschach test, subjects are asked to interpret a series of inkblots with no obvious pattern or meaning. Researchers subsequently examine the subject's interpretations for patterns or themes that dominate the subjects descriptions and, in theory, their general attitudes and beliefs.

While the Rorschach test is widely known, there is also considerable debate about its effectiveness and, importantly, its consistency across researchers. This inconsistency is largely due to the especially vague nature of the test and the amount of interpretation required on the part of the researcher to make sense of a subject's responses. While this would appear to be a major concern for all interpretation-based approaches, recent innovations such as conditional reasoning tests offer more reliable and well-defined interpretation-based measures and have become widely used techniques (James 1998).

In a conditional reasoning test (CRT), a subject is presented with a scenario and asked to select one of (usually) four multiple-choice responses that best characterizes the situation. Of the possible responses, two are usually entirely irrelevant and do not deal with the situation at hand. Of the remaining two, one is worded in such a way that a subject exhibiting the bias of interest would find it especially appealing, while the other is more "pro-social" and does not indicate an underlying bias, or indicates an opposing bias.[50]

For example, in a CRT designed to assess aggression, a subject might be asked to identify the biggest problem with the rule "an eye for an eye."

While many subjects will cite the saying's lack of a peaceful conflict resolution method, subjects predisposed to aggressive behaviors will lament
the fact that one must first be victimized before being able to strike back,
that is, the saying precludes preemptive violence (LeBreton, Grimaldi, and
Schoen 2020).

Taken together, implicit measurement techniques offer considerable
insight into underlying attitudes and can reveal attitudes and beliefs that
diverge considerably from those observed using explicit measurement.
The ability to differentiate between these two forms of attitudes allows
academics to examine the relationships between them and uncover, for
instance, when one dominates the other as a source of a specific behavior. In business contexts, these techniques have been predominantly used
in the context of employees, for instance, to assess and address racial or
gender bias among employees (e.g., Bohnet 2016; McCormick 2016; Staats
2015; Van Bavel and West 2017). In such applications, these techniques
have clear advantages over explicit measurement techniques that are subject to lying and nonresponses due to social desirability. Other applications
can be found in marketing and brand management (Dempsey and Mitchell
2010; Wennekers et al. 2015). But, to the best of our knowledge, they have
not been used in the area of corporate reputation.

Once such measures of implicit attitudes are obtained, one can use them
to develop communication strategies. For example, if Whole Foods scores
higher than other food retailers on sustainability, this finding can be the
basis of a communication or CSR strategy. Alternatively, companies may
be interested in changing implicit attitudes and associations. The ability
to change implicit attitudes has been most extensively studied in the context of workplace bias and stereotyping. Popular bias-reduction techniques
include imagined contact (e.g., Dermody, Jones, and Cummin 2013; Garcia
et al. 2002; Wright et al. 1997), evaluative conditioning (Olson and Fazio
2006), counterstereotype scenarios (e.g., Dasgupta and Greenwald 2001;
Foroni and Mayr 2005), cross-cutting group competition (e.g., Lai et al.
2016; Riek, Mania, and Gaertner 2006), and empathetic identification (e.g.,
Todd et al. 2011).[51]

The evidence for the impact of these strategies, however, has been
mixed at best. For instance, in their review of 492 studies and 11 different bias-reduction techniques, Forscher et al. (2019) find that only
about half of the techniques succeeded in producing reliable changes
in the measured attitude.[52] Further, even among those studies with significant effects, the resulting changes were often small.[53] For instance,

interventions employing counterstereotypical scenarios or empathetic perspective taking succeeded in shifting measured biases by a standardized mean difference of only around 0.30.[54]

In sum, there is only very limited evidence for the sustained impact of bias-reduction strategies. Of course, the domain of racial and gender bias may be particularly resistant to interventions. That said, the available evidence points out that implicit attitudes are likely to be "sticky" and can persist for extended periods of time. This suggests that reputation management strategies should be less focused on changing such attitudes, especially when time is short and resources are limited. Instead, they should focus on designing strategies that are aware of these patterns and take them into account as quasi-constraints that should be assumed as fixed, at least in the short run. This makes a proper measurement of implicit attitudes and associations particularly important.

2.5 Summary

In this part we explored some of the factors that shape opinion formation at the microlevel. Our approach was based on the premise that attitudes and opinions about a company are not stored in a mental database where they can be retrieved from memory, but are constructed in each given instance, such as being prompted by a query or needing to make a decision, for instance, to purchase a certain product. The approach is fundamentally cognitivist. It requires a thorough understanding of how associations are formed, stored, retrieved, and integrated into attitudes. Such an understanding can then be used to shape the development of reputation management strategies. From the growing research on the role of cognitive processes in public perception and attitude formation we identified six major principles.

Repetition

Repeated exposure to entities makes it more likely that such entities are encoded in memory.

Recency

More recent impressions are more likely to be activated and retrieved from memory.

Attention

The greater a person's level of attention, the more likely he or she is to be aware of an impression, to memorize it, and to recall it.

Affect

Affect influences the coding, formation, storage, and retrieval of memories and attitudes.

Consonance

Messages that are consonant with a person's current beliefs or attitudes are more likely to be sought out, received, accepted, and stored in memory. Messages that are inconsistent with a person's current beliefs or attitudes are less likely to be sought out, received, accepted, and stored in memory. Messages that are neutral will tend to be interpreted in line with a person's current beliefs and attitudes.

Online Processing

Evaluations of entities are based on an online tally that, over time, aggregates experienced affect and considerations associated with an entity, while the specific details that originally gave rise to the evaluation are forgotten.

Importantly, these principles operate not only on uninformed observers, but also on well-informed and engaged audiences. Indeed, in many instances the effects are stronger for such sophisticated audiences (Lodge and Taber 2013). This cognitive approach resolves the various methodological problems of survey research in a fruitful way. What appears random and unstable to an observer makes sense once we realize that attitudes are constructed, not simply reported. Opinions and attitudes are not fixed entries in a database, but are the result of complex encoding, storage, and retrieval processes governed by a network of associations stored in long-term memory. These networks change over time due to external factors such as personal experience, media coverage, or peer influence. It is therefore to be expected that answers in a survey change over time, even if there is no "material" change in the issue environment that would explain such changes. Question wording, sequencing, and priming effects can all be explained in this context. Such effects do not constitute mere measurement error but are evidence for the mental processes of attitude formation.

This constructionist perspective can deepen our understanding of the processes of opinion formation, but it also has direct practical consequences. For example, the combination of online processing, affect, congruence, and recency implies that we need to be very cautious when interpreting the reasons given by members of the public for why they like or dislike a certain company. Often the basic attitude about the company is derived from an online tally that aggregates prior experiences and attitudes, while the details are forgotten. If queried, subjects will tend to form their attitudes based on deep-seated online tallies. If an interviewer then asks for a reason for the expressed opinion, subjects will tend to retrieve recent issues, such as those related to current media stories. Yet these issues may be entirely unrelated to the original events that shaped the respondent's attitude and are mere rationalizations of an already existing, affect-laden opinion. Moreover, consistent with the congruence and affect principles, respondents will tend to recall specific issues that are congruent with the experienced affect. That is, if a subject expresses a negative opinion, issues that are congruent with the valence of the expressed opinion will more easily come to mind. But these reasons are mere rationalizations; they did not cause the negative attitude.

If companies naïvely respond to the expressed concerns, for example, by changing their business practices in response to survey data that capture concerns over a given issue, they are missing the deeper reasons for the expressed negative opinion which are rooted in a network of associations expressed in an online tally. A better approach is to map out such association networks using experimental methods and then develop strategies that address specific areas of concern. Such strategies need to be consistent with the constructivist nature of opinion formation. For example, simply providing additional information may backfire in polarized issue contexts and merely intensify existing value orientations, leading to increased polarization. In such cases, using third parties with cultural credibility may be much more effective.

The principles of consonance and online processing also suggest that companies are well advised to engage with emerging issues early in each issue's life cycle. This requires the ability to identify, assess, and track emerging issues (Diermeier 2011). In the last part of this book we discuss how the insights developed here can be used to develop such dynamic issue management capabilities.

The processes captured in the six principles are general in nature. They apply equally to attitudes about issue areas, policies, candidates, products, ingredients, companies, or sports teams. Together they provide an organizing framework and operate on many issue domains. In the next part, we discuss the application of these principles in three domains that are of paramount importance in the context of corporate reputation: moral judgments, risk perception, and trust.

PART II
Perception, Attitudes, and Behavior

CHAPTER THREE

Evaluations, Attitudes, and the Role of Values

In contrast to political domains, attitudes towards companies are not easily summarized by partisan leanings or general ideologies. There is no simple equivalent to the concept of "party identification" widely used to conceptualize public opinion in politics (Campbell et al. 1960; Converse 1966). When it comes to companies, public attitudes seem to be far less stable and more multifaceted. Some appear to correlate with political values (e.g., opinions toward a company's decision to offer benefits to same-sex couples). Others appear to be universal (e.g., concern about food safety) and unconnected with ideological orientations.

Reputational challenges can originate in most, if not all, business contexts. Consider the list of crises mentioned in the introduction.

This list comprises different industries, issues, locations, and products. It contains US and international companies and even some nonprofits. But these cases do have various features in common. Consider, for example, the main emotion associated with each crisis. For example, in many safety crises, the immediate emotion is fear, while in crises triggered by concerns over executive compensation, the primary emotional response is anger or outrage. Sometimes an initial emotion (e.g., fear) is followed by another (e.g., anger), for example, when management in a safety crisis is seen as unresponsive. Let us reconsider our list of crises from this perspective.

TABLE 3.1 **Reputational crises examples**

Company	Issue
Toyota	Unintended acceleration
Goldman Sachs	Improper investment disclosure
J. P. Morgan Chase	Rogue trading
Standard Charter	Money laundering
News Corp.	Phone hacking
BP	Industrial accident
Costa Concordia	Accident
Wal-Mart	Bribery
Mattel	Lead paint in toys
Paula Deen	Racism and discrimination
Chick-fil-A	Position on gay rights
Barilla	Position on gay rights
Susan G. Komen Foundation	Funding cuts to Planned Parenthood
Livestrong Foundation	Cheating by founder Lance Armstrong
AIG	Executive compensation
Netflix	Pricing
Ergo	Paying prostitutes to reward employees
Apple	Labor standards at supplier FoxConn
H&M	Collapse of Rana Plaza garment factory
FIFA	Corruption
Volkswagen	Deception and environmental pollution
Enron	Accounting fraud
WorldCom	Accounting fraud
Arthur Andersen	Faulty audits
Facebook	Privacy and Cambridge Analytica scandal
Texaco	Racism
United Airlines	Dragging customer off plane

As we can see, outrage is almost always present. Even in the Toyota case, initial fear gave way to outrage due to the perceived lack of responsiveness by Toyota management. Interestingly, sometimes the outrage directed at a company comes from the company's stance on a social issue, such as gay rights in the case of Barilla, or a company action that is viewed as violating a universal norm, such as decent labor standards at Apple's supplier FoxConn.[1] Yet in other cases, outrage is triggered by the perception that a promise had been broken, such as the case of Netflix, which significantly increased prices for loyal subscribers.

In sum, our casual review of recent crises hints at two main reputational risk factors.

- Moral outrage: This factor is based on a perceived violation of deeply held norms and values.
- Fear: This factor is based on a perceived danger or threat to oneself or others.

TABLE 3.2 **Reputational crises examples with emotional component**

Company	Issue	Associated emotion
Toyota	Unintended acceleration	Fear
Goldman Sachs	Improper investment disclosure	Outrage
J. P. Morgan Chase	Rogue trading	Both
Standard Charter	Money laundering	Outrage
News Corp.	Phone hacking	Outrage
BP	Industrial accident	Both
Costa Concordia	Accident	Both
Wal-Mart	Bribery	Outrage
Mattel	Lead paint in toys	Both
Paula Deen	Racism and discrimination	Outrage
Chick-fil-A	Position on gay rights	Outrage
Barilla	Position on gay rights	Outrage
Susan G. Komen Foundation	Funding cuts to Planned Parenthood	Outrage
Livestrong Foundation	Cheating by founder Lance Armstrong	Outrage
AIG	Executive compensation	Outrage
Netflix	Pricing	Outrage
Ergo	Paying prostitutes to reward employees	Outrage
Apple	Labor standards at supplier FoxConn	Outrage
H&M	Collapse of Rana Plaza garment factory	Outrage
FIFA	Corruption	Outrage
Volkswagen	Deception and environmental pollution	Outrage
Enron	Accounting fraud	Outrage
WorldCom	Accounting fraud	Outrage
Arthur Andersen	Faulty audits	Outrage
Facebook	Privacy and Cambridge Analytica scandal	Both
Texaco	Racism	Outrage
United Airlines	Dragging customer off plane	Both

For each category, we can identify the main psychological processes that drive an emotional response. This will then allow us to classify issues with respect to their crisis potential and develop effective anticipation and response strategies. While moral outrage is driven by norms and values, risk perception is related to beliefs. Yet, as we will see later, the relationship between beliefs and values is fluid and interconnected. This is especially true for the issue of *trust*, which we will discuss separately. Trust lies at the intersection of ethical norms and belief formation. On the one hand, perceptions of broken promises made by a company constitute a particularly important case of norm violation. On the other hand, trust, like risk perception, involves belief formation. When we trust someone we believe that they will follow through on a given promise, often in situations where we may be vulnerable. For companies, this combination of norms and beliefs creates specific challenges that need to be carefully managed.

3.1 Moral Intuitions and Values

Our first category is moral outrage. Moral outrage is the emotional response triggered by a perceived violation of deeply held norms or values captured by various fundamental ethical principles.

3.1.1 Do No Harm

The first fundamental principle is the *avoidance of harm* (Turiel 1983). Moral judgments in response to human suffering are fundamental. Responses to suffering develop early in life (Hamlin, Wynn, and Bloom 2007) and can even be found in some animals (de Waal 2006). They can already be detected in young children, even before they can verbalize such feelings, and are common across human cultures.[2] When asked to name an "act that is morally wrong," 51 percent of respondents named examples of direct, physical harm (Gray Young, and Waytz 2012; Schein and Gray 2015), and the avoidance of harm frequently prevails in value conflicts (van Leeuwen and Park 2011). The paradigmatic setting for the "do no harm" principle is the care of young children. The moral and emotional response is triggered by expressions of suffering and need (Haidt 2013a). Its corresponding duty is care; its characteristic emotion is empathy.

The emotional mechanism for the do-no-harm principle is the empathic aversion of pain in others (e.g., Hoffman 2001; Preston and de Waal 2001). Moral judgments of blame emerge when empathic aversion to harm is combined with intentionality and causation (Gray, Young, and Waytz 2012). Specifically, judgments of blame appear to be driven by attributions of causal responsibility for harm that has occurred, due to inferences of either not foreseeing probable harm, intending to cause harm, or desiring to cause harm (Lagnado and Channon 2008; Weiner 1985).

In corporate contexts, incidents of harm often emerge from issues related to accidents, safety, or environmental damage, the traditional domains of the corporate function Environment, Health, and Safety (EHS). Product safety crises, for example, lead to reduced sales and undermine a company's position in the marketplace (e.g., Cleeren, Dekimpe, and van Heerde 2017; Pennings, Wansink, and Meulenberg 2002; Rubel, Naik, and Srinivasan 2011; van Heerde, Helsen, and Dekimpe 2007). Barrage, Chyn, and Hastings (2020) study the impact of the 2010 BP oil spill and find a 4.2 percent impact on sales and up to an 18 percent impact on gas station margins, though these effects are mitigated by precrisis advertising.

The do-no-harm principle implies that companies are viewed as having a general duty to avoid harm. This is even true for products that are inherently risky such as cigarettes, motorbikes, or chainsaws. In cases of accidents, even if they were caused by customers' improper handling of products, companies will often be blamed. We can see this clearly in the Toyota example. Even though there was evidence that unintended acceleration was due to the improper installation of floor mats, the public was reluctant to blame the victims.

This pattern can be explained by research that has found that when evaluating a transgression, people rely on a basic cognitive template of perpetrator and victim. For example, when presented with apparently "victimless" offenses, respondents still perceived a victim 89% of the time after they judged the action as wrong (DeScioli, Gilbert, and Kurzban 2012). In the perpetrator-victim template, the perpetrator is powerful and causes harm to the weaker victim. This pattern naturally maps onto the company (the powerful perpetrator) versus consumers or employees (the powerless victims).[3]

It is difficult for people to process a case in which the perpetrator is the one who is harmed or in which the victim is the one who caused the harm (Gray, Young, and Waytz 2012). The difficulty of blaming drivers (and the relative ease in assigning blame to Toyota or Porsche), even in cases where drivers acted carelessly or irresponsibly, is due to the violation of this standard cognitive template. While drivers may have improperly installed the floor mats, they were also the ones who were harmed. Neither party thus aligns with its usual role in the cognitive template related to the do-no-harm principle. Thus, Toyota was blamed because consumers were weaker and harmed, while Toyota was powerful and unharmed. Critically, assessments of harm depend on the extent to which victims are clearly identifiable and seen as experiencing pain and suffering. To the extent that the victims of a transgression are diffuse or abstract, perpetrators of harm usually will not be blamed.[4] This is why the emergency call was so critical in triggering the Toyota crisis: it made the victims salient and identifiable (Jenni and Loewenstein 1997; Small and Loewenstein 2003, 2005).

The expectation of care implies that during a safety concern or after an accident, companies are well advised to express empathy, even if they do not believe they are at fault. Expressions of empathy are a natural consequence of the care paradigm, and if they are absent, the company is viewed as cold and uncaring. Such expressions need to be authentic and fit with the identity of the company and the personality of its CEO or chairman. While it needs to balance such expressions of care with other concerns, such as legal risks, a company must understand that if it chooses to forgo any expressions of regret, care, or empathy and pursue a highly guarded, overly legalistic approach, it will be perceived negatively and suffer reputational consequences.

PRIMUM NON NOCERE. In line with these findings, Minor and Morgan (2011) have argued that the principle "first, do no harm" (*primum non nocere*), known from the Hippocratic Oath, should be the basis of corporate reputation management. While doing good, for example, investing in CSR activities, can have some positive impact, the impact from doing harm is disproportionately higher.[5] In his study of stock prices and the impact of product recalls by S&P 500 companies, Minor (2015) finds that CSR activities can function as "reputation insurance" for companies, that is, the impact of a recall on their stock price is much smaller than that experienced by companies that have not engaged in CSR.[6] Brand equity may also serve as a buffer (Cleeren, Dekimpe, and Helsen 2008; Hsu and Lawrence 2016; Lei, Dawar, and Gurhan-Canli 2012). However, the impact strongly depends on the company's response (Dawar and Pillutla 2000). Moreover, customers with high expectations react more negatively, especially in severe cases (Germann et al. 2014; Liu and Shankar 2015).

The magnitude of sympathy, and thus expectations of care, varies with the specific characteristics of the situation. This provides an intuitive assessment of the reputational risk imposed by the do-no-harm principle. The risk is particularly high in the case of population segments that are considered especially vulnerable. Those include children, the elderly, the sick, injured, and handicapped, but also the indigent and minorities. They may also include animals, especially animals that look "cute," such as baby seals. These categories of victims are seen as especially capable of feeling pain and suffering, while also being seen as largely incapable of having control over their actions and thus unlikely to elicit blame. This means, for example, that a car company that develops a new car designed for young families will face a higher reputational risk than if it develops a new sports car intended for wealthy executives. Companies frequently underestimate these effects, especially when they enter new market segments or introduce new products.

Mercedes's introduction of the A-class, discussed in chapter 2, was such an example. The car was marketed toward families with young children, a significant departure from Mercedes's traditional market positioning as a luxury car. In its advertising campaign, Mercedes even used drawings by young children. When the controversy over the failed Moose Test broke out, Mercedes was surprised by the level of fear and concern conveyed in the media. But the response was a direct consequence of the increased level of perceived potential harm that could be done to young families (Diermeier 2011).

Somewhat surprisingly, the actual number of victims is largely irrelevant for the level of sympathy. Observers feel very little difference between 96 and 97 victims. This effect of "psychic numbing" (e.g., Slovic 2000) is particularly striking for very large numbers of victims, for example, in genocides. People feel little difference if the number of genocide victims turns out to be 400,000 rather than 200,000. Former Soviet leader Joseph Stalin allegedly expressed this phenomenon cynically as follows:

> The death of one man is a tragedy, the death of millions is a statistic.

Conversely, the emotional response to harm is enhanced if there are sympathetic, identifiable victims with a clear sense of suffering. Charitable contributions, for example, significantly increase in the presence of identifiable victims as opposed to abstract statistics (Jenni and Loewenstein 1997; Kogut and Ritov 2005; Small and Loewenstein 2003). Small, Loewenstein, and Slovic (2007) provide evidence that the mere presence of statistics can undermine the sympathetic victim effect. Respondents who were shown a picture of an African girl suffering from hunger contributed twice as much to charity as subjects who were given statistical information. But, strikingly, if both the picture and the statistical information were presented simultaneously, contributions dropped to the same level as when only statistical information was presented. This effect is expressed in the famous quote attributed to Mother Teresa (Small, Loewenstein, and Slovic 2007):

> If I look at the mass I will never act. If I look at the one, I will.

THE TROLLEY PROBLEM.   Recent research by social and cognitive psychologists has indicated that the degree of perceived harm and associated responsibility can vary due to the specifics of the situation. This has been studied extensively in the context of the so-called trolley problem:[7]

> Suppose a runaway trolley is about to run over and kill five people. Suppose further that you can hit a switch that will divert the trolley onto a different set

of tracks where it will kill only one person instead of five. Is it okay to hit the switch?

The trolley scenario was originally introduced as a moral dilemma, an instance where different moral intuitions conflict. Ethical intuitions based on maximizing aggregate welfare, such as utilitarianism, imply that the person has a moral obligation to hit the switch. Though this may conflict with a duty to refrain from killing innocents, most people respond that they would hit the switch. Their response changes, however, with the following variant:

> Now, what if the only way to save the five people were to push a large person (larger than yourself) in front of the trolley, killing him but saving the others? Would that be okay?

Now most people say "no," even though the consequences in terms of life and death are identical. The reason is a basic reluctance to inflict personal harm actively and directly, intuitively capturing the difference between killing and letting die. Subsequent research has established three principles that moderate moral judgment in these contexts (Cushman, Young, and Hauser 2006). The *contact principle* states that using physical contact to cause harm to a victim is morally worse than causing equivalent harm to a victim without using physical contact. In the trolley example, pushing a person onto the track certainly involves physical contact; though, as we will see, the use of physical force is not the only relevant difference between the two scenarios. To isolate the dimension of physical contact, consider a variant of the scenario where a person can be dropped onto the tracks by throwing the person physically over the bridge or by pulling a switch that activates a trap door. Not surprisingly, pulling the trap door is seen as less objectionable. Subsequent research has shown that it is not physical proximity that is most important, but direct physical contact (Greene et al. 2009; Mikhail 2007).

We can also see the contact principle at work in reverse, that is, when an action causes a benefit. The contact principle suggests that executives should bestow such benefits in person if possible. French king Louis XIV, for example, was known to make all military officer appointments in person (Finer 1999).

The *causation principle* states that harm caused by an action is morally worse than an otherwise equivalent harm caused by an omission.[8] Putting poison in someone's drink is worse than failing to tell them it is already there. This phenomenon is also illustrated by the trolley problem above and is often referred to as the omission bias (Spranca, Minsk, and Baron 1991). It has also been widely discussed in moral philosophy and jurisprudence (e.g., Nebel 2015; Prentice and Koehler 2002). To isolate the causation principle, we can again consider a modified version of the trolley problem. Suppose instead that a person is already standing on the tracks with his back to the oncoming trolley. Warning the person of the danger would cause the person to step off the tracks, with the result that five workers are killed. Failing to warn the person, a mere omission, would kill the person but save the others.

We can see the causation principle at work in the Toyota example. Toyota was accused of a safety defect in its vehicles that caused the unintended acceleration. Concern then shifted to the floor mats as the possible cause. These were bought from third-party vendors and installed by vehicle owners. Toyota could have warned customers about the possible danger of improperly installing the floor mats (it did so after the crisis broke), but this (perceived) "omission" played virtually no role in the criticism leveled at Toyota compared to the suspicion that Toyota built an unsafe vehicle in the first place.

The *intention principle* states that harm intended as a means to a goal is morally worse than otherwise equivalent harm that was foreseen as a mere side effect (Royzman and Baron 2002). The intention principle goes back to Thomas Aquinas's justification of self-defense and continues to be an important principle of Catholic ethics. In philosophy and ethics, it also became known as the doctrine of double effect.[9]

One of the paradigmatic cases is a doctor who administers his terminally ill patient a fatal dose of morphine. Most observers find it impermissible if the physician simply intended to bring about the patient's death by administering the morphine, while most observers find it permissible if the doctor intended to alleviate the patient's suffering, while being aware that the patient would die. In this case the patient's death is viewed as a side effect of a laudable goal. The goal, of course, must be praiseworthy. If it is not, the judgment reverses. Indeed, in the case of such a reversal, observers overestimate the harm caused (Pizarro et al. 2006).

The trolley problem is a perfect illustration of this effect. Throwing a person onto the track carries the intention of harm, even if it was as a means of saving the five. But consider the original trolley problem, in which a person is already standing on the second track. This removes the act of

throwing, or physical contact, and the dimension of causation. Now divert-
ing a runaway trolley with the same outcome is seen as permissible, as one
foresees the death of the one as a mere side effect of saving the five, but
one does not intend it. When flipping a switch, the death of the person can
be viewed as a mere side effect of saving the five.

The intention principle can play an important role with products that
customers desire, but that also carry risks or side effects. Examples include
cigarettes and unhealthy foods. In such cases, the negative health consequences are mere side effects of the product; the company is not perceived
as intentionally trying to make the products unhealthy, and their unhealthy
consequences are merely harmful side effects. Many observers give companies a pass in such settings and locate responsibility with the individual who
consumes the product. This perception changes if the company is known
to intentionally add the harmful ingredient, for example, to make the
product more addictive or less healthy, for example, by adding unhealthy
ingredients such as high-fructose corn syrup as a sweetener.

One of the best-known examples of this effect is the history of the US
tobacco industry. The US tobacco industry had faced reputational and
legal challenges for decades, most importantly the publication of the 1964
Report of the Advisory Committee to the Surgeon General on Smoking
and Health, which stated the existence of a causal link between cigarette
smoking and lung cancer and other diseases. Yet, despite growing health
concerns, the industry was able to weather all political, regulatory, and
legal challenges until the mid-1990s. This strategy was successful as long as
the industry, through a sustained PR campaign, claimed that smoking was
a choice made by adults. Hence, any negative health consequences were
the unfortunate side effects of a natural product, tobacco. The industry
claimed that it neither caused the harm nor had any intention of harming
smokers.

We will discuss the history of the tobacco industry in detail in chapter 7,
but it is instructive to see how important developments in the mid-1990s
significantly changed the reputational environment of the industry. A key
component was the leaking of industry documents that pointed to the
intentional manipulation of nicotine content to make cigarettes maximally
addictive.[10] Based on this evidence, the industry was viewed as intentionally causing harm, a development that dramatically increased the legal
and political risks for tobacco companies, eventually forcing the industry
to the bargaining table in a process that culminated in the 1998 Master
Settlement.

Another example is food ingredients believed to be harmful. The products most likely to cause outrage are cases where the company intentionally uses an ingredient, perceived to be unhealthy, for financial gain, for example, using high-fructose corn syrup as a less expensive alternative to sugar. Less blameworthy are cases where companies fail to reduce the unhealthy side effects of existing food products, such as French fries with high fat content. Still, even in those cases, companies may face an uphill battle if such ingredient changes are perceived to be easy, low-cost, and can be made without lowering the quality of the product, for example, by switching to a healthier cooking oil.

In sum, the do-no-harm principle is at the root of many situations that cause outrage and reputational damage. The principle is particularly important in health and safety contexts, and its violation can elicit strong emotional responses of anger and outrage. Recent research on moral intuitions and corresponding emotional responses in various settings has demonstrated the existence of cognitive templates and factors that impact the typical response to perceived violations of the do-no-harm principle. These patterns can serve as the basis for assessing the intrinsic reputational risk of products and business practices.

The duty to avoid harm, however, is not the only moral principle that drives moral perceptions. Jonathan Haidt and his colleagues (Graham et al. 2013; Graham, Haidt, and Nosek 2009; Haidt 2013a; Haidt and Graham 2007; Haidt and Joseph 2004, 2008) have systematized many of these principles as the *moral foundations theory*, which lists five fundamental moral principles that guide moral judgment.[11] The avoidance of harm is the first principle, and the next principle deals with issues of fairness, justice, and rights.[12]

3.1.2   Fairness — Justice — Rights

The second major principle of moral judgment is related to *fairness, justice, and rights*. It is a far more complex and contested domain than the harm principle. Indeed, it has been the main battleground of moral philosophy since Plato. While it is often argued that fairness is a fundamental moral concern of human beings everywhere (Haidt 2007; Turiel 1983), the concrete nature of what constitutes fairness is often unclear. Within the sphere of distributive justice alone, fairness may be based on equality, such that all parties receive an equal amount, or merit, such that each party receives an amount proportional to its input. It may be fair to give the greatest allocation to the most needy, or to the ones who made the largest contribution to the community. Understanding how people determine what is fair in different contexts is key to successfully managing corporate reputation.[13]

Different fairness intuitions can be illustrated by the following decision problem.

THE ULTIMATUM GAME.   Consider a simple bargaining setting, where two negotiators have a fixed amount of money to split, say $100. Now consider the following scenario. One of the negotiators ("the proposer") makes an offer to the other negotiator ("the responder"), who must either accept or reject it, with rejection resulting in a zero payoff for both. Only the proposer can make an offer; there is no opportunity for counteroffers. Now, put yourself in the shoes of a responder who has been offered $1, leaving $99 for the other player to keep for himself. How would you react?

Most people would grow angry and reject the offer, leaving both parties with nothing. Notice that there is something puzzling about this reaction. Should the responder not be rational and accept the $1—which is better than nothing? But this is not what happens. Instead, responders consistently reject offers below a certain threshold. That threshold varies by population but generally ranges from 30 to 50 percent of the total amount (Henrich et al. 2006). Some cultures are more tolerant of unfair distributions than others. Japan and Israel, for example, have lower offer thresholds than the US or many European countries. Moreover, proposers seem to anticipate this reaction and tend to offer proposals close to the acceptable amount, knowing that lowball offers face likely rejection. In most experiments, the modal offer is a 50-50 split, but, consistent with the expected behavior of respondents, the exact allocation varies by population (e.g., Camerer 2003). Indeed, in some cultures, proposers even offer more than half of the pie (Henrich et al. 2006).

Known as the ultimatum game, this choice situation is one of the most studied decision problems in modern experimental economics (Camerer 2003; Güth, Schmittberger, and Schwarze 1982; Henrich et al. 2006; Sanfey et al. 2003; Thaler 1988). In the early years after their publication, many economists were highly skeptical of these findings, dismissing them as artifacts. Various criticisms centered on the responder's ability to know the identity of the proposer, which may trigger concerns in the mind of the proposer about possible retaliation if proposals are too low. But subsequent experiments showed that negotiators leave substantial amounts of money on the table even if it is impossible to establish the identity of the other party (Bolton and Zwick 1995; Hoffman et al. 1994). Others suggested that the amounts used in actual experiments were too small to induce proper incentives. Yet the results broadly persisted even for larger amounts of money (Cameron 1999; Hoffman, McCabe, and Smith 1996). Finally, there were general concerns about the validity of laboratory experiments for understanding economic behavior and attitudes toward fairness (e.g., Camerer 2003; Rai and Fiske 2010; Camerer 2003). Over the years, these criticisms have mostly subsided. Experimental and behavioral economics are now established and rapidly growing subfields in economics, and the ultimatum game has become one of the workhorse models to study fairness concerns in economic exchange.[14]

The ultimatum game offers one of the clearest pieces of evidence for the existence of universal fairness norms.[15] Proposals that responders perceive as unfair trigger anger in respondents (Pillutla and Murninghan 1996) and induce their willingness to engage in costly punishment (Fehr, Fischbacher, and Kosfeld 2005). Interestingly, punishment is not only done by the affected party, the responder, but is also handed out by third-party observers, even if doing so is costly to them (Fehr and Fischbacher 2004). This suggests that fairness operates like a social norm (Bendor and Swistak 2001). It is not just a matter of the two participants, but third parties also feel the need to get involved and enforce the norm through punishment, even if such punishment is costly to them (Descioli and Kurzban 2009).

While the general behavioral phenomena established by the ultimatum game are now widely accepted, what is less clear is what explains the existence of such norms. One possible explanation points to altruistic preferences. Forsythe et al. (1994) designed a variant of the ultimatum game to explore the presence of altruism. In the so-called dictator game, the proposer unilaterally determines the allocation between the two players without any input from the respondent. Forsythe et al. (1994) found that proposers allocated substantial amounts to respondents even when they served as dictators. The allocated amounts, however, are dramatically reduced in double-blind experiments (Hoffman et al. 1994). Since double-blind designs eliminate the risk of being found in noncompliance, they largely eliminate substantial allocations to the responder in the dictator game and somewhat reduce them in the ultimatum game, although, in the latter, substantial amounts are still allocated to the responder and responders still reject insufficient offers. This suggests that the motivation behind fair allocations is not simply altruistic preferences, but is instead the proposer's desire to be seen in compliance with fairness norms (Binmore and Samuelson 1994).

While they are potent drivers of behavior, fairness norms can be quite subtle and can vary depending on the situation. Hoffman et al. (1994) consider the case where the right to propose is earned by performing better on a general knowledge test. When the right to propose is earned, proposers offer less to respondents and respondents are willing to accept these lower offers. Thus, both proposers and respondents appear to settle on a different norm that corresponds to a less equal distribution in cases where the right to propose is "earned," that is, based on performance in a test perceived as fair. These results suggest that fairness norms may not hinge solely on a desire for equality, but may include other moral principles, such as a sense of proportionality to performance or effort that makes more inequality acceptable under certain conditions. Further evidence of this contextual variation can be seen in other experiments. For example, simply calling the proposer a "seller" and the respondent a "buyer," suggesting a market transaction where the seller is entitled to make the offer, leads to reduced offers and more willingness to accept unequal proposals (Hoffman et al. 1994).

The idea of "rights" can be sharpened by considering variants of the ultimatum game, where the proposer and respondent receive unique, nonzero payoffs in the event of a rejection—their respective "disagreement values." This modified game can be compared to the standard ultimatum game where both players have a disagreement value of zero (Diermeier and Gailmard 2003, 2006). For example, in the revised game, the proposers may keep $3 (of the $10 to be allocated) if the proposal is rejected, rather than $0 as in the standard ultimatum game.[16] We can view this as a simplified version of an entitlement or right. Note that, in contrast to the Hoffman et al. results, here the entitlement is not earned, but simply assigned. In this setting, proposers demand more if their own disagreement value is higher and respondents accept more unequal offers, suggesting that the participants interpret even arbitrarily assigned disagreement values of the proposer as an entitlement that deserves to be respected (Diermeier and Gailmard 2006).

Overall, these results suggest the importance of framing in the context of fairness concerns. Simply renaming an interaction or assigning arbitrary disagreement values that can be interpreted as rights changes what is considered fair in a given situation and determines how individuals behave. Developing effective frames is both important and difficult, as we discuss in detail in chapter 7.

PRICING.   Perceptions of injustice are at the heart of many reputational problems, and fairness concerns can lead to severe reputational problems. An important area for fairness concerns is pricing in markets where the customers are seen as particularly vulnerable or having few options. Such transactions are structurally similar to the ultimatum game, where the recipient is in a very weak bargaining position and is confronted with a take-it-or-leave-it offer. One example is pricing for life-saving drugs or medical treatments.[17] In 2001, GlaxoSmithKline's AIDS drug Combivir, for example, sold for $7,000, while the active ingredient could be purchased for only $240 on the international generic market (Peterson 2001). By insisting on the higher price, pharmaceutical companies are often perceived as a "greedy" proposer in the ultimatum game taking advantage of a terminally ill patient.

Drug companies justify high retail prices with the substantial cost of investing in new drug research. They estimate that it costs nearly $800 million to bring a new drug to market (e.g., Goozner 2004). Companies then recoup these development costs over the lifetime of the drug by pricing the drug above the marginal cost for producing it. R&D-driven drug companies therefore need to charge higher prices compared to the price charged by generic manufacturers, which do not need to amortize these same costs of development. In 2000, for example, GlaxoSmithKline spent $4 billion on research (Peterson 2001).

The ability of drug companies to charge higher prices is due to patent protection. A patent gives inventors an intellectual property right to exclude others from making, using, offering for sale, or selling an invention in a given market for a limited time in exchange for public disclosure of the invention. A patent term of 20 years from the date of filing is common. As a consequence, drug companies enjoy a temporary monopoly during the term of the patent which allows them to raise prices accordingly and recover their costs of development.

While this argument is widely accepted among economists, it remains highly controversial among the public and leads to ongoing reputational challenges for the industry. Laypeople have difficulties accepting the R&D incentive argument. A main reason for the public skepticism of R&D incentives is that, contrary to economic principles, the public typically assumes that the amount of wealth is fixed (e.g., Caplan 2002; Róycka-Tran, Boski, and Wojciszke 2015). This so-called zero-sum fallacy then naturally leads observers to focus on a fixed pie and how it should be distributed, rather than how the pie is produced and how it can be grown. Once distributional concerns become central, attention shifts from issues of efficiency and wealth creation to issues of fairness. But, in the context of fair distributions, the company is perceived in the same fashion as the proposer in the ultimatum game, exploiting an unfair bargaining advantage. That is, once we focus on distributional issues, the pricing of drugs seems blatantly unfair, depriving terminally ill patients of life-saving drugs.

In an effort to counteract the reputational damage, some pharmaceutical companies have lowered their drug prices. Bristol-Myers Squibb and Merck both announced significant discounts to their AIDS drug cocktails, with Bristol-Myers Squibb charging patients $1 per day and Merck charging $600 per year. GSK extended its preferential pricing system beyond governments to NGOs, aid groups, churches, and charities, and eased access to various drugs like malarial pills. For example, Trizivir, a combination drug pill costing $27.92 in the US, sold for only $6.60 in developing countries under the new pricing system.[18]

The ongoing debates over pricing and access have severely eroded the reputation of the pharmaceutical industry. In a 2007 survey conducted by PricewaterhouseCoopers, 45 percent of consumers believed drug companies' R&D strategies were largely driven by sales considerations, while 62 percent of stakeholders agreed that pharmaceutical companies suppress negative clinical trials in order to boost sales, and 73 percent of stakeholders agreed that pharmaceutical companies spent excessive amounts of money attempting to prevent competition from generic drug companies (PMLive.com 2007).

The COVID-19 crisis has reignited the issue of patent protection for pharmaceutical companies, now in the context of vaccine access for less developed economies. While vaccine manufacturers have engaged in various strategies to increase vaccine production and access, they have generally remained opposed to patent waivers or the disclosure of trade secrets, such as those related to the complex vaccine manufacturing processes. In May 2021, the Biden administration announced its intention to waive IP protections for US COVID-19 vaccine producers, supporting an initiative started by India and South Africa in October 2020 to allow their manufacturers access to patented vaccines. More than a year later that process has stalled at the World Trade Organization due to the opposition from many developed countries (Rimmer 2022).

These issues are not limited to the pharmaceutical industry. Another example is subprime mortgages (Diermeier 2011). Historically, high-risk borrowers had been excluded from consumer credit markets. However, subsequent financial innovations, such as new models of default risk and securitization, allowed lenders to offer mortgages and other forms of consumer credit to population segments that would not qualify for "prime" rates. While some policymakers praised these new lending tools as important steps toward increasing access to credit for low-income consumers, the industry quickly faced media scrutiny and was attacked by consumer advocacy groups.

First, customers in the subprime segment tended to be poorer than typical borrowers, yet rates were substantially higher. Of course, these higher rates were determined by the corresponding securities markets and largely reflected higher expected default risks. But to observers unfamiliar with risk-adjusted pricing, charging poorer people higher rates simply looks unfair. Such perceptions can become more pronounced in cases in which subprime lenders are highly profitable or compensate their executives lavishly. Second, minorities, immigrants, the less educated, and the elderly are over-represented among subprime customers. This pattern may simply be a consequence of lower credit scores for these population segments, but it also triggers concerns about discrimination and predatory lending practices.

Companies often use efficiency arguments to overcome concerns of justice. That is, they argue that sub-prime lending expands the pool of available consumer financing, which is beneficial to everyone. But such efficiency arguments are often overshadowed by conflicting moral intuitions. Tetlock (2002) has argued that, in ethically charged situations, consumers are much more likely to act like "intuitive prosecutors" who emphasize moral imperatives rather than economic outcomes. Simply reading an unrelated story about harm to an innocent person is sufficient to cause such a shift from an intuitive economist mindset to an intuitive prosecutor mindset (Tetlock et al. 2007). Once an observer is in the mindset of an intuitive prosecutor, arguments made from an economic perspective are perceived as irrelevant and even repugnant. According to Tetlock, this is because moral arguments often tap into "sacred" values that cannot be traded off against economic considerations. To even attempt to place a price on certain moral values taints the value itself. It would be like contemplating the right price for selling your child (Tetlock et al. 2000).

FAIR PROCESS, RIGHTS, AND DISCRIMINATION. Fairness evaluations are not only based on outcomes (i.e., distributive fairness) but can also apply to fairness of processes. In the context of attitudes by employees towards their employer, Lind and Tyler (1988) show that perceived procedural fairness can explain four times as much variance in job satisfaction, supervisor evaluations, and workplace harmony as distributive fairness. In particular, people care about whether authorities have fair intentions, are honest, are ethical, and make good decisions. People also care about whether their own position will be fairly represented and whether there are systems in place to correct errors. Individuals make these judgments independently of the outcomes they receive (Lind and Tyler 1988).

Closely related to procedural fairness are rights. Perceived violations of basic rights can lead to moral outrage. We have already seen the importance of rights in the context of the ultimatum game, where the presence of perceived entitlements moderated the desire for equal allocations. But there are contexts other than bargaining or pricing where rights matter. The most important category here is concern over discrimination. In November 1996, the oil company Texaco made headlines when its top executives were overheard making racially insensitive jokes during a secretly recorded board meeting. News reports of the so-called black jelly beans tape led to public outcry and a class-action lawsuit, which the company eventually settled for $176 million (e.g., Diermeier 2011).

In such cases, the outrage results from the violation of strongly held norms; an evaluation of consequences, financial or other, matters little. For example, in a series of recent experiments, participants strongly preferred a "misanthropic" manager who treated all of his employees badly to an otherwise similar manager who only disparaged his African American employees (Zhu, Uhlmann, and Diermeier 2014).

The perceived violations of fairness norms and rights are a second major source for moral outrage. Concerns range from discriminatory practices and unfair processes to the violation of rights or the unfair exploitation of market power. As in the case of the do-no-harm duty, context and framing can materially shape moral judgments. For example, negotiation proposals that are commonly viewed as unfair, even exploitative, can be viewed as acceptable if they are the consequence of fairly earned bargaining advantages. Fully understanding such context and framing effects is essential to assess reputational risk.

3.1.3   Loyalty—Respect—Purity

These two core moral domains, one centered on the avoidance of harm and the other on the maintenance of rights, justice, and fairness, have long been viewed as covering the domain of moral intuitions (Kohlberg 1958, 1969;

Turiel 1983). This view has recently been challenged. Cultural anthropologists such as Fiske (1991) and Shweder et al. (1997) have pointed out that the moral practices of many traditional societies are poorly accounted for by concerns over fairness or harm. These moral practices include concerns over purity (usually related to food and sexual practices), group loyalty, and authority. Subsequent research has shown that similar moral intuitions can be found in Western cultures as well, particularly among political conservatives (Haidt 2007). Interestingly, in Western cultures, it has been found that subjects may exhibit a strong intuitive adverse reaction to violations of these broader moral concerns, but subsequently struggle to find an explanation for their emotional reaction in terms of justice or harm—a phenomenon referred to as "moral dumbfounding," which we will discuss later (Haidt 2001).

THREE VIEWS OF HUMAN RELATIONS. Shweder et al. (1997) suggest that there are three moral domains based on different views of human relationships and society. The first views human society as consisting of *individuals*, leading to an individualist conception of morality. Of central importance are the principles of avoidance of harm to individuals, fair allocation among members of society, and respect for individual rights.

Other cultures instead focus on the *community* as the central organizing principle. Society is composed of collections of relationships, husband-to-wife, father-to-son, and so on. These relationships are often hierarchical, where each member of the relationship has specific and well-defined responsibilities. Shirking one's responsibility or assuming a responsibility inappropriate for one's role are viewed as severe ethical violations. The corresponding hierarchies are to be obeyed and respected. Disobedience is discouraged and viewed as disrespect. The hierarchical virtues point to the internal organization of a group, but groups also define themselves against other groups. Here the relevant relationship is in-group versus out-group. Members are supposed to defend the group against others; critical virtues are loyalty and contribution to the common good without regard for personal benefit.

Finally, some human societies are based on the relationship with the *divine*. While secular societies may exclude such considerations as external to moral discourse, they are central in more traditional societies. Key distinctions include the sacred versus the profane and the pure versus the impure. Attitudes toward food, sex, and religion are central components of these domains, and may include taboos and rituals. The characteristic emotion is disgust, especially in the domains of food and sex. Chastity, temperance, cleanliness, and piety are important virtues (Haidt and Graham 2007).[19]

Taboos, rituals, and sacred values can play important roles in shaping attitudes and beliefs, even if they are not directly derived from religious beliefs and practices. Functionally, taboos are constitutive of the "sacred" and preclude comparisons, trade-offs, or counterfactual comparisons. If they are perceived to be violated, subjects express moral outrage and engage in "moral cleansing," which involves reaffirmation of core moral convictions and increased desire for punishment of the taboo violators. While sacred values often have a religious foundation, there are secular variants as well, such as prohibitions against selling votes and other civic rights, organs, or children. Indeed, mere contemplation of value violations can trigger moral outrage, for example reading counterfactuals of religious stories or, in a secular context, statistical data that violate firmly held beliefs about racial or gender equality (Tetlock et al. 2000).

MORAL INTELLIGENCE. Western cultures often emphasize individualist forms of morality. To see the potency of community and religious values in the domain of corporate reputations, however, consider the following example (Diermeier 2011). In 2005, a Danish newspaper published a series of satirical cartoons, some of which portrayed the Prophet Mohammed. Within hours, violent protests and riots broke out in various Muslim communities. This was followed by boycotts of Danish products in the Islamic world, leading to a significant drop in sales (Fattah 2006). European commentators focused on the right to free speech and the absence of personal harm, while the outrage in the Muslim world was driven by religious concerns fueled by a sense of insult and disrespect.

Recent research has shown that value orientations based on loyalty, hierarchy, and purity are not restricted to traditional societies. Rather, they are an essential component of the moral universe of political conservatives in western countries (Graham et al. 2011). Examples include resistance to gay marriage or anger at burning the flag or kneeling during the national anthem, among others. Such concerns are virtually absent among political liberals and libertarians. Importantly, liberals and libertarians not only do not have these concerns, but view them as matters of taste or personal preference—outside of legitimate moral discourse.

These issues are especially important when companies need to navigate cultural diversity in a global economy. Consider an executive with a typical liberal value orientation: Morality is conceptualized as a duty to avoid harm and a respect for rights with some additional concern for distributive justice. Now consider the executive operating in a global business environment where community-based or religious value systems are prevalent. Such a decision maker will tend to make two mistakes. First, she will not consider possible violations of authority, purity, or loyalty when making a decision. In other words, an issue that does not harm anyone or violate their rights seems unproblematic. But these omissions constitute a moral blind spot. The case of the Danish cartoons of the Prophet Mohammed is a typical example.

But there is a second and more subtle issue. The executive may not even consider the issue as moral. Rather, she would likely view it as cultural and a matter of conventions. This may seem like a rather minor shift in perception, but it is crucial. Once we view an issue as cultural or as a mere convention, we tend to tolerate and affirm such multiplicity as reflecting equally valued customs; there are multiple ways of organizing matters without one being clearly better than the others. People drive on the left or the right, some eat with knife and fork while others eat with chopsticks, and unless we are bigots, we are comfortable with this diversity.

Viewing something as a convention rather than a moral issue constitutes a very different mental state. Our emotional involvement with a question of right or wrong, accompanied by our immediate and forceful intuitions on what is the right thing to do, is replaced by a detached, perhaps even benevolent, attitude of tolerance. Of course, within a more traditional culture where values like loyalty are a critical component of the moral universe, there is no such detachment. People feel outrage and anger. The Muslims rioting in the street after the publication of the Danish cartoons did not see this as an instance of multiple cultures having different conventions, but as an outrageous, immoral act.

To properly address such issues, we need to move from *cultural intelligence* that appreciates the differences in cultures and values to *moral intelligence* that is fully aware of the emotional agitation that comes with a moral issue, even if we do not share the underlying moral code. Of course, to understand the moral significance of an issue for a particular group or community does not mean to accept or even respect it. The editors of the Danish newspaper may still insist that freedom of speech is a supreme value even if it causes deeply felt moral outrage. But to make such decisions in the first place, leaders need to be aware of the tension between moral principles, understand the significance of the issues, and grasp how they may affect their business.

Together these principles provide a rich structure to analyze the dimensions that shape evaluations. Together, they encompass one version of moral foundations theory (Haidt 2013b). But there are other important moral principles that have been shown to shape attitudes.

3.2 Tells

A "tell" in poker is a tendency in a player's behavior or demeanor that provides information about the player's style of play and thus his current hand and probable next move. Tells are unintentional, but for a skilled player who can recognize them, they can provide a crucial advantage.

Up to this point, we have considered moral judgments and evaluations of corporate actions or inactions, such as a controversial marketing program or product, the use of suppliers with appalling labor or environment standards, and so forth. But there are many cases of evaluating corporate conduct where such an act-focused approach reaches its limits. Consider the example of executive compensation. There are few domains that generate as much public outrage as executive perks (Diermeier 2011). The 2008 financial crisis provided a particularly rich list of scandals. Examples include the infamous trip by the CEOs of the Big Three American automobile manufacturers using their private jets to ask the US Congress for taxpayer support, the outrage over AIG spending over $200,000 in hotel and spa services only a few days after receiving an $85 billion federal bailout and additional multibillion-dollar loan guarantees, and Merrill Lynch CEO John Thainn's $1.2 million redecoration of his personal office, which included an $87,000 rug, a $35,000 toilet, and a $1,400 waste paper basket. In comparison, Thainn's annual compensation of over $83 million hardly raised an eyebrow.

Outrage over executive perks is not limited to times of financial hardship or crisis and can affect even widely admired business leaders. Former GE CEO Jack Welch found himself in the center of a controversy when details of his retirement package became publicly known. Perks included free lifetime use of a company Boeing 737, tickets for major sporting events and the Metropolitan Opera, fresh flower arrangements, and generous tips for the doorman. Welch quickly decided to forgo these benefits (Diermeier 2011).[20]

3.2.1   A Question of Character

These examples have a striking common feature. They made the public's blood boil, even though the actual sums of money were quite small—even insignificant in comparison to what was at stake. In the case of the Big Three automakers, for example, the companies requested $25 billion in additional taxpayer funds to avoid bankruptcy. The cost of the private plane trip from Detroit to Washington, DC, was estimated at $20,000, while commercial flights from Detroit's metro airport ranged from $288 for coach to $837 for a first class ticket (Levs 2009). The CEOs immediately recognized their poor judgments and promised to sell their jets, but that did little to stem the outrage. GM CEO Rick Wagoner resigned at the White House's request, and both GM and Chrysler subsequently filed for Chapter 11 bankruptcy protection.

Since the material impact of each action was insignificant, explaining the degree of moral outrage from any consequentialist point of view, whether it emphasizes aggregate welfare or distributive justice, will be challenging. There may have been some harm caused, but if so, it was very small. And while there is some impact on welfare and income distribution, such effects are nowhere near proportional to the public anger. A US Congressman complained that they were "getting manicures and massages, while the American people were footing the bill," and Merrill Lynch's John Thainn made it onto the infamous "Worst Person of the World" list by US talk show host Keith Olbermann.

A rights-based perspective does not fare much better. There do not appear to be any rights or widely held principles at stake here. In each example, the perks were granted by private entities, such as corporate boards, that had the right to grant them to their executives. Giving and accepting such perks may have been foolish, but it did not violate any rights. Inequality may have increased, but not by much. The CEOs were also legitimate authorities within the context of conventional corporate hierarchies and integral parts of their communities. Hence, issues related to loyalty or hierarchy were unlikely to be at play. Similarly, the actions do not seem to represent violations of purity.

In sum, none of these standard perspectives gets at the root of the moral intuition so powerfully activated in these examples. Instead, the moral outrage in these examples appears to be more like "tells." Intuitively, there is something frivolous, distasteful, or unseemly about these cases—a sense of "What kind of person would do something like this?" This suggests that we are evaluating not the action per se, but the *person* who is committing it, questioning his or her moral character and disposition.

Such tells tend to be involuntary. The agent is usually not aware that he is sending an informative message about his moral character. Indeed, in the context where the decision is made, it may look harmless and routine, yet when put into a different context, it is interpreted as a tell. What looks unproblematic in the meeting room may become highly embarrassing in the glaring spotlight of public scrutiny. What may look like a technical business decision (e.g., offering a new CEO a perk) can later be interpreted as a signal of bad character.[21]

We can sharpen our understanding of this intuition through a controlled experiment (Tannenbaum, Uhlmann, and Diermeier 2011). In one experiment, participants were asked to make a choice between two candidates for CEO of a manufacturing company. The two candidates, John and Robert, had comparable backgrounds and employment histories. One candidate, say John, requested a salary of $2 million per year. Robert requested a lower salary of $1 million per year plus a signing bonus. The nature of the signing bonus was the treatment variable in the experiment. It consisted of either a $40,000 cash bonus (cash only condition), a $40,000 marble table (marble table condition), or a $40,000 marble table engraved with the candidate's portrait (personalized table condition). The intuition was that the cash bonus would be viewed neutrally, that the marble table would be perceived as a frivolous perk, and that the personalized table would be seen as especially jarring and reflective of a poor moral character.

Participants rated the candidates in terms of their relative integrity (e.g., "Who has more integrity?"), anticipated behavior (e.g., "Who would you expect to make more sound business decisions as CEO?"), and hiring preferences (e.g., "Who would you hire as CEO?"). Respondents were also asked how much each candidate's compensation request "revealed about who he really is and what he really is like."

The results were clear. In the cash bonus conditions, participants viewed the low-salary candidate Robert more favorably than the high-salary candidate John. Robert was also believed to have greater integrity and be more likely to behave responsibly in the future. However, when Robert asked for a signing bonus in the form of a $40,000 marble table, participants made the opposite pattern of attributions. They now saw the low-salary candidate as having less integrity and as less likely than the high-salary candidate to behave responsibly in the future. This pattern was most pronounced when the candidate asked for a marble table with his portrait engraved into it—a particularly egregious perk. The difference in judgments across the three conditions was sizable. Respondents also believed that the marble table was more informative about the person than the cash bonus, with the personalized table being the most informative.

This experiment is essentially a controlled version of the executive compensation issues discussed above, located in a hiring context. What we find is that the nature of the compensation request significantly influences respondents' evaluations of the person and may even reverse the (hypothetical) hiring decision, despite the lower overall compensation. The request is not just viewed in isolation but is interpreted as a signal of the person's moral character indicative of his future behavior.

Person-centered judgments can be found in various other business contexts. Short sellers, for example, are often judged very negatively. In his book *The Big Short*, author Michael Lewis highlights a group of traders who predicted the 2007 market crash (Lewis 2010). Consider, for example, the behavior of Greg Lippmann, a trader at Deutsche Bank who advised investors to bet on mortgage defaults. Lippmann's strategy was to purchase financial instruments that were linked to a pool of mortgages and would became far more valuable if those mortgages went into default (i.e., if individual homeowners were unable to make the payments on their homes). Of course, Lippman's bet did not (and could not) cause the subprime mortgage crisis to occur. Neither did Lippman intend for his bet to cause a crisis. He merely sought to benefit from a tragic event that he knew to be beyond his control but believed to be likely. From the perspective of the theories described earlier, there is no basis on which to judge actions like Lippman's as blameworthy, yet people do assign moral blame to short sellers who are perceived to benefit from the misfortune of others.[22]

Inbar, Pizarro, and Cushman (2012) argue that the reason for such negative judgments lies within an aversion of *wicked desires*, that is, an agent desiring or hoping for a bad outcome, even if they do not or cannot bring the bad outcome about. Note that the desire is not to cause harm, merely to benefit from it. Observers judge such individuals to have a bad moral disposition, which then affects their evaluation of the action itself. That is, an action may be considered morally wrong if it follows from a wicked desire.

In one experiment, half the participants were asked to evaluate a money manager who had invested in bonds that became highly valuable in the case of an earthquake "causing great devastation." The other half were presented with the opposite scenario, where the investment became highly valuable if no earthquake struck. Subjects were asked to evaluate the specific action and the manager's moral character. As predicted, participants saw an action that benefited from harm as more blameworthy than an otherwise identical action that did not, even when controlling for negative assessments of the actor's character. Participants also rated the money manager's character as worse when they benefited from harm.

This emphasis on the desires of an actor (regardless of whether those inferences are correct) can have serious practical consequences. For example, following 9/11, the Defense Advanced Research Projects Agency (DARPA) considered creating a prediction market for political instability, in which people could place bets on the likelihood of events such as terrorist attacks across the globe. Previous research had shown that monetarily incentivizing correct predictions increased predictive accuracy in groups, so a properly designed prediction market could possibly have improved the predictability of terror attacks and other negative political events, which could lead to improved prevention strategies and response plans. However, the public was so repulsed by the idea that someone could profit from a terrorist attack that DARPA had to quickly abandon the project (Wolfers and Zitzewitz 2004).

This focus on moral character has an impressive pedigree. In moral philosophy, it has a longstanding tradition often referred to as "virtue ethics" (Anscombe 1958; Aristotle 2009; MacIntyre 2007). Virtue-based approaches evaluate the character of the agent (e.g., "What kind of person would do this?"), rather than the act itself. Recent developments in social psychology suggest that similar considerations influence everyday moral judgment (Pizarro and Tannenbaum 2011; Tannenbaum, Uhlmann, and Diermeier 2011; Uhlmann, Pizarro, and Diermeier 2015). The general idea is that, rather than just evaluating an act in isolation, individuals view the act as a signal about the person's moral disposition.

From a practical perspective, information about character and behavioral dispositions is very important in social interactions. Agents need to know whether another person can be relied on to cooperate in joint endeavors: Who can be trusted, and with whom can we form lasting bonds (Baumard, André, and Sperber 2013; Frank 1988; Gintis et al. 2008; Miller 2007).

Humans are particularly good at evaluating moral traits. It is an effortless, automatic capability that develops early in life and can be found across cultures (Choi and Nisbett 1998; Hamlin, Wynn, and Bloom 2007; Lieberman, Jarcho, and Obayashi 2005; Uleman, Saribay, and Gonzalez 2008; Willis and Todorov 2006). Moreover, traits related to a person's moral attributes (e.g., honesty, sincerity, and trustworthiness) are dominant in forming general evaluations of a person such as warmth and benevolence (Aquino and Reed 2002; Brambilla et al. 2011; Fiske, Cuddy, and Glick

2007; Lapsley and Lasky 2001; Walker and Hennig 2004). In short, social perception is often person perception, and person perception appears to place special weight on moral traits (Goodwin, Piazza, and Rozin 2014).

ACTIONS VERSUS CHARACTER. An important dimension of person-centered morality is the act-person dissociation. That is, in a given context, we may view agent A more negatively than agent B, while at the same time judge agent B's action more negatively than agent A's. We can exemplify this insight in an experiment that captures the Michael Vick scandal. In 2007, Atlanta Falcons star quarterback Michael Vick was exposed for bankrolling a dogfighting ring. Dogs that proved insufficiently violent in test fights were brutally hanged or drowned. Vick was dismissed from the team and suspended by the National Football League. Vick lost a $130 million contract with his team, the Atlanta Falcons, and was sentenced to 23 months in prison, a more severe punishment than requested by the prosecutors. Media coverage and public outrage was enormous. In the US Senate, the late Senator Robert Byrd (D-WV) denounced Vick's acts as follows (Alfano 2007):

> Barbaric! Let that word resound from hill to hill, and from mountain to mountain, from valley to valley, across this broad land. Barbaric! Barbaric! May God help those poor souls who'd be so cruel. Barbaric! Hear me! Barbaric!... I am confident the hottest places in hell are reserved for the souls of sick and brutal people who hold God's creatures in such brutal and cruel contempt.

In this case, the actions by Vick and his associates caused substantial harm. Still, the degree of outrage requires some explanation, especially compared to harm against humans, such as in domestic violence cases. For example, in 2014 Minnesota Vikings star running back Adrian Peterson was charged with felony child abuse for spanking his four-year-old son with a switch, resulting in cuts and bruises all over the boy's body. Peterson eventually pleaded no contest to a reduced charge of misdemeanor reckless assault. The NFL suspended him for one year with a two-year probation period. He was fined $4,000 and performed 80 hours of community service (Belson 2016; Keim 2018).

We can disentangle the dimension of moral judgment towards character and action in the following experiment (Tannenbaum, Uhlmann, and Diermeier 2011). Sixty-eight undergraduates (34 females) were asked to complete an anonymous survey. Participants read a scenario involving two persons, again named "John" and "Robert." Both men had found out that their respective girlfriends had been unfaithful. Upon learning that their respective girlfriends were cheating on them, one man reacted by beating her violently, while the other reacted by beating her cat violently.

Participants were then asked to evaluate whose actions were more immoral on a seven-point scale (1 = definitely John beating up his girlfriend, 7 = definitely Robert beating up his girlfriend's cat). Participants also assessed character attributes, including which person was more empathic, sadistic, "sick and twisted," "screwed up," likely to feel sorry for the homeless, have normal human feelings, and so forth. Participants responded to these items on a seven-point scale ranging from 1 (definitely John) to 7 (definitely Robert). Responses were combined to form an index of moral character evaluations, where higher scores reflected negative reactions toward the cat beater, and lower scores reflected negative reactions toward the woman beater. Participants were also asked which of the two acts was more common, using the same seven-point scale as before.

The results indicated a disassociation between evaluations of acts and evaluations of persons doing the act. Most of the time, moral evaluations of acts and persons correspond with one another; good people are those who engage in praiseworthy behaviors and bad people in blameworthy ones. But this does not need to be the case. That is, while the cat beater's actions were seen as less wrong than those of the woman beater, the cat beater was seen as having worse moral character than the woman beater.[23]

This can be illustrated in the following figure. Figure 3.1 displays a scattergram with participants' moral judgments of behavior on the y axis and trait attributions on the x axis. Higher numbers on the x axis reflect negative attributions about the cat-beater's moral traits relative to the woman beater. Higher numbers on the y-axis reflect negative evaluations of the cat beater's actions relative to the woman beater. The midpoint of 4 on both axes reflects indifference between the two targets. By splitting the scattergram along its diagonal axis, we can get a sense of dissociation between judgments of actions and persons. Data points that fall along the diagonal axis show no dissociation between act and person judgments.

Data points that fall above the diagonal axis indicate dissociation, such that the participant thought that the woman beater had negative moral traits relative to their moral judgments of his behavior. Data points that fall below the diagonal axis indicate the opposite dissociation, such that the participant thought that the cat beater had negative moral traits relative to

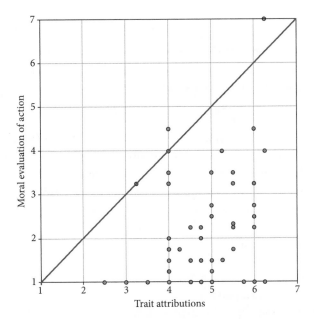

FIGURE 3.1. Higher numbers on the *x* axis reflect negative attributions about the cat beater's moral traits relative to the woman beater. Higher numbers on the *y* axis reflect negative evaluations of the cat beater's actions relative to the woman beater. The midpoint of 4 on both axes reflects indifference between the two targets.

their moral judgments of his behavior (i.e., the predicted dissociation). As seen in figure 3.1, there was a general tendency to view the cat beater as possessing more negative moral traits relative to the moral judgments of his actions.

The finding of act-person dissociation shows that moral judgments of persons are not simply a byproduct of judging the action undertaken by the person. Acts can be evaluated as less wrong by themselves, yet signal worse moral character. An act of violence toward a person was viewed as more blameworthy than violence toward an animal, but animal cruelty signaled more severe deficits in moral character. Respondents thus judged the settings as intuitive virtue theorists who view acts as signals of underlying moral traits such as integrity and empathy for others (Frank 1988; Reeder and Brewer 1979). As a result, acts perceived as unusually informative of poor moral character—such as those committed by Michael Vick—can weigh more heavily in moral judgments than objectively more harmful acts.

Viewing actions as signals about character has immediate consequences. First, negative acts are more informative than positive acts because people often have ulterior motives for prosocial behaviors, such as a desire to create a positive impression on others. Thus, person-centered moral judgment often exhibits the well-known negativity bias, the tendency to pay more attention or give more weight to negative rather than positive information (Baumeister et al. 2001; Klein and Epley 2014; Rozin and Royzman 2001; Skowronski and Carlston 1987, 1989).[24] Second, acts that can be attributed to multiple plausible motives or causes tend to be low in informational value. In particular, having an ulterior motive can undermine praise (Uhlmann, Zhu, and Tannenbaum 2013), while actions that are costly to the agent are better signals (Ohtsubo et al. 2008). Third, behaviors that are statistically rare or otherwise extreme are particularly informative (Ditto and Jemmott 1989; Fiske 1980; Kelley 1967; McKenzie and Mikkelsen 2007; Nelson 2005; Nelson et al. 2010). Fourth, actions that are taken fast, without much deliberation, and are accompanied by genuine emotions are viewed as better signals about character traits (Critcher, Inbar, and Pizarro 2013; Gauthier 1986; Trivers 1971; Verplaetse, Vanneste, and Braeckman 2007).

DIMENSION OF CHARACTER EVALUATION.   A large number of studies indicate that personal integrity and empathy are routinely viewed as core components of moral character (Aquino and Reed 2002; Lapsley and Lasky 2001; Walker and Hennig 2004; Walker and Pitts 1998; Wojciszke, Dowhyluk, and Jaworski 1998). Empathy is particularly informative of future behavior, in part because it tends to be involuntary and difficult to fake (Frank 1988; Hoffman 2008). Therefore, acts that signal a deficit in empathy are a very useful source of social information. Cruelty to animals indicates such a lack of empathy.[25]

But act-person dissociations can also be found in the content of praiseworthy acts. In a study of moral dilemmas, Uhlmann, Zhu, and Tannenbaum (2013) found that participants can evaluate an act positively but the person negatively, or at least less positively. For example, a person who sacrifices an injured person to save many others by throwing the injured survivor off a lifeboat is viewed as deficient in moral character, while the action itself is seen as less problematic than refusing to sacrifice the one injured person to save others. In such situations, two factors that undermine moral praise for the agent seem to be particularly important. First, if the agent benefits himself—for example, if his own chances of survival increase—he is evaluated less favorably. What we have here is an instance of multiple possible explanations that reduce the informativeness of the signal. Sacrificing oneself for the good of others, in turn, is an unambiguous signal of moral character. Second, the suppression of empathy to do the right thing undermines praise. Suppose a hospital administrator can buy expensive equipment to save the life of a child or use the same funds to save the lives of a large number of other patients. In an experiment presenting this scenario, the administrator was viewed negatively after declining to buy the equipment even though respondents found the act of doing so praiseworthy, an effect mediated by a perceived lack of empathy (Uhlmann, Zhu, and Tannenbaum 2013).

This has important practical consequences for some industries. Consider the case of health insurance companies. Health insurers have low levels of public trust and often find themselves criticized for failing to pay for a particularly expensive medical treatment. For example, a 2016 Harris poll found that only 16 percent of respondents believe that health insurance companies put patients over profits (Harris Insights & Analytics 2016).

To defend themselves, health insurers often use consequentialist arguments, that is, that limited funds need to be allocated to the greatest medical need. Such enhanced efficiency would then lead to lower premiums and greater access to health care. Health insurers thus need to deny claims that are not medically necessary. Note that this issue has a structure similar to the social dilemmas studied by Uhlmann, Zhu, and Tannenbaum (2013); it is based on a social welfare argument but is associated with acts that are viewed as blameworthy, in this case denial of coverage to a patient. Note also that health insurers are often perceived by the public to have a financial interest in denying coverage ("make more money"), and sacrificing a particular patient may be interpreted as empathy suppression.[26] This suggests that the public may begrudgingly agree with the decision but may still hold the insurance company in low regard.

A person-centered approach can also help make sense of various puzzling phenomena of moral evaluations. Respondents find some behavior morally reprehensible, for example, the personalized marble table, but have difficulties providing explanations for their strong feelings. Respondents often resort to statements such as "this is just wrong," but cannot give further explanations. Known as "moral dumbfounding," such reactions are often observed in the context of purity violations such as repulsive sexual conduct or improper eating (Haidt 2001; Haidt, Bjorklund, and Murphy

2000; Haidt, Koller, and Dias, 1993), but they can occur in other contexts too. According to a person-centered approach, such reprehensible actions are often highly unusual and "bizarre" and thus provide high informational value about the character of an agent, even though the action itself may not cause harm or violate a general ethical principle.

Evaluations of acts and character can also interact in interesting and complex ways. In the trolley experiment, we have seen that intentionality and assignment of causality are important factors in how an action is judged morally. Acts of omission are judged less harshly than acts of commission (the causation principle), and harm due to side effects is viewed more positively than intentional harm (the intention principle). But the assignment of intentionality or causality to an action may also depend on the assessment of the person's character (Sripada and Konrath 2011). This may be based in the intuition that it "takes a worse person" to actively harm others than to passively allow harm to take place. For example, agents are more likely to be viewed as the cause of a complicated accident if they had a bad motive, such as speeding to consume drugs at home (Alicke 1992, 2000). This has significant practical implications, as in many cases of transgression, intentionality and causality are inherently ambiguous. Inferences of an actor's motives can then be used to disambiguate the evidence. Thus, in the traffic accident example, it may not be clear who is at fault, but if someone was racing home to consume illegal drugs, then that may be viewed as constituting positive evidence of his being at fault. This is one important reason why reputation is so important—it can tip the balance when observers are unsure of how to assign fault.

Person-centered morality can also shed light on another puzzling phenomenon, the "side-effect effect." Suppose a corporate executive launches a new product with a side effect that causes harm to the environment. In this case, the harm is interpreted as intentional. If, however, the product's side effect is beneficial to the environment, the act is not perceived as intentional (Knobe 2006; Leslie, Knobe, and Cohen 2006). Thus we have a tendency to interpret the negative, but not the positive, side effects of an action as intentional (Knobe 2006). Note that, in the case of the negative side effect, the executive could have prevented the harm, but did not do so. This serves as a signal about the executive's character and moral disposition. Based on that assessment, ascribing an intention to do harm is more plausible.[27] This assessment chain does not occur in cases of positive side effects.

Assessment of a person also influences the recollected magnitude or severity of an action. In an experiment presenting an account of a restaurant customer who intentionally left without paying his bill, participants recalled the cost of the meal as significantly greater than in a story where he had merely forgotten to pay (Pizarro et al. 2006). Such processes can also influence the degree of punishment and retribution (Carlsmith 2006, 2008; Carlsmith, Darley, and Robinson 2002).

JOKES AND PRIVATE COMMENTS.   Person-centered morality can also help us understand the tremendous outrage over racist comments, even if they are told in private (Uhlmann, Zhu, and Diermeier 2014). One such example is the Paula Deen controversy. Paula Deen had been a celebrity chef with millions of followers. Known for her Southern-style comfort cooking, she had a successful cooking show, wrote bestseller recipe books, owned multiple restaurants, and became a spokesperson for the Food Network, Wal-Mart, Target, Home Depot, Kmart, J. C. Penney, Sears, Smithfield Foods, and various others. Eventually Paula Deen Enterprises expanded to include a magazine, cruise vacations, casino restaurants, kitchen supplies, and more (Woolner and Gillette 2013). Paula Deen had previously been criticized for her high-calorie, high-fat recipes, a criticism that increased after she was diagnosed with type 2 diabetes in 2012 and began endorsing the diabetes drug Victoza made by pharmaceutical company Novo Nordisk. Critics argued that it was hypocritical to promote and benefit from a cuisine that increases the risk of diabetes and then to profit from diabetes drugs (Piazza 2012).

But these controversies were insignificant compared to what happened in the summer of 2012. In 2012 Paula Deen Enterprises was sued by former employee Lisa Jackson. Jackson had worked for five years as restaurant manager at Uncle Bubba's Oyster House, a restaurant in Savannah, Georgia, owned by Deen and her brother, "Bubba" Hiers. During this time, Jackson claimed to have been "subjected to a hostile work environment full of sexual impropriety, boorish behavior, and racist remarks." The restaurant was run by Hiers and most of the offending behavior was alleged to have been carried out by Hiers, yet Deen, as the co-owner, was held responsible for having created the hostile work environment. Deen refused to settle and, during the subsequent deposition, Deen not only defended her brother as having a good sense of humor, but admitted to having used the N-word in private conversation with her husband in 1987. Later it also became known that, when planning a "Southern-style plantation wedding," Deen spoke longingly of the antebellum days as she described wanting to have African American men representing slaves as servers.

The news of Deen's deposition was greeted with outrage. Media coverage quickly became very critical of Deen. For example, in a widely discussed interview on *the Today Show*, host Matt Lauer observed that, "Right now as we sit here, it seems to me an informal jury of your peers— and your fans and your critics and your business associates are—are weighing the question, 'Is Paula Deen a racist?'"(Moraski 2013).[28] Deen was dropped by most of her major sponsors, although some smaller companies stuck with her, and her future as a national brand was considered bleak (Woolner and Gillette 2013). It is noteworthy that media coverage of the Deen scandal did not focus on the legal issues. Indeed, the lawsuit claiming a hostile work environment was dismissed after the parties reached a settlement. Rather, observers commented on what the racist comment revealed about Deen's character, even if it was uttered in private. The *Los Angeles Times* summarized its assessment as, "Paula Deen lawsuit dismissed, but not before it destroyed career" (Lynch 2013).

Racist or sexist jokes or slurs are powerful signals about a person. For example, when sued over discriminatory hiring and promotion practices in 1996, Texaco defended itself by pointing to possible explanations for the statistical disparities, for example, a small pool of qualified African American applicants. But when audio recordings of executives making racist jokes were revealed, such arguments lost any force. The racist jokes seemed to settle the matter, transforming Texaco's poor record of minority hiring from suspicious to a clear-cut case of racial bias, forcing the company to settle for $176 million (Mulligan and Kraul 1996).

The signaling aspect of racism and bigotry can be seen in the following experiment (Schweinsberg et al. 2016). Participants read about two company managers, John and Robert. John arbitrarily cut the vacation time for all of his employees, while Robert cut the vacation time only for his African American employees. Subjects were asked to evaluate the manager's actions and his character. They were also asked to indicate, "How much does Robert's (John's) decision reveal about who he really is and what he is really like?" Almost all of the respondents agreed that the bigoted manager (Robert) committed a worse act (97 percent), and most (64 percent) agreed that his action was more informative of his character. Thus, even though the misanthropic manager John had caused more aggregate harm than the bigot Robert (in terms of the number of employee vacation days cut), he was perceived more positively.

Uhlmann, Zhu, and Diermeier (2014), in an experiment that captured the Paula Deen story, show that even a racist slur muttered in private can lead to outrage. The same holds for a symbolic gesture, such as privately defacing a picture of civil rights leader Martin Luther King Jr. Again, we find the familiar act-person dissociation. Subjects regarded the private use of a racial slur as a less blameworthy act than physical assault, but the use of the slur was perceived as a clearer indicator of poor moral character. Moreover, once a character judgment had been made, the subsequent act was judged more harshly.

In sum, people use behavior as a cue to make inferences about the person who carries out the act that go beyond their judgments of the act itself. Actions are viewed as signals or "tells" about moral character and may be unrelated to the actual harm caused by the behavior. That is, the character information signaled by a behavior serves as an additional input into moral judgments, over and above evaluations of the act itself. As a result, moral outrage is amplified when acts are perceived to be strong signals of poor character. Act- and person-centered judgments may focus on different moral dimensions. Evaluations of acts are more likely to focus on the extent of harm caused, while person-centered moral judgments are more likely to center on whether the act signals the presence or absence of moral virtues (Tannenbaum, Uhlmann, and Diermeier 2011; Uhlmann, Pizarro, and Diermeier 2015; Uhlmann and Zhu 2014; Uhlmann, Zhu, and Diermeier 2014). Even if such offensive behavior occurs in private or has no discernible direct consequences, moral outrage will follow. Observers ask themselves the question "What kind of person would conduct such an action?" and come to the conclusion that it can only be a person of poor moral character. Jokes or symbolic actions can be particularly potent signals. In contrast to other actions, such as a hiring decision, there are few plausible alternative explanations. The joke is viewed as a pure tell of the person's true moral character.

3.2.2   Companies as Persons

In the context of corporate reputations, an additional question must be answered: What does it mean for a company to have a "moral character?" Are companies judged like people? Such questions have been analyzed in the consumer research literature, but mostly in the context of branding (Aaker 1996). More recent research has added nuance to this picture, indicating that observers frequently assign some, but not all, mental states to collectives including companies (e.g., Gray, Gray, and Wegner 2007).[29] Gray, Young, and Waytz (2012) have argued that the assignments of mental states and moral judgment are closely interrelated and connected. For example, agents with lower or yet undeveloped mental capacities (e.g., children) are viewed as less responsible for their actions, but are also assigned fewer rights.

Gray, Gray, and Wegner (2007) found that, when assigning mental states and capacities to agents, observers rely on two fundamental dimensions. The first dimension, referred to as *agency*, includes attributes related to taking actions, such as capacities for memorizing, learning, remembering, thinking, knowing, intending, and self-control. The second dimension, referred to as *experience*, includes attributes related to feelings and sensations, such as hunger, pain, anger, pleasure, and desire. An entity can be high or low on either one of these dimensions. Adult humans are usually viewed as high on both dimensions unless they suffer from a mental illness or disability. Children are viewed as low on agency, but high on experience. Intelligent machines, such as robots, but also deities, score high on agency, but low on experience. Plants or inanimate objects, such as rocks, are viewed as low on both.

These two dimensions naturally translate into moral qualities (Gray, Young, and Waytz 2012). Agency qualifies an entity as a *moral agent*, capable of doing good and evil, and thus responsible for its actions. Experience qualifies an entity as a *moral patient* capable of feeling pleasure and pain, and thus worthy of empathy and protection from harm. Adult humans exhibit both dimensions, while an infant possesses only patiency and thus should be protected from harm, but not held responsible for its actions, even if they have negative consequences. Finally, kicking a rock is permissible, and we do not blame a rock even if it killed a mountain climber, as these inanimate objects exhibit neither dimension.[30]

Companies score low on experience and high on agency (Knobe and Prinz 2008). Rai and Diermeier (2015) find that both individuals and corporations elicit the same amount of outrage for the same infraction (selling customer data without permission), but corporations receive far less sympathy than individuals when they are struck by the same calamity (a data security breach that leads to bankruptcy). Individuals are also seen as more capable of experiencing pain or suffering, which leads to differences in sympathy. This suggests that, when it comes to person-centered morality, companies can be evaluated like individuals in terms of intentions but not suffering: companies can think but not feel. Hence, we tend to hold them accountable but do not pity their misfortune.[31]

MORAL TYPECASTING. This finding has some important practical consequences. The first is related to the concept of *moral typecasting* (Gray, Young, and Waytz 2012). That is, in a given situation, people are seen as either moral agents (capable of intention and thus worthy of blame or praise) or moral patients (capable of experience and thus experiencing pleasure or pain), but not both. Indeed, suffering moves people firmly into the moral patient category, even if their suffering is "their own fault." Conversely, once an individual is classified as a moral agent, he is perceived to feel less pain from injuries (Gray and Wegner 2009). These judgments are accompanied by matching emotional responses. Emotions such as sympathy and sadness accompany our response to victims; emotional responses to villains are anger and disgust, and to heroes, admiration and gratitude.

This phenomenon becomes especially relevant in the context of safety issues, particularly in those cases where there is the possibility that the consumer was responsible for the injury due to lack of care or preparation, as in the Toyota unintended acceleration case. In such cases, companies may be tempted to blame the customer. Moral typecasting suggests that such strategies are ineffective. Once customers are victims, they become moral patients and are removed from blame. Rai and Diermeier (2019) found that when participants are told that a company and an individual are involved in a dispute with each other, participants expressed greater support for companies when asked to focus on the harm that each side had caused to the other rather than on the harm that each side endured. This is because, while both companies and individuals are capable of eliciting blame for harm, only consumers are capable of eliciting sympathy as victims.

The fact that companies cannot credibly play the role of victims provides a difficult challenge for managers, especially in a reputational crisis where they believe they have done nothing wrong and are unfairly vilified. In such situations, managers may feel individually victimized, but in their role as corporate executives that is not how they are seen by the public. Rai and Diermeier (2015) found that, in contrast to the general public, corporate *executives* do see companies as capable of experience, and as a result they can feel sympathy for them as victims. Perhaps this discrepancy is due to the fact that, in their daily lives, executives do not experience companies as abstract entities, but rather as real workplaces with colleagues and co-workers who exhibit a full range of emotions. Executives, however, need to remember that this more empathetic view of companies is not shared by the public.[32]

The very same agentic qualities that enable companies to be seen as villains deserving of blame, however, also enable them to be seen as heroes deserving of praise (Diermeier 2011; Rai and Diermeier 2015, 2019). In such contexts, therefore, the only relevant question for companies is not how to engender sympathy but how to become the hero. The answer is: save the (perceived) victim. Blaming the victim is not part of the story line.

In a study by Rai and Diermeier (2019), participants were asked to evaluate two kinds of responses to a crisis that involved either an individual entrepreneur or a company. One response involved deflecting blame and claiming to be a victim. The other response involved accepting responsibility for the crisis and working to resolve it and ensure it would never happen again. The results showed that, for both individual entrepreneurs and for companies, taking responsibility for a crisis engendered more positive attitudes among respondents. However, companies benefited much more from taking responsibility instead of deflecting blame than did individual entrepreneurs. In other words, during a crisis companies usually do not elicit sympathy, but they can elicit outrage *as well as* admiration.

These findings also suggest that the perception of companies as lacking feelings may be malleable if they can be viewed more like people. For example, Rai and Diermeier found that, when participants were asked to imagine a company as a person, they ascribed more experience and expressed more sympathy for the company, although still not as much as afforded to individuals. This strategy of anthropomorphizing companies can be seen in efforts to put a "human face" on a company, such as when charismatic CEOs come to represent the company (as in the case of Elon Musk and Tesla) or when companies try to personalize their image and values (as when British Petroleum ran their "I am BP"campaign, in which employees of the company spoke about its values following the Gulf of Mexico oil spill).

DYADIC COMPLETION.   The second important concept is *dyadic completion* (Gray, Young, and Waytz 2012). When we see a blameworthy act, we tend to look for a victim (Gray and Wegner 2009). Conversely, when we see a suffering patient, we look for a blameworthy moral agent. In complex cases where suffering cannot easily be attributed to a specific agent, blame still needs to be assigned. This is true even for natural disasters. Although an earthquake or a pandemic cannot be blamed on a human agent, insufficient preparations or disaster responses can.[33] There is always something a company or its management could have done differently to save additional lives. Companies should expect to be blamed for the consequences, especially if the suffering is profound.

These emotional responses cannot be prevented or explained away, but companies can mitigate their impact. Managing such situations first requires an awareness of the emotional dynamics at work and an empathetic response that acknowledges the suffering in an authentic fashion. Second, disaster preparedness needs to move from a purely operational focus to include an empathetic response to human suffering, such as providing counseling to address the emotional needs of employees and community members. Third, prevention strategies need to be augmented by preparation strategies that limit the reputational impact should a disaster occur. This means that companies need to be able to demonstrate that they "did everything they could" in language that is easy to understand. Sometimes this may involve the use of third parties that can lend their credibility to a company's prevention strategies.

We can use these phenomena to gain a better understanding of the Toyota case discussed in chapter 2. As a multinational corporation, Toyota was not seen as being capable of experiencing "feelings." It could only be seen as a moral agent: a hero or a villain. The 911 call of the Saylor accident triggered empathy in the US public for the victims and firmly placed drivers who experienced unintended acceleration into the victim category. Moral typecasting removed them from being viewed as moral agents. Dyadic completion required a villain and quickly settled on the most obvious candidate: Toyota. Toyota's response was ineffective: it focused on technical expertise, ignoring the moral and emotional dimensions, and tried to shift the blame to perceived victims, violating the moral typecasting frame and leading to widespread public outrage.

WARMTH AND COMPETENCE.   Once companies are viewed as agents, we need to understand how their role is perceived. Social psychologists have argued that two dimensions influence social perception: *warmth* and *competence*. Perceptions of warmth are associated with kindness, generosity, sincerity, helpfulness, and so forth. They suggest a motivation that is other-oriented and driven by moral principles. Competence is driven by the motivation to enact one's intent, and is associated with confidence, effectiveness, skillfulness, and so forth (e.g., Cuddy, Fiske, and Glick 2007, 2008; Fiske et al. 2002; Judd et al. 2005). Perceptions of warmth and competence also affect trust.[34] Warmth is connected with the perception that the other person has one's best interest in mind, while competence relates to the person's ability to follow through on their promises.

The perception of social groups differs along these two dimensions, often resulting in different perceptions (often in the form of stereotypes), affective responses, and associated behavior. Indeed, cognition, affect, and behavior often operate in consonance. For example, the elderly are viewed as high in warmth, but low in competence. This elicits a typical emotional response of pity, which triggers a desire to help. In general, groups that are perceived to be low in competence but high in warmth elicit the signature affect of pity and the signature action of help; groups that are perceived to score high on both dimensions elicit admiration and the desire for cooperation; those that score low on both elicit contempt, often accompanied by neglect; and those that score high on competence and low on warmth elicit envy, accompanied by the desire to harm (Cuddy, Fiske, and Glick 2008).

Such social perceptions also apply to companies and other organizations. Companies score low on warmth, but high on competence (Aaker, Vohs, and Mogilner 2010). Companies are expected to follow through on their commitments and execute, and competence is often a necessary component for a company to be successful. In one study that examined service industry interactions, the effect of employee competence on customer satisfaction was seven times higher than the effect of warmth. Moreover, perceptions of warmth improved satisfaction only if the employee was already perceived as competent. For service interactions, no amount of warmth could compensate for a perceived lack of competence (Grandey et al. 2005). This is in marked contrast to studies of warmth and competence in individuals, wherein the warmth component carries more weight (Cuddy, Fiske, and Glick 2008).

Being perceived as competent has many benefits. Perceptions of competence are associated with expectations of high-quality products (e.g., Goldsmith, Lafferty, and Newell 2000) and an increased willingness by consumers to buy the company's products (Aaker, Vohs, and Mogilner 2010). On the other hand, not fulfilling expectations of competence can lead to disappointment and even a sense of betrayal among customers (Jordan, Diermeier, and Galinsky 2012). Various organizational types vary in how they are perceived. Whereas for-profit companies are seen as relatively more competent than warm, nonprofits are usually perceived as low in competence, but high in warmth (Aaker, Vohs, and Mogilner 2010; Kervyn, Fiske, and Malone 2012). This can lead to a lower willingness to buy a product from a nonprofit. The effect can be induced by simply varying the organization's domain name from .com (usually associated with for-profits) to .org (usually associated with nonprofits) (Aaker, Vohs, and Mogilner 2010). Endorsements by credible sources, such as the *Wall Street Journal*, and priming by using subtle cues to "money," however, removed the difference in perceptions of competence.[35] Indeed, once a nonprofit is seen as competent, willingness to buy its products can exceed the corresponding willingness in the case of a for-profit. Such willingness was accompanied by feelings of admiration, consistent with the typical affect associated with high competence–high warmth organizations (Aaker, Vohs, and Mogilner 2010). Nonprofit hospitals, for example, typically exceed for-profits on perceptions of trustworthiness, fairness, and humane treatment (Schlesinger, Mitchell, and Gray 2004).

The perception of warmth, even if accompanied by a perception of competence, is, however, not only an asset; it also bears risks. At the root are expectations that the respective organization has the customer's best interests in mind. Actions that disappoint this expectation can lead to a sense of betrayal. For example, executive compensation scandals have a far more significant impact on perception in the case of nonprofits. Experiments show that even very minor perks, such as the use of expensive bottled water, can undermine trust and perceptions of integrity in nonprofits (e.g., Schweinsberg et al. 2016). The perceptions of warmth and competence also impact the emotions people feel toward corporations. When companies have bad intentions and are seen as incompetent, they elicit contempt, while consumers feel admiration for companies that have good intentions and high levels of ability (Kervyn, Fiske, and Malone 2012).

In sum, while actions are often evaluated directly with respect to their moral value, actions can also be interpreted as signals about an agent's character. Judgments about an agent's character are not simply derived from judgments about actions, but constitute a different dimension. For example, the dollar value of executive perks is often nonmaterial, but they can elicit strong feelings of moral outrage. The focus here is not on direct harm or the violation of rights and other norms of behavior. Rather, observers ask themselves what kind of person "would do something like this?" Racist or sexist jokes and private comments are particularly strong character signals, as they do not serve any defensible business purpose.

Just as in the case of an individual, a company is also ascribed a character, and its actions are interpreted as signals about its character. There are, however, important differences between the character features of companies and of individuals. While adult individuals are seen as capable of forming intentions and having feelings, companies are viewed as acting with intent but also as not being able to experience emotions. This pattern has the important consequence that in crisis situations individuals can be victims, villains, or heroes, while for companies the victim role is not available; they can only be villains or heroes. To become the hero, companies are well advised to act with competence *and* warmth. Agents that are only competent tend to elicit negative responses such as a sense of coldness and envy, even hatred, while agents that score high on both warmth and competence elicit admiration and a desire to cooperate.

3.3   Social Relations

3.3.1   Exchange and Community

Finally, we consider the view that moral evaluations and behavior emerge out of the norms and expectations associated with particular types of social relationships (Rai and Fiske 2011). The social relationship approach argues that moral evaluations cannot solely be understood by focusing on features of actions (e.g., Did an action cause harm? Was it intentional? Was it fair?) or persons (What was the person's moral character?). Rather, the moral status of an action will be viewed differently depending on the nature of the social relationship in which it takes place (Clark and Mills 1979; Rai and Fiske 2011).

Consider the following two settings for a dinner. If you are served dinner at a restaurant, you pay for the meal, and if you enjoyed the food and service, you leave a tip. Such behavior is appropriate in a commercial relationship (here between the customers—the diners—and the service provider—the restaurant and the server). But the same behavior is completely inappropriate if you are invited for dinner at your neighbor's house. Leaving a tip or asking for the check will likely cause consternation and outrage. Rather, in the case of the dinner invitation, we have a highly ritualized form of gift giving and receiving. The guest brings a bottle of wine or some flowers and, rather than paying for the meal, they may reciprocate with an invitation for a future dinner at their house.

Economists have long pointed out that such forms of gift giving are inefficient. Gifts introduce transaction costs and limit choices. A $50 gift card to a restaurant, for example, restricts a recipient's choice to that restaurant, and, more generally, any gift restricts the recipient's choice to that one object, the gift. From this perspective, the only efficient gift is cash (Waldfogel 1993). Yet, in many contexts, cash gifts are seen as wholly inappropriate.

To make sense of such phenomena, Clark and Mills (1979, 1993) introduced the distinction between exchange and community orientations.[36] The paradigmatic case of an *exchange orientation* is found in market transactions; buyers purchase goods and services for money. There is a clear and explicit expectation of compensation; self-interested behavior and bargaining are expected. Exchange orientations can be long-term and involve personal bonds, for instance, in a business partnership, but such bonds are based on and sustained by mutual self-interest and benefit.

In contrast, *communal orientations* are originally driven by need and caring. Actions are intended to meet another person's need without expecting specific compensation. The paradigmatic examples are caring for children and responding to the needs of members of the community (such as calling an ambulance for an injured person). Such actions may become highly ritualized, such as bringing a dish to share at a pot-luck dinner or volunteering at a school event. The motivations for community-oriented actions may be altruistic, but they do not need to be. Instead, they may be driven by a desire to comply with a communal norm. Sometimes, community orientations carry an expectation of reciprocity ("I help you move your furniture, you help me move my furniture"), but such expectations are not explicit, and stating them is considered inappropriate and a violation of the norm. It is appropriate for a lawyer to send a bill for services, but not to ask one's dinner guests to invite one over to their home the next weekend (Clark and Mills 1993).[37]

We can see the subtleties of this distinction in the following example (Clark and Mills 1993; Mills and Clark 1982): We expect to see price tags in a store, but we remove them when we give a gift. Indeed, it is appropriate and expected for a sales clerk in a store to apologize that a sales tag is missing and also to apologize for having failed to remove the price tag after gift-wrapping an item. The point is that social relations are governed by sets of distinct rules, norms, and conventions. Violating them is as appropriate as tackling the pitcher at a baseball game.[38]

Failing to recognize social orientations can have unintended consequences. An example is a field experiment conducted by Gneezy and

Rustichini (2000) in Israeli daycare centers. Parents were frequently late to collect their children in the afternoon, which annoyed the staff who had to stay after hours so as not to leave the children unattended. To reduce the parents' tardiness, the daycare centers introduced a monetary fine for late parents. To their surprise, the fine systems substantially *increased* the number of late-arriving parents, a feature that persisted even after removing the late arrival fee. Parents originally felt a sense of obligation—a moral norm not to be late—but the introduction of the fee reframed their approach from a sense of communal duty to an exchange orientation. The fine became a price paid for extra service for which many busy parents decided they were more than willing to pay.

3.3.2   Natural Disasters, Terrorist Attacks, and Pandemics

In the daycare example, the center's fee policy caused a change from a communal to an exchange organization. Sometimes external events can trigger such shifts. Among such triggers are natural disasters, terrorist attacks, and pandemics. In each case the community has experienced collective hardship that created urgent need for help and relief.

Disaster relief is one of the few opportunities for companies to improve their reputation on a large scale. Disasters are events with high visibility and attention, where considerations are more fluid and new associations and memories can be formed. The main difference between external events such as natural disasters, terrorist attacks, and pandemics versus corporate crises is that the company is not viewed as a causal agent for the calamity. That does not mean, however, that audiences do not have high expectations for companies during such external disasters. Whether the company was sufficiently prepared, how it handled the event, and so on, quickly take center stage. If the company's efforts are found lacking, accusations that it took shortcuts to save money frequently follow.

A particularly striking example is Tokyo Electric Power Company (TEPCO), operator of the Fukushima Daiichi nuclear power plant. During a devastating earthquake and tsunami in March 2011, the plant's emergency cooling systems were overwhelmed by tsunami waves more than twice the height of those the plant was built to withstand. With the cooling system rendered inoperable, several of the reactors failed, releasing radioactive material and shutting down the entire plant. Both TEPCO and the Japanese government were criticized for a lack of transparency and timely release of information; the company was viewed as both uncaring and incompetent. Indeed, the Fukushima Daiichi meltdown pushed the debate over the safety of nuclear power in Japan to new levels, resulting in a dramatic decrease in the use of nuclear power across the country (Fackler 2012; Normile 2018; Tabuchi 2012).

But leaders are not only in the spotlight for their current conduct; their preceding actions (or inaction) also come under heavy scrutiny. TEPCO's history of safety violations quickly took center stage, while the Japanese government was criticized for a lack of oversight and too cozy a relationship with the nuclear power industry. Similarly, during the COVID-19 crisis the US government under President Trump was accused of lack of preparation, slow and misleading communication, and of political meddling with public health officials.

But natural disasters can also provide opportunities for companies to be viewed as heroes. One such instance occurred in the aftermath of Hurricane Katrina. On October 3, 2005, *Fortune* magazine gave three companies the hero treatment. Under the front-page headline, "When Government Broke Down, Business Stepped Up," *Fortune* highlighted the relief efforts of Wal-Mart, FedEx, and Home Depot in the aftermath of Hurricane Katrina. The coverage in the *Fortune* article highlighted many of the things these companies did right in their responses. For example, Wal-Mart trucks hauled over $3 million in relief supplies to victims (Leonard 2005), FedEx delivered over 400 tons of relief supplies (Kratz 2005), and Home Depot analyzed community needs and sent over 800 trucks filled with carefully selected merchandise intended to provide shelter and rebuild homes. Yet the unusually positive response of these press (and public) accolades prompts the question of why these companies, and not others, received such favorable responses. After all, virtually all Fortune 500 companies were involved in Hurricane Katrina relief efforts, donating approximately $500 million dollars within the first week following the disaster (Hempel and Leak 2005).

Various explanations come to mind. First, all three companies excelled in the effectiveness of their responses, leveraging their respective core competencies in distribution, logistics, and retail. Home Depot, for example, chose only items that would address victims' most pressing needs. But that was not the only distinguishing feature. All three companies' relief efforts were characterized by the direct personal involvement of company employees. Wal-Mart's store managers reportedly gave away much of the store's supplies to residents—in one case even breaking into the pharmacy to provide diabetic victims with life-saving insulin.[39]

These characteristics point to a broader phenomenon. Natural disasters, terrorist attacks, and pandemics trigger a community orientation. It is well known that during natural disasters or after terrorist attacks communities tend to come together (Solnit 2010). For example, following Hurricane Katrina, boat owners from all around the Gulf Coast sailed into New Orleans to save people who had been stranded by the flooding. In such circumstances, companies are now also viewed as members of the community and not simply as providers of goods and services. This creates expectations for companies to respond to their needs in alignment with a community orientation, rather than the exchange orientation that governs day-to-day business interactions. Jordan, Diermeier, and Galinsky (2012) have called this the "Good Samaritan effect." That is, in an external crisis such as a natural disaster or terrorist attack, companies are expected to act as the Good Samaritan in the Bible, and companies offering their help should be motivated by a desire to help rather than by self-interest.

The Good Samaritan effect implies that the help needs to be warm and empathetic but also competent. Indeed, ineffective assistance not only undermines perceptions of corporate competence, but also of integrity. The public then suspects ulterior motives. Actual competence of relief efforts is much more important than the strategic alignment of response efforts with companies' core products or capabilities. Indeed, a response that is too closely aligned with a company's business purpose may even be viewed negatively. For example, if a beauty company were to send skin moisturizer to victims needing clean water, the public would likely severely criticize them, seeing the move as self-serving (Jordan, Diermeier, and Galinsky 2012).

In general, both warmth and competence need to be present for a positive impression during a natural disaster. Having executives assist victims personally is viewed far more positively than just donating money. There are various reasons for this. First, sending money is consistent with an exchange orientation rather than a community orientation. Second, sending money from a distance removes physical proximity, one of the factors that enhances the moral impact of an action. In addition, the causal chain between the action and its positive consequences is longer and less clear.[40] Any action that hints at an exchange orientation, for example, offering discounts for bottled water rather than providing it for free, tend to be viewed harshly. As a consequence, companies need to be especially cautious in their communications approach. Anything that can be interpreted as self-promotion is likely to backfire.

These insights can be confirmed in controlled experiments. Uhlmann et al. (2009), replicated in Schweinsberg et al. (2016), provided subjects with four scenarios. In the "charity only" condition, a fictitious company was reported to have made a donation of $500,000 to support cancer research. In the "publicized charity" condition, the company donated $500,000 to cancer research and subsequently spent $2 million publicizing its charitable contribution. In the "charity and advertising" condition, the company donated $500,000 for cancer research and subsequently spent $2 million on unrelated product advertising. In the control condition, the company did not donate any money to charity. Subjects rated the company that publicized its charity works last, even lower than the control condition where the company had not donated any money to charity whatsoever. The same pattern was found with respect to trust in the company.

Wal-Mart's strategy avoided these pitfalls. Its efforts to help Hurricane Katrina victims in 2005 highlighted the corporation's competence (for example, delivery of water and other supplies well before the federal government's relief effort) and warmth (such as store managers personally distributing emergency supplies), yielding large reputational benefits. Wal-Mart also allowed store managers and truck drivers to talk directly to the media, a highly unusual step for a company that usually tightly restricts media contacts of its employees. Executives, on the other hand, the company's usual public spokespeople, adopted a very low profile. This approach was consistent with a communal orientation of neighbors helping neighbors and played an important role in boosting Wal-Mart's reputation. It also energized the company's employees and provided a sense of pride.[41]

Terrorist attacks similarly induce a community orientation. During the November 26, 2008, terrorist attack on the Taj Mahal Palace hotel in Mumbai, the hotel staff and management performed extraordinary feats of heroism. Hotel staff calmly instructed guests to seek cover and pointed them to escape routes, insisting on leaving last. In one such episode, a 48-year-old waiter, Thomas Varghese, ensured the safety of 50 guests at a hotel restaurant by insisting on staying behind until all the guests were evacuated. Varghese was gunned down by the terrorists before he could escape. The hotel's general manager Karambir Singh Kang lost his wife and children during the attack, but insisted on leading the rescue efforts until noon the next day. Only then did he call his parents to tell them about the death of his family (Deshpandé and Raina 2011).

Such extraordinary efforts are often rooted in a company's values and culture, defined and constantly reinforced by leadership. In the case of the

Tata Group, owner of the Taj Mumbai, extreme customer focus permeates every aspect of its corporate culture, from recruitment to training, rewards, and career development (Deshpandé and Raina 2011).

This culture is exemplified by the company's response to the terrorist attacks. In the immediate aftermath of the attack, the company set up post-trauma counseling centers. Subsequently, Raymond Brickson, chief executive of Taj Hotels Resorts and Palaces, and Ratan Tata, chairman of Tata Group, created a trust to pay the families of the 15 Taj employees who died in the attacks the salaries of the deceased for the rest of their lives, as well as to cover all medical benefits and educational benefits for their children up to age 24. In addition, Taj Hotels would provide immediate relief to all families of those who were killed, whether employees of Tata or not. Staff were recognized in ceremonies and the list of the victims displayed on a commemorative plaque in the hotel's lobby.

Pandemics, such as the COVID-19 crisis, are particularly challenging due to their long duration and persistent uncertainty and fear. Moreover, due to the economic impact of pandemics, companies are often forced to lay off or furlough employees, a process that may undermine expectations associated with a community orientation. These difficulties require leaders to engage in frequent, transparent communication that expresses empathy for the victims of the crisis in an authentic fashion. While the impact on the business may capture most of the leader's attention, this needs to be balanced by concern for the fear and physical well-being of their employees and their families. We discuss the dimension of fear in detail below.

In sum, natural disasters, terrorist attacks, and pandemics are paradigms of communal orientations. They trigger a helper paradigm characterized by warmth and competence. Companies need to conduct themselves in alignment with these expectations. The problem for companies is that they spend most of their existence in only one social orientation, exchange, and then fail to recognize that the social context has shifted. That is less of a problem in the case of natural disasters, pandemics, or terrorist attacks, where the shift is marked by a public and highly salient event, but it becomes more difficult if it is the consequence of a company action or involves management across cultures. Here, a deeper understanding of social contexts can prove highly valuable.

3.3.3   Structures of Social Life

One prominent approach to the study of social contexts, *relational models theory*, distinguishes four basic models that structure human relationships and social interactions: market pricing, communal sharing, authority rank-ing, and equality matching (Fiske 1991; Fiske and Haslam 2005; Rai and Fiske 2011).[42] In *market pricing*, interactions are characterized by expec-tations of return, such as payment for services, efficiency, and the effective allocation of resources. Market pricing often involves the use of a com-mon metric, that is, money, that makes otherwise noncomparable goods and services comparable. Its core principle is *proportionality*, payment according to value. It is the closest analogue to Clark and Mills's con-cept of exchange orientation. However, the principle of proportionality goes beyond market exchange and also influences certain notions of fair-ness, for example, compensation according to the contribution or value added. That is, rather than treating people equally, they are treated pro-portionally. Violations of proportionality thus can mean that a person receives too little compared to what they deserve or too much. Get-ting something for nothing is just as unfair as getting less than what you deserve.

The case of executive compensation is a paradigm for problems of this sort. The public debate over executive compensation often focuses on the level of compensation. Yet high compensation levels alone cannot explain public outrage. High-tech CEOs routinely receive very high compensation packages but face little criticism. We have already seen the importance of perks as a tell of the CEO's (deficient) moral character. Social relations theory adds another dimension: the disconnect between compensation and performance, especially when a CEO is fired or resigns amid controversy, but still walks away with a substantial compensation package. In 2006, for example, Pfizer's CEO Henry McKinnell left the company with an exit package of over $213 million, despite a loss of $137 billion in the company's market value during his tenure (Dash 2007a, 2007b). At the heart of these cases is a difference between what is viewed as fair ex ante and ex post. A contract that may look fair ex ante may look unfair ex post. Deferred compensation is one example. A board may decide to defer a substantial amount of a CEO's compensation, for example, for tax reasons or to pro-vide better incentives. Such incentives may seem reasonable and efficient ex ante, but may lead to outrage when the CEO exits and is now contrac-tually entitled to the deferred compensation. The deferred compensation may have been accumulated over a lifetime of successful service in differ-ent roles at the company. Pfizer's CEO McKinnell, for example, had spent 30 years at the company. However, despite years of successful service, if a CEO's final exit comes after an unsuccessful period, the optics of the case are awful and may trigger public outrage.

A similar dynamic arises in "make-whole payments" that are often needed to attract outside CEOs. In general, the structure of CEOs' compensation is heavily influenced by "comparables," that is, what others at similar rank are making, as well as by incentive structures and tax considerations. These assessments can become especially complicated when a company is pursuing outside candidates who have had successful careers at other companies and, over time, have accumulated various incentives, options, stock purchase plans, pensions, deferred compensation, and so on, a significant part of which will be lost if the executive leaves his current employer. To be attractive, the hiring company will need to "make its desired new CEO whole," that is, offer compensation that accounts for these previously accumulated benefits. Note that make-whole compensation will tend to be guaranteed, since it is intended to compensate for lost income from leaving the former employer rather than as an incentive for future performance with the new employer. To the public such make-whole packages may look outrageously generous, but they are often necessary for the candidate to leave his current employer.

These two features can also be combined. This is the case when paying a make-whole payment is not structured as a cash signing bonus, but as deferred compensation to be paid when the new CEO leaves the company. This can lead to additional difficulties, especially in cases where the new CEO is not successful and departs after only a few months. Given the prior make-whole agreement, the company now needs to make a massive payment, right after it has dismissed its leader for ineffectiveness. Of course, when agreeing on the contract in advance, the board did not know that the CEO would fail. Otherwise, presumably, it would not have hired him. The guaranteed bonus was necessary to attract what seemed to be the most promising candidates, and the candidate CEOs are unlikely to walk away from their accumulated compensation at their previous employers. After all, that money was earned during years of successful service. The problem occurs ex post, when the CEO turns out to be unsuccessful. What looked reasonable and fair ex ante looks outrageous now. Once outrage has been triggered, it is difficult to overcome the emotional response with a detailed explanation of the logic of executive compensation that, moreover, looks self-serving from the point of view of the board. In the mind of the public, the exit payments look like "money for nothing," a fundamental violation of the principle of proportionality.

These phenomena are well illustrated by the following example. In January 2000, Bob Nardelli took over as Home Depot's new CEO. Nardelli came from a long, distinguished career at General Electric (GE), where he started as a stocker and eventually worked his way up to become CEO of the company's power systems business in 1995. He arrived at Home Depot after losing out to Jeff Immelt in a three-way race to succeed Jack Welch as GE's new CEO. Home Depot had been a success story in the retail sector and was named "Most Admired Specialty Retailer" for the sixth year in a row by *Fortune* magazine in 1999 (*Fortune* 1999). However, Home Depot's board believed the company had relied too much on ad hoc expansion and lacked a well-designed growth strategy. Nardelli's task was to develop such a strategy and execute it. His compensation package was substantial and complex, not surprising given his track record at GE and the use of retention bonuses by GE to induce Nardelli and the other potential GE executives to participate in the contest to succeed Welch.[43] In addition to an annual base salary of no less than $1.5 million and an annual bonus at a target of no less than $3 million, Nardelli received a make-whole compensation package to compensate him for foregone stock options and equity compensation at GE. According to his employment agreement dated December 4, 2000, the package included the following: $50,400 in cash, a $10 million loan which was to be forgiven after five years, a 10-year stock option grant of 2.5 million shares that would become vested in increments of 500,000 shares over the following five years, and a 10-year, fully vested stock option grant of one million shares worth $25 million. After the board later agreed to cover the taxes on Nardelli's $10 million loan, his employment package reached a value of at least $50 million, excluding the tens of millions of dollars in future earnings he would stand to gain from his unvested stock option grant (Creswell 2006; US Securities and Exchange Commission 2000).

Things worked well at first. Less than a year after Nardelli's arrival, Home Depot enjoyed a market capitalization of $115 billion, second only to Wal-Mart among retailers and far bigger than its primary competitor Lowe's, which had a market cap of about $30 billion (Deutsch 2001). But this honeymoon did not last. By 2006, Home Depot's shareholders were increasingly weary of Nardelli's autocratic management style and the company's stagnant stock price. While net income had increased by 129 percent and revenue was up 100 percent, Home Depot's stock was up less than 6 percent, lagging behind the S&P 500 at 7.7 percent. By comparison, Lowe's stock had climbed 230 percent over the same period (Jones and Krantz 2007). Moreover, Nardelli's high compensation angered shareholders. Since 2000, he had collected $245 million in total pay, four times as much as Lowe's CEO (Creswell 2006).

Things took a turn for the worse when on May 16, 2006, to the astonishment of analysts and investors, Nardelli announced that Home Depot would no longer report same-store quarterly sales, a key metric in the retail industry (Bhatnagar 2006). This was followed nine days later by a tumultuous shareholder meeting. Investors were irate and prepared to voice their opinions at the meeting (Kavilanz 2007). To their surprise and outrage, Home Depot's board did not attend the meeting. Rather, Nardelli delivered a 30-minute presentation and subsequently used large digital timers to restrict shareholders' questions to one minute each, cutting the microphone if questions exceeded the time limit (Morgenson 2006). Subsequently, 30 percent of shareholders withheld votes from 10 of the 11 directors up for election, far exceeding the average at the time, which was well below 10 percent (Terhune and Lublin 2006). On January 2, 2007, Home Depot's board decided to act and reached a mutual agreement with Nardelli for him to resign (Grow 2007). His departure, however, was not without controversy. In accordance with terms outlined in his hiring contract, Nardelli received a $210 million exit package. The agreement awarded him $20 million in severance pay, a $32 million pension, a $2 million 401(k) retirement plan, $139 million in stock options and deferred equity awards, and $18 million in "other entitlements" which Home Depot did not specify (Dash 2007b). Investors and the general public were outraged at what they considered "golden parachutes" for failing CEOs. "We're aghast at the level of compensation that Nardelli is walking away with—this is money directly out of shareholders' pockets," remarked one investor (Creswell 2007).[44]

Executive compensation is not the only example where ex ante and ex post proportionality notions diverge. Similar problems occurred in the context of subprime lending. Subprime lenders often used lock-in mechanisms, such as significant prepayment penalties, to compensate for the risk of losing their customers due to refinancing at prime rates once their credit score improves. Lock-in mechanisms may lower effective rates and may look acceptable to a borrower when they have no alternative due to a low credit score. However, once borrowers recover their financial health, such mechanisms are likely to be perceived as unacceptable financial handcuffs (Diermeier 2011).

Corporate decision makers need to be aware of these pitfalls. They pose substantial reputational risks, as they clash with fundamental notions of proportionality. However, the possible reputational damage is often not considered in the design or pricing of such contracts. If possible, such arrangements should be avoided. At the very least, the possible reputational consequences need to be part of the decision-making calculus.

Communal sharing relations are characterized by contributions driven by need, gift giving rather than exchange, and are often motivated by an overarching common group purpose or goal. Communal sharing sharply distinguishes between members of the group (in-group), such as families, teams, clans, or military units, and others (out-group). Communal sharing is driven by concerns about *unity*, that is, caring for and supporting the integrity of the in-group. Actions and judgments attempt to respond to needs of in-group members, but also respond to threats or contamination. The desire for unity can manifest itself in virtues such as loyalty and concerns for purity.[45] Group members share equal responsibility for the well-being of the group and are expected to punish or discipline violators. Communal sharing is thus closely related to Clark and Mills's community orientation, but it adds a sharp distinction between in- and out-groups and the need to maintain group unity against transgressions, even through violence. The response to the Danish cartoons discussed in chapter 3 is a paradigmatic example of this aspect of communal sharing. Mutual assistance during natural disasters, as we have seen in the case of Wal-Mart and Hurricane Katrina, are also instantiations of the same principle, though without an emphasis on the in-group/out-group dynamic. Responses to terrorist attacks, in contrast, tend to highlight communal unity and patriotism.

Authority ranking is concerned with creating and maintaining social differentiation. Its predominant concern is *hierarchy*. Critical virtues among followers are respect, obedience, and deference, while leaders are expected to guide, protect, and care for their subordinates. According to the authority ranking model, individuals are not to be treated alike, but differently according to their role or status. Treating people equally despite their difference in rank is viewed as a potentially severe violation. Military hierarchies are paradigms of this social domain, but they occur in many other contexts, including corporations. Some ethical systems, such as Confucianism, are based on hierarchies with well-defined rights and obligations. Hierarchies often come with visual markers, ranging from the large headdress of a Mayan king to the stars of a US general, or the expensive sports car or watch of the successful executive. They serve as signals to others and reaffirm the owner of her own position in the social hierarchy.

Hierarchical relationships are endemic in corporate life. Those with higher status have different expectations than those with lower status. This can also affect moral judgment and the sense of what is permissible. Lammers, Staple, and Galinsky (2010) found that individuals who were primed to feel an elevated sense of power judged their own hypothetical transgressions more leniently. Executive perks often serve as status markers. These may include a private plane, but also smaller perks like separate elevators or dining facilities. In some cases, executive compensation schemes specifically draw a sharp line between senior executives and others, such as when a company covers the executives' co-pay in health plans or other small fees. Despite the very small financial impact on the executive, "receiving special treatment" reaffirms status.

Equality matching, with its corresponding concept *equality*, is concerned with enforcing balance and in-kind reciprocity. It is expressed in phenomena such as turn taking, equal contributions, equal say, equal opportunity, and so forth. It is at the basis of many conceptions of equal rights, nondiscrimination, and equity as fundamental forms of justice. Such concerns motivate people to be more focused on receiving an equal share than a larger share (Bazerman, White, and Loewenstein 1995) or to reject unequal offers in the ultimatum game, as discussed in chapter 3. They underlie solutions such as coinflips or 50-50 splits. Violations include racial and gender discrimination and failures to reciprocate. These ideas are also connected to "eye for an eye" revenge and other forms of reciprocal punishment. Equality matching also occurs in the context of natural disasters. Recall that managers were perceived more positively if they were on the ground, pitching in *like everyone else*. Notice that this gives us a more nuanced view of the disaster response context and, indeed, communal orientations. It involves a rejection of market pricing and authority ranking, but combines communal sharing (responding to needs) and equality matching (equal, direct contributions).[46]

Authority ranking and equality matching can frequently come into conflict as we move from one context where status is endemic and well understood to another context where equality is emphasized. Corporate hierarchies, for example, are potent only inside the corporate context and do not carry over to interactions with the outside world, many of which are characterized by equality matching. New CEOs, for example, are often startled by how they are treated by the press, analysts, or politicians. Inside the company, they are used to an environment of deference and respect. Outside, especially in democratic polities, equality matching prevails and status symbols are greeted with suspicion and hostility. Recall the Big Three car-maker CEOs using private planes to fly to Washington as a classic example of not recognizing these differences. Misunderstanding that one has moved from one social relation to another can have severe consequences, often leading to anger and outrage.

Social relations theory can help us understand when and how people will rely on one set of moral principles than another. For example, once individuals are in a community sharing mindset, certain actions consistent with a proportionality orientation are viewed as despicable. For example, most responders react with outrage when asked how much people should pay to obtain US citizenship (e.g., Fiske and Tetlock 1997; Tetlock et al. 2000).

A particularly interesting conflict occurs in social contexts where market mechanisms are seen as morally wrong but unavoidable, as in engagement gifts, weddings, and funerals (e.g., McGraw, Tetlock, and Kristel 2003; McGraw et al. 2016). Here, because one "cannot put a price on love," consumers tend to overspend or need "guidance" from marketers, as in the traditional US norm to spend two months' salary on an engagement ring.[47] This willingness to pay higher amounts stems from the difficulty people have in mapping a sacred or communal domain, in which goods are not assigned a value, onto a market domain, in which goods must be priced.[48] The morality of the domain has impacts not only on buyers but on sellers as well. In the same manner that people think it is wrong to take advantage of natural disasters, people are uncomfortable with sellers in communal domains engaging in market pricing and profit seeking. For example, people feel greater distress when churches, funeral homes, hospitals, and pharmaceutical companies adopt market pricing-oriented marketing strategies (e.g., McGraw, Tetlock, and Kristel 2003; McGraw, Schwartz, and Tetlock 2011). This distress is particularly pronounced for products related to an urgent need, which triggers community orientations, compared to discretionary items. For example, people express greater distress when pharmaceutical companies engage in market pricing tactics to sell cholesterol medication (a need) compared to wrinkle cream (a luxury) (McGraw, Schwartz, and Tetlock 2011). Distress at mixing communal and sacred domains with market pricing domains may also underlie the distaste people have for high overhead at charities, even though such expenses may attract better talent that ultimately leads to more effective impact, and the money is going to actors who are doing good (Gneezy, Keenan, and Gneezy 2014).

Domain confusions are particularly likely when an agent spends most of her life in one domain, but, in some rare cases, finds herself in a decision context governed by different social rules. Companies mostly live in a world of market pricing, which makes monetary compensation a natural response. But sometimes the social relation changes. Now, the same monetary compensation may look inappropriate, or even offensive. Consider stem cell research, short-selling, prediction markets involving crime or death, and so on. Domain confusion is particularly likely in global business decisions that involve cross-cultural differences with different standards for what is considered sacred or disgusting (e.g., Fiske 1991; Fiske and Tetlock 1997).

An interesting and understudied question is when and under what conditions the various orientations are actualized. We discussed one such example in the context of natural disasters, when we move from an exchange or market pricing orientation to a communal orientation where everyone pitches in to address the community's needs. Fiske (1991) points to various constitutive factors that play an important role in how social relations are regulated. Often these factors are symbolic or ritualized. Authority ranking can be reinforced by a big headdress, a throne on an elevated platform, or an office on the top floor with a private elevator. Similarly, market pricing orientations can be triggered by introducing charges or prices where they did not exist before, as in the daycare example, or by concepts such as "optimal pollution" or a "market for organs." How to induce such orientations systematically is still an open question.

3.4 Summary

Moral outrage is one of the main sources of reputational crises. It is the emotional response to a perceived violation of an ethical norm, value, or principle and frequently leads to direct actions such as protest, boycotts, or even violence, often fueled by intense anger and resentment. Recent advances in moral psychology and cultural anthropology have made these processes more understandable and predictable.

The factors that shape moral judgment are multifaceted. Here we focused on three major approaches. The first, *moral foundations theory* (e.g., Graham et al. 2013; Haidt 2013b), identifies five major moral principles: Care/Harm, Fairness/Cheating, Loyalty/Betrayal, Authority/Subversion, and Sanctity/Degradation.[49] We saw how these principles can explain outrage in many different contexts. They also help in avoiding the main mistake made by managers and executives: the "moral blind-spot," that is, the inability to evaluate corporate actions from the point of view of morality rather than just expediency and efficiency, and the accompanying failure to adjust actions and strategies accordingly.

The second approach, *person-centered morality* (e.g., Pizarro and Tannenbaum 2011; Uhlmann, Pizarro, and Diermeier 2015), adds a different dimension to our understanding of moral outrage. Here actions are not simply evaluated by themselves but serve as signals of a person's moral character. Observers ask themselves, "What kind of a person would do something like that?" While the actions themselves may have little or no direct consequences, they can be highly informative. Managers and executives are often unaware that such actions can serve as powerful "tells" about a person's character, especially when they are considered harmless in the usual social context. Particularly powerful examples are perks, jokes, and unguarded private comments.

The principles of person-centered morality also apply to companies and other organizations, though companies are not simply seen as "persons." Rather, they are ascribed intentions but not emotions. This implies that they are not usually seen as victims, even if they were clearly subjected to criminal activity, such as a cyber attack. Managers and executives rarely elicit empathy from the public and instead need to focus on gaining admiration rather than contempt, that is, acting as the hero rather than the villain. This can be done by acting in a way that conveys both warmth and competence.

The third approach, *social relations theory*, emphasizes the importance of understanding actions and transactions in a social context (e.g., Clark and Mills 1979, 1993; Fiske 1991; Rai and Fiske 2011). For example, having dinner in a restaurant corresponds to an exchange orientation governed by market mechanisms, while being invited to dinner in a private home is governed by a communal orientation. Tipping is expected in the first setting, but would be outrageous in the second. Managers and executives need to realize when social contexts change. For example, regular business interactions are shaped by exchange orientations, and practices like providing a discount for bottled water is a perfectly acceptable business practice. But doing the same thing during a natural disaster would elicit outrage, as natural disasters, like terrorist attacks and pandemics, trigger communal orientations characterized by volunteering and free sharing.

Understanding such principles and integrating them into a properly designed reputational risk management process enables a more sophisticated approach to the assessment of reputational risk and the development of prevention and preparation strategies for reputational crises. How to design and operationalize such processes is the subject of chapter 21.

CHAPTER FOUR

Affective Primacy and Dual-Process Theories of Cognition

4.1 Sentiment and Affect

In the first part of the book we discussed six major principles of opinion formation: repetition, recency, attention, affect, consonance, and online processing. In our discussion of moral outrage we could see some of these principles at work. For example, natural disasters generate significantly higher levels of attention, a feature that makes considerations more fluid. Hence, actions taken during such times of crisis are more likely to be remembered. Wal-Mart was able to improve its reputation during such a crisis, while TEPCO was not. The most important principle in understanding reputational risk, however, whether through outrage or fear, is affect. As we will see, it can provide a unifying foundation for the psychological aspects of reputational risk.

A long tradition in philosophical ethics has viewed moral judgments as the consequence of reason. This basic assumption, which has also dominated business ethics for many decades, has recently been challenged by moral psychologists. As we saw in the previous chapter, their approach highlights the roles of emotions and intuitions in moral evaluations and provides broad evidence that moral reactions are better predicted by emotions than by reasoning (Haidt 2001, 2007; Haidt and Kesebir 2010; Knobe 2006; Sunstein 2005).

This view is not new. It goes back to the moral philosophers of the Scottish Enlightenment such as the Earl of Shaftesbury, Francis Hutcheson, Adam Smith, and especially David Hume. The core concept of this approach is the primacy of "moral sentiment." This is expressed in Hume's famous quote from the *Treatise of Human Nature* (Hume [1739] 2000, pp. 414–415):

> It is obvious, that when we have the prospect of pain or pleasure from any object, we feel a consequent emotion of aversion or propensity, and are carryed to avoid or embrace what will give us this uneasines or satisfaction. It is also obvious, that this emotion rests not here, but making us cast our view on every side, comprehends whatever objects are connected with its original one by the relation of cause and effect. Here then reasoning takes place to discover this relation; and according as our reasoning varies, our actions receive a subsequent variation. But it is evident in this case that the impulse arises not from reason, but is only directed by it. It is from the prospect of pain or pleasure that the aversion or propensity arises towards any object: And these emotions extend themselves to the causes and effects of that object, as they are pointed out to us by reason and experience.... Reason is, and ought only to be the slave of the passions, and can never pretend to any other office than to serve and obey them.

Modern psychology has argued that such "feelings" or "emotions" are based on *affects*, small flashes of negative or positive feeling that prepare the respondent to approach or avoid something (e.g., Haidt 2013a; LeDoux 1998; Wundt 1927; Zajonc 1980, 2000). Affects are not fully developed emotions, they are too fleeting and undifferentiated. They happen first, faster, and with less effort than other forms of cognitive engagement. While emotions include an affective reaction, emotions are more than mere affect and constitute complex mental entities similar to beliefs and attitudes. Emotions, for example, are usually directed: "fear" may be directed at a snake, "disgust" at a cockroach, "anger" at one's boss, and so on.

4.2 Two Ways of Thinking

Over time, this approach led to the development of dual-process theories of cognition (e.g., Damasio 1994; Epstein 1994; Zajonc 1980). According to this approach, people comprehend and judge their environment in two different ways, sometimes called System I (the affective or experiential system) and System II (the deliberative or analytical system).[1] Epstein (1994, p. 710) states this as follows:

> There is no dearth of evidence in everyday life that people apprehend reality in two fundamentally different ways, one variously labeled intuitive, automatic, natural, non-verbal, narrative, and experiential, and the other analytical, deliberative, verbal, and rational.

System I is fast, easy, effortless, connected with affect, and often operates instantaneously with little control. System II is deliberative, analytical, and takes effort and concentration; engaging in System II requires focus and attention, often leading the person to be "blind" to other stimuli.[2] System II processes, such as active self-control and calculations, compete with each other and draw on the same limited resources, an "effort budget." As this budget of mental energy is depleted, self-control is weakened and the tendency for superficial choices increases (e.g., Gilbert 1991; Macrae and Bodenhausen 2000).

Dual-process approaches state that our System I everyday intuitions are an alternative cognitive system to the rational deliberation that we traditionally associate with judgment and decision making. Emotions and affect are not distractions or departures from the ideal of rationality, but work efficiently and reliably in most everyday decisions. Indeed, evolutionary psychologists have argued that System I processes evolved as efficient judgment and decision-making modules well suited to their original prehistoric environment. According to this view, rational deliberation is a much later adaptation, closely connected with the development of language (e.g., Gigerenzer 2007).[3] Recent research has tried to support this view by linking moral attitudes with evolutionary and physiological processes (Batson 1987; Damasio 1994; Greene et al. 2001; Lieberman 2007; Lieberman et al. 2002). For example, concerns for fairness can be linked with evolutionary needs for group collaboration (Cosmides and Tooby 1989), while purity concerns can be linked with avoidance of germs and infectious diseases (Haidt and Joseph 2008). The goal of this approach is to provide a biological grounding for moral intuitions and judgments and to understand them as adaptive solutions to evolutionary pressures in early human history.

When taken out of that original environment and operating in a modern context, however, System I processes can exhibit biases.[4] Indeed, it was these judgment and decision-making biases that propelled the research on System I processes (Tversky and Kahneman 1974).

System I is intimately associated with affect. That is, when experiencing an emotionally engaging event, System I retrieves associated events from memory. If the activated events are positive, they motivate actions and thoughts associated with such feelings. If they are negative, they motivate dissociated actions and thoughts (Epstein 1994). Observations may trigger emotions, and emotions may trigger memories that lead to other associations or physical reactions, such as increased blood pressure. This process of associative activation is associatively coherent; emotional, cognitive, and physical responses mutually reinforce each other (Kahneman 2011; Morewedge and Kahneman 2010). Such associations can be based on causality, temporal or spatial association, category membership, or the relationship between an object and its properties. Zajonc (1980) has argued that such processes serve as quick and efficient orienting and decision mechanisms that help humans navigate a dangerous environment.

An important aspect of System I is its holistic nature. System I is designed to create the most coherent "story" possible given the currently activated ideas. Coherence is accompanied by an experience of cognitive ease. Note that the story is based only on activated ideas; information that is not retrieved from memory plays no role. System I also does not evaluate or assess the quality of input; that is a function of System II. When information is limited, System I will tend to fill in the blanks to make the overall representation more coherent. Unless activated, System II does not control or limit this process, and the activation of System II requires costly effort.

The story constructed by System I will guide subsequent judgment and decision making. System I takes no account that its story is constructed or may be based on limited or faulty information. Rather, it regards it as true and jumps to conclusions. Kahneman (2011) refers to this as "what you see is all there is." For instance, we form immediate impressions of people within just a few seconds of meeting them, as if there were no other relevant information about the person that might currently be unavailable to us. Thus, System I is fast and efficient, but subject to biases. These biases include availability, overconfidence, confirmation bias, framing effects, and many more (e.g., Kahneman and Tversky 1979; Kahneman 2011; Tversky and Kahneman 1973, 1974, 1982). For instance, when using the availability heuristic, we base our decisions on the examples that most easily come to mind. Thus, if asked to estimate the likelihood of an airplane crash, we will provide a higher estimate if we have recently been exposed to media coverage about an airline crash. Similarly, the overconfidence bias, the tendency of agents to have more subjective confidence than is warranted by objective information, follows directly from the "what you see is all there is" principle. Thus, the measure of confidence generated by System I is not based on the quality or quantity of information, but rather on the coherence of a story and its associated cognitive ease.

Framing effects refer to the broad category of effects that reflect how different ways of representing the same information may trigger different associated feelings or memories. Once these associations are activated, the process of activation will lead to associated cognitive, emotional, or physical states. Once these associations occur, the "what you see is all there is" principle interprets this web of associations holistically—as all there is—setting aside the partial and incomplete basis for the web of beliefs.

These processes can also lead to polarization. For different value systems and personal histories, the same stimulus may trigger different associations; the word "technology" will lead to different memories and affects for an engineer than for an environmentalist. Once started, the self-reinforcing chain of associations leads to different affective and cognitive states, leading to different judgments and evaluations.

Another well-known example is reference dependence (Kahneman and Tversky 1979). Rather than evaluating the absolute value of a good, people evaluate the value of a good in relation to some other value, often a reference point. This causes predictable biases in judgments of fairness. For example, as discussed earlier, consumers find it unfair to take advantage of increases in demand by raising prices. However, if people perceive that a good is returning to its standard price rather than raising its price in response to demand shocks, consumers will not be angry. For example, in one study, it was found that if a car dealer was selling a car at list price and then increased the price in response to an increase in demand, most consumers found this action to be unfair. However, if the car dealer had previously been selling the car at a discount below list price and then increased the price of the car to list price in response to demand, most consumers felt that the action was fair (Kahneman, Knetsch, and Thaler 1986).

The differences between System I and System II can be summarized in the following table (Slovic et al. 2004, p. 313).

TABLE 4.1 **Two modes of thinking: Comparison of the experiential and analytic systems (from Slovic et al. 2004, p. 313)**

Experiential system	Analytic system
Holistic	Analytic
Affective: pleasure-pain oriented	Logical: reason oriented (what is sensible)
Associationistic connections	Logical connections
Behavior mediated by "vibes" from past experience	Behavior mediated by conscious appraisal of events
Encodes reality in concrete images, metaphors, and narratives	Encodes reality in abstract symbols, words, and numbers
More rapid processing: oriented toward immediate actions	Slower processing: oriented toward delayed action
Self-evidently valid: "experience is believing"	Requires justification via logic and evidence

4.3   Dual-Process Theory and the Study of Corporate Reputation

In this book, we take the approach that public attitudes toward companies are largely driven by System I processes. Few members of the public will spend the effort to acquire and process the relevant information about a company necessary to form a well-informed judgment. Moreover, most observers have little incentive to do so. This is particularly true for members of the public who are not customers, suppliers, employees, or investors. Yet mass public opinion can lead to immense pressure on companies, especially through its impact on political, regulatory, and legal decisions. Most members of the US public, for example, are not customers of Goldman Sachs and never will be. But once Goldman is widely perceived as the "giant vampire squid wrapped around the face of humanity" (Taibbi 2009), this perception creates incentives for public officials—whether legislators, regulators, or attorneys general—to go after the company to position themselves as the defenders of Main Street.

Even in cases where there is a business relationship and financial incentives are present, the System I processes may play an important role. Customers, especially consumers, rely extensively on System I processes when making many purchasing decisions. Understanding such processes in detail is the task of modern consumer research.[5]

From this perspective, we can then reinterpret the principles of moral psychology discussed in chapter 3. Similarly to David Hume, contemporary moral psychologists have argued that moral judgments originate from emotions, affect, and intuitions rather than being based on deliberation and analysis (Haidt 2001). According to this view, the function of deliberation and argument is not to ground moral judgment, but rather to justify and explain our moral intuitions to ourselves and others (Mercier and Sperber 2011). As expressed in the Consonance Principle, such judgments are justifications or rationalizations of an affective response which shapes the original intuition and judgment.[6]

Moral psychologists have provided various arguments for this view. For example, moral judgments do not require the mental effort characteristic of System II activities and can be made rapidly. In contrast to typical System II processes, they are unaffected if subjects are exposed to heavy cognitive load (Haidt 2013b). Also, moral judgments activate parts of the brain related to emotional processing (Greene et al. 2001).

The phenomenon of "moral dumbfounding" (Haidt 2001) provides additional evidence for the primacy of System I processes in moral judgments. Here, subjects exhibit strong adverse reactions to bizarre and disgusting moral violations, but when asked to explain their judgment, they struggle to find reasons—pointing to harm or justice violations to explain their reactions, even when the experimenter points out that such reasons have no basis in fact. For example, in a case of consensual incest, respondents may point to health risks or lack of consent, even though the scenarios were carefully created to eliminate such concerns. When the experimenters gently point out these fabrications, subjects retreat and look for another justification. When these efforts fail, subjects even invent facts to have them fit their pattern of reasoning. In the end, participants persist in claiming that, for example, the action is "just wrong," even though they cannot articulate why.[7]

Moral dumbfounding was first discovered when a population of well-educated college students was taking part in an experiment. Most students had liberal value systems and thus vainly searched for justifications among the principles that were available to them. As we discussed above, liberals tend to restrict the moral domain to two areas: the avoidance of harm and issues related to justice and rights. Issues that cannot easily be accounted for within these two areas are viewed by liberals as beyond moral judgment; they are viewed as convention, lifestyle choices, or instances of freedom of expression. Subjects felt the need to resolve the tension associated with moral dumbfounding because they were in an affective state (disgust) that was inconsistent with their moral universe; according to their own value system the feeling of disgust should not occur. Since the affect could not be controlled and subjects were not willing to give up their value system, the only viable resolution to this affective-cognitive dissonance was to find a justification for the reaction within the existing structure, even if that meant reconfiguring the scenario, for example, by inventing victims (Haidt 2013b; p. 28).

The reaction to these scenarios is quite different when the experiments are conducted with subjects who have a more conservative value orientation. In such cases, dimensions of purity, loyalty, and hierarchy are part of the moral repertoire. When confronted with a bizarre scenario, their reaction is immediate. But when asked by the interviewer to give a reason, they are dumbfounded why anyone would see the need for a reason when the behavior is despicable and just plain wrong (Haidt 2013b, p. 211). In this case, there is no tension between principles and affect. Rather, as discussed above, respondents interpret the very act of questioning as a signal about the interviewer's suspicious moral character.

Thus, according to the affective primacy approach, the reasons respondents give for their judgments are ex post justifications for their initial judgments generated by affect. In reference to Hume, Haidt (2013b, p. 47) summarizes this position as follows:

> Reasoning was merely the servant of the passions, and when the servant failed to find good arguments, the master did not change his mind.

The consequences of this approach for effective reputation management are profound. First, the explicit reasons given for an attitude toward a company may not reflect the actual moral intuitions, but tend to be post hoc rationalizations or justifications for an evaluation primarily driven by affect. A major implication of this claim is that refuting the stated reasons for consumers' or the public's complaints about corporate conduct may not actually quell their anger if the actual reasons driving their moral outrage differ from their expressed reasons. Companies that react to the surface justification may miss the underlying moral principle. For example, Feinberg and Willer (2011) show that many religious conservatives reject claims about global warming because such a phenomenon violates a deeply held belief in a world created by a benevolent god. But this is not how conservatives typically express their skepticism toward global warming research. Rather, conservatives may point to methodological issues related to climate change research or the political motivations of researchers. While many of these counterarguments may be flawed and fail to survive scientific scrutiny, trying to refute them with better statistical analysis of more data will be ineffective, as it does not address the underlying value conflict. Second, to be effective, strategies need to connect with System I, not just System II. This means that the messages used should connect with the deeper value orientation rather than only with the surface justifications. When using experts as credible third parties, their credibility should be grounded in shared values, not just domain expertise. For example, in a traditional community, religious leaders may have far more credibility than a professor from Cambridge, MA.

Third, peer-to-peer influence will be an important channel of attitude formation. Since people tend to associate with people like themselves, a phenomenon known as *homophily*, their value orientations tend to be aligned (McPherson, Smith-Lovin, and Cook 2001). This is especially pronounced in social networks where entry and exit is virtually costless, such as an online discussion forum. Members of a community will tend to trust each other more than they trust experts. Recent surveys have shown that among the most trusted individuals is "a person like yourself" (Edelman 2019). Indeed, some have argued that it is the opinion of members of a social network that is the main source of attitude change, not new arguments.[8] Haidt (2013b, p. 55) summarizes this view as follows:

> We make our first judgments rapidly, and we are dreadful at seeking out evidence that might disconfirm those initial judgments. Yet friends can do for us what we cannot do for ourselves: they can challenge us, giving us reasons and arguments that sometimes trigger new intuitions, thereby making it possible for us to change our minds.

The importance of the dual process approach, however, is not only limited to moral judgments and evaluations. It also affects the formation of beliefs (Erb, Bioy, and Hilton 2002). We already encountered this phenomenon in the case of global warming in a religious value system. When confronted with evidence that challenges their beliefs in a just, divinely created world, subjects resolve this value conflict not by abandoning their basic beliefs, but by doubting the evidence presented to them. Apparently neutral information is interpreted and evaluated in ways to make it consistent with value orientations and affect. Thus, affect not only shapes evaluations, but also beliefs. This phenomenon is known as "motivated reasoning" (Epley and Gilovich 2016; Mercier and Sperber 2011). There is ample evidence for this phenomenon. Subjects seek out information that questions the validity of an IQ test if they scored low on the test, or interpret an ambiguous symbol in a particular direction to receive a reward (Riccio, Cole, and Balcetis 2013). Respondents still feel the need to justify their attitudes, but rather than reevaluating their fundamental attitudes based on new evidence, they search for the evidence that supports their beliefs. We explore this and related processes of belief formation in the next chapter.

CHAPTER FIVE

Beliefs: Risk, Trust, and Apologies

In chapter 3, our focus was on value-based processes that shape evaluations of companies. As we have seen, many of these phenomena can be accounted for by the dual process theory of cognition, which locates value judgments in System I processes driven by affect rather than deliberated reasoning. Understanding these processes helps us understand the public outcry over executive perks or racial discrimination. It also explains the reputational damage suffered by companies when their pricing models were deemed unfair, as in the case of subprime loans or drug pricing.

We now turn to the process of belief formation. Specifically, we focus on two important types of beliefs about companies: risk perception and trust. Here the issue is not about values and moral intuitions, but instead it involves questions such as whether a particular product is considered safe or whether a service provider can be trusted. In our discussion of risk perception, we will outline the processes that shape over- or underestimations of risk. In our analysis of trust, we will focus on (perceived) trust violations and how to manage them. As we will see, the processes shaping risk perception and trust can also be accounted for by the dual process theory of cognition. Just as we can conceptualize "ethics as emotion" (Haidt 2001) we can view "risk as feeling" (Finucane et al. 2000; Slovic et al. 2002; Slovic and Peters 2006). The process of affective primacy grounds them both.

5.1 Risk and Fear

Scientists and engineers are often surprised by the public's reaction to new technologies or accidents. Often the reaction seems to be out of proportion to the objective risk exposure. Over the last few decades, psychologists and cognitive scientists have gained a much deeper understanding of the processes that shape risk perception. Early research on risk perception showed that laypeople did not perceive risk in line with objective data. They tended to either overestimate or underestimate the risk. Importantly, such misperceptions were not random, but systematic; they could be described by a list of heuristics and biases, similar to other contexts of judgment and decision making (Slovic 1987).

One of the cases that triggered the research program on risk perception was nuclear power. Many scientists and policymakers had supported the peaceful use of nuclear power as a cheap and clean energy source, only to be surprised by intense fear, leading to sustained and powerful antinuclear movements in many developed countries. Such movements effectively halted any new nuclear power construction over the last decades in many Western countries (Peters and Slovic 1996).

In our survey of reputational challenges for companies, we identified risk perception, and its emotional expression as "fear," as the second main source of reputational risk. As we have seen, crises involving fear typically focus on concerns over safety, as in the Toyota unintended acceleration case. Sometimes fears are based on objective risk, but in many cases there is a large gap between objective risk and risk perception. Emotions, heuristics, and biases play an important role in understanding this gap. Phenomena such as confirmation bias and motivated reasoning show that belief formation can be significantly impacted by underlying value orientations and emotional states, and risk assessments often directly reflect such biases.

5.1.1 Risk Factors

While perceptions of risk are driven by a multitude of factors, we focus on seven of the core causes of perceptual biases most relevant to reputational risk (e.g., Fischhoff et al. 1978; Sjöberg 2000; Slovic 1992).[1] The first such bias is *novelty*. Respondents tend to overestimate the risk from unfamiliar processes and technologies, such as biotech, and underestimate the risk from familiar ones, such as X-ray machines or exposure to sunlight (Fischhoff et al. 1978).

The second bias is *lack of control*. People tend to underestimate risks for which they have a sense of control, such as driving accidents, but they overestimate the likelihood of risks for which they are powerless, such as plane accidents or terrorist attacks (Langer 1975). These attitudes affect behavior, causing, for example, a reluctance to wear seat belts or bicycle helmets. They also may lead to consumer panics, like those over potentially harmful food ingredients, especially if such ingredients are not disclosed on the packaging. The fear over GMOs is a particularly potent example.

The third factor is *dread*, which involves the possibility of some very bad consequences such as violent death, for example, due to a shark attack, or a terminal disease, such as cancer. The mere possibility of dreadful consequences tends to lead members of the public to overestimate risks (Fischhoff et al. 1978; Slovic 1992).

The fourth factor is *salience*. Vivid recent instances of a problem or extensive media coverage will exacerbate perceived risk. The fear of dying in an airplane rather than, say, a car crash, will increase after recent widespread coverage of an airplane crash. The salience of the imagery of plane wreckage is easier to access and therefore makes another crash seem more likely to happen in the future (Lichtenstein et al. 1978). Salience is an instance of the availability heuristic discussed earlier. In the Toyota case, it was the horrific recording of the 911 emergency call that made the rather remote and abstract risk of unintended acceleration real, leading to widespread fears. Indeed, some drivers were too afraid to drive their cars to the dealership and had to be towed. Daily calls to Toyota's customer care center increased from about 3,000 a day to 96,000, and driver reports of unintended acceleration skyrocketed (Liker and Ogden 2011, p. 133).

The Toyota case was also affected by the fifth main factor: the presence of identifiable *victims*. Risk perception increases if an event affects identifiable, sympathetic victims such as vulnerable populations (e.g., children) or comparable groups (e.g., "people like me"), especially if the incident seems to unfairly burden these groups (Sandman 1989). The issue of unfair burdens can play an important role in the occurrence of NIMBY ("not in my backyard" movements), such as opposition to building a nuclear power plant or a cellphone tower near one's residence or town (Chapman and Wutzke 2006). Note that here a moral concern, namely, fairness, directly impacts a belief, namely, risk perception.

The sixth factor is the *lack of benefits*. Members of the public tend to overestimate a risk if the associated benefit is perceived to be low (Slovic, Fischhoff, and Lichtenstein 1982). The absence of perceived benefits reduces the sense of usefulness and positive affective orientation, and heightens risk perception (Finucane et al. 2000). On the other hand, the immediate positive feelings associated with imagining desired outcomes increases attention to possible benefits. This lowers risk perception.

The final factor pertains to *losses versus gains*. Individuals are less willing to accept risk in the context of gains (e.g., a guaranteed small reward versus a gamble between a larger reward or nothing) but are more risk tolerant when choices are framed as a loss (e.g., a guaranteed loss versus a gamble between a larger loss or no loss at all).[2] For example, a gain frame for an investment would state, "If you make this investment you will have enough money for your retirement." The corresponding loss frame would state, "If you don't make this investment, you won't have enough money during your retirement."[3]

Fear over nuclear power is one of the early examples of these factors. When nuclear power plants were first built, they represented a novel and unfamiliar technology. Their benefits were largely intangible (e.g., slightly lower energy prices) and constituted possible gains in terms of a cheap, abundant source of energy. However, their potential risks, namely, catastrophic nuclear accidents, were dreadful. Local residents felt that they had no control over these risks, and accidents such as Three Mile Island and Chernobyl dramatically increased fears, despite different technologies and regulatory regimes. These dynamics could be seen at work during the 2011 Fukushima accident, which led Germany to exit its nuclear program.

Compare this to the perceived risk from taking an X-ray. Taking an X-ray occurs in a familiar context and offers substantial benefits; it is also intended to prevent a loss (i.e., illness). Health consequences from too much X-ray exposure typically do not make the news, and many individuals choose to have an X-ray without much concern.

The COVID-19 pandemic is another example of these factors at play. The pandemic was novel, dreadful, and it featured extensive media coverage which often told stories of specific individuals who died due to the infection. Many of these factors are intrinsic to the disease and cannot be changed, though increased familiarity with the pandemic will decrease fear, as over time people will get used to the threat. A particularly interesting factor is the sense of powerlessness during a pandemic. One practical way to decrease fear and anxiety is to ask people to engage and volunteer, as the British National Health Service did in the early days of the pandemic. Similarly, leaders can reinforce a sense of mission and commitment with their team members during a crisis, asking them to step up to the challenge and make it their "proudest moment." Such engagement creates a sense of empowerment that, in turn, decreases fear.

Attitudes toward novel technologies are paradigmatic examples of where risk perception drives public attitude formation. Securing rapid customer acceptance, especially for highly innovative products, is critical. Yet the history of innovative technologies is full of examples where a promising technology encountered not only indifference, but substantial resistance, never reaching its economic potential due to fear. In the most extreme cases, such as that of genetically modified food products in Europe, companies effectively lost their licenses to operate in the marketplace.

The case of biotechnology is especially illustrative of these phenomena. Biotech has faced an uphill battle with public opinion since its inception. Genetic modification meets the all criteria for presenting both "unknown" and "dread" risks, which are perceptions that dramatically increase the perceived potential harm of a technology (Finucane and Holup 2005). Expert analyses of the risks (and benefits) of biotechnology, however, consistently differ from lay evaluations. Experts view biotechnology products as safer and showing more promise of future benefits than do laypeople (Savadori et al. 2004). Biotech also offers an instructive case study in how risk perception can derail a market entry strategy, as in the case of biotech pioneer Monsanto's entry into Europe (Diermeier 2011). Fueled by hostile media coverage and NGO campaigns, fear and concern over GMOs grew, especially in Europe, where major retailers stopped carrying food products with GMOs as ingredients. After widespread protests, the European Union subsequently adopted a moratorium on GMOs, effectively closing access to European markets. Monsanto, one of the biotech pioneers, lost 35 percent of its share price, which eventually led to the retirement of its CEO and a merger with drug company Pharmacia.[4]

Monsanto's market entry strategy in the European agricultural market has been widely criticized for being too technology-focused and for ignoring growing public unrest (Charles 2002; Diermeier 2011). Yet there were no similar protests against *medical* applications of biotechnology in Europe or other markets. The comparison between agricultural and medical applications of biotechnology is instructive. While both applications are novel and unfamiliar, feelings of control differ substantially since patients must actively consent to any therapy, whereas consumers have no control over whether and to what extent biotech products enter the food supply, especially in the absence of labeling requirements. Additionally, medical applications of biotechnology, such as gene therapy, can have substantial dread risks, but these concerns are usually outweighed by the potential benefits. Agricultural applications, however, can also be associated with dreadful consequences, though often to a lesser degree. Examples include concerns about allergic reactions and the emergence of antibiotic resistant bacteria, as well as environmental concerns such as super-weeds, loss of biodiversity, and so forth. To make matters worse, concerns over GMOs were linked to potential harm to Monarch butterfly larvae. This provided the previously rather abstract concerns over biodiversity with a concrete victim (Losey, Rayor, and Carter 1999).[5] There was no similar identifiable victim for medical applications.

All of these comparisons aside, perhaps the biggest difference in the history of these two industries is in the area of benefits. The health benefits of biotechnology—such as saving lives—are usually immediately evident. On the other hand, the main benefit of GMOs is economic efficiency—something difficult for the general public to understand and assess. This is especially problematic in the presence of patented technologies that raise concerns over who captures the benefits from enhanced efficiencies.[6] Indeed, the small economic benefits of agro-biotech that are felt by consumers, such as increased crop yield and lower food costs, are spread over many products or have only a small financial impact on consumers. In sum, the problem in the agricultural setting is that salient, dreadful concerns are not balanced by clear, identifiable benefits. Based on this assessment, it is not too surprising that public opinion on agricultural applications of biotechnology differs sharply from medical applications.

5.1.2 The Feeling of Risk

Recent research has shown that many of these biases can be accounted for by the dual-process theory of cognition. Recall that dual-process approaches view cognition as being composed of two cognitive systems operating concurrently and interactively, each influencing judgments. The first system, the experiential system (System I), allows for quick, intuitive assessments of situations, often driven by affect. The second, the analytic system (System II), involves a more logical method of making a decision, requiring sustained effort and concentration. In the context of risk perception, the approach based on System I is commonly known as "risk as feeling" or the "affect heuristic" (Alhakami and Slovic 1994; Finucane et al. 2000; Slovic 2010; Slovic and Peters 2006). As we have seen above, perceptions of benefits and perceptions of risks are inversely correlated; high benefits are associated with low risks, and low benefits with high risks. But these perceptions are jointly influenced by the affect experienced by a person; if they feel positively towards an activity, they tend to judge the risk as low and the benefits as high, while if they feel negatively about the activity, its risk is judged as high and the benefit as low.

These phenomena can be seen at work in a variety of business contexts. For example, Australia recently introduced extremely graphic labels depicting victims of cancer and other harmful effects on human health on cigarette packages. The purpose of these labels was to create a negative affect which will change risk perceptions and perceptions of benefits. Indeed, smokers immediately complained that the cigarettes did not taste the same and asked the cigarette companies why they had changed the product (Siegel 2013; Skaczkowski et al. 2018; Wakefield et al. 2013). Of course, the companies had done nothing of the sort; all changes were exclusively to the packaging, not the product. Note that the risk-as-feeling approach would predict that following the introduction of the labels, risk perception would increase as well (Slovic and Peters 2006).

This, of course, is nothing else but the phenomenon of affective primacy, characteristic of System I processes, now applied to risk perception.[7] The affect heuristic has been empirically demonstrated to influence risk perceptions in a variety of situations from toxicity and finance to nuclear power (Finucane et al. 2000). Rottenstreich and Hsee (2001) have shown, for instance, that for very strong affect, that is, for highly desirable or aversive outcomes, probability weights are altered such that low probabilities are treated as higher, and high probabilities are treated as lower.

5.1.3   Risk and Values

As in the case of moral judgments, risk assessments are also influenced by values and culture (Adam 2000; Douglas and Wildavsky 1982). Kahan, Braman, et al. (2008) and Kahan, Slovic, et al. (2008b) on nanotech and Druckman and Bolsen (2011) on biotech show that respondents with an individualistic-hierarchical value orientation evaluate emerging technologies as less risky than respondents with communitarian-egalitarian values. Moreover, these evaluations become *more* pronounced after the groups are exposed to neutral information. That is, value orientations not only influence evaluations but also *beliefs*. Traditional decision-theoretic models carefully separate assessments of the likelihood of an event ("beliefs") from attitudes toward the event ("preferences"). Classical decision theory posits that individuals should form those beliefs rationally, for example, following Bayes' rule in updating probabilities, irrespective of their preferences over outcomes. What we see here instead is an interaction between value orientations and beliefs. That is, beliefs over risks (i.e., probability assessments) and value judgments (preferences over outcomes) are not independent, but interrelated. Respondents adjust their beliefs about risk in line with their values.[8] For example, when subjects are presented with the same information about new technologies, perceptions of risks associated with the new technologies are adjusted downward if respondents hold an individualistic-hierarchical value orientation. This orientation is favorably inclined toward private enterprise, commercial activity, and merit, and holds "man's mastery over nature" in high regard. The opposite effect (upward adjustment) occurs for egalitarian communitarians, who view commerce as a cause of increasing inequality and are focused on communal well-being rather than individual merit (Kahan and Braman 2006; Kahan, Braman, et al. 2008). That is, the provided information tends to trigger negative affect for respondents with communitarian-egalitarian value orientations, who tend to associate new technologies with negative consequences, while it tends to trigger positive affect for subjects with individualistic-hierarchical orientations, who generally are positively inclined toward new technologies. Positive affect will tend to lead subjects to perceive the risks as lower and the benefits as higher, while negative affect will have the opposite effect.[9]

5.2 Trust

Trust is at the heart of many business models, especially for businesses whose main asset is a strong brand.[10] Brands are often conceptualized as promises, as in the famous quote attributed to branding pioneer Walter Landor (e.g., Jankowski 2013; Nelson 2008):

> Simply put, a brand is a promise. By identifying and authenticating a product or service it delivers a pledge of satisfaction and quality.

There is extensive evidence connecting consumers' level of trust and their purchase intentions (Agag and El-Masry 2016; Gefen 2000; Gefen and Straub 2004; Hajli et al. 2017; Hong and Cho 2011; Kim, Dirks, and

Cooper 2009; Pappas 2016; Pavlou and Gefen 2004; Pavlou, Liang, and Xue 2007; Ponte, Carvajal-Trujillo, and Escobar-Rodríguez 2015; Wang and Benbasat 2005; Yang, Tjiptono, and Poon 2018), as well as their loyalty and willingness to recommend a product to others (Ball, Simões Coelho, and Marchás 2004; Hong and Cho 2011; Moriuchi and Takahashi 2016; Pizzutti dos Santos and Basso 2012). Additionally, a small number of studies have examined how consumer trust can influence consumers' willingness to pay a premium for a product or service (Ba and Pavlou 2002; Gefen, Kara-hanna, and Straub 2003; Pavlou and Dimoka 2006; Ponte, Carvajal-Trujillo, and Escobar-Rodríguez 2015; Sirdeshmukh, Singh, and Sabol 2002).

5.2.1   The Trust Game

Despite its agreed-upon importance, there are many definitions of trust. In business contexts, trust is often conceptualized as the willingness "to accept vulnerability based upon positive expectations of the intentions or behavior of another" (Rousseau et al. 1998, p. 395). The concept of trust can be captured in the following simple decision problem, the "trust game," from Berg, Dickhaut, and McCabe (1995). The game is known to both players before it commences, and works as follows. There are two players, a sender (trustor, investor) and a receiver (trustee). The sender has a fixed amount of money x, which she can keep or "invest," that is, pass to the receiver. That is, the sender allocates an amount z (between 0 and x) to the receiver and keeps the rest. This amount z, the "investment," earns a return at rate $(1 + r)$. The amount $(1 + r)z$ then is sent to the receiver. The receiver keeps an amount y (between 0 and $(1 + r)z$) and then returns the rest to the sender, namely, $(1 + r)z - y$. This ends the game. The final payoffs are then $(x - z) + (1 + r)z - y = x + rz - y$ for the sender and y for the receiver. For the sender, trusting the trustee is potentially valuable, but risky, since the receiver has no monetary incentive to send any money back to the sender. The sender, however, has no choice but to trust the receiver to get a higher payoff. Variations in the amount passed to the receiver z can thus be used to measure trustworthiness.

Berg, Dickhaut, and McCabe (1995) found that (1) senders are willing to send a considerable amount to receivers, and (2) receivers tend to reciprocate the trust put into them. In their original experiment, x was set at \$10 and r was set at 2. Thus, the amount invested was tripled. On average, senders invested a bit over 50 percent. Only two subjects invested nothing. The average amount returned was about 95 percent of the invested amount z, roughly $\frac{1}{3}$ of the total amount $(1+r)z$. Among the trustees, there was substantial variance. Roughly half sent either nothing or a token amount. In a second experiment, senders who knew the outcomes of the first experiment sent slightly more (about 54 percent), and trustees also returned more (about 121 percent of the invested amount z).

The trust game sets aside many important aspects of social interaction.[11] There is no history, there are no social networks, no communication, and so forth. Indeed, such experiments are designed to control for any influence of social context. They often use "double-blind designs," where players interact through computer screens, are unable to communicate except by transferring money, and even the experimenter cannot observe what an individual player did (to avoid potential contamination by a player's desire to please the experimenter). Players are paid according to performance and so forth. The advantage of these sparse settings is that such games capture what is essential about trust in a pure form: *trusting is valuable but risky*.

5.2.2   Dimensions of Trust

In a business context, the degree of trust placed in a company will naturally depend on the trustor's attitude toward risk and general disposition to trust others.[12] It will also depend on the characteristics of the specific situation. Individuals use a variety of cues, often subtle, to form an assessment of the transaction context and decide whether or not to place their trust in a company (McKnight, Choudhury, and Kacmar 2002). In a business context, consumers' willingness to trust a company will depend on whether it is viewed as *trustworthy*. Following Mayer, Davis, and Schoorman (1995), most attention has been focused on three dimensions of trustworthiness: ability, integrity, and benevolence.[13]

Generally speaking, a company's perceived ability stems from an assessment of whether it is capable of following through on its promises. Consumers can use a variety of cues to assess whether a company has the ability to fulfill its promises, including past experiences, reviews from other consumers, and assessments of the technical capabilities of the company. On the other hand, assessments of a company's integrity concern whether the company is willing to work to uphold its promises. This emphasis on whether the company *wants* to uphold its promises contrasts with assessments of ability that focus on whether a company *can* do so. Separating these two dimensions allows, for example, for the possibility of a company being seen as capable but unwilling to do something for its consumers, and vice versa. Finally, a company is considered benevolent if its preferences and actions reflect a desire to do what is best for consumers and others.

While each of these three dimensions of trustworthiness can apply in any domain of trust, their respective importance may vary by situation and domain. For example, consumers who care about the timely delivery of a product may pay the most attention to a company's ability and integrity, and place little emphasis on the benevolence of a company. For these individuals, receiving the product on time is of primary importance, and as long as this can be largely guaranteed, little other assurance is needed. On the other hand, consumers who place great emphasis on a company's workplace and community practices are less likely to emphasize the company's competence, and instead focus on its integrity and benevolence. For these consumers, the company signaling that it wants to "do good" is important—even if it may not always succeed in doing so. Such consumers may also be willing to purchase products at a higher price in an effort to support a company that shares their values. Finally, consumers preoccupied with privacy and security concerns are likely to strongly emphasize all three of the dimensions of trust. These consumers are especially wary of being taken advantage of and desire assurances that the company wants to protect their data, is willing to make the necessary investments to protect their data, and will ultimately be successful in protecting their data. In these cases, intention or capability alone will not be sufficient to lead a privacy-focused consumer to trust a company; only the convergence of desire, intent, and ability can create such willingness.

Importantly, the general trustworthiness of a company may derive from activities that are not directly related to its treatment of customers, but may influence whether consumers are willing to trust the company in a particular interaction. For example, an insurance company may enhance its general trustworthiness by investing in local communities or by engaging in corporate social responsibility programs. Consumers may view such companies as benevolent and be more willing to trust them when buying life insurance (Park, Lee, and Kim 2014; Vlachos et al. 2009).[14]

5.2.3 Broken Promises

Given the various components that define trustworthiness and the degree of trust one places in another, it should come as little surprise that humans react strongly to trust violations. In the trust game, for example, violations occur when a receiver has been supplied with a significant amount z, but then decides to pocket the money rather than reciprocating by sending over a corresponding amount y. Trust violations lead to anger and the desire for vengeance or retribution. Research across several fields has shown that people favor much harsher punishments for crimes that involve a betrayal, such as a theft committed by a trusted employee (Koehler and Gershoff 2003), and trust violations can be difficult to repair (Schweitzer, Hershey, and Bradlow 2006). Evolutionary psychologists have shown that humans are very good at detecting cheating and norm violations. Some have even posited the existence of a mental "cheater detection module" (Cosmides and Tooby 1989).

In general, brands require trust, but trust can be fragile. When trust is violated (or perceived to be violated), trust quickly turns to feelings of betrayal, and passionate support can turn to rage. The case of Netflix provides an instructive example. In July 2011, Netflix was on top of the business world. In 2010, its cofounder and CEO Reed Hastings was named "Business Person of the Year" by *Fortune* magazine (Newcomb 2010). During the same year, Netflix's stock rose more than 200 percent compared to a more modest gain of 14 percent for the S&P 500 (MacroTrends.com 2021). At the beginning of July 2011, the company was valued at over $16 billion, had 24.6 million subscribers in the United States, and had begun expanding its services abroad (Wingfield 2011). Netflix's success came as a surprise to many observers, who expected that larger and established competitors such as Blockbuster, Wal-Mart, and Amazon would have significant advantages due to their economies of scale (Copeland 2010). However, Netflix generated tremendous customer loyalty through outstanding customer service, low prices, and access to a wide variety of movie titles and genres. Netflix offered users unlimited streaming of online movies and the ability to rent one DVD at a time by mail for a total of $9.99 per month with no late fee or other hassles. Customers simply created a rental queue and were sent the top entry once the DVD had been received by Netflix. None of Netflix's competitors were able to match its approach. Indeed, the previous incumbent market leader Blockbuster filed for bankruptcy in early 2010.

On July 12, 2011, in the wake of this success, Netflix made a surprise announcement. Instead of continuing to bundle the DVD and streaming content into one subscription, the company decided to separate them into two different price structures. The statement stressed that the previous price structure did not adequately account for the additional costs of mailing and the rising consumer demand for streaming content. Instead, customers would now have the following options (Becker 2011): (1) Purchase a streaming-only subscription (no DVDs) for $7.99 per month; (2) Purchase a DVD-only subscription (no streaming), one DVD out at a time for $7.99 per month; (3) Purchase both streaming and DVD subscriptions for $15.98 per month ($7.99 + $7.99). The $15.98 cost of the bundled subscription represented a price hike of 60 percent and outraged Netflix's 24.6 million customers (Goldman 2012). Within hours of the announcement, thousands of irate Netflix users had commented on the blog post making the announcement—with most threatening to cancel their subscriptions. "Your [Netflix's] nominal price increase, while unexpected, does not deter my loyalty. However, your ... presentation of this upcharge—as an added choice for my own benefit—insults my intelligence and reveals the breadth of your arrogance," one user remarked. "How sad that after years of holding a subscription ... we are stopping the use of your services. Greedy, greedy, greedy ... Goodbye Netflix, hello Red Box!" commented another (Hastings 2011).

To complicate matters further, two months later on the company blog, Netflix CEO Reed Hastings apologized for the July price hike and went on to explain that the by-mail DVD and streaming content were now going to be divided into two entirely separate businesses. Netflix would shift its focus to streaming-only content, while a new entity, called Qwikster, would handle the mailing of DVDs. Netflix and Qwikster would operate autonomously, and customers who wished to enroll in both services would be required to browse two different websites, create two user accounts, and receive two billing statements. Moreover, the ratings and preference algorithms that supplied individual users with suggested films would not be linked across the two businesses. "We realized that streaming and DVD by mail are becoming two quite different businesses with very different cost structures, different benefits that need to be marketed differently, and we need to let each grow and operate independently," Hastings explained.

Customers were outraged again. Many complained about the inconvenience of two different websites: the fact that ratings and preferences do not show up in both locations, having to check both websites to see whether a particular title is available in one way or the other, and two different charges showing up on one's credit card statement. Hastings's September blog post received nearly 10,000 comments in less than 24 hours (Chansanchai 2011). Most comments came from irate users who stated that they would end their subscriptions. Customers were also angry that, aside from Hastings's short statement, Netflix provided little immediate guidance to address customers' concerns, such as an FAQ sheet or Twitter handle. On October 10, Hastings announced that Netflix would abandon the Qwikster idea and remain one company. Yet this announcement did not stem the tide. By the end of the third quarter of 2011, Netflix had lost 800,000 subscribers, and by December its stock had fallen to just under $70 a share (down about 75 percent from its high in July), erasing roughly $12 billion in shareholder value—from $16 billion to $4 billion (Pepitone 2011). Netflix's stock finally bottomed out at around $55 a share in September 2012—a year after the Qwikster announcement.[15]

The issue with Netflix was not that customers were unable to pay the few extra dollars for a Netflix subscription, but that it appeared the company was taking advantage of its loyal customers and breaking its promises. Even loyal subscribers were outraged and aghast at the company's actions. A loyal customer since 2004 expressed this as follows: "No matter what you say, you cannot explain away the inconvenience of what you've done. I can no longer stand by your decision as it is purely business related, and in no way are you thinking about your customers." Another comment echoed that sentiment: "This [blog post] is disingenuous. You are offering an apology for not doing a good job of explaining the new structure, but it is all about the needs for your corporation. What about the needs of the customer?" Another user tried to reason with Hastings: "My interaction with your brand is for the sole purpose of watching films. How the film is delivered isn't that important to [users]. It's sounding like ... my pricing and user experience are getting more complicated. And I think that's ... the essence of why people are so angry. Because they feel like they are paying for a corporate decision, and not for what they want. Movies." (Hastings 2011).

As the customer comments make clear, the anger observed in the Netflix case is based on a sense of betrayal. Betrayal leads to a desire for retribution, and such desires are deeply rooted. Experimental studies of jury decision making, for example, show that only retribution-related factors significantly influence recommended punishments (e.g., Carlsmith 2006, 2008; Carlsmith, Darley, and Robinson 2002; Carlsmith and Sood 2009). Consequentialist factors, such as whether punishment will deter future acts, play little role. However, when asked explicitly, most respondents will state that the primary function of punishment is to deter wrongdoing. Nevertheless, their actions are consistent with the "intuitive prosecutor" who delivers just retribution (Carlsmith, Darley, and Robinson 2002; Tetlock et al. 2007).[16]

In addition, betrayals are treated as norm violations. That is, they not only lead to retribution by the cheated party, but they may also trigger punishment by uninvolved third parties who have observed the trust violation (Fehr and Fischbacher 2004; Fehr and Gächter 2002). These third-party dynamics have been explored using experimental methods. In these games, third-party players can use some of their monetary compensation to punish other players. For example, consider a version of the trust game in which a third party can spend a portion of their own allocation in order to take money away from players who do not cooperate. In this scenario, there is no monetary incentive for a third party to punish, as they are completely unaffected by the actions of the first two players and will never interact with them as players in the future. As such, there is no rational reason for the first two players to alter their behavior based on the presence of the third party. Yet third parties do pay a portion of their own allocation to punish noncooperation in the trust game, and expecting this, players engage in more cooperative behavior in the presence of third party punishment (Fehr and Fischbacher 2004).

Bendor and Swistak (2001) have provided an evolutionary argument for the role of third-party enforcement in maintaining social cooperation. Cooperative outcomes that fail to be evolutionarily stable under direct enforcement by one of the parties involved can become stable under third-party enforcement. While the adaptive purpose of third-party punishment is to increase cooperation in future interactions, its proximate psychological cause is based in large part on retributive moral outrage at past transgressions (Crockett, Özdemir, and Fehr 2014). It is for this reason that third-party punishment occurs even in the absence of any future social interaction.

If a company is perceived to have violated the trust of its customers or other constituencies, trust needs to be repaired (Dirks et al. 2005; Kim et al. 2004). Research on close private relationships shows that even severe forms of betrayal can be forgiven, provided that the partners are strongly committed to the relationship (Finkel et al. 2002).[17] Unfortunately, most companies cannot count on such strong relationships, let alone a sense of commitment.[18] Thus, trust needs to be actively reconstituted.

Not all trust violations are treated alike; both the context and the content matter. A good prior reputation is an important asset if a company is accused of a trust violation. Because violations are often ambiguous, a company's reputation can be used to disambiguate a potential violation, as actors with poor reputations are more likely to violate trust than actors with good reputations. Determining level of intent, for example, is critical to assigning blame, and when a situation is ambiguous, an actor's character or reputation can bias judgments of intent and blame in either direction.[19]

In the context of companies, positive beliefs about a company can lead consumers to interpret ambiguous information in its favor (Ahluwalia, Burnkrant, and Unnava 2000; Coombs 2012; Coombs and Holladay 2006). Indeed, participants strongly committed to a brand spontaneously generate counterarguments when reading negative evaluations of relevant products (Ahluwalia, Burnkrant, and Unnava 2000). Companies with good reputations are given the benefit of the doubt during a safety crisis when they give an ambiguous response (Dawar and Pillutla 2000) or when they say nothing (Uhlmann et al. 2010), whether such a good reputation was directly related to the crisis (such as a good safety record) or only indirectly related (for example, from charitable contributions). In general, a company's record of social responsibility improves its reputation and that of its products, but only when such acts are perceived as sincere (Yoon, Gürhan-Canli, and Schwarz 2006).[20] Actions that are inconsistent with the prior reputation, however, will lead to strongly adverse reactions that may lead the company to be worse off than if they had not engaged in beneficial actions at all.

It is misleading, however, to interpret this phenomenon as a "trust bank account," a concept suggested by Alsop (2004a, 2004b), where companies can simply withdraw previously deposited trust assets. Rather, through poor decisions during a crisis, companies can destroy their hard-earned reputations quickly. A defensive posture will undermine trust even if a company has previously engaged in virtuous acts. For example, a company that funded cancer research would still be viewed negatively if it responded in a defensive fashion. A company is still best served by an engaged response, regardless of a record of prior good deeds (e.g., Coombs and Holladay 2002, 2006; Dawar and Pillutla 2000; Uhlmann et al. 2010).

Personal relationships provide an instructive analogy. When we "invest in a relationship" we do not mean that, after a period of virtuous and caring behavior, we can now "spend" some of our trust bank account by acting like a jerk for a while. Rather, to use another financial metaphor, trust works more like a currency. Strong currencies act like multipliers. That is, when a currency is strong, purchasing power increases for all sorts of tradable goods and services. Thus, the same statement is likely to carry more weight if it comes from a trusted company. Or alternatively, a company with a strong record of trust ("strong currency") will need to do less than a company with a lower record of trust ("weak currency") to accomplish the same effect.

Some survey evidence from the 2011 Edelman Trust Barometer (Edelman 2011) supports this intuition. In the case of "low trust," a negative message about a company has roughly four times as much impact as a positive message, a finding consistent with the general negativity bias discussed above. The situation is reversed in the "high trust" case; now a negative message has only half as much impact as a positive one. So, by moving from low to high trust, a company enjoys an eight fold increase in positive impact.

Finally, the type of trust violation matters. As discussed above, trustworthiness depends on three main factors: capability, integrity, and benevolence (Mayer, Davis, and Schoorman 1995). A company must be both *able* and *willing* to keep its promises. *Capability* captures a company's expertise and competence that allows it to function effectively. *Integrity* means adherence to widely accepted moral principles such as honesty, fairness, and respect that motivate a company to keep its promises—even if it has no short-term incentive to do so.

Consider the case where a company exposed private customer data after having promised to keep these data secure. A lack of proper data security processes is a competence violation; the company may have intended to keep the data safe, but was unable to do so, perhaps because of an oversight, or perhaps because of insufficient investment in data security technology. Selling customer data to a third-party vendor without customer consent is an integrity violation, as the company was able to protect customer data, but decided to reveal them anyway.

In general, integrity-based trust violations are much more difficult to repair, especially if they were accompanied by deception (Ferrin et al. 2007; Kim, Dirks, and Cooper 2009; Schweitzer, Hershey, and Bradlow 2006). Overall, blame will increase if an agent is viewed as the *cause* of experienced harm, as well as when the harm is believed to be the result of their *intentions* and desires (Bratman 1989; Tomlinson and Mayer 2009; Weiner 1985).[21] Deception and other integrity-based violations usually score high on all of these dimensions. Importantly, they also serve as a tell about a person's character, as seen in person-centered approaches. That is, a trust violation is interpreted as a signal about an agent's type, reducing future willingness to trust.

Particularly problematic are trust violations of moral principles previously endorsed by companies. Rather than being given the benefit of the doubt, the company may be viewed as hypocritical. People condemn hypocrites even when they disagree with the values being betrayed. Experiments by Uhlmann, Tannenbaum, and Diermeier (Schweinsberg et al. 2016) showed that participants condemned the leader of an animal rights organization who was caught hunting, even when the participants supported hunting. The hypocritical animal rights leader was deemed untrustworthy and unethical. Similarly, a company that donated money to cancer research, but then spent an even larger amount to promote its activities, was viewed more negatively than a company that donated no money at all.

The same effect can be seen in the case of nonprofits, which are generally seen as more caring than companies (Aaker, Vohs, and Mogilner 2010). A small perk, but not a large one, was tolerated for a corporate executive. However, for the head of a charity, even a small perk was perceived as an unacceptable betrayal.

The critical question, then, is how an audience whose trust has been broken interprets such a violation. The more a trust violation is treated as a signal about the agent's type rather than something that was a mistake, that is, an action that was out of character and can easily be fixed by paying more attention in the future, the more future trustworthiness will decrease. Thus, the key question is whether the trustor believes that the trustee is willing and able to refrain from the offensive conduct in the future (Kim, Dirks, and Cooper 2009; Tomlinson and Mayer 2009).

Violated trust can be repaired by material restitution through penance (Bottom et al. 2002) or through a sequence of trustworthy actions (Schweitzer, Hershey, and Bradlow 2006).[22] Effective penance needs to be consistent with fundamental fairness intuitions, such as "an eye for an eye" or causal attribution. In one experiment, subjects preferred that a polluting company clean up its own waste rather than some other waste site, even if the other waste site was considerably more toxic (Baron, Gowda, and Kunreuther 1993).

But verbal acknowledgments of the harmful act and apologies can also be effective, even in fully anonymous settings, as in the trust game (Schniter, Sheremeta, and Sznycer 2012). Indeed, failing to communicate can further erode trust and goodwill. In general, a "no comment" response is treated negatively, almost tantamount to an admission of guilt (Ferrin et al. 2007). The same holds for responses that are defensive (Dawar and Pillutla 2000). In contrast, an engaged response (i.e., by expressing serious concern and proactive intentions to safeguard the well-being of consumers) often leads to positive evaluations of the company.

These effects can be seen in the following experiment (Schweinsberg et al. 2016; Uhlmann et al. 2010). Subjects read little vignettes of fictitious newspaper articles that each describe a fictitious crisis. In one case, a food manufacturer is accused of using a potentially harmful food additive. In the other case, the company is involved in a nasty sexual harassment lawsuit. The company responded in one of three ways. In the case of an "engaged response," the company voiced concern about the allegations, expressed its empathy toward customers, and committed itself to conduct an investigation into the allegations. In the case of a "defensive response," the company disputed the allegations, showed no empathy, and highlighted its expertise. Subjects were then asked to express their opinions of the company. The subjects responded as predicted, viewing the engaged company significantly more positively. Interestingly, their responses exhibited no significant difference between a "no comment" and a defensive response. In other words, when a company is silent, subjects view it as defensive and judge it negatively (Uhlmann et al. 2010).[23] Negative reactions were not limited to the corporate image, but also applied to the evaluations of logos, bottle designs, and products. An engaged response also increased the respondents' beliefs that the company was warm and caring toward others, although it did not increase their trust that the company was competent and reliable.

Perhaps the most striking example occurred in a variant of the experiment with a bottled water company. Subjects were given the same fictitious vignettes and responses, and then tasted the water from the company in trouble and compared it to a competitor. Of course, the water in both cases was identical. The results showed that the mere accusation of sexual harassment led customers to rate the taste of the company's product lower. Even more strikingly, subjects drank less water from the company in crisis, suggesting that the response was visceral and went beyond a conscious evaluation. Psychologists call this a "contagion effect" (e.g., Nemeroff and Rozin 1994). Negative contagion effects are often associated with the emotion of disgust (Morales and Fitzsimons 2007; Nemeroff and Rozin 1994). This also holds in the water bottle case: negative evaluations are mediated by disgust. As before, the style of response (engaged, defensive, or no comment) mattered. Taste evaluation and quantity consumed were higher for a company with an engaged response, while there was no significant difference between companies offering defensive or no-comment responses.

What makes these findings important is that a corporate response, even to an unrelated event such as a sexual harassment accusation, can have a direct and measurable impact on the evaluation of core product attributes, such as taste, and consumption behavior, even if such behavior may not be conscious or intended.

Corporate executives are only partially aware of these effects. When corporate executives were asked to predict how public attitudes would respond to these same scenarios, the executives correctly predicted that an engaged response would be viewed more favorably than a defensive response, but they were overly optimistic about the public's ability to refrain from forming opinions when the company offered "no comment." That is, executives assumed that such a response would be viewed more positively than a defensive response, when in fact this is not the case. Executives thus appear to believe that laypeople are more willing to withhold judgment and give corporations the benefit of the doubt than they actually are.

Indeed, companies in general do not enjoy the public's benefit of the doubt. Companies are among the least trusted institutions in the United States (Argenti 2007; Edelman 2019; Peters, Covello, and McCallum 1997). In an experiment by Heinze, Uhlmann, and Diermeier (2009), later replicated by Schweinsberg et al. (2016), subjects read the same fictitious news story about a company accused of using an unhealthy food additive. Then, depending on the treatment, they read either that the company had been found guilty or found innocent, or they were given no further information about the outcome of the case. Participants in the no-further-information condition were just as likely to condemn the company as participants in the guilty condition. Interestingly, corporate executives were not aware of this "guilty until proven innocent effect" and gave the company the benefit of the doubt.

In part, these judgments are a consequence of general psychological tendencies. Humans weigh negative acts more heavily than positive acts when forming impressions of others (Baumeister et al. 2001; Jones and Davis 1965; Klein and Epley 2014; Reeder and Brewer 1979; Rozin and Royzman 2001; Skowronski and Carlston 1987, 1989; Ybarra 2002). In part, such attitudes may reflect incorrect stereotypes about companies, such as their profitability. For example, consumers overestimate corporate profits by a factor of 10, underestimate manufacturing costs, and believe rises in prices are due to gouging rather than supply and demand (Bolton and Alba 2006; Bolton, Warlop, and Alba 2003). But whatever the underlying factors are, in general companies do not carry a trust reservoir that can be used during a crisis.

There are some settings, however, where silence can be golden. One such example occurs when a company is negatively affected by the actions of a competitor (Borah and Tellis 2016; Cleeren, van Heerde, and Dekimpe 2013). Reports about contaminated meat at one restaurant, for instance, may raise food safety concerns at other restaurants. Such industrywide spillover effects are more likely when both companies are typical members of the industry (e.g., both are hamburger restaurants) and the crisis-provoking product (e.g., contaminated hamburger meat) is typical of the industry (Roehm and Tybout 2006, 2008). That is, contaminated hamburger meat at Burger King negatively impacts perceptions of hamburgers at Wendy's (another hamburger chain), but not hamburgers at Dairy Queen (mainly known for dairy products). Roehm and Tybout show that, when a crisis at a first company has not yet reached a second company, the second company should not comment at all, rather than issue a denial of its involvement. A public denial will only link the innocent second company to the crisis and lead consumers to believe it "doth protest too much" and is potentially guilty of wrongdoing. The underlying principle here is lack of awareness. If a company is not directly connected to the incident, any action, even a denial, may trigger unwanted attention. That said, as we have seen, once a company is in the spotlight, silence or "no comment" responses are rarely effective, and a denial is more effective than not commenting on the crisis.

5.2.4   Restoring Trust

The ultimate goal of response strategies is to maintain or restore trust. Kim, Dirks, and Cooper (2009) provide a useful three-level typology of trust repair strategies.

> Level 1: "I didn't do it. It didn't happen" (denials and refutations);
> Level 2: "It wasn't my fault" (excuses and justifications);
> Level 3: "I am sorry. It won't happen again" (apologies and commitments).

DENIALS AND REFUTATIONS.   Level 1 strategies deny that the perceived transgression occurred in the first place. They deny the underlying fact pattern. Such strategies appear promising, as they may have the broadest effect. If the audience becomes convinced that no transgression occurred or that the alleged transgressor did not commit the transgression, the situation should be resolved. In practice, perceived trust violations are not always easy to disprove, especially when the alleged transgressor, such as a company, already operates from a low level of trust. Research on jury perception, for example, has found that people are willing to believe unsubstantiated allegations even in the absence of supporting evidence (e.g., Ross et al. 1994). Moreover, the public often expects the suspected party to remove the shadow of a doubt (Hendry, Schaffer, and Peacock 1989). Failing to do so further undermines trust. That is, *in the court of public opinion, the principle "innocent until proven guilty" does not apply.*

A Level 1 defense is analogous to a legal defense that denies culpability. There are two salient Level 1 strategies: *denials* and *refutations.* Mere denials have limited effectiveness at restoring trust (Kim et al. 2004).[24] Moreover, if subsequent incriminating information comes to light, a denial is interpreted as a lie. This lie further erodes trust and triggers an integrity violation, even if the original issue was merely related to competence. Rather, at Level 1, an effective defense needs to be a refutation: providing exonerating evidence which shows convincingly that either there was no problem in the first place, or that the company did not cause the alleged problem. Two examples from the car industry illustrate this approach.

On February 8, 2013, *New York Times* journalist John Broder planned to take a test drive from Washington, DC, to Groton, Connecticut, in a Model S electric car developed by Tesla Motors. The trip was intended to highlight the new ultrafast charging stations installed by Tesla, but, as Broder elaborated in his column "Stalled on the E.V. Highway" two days later, things did not turn out as planned. Completing the 80-mile trip from Washington to Newark should have been easy enough, given that the fully charged Tesla battery can reach 270–300 miles depending on driving conditions. In his article, Broder reported that, after a recharge, the battery erratically showed rapidly falling capacity despite recharges and attempts to conserve power, for example, by turning down the climate control and slowing the car to cruise control at 54 mph under advice from the Tesla customer service office. After an overnight stop, the battery had only 25 miles of remaining range—not enough to get Broder to his intended destination. After an emergency recharge, Broder "limped along" in the car at 45 mph before the battery finally died. Tesla sent a tow truck, whose driver was unable to dislodge the electrically activated parking brake. Broder reached his destination five hours later. Broder summarized this experience in a scathing article accompanied by photos of the car on the tow truck flatbed.

The article appeared less than two weeks before Tesla's quarterly earnings call with Wall Street analysts.

On the day after the publication of Broder's article, Tesla's CEO Elon Musk struck back on Twitter writing, "NYTimes article about Tesla range in cold is fake. Vehicle logs tell true story that he didn't actually charge to max & took long detour" (Hull 2013). The following day, Musk continued his attack on Broder, stating on Fox Business Network: "I think this was a deliberate attempt to gain a picture of the Model S being put on a flatbed truck. I don't think there is any other possible interpretation for what this reporter did" (Money 2013). Musk followed the interview with an all-out online attack on Broder and the *New York Times* on Tesla's blog with his post "A Most Peculiar Test Drive." In particular, Musk pointed out that, unbeknown to Broder, Tesla had begun installing monitoring software in its cars in 2008 after concerns that the automotive show *Top Gear* had publicized a deceptive product review that allegedly was aimed at sabotaging the company. Among other things, Musk showed that Broder had actually set cruise control at a higher level than claimed, had turned up the car's heater while on low battery, and charged the car less and less with each stop. He also claimed that Broder had driven the car in circles with near-depleted battery "for over half a mile, in a tiny 100-spot parking lot" instead of charging it (Musk 2013a). Moreover, the post hinted that Broder may have had ulterior motives and biases, citing a 2012 article in which he dismissed electric cars as "the victim of hyped expectations" (Broder 2012). Musk's post concluded with an appeal to the *New York Times* to "please investigate this article and determine the truth" (Musk 2013a).

In less than 24 hours, Musk's post had generated over 250 comments from loyal Tesla owners and supporters who felt vindicated in their love for the car and who saw Broder's article as yet another attempt to derail the budding electric vehicle industry. "I salute you. For the first time in my life I've submitted a Letter to the Editor of the NY Times, asking for a full review of the facts in this case," remarked one inspired owner. "I must admit when I first read [Elon's] tweets I thought they were overly emotional. . . . But now I understand why he reacted as he did," commented another. Yet another stated "there's a lot of profit to be made by 'smoking the planet' . . . I wonder if any of that money is making its way to members of the media" (Musk 2013a).

A day after Musk's post, Broder posted his own rebuttal in the *New York Times* entitled "That Tesla Data: What It Says and What It Doesn't." Feeling that Musk was attacking his journalistic integrity, Broder stressed that any of his charging missteps were due to misinformation he received during about a dozen phone conversations with Tesla. Likewise, he said maintaining a comfortable temperature within the car despite frigid outdoor temperatures was a trade-off he struggled with. Though he was not able to explain his claim of maintaining 54 mph cruise control, Broder stated that the car's tires—which were larger than the expected factory default—may have altered the speed. He also claimed that he was driving in circles in the parking lot looking for the poorly identified charging station, not to run down the battery as Musk claimed.

In the days after, CNN, CNBC, and *Consumer Reports* replicated the trip with no difficulties. The CNN report called the car "phenomenal" (Goode 2013a; Valdes-Dapena 2013). A few days later, a group of nine Tesla owners sought to debunk Broder's article by retracing his steps with their own cars and tweeting their experiences (Goode 2013b).

New York Times public editor Margaret Sullivan entered the debate 10 days after Broder's initial article in response to hundreds of angry emails and blog comments. In the article, she detailed interviews she had conducted with Broder, Musk, Tesla employees, *New York Times* journalists, the tow truck driver, and Tesla car owners. While Sullivan affirmed that Broder "took on the test drive in good faith, and told the story as he experienced it," she stated that he did not show good judgment in his fuel management (Sullivan 2013). The following day, a vindicated Musk again posted to Tesla's blog thanking the *New York Times* for "reversing its opinion" and gave a nod to Tesla's loyal customers "who rallied immediately to the defense of Tesla and the electric car revolution" (Musk 2013b).

Musk's strategy is a clear example of a refutation. Its goal was to refute the alleged facts and details of the event as reported by Broder. Such strategies are risky, as they need to provide convincing evidence that the event did not unfold as stated by the journalist. Musk was able to do this due to the sophisticated monitoring technology deployed by Tesla. Musk's cult-like status as Tesla's visionary CEO brought additional credibility, especially with its existing customers who leapt to the company's defense.

Twenty years earlier, General Motors (GM) was able to accomplish a similar turnaround (Krehbiel 1994). On November 17, 1992, the NBC news program *Dateline* aired a 15-minute segment entitled "Waiting to Explode?" *Dateline* showed footage of a side-impact collision of a GM truck hit by an unmanned car. Upon impact, both the car and the truck burst into flames. The collision was shown in slow motion and accompanied by the narration of *Dateline* reporter Michelle Gillen. "The pressure of the collision and the crushing of the gas tank forced gasoline to spew from the gas cap," Gillen stated. "The fuel then erupted into flames when ignited by the impacting car's headlight" (Weiser 1993). The *Dateline* segment had been produced in response to concerns by the consumer advocacy group Center for Auto Safety and others that certain GM pickup truck models were responsible for 300 deaths in fire-related collisions (Tolchin 1993).

One such collision, involving 17-year-old Shannon Moseley, gained substantial media attention. In 1989, Moseley died after his 1985 GM pickup truck was struck by a drunk driver. Moseley's parents refused to settle out of court and sued GM, claiming that their son died due to the fire resulting from the fuel tanks, while GM asserted that his death was instant upon collision and not due to the truck's design.[25] At issue was the location and design of gasoline tanks. The GM trucks were designed with dual "side-saddle" gasoline tanks that were mounted outside the truck's main frame rather than inside. While GM asserted that the tanks posed no safety risk, critics contended that the outside placement made them more vulnerable and likely to cause fires during collisions. As of October 1992, GM was engaged in over 100 lawsuits in connection with the tank design, several of which GM settled with payments exceeding $1 million (Meier 1992). Reaching approximately 11 million viewers, the *Dateline* coverage fueled the growing perception that the side-saddle tanks were unsafe (Kurtz 1993).

From the very beginning, GM doubted the report's validity and began an investigation, writing to NBC producer Robert Read two days after the "unfair [and] misleading" broadcast to request the collision data. When Read refused to comply, GM's head of public affairs, William O'Neill, wrote that his team wanted to inspect the crash test vehicles. Read responded that they were "junked" and therefore "no longer available for inspection" (Weiser 1993). GM caught a break on January 15, 1993, when the company received a call from editor of *Popular Hot Rodding* magazine Peter Pesterre. Pesterre had been contacted by a firefighter who was present during the *Dateline* tests and had independently filmed the event. Upon reviewing the new footage, GM reached two startling conclusions: (1) *Dateline* had understated the velocity of the test car by 9 mph in the first test and 7 mph in the second, and (2) puffs of smoke appeared beneath the truck prior to impact, seeming to indicate the use of incendiary devices. When GM eventually tracked down the trucks used in the test in an Indiana junkyard, the presence of flare marks and duct tape remnants on the trucks' exteriors confirmed their suspicions (Weiser 1993). When pressed on the issue, NBC asserted that the devices were meant "to simulate sparks which could occur in a collision," but that they did not cause the fire (Kurtz 1993). Later, NBC admitted that this should have been "described to our viewers" (Weiser 1993).

GM revealed its findings during a two-hour press conference and announced that it had filed a defamation lawsuit against NBC for "outrageous misrepresentation and conscious deception" (Weiser 1993). The next day, *Dateline* anchors Stone Phillips and Jane Pauley publicly apologized, cited GM's findings, and refuted the show's original claims. "We acknowledge and take responsibility for the problems that GM had identified in the demonstration crash," Phillips stated. "We deeply regret we included the inappropriate demonstration in our Dateline report. We apologize to our viewers and to General Motors" (Weiser 1993). News division president Michael Gartner along with three other producers were fired following the incident.

As in case of Tesla, GM's Level 1 defense was successful, as it provided convincing evidence that *Dateline*'s report had been based on a tampered simulation and was deeply misleading. This demonstration was followed by an apology by NBC News that effectively acknowledged GM's refutation of the original report.

A Level 1 rebuttal strategy is a tempting approach for companies that feel they are being attacked unfairly by the media. However, there are various limitations to this approach. First, it is rare that companies have the time and resources to fully refute a claim in time to limit reputational damage. If they miss their window of opportunity when the public is paying attention, the audience is left with a "no comment" impression while the company is trying to get to the bottom of the allegations.

Second, collecting and assembling the relevant evidence takes time, effort, and, at least in the case of GM, a lucky break. Effective refutation strategies require tremendous technical expertise (GM) or extensive preparation (Tesla). In both cases, the companies could rely on preexisting knowledge and technologies that could quickly be mobilized for the purpose of forcefully discrediting the allegations. It is rare that companies have detailed data not known to a journalist that can be used to devastating effect. Using such secret data could cause other problems as well; for instance, the revelation of secret monitoring technology used by Tesla may raise privacy concerns with some drivers.

Such fortuitous circumstances will rarely be present, especially if the allegations come out of the blue. Both GM and Tesla had some advance warning of the imminent allegations, and the respective issues, gas tank safety and battery life, were already core concerns for both companies. GM also enjoyed some good luck when it received the call that pointed to the doctored test. Such lucky breaks are rare.

Third, the exonerating evidence needs to be easily understood by laypeople. Just as in a jury trial, evidence needs to convince laypeople, not experts. But, in contrast to criminal trials, there is no presumption of innocence. In both the Tesla and the GM cases, the evidence supporting the companies was easy to understand and aggressively and convincingly presented to the public. In general, this can be difficult if an audience has already formed an opinion. In such cases, ambiguous or hard-to-understand evidence will tend to be interpreted in line with preexisting beliefs. Companies will usually fail to get the benefit of the doubt. Finally, the journalists, at best, had acted sloppily, at worst, unethically, and effectively retracted their stories. Companies cannot count on such good luck.

EXCUSES AND JUSTIFICATIONS.   In contrast to these Level 1 approaches, Level 2 strategies do not deny that an event took place. Rather, they attempt to deflect culpability by shifting responsibility to other actors or circumstances by providing explanations for the event that either limit the blame put upon the company or justify its actions. Two strategies figure most prominently: *excuses* and *justifications*. Excuses grant that the conduct was blameworthy but deny that the company was responsible. Justifications admit that the company was responsible but assert that its conduct was justified.

One intuition for Level 2 strategies is that there is a fixed amount of blame. Therefore, if more blame is assigned to situational factors, less is left for the company and its leadership (Kelley 1973; McClure 1998). In workplace settings, for example, supervisors tend to be more forgiving of mistakes by their subordinates when they are given an explanation that refers to external circumstances (Weiner et al. 1987). In corporate settings, a common strategy for companies is to blame suppliers. For example, in the aftermath of the BP oil spill, BP blamed contractor Transocean, arguing that its oil rig was to blame. Similarly, when faced with controversy over sticky gas pedals, Toyota pointed its finger toward CTS Corporation, the supplier of its electronic accelerator pedals.

Blaming suppliers is tempting, especially if the supplier truly was at fault. The problem is that such strategies are either immediately discounted by the public as "making excuses," or the concern shifts from the specific incident to the more general questions of vendor selection and supply-chain management. That is, when told that a supplier is at fault, the media and the public may ask why the company chose such suppliers in the first place, or may question the underlying business rationale for outsourcing. This is a particularly potent problem if outsourcing decisions and supplier selection were largely undertaken in order to lower operating costs. This may lead to suspicions that safety or quality was sacrificed to increase profits, which may then lead to concerns about the company's integrity. In the end, in the face of complex global supply chains, the company that made the promise to its customers, usually the well-known brand, is the one that will be held accountable, even if the operational or legal responsibility lies elsewhere. Finally, suppliers may fight back and dispute the factual basis for the company's statement. CTS Corporation, for example, pointed out that Toyota had received reports of unintended acceleration years before CTS Corporation became its supplier (CTS Corporation 2010). These disputes can easily escalate into mutual finger pointing, to the great delight of the company's critics and plaintiffs' attorneys.[26]

Along with allocating responsibility to corporate partners, some companies also try to shift blame to external events beyond their control, such as natural disasters or macroeconomic and political events. The problem with this approach is that concern then tends to shift toward the quality of the company's crisis response and preparedness. In the case of Hurricane Katrina, blame quickly shifted to local government and the Federal Emergency Management Agency (FEMA), alleging a lack of preparation and responsiveness. Companies are usually better off when they provide competent support for the affected community, delivered with empathy and warmth (Jordan, Diermeier, and Galinsky 2012).

Particularly problematic are situations where customers were harmed, but arguably share some or most of the blame. Some examples are driver error or reckless driving in car crashes and home foreclosures, where borrowers took on too large a debt burden. Here, no amount of blame shifting will easily deflect attention away from the company. The public will almost always side with the victim, that is, the hurt consumer, leaving the company in the role of the villain (Rai and Diermeier 2015, 2019).

All of the aforementioned strategies rely on excuses and attempts to shift blame to alternate entities or events. An alternative category of Level 2 strategies is *justification*. Here the goal is not to shift responsibility, but to show that the action does not deserve blame because it was in accordance with widely accepted principles and values.[27] Successful justification strategies are very difficult to develop. For example, denial of coverage by health insurance companies is often viewed as a severe trust violation accompanied by outrage. Such outrage will be particularly vocal if there are identifiable, sympathetic victims, such as a child who is denied a medical procedure. Insurance companies often use scientific arguments ("the procedure has not been proven to be safe and effective") or economic arguments ("the procedure is very expensive and its expected medical benefits are limited"). The problem with such justifications is that they are far less persuasive than the original concern, which is often based on strong moral intuitions like the avoidance of harm to innocent victims.

Other examples are the marketing and advertising of potentially harmful products. Here companies will tend to argue that customers voluntarily engaged in the contract and that all risks were fully disclosed. Examples include subprime lending, and alcohol and tobacco products. The appeal here is to the fundamental principle of the freedom of contracts. Similarly, in the case of executive compensation, a common defense of such arrangements is that they were made between private parties. The additional issue of fiduciary responsibility to shareholders is usually addressed by providing an economic argument about market rate compensation and the superior experience or qualifications of the senior executive.

In general, justification strategies are rarely successful; they work only if the strategy can draw on intuitive, easy-to-understand arguments and connect with deeply held convictions. However, executives will often be tempted to use such strategies, especially if they believe that they have been criticized unfairly.

Moreover, there are various factors that generally limit both Level 1 and Level 2 strategies. First, there is the phenomenon of the "fundamental attribution error" (Jones and Harris 1967; Nisbett et al. 1973). When observers make assessments about an agent, they tend to discount situational and contextual factors, and focus instead on dispositional and intrinsic features. Second, as discussed in chapter 3, in cases where there is a victim, for example, after an accident, companies tend to be blamed even though the victim may have been at fault. As we saw, this is the consequence of three interconnected effects. The first is moral typecasting (Gray, Young, and Waytz 2012). That is, agents are either seen as moral agents (capable of intention and thus blame or praise) or moral patients (capable of experience and thus experiencing pleasure or pain), but not both. Moral typecasting implies that when we have a victim who is responsible for their own misfortune, we classify them either as a victim without responsibility, or as a responsible party undeserving of sympathy. This usually tips the balance toward viewing an injured party purely as a victim. Moreover, as we saw in chapter 3, companies are believed to have intentions, but not to experience pain (Gray, Gray, and Wegner 2007; Gray, Young, and Waytz 2012; Knobe and Prinz 2008; Rai and Diermeier 2015).[28] As a consequence, companies receive far less sympathy than individuals when they are struck by the same calamity, but they tend to be blamed more.[29] Finally, when we see a blameworthy act, we tend to look for both a victim and and a villain (Gray, Young, and Waytz 2012; Schein and Gray 2015). Since companies are unlikely victims, they must be villains.

In summary, both denials and refutations (Level 1 strategies) as well as excuses and justifications (Level 2 strategies) are often ineffective or difficult to execute, yet they are widely used.

One explanation for this discrepancy is the impact of the daily experiences of executives. Executives are usually engaged in problem solving, where fact- and data-based arguments carry the most weight. Establishing what is and what is not the case is a basic desideratum of effective decision making, as is understanding processes and causal patterns. Moreover, managers will be much more familiar with the intricacies of a product or service, its risks, benefits, and limitations, and will have a better understanding of the importance of contextual factors. This familiarity will make such factors more salient and thus focus attention (Jones and Nisbett 1971; Kim, Dirks, and Cooper 2009). In addition, the desire to refute an allegation or provide a justification may be driven by a sense of injustice at being unfairly singled out or misunderstood, and thus may bolster self-esteem (Kim, Dirks, and Cooper 2009; Snyder and Higgins 1988). Together, these factors imply that a company's self-perception and its perception by others may be far apart (Rai and Diermeier 2015). That makes understanding the process of how companies are being perceived especially valuable.

APOLOGIES AND COMMITMENTS. The primary goal of all trust-related strategies is to make the company more trustworthy in the future. One way this can be done is by reducing perceptions of past culpability, which is the primary purpose of Level 1 and Level 2 strategies. Both strategies are intended to reduce the blame placed on the company. Yet assuming *more* responsibility and thus, potentially, *more* blame can actually be more effective in reestablishing trust. Level 3 strategies do not deny flawed behavior in the past, but instead focus on addressing concerns about future behavior. The restitution of trust usually involves an acknowledgment of the harmful act, often accompanied by an apology and some promise of repentance or restitution, even if the restitution is only symbolic.[30]

The success of such strategies depends on engendering beliefs in the audience that the behavior was not typical or that the company can and will improve its conduct in the future. The two main Level 3 strategies are *apologies* and *commitments* to do better. Commitments are future-oriented; they convey an assertion about future acts that are beneficial to the trustor. If believed, they can restore positive expectations about the trustee's future behavior (Schweitzer, Hershey, and Bradlow 2006). Apologies are oriented toward the past. They consist of "an admission of blameworthiness and regret" for an undesirable event (Schlenker and Darby 1981; p. 271). Apologies have been shown to reduce negative affect (Ohbuchi, Kameda, and Agarie 1989) and reduce punishments (Schwartz et al. 1978).[31] Apologies that contain an internal attribution ("I overslept") tend to be more effective in repairing relationships (Tomlinson, Dineen, and Lewicki 2004) than those that refer to external causes ("My alarm didn't ring"). A proper apology contains most of the following components (Schlenker and Darby 1981; Schweitzer, Hershey, and Bradlow 2006):

1. A statement of apology: "I am so sorry."
2. An expression of remorse: "I feel bad."
3. An offer of restitution: "I will make it up to you."
4. An expression of self-castigation: "I was thoughtless."
5. A request for forgiveness: "Can you forgive me?"
6. A promise regarding future behavior: "I won't do it again."
7. An explanation for the transgression: "I was so busy. It slipped my mind."

Apologies play different roles in different cultures (Maddux et al. 2011, 2012). They are very prevalent in many East Asian cultures, such as Japan, but far less prevalent in Europe or the United States. Moreover, they have different significance in different cultures. In individualist cultures, such as the United States, responsibility for an action is primarily located inside the individual (Nisbett et al. 2001). Therefore an apology is viewed as an admission of blame, and these cultures put a premium on sincerity and authenticity. In Japanese culture, where people tend to define themselves more in terms of their social relationships, their main function is to express remorse with the goal of repairing relationships, often in a ritualized form that prescribes practices such as bowing at a certain angle. Things go wrong when these cultural differences are not understood. The Japanese public, for example, may expect an apology as a ritualized step to repair a relationship, while US companies may refrain from an apology because they do not feel a sense of individual wrongdoing (Markus and Kitayama 1991). Similarly, to Western eyes a highly ritualized apology may appear insincere and inauthentic.

Apologies, explanations, and promises of future cooperation can help to restore trust after trust violations (Schniter, Sheremeta, and Sznycer 2012). However, if the same trust violation was accompanied by deception, trust never fully recovers (Schweitzer, Hershey, and Bradlow 2006). In other experiments, Kim et al. (2004) show that apologies have little effect in trust violations based on integrity. Similarly, Ferrin et al. (2007) show that, while apologies are effective at restoring trust in competence-based trust violations, they do not work in integrity-based cases. Indeed, the damage done in integrity violations is so severe that casting any doubt on the culpability of the party may be helpful. For example, denial can outperform apologies in an integrity-based crisis. Yet reticence to address the violation ("no comment") is never effective. Similarly, in integrity-based violations, apologies that point to an external explanation, such as the direction of senior management, and thus only partially assume responsibility, are more effective than apologies where the trustee assumes full responsibility.

The opposite holds for competence-based violations. Here, assuming full responsibility is more effective at restoring trust than pointing to external circumstances. Companies sometimes believe that apologies need to be avoided, as they constitute an admission of guilt which may lead to legal ramifications. Such concerns are often overstated. First, the relevant question is not whether legal liability can be fully avoided—this is often impossible, especially in the case of actual harm to a victim—but whether risk would *increase* due to an apology. That is, starting from a baseline of "no comment," how much would the legal risk increase if a company or executive apologized? Second, there is evidence from the domain of medical malpractice that maintaining a personal connection to patients and expressing regret actually *lowers* liability exposure (Kachalia et al. 2010). Whether such findings generalize to other domains, such as product safety, workplace discrimination, or shareholder lawsuits, however, is an open question. That said, the widely held belief that apologies increase liability does not hold in general. Third, the trust violation itself also constitutes a risk that needs to be compared with other risks. Suppose that issuing an apology was indeed found to increase legal risk. In that case management has to weigh the two types of exposure, reputational versus legal risk, and make a decision based on the best available assessment of their relative magnitude. Often there are more than these two types of risks. Additional risks include regulatory concerns as well as the company's perception among investors, employees, and business partners. Apologies may be well received by employees, but less so by investors. In general, management decisions on whether to apologize should be based on a careful assessment of the likely consequences among the various constituencies.

Other than apologies, effective Level 3 strategies to repair trust include expressions of empathy, the commitment to do better in the future, and concrete steps to improve (Schniter, Sheremeta, and Sznycer 2012; Schweitzer, Hershey, and Bradlow 2006). Such strategies are especially important if an apology is not advisable, for instance, for legal reasons. From the point of view of the audience, the key question is whether trust can be restored. Indeed, inauthentic or overly legalistic apologies, such as the infamous "mistakes were made," may backfire and trigger additional outrage.

Competence-based violations, if accompanied by a proper apology and the assumption of responsibility, are more likely to be understood as missteps rather than signals about the trustee's type. To be sure, if an action signals fundamental incompetence, even a full apology is unlikely to have any effect. However, in more moderate instances trustors will likely maintain the belief that the person or organization can change, especially if the apology points to circumstances that can easily be addressed, for example, by an upgrade to a state-of-the art technology.

For integrity-based violations, the key question then is whether the trustor believes that the trustee's moral character can change over time, or whether it is permanent (Chiu, Hong, and Dweck 1997). Haselhuhn, Schweitzer, and Wood (2010) show that these beliefs mediate trust recovery. Such beliefs can be malleable, and once they are present, trust recovery and forgiveness become easier. Indeed, even a simple message by the trustee to the (betrayed) trustor that contains a promise to change can have a positive effect on trust repair (Schniter, Sheremeta, and Sznycer 2012). Again cultural differences matter. Heine et al. (2001) show that Japanese audiences have stronger beliefs in malleable selves that Americans. This suggests that Japanese trustors should be more forgiving of integrity-based trust violations after an apology compared to Americans. This is indeed the case (Maddux et al. 2012), but the opposite is true of competence-based violations. Here an apology is more effective for American audiences (Maddux et al. 2011).

For companies, this means that after an integrity-based violation, the main goal is to convince the audience that the company is not only willing but capable of making the necessary changes. In the corporate context, integrity-based violations are often the consequence of a dysfunctional culture, ineffective leadership, or the lack of effective compliance processes. Therefore, to restore trust after integrity-based violations, companies should take concrete steps to reform their culture and values, and significantly improve their internal control and compliance processes. Often this requires a change in leadership, the involvement of credible third parties, and the commitment to a sustained process of cultural change.

5.2.5 The Need for Speed

Just as important as the content of a response is its speed (Diermeier 2011). One reason to strive for a timely response is the shortness of the news cycle (Leskovec, Backstrom, and Kleinberg 2009).[32] As discussed in chapter 2, members of the public rarely pay attention to companies in their daily lives other than during a corporate crisis. If this pivotal moment is missed, audiences will remember that the company did not respond when it was "on stage." Subsequent efforts are likely to go unnoticed. The net effect is similar to a "no comment" response and will likely further erode trust. Even if the company has an effective response strategy, it will have little effect if the public is no longer paying attention. Considerations are frozen again, this time at a lower level of trust. Taking advantage of pivotal moments to leave a lasting, positive impression in the minds of customers should therefore guide decision making, rather than the goal of ending a crisis as quickly as possible. Simply exiting the headlines quickly is a very bad idea if the last thing customers remember about a company is that it doesn't care about them.[33]

The second reason for urgency is that audiences use speed as an indicator of sincerity.[34] Subjects in experiments judge decision makers as increasingly less moral the longer they take to reject a clearly unethical option. Recent research has shown that decision speed is used as a cue to infer moral character. Thus, in trust games, people trust partners more when they decide quickly, as it indicates that they are cooperating because it is the right thing to do, rather than because they have calculated that it is most beneficial (Rand, Greene, and Nowack 2012). In effect, merely taking the time to consider acts that are perceived to be unethical rather than taking immediate action leads to moral outrage, even when the decision-maker makes the "right" moral decision eventually (e.g., Critcher, Inbar, and Pizarro, 2013; Tetlock et al. 2000; Trivers 1971).

A clear example of this phenomenon can be seen in the case of the Equifax data breach. When Equifax was hacked and the personal data of millions was stolen, much of the resulting anger was in response to Equifax's delay in revealing the information. While Equifax may have been waiting to make sure it had all of the facts, it left an impression with consumers that it was trying to hide the attack, an impression that was only strengthened when three Equifax managers sold Equifax stock prior to the company publicly revealing the breach. Even if the timing of the sale was a coincidence, the appearance of foul play could have been avoided with a more immediate response (Cowley 2018, 2019; McCrank and Saxena 2017).

The need for speed creates a serious quandary. On the one hand, a slow response by itself will further undermine trust, especially if the company misses its window of media attention. On the other hand, it is practically impossible to obtain even a rudimentary assessment of a situation during the few hours when audiences pay attention. How should companies respond? Reputational crises are almost always about trust, so the primary goal during the first few hours should be to reassure customers and other constituencies in order to maintain and enhance trust in an environment of fear and skepticism. Any delay will erode the public's trust in the company.

Management's first instinct will often be to find a solution during this period. Given the short time frame, this is likely a futile attempt and may distract from the main focus of restoring trust. Eventually, companies have to find a solution to a perceived problem, but the initial goal is to restore trust. Indeed, maintaining trust will give companies much needed room to maneuver to resolve the problem, and a more receptive audience once a solution is found.

5.2.6   Building Trust during a Crisis

From a practical point of view, companies should emphasize four major factors to maintain and increase trust during a crisis: transparency, expertise, commitment, and empathy (Diermeier 2011).[35]

Little undermines trust as much as the suspicion that a company is hiding something or is willfully withholding relevant information. Full *transparency* is reached when, in the mind of the audience, all relevant questions have been addressed. What matters is what the audience considers to be relevant—not the company. Yet, what is considered relevant will vary for different audiences. What is transparent to an investor may not be transparent to a customer. What is important to a faculty member may be irrelevant to a parent or a student. It is essential to understand what is "in the head" of the respective audience members and address it in a language and style that resonates with them.

Transparency is not the same as full disclosure, and transparency may be reached without full disclosure. This will be the case if the leader conveys a rationale for limiting disclosure that reflects concerns shared by the relevant audience. For example, in the case of a health crisis, privacy concerns may limit what can be disclosed (e.g., not revealing the identity of an individual who has tested positive for COVID-19). Rather than simply declining to comment, leaders can emphasize the importance of patient privacy, a concern shared by the audience, as a clear and understandable reason for limiting disclosure. In other cases, relevant information may not yet be available (e.g., the number of people who may have had direct contact with an infected person or the likely infection rates). As a general rule, the rationale for limiting disclosure must pass the "reasonable person test," meaning that it will seem justifiable to most people.

It is also possible that transparency will not be achieved despite full disclosure. That will be the case when the leader, in the attempt to fully disclose an issue, fails to be understood. Technical mumbo-jumbo, a complex explanation, or legalese—even if it involves disclosing relevant information—will not be considered transparent by the general public. Rather, an audience will assume that a company is hiding behind incomprehensible jargon rather than speaking plainly and in a straightforward manner. This is a common trap for leaders who have highly specialized knowledge, such as physicians during a health crisis. It is important to remember that what is obvious to an expert may not be obvious to the general public.

Furthermore, holding back information can lead audiences to doubt the veracity of what they are being told. There may be times when leadership does not want to release known information. If this is the case, it is important to anticipate the reaction of audiences if the information is brought to light through means other than direct communication from leadership. Will the rationale for not disclosing the information pass the reasonable person test? Most often, it is better to release bad information all at once rather than withholding information that will continue to trickle out over time.

A perceived lack of *expertise* can undermine trust quickly. This is particularly important during health crises and natural disasters. The reputational catastrophe suffered by the FEMA because of its bungled response during Hurricane Katrina was not driven by the belief that it had bad intentions, but rather that it was incompetent.

In the United States, companies are usually viewed as competent, which is not generally true in other countries. On balance, this is a benefit to a company. It also implies, however, that if things go wrong, the public may not doubt corporate ability but may doubt its willingness to do the right thing. That said, for companies the expectation of competence often has a threshold structure. Companies get little credit for exceeding expectations but are heavily criticized if they fail to meet them. This is particularly problematic when the public has unrealistic expectations of what companies can do.

In contrast, nonprofits are usually viewed as less competent than profit-making companies, but more caring (Aaker, Vohs, and Mogilner 2010). This means that their audiences may be more forgiving when things do not work out as planned. However, this goodwill does not apply to problems within a nonprofit's core competency. The Red Cross will likely be forgiven for a cybersecurity breach, but not for a contamination of its blood supply. Moreover, given their reputation for warmth and caring, nonprofits will experience a serious backlash if their actions are viewed as self-serving or financially motivated.

Leaders can address a perceived lack of expertise by bringing in third-party experts with high credibility. Experts with knowledge well outside of the expected expertise of management are not likely to cause a perception of management incompetence. For example, a well-respected physician or public health expert from the Centers for Disease Control, a prestigious university, or the local health department will have medical knowledge about diseases that management would not typically be expected to have.

Crisis preparedness is a particularly important aspect of competence. The reputation of an organization and trust in its leaders will diminish significantly if the company seems unprepared. First, audiences will ask, "What did the organization do to prevent this crisis?" When it is humanly possible to prevent or significantly decrease the likelihood of harm occurring, the widely held belief is that preventive action should have been implemented. If the company appears negligent, dismissive, or incompetent, then outrage will occur. These concerns are less common during new threats like the COVID-19 pandemic, but are important for crises that are

more familiar. Second, customers and other constituencies expect an organization to be prepared and "ever ready" to manage a crisis effectively
when it occurs, especially when the crisis is considered foreseeable. The
excuse that "we didn't think it would happen to us" holds little credibility.

Lack of crisis management expertise will cause outrage and diminished
reputation for unprepared organizations. People expect leaders and their
organizations to have the expertise to take full preventive action and to be
prepared to respond quickly, decisively, and effectively when crises occur.

At the end of the day, stakeholders want to make sure that a crisis is
resolved and that those affected are "made whole," if at all possible. One
problem with this expectation is that early in a crisis it is impossible to
establish even the most basic facts, let alone find a solution. This is particularly true during pandemics in which the situation is highly dynamic and
fluid, and easy solutions are not available. So, what are we to do? This is
where commitment, our third factor, can play an important role.

The most powerful and direct way to signal *commitment* is for leaders
to show up in a highly visible manner and take charge. This demonstrates
accountability and sends the message that nothing is more important than
resolving this particular crisis. When a Virgin train from London bound for
Glasgow crashed after derailing because of a line defect, CEO Sir Richard
Branson not only cut short a family vacation to help handle the situation
personally, he also visited crash victims in the hospital and praised the train
driver's courage and actions that potentially saved more lives (Diermeier
2011).

To an efficiency-minded leader, such a crisis response ritual may look
like a waste of time, the most precious resource during any crisis. Ironically,
it is exactly this "inefficiency" that creates the strong symbolic value. A
leader signals that nothing is more important than taking care of this crisis
by showing up with the full resources of the company. This creates a sense
of commitment.

Does the company's representative always have to be the CEO? No;
the right level of commitment depends on the perceived magnitude of
the crisis. If in doubt, companies should use someone sufficiently senior
in the management hierarchy, even if the executive is not directing the
operations. The importance of perceived commitment also casts doubt
on the extensive use of public relations professionals as spokespeople.
The problem with spokespeople is that they do not have operational
responsibilities—they are not in charge and audiences know it. People
want to hear from leaders in a crisis. Depending on the crisis, it is best to

use skilled media spokespersons for ongoing briefings in conjunction with the highly visible presence of the leader of the organization.

Another important commitment device is process clarity. The definition and communication of a decision process is particularly important during crises that may last a long time, yet evolve rapidly. Ideally, the details of the process are clearly communicated to the relevant audiences, followed by regular updates.

The final component, *empathy*, is often the most important factor of the four and the easiest to miss. Showing empathy is not the same thing as apologizing. Leaders show empathy with colleagues at work, neighbors, and family members, even if they do not feel responsible for a problem. During pandemics or natural disasters, stakeholders do not see the company or organization as an anonymous provider of goods or services, but as a member of the community. And a member of the community is expected to care and show empathy. In many crises, if there is a perception that the company or organization mishandled a situation, stakeholders expect a sincere apology, but the apology must be authentic. An apology that appears formulaic, insincere, or calculated is worse than useless.

A leader's reaching out to perceived victims with warmth and authenticity can be very effective, even without an apology. In response to Virgin's train accident, Sir Richard Branson expressed both sorrow for the loss of life and support for the driver who helped the vast majority of passengers survive the crash. People want to know leaders and their organizations care when there is real or perceived harm. Caring is behavioral, not just a passive feeling. An effective crisis manager engages in behaviors that encourage people to believe that the organization truly cares.

5.3 Summary

This chapter analyzed reputational challenges based on beliefs. We particularly focused on risk and trust. The modern literature on risk perception has identified multiple biases in how people perceive risks. Recently, Slovic's concept of "risk as feeling" (Slovic 2010) has provided a common framework that can account for many such biases. Hence, both moral judgment and risk perception are grounded in affect and emotions. Beliefs and values do not operate in isolation, but influence each other.

We then turned our attention to trust and trustworthiness. Trusted relationships are crucial for business success, whether they involve customers, investors, employees, or suppliers. In a trusted relationship, one party (the trustor) puts themselves at risk with respect to the other party (the trustee). If such trust is violated, or perceived to be violated, trustors react with anger, disappointment, and outrage. Companies that need to address perceived trust violations face an uphill battle. Unless the factual basis is clear and easy to understand, strategies that involve denials, refutations, excuses, or justifications are rarely effective. In such cases, companies should instead consider apologizing and committing to do better in the future. We show that the effectiveness of apologies varies by the type of trust violation and often involves moral judgments. This interconnection between beliefs, here in the context of trust and credibility, and moral judgment further highlights the interconnection of moral judgment and beliefs and their foundation in affect and emotion. These issues are particularly highlighted during a crisis, when fostering trust is essential.

CHAPTER SIX

Open Questions and Future Directions

Our review of the psychological processes that drive evaluations of corporate conduct has uncovered a rich set of principles. Value orientations and character assessments are as important as cultural context and the nature of social relationships. Risk perception and trust are often influenced by moral judgments. Many of the evaluations of companies are not based on careful deliberation, but on affect and emotion. Rather than investigating an issue carefully, members of the public listen to their gut feeling. This creates a complex and challenging environment for companies. We discussed these processes in detail and derived lessons for effective strategies.

That said, the approach also points to various open questions that need to be addressed in future research. First, we have seen various examples where the value orientations that people use in everyday life are simply applied to the corporate domain, ranging from pricing decisions to emerging technologies. Where we have empirical research, for example, in the case of new technologies, evaluations in the corporate domain closely follow evaluations in everyday judgments. However, there are potentially important differences between everyday moral judgments and the evaluation of companies. Companies are embedded in a complex web of competitive and cooperative relationships with customers, suppliers, distributors, and so forth. Our survey of company evaluations suggests that the public takes little to no account of such complexities. For example, the

public tends to equate revenue with profits.[1] A price increase of an airline ticket is interpreted as the airline making more money. Indeed, public
estimates of profitability are much higher than the actual numbers. According to the Survey of Americans and Economists on the Economy (SAEE),
the average respondent estimated corporate profit rates at 46.7 percent,
while the true number is closer to 3 percent (*Washington Post*, Kaiser Family Foundation, and Harvard University 1996). This and related evidence
suggests that laypeople perceive market interactions in a highly biased
fashion, effectively using a form of "folk economics" to make sense of the
world of commerce (Blendon et al. 1997; Caplan 2002).[2] Yet little is known
about the underlying cognitive processes that shape such folk economics.

To see the practical relevance of these issues, consider the case of obesity. Fast food and soda companies have been the subject of hostile media
and attacked by activists. But a lay theory that obesity is caused by lack of
exercise rather than high-calorie food consumption will not see companies
as the main culprits, but will place the responsibility on consumers. Notice
that the value orientation in both cases is the same; it is a straightforward
application of the do-no-harm principle. The question is, who has the duty
of care? In the context of childhood diabetes, for instance, it can lie with
companies that market high-calorie food products to children or with parents who fail to model a healthy lifestyle. The difference is not values, but
different beliefs about the way that the world works.

The general point is that folk theories and general perceptions, not just
value conflicts, can determine whether a company faces reputational challenges or regulatory pressure. They make certain policies plausible and
others implausible. If food companies are viewed as the culprit for obesity,
restrictions on marketing or portion sizes become plausible. When confronted with high local rents, most people will look for rent control as the
obvious solution, while temporary subsidies for developers, rezoning, or
the removal of regulatory hurdles that delay construction may not come
to mind. Combined with strong fairness intuitions ("giving money to rich
developers is wrong"), this may lead to a hostile business environment for
real estate developers, which may further limit housing stock.

A second set of questions pertains to the degree of similarity between
people and companies as objects of moral judgment. As an example, recall
the importance of person-centered evaluations in moral judgment. Actions
are often interpreted as signals of character and virtue. We have seen
that corporate decisions, for example, in the area of compensation, are
evaluated by similar processes. But how far does this similarity reach?
Does the person-centered approach mean that all the processes that we

apply to individuals are wholeheartedly used to evaluate companies as well?

We can see some immediate differences. For example, in our review of moral judgments the do-no-harm principle loomed large. We saw that it is a powerful driver in shaping the perception of companies. But these examples focused on the company as the cause of harm, inflicted onto the public. What about the reverse, when a company experiences harm? Do we have empathy with companies? Our analysis showed that we do not. The loss of revenue or profits, even a bankruptcy, does not cause the same reaction as a family losing its home. Of course, we have empathy with the individual losing her job, but not with the abstract corporation suffering a drop in market cap. Shareholders do not fare much better. They tend to be perceived as rich, greedy, and anonymous, attributes that rarely attract sympathy. Yet, in other regards, we treat companies like persons. Companies are said to have rights; we ascribe intentions to them, hold them accountable for their conduct, and so on.

This asymmetry deserves to be explored further. For example, we do not have a clear understanding of whether this assessment of companies holds in general or can vary by company or segment. What we do know is that companies are viewed differently from nonprofits. Aaker, Vohs, and Mogliner (2010) have shown that companies are usually viewed as competent, while nonprofits are viewed as warm and caring. Being viewed as competent may be seen as an asset, but it also leads to higher expectations. Indeed, as shown by Jordan, Diermeier, and Galinsky (2012), when companies fail to act competently, e.g., in a natural disaster, they are viewed negatively not only on dimensions of competence, but also on integrity and trustworthiness. Similarly, being seen as caring is usually an asset for nonprofits, but if this perception is violated they suffer more than for-profits. Research by Uhlmann et al. (2009), later replicated in Schweinsberg et al. (2016), for example, shows that even very small executive perks, such as expensive bottled water, can undermine trust in nonprofits, while having no impact on for-profit companies.[3]

A fruitful direction for further research is to study whether similar heterogeneities can be observed across industries or across companies. For example, are start-ups viewed the same as large, established corporations? Does it matter if the CEO has a strong public profile and is well known? And how does the CEO's personal reputation interact with the reputation of the company?

We would surely expect that the overall reputation of an industry matters. In addition, there is the question of whether a given issue is closely related to a core competency. A loss of vendor data is a big deal for American Express, but is presumably less important for Burger King, while a case of food poisoning in the executive cafeteria has the reverse effect.

Of particular importance is the relationship to CSR and other firm differences such as strong brands. Minor and Morgan (2011) argue that CSR activities can buffer a company from adverse stock effects in cases of product recalls. However, they also find that CSR activities can backfire if the company is perceived to cause direct harm. Understanding such relationships in more depth will help us understand the effectiveness and risk of reputation-building strategies.

Finally, we saw the importance of social relationships in shaping evaluations. As with the other principles, we discussed evidence that in certain contexts the public simply transfers these dimensions when evaluating companies. In the case of natural disasters, terrorist attacks, and pandemics, for example, people switch from an exchange to a community orientation and evaluate corporate conduct accordingly. While such findings are promising, the existing categories supplied by social relations theory are likely too coarse. Individuals relate with companies in all sorts of ways: as customers, as employees, as investors. Subsuming all of these relationships as market interactions does little justice to the difference between relationships like working for Wal-Mart versus shopping at Wal-Mart.

In sum, the application of the methodologies of social and cognitive psychology as well as behavioral economics to the study of corporate reputation has generated rich insights into how companies are perceived by various constituencies and what this means for corporate strategies. We have already seen that how audiences view a particular issue can matter for who is held responsible and who gets a pass. It is to these questions that we turn next. This focus will also allow us to discuss a new set of methodologies.

PART III

Salience and Attention

CHAPTER SEVEN

Framing

7.1 Tobacco

The history of the US tobacco industry is perhaps the best example of the reputational collapse of an entire industry. Not only did it lead to fundamental changes in attitudes toward smoking, but also to sweeping regulatory changes such as severe advertising restrictions, smoking bans in restaurants and public spaces, and, eventually, regulatory oversight by the US Food and Drug Administration (FDA).[1]

A thriving industry for most of the last century (tobacco contributed $12.9 billion in federal and state taxes in 1995 from cigarette sales alone [Jones 1997]) and an important part of popular culture, in the midcentury the industry started to face concerns over adverse health consequences. Possible links to lung cancer were identified as early as the late 1930s (Müller 1939). Mounting evidence over the next decades led to the publication of the 1964 Report of the Advisory Committee to the Surgeon General on Smoking and Health. Having studied more than 7,000 articles on smoking and disease, the authors of the report concluded that a causal link existed between cigarette smoking and lung and laryngeal cancer in men, that cigarettes were a probable cause of lung cancer in women, and that cigarette smoking was the single most important cause of chronic bronchitis. The committee also stated that cigarette smoking constituted a health hazard of sufficient importance in the United States to warrant appropriate remedial action. The report constituted a watershed event for public awareness of the health risks of smoking.

Yet, strikingly, despite broad consensus within the medical and scientific community about the dangers of smoking, the business environment for tobacco companies hardly changed during the next 30 years. Cigarette sales fell by 1.6 percent in 1964, but climbed to a new record in 1965. As late as 1992, Phillip Morris's flagship brand Marlboro was named the most valuable brand in the world. While customer attitudes did change over the subsequent decades, such change was slow and hardly left a dent in the fortunes of the industry.

Moreover, political and legal challenges to the industry were largely unsuccessful. The main restrictions were labeling requirements and, later, some advertising restrictions. But even those were heavily contested by the industry, often watered down, and had little effect. For example, the 1965 Federal Cigarette Labeling and Advertising Act required that the warning "Caution: Cigarette Smoking May Be Hazardous to Your Health" be placed in small print on one of the side panels of each cigarette package. However, the act also prohibited additional labeling requirements at the federal, state, or local levels. In addition, the final wording of the warning was weaker than anti-tobacco activists had wanted and applied only to cartons and packs, but not advertising copy. Tobacco opponent Philip Elman, a member of the Federal Trade Commission (FTC), branded it "one of the dirtiest pieces of legislation ever," while the *New York Times* proclaimed it to be a "shocking piece of special interest legislation ... a bill to protect the economic health of the tobacco industry by freeing it of proper regulation" (Derthick 2002).[2] Furthermore, despite a 1970 federal law that banned cigarette advertising on television and radio, cigarette sales were largely unaffected (Steward 1993).

On the legal front, the first individual tort cases against the cigarette companies arose in the mid-1950s, with the plaintiffs claiming both negligence and a failure to warn on the part of the tobacco companies. However, in all of these cases, the courts ruled that the risks were unknowable in advance and that the tobacco companies had exercised due care. Subsequent cases were hardly more successful. Of the 813 cases filed up to 1996, only 23 were tried, and all but two were won outright by the industry, with no compensation being paid.

Juries, on the whole, were heavily predisposed toward holding individual smokers, not tobacco companies, responsible for the negative health effects of smoking. The concept of "comparative fault" used in most states meant that juries could allocate damages in the proportion to the degree of fault assigned to the defendant. If a company's responsibility was below a certain threshold, no damages could be awarded. Moreover, plaintiff's attorneys could not compete with the financial resources available to the tobacco companies.

The industry's success in preventing additional regulation and winning in the courtroom was due to a pervasive, well-funded public relations campaign that started in late 1953 with a meeting of executives of the six leading US tobacco companies. The subsequent campaign was developed by John Hill of the public relations firm Hill & Knowlton. At its core was the decision to move from their traditional reactive approach of defending the industry to one that was both proactive and "ferocious." The approach was stated most directly in a company memo: "We have one essential job—which can be simply said: Stop public panic.... There is only one problem—confidence, and how to establish it; public assurance, and how to create it.... And, most important, how to free millions of Americans from the guilty fear that is going to arise deep in their biological depths— regardless of any pooh-poohing logic—every time they light a cigarette" (Hill & Knowlton 1953).

The industry's strategy was based on the following three components: stressing contradictory evidence and knowledge gaps to maintain that the causal connection between smoking and ill-health remained unproven; finding loopholes in arguments advanced for legislation and influencing researchers to not publish unfavorable research; and, finally, funding research that would cast further doubt on the antismoking movement's assertions. Many of these activities were coordinated by the Tobacco Industry Research Committee (TIRC), later to be renamed the Council for Tobacco Research (CTR), founded to aid the "research effort into all phases of tobacco use and health," (Brandt 2012; Tobacco Tactics 2020).

Throughout the debates over the health effects of tobacco, the role of personal choice was of critical importance. Smoking was viewed as a choice by adult individuals who were aware of the health risks, but who chose to smoke anyway for personal reasons including relaxation and enjoyment. In the current era of pervasive bans on smoking and the advertising of tobacco products, these views may appear implausible but, decades ago, they were widely shared. This perspective is evidenced by the position of the American Cancer Society, which stated in its 1957 annual report: "The society believes that at our present state of knowledge, the question of whether to start smoking or to give it up must be left to the judgment of individuals. For intelligent decisions everyone should know the facts: There is a definite association between cigarette smoking and cancer"(p. 19; cited in Nathanson 1999, p. 446).

Despite the industry's efforts, the regulatory and legal environment significantly worsened for it during the mid-1990s. These developments were the result of a variety of factors, including a newly assertive FDA under the leadership of David Kessler and new legal strategies such as the so-called Castano class-action lawsuit, as well as state lawsuits trying to recoup health system expenditures used for the treatment of tobacco-related illnesses. In addition, highly embarrassing tobacco company internal documents had reached the public through whistle-blowers, despite desperate attempts by tobacco companies to keep them confidential.[3]

Eventually, these developments led to the Master Settlement Agreement of 1998 between 46 US states, the District of Columbia, and the five US territories, on the one side, and the major tobacco companies, on the other. The agreement aimed to settle all the state lawsuits seeking to recover Medicaid costs related to smoking. The final outcome included a payout of $246 billion to states and various other funds, as well as significant marketing restrictions. The battle between tobacco companies and antismoking advocates continued for another two decades. Finally, on June 21, 2009, US president Obama signed into law legislation that gave the FDA regulatory oversight over tobacco products, a key objective of the antitobacco movement.

7.2 Cognitive and Issue Frames

While these events were highly complex and shaped by many interconnected developments, among the most important factors that turned the tide was a significant shift in the public perception of smoking and its relationship to public health. Originally, the public had viewed smoking as a matter of personal choice. But, over time, this changed to viewing smoking as an "epidemic," a term borrowed from public health.

What changed was *how* the public viewed smoking. The factors that shape how an issue is viewed are commonly known as *frames*. The concept of *framing* was made famous by Kahneman and Tversky (1979, 2000). The idea is that individuals will change their attitudes (judgment) and behavior (decision making) in response to changes in how the same information is presented. For example, snacks that are described as "90 percent fat free" evoke a different emotional reaction and attitude than if they are described as "10 percent fat" (Kahneman 2011, p. 88). We may call these *cognitive frames*.

We have already encountered cognitive frames in the context of risk perception (Slovic 2000, 2010), for example, in the example of gain versus loss frames. People who suffer (or are worried about a loss) tend to be more accepting of risk, while those who experienced a gain tend to be risk averse. There is now a vast literature on framing effects, especially in the context of judgment and decision-making under uncertainty (Kahneman 2011; Kahneman and Tversky 2000).[4] But there is a second type of framing, particularly important in the context of public opinion: *issue framing*.[5] Issue framing is most relevant in the context of evaluating complex issues where there are different possible points of view or where it is difficult to establish which side is correct. For example, is the rise in obesity due to a lack of personal responsibility and self-control, or is it due to irresponsible marketing practices by food companies (Lawrence 2004)? How we view an issue shapes our attitude. If obesity is viewed as caused by a lack of self-control, there will be less pressure on companies to change their marketing practices. In other words, once people view an issue through a certain frame, some policies become more plausible and intuitive than others.

"Framing" is distinct from "priming," although both influence opinion formation. In short, *priming* operates on memory and access, while *framing* operates on attention and salience. Priming refers to a cognitive process where a stimulus temporarily increases the accessibility of certain knowledge units in the memory of an individual, which makes it more likely that these knowledge units are used in the reception, interpretation, and judgment of issues and events. Hence, priming makes certain considerations more accessible and thus influences opinion formation and expression. Iyengar and Kinder (1987) were able to demonstrate, for example, that after being exposed to stories about national defense, subjects will judge the performance of the US president largely on defense-related issues. When primed by stories about inflation, on the other hand, citizens evaluated the US president on economic performance.

Framing refers to the processes that influence how individuals view a complex issue; it explains which dimension or aspect of an issue is front and center.[6] For example, the debate over mandatory funding of contraceptives can be interpreted as being about access to contraceptives, compliance with federal law, or religious freedom. Framing plays a crucial role in political debates (Chong and Druckman 2007c; Gamson and Modigliani 1987), but is equally important in the context of corporate reputations, especially in the context of corporate campaigns where a company is criticized by an NGO. In those cases, we may also find instances of competitive framing, where two opposing sides promote alternative frames to shape how the public views an issue.

7.3   A Model of Framing

In part 1 we discussed the model of opinion formation from Zaller (1992) and Zaller and Feldman (1992). In the Zaller model, individuals do not have well-formed attitudes on a given issue, but rather construct responses on the fly as functions of immediately accessible *considerations* retrieved from long-term memory. Considerations are defined as "any reason that might induce an individual to decide a political issue one way or another" (Zaller 1992, p. 40). Considerations are not cold calculations, but a "compound of cognition and affect." Which considerations are top of mind for respondents depends on their personal histories and external factors such as media coverage. Opinions are then formed by averaging over the set of accessed considerations.

We can apply these ideas in a model of framing (Ajzen and Fishbein 1980; Nelson, Oxley, and Clawson 1997). We denote the object of an attitude as x. This can be a company, a product, an industry, a proposed regulation, and so forth. Individual i's attitude toward x is a real number denoted $a^i(x)$, for which a positive number indicates a favorable attitude. Suppose there are K issue dimensions indexed by k. For example, soda vending machines in schools may be evaluated on the dimensions of health (i.e., nutritional impact on children), financial support for schools (i.e., a portion of sales may be used for funding after-school advancement activities), marketing to children (i.e., the ethics of advertising directed at children), and so forth. Then we denote $c_k^i(x) \in \Re$ as individual i's evaluation of the object according to issue dimension k. These are our (simplified) considerations. They constitute the set of considerations C^i for individual i.

The set of considerations may change over time and will vary across individuals. At any given time, some of these considerations are top of mind. This can be modeled by defining relative weights w_k^i over the set of considerations. That is, we have $w_k^i \geq 0$ for all k and i with $\sum_k w_k^i = 1$. These weights can capture a process where more than one consideration is accessed with different levels of salience, or they may correspond to the probability that any one consideration is activated. Individual i's overall attitude toward an object is then given by $a^i(x) = \sum_k c_k^i(x)w_k^i$.

In the case of vending machines in schools, for instance, an individual may not think of the ethical issue of marketing to children, but may consider the other two factors (nutritional impact versus funding of after-school programs). That is, we have $w_{funding}^i > 0$ and $w_{nutrition}^i > 0$, but $w_{marketing}^i = 0$. An individual may have a positive attitude toward the dimension of funding after-school programs, that is, $c_{funding}^i(x) > 0$, but a negative attitude toward the dimension of nutrition, $c_{nutrition}^i(x) < 0$.

A firm can try to change attitudes by attempting to "persuade" the public, that is, by increasing any of the c_k^i. For example, the company can try to convince the public that public health research that links soda consumption with childhood obesity is methodologically flawed, or that the real driver in increasing childhood obesity is lack of physical exercise. We call messages that are intended to change any of the considerations *persuasive*. If accepted, they may modify given considerations or add new considerations to the set C^i.

But this not the only way by which a company or an interest group can try to effect opinion change. Note that the overall attitude toward the company does not depend simply on the relative magnitude of $c_{funding}^i$ and $c_{nutrition}^i$, but also on the relative magnitude *weighted* by $w_{funding}^i$ and $w_{nutrition}^i$. That is, i will have a favorable attitude toward x (i.e., $a^i(x) > 0$) if $c_{funding}^i(x) \cdot w_{funding}^i > c_{nutrition}^i(x) \cdot w_{nutrition}^i$. This can be accomplished by sufficiently increasing $w_{funding}^i$ while all the other components stay the same. The idea is to make the consideration more easily accessible in the mind of the audience. This can be done through advertising, such as by buying ads explicitly sponsoring after-school programs, or by making that consideration particularly salient, such as by involving well-known celebrities or using symbols such as colored wristbands to keep the issue top of mind. A more subtle strategy may want to try to lower $w_{nutrition}^i$. This can be done by "complexifying" an issue to make it less likely to be easily accessible in the mind of the public.

The important insight of this approach is that attitude shift does not require that an individual changes her mind on a given dimension, for example, by changing her attitude on $c^i_{nutrition}$. Rather, attitude shift may occur simply by shifting the weights w^i_k that capture the intuitive concept of salience. Hence, shifting salience leads to attitude shift.

We call messages that are intended to activate certain considerations or shift the relative likelihood of activation *cueing messages*. Cueing messages do not operate on the considerations themselves but on the distribution of considerations and their respective accessibility in memory.

This point deserves some emphasis. Much of the discussion in the last chapter was focused on understanding how considerations are formed, such as through the processes of moral judgments or trust. But attitudes do not simply express considerations; that was the flaw in the "database" model of opinion formation. Rather, at any given moment, attitudes are constructed through a complex process that involves access to memory, associations, and attention. People have a set or network of considerations, but which of these considerations are accessed or activated depends on the psychological processes of memory access (e.g., priming) and attention (e.g., framing).

This insight has important consequences. First, a change in considerations is not necessary for attitude change. Rather, any factor that shapes the *distribution* over considerations and the retrieval process may lead to attitude change. People don't have to change their mind—that is change their considerations—they can also change what they pay attention to. Second, two people with the same set of considerations, shaped by the same set of values and preferences, may express different attitudes if they are exposed to different stimuli, (e.g., through different types of media coverage) if such stimuli lead to differences in memory retrieval or attention. It follows that attitudes are not well-formed, consistent, or constant evaluations. Rather, they may be constructed in the moment, shifting, inconsistent, and change in response to stimuli.

Framing effects occur when individuals shift their attitudes in response to being exposed to a frame. A large number of empirical studies have found evidence of such framing effects (Chong and Druckman 2007a, 2007b, 2007c).[7] In such studies, subjects are randomly assigned a stimulus, usually a text like a newspaper article or commentary, that encapsulates a particular frame. After being exposed to the frame, researchers measure attitude shift, usually by administering a short opinion survey. In some designs, the attitude of a treated group is compared to a control group that is not exposed to any frame. In other designs, one subsample is assigned to one frame and another group to a different frame. In yet other designs, the

same group of subjects is exposed to competing frames. The general finding in these studies is that when subjects are exposed to a given frame, their
opinion shifts in the direction of the frame represented in the stimulus.

As an example, consider a study of attitudes toward genetically modified food products (Druckman and Bolsen 2011). In this experiment the
researchers conducted exit polls on Election Day in 2008. Twenty teams
of pollsters were randomly assigned to polling stations in northern Cook
County, Illinois. Pollsters asked every third voter to complete a survey, and
respondents were paid $5. All subjects were provided with a brief descrip-
tion of genetically modified food. In addition, subsamples were randomly
assigned to various experimental conditions that captured commonly used
frames in the GMO debate. Specifically, two frames were used: a pro frame
focused on biotech's role in combating world hunger, while a con frame
elucidated its negative effects on biodiversity. These two frames had commonly been used in the GMO debate[8] and emerged from pretests as the
most potent frames. In the control condition, subjects were provided with
only background information. After exposure to background information
and frames (if applicable), subjects answered questions about their support for biotechnology measured on a seven-point scale regarding the
"production and consumption of GM foods," with higher scores indicating increased support. Compared to the control group, support for GM
foods significantly increased by 6.8 percent for subjects exposed to the pro
frame and decreased by 11.2 percent for the con frame. So opinions toward
genetically modified food shifted, as expected, in response to frames. Interestingly, adding further facts to the frames had no significant effect on
opinions. What seems to matter more is whether subjects pay attention to
a particular aspect of the issue, irrespective of whether this attention shift
is driven by additional facts or just by the expressed opinions of others.

7.4 Competitive Frames and the US Tobacco Industry

We can now revisit the changes in the US tobacco industry through the
lens of framing theory. What we see is a reframing process from an indi-
vidualized frame that assigned responsibility to adult consumers, that is,
smokers, to a systemic frame that shifted responsibility to companies and
public actors, which opened the door to stringent policy interventions justified by public health concerns (Lawrence 2004; Nathanson 1999). Public
health policies may involve rather drastic interventions, such as mandatory

vaccinations or quarantine. Thus, they are often met with considerable and strongly voiced resistance, often framed in terms of individual liberty and choice (Garrett 2000).

Nathanson (1999) has proposed a list of three dimensions of frames in the context of health policy. The first dimension captures individual culpability versus innocence. The question is whether the health risk or condition was acquired deliberately or involuntarily. A sexually transmitted disease that could be prevented, for instance, by the use of a condom, would fall in the voluntary category, but a smallpox epidemic would be considered involuntary. The second dimension pertains to whether the risk is universal or is restricted to a particular, identifiable group. Contagiousness of a disease, for example, shifts the issue toward universality. The third dimension is whether the health risk is viewed as arising from within the individual or from the environment. Compare, for example, exposure to toxic emissions with exposure to illegal drugs.

We can then distinguish two different frames. On the one hand, we have the "individual responsibility" frame. It accentuates personal culpability, group specificity, and individualism. Within this frame, choice-based policies are most plausible. These may include warning labels and education measures. However, prohibition, serious restrictions, or penalties for companies will tend to garner less support. On the other hand, there is a "systemic" frame. It will highlight innocence, universality, and systemic factors. In the context of this frame, bans and other severe restrictions will be viewed as more plausible. Moreover, if companies are viewed as intentionally causing harm or increasing risk (rather than merely failing to prevent the harm or risk), blame will shift toward the companies, and proposed policy solutions that target firms are more likely to be supported.

Until the mid-1990s, the tobacco industry and its allies were successful in maintaining an individual-choice frame. First, smoking was viewed as a voluntary activity by adult consumers who were reasonably cognizant of the associated risks. Second, the risk was limited to smokers. Third, the health risk was viewed as arising from the decisions of smokers rather than environmental factors. Consequently, proposed public health measures such as severe marketing restrictions, tax increases, smoking bans, and FDA oversight received little public support. Indeed, early regulation exclusively focused on labeling, a policy consistent with an individual responsibility frame. An example is the Federal Cigarette Labeling and Advertising Act of 1965, mentioned above, which required that the warning "Caution: Cigarette Smoking May Be Hazardous to Your

Health" be placed in small print on one of the side panels of each cigarette package.

All three dimensions underwent dramatic changes in the early 1990s. The first major development was the growing awareness of health risks from secondhand smoking, beginning in the mid-70s. In 1992, the *Journal of the American Medical Association* estimated that secondhand smoke exposure was responsible for 35,000 to 40,000 deaths per year in the United States due to heart disease. Additional risks included cancer and lung disease. In 1993 the Environmental Protection Agency (EPA) classified secondhand smoke as a human lung carcinogen. Importantly, the research also pointed to increased risk to children, including asthma, sudden infant death syndrome, allergies, and learning disabilities. The US public quickly became aware of the potential dangers of secondhand smoking. Between 1974 and 1987, the percentage of survey respondents who stated that smoking is hazardous for the health of nonsmokers increased from 46 to 81 percent (Nathanson 1999). Surveys conducted by the US National Cancer Institute and Centers for Disease Control found widespread public awareness that secondhand smoke is harmful. In a 1992 National Health Interview Survey (NHIS), more than 80 percent of respondents agreed with the statement that secondhand smoke was harmful. Similarly, a 2001 study found that 95 percent of adults agreed that secondhand smoke was harmful to children, and 96 percent considered tobacco industry claims that secondhand smoke was not harmful to be untruthful (US Department of Health and Human Services 2006). These shifts in attitudes led to regulatory changes, largely at the local level, for example, restaurant nonsmoking ordinances. The adoption of such ordinances was strongly correlated with the presence of grassroots activist groups concerned about passive smoking (Nathanson 1999, p. 461, fig. 8). Companies responded as well. For example, in 1994 McDonald's Corporation announced its decision that all nonfranchised outlets would be smoke-free.

The second development saw a slew of media reports that claimed that tobacco companies had intentionally manipulated the nicotine content of cigarettes to make them more addictive.[9] Many of the relevant materials were supplied by whistleblowers such as Jeffrey Wigand, former vice president of research and development at Brown & Williamson.[10] The tobacco industry vehemently denied these allegations and backed up their position by filing various lawsuits. A particularly dramatic instance was the case of Merrell Williams, a former drama teacher and paralegal at the law firm Wyatt, Tarrant & Combs, which had been hired in connection with the

Castano class-action lawsuits. While at work, Williams had secretly copied and taken thousands of confidential Brown & Williamson documents. Despite desperate attempts by Brown & Williamson lawyers to recover the documents and prevent any publication, the documents were obtained by antitobacco lawyers and congressional staffers. On May 7, 1994, the *New York Times* published the first of several articles on the secret industry documents. A week later, 4,000 pages of the documents were sent to Professor Stan Glantz, a medical school professor and leading antitobacco activist. Glantz eventually gave them to the library of the University of California at Berkeley. After an intense legal battle, on June 29, 1994, the California Supreme Court allowed the library to make the documents available to the public. The library immediately put them on the web and issued a CD-ROM. The collection also included company documents that pointed to the connection between smoking and cancer, and it contained strategy papers and memoranda that outlined marketing campaigns specifically targeting underage smokers. Concerns over tobacco companies marketing to children had been expressed before; in February 1994, the US Surgeon General had released a report stating that the tobacco companies had been targeting underage smokers (US Department of Health and Human Services 1994). The internal documents, however, added evidence of strategic intent.

Finally, the lawsuits brought by the states argued that all states were harmed by smoking due to increased health expenses of smoking-related illnesses. The states claimed that tobacco companies enjoyed "unjust enrichment," that is, they had not borne the full costs of the by-products of their enterprises, and that the states were entitled to compensation for their share of Medicaid expenses.[11]

These developments fundamentally altered the public perception of smoking and the tobacco industry. Through the lens of framing theory, we see a significant shift from the individual-responsibility frame to the systemic frame. On the first dimension (deliberate versus involuntary), both passive smoking and increased healthcare expenditures pointed to increased health risks and costs to innocent third parties. The impact on minors and children was particularly significant, as both are commonly considered passive victims who were exposed to harm without their consent. It also added another dimension of moral outrage since children are viewed as a particularly vulnerable group entitled to special protection.

A unique, additional dimension is presented by the issue of addiction. Nicotine had long been considered addictive, though the level of addiction changed from a comparison with coffee in the US Surgeon General Report from 1964 to comparisons with heroin in a 1988 report by the Department of Health and Human Services (Nathanson 1999). According to the individual-responsibility frame, smokers were largely responsible for managing this risk, similar to dealing with other habits. The responsibility of tobacco companies thus was limited. They were viewed as enablers and promoters, but did not "cause" nicotine to be addictive. Rather, the addictiveness of the product was considered an unavoidable, natural feature of smoking tobacco.

The evidence of intentional manipulation of nicotine levels by tobacco companies changed all that. The addictiveness could now be viewed as "caused" and "intended" by tobacco companies. This not only further undermined the individual-responsibility frame, it also significantly increased the moral blame assigned to tobacco companies. As we saw in chapter 3, for example, in the context of the trolley problem, the attribution of causality and intent to an actor is an important component in the moral evaluation of actions (Cushman and Young 2011; Cushman, Young, and Hauser 2006; Greene and Haidt 2002). First, harm that is caused by action is considered worse than harm due to mere omission, even if the consequences in both cases are the same. For example, giving a terminally ill patient a lethal injection is typically judged as morally worse than deliberately withholding life-prolonging treatment. This judgment primarily rests on an attribution of causality (Cushman and Young 2011).[12] Second, intended harm is viewed as morally worse than if the harm was due to a side effect. For instance, bombing civilian targets in order to break an enemy's will is judged worse than bombing military targets to break its infrastructure with the foreseeable side effect that an equivalent number of civilians will die. In this case, the moral judgment is based on an attribution of intentionality (Cushman and Young 2011). Manipulating nicotine levels was viewed as both causal and intentional, which triggered both evaluative mechanisms and significantly changed the public's view of tobacco companies, which were now increasingly being held responsible for the harm due to smoking.

The attribution of blame is of particular importance in policy debates. Stone (1997) has argued that identifying who is responsible, and thus who needs to be punished, is a crucial component of many policy debates on social issues. In the case of smoking, the shift in public opinion toward assigning responsibility undermined the individual-responsibility frame and provided additional plausibility to viewing smoking as a systemic public health crisis caused and intended by unscrupulous tobacco companies.

The first dimension of public health frames (individual culpability versus innocence) shifted from the smoker as a responsible individual to people harmed who were either innocent, as in the case of secondhand smoking, or were viewed as not fully responsible for their actions, as in the case of underage smokers. Even adult smokers are more likely to be viewed as less responsible if they are subjected to the manipulation of nicotine levels unbeknownst to them. The second dimension of the public health frame pertains to whether the risk is universal or is restricted to a particular, identifiable group. Passive smoking from secondhand exposure decisively shifted the issue toward universality. The third dimension focuses on whether the health risk is viewed as arising from within the individual or from the environment. Marketing to children as well as the manipulation of nicotine levels shifted responsibility from individual smokers to their "environment," the tobacco industry. Moreover, since the industry was viewed as intentionally causing harm, blame further shifted toward it, and moral outrage increased.

As a consequence, public support for drastic public health interventions grew. These included widespread smoking and advertising bans and punishments for the tobacco companies in the form of payments to the US states as part of the Master Settlement Agreement or to other plaintiffs for punitive damages. Finally, in 2009 new legislation gave the FDA broad oversight over tobacco products, including the authority to regulate tar and nicotine levels in tobacco products, set national disclosure standards about how tobacco products are manufactured and labeled, and wage a public information campaign to address issues such as youth smoking, smoking cessation, and tobacco-related health issues.[13]

Framing theory thus helps us make sense of some of the dramatic shifts in attitudes toward the tobacco industry. It can account for the observed changes in public opinion as well the tougher political, regulatory, and legal environment. Note that it can explain not only the overall increase in regulatory actions (e.g., the rise of local ordinances that ban smoking in public places and restaurants) but also the changes in their content, that is, a shift from labeling and education to bans and punishments. This shift away from a focus on personal behavior toward policy solutions that focus on systemic factors is even more noteworthy if we keep in mind the prevalence of individual frames in US political culture that frequently undermines support for community-oriented policy solutions (Garrett 2000) and favors approaches that focus on personal behavior or lifestyles (Lawrence 2004; Tesh 1988). Add to that the so-called fundamental attribution error, that is, the tendency to overestimate the effects of personal features such as personality traits or character and underestimate the effects of social context in explaining the behavior of others (Jones and Harris 1967; Jones and Nisbett 1971), and the success of the antitobacco movement in overcoming these obstacles becomes even more remarkable.

It also suggests that much had to go right for the antitobacco movement to succeed. There is little doubt that a combination of a newly aggressive FDA stance under commissioner David Kessler, plus the innovation of a new legal strategy by the US states in conjunction with the leaked documents, put the tobacco companies on the defensive. Moreover, the shift in attitudes and policy solutions took place over many years and required the sustained efforts of multiple dedicated and well-organized antismoking advocacy groups (Nathanson 1999).

7.5 Obesity

To assess whether these accounts can be generalized to other products and industries, let us consider the issue of obesity (Lawrence 2004). Obesity has many similarities with smoking. It has been called a public health epidemic (Ebbeling, Pawlak, and Ludwig 2002) with the potential for substantial human suffering and economic costs. Obesity rates in the United States are among the highest in the world. According to data compiled by the Centers for Disease Control and Prevention (CDC), in 2009–2010, 35.7 percent of adults and 16.9 percent of children and adolescents were obese in the US. Among these obese adults, 6.3 percent of them were extremely, or "morbidly," obese. The prevalence of obesity in the United States has increased sharply during the last few decades, going from 13.4 percent in the 1960s, to 23 percent in 1990s, up to around 35 percent in the 2010s (Fryar, Carroll, and Ogden 2012). Obesity significantly increases the risk of numerous health problems. Obese adults are more susceptible to suffer from high blood pressure, high cholesterol, type 2 diabetes, coronary heart disease, stroke, gallbladder disease, osteoarthritis, sleep apnea, and respiratory problems, as well as endometrial, breast, prostate, and colon cancers. According to the US Department of Health and Human Services (2010), obesity contributes to an estimated 112,000 preventable deaths per year. In addition to being associated with many health problems and deaths,

obesity is extremely costly. Recent estimates of annual medical costs associated with obesity are as high as $147 billion. In other words, the medical
costs of a person who is obese are $1,429 per year higher than those of a
normal-weight person (Centers for Disease Control and Prevention 2010,
2013).

Despite these similarities, there are also important differences between
the two domains. First, there is no equivalent of passive secondhand smoking or the manipulation of nicotine levels. There are some recent attempts
to highlight the addictive quality of processed food and the intent of
companies to make them addictive, as in a recent book by former FDA
commissioner and leading antitobacco advocate David Kessler (2012),
but there is not yet an equivalent to proof of intent like the Brown &
Williamson memoranda.[14]

Second, in contrast to tobacco, there is an apparent alternative to the
regulation of food production: exercise and physical activity. That is, in
public perception, obesity is the consequence of too many net calories,
so eating too many calories can be compensated by additional physical
activity. This idea is at the root of various campaigns by companies, such
as McDonald's "balanced lifestyle" initiative. There is no such "compensation" for the negative health effects of smoking; the only way to avoid
harm is to stop smoking.

Third, there is no equivalent to the well-organized advocacy environment in the antismoking movement. Victims of obesity are not well
organized. One may argue that the lack of an effective advocacy environment is a consequence of how the issue is perceived or simply a reflection of
the early state of the movement. But it may also point to deeper issues. For
example, there are some advocacy groups that focus on increased public
acceptance of obese individuals, further undermining support for antiobesity policies. The frame here is an antidiscrimination frame known from
racial and gender politics. This emerging social movement is at odds with
antiobesity advocates who use the public health frame of "obesity as an
epidemic."

This is in contrast to the case of tobacco, where attempts to set up
"smokers' rights" groups were largely ineffective. Such attempts were
hampered by the fact that secondhand smoking not only put the blame
on tobacco companies, it also stigmatized smokers, who through their
behavior appear to directly harm innocent bystanders, a particularly powerful charge if the victims are children or pregnant women. This feature
undoubtedly undermined support for any notion of smokers' rights.[15]

Finally, there is ongoing, widely publicized research to identify a genetic pathway for obesity, popularly known as a "fat gene" (e.g., Blackstone 2017). Such an approach would suggest private solutions such as drug treatments which would not require any policy intervention other than the usual drug approval process.

As in the case of smoking, we have both an individual-responsibility and a systemic frame (Lawrence 2004). According to the individual-responsibility frame, the problem is rooted in personal choice and lifestyles, and is best solved by individuals. Proper policy responses focus on information provision, for example, package labeling and nutritional education such as the US Department of Agriculture's "food pyramid." The promotion of physical exercise and other healthy lifestyle choices also falls into this category. The systemic frame, in contrast, treats obesity as a disease that is the consequence of an unhealthy environment, ranging from the pervasive marketing of unhealthy foods, to ill-conceived policies like trade policies or subsidies that favor unhealthy ingredients such as high-fructose corn syrup (White 2009), to the lack of exercising facilities and the availability of affordable food items with good nutritional properties, especially in low income communities (US Department of Health and Human Services 2010). Under the systemic frame, acceptable solutions include ingredient bans and advertising and marketing restrictions, as well as changes to tax treatments or other economic incentives for food producers. Finally, we have a third frame, which was largely absent from the issue of smoking. This "biological frame" is based on medical research that points to a biological, that is, genetic or epigenetic, basis for obesity, which indicates that dieting and exercise may be ineffective for many individuals (Blackstone 2017). Such frames suggest medical solutions such as drug therapy or bariatric surgery rather than policy solutions.

Among these options, the individual-responsibility frame naturally had the upper hand for several reasons. First, as in the early years of the debate on smoking, individual culpability was largely seen as the driving force behind obesity. This view is often manifested in perceptions of a lack of self-control or weakness of will. The association with the traditional sin of gluttony further strengthens this association. Second, the consequences of obesity are seen as affecting only a specific group, the obese. Third, causality is still largely viewed as resting within the individual and her food choices, rather than the social or economic environment, despite increasing criticism of food companies by various activist groups.

Consequently, as in the case of tobacco, a prevalent individual-responsibility frame will lead to public support for policy solutions that favor personal choice, such as labeling, education campaigns, and the promotion of healthy lifestyles. In contrast, public support for more interventionist policies, such as ingredient bans, serving size restrictions, taxes, or advertising restrictions, are expected to be more limited.

Additional factors continue to point in the same direction. First, there is not yet an equivalent to passive smoking, which would broaden the group of affected individuals, or the manipulation of nicotine levels, which would undermine the notion of individual responsibility. Second, some of the obese resist being labeled as "sick" and consider this view a form of discrimination. Third, there are medical alternatives to bans and restrictions, such as exercise, dieting, bariatric surgery, and the promise of drug treatments.

The one area where more interventionist policies have found widespread success is with respect to childhood nutrition, for example, in bans of soda and candy vending machines in schools. In 2010, for example, the US Congress passed the Healthy, Hunger-Free Kids Act, which required the US Department of Agriculture to set nutritional standards for all foods sold in schools. On June 27, 2013, this led to the ban of the sale of snack foods and sugary drinks in vending machines (Strom 2013). Based on our analysis of public health frames, this should come as no surprise. Again we see that a focus on children, in their role as victims, invalidates the individual-responsibility frame. Coupled with concerns over the advertising of food products to children, marketing and sales restrictions become plausible and reach higher levels of support.

In sum, the persistent prevalence of the individual choice frame not only undermines systemic public policy solutions, but will also limit the perceived culpability of food companies. Despite some severe attacks by various advocates (e.g., Brownell and Horgan 2003; Kessler 2012; Schlosser 2002), blaming food companies is likely to be more difficult than blaming tobacco companies.[16]

7.6 The Effectiveness of Frames

The examples of smoking and obesity illustrate the potential impact of framing on public perception. They also highlight the conditions under which individual-responsibility versus systemic frames are more likely to dominate public opinion. A key insight is the importance of value congruence. Individual-responsibility frames, for example, resonate more in a social and political context that views smoking as an individual right. The importance of general value orientations also holds for other predispositions, such as trust in science and political conservatism. In the case of new, shifting, or complex issues, establishing such connections firmly constitutes an example of successful framing.

These insights generalize to other domains. Frames are more effective if they evoke widely held cultural values (Chong 2000; Gamson and Modigliani 1987), while the impact of frames can be severely limited if they are at odds with the audiences' firmly held values (Edwards 2003; Shen and Edwards 2005). Indeed, frames that are at odds with fundamental value systems may backfire and shift beliefs and attitudes in the opposite of their intended direction.

We can see this in the case of climate change. Many members of the public hold a deep-seated belief that the world is just, orderly, and stable (Lerner 1980). Feinberg and Willer (2011) find evidence that such "just world" believers are less likely to believe in global warming. Moreover, after being exposed to a particularly dire message about climate change, respondents with just-world beliefs tend to become more skeptical of the accuracy of the message and decrease their intent to reduce their carbon footprint. That is, the factual content of the message tends to be dismissed if it clashes with their deeply held belief that this world is fundamentally just, while the propensity to take a certain action shifts in the opposite direction than the one favored by the suggested information.

Sometimes the connection to values is indirect. In a study on genetically modified foods, the general value orientations of subjects significantly influenced their respective support for genetically modified foods. Specifically, value orientations were measured through a survey on a seven-point scale on the dimensions of hierarchical versus egalitarian and individual versus communitarian value orientations. Increasing the value orientation from 1 (most egalitarian) to 7 (most hierarchical) leads to an 15 percent increase in support for GM foods. The corresponding increase for a change from most communitarian to most individualistic produced an increase of 8 percent (Druckman and Bolsen 2011). Similar results could be obtained for attitudes toward nanotechnology (Druckman and Bolsen 2011).

In addition to shaping attitudes, frames can also impact beliefs, for example, on risk perception. Kahan, Braman, et al. (2008b) show that frames designed to correspond to a value orientation can shift risk perception in the intended direction. In an experimental study on the perception of the risks of nanotechnology, subjects were exposed to fictitious newspaper articles that each highlighted a particular benefit of the technology. One such frame highlighted the benefits of nanotechnology for consumer goods. Kahan et al. (2008b) hypothesized that the consumer frame would particularly resonate with respondents who had a hierarchical-individualist value orientation and would lower their risk perception. This was indeed the case for male respondents with a strong hierarchical-individualist value orientation. A corresponding effect for egalitarian-communitarian value orientations could be established with a frame that highlighted the potential of nanotechnology to improve the effectiveness of regulating industrial pollution. It also lowered risk perception, but now for respondents with an egalitarian-communitarian value orientation.

That said, other frames did not turn out to be effective. A "green to gold" frame, for example, highlighted how nanotechnology could be used to commercially develop devices that could help clean up the environment. The intuition was that such a frame would both appeal to hierarchical-individualists through its references to the technology's commercial potential, and to egalitarian-communitarians through its emphasis on environmental benefits. This effect did not materialize.[17]

Frame coherence with moral value orientations can have profound effects even in highly contentious domains, such as global warming and environmental policy (Feinberg and Willer 2013). Debates on environmental policy are often couched in moral language, using terms such as "duty," "responsibility," and so forth. Using content analysis of popular YouTube videos and newspaper op-eds, Feinberg and Willer (2013) show that environmental discourse is heavily shaped by moral vocabulary. Specifically, such vocabulary predominantly draws from the harm/care moral domain identified by Haidt and Joseph (2004).

Recent research by Graham, Haidt, and Nosek (2009) has found evidence that the moral dimension of harm/care predominantly resonates with political liberals (in the US sense of the word), while a purity/sanctity dimension was more characteristic of political conservatives. This implies that environmental frames that focus on harm/care would resonate more strongly with liberals than conservatives (Feinberg and Willer 2013). More surprisingly, Feinberg and Willer (2013) show that frames that emphasize the purity/sanctity dimension, such as references to "pollution" and "God's creation," can significantly increase proenvironmental attitudes and support for environmental legislation among conservatives compared to a neutral baseline case or the harm/care frame. Importantly, exposure to the purity/sanctity frame also elicited the emotion of disgust among conservative respondents, a common response to purity/sanctity violations (Haidt 2013b). This evidence suggests that to reach political conservatives on issues related to environmental issues, purity/sanctity frames will be more effective than economic opportunity frames, such as the "green to gold" frame used in in the context of nanotechnology. While these findings are intriguing, more research is needed to see whether purity/sanctity value orientations can be systematically activated across issue domains, and whether appropriately constructed frames indeed have the predicted impact.

The debate over mandatory masking requirements during the COVID-19 pandemic exhibits similar characteristics. Again, we see two competing frames. On the one hand, there is a public health frame, which focuses on the involuntary nature of being infected, the universal contagiousness of the disease, and the risk of exposure due to the presence of infected individuals not wearing masks. The focus here is on the person being infected, the victim; the risk of being infected is involuntary, universal, and external. The competing frame focuses on individual rights and the choice of the mask wearer. It emphasizes differential risks to certain groups, such as the need to protect nursing home patients but not young adults. Proponents of masking naturally ground their approach in the do-no-harm principle, emphasizing the duty to protect others from harm, even if masks were to provide no benefit to the mask wearer. Opponents of masking requirements emphasize notions of individual freedom and responsibility and a general opposition to government mandates. Opponents of mask mandates also tend to question existing evidence in support of masking.

Such opposition to public health health measures is often incomprehensible to proponents. How can anybody be opposed to the reduction of harm to the public? From their perspective, such opposition seems "irrational" or "contrary to science." Yet, these views presuppose that such policy debates are exclusively grounded in the do-no-harm principle and are devoid of competing value systems that may serve as alternative foundations for public policy, such as concerns over individual freedom and a general skepticism toward government. Indeed, the prevalence of individual frames in US political culture makes the adoption of community-oriented policy solutions, such as mask mandates or mandatory vaccination, particularly challenging and instead favors solutions that emphasize individual choice (Garrett 2000; Tesh 1988).

The presence of motivated reasoning further muddles the debate, as opponents of masking may not explicitly state value conflicts, but rather question the evidence in support of masking, even if such evidence is pervasive. This dynamic parallels the debate on climate change; underlying value conflicts are obscured by debates on evidence. Opponents of environmental policies do not simply state their belief in a just world, but they question the proposed evidence for climate change. Available data and facts are evaluated and interpreted to justify an opinion grounded in values, not dispassionate reasoning.

But arguments for masking do not need to rely solely on the do-no-harm principle. For example, messaging may also emphasize the health benefits to the mask wearer, even if such benefits are limited. Such appeals are consistent with individual responsibility frames. In addition, other value systems can be activated. In our discussion of moral foundations theory in chapter 3, we saw that political conservatives often exhibit value orientations that emphasize group loyalty, hierarchy, and purity, while political liberals tend to limit themselves to do-no-harm and justice/fairness concerns. We can easily see how frames in support of masking can be constructed for each value orientation. The do-no-harm principles would emphasize the protection of potential victims, justice and fairness concerns would highlight the differential impact on the most vulnerable (the elderly and the poor), group loyalty concerns would frame mask wearing as a patriotic duty, hierarchical orientations could be activated through role modeling of respected authority figures (e.g., spiritual or military leaders), while purity orientations would emphasize personal hygiene and protection from "germs."

Yet, frames that would resonate with political conservatives have been largely absent from the public debate. While there are political reasons for their absence, rooted in the partisan polarization of the debate and political positioning in the context of a presidential campaign, the issue of mask wearing also highlights a general blind spot in policy debates. Proponents of systemic measures tend to rely exclusively on scientific data that emphasize universal harm or harm to the most vulnerable. Such frames are convincing to population segments with a liberal value orientation, but less so to political conservatives, especially if the proposed policy measures restrict individual freedoms. Restrictions on fossil fuel consumption, food ingredients, and portion sizes, as well as public health measures, all fall into this category. In such debates proponents often point to overwhelming evidentiary support for their policies, while opponents often question the proposed evidence or highlight dissenting voices. Proponents are often perplexed why opponents refuse to agree with the recommendations of the mainstream scientific community and view opponents as "irrational" or "opposed to science."

But an exclusive focus on the surface-level features of standards of evidence and scientific reasoning misses the mark. Rather, the policy debate is not necessarily grounded in different attitudes to science, but in value conflicts. Such value conflicts express themselves, via motivated reasoning, in different interpretations of existing scientific evidence. Opponents with different value orientations will neither be convinced by more forceful appeals to follow the mainstream scientific consensus, nor by attacks on their lack of rationality. A more promising approach is to ground frames in congruent value orientations and use spokespeople who have cultural credibility with the relevant population segment, such as military or religious leaders.

One such example occurred in March 2021, when country music star Dolly Parton was vaccinated with the Moderna vaccine at Vanderbilt University Medical Center. Parton distributed a video with her getting the shot, and encouraged everybody to get vaccinated by singing a version of her hit "Jolene," with the new lyrics "Vaccine, vaccine, vaccine, vaccine, I'm begging of you please don't hesitate. Vaccine, vaccine, vaccine, vaccine, 'cause once you're dead then that's a bit too late." The singer and songwriter had previously provided financial support in the early development of the vaccine at Vanderbilt (Treisman 2021).

A particularly important question in the understanding of frames is the role of information and knowledge. This relationship turns out to be complicated. On the one hand, the availability of other sources of information may limit framing (Price and Na 2000), but, on the other hand, predisposed individuals may seek out confirmatory rather than conflicting information (Druckman, Fein, and Leeper 2012). Similarly, preexisting knowledge may not affect the impact of frames significantly. There is some evidence that better scientific knowledge by the audience increases support for new technologies such as GM foods and nanotech, although more factually supported frames do not seem to have a stronger impact (Druckman and Bolsen 2011).

One complicating factor in disentangling the effect of knowledge is that more knowledgeable individuals also tend to have more firmly held predispositions (Zaller 1992). Druckman and Nelson (2003) provide evidence that, once we control for predispositions, more knowledgeable individuals may be *more* susceptible to framing. This may be due to the fact that more knowledgeable individuals are more likely to satisfy some of the basic cognitive preconditions for understanding a frame (Chong and Druckman 2007c). For example, an individual must know what the word "obesity" means and understand that issues like regulatory jurisdiction can be relevant dimensions in evaluating a given policy. Alternatively, more knowledgeable individuals may also have more relevant considerations at their disposal that can then be actualized by a frame (Zaller 1992).

In addition to value congruence and knowledge, the credibility of the source is a third factor that impacts the effectiveness of frames. Frames are more impactful if they come from sources that the audience considers credible (Druckman 2001a, 2001b).

A fourth set of factors pertains to the issue of memory. To be efficacious, a frame must be accessible. This means that, unless the frame is present at the very moment when the opinion is formed, it must somehow be stored in long-term memory. Thus, repeated exposure to a frame will increase its accessibility (Chong and Druckman 2007a). More generally, factors that enhance memory encoding and recall will influence the effectiveness of frames.

Of particular importance in the context of reputation management are competing frames, as we saw in the contexts of the tobacco industry and the issue of obesity. Understanding competitive frames is particularly important when activists, such as NGOs or journalists, attack a company and the company tries to defend itself. Early research on competing frames pointed out that alternative frames tend to cancel each other out, leading to a net effect that leaves attitudes unchanged (Sniderman and Theriault 2004). The same effect could be found in the case of GM foods. Once subjects were exposed to both the pro and the con frames, there was no discernible net shift in attitude.

Subsequent research, however, has pointed out that this cancellation effect occurs only when the competing frames are of similar strength. Otherwise, a strong frame will dominate a weak frame, even if the weak frame is repeated (Chong and Druckman 2007a, 2007c, 2010). On a practical level, a frame's strength is measured by a survey of typical subjects in a pretest. An example of this approach is Druckman's (2009) analysis of public funding for casinos. Druckman constructs two strong frames: one pro-casino frame focusing on economic benefits and the use of casino-related revenues for public education funding, and a con frame that highlights the social costs of gambling. Druckman then compares these frames with others that pretested as "weak" frames. Those included a pro frame focusing on the entertainment benefit from having a casino, and two weak con frames, a corruption frame and a moral values frame. As expected, the weak frames have no effect, whether used alone or matched with an opposing weak frame. Strong frames have a significant impact on attitudes toward publicly funded casinos in the expected direction, but cancel each other out when paired against each other. However, a strong frame continues to have a significant effect even if paired with one or more weak frames, sometimes even stronger than when it is presented alone. For example, the strong pro-casino frame based on economic benefits shifted opinion by 41 percent when combined with two weak con frames versus a shift of 24 percent when presented by itself.

Competing frames also highlight the importance of dynamic framing. For example, will early or late exposure to frames have a bigger effect? From a practical point of view, should a company with a limited budget focus on getting its messages out early or late? This is particularly important if maintaining public support is crucial for a particular decision, such as winning a popular referendum, as in the casino example. The fact that frames need to be accessible in memory to impact opinion formation suggests the importance of recency effects; individuals give greater weight to frames received more recently. That is, the accessibility of frames is expected to decay over time, giving an advantage to messages received more recently (Chong and Druckman 2010).

However, recent research has pointed out that framing dynamics are more complex, especially when individuals can seek additional sources of information while receiving competing frames. That is, successful early framing may shape attitudes that then influence the selection, evaluation, and memorization of subsequent information, an instance of motivated reasoning. Druckman, Fein, and Leeper (2012) show that, under these circumstances, the effects are exactly reversed; *early* messages dominate later messages. What we have is a *primacy* rather than a *recency* effect. The data are supportive of an underlying mechanism of motivated reasoning, rather than a simple memory decay effect. That is, once subjects have formed an opinion, they will process information in a way that supports their initial opinion and seek out information that further supports it, rather than challenge it with contrasting points of view. This is an instance of the Consonance Principle, now applied to frames.

In the context of competitive framing, a motivated reasoning perspective means that the subject will discount later frames if they have formed a sufficiently strong opinion early on. Experts and new information will be interpreted in such a way as to support the initial belief. Primacy effects can result because of the early repetition of strong frames, or because subjects seek out information selectively. In the context of healthcare reform, Druckman, Fein, and Leeper (2012) showed that subjects systematically chose to predominantly read additional articles that reinforced the frame that they were exposed to earlier. This leads to a feedback effect that renders later counter-frames ineffective. The point is that, once opinions are sufficiently ingrained, either due to exogenous factors (repetition) or because of endogenous behavior (selective search), changing opinions can be a tall order. This holds both for the direction of the opinion shift and for its intensity (Druckman, Fein, and Leeper 2012).

The practical consequences of these findings are profound. Companies do not have the luxury to wait until an issue has matured. They need to engage early. Otherwise the positive feedback loop of selective search and motivated reasoning will result in hardened opinions that are difficult (and expensive!) to shift. This provides a strong argument for a well-designed issue identification and management process. The properties of such processes are the subject of the concluding section of this book.

7.7 Summary

The empirical literature on issue frames has demonstrated the potential impact of *framing* processes that influence how individuals view a complex issue and what they pay attention to. In this section, we discussed the potentially far-reaching consequences of framing in the context of the history of the US tobacco industry, which was able to avoid regulation or significant legal liability for decades, despite mounting evidence for the severe health risks associated with smoking. The industry's success was, in large part, due to a framing strategy that focused attention on smokers' individual responsibilities. The effect of this strategy only waned with the discovery of the consequences of passive smoking as well as the release of internal industry documents that demonstrated systematic efforts at marketing to children and teenagers and the intent to manipulate nicotine levels. Such findings undermined an individual-responsibility frame and provided an opening to reframe smoking as a public health issue, which eventually led to FDA oversight, penalties, and severe marketing restrictions.

Using events surrounding the tobacco industry as a guide, we then discussed the factors that shape the success of frames. The first such factor is *value congruence*. Frames are more effective if they align with the public's value orientation. This finding was illustrated by the history of the US tobacco industry, but can be found in many other domains. Second, *source credibility* can enhance the impact of frames. Third, any factors that aid storage in long-term memory are important, such as *repetition* and *recency*. That said, if a company has to decide whether to address an issue early or late, it is advisable to *engage early*. This follows from processes related to motivated reasoning, captured by *consonance*. Once respondents form an impression, they tend to seek out information that confirms their existing opinion and interpret new information in light of old attitudes. This emphasizes the practical need for companies to identify issues early and engage in appropriate communication strategies.

The importance of framing naturally leads to questions about the role and impact of the media, both social and traditional, since media coverage plays an essential role in determining which frames and issues receive broad attention and when. It is these questions that we turn our attention to next. First, we discuss the broadcast media in the context of corporate reputation. Social media is discussed in the subsequent chapter.

CHAPTER EIGHT

Models of the Media: Bias and Influence

8.1 The Roles of the Media

The phenomenon of media influence appears so clear and unambiguous that there seems to be little left to explore or explain. After hostile media coverage of Toyota's unintended acceleration crisis, for example, the company's stock price dropped by as much as 17 percent, reducing its market cap by about $25 billion, more than the entire value of American Express at the time.[1]

In a study of toy recalls, Freedman, Kearney, and Lederman (2012) find a significant impact of safety recalls on sales. The impact is significantly larger for recalls that attract widespread media coverage. In one famous case, the recall of Thomas the Tank Engine by manufacturer RC2 in 2007, adjusted Christmas season sales dropped by 58.5 percent.[2] Moreover, competitors that sold similar toys also experienced significant sales declines due to industrywide spillover effects, while the sales of dissimilar toys made by the company that issued the recall were not affected.[3]

These findings suggest strong media effects. But, on closer inspection, some questions remain. Did it matter *how* the media reported the incident, or were these consequences simply due to the event itself? Perhaps the media simply reported the facts truthfully and the company suffered the consequences.

But that is not how the public views the media. The belief that the media is biased is widespread. Accusations of media bias are particularly common, especially in political domains (Groseclose 2011). Indeed, a 2020 national Gallup found that 60 percent of the American people have "not very much" trust or "none at all" that the media will report the news "fully, accurately, and fairly" (Brenan 2020). This skepticism is especially pronounced among Republicans, among whom less than 25 percent trust the media and nearly 50 percent believe the media is the "enemy of the people" (Bump 2018).

In the Toyota case, for example, media coverage focused on the horrific accident and the emergency phone call. It did not, for example, compare Toyota's safety record to that of other car companies. Second, Toyota is rarely covered by the mass market media. Like many corporations, if it is covered, then the coverage tends to be negative. But since such negative coverage is not balanced by positive coverage on other topics, the net impact on public perception is likely to be negative.

For Toyota, this imbalance was particularly striking. As the case unfolded, Toyota resisted any admission of a safety-related defect responsible for unintended acceleration problems. These claims received additional support when a government report from NASA could not find any evidence of electronic malfunctions, a finding publicly endorsed by US transportation secretary Ray LaHood (NHTSA 2011).

Yet this remarkable turnaround hardly received any media coverage.

Media influence may work through various mechanisms.[4] **Slant** is the most frequently discussed form of media influence (e.g., Groseclose and Milyo 2005; Ladd 2012). It may work through several different mechanisms. For example, slant may operate through explicit persuasion, as found in an editorial, or indirectly by misrepresenting facts, mixing opinion with reporting, quoting biased experts in a feature, and so forth.[5] Slant may also operate via priming by triggering certain associations and not others, or through framing by consistently favoring a certain perspective on an issue. In sum, slanted coverage presents a given issue in a particular way that favors one side over the other; it shapes *how* an issue is covered. In the Toyota case this may have consisted of a negative editorial or a focus on the accident victims rather than overall safety statistics.

Agenda setting pertains to *which* issues are covered rather than how they are covered; it occurs when media coverage influences which issues are considered important and which are not. It can be an important source of bias by focusing public attention on particular sets of issues and topics while ignoring others (McCombs and Shaw 1972, 1993).[6] For example, the media may focus on certain policy areas but not others. Note that the dimension of agenda setting is orthogonal to other dimensions of media influence. Even if the content and style of media reporting were completely accurate, bias could still occur by favoring some topics over others. Agenda setting is particularly important in the context of corporate news coverage. In contrast to major political events, electoral campaigns, major trials, or wars, which are covered continuously, coverage of companies in the mainstream press is sporadic and much shorter in duration (Boydstun, Hardy, and Walgrave 2014; Leskovec, Backstrom, and Kleinberg 2009). Even the coverage of major crises usually does not last longer than a day or two. Moreover, much of this coverage is newsworthy only if it is negative. This means that public attention paid to companies is rare, short-lived, and often negative. This has important consequences for the management of reputational crises (Diermeier 2011).

While the perception of media bias is widespread, there are significant conceptual and methodological problems with studying it in a rigorous fashion. For example, on its op-ed page the *Wall Street Journal* expresses more conservative opinions than the *New York Times*. But that is not necessarily evidence of media bias, as such opinions may be limited to the editorial page and not affect news coverage. For example, suppose the *Wall Street Journal* and the *New York Times* were to cover exactly the same news items in exactly the same way; would we consider either one biased? After all, the editorial section is clearly separated from the news sections, and readers are generally aware of this distinction.

Of course, both topic selection and the way issues are covered does vary between the *Wall Street Journal* and the *New York Times*. But even that is not necessarily evidence of bias. The *Wall Street Journal* may be more conservative for the simple reason that the *Journal*'s readership expects it. The point here is that, in a competitive media market, readers and viewers may sort into various media outlets according to their preferences.[7] If sorting is prevalent, what looks like media bias may be nothing other than a particular news outlet giving its customers exactly what they want.[8]

Note also that the concept of "media bias" is distinct from the concept of "media influence." The former suggests a misalignment between the preferences of the public and positioning of the media, while the latter simply points out that media coverage influences attitudes and beliefs. Such influence can occur irrespective of any claim of media bias. For example, sports fans may feel more pessimistic after sports journalists give a grim assessment about their favorite team's prospects for next season, opera fans may avoid the current production after a negative review, and investors may invest in a certain stock because of an impressive interview with the CEO. Bias plays no discernible role in any of these cases, but influence may still be present and important.

8.2 Bias

The belief that the media is biased is widespread (Goldberg 2001; Groseclose 2011; Ladd 2012). This is particularly true of political contexts, the main area of focus of research on media bias. A survey by the Pew Research Center for the People and Press (Pew 2011) found that 77 percent of survey respondents in the United States believe that news stories "tend to favor one side," while 63 percent say that news organizations are politically biased. The intuition here is not that any given news source may have a particular point of view or ideological positioning, but that the *media as a whole* is leaning in one direction. Interestingly, respondents on the left tend see an bias to the right, while those on the right see a bias to the left.

By media bias we mean a mismatch between the preferences and ideological positioning of the public and the ideological distribution of the media.[9] Note that this does not mean that *each* publication needs to be "fair and balanced," but that the distribution of coverage roughly corresponds to the distribution of political alignments in the public.

As briefly discussed above, in a competitive media market, readers and viewers may sort into various media outlets according to their preferences. Such sorting will lead to publications with particular ideological leanings, but such diversity across the political spectrum is simply a consequence of supply matching demand in a competitive market equilibrium, where a profit-maximizing publisher will match positioning (supply) with political leanings of the readers (demand).

It follows that, in competitive media markets, any form of media bias imposes a financial cost on media companies. Media bias is a mismatch between producers and consumers of media content, reducing the demand for any particular media source, leading to lower profits for its owners.

Owners, of course, may not simply be profit maximizers. They may be willing to sacrifice economic gains for ideological goals. We refer to this phenomenon as "ownership bias."

Bias may also reside within journalists. Baron (2006) considers a model with biased journalists but profit-maximizing media owners. Journalists may be biased due to career concerns (the author of a negative story about Monsanto would see their work make it to the front page, while a more nuanced story may be found on page 15) or due to ideological concerns (the journalist may be opposed to genetically modified food products). But journalists need to find employment. Baron argues that profit-maximizing owners will employ biased journalists only if this allows them to pay lower wages. The reason is that biased coverage will reduce the demand for news and thus decrease the profitability of ownership. In both cases, media slant reduces the profitability of media ownership. These costs must be borne either by the owner (through lower profits) or by the journalist (through lower wages).

The questions of whether there is media bias or not, and whether it is due to ownership bias, are ultimately empirical ones. The problem is how to measure the ideological content of media coverage and compare it to the ideological leanings of the public. Groseclose and Milyo (2005) used quotes from think tanks, such as the American Enterprise Institute or the Brookings Institute, as measures of ideological positioning. The approach works as follows. Start by noting that political scientists have, over many years, developed reliable measures of the ideological positioning of members of the US Congress based on their voting record (Poole and Rosenthal 1985). Members of Congress can then be ranked from the most liberal to the most conservative. Using these methods, Groseclose and Milyo (2005) identify the think tanks that legislators frequently cite in their speeches. For example, a conservative member of Congress will cite the American Enterprise Institute more frequently than the Brookings Institution. By counting up the average citation frequency of a think tank by members of Congress, one can assign an ideological position to think tanks derived from the ideological positions of the politicians who cite them. Now media outlets can be assessed on ideological positioning based on the average frequency with which they cite the various think tanks. So the *Wall Street Journal* would be expected to cite the American Enterprise Institute more often than the Brookings Institute. Using this approach, Groseclose and Milyo (2005) then compared the ideological positions of major news outlets and found a significant liberal bias in news coverage: 18 of the 20 major news outlets investigated are to the left of the mean member of the US House of Representatives.

There are various difficulties with this approach. First, this interpretation of media bias rests on the assumption that the US House is broadly representative of the US, a view that has been heavily criticized by many political scientists (Cox and Katz 1999; Fiorina and Abrams 2009). Subsequent work has also challenged some of the underlying methodology used by Groseclose and Milyo. Reanalyzing Groseclose and Milyo's data, Gasper (2011), for example, finds liberal slant in the early 1990s, but conservative slant during the early 2000s.[10]

An alternative approach to assess media slant was recently proposed by Puglisi and Snyder (2015). They used newspaper endorsements of ballot propositions. The idea is as follows: Suppose we line up voters from left to right on an ideological spectrum and a majority of voters supported a given ballot initiative, say a local ordinance to prohibit smoking in public places (typically a liberal position). Suppose the local newspaper recommended to vote "no" on the ordinance. In doing so, that newspaper revealed itself as more conservative on that issue than the majority of the population. Note that if the paper recommended a "yes" vote, nothing can be inferred, as the paper may be more conservative than the median voter but still support the ordinance. Particularly informative are ballot propositions that split the electorate in half. To estimate the position of a paper, Puglisi and Snyder averaged over all ballot propositions on which a newspaper made an endorsement.

One possible concern is that a newspaper may strategically select the ballot issues on which it takes a position, perhaps avoiding the most "controversial" one. Puglisi and Snyder, however, argue that sample selection is not much of a concern since newspapers usually take a position on almost all ballot initiatives. A more serious problem is that the newspaper endorsement may influence voters. Puglisi and Snyder point to existing literature that found little net evidence of the influence of newspaper endorsements. They also argue that, even if endorsements had an influence, the resulting bias would be toward finding newspapers to be more extreme than they really are. This is not what Puglisi and Snyder find. Rather, their main finding is that newspapers are almost exactly located at the median voter of their state; newspapers are an almost perfect ideological match for their readers. Indeed, newspapers are more moderate than interest groups and political parties.[11]

Gentzkow and Shapiro (2010) developed yet another approach. They used text-analytic methods to measure the similarities between speeches given by members of the US Congress and the news content of media outlets (excluding editorials).[12] Specifically, Gentzkow and Shapiro identified partisan phrases in the 2005 *Congressional Record*, such as combinations of words that are used more frequently by one party than the other. Examples of "Democratic phrases" are "estate tax" or "tax break" and "war in Iraq," while "death tax," "tax relief," and "war on terror" were predominantly used by Republicans. Gentzkow and Shapiro then created a "slant index" by measuring the relative frequencies with which the expressions appeared in a sample of over 400 newspapers in 2005.[13]

Gentzkow and Shapiro used these measures to investigate if the ideological positioning of news outlets is driven by the audience or by the ideological positioning of their owners. Gentzkow and Shapiro first showed that there is a close match between the ideological positioning of a newspaper (measured by the language similarity to politicians) and a local constituency (measured by donations to political campaigns). In other words, in a district where most donations go to Republican candidates, the language of the newspaper will match the language used by Republican members of Congress. Second, they showed that there is no evidence of ownership bias. This was done by comparing various newspapers belonging to the same chain, that is, having the same owners. Gentzkow and Shapiro showed that, once local factors have been taken into account, the ideological positioning of a newspaper is largely accounted for by the ideological positioning of its readership.[14] This suggests that newspapers follow a profit-maximizing approach, where the ideological positioning of the paper matches its readership. Indeed, Gentzkow and Shapiro computed the positioning that each newspaper would choose if it maximized its own profits. The average profit-maximizing position was found to be close to the newspapers' actual one.

A nice illustration of the importance of sorting is given by Durante and Knight's (2012) study of Italian broadcast news. In Italy television news coverage is provided by state-owned networks (RAI) as well as by privately owned networks, the biggest one owned by former prime minister Silvio Berlusconi. Durante and Knight found that after Berlusconi became prime minister in 2001, the content of state-controlled news coverage shifted to the right, suggesting political influence by the Berlusconi government. However, this ideological shift was offset by sorting. Right-wing viewers started watching state-owned news channels, while viewers with a more leftist ideology changed their allegiance to a more leftist privately owned channel.

It is important to note that sorting depends on a competitive media market. In a media market controlled by the government, or in areas where entry and exit are severely constrained, sorting by ideology cannot occur. Moreover, sorting can itself be problematic if markets are not perfectly competitive. Mullainathan and Shleifer (2005) argue that if the news audience exhibits confirmation bias, that is, the desire to receive news content consistent with their prior beliefs, news outlets can avoid price competition by presenting biased news that reinforces the worldviews of their audience. This results in less informative news coverage overall. Gentzkow and Shapiro (2006) showed that similar effects can also occur in a world where all readers are fully rational and do not exhibit confirmation bias. In their model, the driver is the desire of newspapers to build a reputation for being knowledgeable, which leads to incentives to suppress news items that contradict common expectations.

In summary, the evidence for media bias, conceptualized as a mismatch between the ideological positioning of news sources and their audiences, is mixed at best. More recent studies have found no evidence of media bias at all. Rather, the ideological positioning of newspapers seems to be largely driven by audience demand and sorting. However, a few caveats are in order. These studies were conducted on political attitudes, not attitudes toward companies and their activities. While political attitudes on a left-right spectrum are a decent approximation of general opinion toward business, the validity of this comparison is far less clear when considering specific issues, industries, firms, or products. It is entirely possible that a media outlet broadly matches the ideological profile of its audience, but offers slanted coverage on certain issues or industries. Indeed, Puglisi and Snyder (2015) found that newspapers are more liberal than their audience on social issues such as gay marriage or affirmative action, but more conservative on economic issues, such as minimum wage, environmental pollution, smoking, animal rights, or health care. So this evidence would suggest that, if there is any slant at all, it is the direction of a *probusiness* bias.[15] That said, research on news coverage on specific companies, products, or industries is almost entirely lacking.

8.3 Media Influence

The literature on media bias has shown little evidence for a mismatch between the ideological positioning of news outlets and their audiences.

The matching of media sources to audiences could be due to various mechanisms. It could be the result of very effective media influence, causing audiences to reflect the views of the media outlets. Or, as the existing studies suggest, the ideological match can be due to sorting in a competitive media environment. The presence of sorting, of course, does not mean that there is no media influence; it just implies that the public is seeking out sources of information that match their ideological positioning. The evidence of sorting does, however, create important methodological challenges for those studying media influence.

Recall that media influence can operate through various mechanisms. The media can influence how an issue is covered, that is, impacting perceptions through slant, or which issues are covered, that is, affecting views through agenda setting.

To identify the causal effect of media coverage, one would need to pick a set of issues and then assign media coverage in a randomized fashion to see whether it has the anticipated effect on its audience. For examples, readers would need to be randomly assigned to, say, the *Wall Street Journal*, the *New York Times*, and perhaps a control group. Then one would measure their attitudes before and after the media exposure and see whether such exposure shifted their attitudes significantly.

The random assignment here is critical. If readers are free to choose their preferred source of news, they may choose news sources depending on their ideological preferences. This selection process will determine what media coverage they hear, and as a result, it will create a high level of alignment between their ideological position and that of the media outlet. If researchers do not control for this sorting process, the high degree of ideological alignment would mistakenly lead one to believe that media messages influence ideological positions. As a result one may falsely infer a very high level of media influence, when, in actuality, the apparent relationship was due to audience sorting.

This problem is an example of the well-known statistical problem of selection bias, wherein subjects self-select into the groups the researcher ultimately observes (Heckman 1979).[16] If left unaccounted for, selection bias will lead to statistically biased and inconsistent estimates. This problem is particularly severe in the study of media influence, given the strong theoretical and empirical support for sorting.

There are three methodological solutions to this problem: (1) laboratory experiments, (2) field experiments, and (3) carefully constructed empirical studies that control for self-selection. In laboratory experiments, random assignment is done explicitly by the researcher, who has broad freedom to vary the media stimuli. Random assignment eliminates any inference problems due to sorting. The limitation of this approach lies in the questionable external validity of any results. In other words, do the findings still apply outside of a laboratory setting? In contrast, field experiments provide a greater level of external validity, but are limited to a specific context which may not generalize (Gerber and Green 2012). It is also more difficult to manipulate variables and identify causal mechanisms given the practical and financial limitations of many field experiments. Finally, properly specified statistical models can alleviate some of the most obvious biases. The main approach here is the use of instrumental variables (e.g., Enikolopov, Petrova, and Zhuravskaya 2011). This requires the careful selection of data and design of the statistical model.

In general, instrumental variable models are useful in situations where an unobserved confounding variable influences both the independent and dependent variables under examination (Angrist and Pischke 2009; Heckman 1979). This is the case in the media influence example, since ideological sorting influences both which messages a subject sees and the level of ideological alignment we observe. Using traditional regression methods in the face of these relationships will result in biased estimates of the relationship between media messaging and alignment and cause us to incorrectly infer media influence. To resolve this problem, we seek out an additional variable known as an "instrument." To be suitable, this instrument must be correlated with the independent variable (e.g., messaging) but uncorrelated with the confounding variable (e.g., sorting).[17] The basic intuition behind the estimation of instrumental variable models is that the instrument can be used to create a "replacement" for the values of the independent variable (Angrist and Pischke 2009; Dougherty 2011). If the assumptions of the technique are met, these new, estimated values of the independent variable can be considered independent of the confounding variable and can then be used to obtain unbiased estimates of the relationship between the independent and dependent variables.[18]

While the technical details of this method are straightforward and can be readily extended to cover a variety of scenarios (Greene 2012), its usefulness is often limited by the difficulty in finding a suitable instrument. As we shall see, in the case of understanding media influence, it can be difficult to find reliable variables that are clearly unconnected to ideological sorting yet are connected to the media messages one is exposed to. Nevertheless, some scholars have proposed innovative models that use instruments to assess media influence (e.g., Enikolopov, Petrova, and Zhuravskaya 2011). We discuss such approaches below.

8.4 Slant

First, we discuss media influence through slant, that is, how a given issue is covered. As discussed above, this can be done through explicit position taking, such as in an editorial or by quoting expert opinion, or through priming and framing. As before, we will focus on political contexts where we have explicit measures of beliefs, attitudes, and outcomes.[19]

Let us begin by considering a randomized field experiment conducted by Gerber, Karlan, and Bergan (2009) in the 2005 Virginia gubernatorial election. Voters were randomly assigned to one of three conditions. One treatment group received a free subscription to the *Washington Post*, a newspaper with a liberal orientation. The other treatment group received a free subscription to the *Washington Times*, a conservative newspaper. The third group served as a control and received no subscription. At the conclusion of the experiment, there was no effect of either treatment on political knowledge or on stated opinions. Interestingly, receiving the *Washington Post* increased support for the Democratic candidate (by about 7 percent), but so did receiving the *Washington Times* (by about 6 percent). The difference between these two effects, however, was not significant. In other words, there is no evidence that media slant (receiving the *Washington Post* over the *Washington Times*) impacted support for Democratic candidates, while there is some evidence that media exposure (i.e., receiving either newspaper) improved support for Democratic candidates. In addition, the researchers found some evidence that media exposure improved turnout.

In another study, DellaVigna and Kaplan (2007) examined the entry of Fox News into US cable markets between 1996 and 2000. They find that, in towns with access to Fox News, Republican candidates gained between 0.4 to 0.7 percentage points in US presidential elections. One problem with this approach is that the entry of Fox News is not random, but driven by strategic decisions by News Corp., Fox News's parent, about which markets are most attractive. These decisions are not public information, but may be driven by the prevalence of Republican-leaning voters. It is therefore difficult to determine whether the identified effect is due to slant or to media exposure as observed by Gerber, Karlan, and Bergan (2009).

Using a similar approach, Gentzkow, Shapiro, and Sinkinson (2011) analyzed entry and exit data of US newspapers between 1869 and 1928, a period when newspapers were of particular importance as sources of information and often had explicitly partisan orientations. They found a significant effect of newspaper entry and exit on turnout of about

0.3 percentage points, but no effect on party vote shares. Moreover, the effect on turnout waned after the introduction of radio and television.

In sum, in the context of elections there is, at best, mixed evidence for the impact of media slant on political attitudes and voting behavior. Moreover, in cases where we find some evidence, the effect seems to be driven by media exposure rather than by slant. While there is more robust evidence for an impact on turnout, even here the impact is small.

Such lack of evidence may be explained by the presence of sorting in competitive media markets. An audience may simply expect a particular ideological position from a given news outlet and gravitate toward those outlets that are consistent with their own views. Alternatively, an audience may be aware of the ideological position of a media outlet and able to "filter out" the bias. For example, Chiang and Knight (2011) found an effect of "surprising" newspaper endorsements on candidate support, but no effect of "predictable" endorsements.

To explore this phenomenon more directly, it is useful to consider media environments that are not fully competitive. For example, DellaVigna et al. (2014) used statistical variation in the reach of the radio signal by Serbian public radio stations to study their impact on voting behavior and anti-Serbian nationalist sentiment among Croats in a border region close to Croatia. The idea is that nationalist Serbian coverage, intended for Serbians in Serbia, would trigger anti-Serbian nationalist sentiment among Croats across the border. Since the radio signal reached only some regions, this can be interpreted as a natural experiment where only certain regions were (quasi-randomly) exposed to the treatment ("nationalist coverage"). Consistent with their argument, DellaVigna et al. (2014) found an increase in the vote for nationalist Croatian parties as well as an increase in nationalist graffiti in Croatian villages.[20]

In another examination of radio broadcasts, Adena et al. (2015) explored the impact of pro-Nazi radio in Germany in the 1920s and 1930s. Exploring variation in access to radio, they showed significant effects on electoral support for the Nazi party during the late Weimar Republic. After the full consolidation of Nazi power in 1933, they highlight the impact of radio coverage of denunciations of Jews by anti-Semitic open letters as well as the number of Jews deported to concentration camps.[21]

In a study of the Russian media market, Enikolopov, Petrova, and Zhuravskaya (2011) showed that the entry of the first privately owned television news channel NTV significantly shifted voting in elections for the 1999 Russian Duma. At the time, NTV's owner supported Russia's opposition. Enikolopov, Petrova, and Zhuravskaya found that, in the areas where NTV coverage was available (about three-quarters of the country), the aggregate vote share for the government dropped by almost 9 percent.

In a recent paper on China, Qin, Strömberg, and Wu (2018) directly studied the impact of variations of market competition on slant, here measured by the relative frequency of government propaganda relative to commercial content. They found that a regulatory reform that reduced competition among media outlets let to increased product differentiation among news outlets, with some becoming more progovernment, while others focused more on commercial content. Overall, increases in competition led to more product differentiation and less exposure to government propaganda.[22]

8.5 Agenda Setting

How an issue is covered is not the only way that media coverage can have an impact. The second form of media influence can come from the determination of which issues are covered, an area known as "agenda setting."

The role of agenda setting was already recognized by Lippmann ([1922] 1992, p. 229) when he described the media as "the beam of a searchlight that moves restlessly about, bringing one episode and then another out of darkness into vision." Agenda setting thus operates on shaping attention, influencing which issues matter at a given time. A recurring concern with the agenda-setting role of the media is that the differential attention paid to some issues and not others biases public attention and, eventually, election and policy outcomes.[23] So, while the media may not succeed in changing people's minds on an issue, it may influence what they pay attention to.[24] The classical version of this concern is from Cohen (1963, p. 13):

> The press is significantly more than a purveyor of information and opinion. It may not be successful much of the time in telling its people what to think, but it is stunningly successful in telling readers what to think about.

There is extensive empirical research on the effects of agenda setting, originating with the work of McCombs and Shaw (1972). A typical McCombs and Shaw study would conduct a survey among randomly selected undecided voters and ask them what the key issues of the day were. This provided a rank order among issues based on the percentage of voters who mentioned a given issue. Concurrently, the news coverage of the relevant media outlets (newspapers, television stations, etc.) would be collected and content analyzed. The results would then be used to calculate a rank order among the issues ordered by coverage frequency. Finally, the correlation between the two rank orderings would be calculated and interpreted as agenda setting influence. There are now hundreds of studies following this format (McCombs and Reynolds 2002; McCombs and Shaw 1993). While these findings support the idea of agenda setting by the media, they do not establish a causal impact of media coverage on audience attention. This is because readers are not randomly assigned to a newspaper. Rather, they have a choice of what to read and what to watch. This means that they may gravitate toward news outlets that talk about the events that match their interests. Similarly, newspaper outlets will have an incentive to serve the needs of their audience, especially in a competitive media market. We would then have the same sorting mechanism discussed in the previous section, with the only difference being that here sorting occurs on interest, not on ideology, although interest and ideology, of course, may themselves be correlated.

Expanding on this idea, Gentzkow, Glaeser, and Goldin (2006) developed a simple model of an outlet's decision processes. In this model, a media outlet can acquire a newsworthy story at a cost. A profit-maximizing outlet will always publish the story, but an ideological paper may refrain from publishing it if it conflicts with the media outlet's political leanings. The incentives to pay the costs of investigation depend on the incentives to suppress unfavorable stories, which depend in turn on how much advertising and circulation revenue would be lost by not publishing them. The bottom line is that, in a competitive media market, media outlets will face reduced profits if the covered issues do not match the interests of the audience. Of course, ideological outlets may be willing to pay this cost, but it is a disincentive nevertheless.

This type of attention differential, i.e., media outlets focusing on the stories their audiences are interested in, is also what Puglisi and Snyder (2011) found in their study of coverage of political scandals by newspapers. They classified a newspaper as "Democratic-leaning" if it has a higher propensity to endorse Democratic candidates in elections. The definition of "Republican-leaning" is analogous. They found that Democratic-leaning newspapers give significantly more coverage to scandals involving Republican politicians than scandals involving Democratic politicians, while Republican-leaning newspapers do the opposite. On average, a Democratic newspaper devotes about 26 percent more coverage to Republican scandals over Democratic scandals. This bias in coverage of scandals affects not only editorials but also the news section, and persists even if one controls for the partisan leanings of the electorate.

Larcinese, Puglisi, and Snyder (2011) used a large sample of US newspapers from 1996 to 2005 to assess the correlation between the endorsement policy of newspapers and the differential coverage of economic news as a function of the president's political affiliation. They found that Democratic-leaning newspapers gave more coverage to high unemployment when the incumbent was a Republican.[25]

Note also that there may be underlying issue characteristics (i.e., what makes an issue interesting) that will influence both news coverage and what an audience pays attention to. News outlets will not stay in business long if they do not publish stories that their audience cares about. The Deepwater Horizon oil spill, for example, was likely to both trigger public interest and influence newspaper coverage. To address these issues, Eisensee and Strömberg (2007) studied over 5,000 natural disasters and subsequent relief efforts by the US government. News coverage and disaster relief are clearly correlated, but this does not provide evidence that news coverage influences disaster relief, as both coverage and the policy response may be influenced by issue salience or other factors (e.g., political agendas and ideologies). To disentangle these effects, one needs to find a proper instrument that influences news coverage but has no other impact on policy. The idea is that media attention is a limited resource (not all events can be covered on the front page). Thus, a given disaster is less likely to be covered in the news if other events with higher audience interest take center stage. Eisensee and Strömberg (2007) used the Olympic Games as such an event competing for attention. Since the Olympic Games run on fixed cycles (summer games and winter games are held every four years), the presence of an Olympic year can be used as an instrument. Natural disasters of a comparatively moderate scale may be covered in a non-Olympic year, but may be crowded out by news coverage related to the Olympics in a year when the games are held.

Using this intuition, Eisensee and Strömberg found that, indeed, Olympic games may crowd out natural disasters. To receive the same amount of news coverage during the Olympics, a disaster must have three times as many casualties, while the likelihood of receiving relief efforts for comparable disasters is decreased by about 6 percent. Furthermore, with this approach one can now also identify other factors that shape coverage and the provision of relief. For instance, the effect of news coverage on the likelihood that an event will receive relief is 16 percent. But the effect is much larger for events that are marginal, that is, those that are likely to receive aid only if they are covered. Here the estimated effect is 68 percent. In general, short-term, highly dramatic disasters such as volcanic eruptions or earthquakes are more likely to receive both coverage and support than droughts or famines. For example, a famine must have more than 40,000 times as many casualties as a volcano eruption to have the same likelihood of being covered. Similarly, to receive television coverage, a disaster in Africa must have 45 times as many deaths on average as an otherwise comparable disaster in Europe. These biases in coverage have direct consequences for disaster relief. For example, they bias relief efforts for famines in Africa downward.[26]

While both the Snyder and Puglisi and the Eisensee and Strömberg studies provide evidence of coverage bias, they do not directly investigate the effects of coverage on public attention, which is the key feature of the agenda-setting model. Establishing such an effect directly is difficult since measures of public attention are hard to come by and because we face the statistical problem that both coverage and attention may be directly influenced by the same characteristics of an issue.[27]

That said, the main contributions of Eisensee and Strömberg are (1) a clear statement of the statistical problem (both media coverage and disaster response may be influenced by the same event characteristics) that is germane to many empirical investigations of media influence, and (2) an innovative and convincing estimation approach through the novel use of the Olympics as an instrumental variable that provides a solution to the statistical difficulties. In a different application, these problems will be similar, but new statistical solutions will have to be found.

The statistical difficulties generated by the lack of randomized treatment effects suggest that experiments may be useful for solving these issues, as in the Iyengar and Kinder studies on the effects of television (Iyengar and Kinder 1987). In a typical Iyengar and Kinder study, volunteer subjects were recruited and asked to watch specially edited television news coverage. The news coverage was taken from real newscasts a few months prior to the experiment. Clips from these newscasts were carefully combined and edited to make them appear like regular news broadcasts. News clips were highly varied, from different times of year (avoiding specific dates), and with different styles: some with features, some with "talking heads." The treatment stories were inserted into the middle of the broadcast and ran for between two and four minutes. For example, in one such study, over four days subjects saw four stories on defense, totaling 17 minutes of news coverage. As a control condition, the other half of the sample watched news content with no defense content. Prior to the treatment, subjects were asked to fill out a questionnaire containing eight national problems and rate the importance of these problems by assigning a score between 0 (no importance) and 100 (extreme importance). In a variant of the experiment, subjects were asked to name the "three most important problems." By comparing the answers before and after the treatment and comparing them to the control group, Iyengar and Kinder could thus measure the impact of television news coverage. For example, in the case of defense coverage in the treated group, average importance for defense increased by 10 to 20 points, and the likelihood of being named among the top three problems increased by 20 percent. Similar effects could be seen in other policy areas. Importantly, such effects persisted over weeks. This suggests that issues that the audience pays attention to at a given time are encoded more reliably in long-term memory and accessed more easily, consistent with the principles of opinion formation discussed in chapter 2.

The main advantage of experimental treatments is that they permit proper random assignment and the detailed design of stimuli. But, there are also disadvantages. First, experimental participants usually know that they are participating in an experiment. This may lead to a desire to please the experimenter or to guess what the purpose of the experiment is. Such problems can be alleviated by proper design, for instance, by asking various nongermane questions in a survey to conceal the true purpose of the experiment, or using double-blind designs. But there is no solution to the basic problem that participants may inadvertently alter their attitudes or behaviors when asked to participate in an experiment. For example, they may be more or less engaged in the task than in "real life." These considerations are particularly important in the context of the Iyengar and Kinder experiments, which explored mechanisms relying on attention and the subsequent encoding into long-term memory. Second, many experiments are conducted with populations that are convenient, such as college students or participants in Amazon's Mechanical Turk.[28] Assembling representative samples is more expensive and difficult to administer.[29] Finally, there is the recurring question of how the specifics of the design generalize to other settings, that is, whether the experiment is externally valid.

In sum, there is empirical evidence that (1) newspapers vary systematically in their coverage of issues in understandable ways, (2) variation in coverage impacts policy outcomes, (3) audience members pay attention to different issues depending on media coverage, and (4) such effects tend to persist over time.[30]

8.6 Public Attention and the Media Cycle

Our discussion of the principles of opinion formation in chapter 2 pointed to the importance of audience attention. Members of the public are more receptive to messages when they are engaged and paying attention. Such messages then have a higher likelihood of changing considerations or the distribution of considerations. Even in an age of social media, many of the messages received by the public come from broadcast media, whether in the form of newspapers, television, radio, or online. But the media agenda is limited. Newspapers have space constraints, especially for the front page, and television and radio programs have time constraints. Even online news sources face constraints, although they operate differently. An online audience will attend to only a small subset of the provided content. To find interesting content, users rely on search engines, but will pay disproportionate attention to pages displayed early, especially the first page. In other words, what for newspapers is the front page is the first page of Google for online news (e.g., Cho and Roy 2004; Jacob 2018; Pan 2015).

Newspapers will use different headlines for their print and online editions to adjust to these different constraints.[31] In a story about US President Obama's redecoration of the Oval Office in the White House, the *New York Times*'s online version of the story had the headline "The President's New Office," easy to find, but a bit boring. The print version had the headline "The Audacity of Taupe," much more creative, but hopeless for a search engine (Boydstun 2013). These space and attention constraints imply that understanding what drives newspaper coverage is crucially important.

In the last section, we saw that (1) the media engages in agenda setting through the selection of issues, and (2) issue selection influences beliefs and attitudes as well as policy and electoral outcomes. Now we are interested in understanding in more detail which issues are covered by the media. First, we will investigate the issue of selection: What determines which issues make it into a newspaper or television program? Second, we want to understand the dynamics of news coverage: How long does the media pay attention to an issue, and what is the interaction between different sources?

Each question has a general answer, well supported by empirical evidence. News coverage is *highly skewed*, and news coverage is *punctuated* (Baumgartner and Jones 2009; Boydstun 2013; Jones and Baumgartner 2005).[32] By "skewed" we mean a massive overrepresentation of a small number of events covered in the media compared to the universe of events that occur on a daily basis.

A telling example is the case of Terri Schiavo (Boydstun 2013). In 1990, Terri Schiavo suffered full cardiac arrest that led to massive brain damage and put her into a deep coma, with no chance of recovery. She was kept alive by a feeding tube and other life-prolonging measures. In 1998, her husband Michael petitioned a Florida court to have the feeding tube removed, which led to a legal battle with Terri Schiavo's parents. In February 2005, a Florida judge ordered the tube removed. A long battle in federal and Florida courts and legislative arenas (including the US Congress) followed, involving both the then-governor of Florida, Jeb Bush, and his brother, US President George W. Bush. After all was said and done, Terri Schiavo's feeding tube was removed, and she died from dehydration on March 31, 2005.

The Terri Schiavo case generated massive media coverage. For example, the *New York Times* ran 16 headlines during March 2005, on average one every two days. To see the disproportionate attention paid to the Schiavo case, consider some of the other stories during March 2005 and their number of headlines (Boydstun 2013):

- President Bush advocates his plan for private social security accounts (four headlines).
- The US Supreme Court declares the application of the death penalty to juveniles unconstitutional (one headline).
- 40 US servicemen and -women die in Iraq and Afghanistan (two headlines).
- More than 200 people die in a flood in Afghanistan (no headlines).
- Ukrainian officials reveal smuggling of 18 nuclear-capable missiles into Iran and China by Ukrainian arms-dealers (no headlines).
- The US Senate rejects proposals to raise the minimum wage (no headlines).

The level of skew does not necessarily mean that the coverage of the *New York Times* is biased. The distribution of headlines may well fit the interests of its readership or the US public in general. It simply points out a peculiar distribution of topics on its front page. Issue skew is not unique to the *New York Times* or to newspapers in general. Both local newspapers and online news media have higher levels of skew, with television news having the highest (Boydstun 2013). Skew can also be found in other policy-relevant institutions such as bills, hearings, court cases, and measures of public concern (Jones and Baumgartner 2005).[33]

Second, front-page coverage is "punctuated" (Jones and Baumgartner 2005) or "explosive" (Boydstun 2013). That is, the rate of change is not gradual but rapid, much more rapid than if change were distributed normally.[34] Intuitively, this means that an issue suddenly appears on the front page and then disappears again.[35] The media cycle is very short. Various accounts of these phenomena have been proposed. Many traditional accounts of the media have portrayed it as a "watchdog" surveying various issues, engaged in investigative journalism until a story is deemed important enough to make it onto the front page. While there are some stories that fit this mold, most famously the Watergate stories by Bob Woodward and Carl Bernstein, various scholars have criticized this view as inaccurate. Zaller (2003) argues that the media operates as an "alarm system," quickly reacting to events that it deems important and elevating them into public consciousness. This means that only those events that are considered important by the media will be attended to.[36] Others have suggested that the media exhibits a herding mentality, where various news organizations latch onto newly broken stories and amplify them, creating a positive feedback loop (e.g., Bennet 2003; Boydstun and Russell 2016; Kepplinger 2007). There is recent evidence that these positive feedback effects are particularly strong for television coverage and online news cycles (Boydstun, Moody, and Thomas 2010).

While these accounts may explain the explosive growth of a particular story, they do not account for its equally rapid decline and replacement by the next "big story." What we have here is a second, countervailing force, the tremendous importance placed by journalists and editors on the "scoop," that is, breaking an important story before everybody else does. Once the story has broken, attention shifts to the next one.

The punctuated nature of news coverage has important practical consequences for companies, as the window to respond to a story is very short, often no longer than one 24-hour news cycle. Once media attention has shifted, even a well-crafted company response will not reach its intended audience, since this audience is now occupied with a new story. This means that the audience either will only be left with the impression generated by the original coverage or, even worse, will interpret the company's lack of response as an admission of guilt or lack of caring (Ferrin et al. 2007; Heinze, Uhlmann, and Diermeier 2014; Schweinsberg et al. 2016; Uhlmann et al. 2010).

Finally, there is a third factor that influences media coverage: issue adjacency. That is, once a story has brought an issue to public attention, other stories on the same issue or closely related issues become newsworthy and are actively sought out by journalists (Boydstun 2013). For example, a report about contaminated toothpaste made in China may lead to additional stories about unsafe manufacturing practices more generally. This feature of news coverage has the important practical consequence that, after a big story about a company in a given industry, the reputational risk to adjacent industries, companies, and products increases. In other words, a story about contaminated toothpaste made in China increases the reputational risk not only for the toothpaste business but also for food companies, toy companies, and pharmaceutical companies that have a Chinese supplier or manufacturing base.

In sum, we have three different factors that jointly drive the dynamics of news coverage. First, the scoop effect puts a significant premium on being the first to break a story. Second, once a story is broken, other media outlets will jump onto the hot topic, until it is replaced by a new one. Third, adjacent or related issues may also become newsworthy.

8.7 The Media as Amplifier

Much of the empirical literature on media influence has focused on the factors that shape individual beliefs and attitudes. So far, all our findings were focused on the individual and the processes of belief and attitude formation. This was also true of slant and agenda setting, which focused on how individual attitudes are shaped by how issues are covered and by which issues are covered. That is, the emphasis has been on a directed, bilateral relationship between a sender (a news organization) and a receiver (a typical member of the public). But news stories do not just reach one individual, but (large) groups of individuals. This has important consequences.

Consider the decision to buy a car. You may read a review or article that favors the Toyota over the Ford (slant); or a feature reviewing cars may fail to mention the Ford (agenda setting). But suppose we set aside any form of slant and agenda setting, and assume you read a purely factual story, such as a listing of current car sales. Suppose you are considering buying a car, say a Ford Escort, but hear on television that the bestselling car in America is the Toyota Camry. Based on that news story, you may change your mind and buy the Toyota instead. This is not an issue of framing, rhetoric, or selection bias. The media did not recommend the Camry or forget to mention the Ford. It simply and accurately reported sales numbers. But that report changed your mind and perhaps the minds of many others. What we have is an example of *social influence*, that is, the shift in attitudes, opinions, and behavior due to exposure to the attitudes, opinions, and behavior of others.

The issue of social influence comes into play when the media reports on events that involve the actions of other people. For example, a news report that the Toyota Camry is the bestselling car may change a buyer's mind not because of slant or agenda selection, but because knowing that other consumers have bought a certain vehicle may change buying behavior. This might occur because knowing that others have purchased a certain product may be informative (Bikhchandani, Hirshleifer, and Welch 1998), or because of a basic inclination to emulate the behavior of others (Bandura and Walters 1963; Miller and Dollard 1941).[37] Studying these effects in detail will require the introduction of formal models.

The presence of social influence has been confirmed in various laboratory and field experiments (Anderson and Holt 1996, 1997; Lorenz et al. 2011).[38] A nice example is an experiment on music downloads (Salganik, Dodds, and Watts 2006). The researchers created a new download site for songs by unknown artists with over 14,000 participants. In some versions, the participants could see previous downloads, but in others they could not. Initial popularity of songs (measured by previous downloads) clearly influenced subsequent participants' behavior, and various different rankings emerged with different starting conditions. Other research on the success of cultural products (e.g., music and movies) now supports the idea that information cascades, herding, and the dynamics of "buzz" are major reasons for the unpredictability of success for movies, music, books, and so on (e.g., Aral and Walker 2012; Balter 2008; Centola 2011; De Angelis et al. 2012; Dubois, Rucker, and Tormala 2011; Keller and Libai 2009; Salganik, Dodds, and Watts 2006).

Some researchers have pointed out that social influence can reflect rational decisions by members of the public. The most influential approach is the idea of "information cascades" and "herding" (Anderson and Holt 1997; Bikhchandani, Hirshleifer, and Welch 1992). This idea is that rational agents understand that purchase or download tallies reflect the choices of rational agents who base their information on some (noisy) information about the product. It is therefore reasonable to take this information into account when making one's own decision. Indeed, if the evidence is overwhelming, agents may rationally ignore their own private information and follow the crowd.[39] Under some conditions such herding behavior may lead to bad outcomes, as the crowd may coordinate on the "wrong" option.[40]

Once we recognize the importance of social influence, we can see the potentially important impact of the media as reporters of events involving social actions: the media can serve as an *amplifier*. The point is that, through its reports of public reactions to an event—such as through interviews with outraged citizens, impromptu protests at a company's headquarters, and the like—others may be induced to participate as well. The media thus serves as a crucial channel for social influence. Note that this influence may not be intended by the media. Yet, by simply reporting on an event, the media can change the attitudes and behavior of others. As we will see, this function of the media plays a critical role in explaining the dynamics of reputational crises.

8.8   Crisis Dynamics and the Media

Having examined the various roles that the media can play and the way media outlets can shape opinions, we now investigate in more detail the consequences of media influence for reputational crises. Formal modeling will be particularly helpful for understanding these dynamic relationships. We introduce the model step by step.[41]

Let S be the finite set of consumers of size s. We assume that an individual $i \in S$ can hold one of two opinions, $+1$ or -1. We assume that in each (discrete) period t, exactly one agent i is selected randomly with probability $1/s$. Only that individual will adjust his opinion. Such periods can be arbitrarily short. The model has three key parameters.

Media bias is given by a real number $a \neq 0$, which represents the (net) media bias on all citizens. If $a > 0$ there is a bias toward $+1$; if $a < 0$, there is a bias toward -1. The parameter a captures both slant and agenda setting, that is, which issues are covered and how they are covered. Note that there is no assumption that there is a single media source. For example, there may be multiple outlets on opposite sides of the spectrum. Also, some media outlets may engage in trying to directly influence citizens, while others strictly report. The parameter a will capture the net influence of the total media coverage on a given individual. Recall that the empirical literature found little evidence for such media bias. So, a may be very small.

Note that this model captures individuals who do not intrinsically favor one side over the other because of individual preferences or ideologies. That is, in the absence of any influence, they are equally likely to hold either of the two opinions. This is a reasonable assumption in a business context but less in the case of political debates or an electoral campaign, where members of the public naturally have a preference for one side.[42]

Social influence is given by a positive real number $b > 0$. It will capture the magnitude of influence on a given individual by the attitudes of other individuals. In our first model, we will consider the impact of the mass media, which reports the average opinion on a given issue. Here, reporting by the mass media constitutes the sole channel of influence. The impact of social media is discussed in a later section.

Finally, we will specify an *attention parameter* $\lambda > 0$. The parameter λ captures the degree to which individuals pay attention to an issue. Factors that have an effect on λ include the amount of media coverage, but also placement, such as location within a news broadcast or page number in a newspaper. A low λ corresponds to the case where citizens do not pay attention; their attitudes are not strongly influenced by either media bias or social influence; for $\lambda = 0$ attitudes are completely random. As λ increases, individual opinions increasingly respond to media bias and social influence.

In sum, the model captures the following aspects of media coverage: (1) media bias through parameter a, (2) media reporting of current attitudes and their influence through parameter b, and (3) media volume and reach through parameter λ. Now we will investigate how these factors interact.

It will be convenient to have an even number of audience members of size $s = 2N$. We can then summarize the current state of opinion at any given point in time by

$$n = \frac{n_+ - n_-}{2},$$

where n_+ and n_- denote the number of consumers in state $+1$ and -1, respectively. The state variable n then ranges from $-N$ to N. We will assume that, when selected, agents adjust their states probabilistically according to a log-logistic functional form. Intuitively, this means that the probability of adjusting their opinion is proportional to the strength of influence. Suppose that the initial state of public opinion is n and the selected individual is initially in state -1. The probability that she will switch opinion from -1 to $+1$ is given by:

$$p[- \to +] = \frac{\exp\left[\lambda\left(a + 2b\frac{2n+1}{2N-1}\right)\right]}{\exp\left[\lambda\left(a + 2b\frac{2n+1}{2N-1}\right)\right] + \exp\left[-\lambda\left(a + 2b\frac{2n+1}{2N-1}\right)\right]}.$$

Note that $p[- \to +]$ is increasing in media bias for state $+1$, which we denoted by a. The parameter b captures the strength of social influence via media reporting. First note that $2n + 1 = n_+ - (n_- - 1)$. This implies that $\frac{2n+1}{2N-1}$ is the average opinion among all agents other than the one currently updating her state. If there are more supporters of $+1$ than -1 among these agents, the average opinion is positive. When $b > 0$, the updating agent thus is more likely to adjust his opinion in accordance with the majority opinion. Since $p[- \to +]$ is increasing in $\frac{2n+1}{2N-1}$, this effect will be larger the more the average opinion favors $+1$.

Now suppose that the selected agent is initially in state $+1$. The probability that he will switch opinion from $+1$ to -1 is then given by:

$$p[+ \to -] = \frac{\exp\left[-\lambda\left(a + 2b\frac{2n-1}{2N-1}\right)\right]}{\exp\left[-\lambda\left(a + 2b\frac{2n-1}{2N-1}\right)\right] + \exp\left[\lambda\left(a + 2b\frac{2n-1}{2N-1}\right)\right]}.$$

$p[+ \to -]$ is now decreasing in a, consistent with the interpretation of a of as media bias favoring $+1$. With $b > 0$, $p[+ \to -]$ is also decreasing in the average opinion, now given by $\frac{2n-1}{2N-1}$, which drives the updating agent toward the majority opinion.

The selection rule combined with the switching probabilities define a stochastic, dynamic process. It can be shown that this process has a unique limiting distribution which corresponds to the steady state of the system (Diermeier and Andonie 2007). Moreover, the properties of the distribution depend on the parameters a, b, and λ.

Specifically, there are two distinct regimes. The first is the case where λb is small. Let us call this the *ordinary regime*. Members of the public pay little attention to companies, and media coverage is relegated to the pages of the business section. In this case the limiting distribution will be unimodal. Public opinion will be centered on the average opinion, change is gradual, and average opinion will modestly shift in response to increased media bias a or increased media attention λ. Figure 8.1 is a typical time series of such opinion dynamics.

Public attitudes toward a company will ebb and flow and will be tightly clustered around the average opinion. That average opinion will gradually

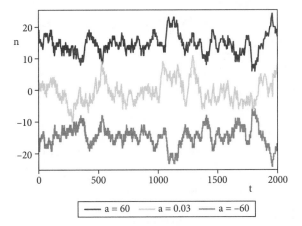

FIGURE 8.1. The ordinary regime: Opinion dynamics for different values of media bias. $\lambda =$ 0.01, $b = 0.9$, $N = 25$, $T = 2,000$; $a = -60, 0.03, 60$.

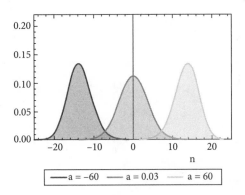

FIGURE 8.2. The ordinary regime: Unimodal distributions. As a increases, the distribution shifts toward $+1$.

shift up or down in response to media bias. Figure 8.2 is another representation of the same three cases, now represented as distributions rather than as sample time series lines.

The distributions are unimodal, and each mode gradually shifts to the right as a increases while keeping the other values constant.

In figure 8.3 we slowly increase λ while keeping the other values constant. The time series shifts accordingly. In the ordinary regime, a higher λ gradually increases the impact of media bias. Intuitively, this means that, as consumers pay more attention to media coverage, they are more susceptible to media bias.

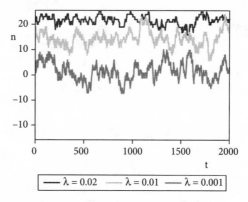

FIGURE 8.3. The ordinary regime: Opinion dynamics for different values of attention. $a = 60$, $b = 0.9, N = 25, T = 2{,}000$; different values of $\lambda = 0.001, 0.01, 0.02$.

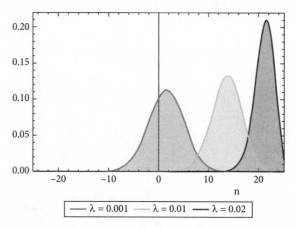

FIGURE 8.4. The ordinary regime: Unimodal distributions. As λ increases, the distribution shifts toward $+1$ (the state favored by a), while the variance of the distribution decreases.

When we consider the distributions directly, the maximum in the phase diagram slowly shifts toward the state favored by a. Note also that the distribution tightens. Intuitively, this follows because as λ increases, individuals pay more attention, which reduces the variance of public opinion. This is portrayed in figure 8.4.

The situation, however, is fundamentally different when λb suddenly increases beyond a critical threshold.

In figure 8.5 we depict the corresponding opinion dynamics for the cases of high and low attention. Specifically, suppose we start out in the ordinary regime at time $t = 0$ with $\lambda = 0.1$. With modest media bias, here at

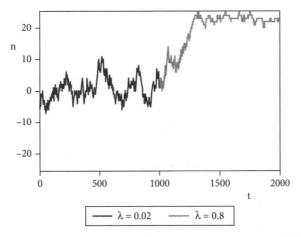

FIGURE 8.5. The crisis regime: Opinion dynamics. $\lambda = 0.8, a = 0.03, b = 0.9, N = 25, T = 2{,}000$.

$a = 0.03$, average opinion moves around but is hovering slightly above 0 on the y-axis the majority of time (as shown by the dark gray line). Now suppose at a point in time, say $t = 1000$, through a scandal involving, say, celebrities, media coverage increases significantly, leading to an increase in public attention at, say, $\lambda = 0.8$, while keeping $a = 0.03$ (shown by the light gray line). Public opinion now suddenly shifts toward almost unanimous support for opinion "1."

This is the *crisis regime*. This regime is characterized by sudden shifts in public opinion. Importantly, these shifts are not driven by changes in media *bias*, but are generated by changes in media *attention* λ. The corresponding limiting distribution is now bimodal with both maxima close to the extremes, as illustrated in figure 8.6.

Now the most likely states are those where almost all agents have the same opinion. Notice also that most of the probability mass is tightly concentrated around the peaks, especially the peak favored by media bias a, which also constitutes the absolute maximum. The bimodal distribution introduces not only sudden shifts but also a sense of unpredictability. It is possible that the public will coordinate on the smaller maximum, that is, the opinion not favored by the media, but this will be less likely, increasingly so as λb or a grow.

One of the important features of the crisis regime is that, assuming the public settles on the opinion favored by media bias, the actual support for an issue may be overstated compared to the ordinary regime.

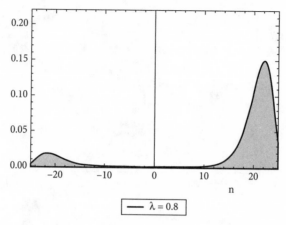

FIGURE 8.6. The crisis regime: Bimodal distribution. $\lambda = 0.8, a = 0.03, b = 0.9, N = 25$.

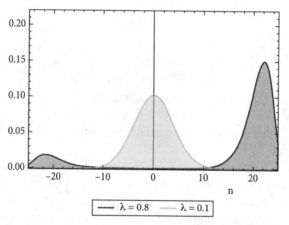

FIGURE 8.7. Opinion dynamics with low and high attention. $a = 0.03, b = 0.9, N = 25, T = 2,000$; $\lambda = 0.8, 0.1$.

Social influence via media coverage thus generates a positive feedback system which leads to artificially homogeneous public opinion. That is, public opinion consists of individual attitudes, which, via the mechanism of social influence, are themselves influenced by public opinion. Figure 8.7 compares the ordinary and the crisis regime.

As an example, consider the issue of offshore oil drilling and assume that there is a slight media bias that supports further restrictions on offshore drilling (call this option "+1"). Also, assume that the media, from time to time, reports on opinion surveys on the issue of offshore drilling. This situation corresponds to the ordinary regime. That is, with moderate social influence, opinion will shift in the direction of media bias in a proportional fashion. As long as media bias is moderate, public support may not be enough to have a significant impact on government policy, leaving the current set of regulations in place.

Now consider BP's Deepwater Horizon crisis. Due to the dramatic nature of the accident and the powerful visuals, media coverage increased dramatically, leading to an increase in public attention, that is, λ. The parameter λ will be influenced by the amount and intensity of media coverage. A substantial increase in the amount of coverage *by itself* will be enough to trigger a dramatic shift in opinion, most likely in the direction of media bias, even if media bias (or the degree of social influence measured by b) did not change at all. Of course, we may also see an increase in media bias in the direction of additional restrictions. But such an increase in a (or social influence b) would only reinforce the dynamic driving the increase in attention. Once media coverage, and thus attention, wanes, we revert to the ordinary regime.

The crisis regime thus creates a (usually brief) window where public opinion dramatically shifts in one direction through the mechanism of social influence, that is, the media reporting on current public attitudes. Such windows correspond to the policy windows described by Kingdon (1984) as well as by Jones and Baumgartner (2005). Jones and Baumgartner show that the dynamic of such shifts is highly skewed and punctuated. In business areas, such phenomena tend to occur in the context of crises or scandals, as such events tend to be the only issues that generate sufficient media attention.

These insights have important practical consequences, especially in a crisis context. If, as is usually the case during a crisis, media bias is unfavorable to a company, senior management has various strategic options. First, the company's leadership can try to shift the tone of media coverage in the opposite direction (from $a > 0$ in favor of additional offshore restrictions toward $a < 0$ supporting BP). The problem with this strategy is that, during the short window when the general public is paying attention to a corporate event, such a shift is very difficult to accomplish, especially if the company has been blindsided by the event. Second, a company can try to "wait things out" until media coverage and public attention subside to subcritical levels. The downside of this strategy is that attitudes tend to be coded into long-term memory during periods of high attention. Hence, simply waiting things out may lead to long-term reputational damage. Therefore, waiting strategies tend to be more successful when companies are primarily concerned about political or regulatory change. Regulatory change, especially if it is substantial, often requires sustained public support, support that can evaporate as attention decreases. In such situations, companies will often use delay tactics or attempts to complexify an issue, which often decrease media interest and attention. In cases where companies are confronted by social activists and NGOs, this can lead to a complex strategic game, where companies try to delay and increase complexity while activists try to create a sense of urgency and frame the issue in emotionally evocative terms that are easy to understand. We discuss the interaction between firms and activists below.

8.9 Appendix

The public opinion model was fully analyzed in Diermeier and Andonie (2007). Here we summarize the main steps. Recall that the conditional probability that a recognized agent will switch her opinion from -1 to $+1$ is given by:

$$p[- \rightarrow +] = \frac{\exp\left[\lambda\left(a + 2b\frac{2n+1}{2N-1}\right)\right]}{\exp\left[\lambda\left(a + 2b\frac{2n+1}{2N-1}\right)\right] + \exp\left[-\lambda\left(a + 2b\frac{2n+1}{2N-1}\right)\right]}.$$

Similarly, the probability that she will switch opinion from $+1$ to -1 is given by:

$$p[+ \rightarrow -] = \frac{\exp\left[-\lambda\left(a + 2b\frac{2n-1}{2N-1}\right)\right]}{\exp\left[-\lambda\left(a + 2b\frac{2n-1}{2N-1}\right)\right] + \exp\left[\lambda\left(a + 2b\frac{2n-1}{2N-1}\right)\right]}.$$

Since our selection rule is stationary and since the log-logistic response rule depends only on n, and not explicitly on time, we have a Markov chain with stationary transition probabilities. Because at most one player can adjust her opinion in a given period, the Markov chain is a birth-death process. A "birth" corresponds to an agent switching her opinion from -1 to $+1$, whereas a switch in the opposite direction corresponds to a "death."

Suppose that the initial state of play is n. The probabilities of selecting an agent in state -1 (respectively, $+1$) are then:

$$p_- = \frac{n_-}{2N} = \frac{N-n}{2N} \quad \text{and} \quad p_+ = \frac{n_+}{2N} = \frac{N+n}{2N}.$$

A transition from n to $n+1$ (or "birth") means that the number of supporters of $+1$ increases by one. This requires that an agent in state -1 be selected and that he switches his opinion to $+1$. The selection probability is then p_- and the individual transition probability is $p[- \to +]$. To calculate the birth probability (denoted γ^n), we simply multiply the two probabilities:

$$\gamma^n = p_- \cdot p[- \to +]$$

$$= \frac{N-n}{2N} \frac{\exp\left[\lambda\left(a + 2b\frac{2n+1}{2N-1}\right)\right]}{\exp\left[\lambda\left(a + 2b\frac{2n+1}{2N-1}\right)\right] + \exp\left[-\lambda\left(a + 2b\frac{2n+1}{2N-1}\right)\right]}.$$

Now consider the transition from n to $n-1$ (or "death"), when the number of supporters of $+1$ decreases by one. This requires that an agent in state $+1$ be selected and that he switches his opinion to -1. The selection probability is then p_+ and the individual transition probability is $p[+ \to -]$. To calculate the death probability (denoted μ^n), we can again multiply the two probabilities and obtain:

$$\mu^n = p_+ \cdot p[+ \to -]$$

$$= \frac{N+n}{2N} \frac{\exp\left[-\lambda\left(a + 2b\frac{2n-1}{2N-1}\right)\right]}{\exp\left[-\lambda\left(a + 2b\frac{2n-1}{2N-1}\right)\right] + \exp\left[\lambda\left(a + 2b\frac{2n-1}{2N-1}\right)\right]}.$$

With the remaining probability $1 - \gamma^n - \mu^n$ the state of the process is unchanged at n. Since the stochastic process described above is a birth-death process, it has a unique limiting distribution that satisfies the detailed balance equations:

$$\pi^n \mu^n = \pi^{n-1} \gamma^{n-1}.$$

Plugging in the expressions for γ^{n-1} and μ^n and rearranging we get:

$$\frac{\pi^n}{\pi^{n-1}} = \frac{N-n+1}{N+n} \exp\left[\lambda\left(2a + 4b\frac{2n-1}{2N-1}\right)\right].$$

By chaining the above equations together and rearranging terms we can express any π^n as a function of π^0:

$$\pi^n = \pi^0 \frac{(N!)^2}{(2N)!} \binom{2N}{N+n} \exp\left[\lambda\left(2an + \frac{4b}{2N-1}n^2\right)\right].$$

Finally, we can solve for π^0 from the condition that the π^n's sum up to one. Plugging the solution into the expression for the values π^n yields finally:

$$\pi^n = \frac{\binom{2N}{N+n} \exp\left[\lambda\left(2an + \frac{4b}{2N-1}n^2\right)\right]}{\sum_{n'=-N}^{N} \binom{2N}{N+n'} \exp\left[\lambda\left(2an' + \frac{4b}{2N-1}(n')^2\right)\right]}.$$

Thus we have proved the following:

Proposition 1 *The limiting distribution of the public opinion model is given by:*

$$\pi^n = \frac{\binom{2N}{N+n} \exp\left[\lambda\left(2an + \frac{4b}{2N-1}n^2\right)\right]}{\sum_{n'=-N}^{N} \binom{2N}{N+n'} \exp\left[\lambda\left(2an' + \frac{4b}{2N-1}(n')^2\right)\right]}.$$

Our intended application is large populations. Therefore we will consider the limit case of $N \to \infty$. We then have the second result of this chapter.

Proposition 2 *Suppose $b > 0$. Then as $N \to \infty$, the extrema of the limiting distribution depend on the values of parameters a, b, and λ as follows: (1) If either $b \leq \frac{1}{2\lambda}$, or $b > \frac{1}{2\lambda}$ and*

$$a > \left|\frac{1}{2\lambda}\left[4\lambda b\sqrt{1 - \frac{1}{2\lambda b}} - \log\frac{1 + \sqrt{1 - \frac{1}{2\lambda b}}}{1 - \sqrt{1 - \frac{1}{2\lambda b}}}\right]\right|,$$

the distribution is unimodal. *The maximum is attained at positive n if $a > 0$, and at negative n if $a < 0$. 2) If $b > \frac{1}{2\lambda}$ and*

$$a \leq \left|\frac{1}{2\lambda}\left[4\lambda b\sqrt{1 - \frac{1}{2\lambda b}} - \log\frac{1 + \sqrt{1 - \frac{1}{2\lambda b}}}{1 - \sqrt{1 - \frac{1}{2\lambda b}}}\right]\right|,$$

the distribution is bimodal. *The global maximum is attained at positive n if a > 0, and at negative n if a < 0.*

As λ grows, probability mass will shift more and more to the most likely state, reaching 1 in the limit. As λ goes to infinity, the distribution collapses on a Dirac distribution (a "spike") that puts positive probability mass only on states where all agents have the same opinion. That is, public opinion reaches consensus. Which opinion is favored depends on the direction of media bias. This is stated more formally in the following corollary.

Corollary 3 *As $\lambda \to \infty$, then $\pi^N = 1$ if $a > 0$, and $\pi^{-N} = 1$ if $a < 0$.*

CHAPTER NINE

Social Media — Social Networks

9.1 The Rise of Social Media

Our analysis has focused on the mass media, exemplified by broadcast media, newspapers, and websites. But individuals are not influenced only by mass news coverage. As part of social networks, individuals interact, share views, and influence each other. Social networks have long been known to be important channels for opinion formation. Early examples of social networks include neighborhoods, workplace environments, community groups, religious communities, and so forth (Berelson, Lazarsfeld, and McPhee 1954; Friedson 1953; Sinclair 2012; Steiner 1954). The rise of social media such as blogs, Twitter, and Facebook, among others, has accelerated interest in understanding the role of social networks in shaping public opinion (Lazer et al. 2009). Existing research has analyzed blogs (e.g., Adamic and Glance 2005; Farrell and Drezner 2008), Twitter (e.g., Gayo-Avello, Metaxas, and Mustafaraj 2011; Tumasjan et al. 2010), Facebook friendship networks (e.g., Bond et al. 2012), and web pages (e.g., Esterling, Lazer, and Neblo 2013).[1]

Networks are a common tool to model social interactions. The use of networks has a long tradition in the social sciences, especially in sociology. Classic treatments are due to Milgram (1967) and Granovetter (1978), who also originated some of the key terminology in network analysis, such as "six degrees of separation," "cliques," "small worlds," and "weak ties."

In recent decades, research on networks has seen path-breaking developments. Many complex networks exhibit universal properties irrespective of their constituent parts. Perhaps the best-known such property is the *small-world phenomenon*, which is characterized by the coexistence of two apparently incompatible conditions: (1) short "path lengths" between any two nodes, as in random graphs, and (2) the presence of local "cliques," interconnected groups of nodes, as in ordered lattices (Albert, Jeong, and Barabási 1999; Ebel, Mielsch, and Bornholt 2002; Newman 2002; Onnela et al. 2007; Palla, Barabási, and Vicsek 2007; Watts and Strogatz 1998).[2] Social networks are also *scale-free* (Albert, Jeong, and Barabási 1999; Barabási and Albert 1999). There is no typical number of social connections; most individuals have very few connections, while some have a lot. Social networks also tend to be highly clustered and exhibit assortative mixing. That is, nodes with many links tend to be linked with other nodes with many links (Newman and Park 2003).

A powerful example of the impact of social media was the backlash against the advocacy group Susan G. Komen for the Cure in early 2012. The Komen foundation, widely known for its pink ribbon symbol, is the largest and most widely known breast cancer charity in the United States (Susan G. Komen for the Cure 2013). In January 2012, the Komen foundation decided to cut its financing of breast cancer screenings and other related programs run by Planned Parenthood, a leading nonprofit provider of sexual health care and sex education, which includes abortion services and referrals. Planned Parenthood immediately sent news releases about the decision via email and Twitter and posted information and links to share on its Facebook page (Sun and Kliff 2012).

Within a few hours, the controversy went viral. Within a day, Twitter messages about Komen increased from a handful before the crisis to over 50,000 a day, reaching 215,000 on the day of the reversal, and then rapidly declining again to 30,000 after the reversal. Komen's initial Facebook post about the new policy received as many as 10,000 comments (Hagey 2012). The overwhelming majority of online expressions were negative. Komen's Facebook wall was flooded with negative comments. The average number of "likes" per comment dropped from 52.4 to 0.3 per post, whereas the number of comments increased significantly, going from 17.5 to 5,515 per post (Fleming and O'Connor 2012). About 75 percent of all social media posts were opposed to Komen's new policy according to social media analytical tool PoliPulse. Indeed, the dramatic increase in social media activity became a news story in itself (Preston 2012). GreatNonprofits.org, a website that allows participants to rate nonprofits, reported a 300 percent increase in negative reviews of Komen in the days following the initial announcement (Lopatto and Armstrong 2012).

After first defending the decision on procedural grounds, Komen's founder and CEO Nancy Brinker announced a few days later that the charity was reversing its decision (Belluck, Preston, and Harris 2012). This mollified Planned Parenthood proponents, but was conversely met with sharp disapproval from pro-life groups and lawmakers.

The fallout from the crisis lingered for months. Attendance at the foundation's signature "Race for the Cure" events declined by more than 25 percent (Lagos 2012; Singer 2012). In August 2012, Komen's founder and chief executive Nancy Brinker announced that she would step down to take on a new management role as chairman of the board's executive committee (Strauss 2012).

9.2 Measuring Social Influence

The Susan G. Komen Foundation case provides a compelling example of the power of social media. The ability of social networks to shape attitudes and behavior is now widely accepted. Popularized by Malcolm Gladwell's *The Tipping Point* (2000), terms such as "connectors," "hubs," "contagion," and "going viral" have entered common vocabulary. Measuring the impact of social media on attitudes and behavior, however, is a lot more difficult.

Most of the studies in the social network area use a regression framework to assess the degree of social influence (e.g., Fowler and Christakis 2008; Pattison and Wasserman 1999; Sinclair 2012; Wasserman and Pattison 1996). In a typical example, to test a social influence model one specifies a regression equation where the outcome variable of interest (some measure of opinion, attitudes, or behavior) may depend on a list of regressors, including a set of variables capturing social influence. If the dependent variable is roughly continuous (e.g., an approval scale), linear regression models are the most common specification. Alternatively, if the focus is on a binary outcome, such as whether a consumer intends to buy a product, a discrete choice model is often preferable.

To ensure that the impacts of the social network variables are isolated from other confounding factors, researchers often include various control variables like demographic information. For example, Soderstrom et al. (2016) use a linear regression model to examine the independent effect of positive word of mouth recommendations on movie box office returns. Here, word of mouth (measured through a survey of respondents) is included alongside control variables covering features of both respondents (e.g., how frequently they see movies) and the movies (e.g., how big was its budget).

While this and similar examples point to the tremendous impact of social media, some caution is in order. In addition to the usual problems encountered when working with field data (for example, measurement error, model misspecification, and missing data) there are specific problems with analyzing social influence. The root issue is that the observed behavioral correlation may be due to other factors such as homophily (the tendency of individuals to link with people like themselves, which leads to similarity in preferences and tastes), confounding effects (the tendency of connected individuals to be exposed to the same stimuli), and simultaneity (the tendency of connected individuals to influence each other).

These features lead to various statistical problems. One such problem is the issue of *identification*. A statistical model is identifiable if, using a hypothetical infinite amount of data, one can obtain the true value of the model's underlying parameters (Fisher 1966; Hsiao 1983; Koopmans 1949). Note that the identification problem is not due to a lack of data, but due to peculiar properties of the statistical model itself. In other words, identification is lacking when a statistical model has more than one set of parameters that can generate the same distribution of observations.

In the context of network models, identification problems may occur because the mechanism through which peer influence is supposed to occur cannot be distinguished from other channels of influence. For example, in the Komen Foundation case, Planned Parenthood launched its social media campaign in response to an article in the Associated Press. While we may feel confident that Planned Parenthood's campaign was instrumental in changing the Komen Foundation's policies, we are unable to determine whether the shift was due to traditional media coverage or due to the social pressures we focused on earlier. This alternative explanation would be true, for example, if users of social media like to post new tweets or Facebook messages in response to news articles, but do not read posts made by others.

In a seminal paper, Manski (1993) showed that the linear model of social influence is not identified without additional restrictions. Manski listed three different types of effects that can account for similar behaviors or opinions in a group. The first are social influence effects: individuals adopt the opinions of others with whom they are connected.[3] The second are shared characteristics of members of a network other than their opinions, for example, demographic characteristics. Finally, members of a network may be subject to similar influences such as the same news coverage by traditional media. This difficulty—also known as the "reflection problem"—can be resolved by carefully adjusting the specification of the statistical model (Bramoullé, Djebbari, and Fortin 2009; Brock and Durlauf 2001a, 2001b, 2006; Goldsmith-Pinkham and Imbens 2013; Jackson 2010).

A second set of problems pertains to the difficulty of specifying the structure of social influence. One common solution is to assume that each agent's expectations of the aggregate choice in the agent's reference group corresponds to the conditional expectation of the average individual state (e.g., Blume and Durlauf 2005; Manski 2000). This property, also known as "self-consistency," effectively imposes a mean field model of influence similar to the model of media influence discussed above. The difference is one of interpretation. Above, social influence was generated by (traditional) media coverage of the current state of public opinion. In the social media context, this corresponds to a model of random interaction, which is at best a rough approximation of the structure of social networks and does not take into account their topological properties, such as local interaction, the small-world property, or scale-free networks.

A third problem is the possible presence of *homophily* (McPherson, Smith-Lovin, and Cook 2001). People tend to associate with others who are similar. This means that preferences, tastes, interests, and other characteristics of connected individuals are likely to be highly correlated (Crandall et al. 2008). The problem then is to determine whether the correlation among connected individuals is due to network effects (social influence) or homophily (linked individuals having similar characteristics and interests). In addition, once a social network is in place, people who are connected may be more likely to be exposed to similar external stimuli. Facebook friends may develop similar interests and pay attention to similar issues. Connected bloggers may be exposed to similar news events. Such correlated exposure to external events may lead to correlated opinions or correlated behavior. Finally, individuals may be more likely to try to influence others who are more similar, because they may believe that those others are more susceptible to their message. Statistically, this means that, unless it is accounted for, homophily may lead to selection bias, which creates biased and inconsistent parameter estimates.

The magnitude of such biases can be substantial. Aral, Muchnik, and Sundararajan (2009) find that methods that do not account for homophily may overestimate social network effects by 300–700 percent. They estimate that homophily alone can account for more than 50 percent of the observed correlation among linked individuals. These effects are likely to be amplified in social networks such as Twitter or Facebook, where users can easily segment into communities with similar interests.

These issues are difficult to address. One approach is to try to modify existing statistical models to control for homophily (e.g., Lazer et al. 2010; Soetevent 2006). Aral, Muchnik, and Sundararajan (2009), for instance, use a dynamic matched sample framework based on a variety of observable individual characteristics. However, that approach can only account for homophily based on observed characteristics, and it also assumes that network structure and behavior do not coevolve.

An alternative approach is the use of randomized field experiments. Bond et al. (2012) use Facebook friendship networks to study network effects on voting. In the treatment condition, randomly selected Facebook users were exposed to randomly selected pictures of their Facebook friends who claimed to have voted. Within a population of about 61 million Facebook users, a message that a friend had voted generated over 886,000 additional self-expressed votes, with an additional 559,000 self-expressed votes if the message came from a close friend, as measured by the degree of Facebook interactions. For a subsample of self-expressed votes, voting could be validated with matches with publicly available voting records. In this case, a total of 282,000 validated votes could be attributed to receiving an "I voted" message from a close friend.[4]

Randomized field experiments can also be used to tackle the difficult problem of differentiating "influentiality" from "susceptibility." In other words, when we see agent i changing her attitude or behavior after receiving a message from agent j, is agent i's change due to j's influence (i.e., i is more likely to change her behavior when receiving a message from j than from a randomly selected member of the network), or due to i's susceptibility being higher (i.e., i is more likely to change her behavior compared to a randomly selected member of the network, no matter who the sender is)?

To address these issues, Aral and Walker (2012) created a randomized field experiment in the context of product adoption decisions among 1.3 million Facebook users for an app that lets users share information and opinions about movies, actors, directors, and the film industry. As users adopted the product, automated notifications of their activities were sent to randomly selected members of their Facebook network. These messages contained information like a movie rating, plus a link to a page where the app could be downloaded. In other words, treated and untreated peers differed *only* by the number of messages they received. This approach has various advantages.

First, since messages are sent randomly, the approach avoids selection bias (here driven by the fact that a sender may be more inclined to send a message to his friends who are perceived to be more susceptible). Second, the approach controls for homophily, including latent homophily. Third, the approach controls for confounding influences. Fourth, the automatically generated messages avoid problems of uncontrolled message valence and content. Overall, the approach allows the authors to precisely compare messages induced from spontaneous adoptions (e.g., due to correlated exposure to external events) and estimate the moderating impact of an individual's attributes (age, gender, and relationship status) on influence and susceptibility.

Aral and Walker found that susceptibility and influentiality are orthogonal. That is, both influential and noninfluential individuals have approximately the same distribution of susceptibility among their peers; being influential is not simply a consequence of having susceptible peers. Also, susceptibility decreases with age; men are more influential, but also more susceptible. Susceptibility also increases with increasing relationship commitment, and women influence men more than other men do. There are also various results on characteristics of dyadic connections and network structures. For example, influential individuals tend to cluster, but not susceptible individuals.

A similar approach (Muchnik, Aral, and Taylor 2013) can be used to separate network effects from the valence or content of a message. That is, how persuasive the content of a message is can be separated from the social influence of its sender or susceptibility of its receiver. The idea is to use randomly generated "likes" and "dislikes," and comments in randomized treatment and control conditions to test for social influence effects. Topics include business, politics, and culture. Specifically, the authors wanted to know how the first like or dislike tag, which was randomly generated, affected subsequent, user-generated likes or dislikes. Their findings show that social influence greatly affects the rating of the second vote; an initial (random) positive rating increases the chance of a subsequent positive vote by 32 percent over a baseline control group. Negative votes are also increased significantly by initial dislikes, but not

as substantively. Furthermore, once the social positivity or social negativity trend begins, it cascades. In the positive initial vote treatment, this
effect accumulates and leads to final ratings that are 25 percent higher on
average than those in control conditions. Thus, slight differences in initial
conditions are amplified through social media. In sum, these results provide substantial evidence for the social influence effect and indicate that
their accumulation, though initiated with the first statement, can lead to
highly biased social ratings.

Randomized large-scale field experiments offer a promising route to
carefully identify and assess patterns of influence in social networks.
But conducting such studies is difficult and resource-intensive. Some of
the best-designed studies show considerable influence of social networks,
but in domains other than opinion formation (i.e., product adoption or
turnout). Whether similar effects can be broadly established in the context
of opinion and attitude formation remains to be seen.[5]

In the next section we provide a theoretical perspective on social
network influence. This section is the "social media" companion to our
discussion in chapter 8, where we modeled social influence via mass media
reporting.

9.3   A Model of Peer Influence

In this section, we generalize the model of social influence introduced in
chapter 8 to the case of social media. Recall from chapter 8 that the set
of agents is S. Each agent i can hold two possible opinions, $+1$ or -1. We
denote the current opinion held by agent i as ω_i. So $\omega_i \in \{+1, -1\}$. The
entire population then can be described by a vector $\omega = (\omega_i)_{i \in S}$. We call
each such ω a *configuration* and Ω the set of configurations. Note that this
is a more granular representation of the state of a population than just
keeping the relative proportions of the population holding an opinion. This
level of granularity is important to capture social interaction via network
topologies.

Next we need to capture social networks. To do this we simply list all the
(nonempty) subsets of agents $\Xi \subseteq S$ and then specify how they influence
an agent. We can then define an *influence network* Φ that captures each
interaction component for all (nonempty) subsets of agents Ξ. As before,
a captures bias in one direction or another, while b represents the strength
of social influence, with $a \neq 0$ and $b > 0$.

In the media model, social influence was generated through reporting. In the social network setting, we instead have a peer-to-peer influence component b. However, we can easily see how the media influence model is a special case of this more general set-up:[6]

$$\Phi = \left\{ \begin{array}{cc} a\omega_i & \text{if } \Xi = \{i\} \\ \frac{1}{s-1}\sum_{j\neq i}b\omega_i\omega_j & \text{if } \Xi = S/\{i\} \\ 0 & \text{otherwise} \end{array} \right\}.$$

This new approach, however, is far more general and can account for a variety of network structures. In general, an *influence network* is simply a family $\Phi = (\Phi_\Xi)_{\varnothing\neq\Xi\subseteq S}$ of functions $\Phi_\Xi : \Omega \to \mathfrak{R}$.

To close the model we need to define transition probabilities between states. As before, we assume that in every (arbitrarily short) period at most one person changes her opinion. That person is selected with probability $\frac{1}{s}$. Conditional on being selected, individuals adjust their opinion probabilistically in response to social influence. As before, we want the probability that an individual adopts a new opinion to be proportional to the strength of social influence. We can capture the strength of social influence as follows. For a given influence network Φ and $\omega \in \Omega$ the sum

$$H^\Phi(\omega) = \sum_{\varnothing\neq\Xi\subseteq S} \Phi_\Xi(\omega)$$

is called a *social influence function*.[7] For example, the social influence function for the media influence model discussed in the previous chapter has the following social influence function:

$$H^\Phi(\omega) = a\sum_i \omega_i + \frac{b}{s-1}\sum_i\sum_{j\neq i}\omega_i\omega_j.$$

This framework is quite flexible and allows us to capture even complex social networks. For example, we can define a square matrix M of size s that captures which individuals are connected. An element of the matrix m_{ij} is equal to 1 if individuals i and j are linked, otherwise we have $m_{ij} = 0$. Note that this formalism allows us to capture directed networks. i may influence j ($m_{ij} = 1$), but j does not influence i ($m_{ji} = 0$). To capture different strengths of influence between connected individuals, we can introduce parameters J_{ij}. Note that influence strength need not be symmetric. For example we can have $J_{ij} > J_{ji}$ to capture the concept that in the relationship between j and i, individual j is more influential. At the social level, this allows us to define concepts such as "influencers" and "susceptibles." Finally, media bias may vary at the individual level. So we may want to specify a_i rather than a common a. This yields the following social influence function

$$H^{\Phi}(\omega) = \sum_i a_i \omega_i + \frac{1}{2} \sum_i \sum_{j \neq i} J_{ij} m_{ij} \omega_i \omega_j.$$

The factor of $\frac{1}{2}$ multiplying the first sum accounts for the fact that each connected pair of nodes will be counted twice in this framework.

With this definition of the social influence function, we can now derive state transition probabilities, that is, the probability that an individual changes his opinion based on social influence. As in the model of media influence, we will specify an *attention parameter* λ, and transition probabilities will be proportional to the strength of the social influence function. A low λ corresponds to the case where a transition probability is not heavily influenced by the social influence factors specified in the model; for $\lambda = 0$ transition is completely random. That is, for all possible configurations, any possible transition will occur with equal probability. For $\lambda \to \infty$, dynamics are entirely determined by the social influence function. Since only one individual can change her opinion in any given period, we have only one-step transitions. That is, for any state ω, only states that differ by one component are reachable. Conditional on being selected with probability $\frac{1}{s}$, the probability of moving from state $\omega = (\omega_i, \omega_{-i})$ to $\omega' = (\omega_i', \omega_{-i})$ is then given by:

$$p[\omega \to \omega'] = \frac{\exp(\lambda H^{\Phi}(\omega_i', \omega_{-i}))}{\sum_{\omega_i'' \in E} \exp(\lambda H^{\Phi}(\omega_i'', \omega_{-i}))}.$$

For a given influence network Φ we can then derive the unique limiting distribution as[8]

$$\pi^{\omega} = \frac{\exp(\lambda H^{\Phi}(\omega))}{\sum_{\omega' \in \Omega} \exp(\lambda H^{\Phi}(\omega'))}.$$

The main advantage of this formulation is that in one fell swoop we can characterize the behavior for any model of social influence that can be formalized via a social influence function $H^{\Phi}(\omega)$, whether the network is a grid, a small-world network, an island network, or whatever its characteristics may be.

The limiting distribution that characterizes the dynamics of opinion formation has a natural interpretation. States with a higher social influence value $H^\Phi(\omega)$ are more likely to occur. The social influence function thus defines a landscape where the peaks are the most likely outcomes.

Next, we can show that peer-to-peer interaction by itself can trigger reputational crises, in the same way as media coverage. Specifically, we have the following result:[9]

Proposition 4 *Suppose*

$$H^\Phi(\omega) = \sum_i a_i \omega_i + \frac{1}{2} \sum_i \sum_{j \neq i} J_{ij} m_{ij} \omega_i \omega_j$$

and for all i and j, $a_i > 0$ and for all $m_{ij} > 0$, we have $J_{ij} > 0$, then there exists a finite λ_c such that all $\lambda > \lambda_c : \pi^\omega(\omega \in \Omega : \omega_i = +1) > 1/2$. Moreover, as $\lambda \to \infty$, π^ω converges to a degenerate distribution that puts probability one on $+1$.

That is, we see the same self-reinforcing feedback loop driven by social influence we saw in chapter 8. What is different is that social influence is not due to media reporting, but arises from peer-to-peer influence. This may mean, for example, that the likelihood and speed of a crisis may depend on the channel of social influence and on the exact structure of social influence. For example, it can be shown that local interaction increases the speed of reaching consensus (Ellison 1993). Moreover, the smaller the size of neighborhood groups and the more connected they are, the faster the transition times are (Young 1998).[10]

As in the case of mass media coverage, the model of social networks has important practical consequences. As before, companies (or their critics) can try to shift the tone of social media postings in a more favorable direction. They can also try to complexify the issue or try to delay any decision in the hope of lowering public attention. But, in the case of social networks, additional strategies are available.[11] If the hubs of social networks can be identified, companies can target social influencers and try to convince them to change their point of view, as individuals with many connections have a disproportionate impact in spreading opinions and information, and the transmission process is faster (Goldenberg et al. 2009).

Interestingly, strong ties are more likely to spread information, but weak ties are more likely to transmit *novel* information (Bakshy et al. 2012). Kitsak et al. (2010) show that the most influential individuals are located in the core of a network.[12] Morris (2000) shows how cohesive subgroups can block the spread of opinions. When hubs cannot be identified, a good strategy is to randomly select individuals and inquire about their links. Such ties are more likely to be hubs if the distribution of links follows a power law.

9.4 Appendix

Recall that in any (arbitrarily small) period only one individual can change his opinion. Individuals are selected with equal probability $\frac{1}{s}$. Then the probability of moving from state $\omega = (\omega_i, \omega_{-i})$ to $\omega' = (\omega'_i, \omega_{-i})$ is given by:

$$T[\omega \to \omega'] = \frac{1}{s} p[\omega \to \omega'] = \frac{1}{s} \frac{\exp(\lambda H^\Phi(\omega'_i, \omega_{-i}))}{\sum_{\omega''_i \in E} \exp(\lambda H^\Phi(\omega''_i, \omega_{-i}))}.$$

We now show that a unique limiting distribution exists.

Theorem 5 *Let Φ be an influence network Φ with Hamiltonian $H^\Phi(\omega)$. Suppose the probability of moving from state $\omega = (\omega_i, \omega_{-i})$ to $\omega' = (\omega'_i, \omega_{-i})$ is given by:*

$$T[\omega \to \omega'] = \frac{1}{s} \frac{\exp(\lambda H^\Phi(\omega'_i, \omega_{-i}))}{\sum_{\omega''_i \in E_i} \exp(\lambda H^\Phi(\omega''_i, \omega_{-i}))}.$$

Then for every $\lambda > 0$ the limiting distribution of the stochastic process is given by

$$\pi^\omega = \frac{\exp(\lambda H^\Phi(\omega))}{\sum_{\omega' \in \Omega} \exp(\lambda H^\Phi(\omega'))}.$$

Proof. The adjustment process is a discrete time, finite state, Markov process. Since all states communicate, the process is also ergodic (Feller 1950). Therefore, it has a unique limiting distribution (which is also stationary) independent of the initial starting state. Let $(\pi^\omega)_{\omega \in \Omega}$ denote that distribution. The distribution is characterized by the global balance equations:

$$\sum_{\omega' \in \Omega} \pi^{\omega'} T[\omega' \to \omega] = \sum_{\omega' \in \Omega} \pi^\omega T[\omega \to \omega']$$

for each state $\omega \in \Omega$. In one-step processes, that is, when only one agent can change his behavior at in a given period, the limiting distribution must satisfy the detailed balance equations:

$$\pi^{\omega'} T[\omega' \to \omega] = \pi^\omega T[\omega \to \omega']$$

for any states $\omega, \omega' \in \Omega$. Clearly, if the detailed balance equations admit a solution, then that solution must also satisfy the global balance equations. Moreover, since the limiting distribution is unique, it then follows that the solution to the detailed balance equations must be the unique stationary distribution of the adjustment process. We will show that the distribution π satisfies the detailed balance equations. Take two arbitrary states that communicate. Thus the transition probabilities are

$$T[\omega \to \omega'] = \frac{1}{s} \frac{\exp(\lambda H^{\Phi}(\omega'_i, \omega_{-i}))}{\sum_{\omega''_i \in E_i} \exp(\lambda H^{\Phi}(\omega''_i, \omega_{-i}))}$$

and

$$T[\omega' \to \omega] = \frac{1}{s} \frac{\exp(\lambda H^{\Phi}(\omega_i, \omega_{-i}))}{\sum_{\omega''_i \in E_i} \exp(\lambda H^{\Phi}(\omega''_i, \omega_{-i}))}.$$

The detailed balance equations corresponding to a transition between ω and ω' are

$$\pi^{\omega'} T[\omega' \to \omega] = \pi^{\omega} T[\omega \to \omega'].$$

Substituting for $T[\omega' \to \omega]$ and $T[\omega \to \omega']$, the equation is equivalent to:

$$\pi^{\omega'} \exp(\lambda H^{\Phi}(\omega)) = \pi^{\omega} \exp(\lambda H^{\Phi}(\omega'))$$

which obviously is satisfied by the distribution π in the theorem. ∎

As an application we show that the media influence model from chapter 8 can be captured within this framework. With $s = 2N$, we had a social influence function of the form

$$H^{\Phi}(\omega) = a \sum_i \omega_i + \frac{b}{2N - 1} \sum_i \sum_{j \neq i} \omega_i \omega_j.$$

Using Theorem 5 the limiting distribution is

$$\pi^{\omega} = \frac{\exp[\lambda H^{\Phi}(\omega)]}{\sum_{\omega' \in \Omega} \exp[\lambda H^{\Phi}(\omega')]}.$$

Let us denote $\sum_i \omega_i =: 2n_\omega$. Note that we have:

$$H^\Phi(\omega) = a \sum_i \omega_i + \frac{b}{2N-1} \left[\left(\sum_i \omega_i \right)^2 - \sum_i \omega_i^2 \right]$$

$$= 2an_\omega + \frac{b}{2N-1} \left[4(n_\omega)^2 - 2N \right]$$

$$\equiv H^\Phi(n_\omega).$$

Therefore we can write the limiting distribution π^λ as:

$$\pi^\omega = \frac{\exp[\lambda H^\Phi(n_\omega)]}{\sum_{\omega' \in \Omega} \exp[\lambda H^\Phi(n_{\omega'})]}.$$

Switching from the state variable ω to n requires that we combine the probabilities for all configurations ω with the same value of n_ω. That is, all states ω with the same value $H^\Phi(\omega)$ are grouped into equivalence classes given by n_ω. The number of such configurations is, for any given n, equal to $\binom{2N}{N+n}$. Therefore we must have:

$$\pi^{n_\omega} = \sum_{\omega: \sum_i \omega_i = 2n_\omega} \pi^\omega = \binom{2N}{N+n_\omega} \pi^\omega$$

and for $n_\omega = n$ this is equivalent to the limiting distribution derived in Proposition 1:[13]

$$\pi^n = \frac{\binom{2N}{N+n} \exp[\lambda H^\Phi(n)]}{\sum_{n'=-N}^{N} \binom{2N}{N+n'} \exp[\lambda H^\Phi(n')]}.$$

Note also that using the Hamiltonian notation we can write the public opinion model's individual transition probabilities directly as:

$$p[- \rightarrow +] = \frac{\exp[\lambda H^\Phi(n+1)]}{\exp[\lambda H^\Phi(n+1)] + \exp[\lambda H^\Phi(n)]}$$

$$p[+ \rightarrow -] = \frac{\exp[\lambda H^\Phi(n-1)]}{\exp[\lambda H^\Phi(n-1)] + \exp[\lambda H^\Phi(n)]}.$$

Using ω as the state variable instead of n, the above individual transition probabilities can be obtained as special cases of the following log-logistic rule:

$$p[\omega \to \omega'] = \frac{\exp[\lambda H^{\Phi}(\omega_i', \omega_{-i})]}{\sum_{\omega_i'' \in E} \exp[\lambda H^{\Phi}(\omega_i'', \omega_{-i})]}$$

where, as before, $\omega = (\omega_i, \omega_{-i})$ and $\omega' = (\omega_i', \omega_{-i})$. But that means that our transition probability is nothing other than the product of the recognition probability $\frac{1}{s}$ and the conditional transition probability given by the log-logistic rule.

$$T[\omega \to \omega'] = \frac{1}{s} \frac{\exp(\lambda H^{\Phi}(\omega_i', \omega_{-i}))}{\sum_{\omega_i'' \in E} \exp(\lambda H^{\Phi}(\omega_i'', \omega_{-i}))}.$$

CHAPTER TEN

Media Influence: An Assessment

The literature on media influence has found substantial evidence for media influence through slant (how an issue is covered), and more importantly, through agenda setting (which issues are covered). However, the evidence for systematic media bias, especially ideological bias, is much more limited. Based on the current state of research, there is at best mixed evidence, and even if bias can be detected it seems to be moderate in magnitude, provided that media markets are competitive. This lack of ideological bias seems to be due to sorting. That is, audiences seek out their information from news sources that match their ideological predispositions. In a competitive media market this leads to close matches between news outlets and their audiences.

There is also growing evidence of the impact of social media. However, rigorous studies that are able to precisely identify the impact of social media on beliefs and attitudes are still quite limited, in part because of the methodological difficulties in separating social influence from homophily or the impact of external factors.

Recent research has also provided a good understanding of the dynamics of media coverage. In general, news coverage is highly skewed, that is, coverage massively favors a very small sample of events, and punctuated, that is, most events are covered for only a very short time. This dynamic, which also occurs in online sources, is driven by the severe limitations of prominent placement, whether on a title page or the first page of a search engine. Much less is known about why certain issues are covered, especially in business contexts. A connection with the intrinsic risk factors associated with moral outrage or fear seems particularly promising.

In general, properly identifying media effects, whether traditional or social, is methodologically quite challenging and usually requires the use of advanced statistical techniques or the use of randomized controlled experiments, whether in lab settings or as field experiments. In the absence of such advanced methodologies, the impact of the influence of broadcast and social media can be dramatically overstated.

The rise of social media has led to an increased interest in social influence. Social influence can occur through traditional media when a news story reports on public attitudes, or directly through social media. Using formal modeling, we could show that media influence is manifested through two different regimes. In the ordinary regime, characterized by limited public attention, public attitudes respond to changes in media coverage in a gradual fashion. In the crisis regime, characterized by high attention, opinions are adjusted rapidly, leading to an "artificial consensus," where individual attitudes and collective attitudes reinforce each other. Here, the media works as an amplifier. However, the instances where business issues capture mass attention, whether through a social media storm or the front page of a newspaper, are rare and the corresponding news cycles are very short.

Strategies can operate on both media influence and attention. Persuasion strategies focus on slant and framing, while attention-based strategies use delays or add complexity. In the case of social media, companies can also try to target social influencers, provided that there is some information about the network structure. These dynamics can lead to an intricate strategic game between social activists, who benefit from crisis regimes and thus will try to simplify the issue and create a sense of urgency, and companies, which want to return to the ordinary regime. We will discuss these and related issues in the next part.

PART IV

Stakeholders and Strategies: Firms, Activists, and Corporate Campaigns

CHAPTER ELEVEN

The Rise of Strategic Activism

Many reputational challenges for companies are triggered by (perceived or real) quality problems, accidents, ethical and legal issues, or mismanagement. But some result from deliberate attacks by political and social activists, such as NGOs, interest groups, politicians, regulators, or attorneys general, who have the goal of changing specific business practices at the firm or industry level. These changes may include corporate taxation, executive compensation, product safety, labor conditions, environmental protection, animal rights, and so forth.

At the core of these examples lies the activists' desire to change firm conduct and general business practices. Traditionally, concerned citizens and interest groups have relied on public institutions such as legislatures, executive agencies, and courts to accomplish these goals through legislation, regulation, and judgments. In recent years, however, many activists have concluded that public processes, whether legislative, regulatory, or judicial, respond too slowly and can be blocked too easily by corporate strategies. In response, they have turned to *private politics* instead. Private politics refers to actions by private interests, such as activists and NGOs, that target private agents, typically firms, by trying to create a reputational crisis or boycott (Abito, Besanko, and Diermeier 2016, 2019; Baron 2002, 2003a, 2003b; Baron and Diermeier 2007; Feddersen and Gilligan 2001; Ingram, Yue, and Rao 2010; King and Pearce 2010). The activists' explicit or implicit goal is *private regulation*, i.e., the "voluntary" adoption of rules that constrain certain company conduct without the involvement of public agents.[1] This sentiment is captured in the quote by Paul Gilding, former head of Greenpeace (Friedman 2001, p. 19):

> The smart activists are now saying, "OK, you want to play markets—let's play." [Lobbying government] takes forever and can easily be counter-lobbied by corporations. No, no, no. They start with consumers at the pump, get them to pressure the gas stations, get the station owners to pressure the companies and the companies to pressure governments. After all, consumers do have choices where they buy their gas, and there are differences now.

Private regulation occurs in countries with well-developed regulatory capacity as an alternative path to change corporate conduct (Vandenbergh 2013), but it is particularly important when public institutions are missing or governance processes are underdeveloped, such as with attempts to reduce the availability of "conflict diamonds," which are used to fund civil wars in West Africa. A recent example was the global media outrage after the collapse of a garment factory building in Bangladesh in April 2013, which killed more than 1,100 workers, many of them women, due to grossly inadequate building safety standards. Advocacy groups quickly called for multinational companies such as Wal-Mart, The Gap, H&M, and Disney to improve safety and monitoring standards at their Bangladeshi suppliers. In response, many companies, such as H&M, committed to improving safety standards, while others, such as Disney, withdrew from Bangladesh. Eventually, the campaign led to the adoption of two industrywide standards: the Accord on Fire and Building Safety in Bangladesh, which has over 150 members, mostly European companies (e.g., H&M and Carrefour), and the Alliance for Bangladesh Worker Safety, which has 26 members, mostly US companies (e.g., Wal-Mart, The Gap, and L. L. Bean). While the accord included legally binding commitments, the alliance members only made voluntary commitments, a distinction largely driven by the differences in corporate law between European and US companies (Kaeb 2013). Note that in this example, public institutions, whether national or global, played hardly any role. Rather, companies adopted voluntary changes to their business practices in response to media outrage and activist pressure.

At the core of these interactions lies the *corporate campaign* (Baron and Diermeier 2007; Manheim 2000). The activist strategy consists of creating a reputational crisis for a company, which forces management to abandon controversial business practices. The campaign may target an individual company, but often the goal is to change the behavior of entire industries. Companies, in turn, may employ both proactive and reactive strategies to safeguard their reputations and respond to activist threats. Similar to political campaigns where candidates compete to influence the electorate's opinions, corporate campaigns compete over the public perceptions of products, business practices, companies, and industries. That is, firms and activists take the processes of opinion formation described in the earlier chapters as given, and formulate strategies and counterstrategies to move the opinions of customers and other stakeholders into their favored directions.

In a corporate campaign, the role of the media is crucial. Most successful boycotts, for example, involve heavy media coverage (Friedman 1999; Vasi and King 2012).[2] To gain attention for an issue on a crowded public agenda, activists need to attract media coverage that frames the issues favorably and triggers psychological processes that are advantageous for activists, such as anger and outrage.

Media coverage offers activists at least four distinctive advantages:

1. Media coverage provides a cheap means of communicating the activists' message and concerns to the public. Since activists compete for scarce public attention, this dimension is of major importance.
2. Coverage by respected media outlets gives the campaign some prima facie credibility and puts it on the public agenda. It generates attention and makes the issue salient. Companies are expected to respond, and other players (for example, politicians or public officials) have an incentive to get involved.
3. Coverage, especially if it is visual, provides a cognitive and issue frame for viewers. For example, the use of water cannons or other heavy-handed corporate security measures may remind viewers of authoritarian regimes and reinforce a "David vs. Goliath" storyline. Media coverage that focuses on individual victims or questions the benefits of a product, for example, will increase the perceived level of risk (Slovic 2000, 2010) and may even lead to widespread fear, even though the objective risk of an ingredient or technology may be quite low.
4. Media reports about campaigns and boycotts provide information about current participation rates and thus may encourage additional participation. As we have seen in chapter 8, reporting on the attitudes and opinions of the public is an important channel of social influence and an amplifier.[3]

Sophisticated activists are keenly aware of these factors. As an example, consider the media strategy used by San Francisco tenant activists

(Shaw 1996, pp. 154–155):

> To keep the media, especially television, pushing for stronger heat laws, tenant advocates had to make the legislative process unusually interesting. We accomplished this by attracting a large turnout of hotel residents to the first Board of Supervisors hearing on the proposed legislation and stationing a person dressed in a polar bear costume to hand out flyers demanding heat. Costumed protesters at hearings garner so much press attention that it's a wonder activists do not use this tactic more frequently. The polar bear gave television cameras some eye-catching footage, something other than the typical clips of speeches.... We followed up our polar bear appearance at a subsequent hearing by distributing badges that showed penguins marching to demand heat. Our emphasis on visuals, combined with the media's sudden interest in running "day in the life" profiles of elderly hotel residents, kept the heat legislation on the media's front burner for over a month.

This shrewd use of the media points to the strategic nature of corporate campaigns, a key feature that is often overlooked. For example, many observers interpret activist campaigns solely as spontaneous expressions of outrage, triggered by corporate practices that are considered offensive or in violation of widely held ethical standards. Examples include violent entertainment products (for instance, the National Association of Women's punitive boycott against Alfred Knopf, Inc., for publishing the book *American Psycho*, with its extensive graphic descriptions of violence against women), the breaking of religious taboos (such as the protests against Martin Scorsese's film *The Last Temptation of Christ* or the 2005 boycott of dairy products from Denmark in many Muslin countries after a Danish newspaper had published cartoons of Prophet Mohammed, which many Muslims considered offensive), or highly charged political wedge issues such as abortion or same-sex marriage (as in the boycott of US fast-food chain Chick-fil-A after the company's president stated that Chick-fil-A supported "the biblical definition of the family unit"). Punitive boycotts are frequently triggered by outrage and intense emotions; they are mainly reactive, and the initial point of attack is usually the company that caused the concern. But many corporate campaigns are proactive. They are designed to engender change in business practices at companies and entire industries.

The immediate objective of a corporate campaign is to trigger a reputational crisis for companies that will force them to change their business practices. This is a crucial difference compared to the reputational crises discussed so far. Rather than being triggered by a business problem, accident, or external event, activist-driven crises result from deliberate actions of strategically motivated activists, mostly NGOs but also politicians and public officials like attorneys general. The underlying issues would not usually have made headlines had it not been for an activist campaign. Companies often appear perplexed by this type of strategic targeting. A spokesperson for Gap expressed surprise and annoyance over why they were singled out after the Bangladeshi factory collapse: "It is perplexing that they're targeting us when we're a leader in taking action on the ground while many others are passively sitting on the sidelines." The answer was given by Alex Wilks, campaign director of the advocacy group Avaaz, which had collected more than 900,000 signatures for a petition aimed at the chief executives of Gap and H&M. "We feel that H&M and Gap are well placed to turn what have become death traps into safe factories.... We're targeting these two companies because they've made commitments to ethics, and we feel that this leadership makes them well placed to not only lead their own companies but also to lead the rest of the industry to sign up to these strong and enforceable agreements" (Greenhouse 2013).

This quote also points to one of the many subtleties of corporate campaigns. If it is true that activists target companies that have made commitments to responsible business practices, then adopting such practices becomes risky for companies, as it may make the company a likely target for subsequent campaigns (Argenti 2004). But this would create an incentive for companies not to change their business practices in the first place, leading to worse outcomes for activists. Targeting responsible companies thus seems to be a self-defeating strategy. This intuition, however, does not hold. As we will see below, targeting responsible companies repeatedly can be a highly effective strategy for activists (Abito, Besanko, and Diermeier 2019).

To understand these incentives in detail, we will need to move from verbal description to mathematical models, using noncooperative game theory, a modeling approach uniquely suited to studying complex strategic interactions (e.g., Myerson 1991). Failing to realize the strategic nature of corporate campaign crises leaves companies unaware and unprepared. Understanding the complex nature of corporate campaigns and activist-driven reputational crises is the goal of this part. We begin with the paradigmatic example of a corporate campaign: the consumer boycott.

The Boycott Game

Consumer boycotts are frequently used by political activists with various agendas, from concerns over the environment, global labor standards, and animal welfare to opposition to genetically modified food products (Baron 2003a; Baron and Diermeier 2007; Friedman 1999; King and Pearce 2010). They are also increasingly used by unions in lieu of strikes (Manheim 2000). Boycotts critically rely on the participation of consumers who care about the social dimensions of a product, such as its environmental impact or the way the product is manufactured or marketed. Such consumers are an increasingly important segment of the market. They may be willing to pay a higher price for a socially responsible product or they may switch to alternative products if their preferred products are considered socially unacceptable. For example, in a 2014 Nielsen survey 55 percent of respondents stated that they would pay extra for goods or services provided by companies committed to positive social and economic impact, while 67 percent stated that they preferred to work for such companies (Nielsen 2014).

To see these ideas at work, consider the well-known example of the confrontation between Shell and Greenpeace over the decommissioning of the Brent Spar oil storage facility (e.g., Diermeier 1996, 2011; Jordan 2001). In 1991, Shell UK, the British operating company of multinational Royal Dutch/Shell Group, was facing the necessary disposal of the Brent Spar, an aging North Sea oil storage facility and tanker loading buoy. Regulatory guidelines (in this case from the UK Ministry of Energy and Environmental

Affairs) govern petroleum companies in the process of offshore facilities disposal; companies are required to rigorously evaluate disposal options and submit their preference, the Best Practical Environmental Option (BPEO), for government approval. Two options survived Shell's screening process: onshore dismantling and deepwater disposal. The former required the transport of the buoy to shore for dismantling, while the latter involved towing the structure to a deepwater disposal site for sinking. Shell UK submitted deepwater disposal as their BPEO, concluding that it was both less costly and less likely to result in an accident that could be dangerous to the environment and the workers. In February of 1995, the British government accepted Shell's BPEO of deepwater disposal.

Meanwhile, one of the world's largest environmental groups, Greenpeace International, had become aware of Shell's plan and had commissioned their own study concluding that removal to shore was a better option than deepwater disposal. Greenpeace subsequently acquired satellite communications and video equipment, and on April 30, 1995, 14 activists and nine journalists boarded the Brent Spar rig. After a three week occupation, the activists were expelled by Shell and local authorities using water cannons, an act that one Greenpeace official, Harold Zindler, characterized as having "portrayed Shell as unresponsive and inconsiderate big business." In response, German motorists engaged in an informal boycott of Shell stations, which led to a drop in sales of up to 40 percent.

On June 20, Shell announced that it would abandon the sinking of the Brent Spar rig. The chairman stressed that while Shell still believed deepwater disposal to be the best environmental option, Shell UK was in an "untenable position" because of its failure to convince stakeholders in the North Sea. Shell also started an advertising campaign admitting mistakes and promising change, despite a University of London study arguing that deep-sea disposal would likely have been less dangerous to the environment than onshore dismantling. Shell's additional costs were estimated at around $60 million.[1]

12.1   A Model of Boycotts

The decision by consumers about whether to participate in a boycott can be modeled using the approach of noncooperative game theory. Suppose concerned Shell customers would like Shell to abandon deepwater disposal.[2] They now need to decide whether to participate in a boycott of Shell, that is, to decide whether to switch their consumption decision to some other gas station in order to force Shell to abandon deepwater disposal of the Brent Spar. Suppose that on the consumption features of the product (quality, price, location of nearest gas station, etc.), these consumers have a preference for buying from Shell; otherwise they already would have bought from competitors instead. That is, if they switch to a competitor they will pay a private cost $c > 0$. If the competitor offers a cheap substitute (such as conveniently located gas stations with similar quality and price), c will be low. We also assume that, on the social dimension, all concerned customers believe that onshore disposal is better for the environment than deepwater disposal. A boycott thus results in a drop of sales for Shell. We assume that, if the drop is substantial enough, Shell will yield to pressure and choose onshore disposal. This social benefit to concerned consumers is denoted $b > 0$.[3] This benefit has the features of a public good. If Shell decided to change its decommissioning strategy and abandon onshore disposal, all concerned consumers would benefit from the decision whether they participated in the boycott or not.

Structurally, boycotts constitute collective action problems among concerned customers (Olson 1965). For Shell customers who are concerned about the company's disposal plans, it is only worthwhile to participate in the boycott if enough other customers participate as well. Such problems can be modeled as N-player ($N \geq 2$) discrete public goods games (Palfrey and Rosenthal 1984), where c stands for the (net) opportunity cost of participating (such as the extra distance a driver has to drive to buy his gasoline from a competitor rather than Shell), while b ($0 < c < b$) represents the (collective) benefit of stopping the Brent Spar from being sunk. If (and only if) a sufficient number of consumers k (with $1 < k \leq N$) boycott the product (Shell gasoline), Shell's management will decide to dismantle the Brent Spar onshore.

Agents have two choices z: they can either boycott ($z = 1$) or decide not to participate in a boycott ($z = 0$). Let X denote the number of agents participating; similarly, let X_{-i} denote that number excluding agent i. Since an agent's payoff depends only on his action and on the number of other players participating, we can write an agent i's payoff as $u(z_i; X_{-i})$, where $z_i \in \{0, 1\}$ represents the agent's choice. Agent i's payoffs can be summarized by the following matrix:[4]

Payoffs $u(z_i; X_{-i})$	$X_{-i} < k-1$	$X_{-i} = k-1$	$X_{-i} \geq k$
$z = 0$	0	0	b
$z = 1$	$-c$	$b - c$	$b - c$

The game has many Nash equilibria. Intuitively, Nash equilibria are stable outcomes in a game. A Nash equilibrium is a combination of strategies where no player has an incentive to deviate to a different strategy from the one prescribed by the equilibrium.[5] Specifically, there are $\binom{N}{k}$ pure strategy equilibria (each with exactly k boycotting consumers), and one pure strategy equilibrium where no boycott takes place.[6]

The core model shows how boycotts can occur as equilibrium phenomena even if there is only a single interaction. However, the game-theoretic approach also faces some limitations. First, the Palfrey-Rosenthal game has many equilibria, some with a protest level of zero. A Nash equilibrium, however, only specifies which outcomes are consistent with the incentives specified in the game. It does not indicate which one is more likely. Specifically, for large populations, the Palfrey-Rosenthal model implies that either boycotts will not occur with probability 1, or (also with probability 1) they will occur at exactly the efficient level. In the game-theoretic context, we are thus left with an equilibrium multiplicity problem. Note that the two types of equilibria exist for all $k > 1$ and $0 < c < b$. Second, for protests to occur, agents must be able to solve a complex coordination problem (especially in large populations) with no apparent coordination device, because all equilibria where the collective good is provided are asymmetric if $k < N$. That is, although the game is symmetric in payoffs and actions, the predicted behavior is not: some agents participate, while others free-ride. This leaves us with a puzzle: how do large populations manage to overcome a stark coordination problem, especially if there is no apparent coordination device like previous experience or existing social structures?

A common solution to the problem of many equilibria is to invoke the theory of "focal points" (Schelling 1960) based on the observation that agents use salient features of a particular equilibrium to coordinate. However, many focal mechanisms such as prior experience or related conventions (for example, Schelling's famous example of meeting in a foreign city at the train station at noon) are not available in the case of boycotts. Extensive media coverage may be interpreted as providing a focal point. However, the mechanism by which coordination is achieved through the media remains unclear.

12.1.1   Incomplete Information

To address these issues, it is useful to consider an incomplete information version of the model. There are various reasons to consider boycotts as an incomplete information environment. First, consumers may not share common beliefs about the desirability of onshore versus deepwater disposal due to its technical nature and their exposure to different media sources. Similarly, costs of participation may vary and may not be common knowledge. Switching costs, for example, may be private information and depend on the idiosyncratic determinants of consumption decisions, such as the distance to an alternative gas station. This makes it appropriate to assume incomplete information about both the benefits and the costs of participating in a boycott. Second, as discussed above, media coverage frequently plays a critical role in successful boycotts. Since one of the roles of the media is to provide information about an issue, it is worthwhile to investigate the role of information in boycotts in more detail.

We do not know the exact structure of such beliefs held by the population of agents. To avoid making detailed assumptions, we will establish our role for a whole class of incomplete information environments called "canonical elaborations" (Ui 2001).[7] Canonical elaborations are incomplete information games where, in addition to the agents specified in the complete information's normal form, types of agents exist who have a strictly dominant strategy to play a given action ("committed types"). We can interpret some of them as "zealots," who participate in a boycott no matter what, and others as "apathetic," those for whom the benefit-cost ratio is never sufficient to lead them to action. The existence of committed types can be motivated by assuming that boycott costs and benefits are privately drawn from a suitably defined common prior distribution.[8] The exact details of the distribution or any other aspects of the incomplete information model do not matter for our result. This approach will allow us to assess the robustness of the equilibria of the boycott game and sharpen its predictions. As we formally prove in the appendix, we can derive a condition that depends on only k, c, and b. The condition will specify exactly when boycotts will be successful. We can summarize this insight in the following result.

Theorem 6 *A successful boycott will occur if and only if $b > kc$.*

Thus, if boycott decisions are made under incomplete information, a boycott attempt will be successful if switching costs are sufficiently low (c is small), if the target firm cannot afford a large drop in sales (k is low), or if the perceived social benefits of the boycott are substantial (b is high). These features have previously been identified as key factors of boycott success (Eesley and Lenox 2006; Friedman 1999; Lenox and Eesley 2009).

The uniqueness condition has another interpretation. Intuitively, it captures the case where, even if the benefit of unit b was a private good (not a public good as assumed in our model), it could be redistributed among the k participants needed for a successful boycott to compensate them for their participation cost c. Intuitively, the long-term savings due to lower product prices need to outweigh the short-term costs of participating in a boycott. Examples are boycotts with economic goals, such as the consumer boycotts against high grocery prices reported in Friedman (1999) or the 2011 Israeli cottage cheese boycott (Hendel, Lach, and Spiegel 2017).

This result may surprise readers familiar with Olson's (1965) seminal work on collective action. Olson's central thesis was that large groups are much less likely than small groups to solve the free-rider problem. Subsequent work, however, has challenged Olson's thesis (e.g., Oliver 1993; Oliver and Marwell 1988). In her comprehensive survey of the literature, Oliver (1993, p. 275) concludes:

> Put simply, in some situations the group size effect will be negative, and in others positive. You have to know the details of a particular situation before you can know how group size will affect the prospects for collective action.

The model shows that collective action, here in the form of boycotts, may occur even for arbitrarily large populations.

12.1.2   A Behavioral Model

Some readers may be concerned with the use of game theory as a framework to model consumer boycotts. After all, game-theoretic models assume actors who maximize utility functions, follow Bayesian rationality, and possess common knowledge of the game form. Indeed, theoretical sociologists have developed an alternative formal methodology to study mass collective action: so-called threshold or critical-mass models (Granovetter 1978; Macy 1991; Oliver and Marwell 1988), similar to our models of social influence in chapters 8 and 9.[9]

Individuals in a population are assumed to vary in their willingness to participate in collective action such as a boycott. These variations may stem from differences in costs and benefits (Oliver and Marwell 1988), or may be directly specified as propensities to act as a function of the number of others who are already acting (Granovetter 1978). Collective action will occur only if there is a sufficiently large critical mass of agents who are willing to take the first step and thus trigger mass participation. Whether collective action occurs thus depends on the distribution of individual participation thresholds in the population. This dynamic structure is intuitively appealing, but has proven rather difficult to analyze.[10]

Fortunately, the gap between the two modeling traditions can be bridged. Diermeier and Van Mieghem (2008b) embed the boycott model in a dynamic adjustment process similar to the threshold models used in sociology. In their model, distributions of thresholds are not assumed, but are derived from a dynamic version of the boycott model. The model works as follows. In each period a consumer is selected and finds out about current boycott participation (for instance, by media reports). He then decides on whether to participate in a boycott. Cost and benefits vary randomly, but on average are the same as in the boycott model. For each consumer, this induces a probabilistic participation process, where the likelihood of participating is proportional to the net benefits from joining the boycott. At the population level, this induces a Markov process with the participation rate as the state variable. Since at most one individual can change his decision at any given time, it is a birth-death process, and a unique limiting distribution over the state variable can be derived.

The distribution will have two maxima corresponding to the two types of equilibria. In the "low participation" state all boycott participation is entirely driven by random fluctuations; it corresponds to the zero-participation case in the game-theoretic model. The "high participation" state corresponds to the second type of equilibria in the boycott model, where exactly k consumers participate. But, due to the stochastic nature of the process, there will be some random fluctuations around these values. Intuitively, the two maxima correspond to the basins of attraction of the stochastic process. It can then be shown that the relative size of these two basins depends on the parameters k, c, and b in the same way as in the incomplete information model. That is, "high participation" is more likely if and only if $b > kc$. Indeed, in the limit (as the random fluctuations go to zero) we recover exactly the same condition as proved in Theorem 6.

The condition $b > kc$ thus does not depend on whether we use a game-theoretic formulation under incomplete information or a behavioral model.[11] It is a robust characteristic of the social dilemma faced by the consumer in the context of a boycott. Importantly, the condition specifies when a boycott is likely to be successful. Sophisticated activists will take such conditions into account and design their strategies accordingly. Let us consider some of the implications of the model for activist strategies.

12.2 Strategic Implications

The fact that activists choose their targets strategically is well documented in the empirical literature (Lenox and Eesley 2009; King and McDonnell 2015; McDonnell, King, and Soule 2015). The boycott game can help us understand why. One core finding of the literature is that consumer brands are more likely to be targeted (Baron and Diermeier 2007). Such companies are already more present in the public's mind and are also more likely to attract media coverage, even if they are not the worst offenders. Companies with large market shares are particularly attractive targets since a decision to change business practices has a larger relative impact on the industry as a whole and may even set a new standard (Abito, Besanko, and Diermeier 2019; Baron and Diermeier 2007; King and McDonnell 2015). All of these features increase the perceived benefits of a boycott (high b).[12]

The same logic explains why activists may target unrelated ("innocent") business units of the same company. In the Shell and Greenpeace example, Greenpeace's strategic purpose was not only to punish Shell specifically, but also to increase the decommissioning costs for the entire European oil industry. To accomplish this goal, Greenpeace targeted Shell Germany (not Shell UK), even though Shell Germany had nothing to do with the initial decision to seek approval for deepwater disposal (Diermeier 1996, 2011). The reason? Greenpeace expected a better strategic environment in Germany, where global environmentalism had wide appeal and recycling was a national passion. In the boycott game, such considerations can be captured by differences in the collective benefit driven by stronger environmental concerns in Germany rather than the UK. That is $b_{Germany} > b_{UK}$. Everything else equal, this means that a boycott is more likely to be successful in Germany than in the UK. Therefore, strategic activists should target Germany, even if operational responsibility rests with Shell UK.

Note that Shell was particularly vulnerable to this approach because of its status as a widely recognized global brand. Customers would view Shell as one entity and would be unaware of its decentralized decision-making structure. This, of course, is exactly the way Shell wants consumers to perceive the company—in good times. But in the case of a reputational crisis, the common brand becomes a liability that can exploited by strategic activists: companies that live by the brand die by the brand.

The parameter k captures the critical participation rate that determines when a company will acquiesce to activist demands. Companies with lower k will naturally make better targets. Various firm characteristics can influence k. If complying with the activist demands is very costly for firms, for example, if they have to abandon expensive capital investments, k will be high (Abito, Besanko, and Diermeier 2019; Diermeier 2007). On the other hand, companies with narrow margins that can ill afford even a moderate drop in sales will have a lower k.

The model can also shed some light on why certain industries are better targets than others. A higher benefit b reflects a higher level of public concern or awareness, but differences in participation costs c also play a role. Industries where customers have many cheap substitutes present a lower participation cost c. Retailers are particularly vulnerable to boycotts, as customers have many alternatives. The highly competitive, low-margin environment of most retail segments also means that the industry is characterized by a low k.

This may explain why retailers are frequent targets of corporate campaigns, as in the case of working conditions in Bangladesh. The model also suggests that activists who seek to change industry practices should, everything being equal, target a *single* firm in the same industry. This will minimize switching costs for customers. That single firm should have a large market share and be highly visible, ideally a consumer brand. The issues should be newsworthy and have cultural or symbolic resonance. All this increases b. Consumers should have low switching costs (low c), as characteristic of most retail operations, and companies should have a low critical threshold k, meaning that a change in business practices should not be too costly for the company. Given these considerations, it is no accident that Greenpeace's campaign against Shell now serves as a textbook example of how to use consumer boycotts to change company practices.

12.2.1   Secondary Targeting

A particularly prominent feature of many corporate campaigns is secondary targeting. Secondary targeting focuses activity not on the business entity that engages in the offensive practice, but on some other entity in the value chain, frequently a retailer or other customer-facing entity, often with a strong consumer brand. The targeting of Western retailers over building standards in Bangladeshi garment factories is an example of secondary targeting. Other examples include the boycott of Campbell's soups over labor conditions of tomato pickers (Associated Press 1986) or the Environmental Defense Fund's campaign against McDonald's in the 1990s over the use of Styrofoam containers (Livesey 1999).[13]

Another recent example is the controversy over labor conditions at the giant Chinese electronics manufacturer Foxconn (Pepitone 2012; Xu and Li 2013). After poor labor conditions and a string of employee suicides rose to public attention, various news organizations and NGOs began calling for change. But, as our strategic targeting perspective would suggest, the bulk of scrutiny was not focused on Foxconn directly. Instead, activists targeted Foxconn's best-known customer, Apple, which quickly agreed to new labor standards and a monitoring regime (Greenfield 2012).

Sometimes secondary targeting is necessary because only the secondary target is a consumer goods company or will provide the necessary media coverage to engage concerned consumers, such as in the McDonald's Styrofoam example discussed above. Secondary targeting, however, can be the key to success even in the case of a consumer goods company and high media coverage. A well-known example is the boycott of Calvin Klein over its controversial advertising, in which apparently underage models were depicted in sexually suggestive scenarios. Accusing Calvin Klein of softcore child pornography, boycott organizers did not limit their boycott to Calvin Klein products, but also targeted over 50 department stores where Calvin Klein jeans were sold, as well as various magazines that traditionally ran Calvin Klein advertising such as *Seventeen*. Calvin Klein subsequently pulled the ads (Elliott 1995).

The strategic insight provided by this campaign is that, while switching costs for Calvin Klein customers may be high due to brand loyalty, switching costs for department store customers or magazines (and their advertisers) are much lower.[14] Note that one of the key advantages of secondary targeting is the reduction of switching costs for consumers, c, *and* the critical threshold k for the targeted business (here the retailers). A boycott of, say, Nordstrom because of Calvin Klein's advertising would not be limited to Calvin Klein products, but would affect *all* products sold at Nordstrom. But this lowers the critical threshold for Nordstrom, as even a fairly moderate participation rate will have a significant impact on its bottom line. Add to that the high level of visibility and outrage as well as low switching costs typical of retail customers, and we have a corporate campaign that is likely to succeed.

Note that this argument also suggests that fashion companies that are vertically integrated, that is, those that own their own retail outlets, are less likely to be vulnerable to boycotts. Examples include Abercrombie & Fitch and Benetton. Indeed, in such cases shock advertising may be used as a strategic marketing tool to generate additional customer interest and media attention, with the goal of developing an "antiestablishment" brand that may appeal to younger customers (Barela 2003; Tinic 1997). Vertical integration immunizes companies from secondary boycotts. In general, if activists target members of the value chain (such as retailers), they also need to understand the company's cost of switching suppliers and the consequences for their competitive position.

Of course, targeting may not stop at secondary targets. This is already obvious in the Calvin Klein example. If a magazine (secondary target) refuses to participate in the boycott, *its* advertising customers can be targeted (tertiary target), and so forth. This can lead to complex target chains. A well-known example was the Rainforest Action Network's (RAN) campaign for the protection of old-growth forests (Baron and Yurday 2004). The primary targets were forestry product companies such as Georgia Pacific and Weyerhaeuser. Such companies do not constitute attractive targets since they are largely unknown to the general public and have a business-to-business (B-to-B) model. RAN therefore targeted the customers of forestry companies, including home improvement stores such as Home Depot and Lowe's.

Of course, by now such targeting of retailers should be entirely unsurprising. But RAN did not stop there. To gain leverage over forestry companies operating in emerging countries, RAN went *up* the value chain and targeted providers of capital, that is, global investment banks. Among the possible targets RAN selected was Citigroup, in part because of Citi's large retail presence (Citi customers were asked to switch their bank accounts and cancel their credit cards), and in part because Sandy Weill, Citi's chairman and CEO at the time, had been embroiled in a personal scandal which generated additional media interest and undermined his credibility. Note that this strategy combines two types of targeting. RAN used higher-order targeting in that the secondary target was the provider of capital Citi, while the tertiary target was its chairman and CEO. RAN also employed business segment targeting like the Shell-Greenpeace case, as the cause of concern was Citi's investment banking business, but the target was its retail business.[15]

As the Citigroup example indicates, attacking a firm's sources of capital can be effective. This may involve campaigns against pension funds, university endowments, or socially responsible investors. It may also include communication with investors and analysts to convince them that an investment in an "irresponsible" company carries additional risks. Labor unions often leverage their large pension holdings to influence company conduct. This can be accomplished by threatening to withdraw money, exercising voting rights, and forming coalitions with institutional investors with similar goals.[16]

Activists do not always get secondary targeting right. A well-known example is the 2003 controversy surrounding the Augusta National Golf Club regarding the admission of female members. Augusta, home of the Masters Golf tournament, traditionally had an all-male membership. To put pressure on the club, Martha Burk, head of the National Council of Women's Organizations, targeted CBS, the network that has historically covered the Masters (De Figueiredo 2006).

Rather than asking CBS's customers (i.e., golf fans, many of them male) to boycott the network, a far more promising strategy would have been to target companies that advertise on CBS, in particular on programs with a predominantly female audience. The rationale is clear: While CBS viewers may have high switching costs (they may be loath to abandon their favorite television show or sporting event), advertisers' switching costs are much lower. Moreover, secondary targeting has a multiplier effect. Any given targeted company may switch its *entire* portfolio to a different network, not just its Masters' advertising, significantly increasing the cost to the targeted network. Ceteris paribus, this would lower the threshold k necesary for boycott success. Note that this would be an example of tertiary targeting. The goal was to change Augusta National Golf Club's membership policy. The secondary target was CBS, and the tertiary target was companies advertising on CBS's programs.

12.2.2 Labor-Organized Boycotts

An illustrative example of the strategic incentives indicated by the model is provided by the late-nineteenth-century consumer boycotts organized by the Knights of Labor union (Friedman 1999; Fusfeld 1980; Wolman 1914). The Knights of Labor was founded in 1869 as a secret organization. After a spontaneous strike by unskilled workers in 1877, it became an open nationwide organization that represented skilled and unskilled workers from all industries. The Knights' importance for our context lies in the fact that the organization ultimately used boycotts as its main tool instead of strikes. The Knights' boycotts in the later nineteenth century were spectacularly successful. Based on historical sources, Friedman (1999) reports that 72 percent of the concluded boycotts were successful in attaining the stated objective, like a change in labor practices.

The Knights was subsequently replaced by the better-organized American Federation of Labor, which continued the Knights' tradition by publishing a "We do not patronize" list. Such boycotts included both primary and, overwhelmingly, secondary boycotts. For example, in the Danbury Hatters' boycott in 1902, labor activists targeted primarily retail outlets, including well-known department stores such as Macy's (Friedman 1999). The success of this new tactic predictably led to counteraction by the employers, who founded the American Anti-Boycott Association in 1902. Increasingly, employers also used legal strategies to defend themselves against boycotts, especially if they were secondary targets. Mostly, employers tried to obtain legal injunctions against picketing and other forms of protest. When one of the founders of the American Anti-Boycott Association, the nonunion hat manufacturer Dietrich Loewe, was boycotted, he sued the union in an attempt to recover damages. The suit went all the way to the Supreme Court, which in 1908 found the hatters' union's boycott tactics to be illegal in the *Danbury v. Lawlor* case. In a later decision, the Supreme Court permitted the collection of treble damages from the union. These decisions, in conjunction with federal legislation such as the Taft-Hartley Act (1947) and the Landrum-Griffin Act (1959) which outlawed "coercive" secondary boycotts, created significant legal obstacles and led to a significant decrease in labor-organized boycotts (Friedman 1999).[17]

Labor-organized boycotts are an important test case for our model since they allow us to compare the use of boycotts with another closely related form of collective action: the strike. Like boycotts, strikes can be modeled as collective action problems, but with some significant structural differences, such as a clearly identified group of actors, repeated interaction among the members of the group, and selective incentives such as strike funds or linkage of strike participation to other social activities (Olson 1965).[18] Participating in a strike is a high-cost activity, yet strike participation usually needs to be substantial to have an effect. Thus, in terms of our simple model, strikes are characterized by high c and high k. Unions try to compensate for these problems by creating selective incentives and punishments, such as picket lines and social ostracism of strike-breakers. They also critically rely on frequent, repeated interactions across various issues important to workers.[19]

In the historic circumstances of the Knights of Labor, however, none of these conditions for success were present, since a large segment of the Knights' constituency represented unskilled labor with high turnover. This had two effects. First, workers were not unionized locally, which would have facilitated, for example, the strategic use of repeated inter-action across issues and selective incentives. Second, striking workers, especially when they were unskilled, could easily be replaced at low cost by unemployed workers. These circumstances made strikes ineffective, with consumer boycotts presenting an attractive alternative. The strategic trade-off here is between a comparatively small group of striking workers with high costs of participation and a high threshold versus a very large group of consumers with low costs of participation and a low threshold. The model suggests that in the absence of repeated interactions or selective incentives, consumer boycotts can serve as an attractive substitute for unions. Note that, once the goal is a consumer boycott, it is essential that both k and c must be low, but the actual size of the participant group plays no role once we control for k. This explains the strategic choice of secondary boycotts.

The same features account for a second example of the successful use of consumer boycotts in labor disputes: the United Farm Workers Organizing Committee (UFWOC), led by Cesar Chavez in the late 1960s (Friedman 1999).[20] The UFWOC was formed to organize migrant farm workers. As in the case of the Knights of Labor, this constituency was characterized by high turnover and mobility, the ease of hiring strikebreakers and replacements, and the absence of strike funds. The key to the successful strategy devised by Chavez was to use consumer boycotts of table grapes, a highly appropriate choice because at the time it constituted a discretionary purchase for most consumers, corresponding to a low c.[21] Consistent with the logic of indirect corporate campaigns, action exclusively focused on retailers such as A&P supermarkets in New York, where UFWOC activists picketed fewer than 30 stores. After store managers complained to their division heads, A&P pulled table grapes from all of its 430 stores (Smith 1990).

Both the Knights of Labor and the UFWOC indicate another key requirement of successful union boycotts. They critically depend on the existence of concerned consumers, that is, a sufficiently high b. Thus, union causes need to appeal to the social conscience of consumers, for example, about the perceived violation of rights (like the right to be organized as a union) or deplorable living and working conditions.[22] Union-led consumer boycotts are less likely to work in wage disputes.

12.2.3   Boycotts and Buycotts

Traditionally, boycotts have focused on corporate conduct widely believed to violate commonly held moral standards. Allegations of unsafe business practices, child labor, discrimination, or environmental pollution tend to trigger widespread outrage rooted in common values and shared norms. But some boycotts aim to force companies to take positions on partisan and polarized issues, or they are a reaction to companies having taken such controversial stances. Recent examples include boycotts of Chick-fil-A over its opposition to same-sex marriage, Nike over its support of former NFL quarterback Colin Kaepernick kneeling during the national anthem to protest police abuse and racial injustice, and Goya Foods, the United States' largest Hispanic-owned food company, after its CEO praised US President Trump during a White House visit. In each case, calls for boycotts from one side of the political spectrum triggered "buycotts" from the other side, that is, appeals to customers who share the company's position to increase their purchases to signal their support for management.

We can model the dynamics of such competitive boycotts/buycotts using a variant of the behavioral model of boycotts discussed above (Diermeier and Van Mieghem 2008a). Now we assume that there are two types of consumers with strictly opposed preferences over company conduct. We will refer to them as supporters and opponents. For example, in the case of Goya Foods, some consumers supported the company's position, while others opposed it. To focus on the dynamics of boycotts/buycotts, we assume that the company maximizes shareholder value and has no intrinsic preferences on a given issue. It thus adopts the position supported by a majority of its customers. That is, if there are more boycotters than buycotters, the company yields to the boycott, otherwise it stays firm. This assumption is likely violated in some instances, especially with privately held companies or in the case of public companies with influential and opinionated founders. In such cases, we can modify the model so that it takes a supermajority of boycotters for the company to change its position. The magnitude of the supermajority will depend on the importance of the particular issue for management. While it may take a lot more boycotters than buycotters to force a change in cases where management feels strongly about an issue, it is highly unlikely that a company is willing to maintain its stance even if it loses *all* of its customers during a boycott.

As before, concerned consumers receive a benefit $b > 0$ if the company's stance aligns with their values and incur a private cost of participation c. For participants in a boycott this cost represents the foregone consumption of a desired product. For participants in a buycott it represents the monetary cost of purchasing a product that they would not have bought otherwise, had it not been for the buycott; it represents the cost of purchasing a unit of a product to signal support for the company, rather than because the purchased unit is desired. Simply put, a customer of Goya Foods may usually buy one can of beans a week. Now, to support the company's position, she buys an unneeded extra can. For simplicity, we assume that the costs are equal for both groups. Thus, in sum, whichever side has the larger participation level receives a benefit of $b > 0$, while the minority gets nothing (payoff $= 0$). Independent of the outcome, there is an additive and private cost of participation c, where $\frac{b}{2} > c > 0$.

As in Diermeier and Van Mieghem's (2008b) model of boycotts, one consumer is selected in each period and receives information about the current participation level through an opinion poll. If the cost-benefit ratio for consumers is sufficiently low, participation rates in boycotts/buycotts can be very high, reaching 100 percent if both factions are equal in size. In such cases, consumers are completely segmented by their social and political concerns. All supporters participate in the buycott, and all opponents participate in a boycott. Intuitively, this will be the case if consumers care a lot about an issue and the cost of participation is small. If the two factions are unequal in size, a subsegment of the larger group matches the smaller group until an approximate balance in reached. The exact participation levels depend on the relationship between cost-benefit ratios and the available information about participation levels (Diermeier and Van Mieghem 2008a).[23]

The study of competitive boycotts is still in its infancy, but the increasing willingness of companies to take positions on polarized issues will likely make such phenomena more prevalent and important in the future. Whether such position taking is advantageous for companies is an open question and will depend on the alignment of customers' political views with the value proposition of the company.

12.3 Summary

Consumer boycotts are the paradigm of corporate campaigns. In this chapter, we modeled boycotts as a collective action problem among concerned customers. Specifically, we used an incomplete information version of the discrete public goods model from Palfrey and Rosenthal (1984). We showed that this model yields a unique equilibrium. The type of equilibrium depends on the switching costs, the threshold for success, and the importance of the social dimension of the boycott to concerned consumers.

We then discussed the model's consequences for activists' strategies. Here are some of the most important insights:

1. Activists select their targets strategically. Attractive targets are high-profile, well-known consumer brands with a large market share in a competitive industry with cheap substitutes.
2. In cases where activists try to change industry practices, they will not target the firm that caused the most egregious offense, but the most vulnerable. Activists will also tend to limit their actions to a single target to make boycott participation easier.
3. Activists frequently rely on secondary boycotts, that is, boycotts where the target is not the business entity engaged in the offensive practice. Targeting is predominantly driven by switching costs and multiplier effects. This can lead to complicated targeting chains.
4. Union-sponsored boycotts will occur predominantly in cases where the conditions for successful strikes are not present and where the issue is a social or political issue with widespread public support, such as rights violations or exploitative working conditions. They will be less likely in wage disputes.
5. On polarized issues boycotts can be matched by "buycotts," that is, campaigns in support of a company through additional purchases. The competition between opposing factions of consumers can lead to complete customer segmentation based on their social and political values, especially when the stakes are high and participation costs are low.

Throughout this chapter we have seen that activists are highly strategic. But what about firms? Should they engage in proactive measures like corporate responsibility initiatives? Should they ignore the issue? Should they reach out to third parties that are more credible than the company, such as scientists or moderate advocacy groups? This interaction between companies and activities is rich in strategic complexity and requires additional modeling efforts. It is to this task that we turn next.

12.4 Appendix

12.4.1 The Model with Incomplete Information

In this appendix we first prove Theorem 6. We must first define canonical elaborations as in Ui (2001). Consider any complete information game **g** with the set of players N and the set of actions A. We will review basic definitions of incomplete information games and the corresponding solution concept of Bayesian Nash equilibrium. Let T_i be a countable set of types of players $i \in N$. The state space consists of all type profiles, $T = \Pi_{i \in N} T_i$. We write $T_{-i} = \Pi_{j \neq i} T_j$ and $t_{-i} = (t_1, \ldots, t_{i-1}, t_{i+1}, \ldots, t_n) \in T_{-i}$. Let $P \in \Delta(T)$ be the prior probability distribution on T with $P(\{t_i\} \times T_{-i}) > 0$ for all $i \in N$ and $t_i \in T_i$. Denote an incomplete information game by $(\mathbf{u}, P)$. A (mixed) strategy of player $i \in N$ is a function of $\sigma_i : T_i \to \Delta(A_i)$, where $\Delta(A_i)$ is the set of probability distributions on A_i. We write Σ_i for the set of strategies of player i, and write $\Sigma = \Pi_{i \in N} \Sigma_i$, $\sigma = (\sigma_1, \ldots, \sigma_n) \in \Sigma$, $\Sigma_{-i} = \Pi_{j \neq i} \Sigma_j$, and $\sigma_{-i} = (\sigma_1, \ldots, \sigma_{i-1}, \sigma_{i+1}, \ldots, \sigma_n) \in \Sigma_{-i}$. We use $\sigma_i(a_i | t_i)$ as the probability of action a_i given $\sigma_i \in \Sigma_i$ and $t_i \in T_i$. Next, we denote $\sigma(a | t) = \Pi_{i \in N} \sigma_i(a_i | t_i)$ and $\sigma_{-i}(a_{-i} | t_{-i}) = \Pi_{j \neq i} \sigma_j(a_j | t_j)$. We set $\sigma_P(a) = \sum_{t \in T} P(t) \sigma(a | t)$. A strategy profile $\sigma \in \Sigma$ is a *Bayesian Nash equilibrium of* (u, P) if, for each $i \in N$,

$$U_i(\sigma) \geq U_i(\sigma_i', \sigma_{-i})$$

for all $\sigma_i' \in \Sigma_i$. We can now define an (incomplete information) elaboration for each complete information game $\mathbf{g}$. We consider the following subset of T_i:

$$T_i^{u_i} = \{t_i \in T_i | u_i(a, (t_i.t_{-i})) = g_i(a) \text{ for all } a \in A, t_{-i} \in T_{-i} \text{ with}$$

$$P((t_i, t_{-i})) > 0\}$$

When $t_i \in T_i^{u_i}$ is realized, payoffs of player i are given by g_i, and he knows his payoffs. We write $T^u = \Pi_{i \in N} T_i^{u_i}$.

Definition 7 *An incomplete information game* $(\mathbf{u}, P)$ *is an* ε *– elaboration of* $\mathbf{g}$ *if* $P(T^u) = 1 - \varepsilon$ *for* $\varepsilon \in [0, 1]$.

Note that the payoffs of a 0-elaboration are given by $\mathbf{g}$ with probability 1 and every player knows his payoffs. Thus, if $a^* \in A$ is a Nash equilibrium of $\mathbf{g}$, then the 0-elaboration has a Bayesian Nash equilibrium $\sigma \in \Sigma$ with $\sigma(a^* | t) = 1$ for all $t \in T$, that is, $\sigma_P(a^*) = 1$. We say that a^* is *robust* if, for small $\varepsilon > 0$, every ε-elaboration of $\mathbf{g}$ has a Bayesian Nash equilibrium $\sigma \in \Sigma$ with $\sigma_P(a^*)$ close to 1. We call $t_i \in T_i \setminus T_i^{u_i}$ a *committed type* if player i of type t_i has a strictly dominant action $a_i^{t_i} \in A_i$ with

$$u_i((a_i^{t_i}, a_{-i}), (t_i, t_{-i})) > u_i((a_i, a_{-i}), (t_i, t_{-i}))$$

for all $a_i \in A_i \backslash \{a_i^{t_i}\}$, $a_{-i} \in A_{-i}$, and $t_{-i} \in T_{-i}$ with $P((t_i, t_{-i})) > 0$. Here, we focus on the following special set of ε-elaborations.

Definition 8 *An ε-elaboration of **g** is said to be* canonical *if every $t_i \in T_i \backslash T_i^{u_i}$ is a committed type for all $i \in N$.*

Definition 9 *An action profile a^* is* robust to canonical elaborations *in **g** if, for every $\delta > 0$, there exists $\bar{\varepsilon} > 0$ such that, for all $\varepsilon \leq \bar{\varepsilon}$, every canonical ε-elaboration of **g** has a Bayesian Nash equilibrium σ with $\sigma_P(a^*) \geq 1 - \delta$.*

To prove the main result, we proceed in three steps. First, we show that the boycott game is a potential game (Monderer and Shapley 1996). This is done in Lemma 11. Then, we show that the (generically) unique global maximum of the potential is parameterized by k, c, and b (Lemma 12). Finally, we apply a theorem by Ui (2001) to show that only action profiles that maximize the potential function will be robust to canonical elaborations.

Definition 10 *(Monderer and Shapley 1996). A complete information game **g** with actions sets A_i and payoff function $u_i : A \to \Re$ for each $i \in N$ is a* potential game *if there exists a potential function $G : A \to \Re$ such that*

$$u_i(a_i, a_{-i}) - u_i(a_i', a_{-i}) = G(a_i, a_{-i}) - G(a_i', a_{-i})$$

for all $i \in N$, $a_i, a_i' \in A_i$, and $a_{-i} \in A_{-i}$.

Potential functions are unique up to a constant (Monderer and Shapley 1996).

Lemma 11 *The Boycott Game is a potential game.*

Proof. Let X be the number of consumers participating in a boycott. Let a_X be an action profile with X participants. The following function $G(a_X)$ constitutes a potential:

$$G(a_X) := \begin{cases} -Xc & \text{if } X < k, \\ b - Xc & \text{if } X \geq k. \end{cases} \tag{12.1}$$

Consider an agent d, and let X_{-d} the number of agents participating, excluding d. We need to consider three cases: (1) $X_{-d} < k - 1$. Then $u(1; X_{-d}) - u(0; X_{-d}) = -c$ and $G(a_{X_{-d}+1}) - G(a_{X_{-d}}) = -(X_{-d}+1)c + X_{-d}c = -c$; (2) $X_{-d} = k - 1$. Then $u(1; X_{-d}) - u(0; X_{-d}) = b - c$ and $G(a_{X_{-d}+1}) - G(a_{X_{-d}}) = b - kc + (k-1)c = b - c$; (3) $X_{-d} \geq k$. Then

$u(1; X_{-d}) - u(0; X_{-d}) = -c$ and $G(a_{X_{-d}+1}) - G(a_{X_{-d}}) = b - (X_{-d}+1)c - b + X_{-d}c = -c$. ∎

We can then solve for the maxima of $G(a_X)$. This is formally stated in the following Lemma.

Lemma 12 *In the Boycott Game we have for any potential function $G'(a_X)$: (i) $\{a_0\} = \arg\max_{a_X \in \mathbb{N}_0} G'(a_X)$ if $b < kc$, and (ii) $\{a_k\} = \arg\max_{a_X \in \mathbb{N}_0} G'(a_X)$ if $b > kc$.*

Proof. Let $G'(a_X)$ be a potential function. Then $G'(a_X) = G(a_X) + h$ where h is an arbitrary constant (possibly equal to 0). Then $G'(a_X)$ has two local maxima, the first at $a_X = a_0$ where $G'(a_0) = h$, the other at $a_X = a_k$ where $G'(a_k) = b - kc + h$. Hence, a_0 is a global maximum if $b < kc$, and a_k is a global maximum if $b > kc$. ∎

An action profile is *robust to canonical elaborations* if it corresponds to a Bayesian Nash equilibrium in any sufficiently "close" canonical elaboration.[24] Our results then follows directly as a corollary to the following theorem.

Theorem 13 *(Ui 2001): Let g be a potential game with a potential function G. Suppose that $\{a^*\} = \arg\max_{a \in A} G(a)$. Then a^* is robust to canonical elaborations in g.*

Proof. In the Boycott Game we have for any potential function $G'(a_X)$: (1) a_0 is robust to canonical elaborations if $b < kc$, and (2) a_k is robust to canonical elaborations if $b > kc$. ∎

12.4.2 The Behavioral Model

As in chapter 9, we model boycott participation as a stochastic dynamic process where individuals are recognized with probability $\frac{1}{N}$ and adjust their actions, that is, whether to participate in a boycott or not, according to the log-logistic rule:

$$p[\omega \to \omega'] = \frac{\exp[\lambda H^\Phi(\omega'_i, \omega_{-i})]}{\sum_{\omega''_i \in E} \exp[\lambda H^\Phi(\omega''_i, \omega_{-i})]}.$$

Rather than keeping track of each agent's action at each time t, all we need to consider is the number of agents participating, which we denote as n, so our state variable is $n \in \{0, 1, 2, \ldots, N\}$. We know from Lemma 11 that the boycott game has a potential function which can be used to define a

Hamiltonian. That is, we have

$$
H^{\Phi}(n) := \begin{cases} -nc & \text{if } n < k, \\ b - nc & \text{if } n \geq k. \end{cases}
$$

Then, by Theorem 5, we have the following result

Proposition 14 *The limiting distribution for the boycott model is:*

$$
\pi_n = \begin{cases} \binom{N}{n} e^{-\lambda nc} \pi_0 & \text{if } n < k, \\ \binom{N}{n} e^{-\lambda nc} \pi_0 e^{\lambda b} & \text{if } n \geq k, \end{cases}
$$

where π_0 is a normalization factor such that $\sum_{n=0}^{N} \pi_n = 1$.

Proof. Observing that there are $\binom{N}{n}$ possible configurations corresponding to any state characterized by n participants, a direct application of Theorem 5 yields the claim. ∎

Diermeier and Van Mieghem (2008b) show that the limiting distribution may have one or two maxima depending on the parameters of the model. Specifically, boycotts are likely to succeed, that is, k is the most likely long-run state, if and only if

$$
g(k) := \left(b - \left(k - n^*\right) c\right) \lambda + \sum_{i=n^*}^{k-1} \ln \frac{N-i}{i+1} > 0,
$$

where

$$
n^* := \max \left\{0, \frac{Ne^{-\lambda c} - 1}{1 + e^{-\lambda c}}\right\}.
$$

Otherwise, the most likely long-run state is n^*. Intuitively, n^* represents random participation close to 0. Indeed, as $\lambda \to \infty$, $n^* \to 0$ and thus $g(k)$ is positive if $kc < b$ and negative if $kc > b$. This yields Theorem 6. Thus, boycotts will be successful if and only if $b > kc$, whether we base our analysis on a game with rational actors under incomplete information or a behavioral model.

CHAPTER THIRTEEN

The Logic of Campaigns

A t the heart of activist strategies lies the campaign, the organizational framework for satisfying activists' goals. The goal of corporate campaigns is to influence business practices, both at the firm and at the industry level. Frequently, activist campaigns for change are motivated by social, political, or ethical concerns. Such goals will be different for an NGO, a union, or a public official and may be highly domain specific, but the object is to change the way a company or an industry does business. As we saw in our previous chapter on boycotts, such campaigns are not always successful, but sophisticated activists can increase the odds by strategically selecting campaign targets, objectives, and tactics. Corporate campaigns may not always aim at a boycott. In general, their goal is to create a reputational crisis for the company that forces the company to change its business. Well-managed companies may expect some of these activist strategies and adopt countermeasures. This may lead to complex strategic interactions that influence the outcome and consequences of corporate campaigns.

The first step in the campaign is to identify an *issue*. While this may seem as simple as choosing a cause most closely aligned with the activists' goals and beliefs, many other factors come into play. For example, because the market for activist support is extremely competitive, groups choose issues that are most likely to attract the public to their causes. Additionally, the issue that most aligns with the activists' true goal may be viewed as idiosyncratic, narrow, or remote. Therefore, groups often choose to bundle their campaign with a larger socially relevant issue in an attempt to broaden support for their desired outcome. For example, in its confrontation with Shell over the Brent Spar, Greenpeace framed the rather technical question of the appropriate disposal of an oil storage buoy as a recycling issue, thus guaranteeing it would resonate with a German public where recycling was viewed as a moral responsibility and environmental studies were already part of the school curriculum. In the case of the Bangladeshi garment factories, issues related to building codes were discussed in the context of social justice, not just narrow safety and monitoring concerns. As we saw in part 2, issues that invoke moral outrage or fear are particularly effective.

Next a campaign must identify a *target*, either a particular firm or an industry. As we saw in chapter 12, target selection is a key piece of any successful corporate campaign; it follows directly from understanding the success factors of boycotts. While the worst offender may seem to be the obvious target, activists may choose to attack more vulnerable firms that will concede more easily. These easy wins can lead to a domino effect of success, as effective advocacy attracts additional supporters and puts industry pressure on larger firms. Aside from vulnerability, activists also favor firms with high visibility. Increased news coverage from a campaign against a well-known brand can put tremendous pressure on a firm. Additionally, activists prefer to target firms with low product switching costs and close substitutes; if consumers do not have to make major changes in their daily habits, they will be more likely to support a campaign.

The third component of a campaign is a *demand* (Baron and Diermeier 2007) accompanied by threatened *harm* and promised *reward*. Activist campaigns are usually structured as take-it-or-leave-it offers of the form, "If you meet our demand x_D, you will receive a reward r. If you do not, you will incur harm h."[1] The threat of harm to the target is at the center of a campaign. Harm could result from a boycott organized by activists as discussed in chapter 12. Many activists, however, do not necessarily try to organize a boycott, but attempt to hurt the target's reputation and the brand equity the targeted company has built over time. Harm can take a variety of forms. The harm could be public criticism, the staging of events such as demonstrations to attract media coverage, mobilizing students to impede the target's hiring, damage to the target's ability to attract capital (whether from institutional investors or socially responsible investment funds), and, in some cases, violence against employees or property. Rewards can take the form of public statements or advertisements, endorsements, and certifications.

One of the striking features of activist campaigns is that they tend to rely on threats and negative tactics (Friedman 1999). There are many more attacks on corporations than endorsements. There are various reasons for this finding. First, in many cases, threats are easier to administer than rewards. For example, credible endorsement may require investments in verification, certification, and auditing processes, capabilities that are well beyond the means or expertise of many activists. Second, rewards alone could increase the profit of the target. In industries where activists are opposed to the product itself, such as oil exploration, mining, logging, tobacco, or guns, threats will be used almost exclusively. In other industries, where the product itself is not the problem but activists object to labor or environmental conditions, such as coffee, chocolate, iPhones, and soccer balls, we may expect some use of rewards depending on the relative costs of imposing harm or providing rewards. Such rewards are commonly structured as certificates for responsible conduct, like labeling for shade-grown or fair-trade coffee.

13.1 Activist Strategies

We can model corporate campaigns as follows.[2] Suppose an activist organization (hereafter referred to as "the activist") has targeted a firm. The firm engages in an activity x. The variable x can be thought of as paying above-market wages to workers, perhaps as part of a "living wage" campaign, or it can represent investments in safety standards that go beyond what is required by law or in abatement technologies to reduce pollution more than is required by regulators. Denote the current activity of the firm by x_0. The value x_0 is the activity the firm would consider optimal in the absence of an activist, that is, it would maximize long-term profits for a profit-maximizing firm. The goals of the firm and the activist are assumed to be opposed on x. Activists gain if firms invest in these activities, while firms lose. We can interpret this as the residual disagreement between firms and activists after the mutual gains have been realized.

The activist chooses a campaign defined by a demand x_D, a promised reward r, and threatened harm h. A firm's value, that is, its profits, is given by a function $\pi(x)$. For simplicity we assume that $\pi(x) = \bar{\pi} - \eta x$, where $\bar{\pi}$ is some (sufficiently large) positive constant and η is the marginal cost of conceding to the activists' demand. So, $\pi(.)$ is decreasing in x. Similarly, the activist assigns a value to the campaign, given by $v(x)$. The function is assumed to be increasing in x. For simplicity we assume that $v(x) = \gamma x$. Providing harm h and rewards r are costly to the activist. We assume that the cost to the activist of providing rewards is αr^2, while the cost of providing harm is given by βh^2. So, in both cases, cost functions are strictly convex.

Once a campaign is initiated by the activist, it succeeds with probability p and fails with probability $1 - p$. The probability p can be viewed as the company's recalcitrance, perhaps driven by the resolve of the owners or managers to never make concessions to activists. Alternatively, it can be derived from a dynamic contest where both the firm and the activist invest resources to win the campaign. With probability p the firm will be accommodating. That is, it will concede to the activist's demand if

$$\pi(x_D) + r \geq \pi(x_0) - h, \text{ or}$$
$$-\eta x_D + r \geq -\eta x_0 - h.$$

With probability $1 - p$ the firm will be recalcitrant and stick with x_0. Then the expected utility to the activist from a campaign with parameters (x_D, r, h) is given by

$$U_a(x_D, r, h) = p[\gamma x_D - \alpha r^2] + (1 - p)[\gamma x_0 - \beta h^2].$$

The optimal campaign x_D^* is then given by[3]

$$x_D^* = x_0 + \frac{\gamma(p\alpha + (1-p)\beta)}{2\eta^2 \alpha \beta(1-p)}.$$

with optimal reward r^* and harm h^* given by

$$r^* = \frac{\gamma}{2\eta\alpha}$$

and

$$h^* = \frac{p\gamma}{2\eta\beta(1-p)}.$$

The model has the following direct implications. First, demand, reward, and harm are all increasing in the value of the campaign to the activist γ. Recall from the introduction that one of the suggested drivers of reputational risk is higher expectations about corporate conduct. In our model this is reflected by an increase in γ. This leads to more high-stakes campaigns, characterized by higher rewards, costs, and demands.

Second, the activist's demands are decreasing in the cost of the campaign given by α and β. So lower costs lead to increased demands. We can interpret the rise of the internet and social media as lowering the cost of conducting campaigns and inflicting harm on companies. Hence, campaigns would be more aggressive (higher x_D) following the availability of social media.

These findings are consistent with our analysis of the boycott model. Consumer goods companies with well-known brand names are more likely to attract public attention and media coverage, which lowers α and β. This may also make consumer goods companies better targets than industrial products companies and lead to secondary targeting. Changes in costs will also affect the respective use of sticks versus carrots. The ratio of harm to reward is given by

$$\frac{h^*}{r^*} = \frac{p\alpha}{(1-p)\beta}.$$

Thus, if rewards are more expensive to deliver than harm, the campaign will emphasize harm. Creating and maintaining an infrastructure that can deliver meaningful endorsements, that is, those that shift demand toward the endorsed company, is challenging and costly. This implies that campaigns will emphasize harm. Note also that profits of the targeted firm are reduced by a campaign, whether it concedes or not. That is,

$$\pi(x_D^*) + r^* = \pi(x_0) - h^* < \pi(x_0).$$

But lower profits discourage investment in an industry.[4] So, if activists wish to reduce the scale of an industry, for example, because of negative externalities such as pollution, using harm becomes attractive. Third, both harm and activist demands are increasing in p. That is, the campaign becomes more aggressive for more accommodating targets.

Previous research has also provided evidence that activists will target more accommodating firms (King and McDonnell 2015). A well-known example is when Starbucks found itself targeted after adopting more responsible business practices (Argenti 2004): the so-called Starbucks effect. This finding is implied by the model. To see why, note that the expected utility from the optimal campaign is given by

$$U_a(x_D^*, r^*, h^*) = p[\gamma x_D^* - \alpha(r^*)^2] + (1-p)[\gamma x_0 - \beta(h^*)^2]$$

$$= p\left(\gamma\left(x_0 + \frac{\gamma(p\alpha + (1-p)\beta)}{2\eta^2\alpha\beta(1-p)}\right) - \alpha\left(\frac{\gamma}{2\eta\alpha}\right)^2\right)$$

$$+ (1-p)\left(\gamma x_0 - \beta \left(\frac{p\gamma}{2\eta\beta(1-p)}\right)^2\right)$$
$$= \frac{p\gamma^2(p\alpha + (1-p)\beta)}{4\eta^2\alpha\beta(1-p)} + \gamma x_0.$$

Note that $U_a(x_D^*, r^*, h^*)$ is increasing in p. Thus, everything else being equal, activists will target accommodating firms. Therefore, an ideal target is a strong brand with problematic business practices (high γ) that is likely to yield to pressure (high p). In its global climate change campaign, RAN targeted US automaker Ford rather than its rival General Motors (GM) (Baron and Diermeier 2007). The model can help us understand why. First, Ford is a well-known consumer brand, while GM operates a larger number of brands. This means that Ford was easier to harm (lower β). Second, Ford had the most inefficient vehicle fleet of all US car makers. Third, Ford's chairman and CEO Bill Ford had been a longtime supporter of environmental causes and was expected to be less recalcitrant than other US car makers.

13.2   Firm Strategies

The counterpoint to activists' targeting strategies is firms' strategies. Once a firm is targeted, its options are limited. A first option is to simply accept the activists' demands. This may be attractive to a firm if the cost of acquiescence is small or if the firm has other urgent issues to attend to that could be harmed by distractions and public criticism, such as a pending merger that requires regulatory approval. Companies may also benefit from rewards promised by activists, but as we have seen above, most campaigns will emphasize harm.

A second strategy is to negotiate with the activist to reach an acceptable outcome that is less extreme than the activist's demand. In the model of corporate campaigns, bargaining was simplified as a take-it-or-leave-it offer by the activist, but bargaining between companies and activists does take place.[5] In its campaign against Citigroup, RAN was willing to accept less than its demands but more than what was in the Equator Principles, a set of industry guidelines for the financial industry in regard to the social and environmental impact of project financing. When Global Exchange targeted Starbucks demanding that the company sell fair-trade coffee, they reached an agreement in which Starbucks would sell the coffee in its company-owned stores for one year and then evaluate whether to continue, expand, or discontinue its sale of fair-trade coffee (Argenti 2004). The negotiated outcome will depend on the respective bargaining power of the two parties and is further complicated by the reluctance of many firms, especially if they are based in the US, to sign binding agreements with activists. The lack of legal enforcement can create commitment problems which may undermine negotiated outcomes.

A third strategy for addressing a campaign is to simply stonewall or delay, with the hope that the activist will turn to other issues or targets. For two years Citigroup conducted discussions with RAN without making concessions or agreeing to negotiate. Eventually, however, it did agree to concessions. Stonewalling and other forms of costly delay can also reveal information about how effectively the activist can deliver harm or about the likely resolve of the company.

Companies can also fight back by engaging in a PR and media campaign (McDonnell and King 2013). Such strategies are often complex, as various constituencies need to be reassured. Companies can use internal newsletters or intranets to reassure their employees, a strategy used by Weyerhaeuser when it was targeted by RAN. They may use shareholder communication and press releases to connect with the investor community and use advertisements and social media to defend their positions to their customers and the public. Companies that have a direct relationship with their customers and can reach them by email or letters, for example, credit card companies, have an advantage compared to companies whose customers are anonymous, for example, a consumer packaged goods company whose customers tend to pay in cash. Loyalty programs, mailing lists, call centers, and customer databases can be repurposed for such activities.

Companies may also be inclined to sue activists, for instance, charging them with trespassing, trademark infringement, libel, or slander, as well as racketeering. While the facts may support a company's legal position, an aggressive strategy can easily backfire. A classic example is the so-called McLibel case. In 1990, McDonald's brought a libel suit against two British activists. Both defendants were unemployed and penniless and were eventually forced to defend themselves. McDonald's was believed to be in a strong legal position, because free-speech protections in the United Kingdom are less stringent than the rights protected by the First Amendment in the United States. However, the decision of McDonald's to file suit led to extensive coverage of the case in the London media and, eventually, pro bono legal counseling by some of London's premier barristers. What began as a minor campaign then turned into the longest civil suit in British history and a public relations nightmare for McDonald's (Diermeier 2011; Vidal 1997).

The difficulties of effectively contesting a campaign make proactive strategies attractive. As we saw in chapter 7, companies can build relationships with credible third parties to maintain trust with customers and other stakeholders. They can prepare contingency plans and communication strategies, including dark sites and readily executable social media strategies. Such strategies will reduce the likelihood p of campaign success. Notice that lowering p has a direct effect; it makes it less likely that a campaign succeeds once it is initiated. It also has various indirect effects. It makes the company a less attractive target, reduces harm, and lowers the activist's demands. For these indirect effects to occur, however, activists must be aware that the company has engaged in such preparatory measures. Only then can they exhibit their deterring effect. Thus, companies would benefit from publicly building relationships with credible third parties that can support them during a campaign, for example, by forming advisory boards or by openly discussing their countercampaigning capabilities.

Companies may also want to forestall a campaign by engaging in proactive self-regulation, for example, by increasing their corporate social responsibility (CSR) activities (Abito, Besanko and Diermeier 2019; King and McDonnell 2015; Maxwell, Lyon, and Hackett 2000; McDonnell and King 2013). A company may want to modify its business practices by shifting from x_0 to $\hat{x}$ to forestall a campaign. For this to work, two conditions must be satisfied. First, the activist must prefer $\hat{x}$ to engaging in a campaign. That is, their expected utility from an optimal campaign must be lower than their utility from the firm engaging in self-regulation. Formally

$$U_a(x_D^*, r^*, h^*) = p[\gamma x_D^* - \alpha(r^*)^2] + (1-p)[\gamma x_0 - \beta(h^*)^2] \leq \gamma \hat{x}.$$

Recall that

$$U_a(x_D^*, r^*, h^*) = \frac{p\gamma^2(p\alpha + (1-p)\beta)}{4\eta^2\alpha\beta(1-p)} + \gamma x_0$$

$$= \gamma \left[\frac{p}{2} \frac{\gamma(p\alpha + (1-p)\beta)}{2\eta^2\alpha\beta(1-p)} \right] + \gamma x_0$$

$$= \gamma \left[\frac{p}{2}(x_D^* - x_0) \right] + \gamma x_0.$$

Thus for $\gamma\hat{x} \geq U_a(x_D^*, r^*, h^*)$ we must have

$$\hat{x} - x_0 \geq \frac{p}{2}(x_D^* - x_0).$$

Notice that self-regulation will move a firm by no more than half the distance of the shift induced by an optimal campaign. Second, the firm must prefer $\hat{x}$ to a campaign. The firm's expected utility from an optimal campaign is given by $p[\pi(x_D^*) + r^*] + (1 - p)[\pi(x_0) - h^*]$. Recall that in equilibrium we must have $\pi(x_D^*) + r^* = \pi(x_0) - h^*$. Hence the firm's expected utility from a campaign is simply $\pi(x_0) - h^* = \bar{\pi} - \eta x_0 - h^*$. Thus, for a firm to prefer self-regulation we must have

$$\bar{\pi} - \eta\hat{x} \geq \bar{\pi} - \eta x_0 - h^* \text{ or}$$

$$\frac{h^*}{\eta} \geq \hat{x} - x_0.$$

Putting these inequalities together, we have

$$\frac{h^*}{\eta} \geq \hat{x} - x_0 \geq \frac{p}{2}(x_D^* - x_0).$$

Such an $\hat{x}$ exists if and only if

$$\frac{1}{2}\frac{p}{\beta}\frac{\gamma}{\eta^2(1-p)} \geq \frac{p}{2}\frac{\gamma(p\alpha + (1-p)\beta)}{2\eta^2\alpha\beta(1-p)} \text{ if and only if}$$

$$\frac{1}{2}\frac{p}{\beta}\frac{\gamma}{\eta^2(1-p)} \geq \frac{1}{2}\frac{p}{\beta}\frac{\gamma}{\eta^2(1-p)}\frac{(\beta + p\alpha - p\beta)}{2\alpha} \text{ if and only if}$$

$$\frac{2-p}{1-p} \geq \frac{\beta}{\alpha}.$$

Note that $\frac{2-p}{1-p}$ is increasing in p. So, the higher the probability that a campaign will be successful, the wider the range will be where self-regulation can forestall a campaign. Similarly, as harm is emphasized over rewards, and a campaign becomes more negative, the scope for self-regulation increases. For sufficiently negative campaigns, that is, if $\beta \leq 2\alpha$, self-regulation is always feasible.

This argument provides an alternative approach to understanding corporate social responsibility. Investment in CSR activities is often justified by competitive advantage (Porter and Kramer 2006), for example, by adopting a product differentiation strategy along a socially responsible dimension. The classic example here is the Body Shop and its (widely advertised) refusal to use animal testing. But few companies brand themselves as socially responsible, even if they engage in substantial CSR activities. Wal-Mart engages in a variety of responsible business practices from energy-efficient light bulbs to conflict-free diamonds, but its marketing continues to emphasize low prices. Using our model, we can now interpret such strategies as defensive attempts to forestall corporate campaigns; they are forms of proactive self-regulation, not attempts to seek competitive advantage.

13.3   Multiple Firms

Self-regulation may also switch an activist campaign's focus to another firm. This effect is particularly important if the activist can target only one company in a given campaign due to budgetary and capacity constraints.[6] Suppose firm 1 engages in self-regulation by adopting $\hat{x}_1$, but firm 2 does not. Then an activist will target firm 2 rather than firm 1 if the following condition holds

$$U_{a1}(x^*_{D1}, r^*_1, h^*_1) - \gamma \hat{x}_1 \le U_{a2}(x^*_{D2}, r^*_2, h^*_2) - \gamma x_{02}.$$

This can be simplified to

$$\gamma \left[\frac{p_1}{2}(x^*_{D1} - x_{01}) \right] + \gamma x_{01} - \gamma \hat{x}_1 \le \gamma \left[\frac{p_2}{2}(x^*_{D2} - x_{02}) \right] + \gamma x_{02} - \gamma x_{02} \text{ or}$$

$$p_1 \frac{\gamma(p_1\alpha_1 + (1-p_1)\beta_1)}{4\eta_1^2\alpha_1\beta_1(1-p_1)} + x_{01} - \hat{x}_1 \le p_2 \frac{\gamma(p_2\alpha_2 + (1-p_2)\beta_2)}{4\eta_2^2\alpha_2\beta_2(1-p_2)}.$$

Firm 1 will have an incentive to indeed self-regulate by adopting $\hat{x}_1$ if and only if

$$\pi_1(\hat{x}_1) \ge \pi_1(x^*_{D1}) + r^*_1 = \pi_1(x_{01}) - h^*_1 = \bar{\pi}_1 - \eta_1 x_{01} - \frac{p_1\gamma}{2\eta_1\beta_1(1-p_1)}.$$

For such an $\hat{x}_1$ we must have, as above,

$$\frac{h^*_1}{\eta_1} \ge \hat{x}_1 - x_{01} \ge \frac{p_1}{2}(x^*_{D1} - x_{01}).$$

This holds if and and only if

$$\frac{2-p_1}{1-p_1} \geq \frac{\beta_1}{\alpha_1}.$$

So we have the same condition as above. In the special case where the two firms have the same parameter values, we get

$$x_{01} \leq \hat{x}_1,$$

which is always true. Therefore, firm 1 will self-regulate under the same conditions as in the single-firm case.

In this analysis, firm 2 was passive, but suppose that both firms can self-regulate, and as before the activist can target only one firm. For simplicity consider the case of two homogeneous firms with identical parameter values. Each firm will try to adopt tougher self-regulation than the other to avoid being targeted. This will be the case as long as $\pi(\hat{x}) \geq \bar{\pi} - \eta x_0 - \frac{p\gamma}{2\eta\beta(1-p)}$. Now, denote the maximal level of self-regulation that satisfies this inequality as $\bar{x}$. Then both firms will compete until they both reach level $\bar{x}$. So, we have

$$\bar{\pi} - \eta\bar{x} = \bar{\pi} - \eta\hat{x}_1 = \bar{\pi} - \eta\hat{x}_2 = \bar{\pi} - \eta x_0 - \frac{p\gamma}{2\eta\beta(1-p)} \text{ or}$$

$$\bar{x} = \hat{x}_1 = \hat{x}_2 = x_0 + \frac{p\gamma}{2\eta^2\beta(1-p)}.$$

This means that activism can have a multiplier effect. Both firms will engage in CSR activities to avoid being targeted, even if a campaign can target only one firm. Overall, activists will benefit from having firms compete in a "race to the top" compared to deciding on a single firm.[7] This creates a collective action problem for firms in that they have an incentive to act collectively as an industry to avoid a race to the top, where companies adopt increasingly tougher standards to avoid being targeted. This can be accomplished by adopting industrywide standards. An example is the Sustainable Forest Initiative established by the US forest products industry (Baron and Diermeier 2007). Over 90 percent of all US firms participated in the initiative.

The ability of firms to solve this collective action problem will depend on industry structure and firms' ability to leverage existing assets such as industry associations. Since such industry agreements are voluntary, ensuring industry participation and compliance can be challenging. In some cases, an industry may benefit from eventually transitioning from voluntary agreements to legally binding government regulation to solve collective action problems. Companies also need to understand that establishing such agreements will not necessarily end activist campaigns, as agreements acceptable to the industry will usually fall considerably short of the goals of activists. That said, self-regulation, whether at the industry or firm level, lowers the net benefit of continuing a campaign (the b in chapter 12), and thus will tend to make future campaigns less effective.

13.4 Commitment and the Activism Paradox

Global activism has emerged as a potent source of reputational challenges for firms. Taking proactive steps, whether at the firm or industry level, can lower reputational risk. But the desirability of concessions, whether during a campaign or as a form of proactive self-regulation, may depend on how credibly the activists can commit to not demanding more from the firm (Baron and Diermeier 2007). The problem is that, once a firm makes a concession, the activist can consider this as the new status quo x_0 and demand more. But, anticipating the future demands of activists, the firm will not make concessions in the first place.[8] The inability to credibly commit thus may undermine the effectiveness of activism. To solve this problem, activists may want to build a reputation for trustworthiness through the conduct of their campaigns. But this will be difficult if companies face multiple activist groups, as making concessions to avoid a campaign by one activist may not satisfy a more aggressive or radical activist. Activists compete for donations, volunteers, and other forms of support, and strive to develop their own "brand." This may create an incentive for radical activists to outflank more moderate NGOs. The use of self-regulation, intended to shift an activist's focus to another potential target, may instead shift the firm from being targeted by a moderate activist to facing a more radical activist. For example, a firm that demonstrates that it is responsive to activist pressure may reveal itself as accommodating and become a better target for future campaigns, as was the case for Starbucks (Argenti 2004). Moreover, if chosen as a target in the future, a target that reveals that it is soft may face a more aggressive campaign with stronger demands and threats (Abito, Besanko, and Diermeier 2019; King and McDonnell 2015). Therefore, building a reputation for toughness may be in the interest of the firm, which is counterproductive for activists

(Baron and Diermeier 2007). These paradoxes can be resolved only in a dynamic framework of corporate reputation, which we turn to next.

13.5   CSR, Activists, and the Dynamics of Corporate Reputation

These considerations suggest that a fuller understanding of the reputational risk from activism requires a dynamic perspective that models corporate reputation directly. This will also allow us to gain a more nuanced understanding of corporate campaigns, especially for large companies with strong brand equity. It will also provide a new approach to CSR. As discussed above, many traditional explanations for CSR activities point to a competitive advantage for companies (Porter and Kramer 2006; Maxwell, Lyon, and Hackett 2000). In addition to reaching consumers through socially responsible brands, researchers have tried to identify alternative benefits from investing in socially responsible business practices, such as better ability to attract and retain talent, better employee engagement leading to higher productivity, better access to socially responsible investors, and many more.[9] However, the evidence that CSR activities are correlated with a positive financial impact is mixed at best (Margolis and Walsh 2001; Vogel 2006). Indeed, investing in CSR activities may have a (moderately) negative impact (Fisher-Vanden and Thorburn 2011; Jacobs, Singhal, and Subramanian 2010).

These findings have been viewed as puzzling and have led to alternative explanations for CSR activities rooted in motivations other than shareholder value maximization. Such approaches have focused on agency problems where senior managers spend company resources to advance their own goals, for example, a specific social agenda or the desire to improve their personal reputation, without any benefit for shareholders. According to this view, corporate citizenship is simply a form of non-monetary compensation to management, similar to a perk (Baron 2008, 2009).

An alternative approach, discussed above, views CSR activities as defensive in nature and intended to forestall a campaign or shift activist attention to a competitor. But such accounts become more problematic once we take the dynamic aspect of corporate reputation seriously. Unless activists can commit to refrain from repeated targeting, proactive self-regulation is not in the interest of companies. Activists can simply demand further, more costly changes, and companies that have accepted activist demands are revealed as "soft," which leads to increased targeting and more aggressive demands. Indeed, repeated targeting of firms by activists is quite common. Examples are campaigns against Starbucks, Wal-Mart, Coca-Cola, McDonald's, and Gap. Yet these firms continue with multimillion-dollar investments to address social problems year after year that have little to do with their brands and are unlikely to further increase brand equity.

A dynamic account of corporate reputation, however, can explain such puzzles while maintaining a perspective where companies maximize shareholder value.[10] Specifically, here CSR activities are modeled as the private provision of a public good or as a form of private regulation (Baron 2008; Besley and Ghatak 2007; Kotchen 2009). We also assume that engaging in CSR activities provides a (moderate) benefit for firms by improving their reputations. As discussed above, whether such a benefit can be empirically identified is hotly debated in the literature, but it is certainly widely believed by practitioners (Porter and Kramer 2006).

In our context, we are less interested in taking a side in this debate, but by making these assumptions we can clearly separate two kinds of CSR activities: "offensive" activities which provide benefits for the company as argued in much of the CSR literature, and "defensive" activities which are intended to forestall corporate campaigns or at least mitigate their impacts, as discussed in the Baron and Diermeier (2007) model. Offensive CSR activities are based on seeking competitive advantages in market competition for customers, talent, or capital by improving the company's reputation, while defensive CSR activities are intended to mitigate the impact of corporate campaigns.[11] Defensive CSR activities are not rooted in the desire to gain a competitive edge, but in risk management, that is, to protect corporate reputations in the presence of activists.

We can model this as follows. We consider a single firm and an activist organization ("the activist") that may engage in a corporate campaign against the firm.[12] The firm's operations are assumed to contribute to a social harm, such as a negative environmental externality or unsafe conditions in an upstream supplier's plant. The harm-producing activity is not regulated due to factors like a lack of regulatory capacity, the absence of legal jurisdiction, or political gridlock. To fix ideas, consider examples such as conflict diamonds, the lack of safety standards among suppliers as in the case of the collapse of the Rana Plaza factory in Bangladesh, or the destruction of tropical rainforests due to palm oil plantations.

Firms can invest in costly CSR activities x, for example, by requiring safety standards that increase the costs of production or by switching to more expensive but more environmentally responsible business practices. The activist can launch a campaign against the firm. The intensity of the activist's campaign against the firm is denoted by y. The actions by the firm x and the activist y jointly determine the stochastic evolution of the firm's reputation r.

Reputations are understood as general evaluations of a company, as in the online processing model (Anderson 1965; Hastie and Park 1986; Lodge 1995; Lodge, Steenbergen, and Brau 1995; Lodge and Taber 2013), our fifth principle of opinion formation. That is, reputations are interpreted as running tallies that aggregate the sequence of impressions and evaluations of a company stored in long-term memory. Recall that, while such online tallies aggregate experienced affect and considerations associated with an entity, the specific details that originally gave rise to the evaluation tend to be forgotten.[13]

Here, online tallies, and thus reputations, are influenced by the actions of activists through corporate campaigns, and by companies through CSR activities. Corporate campaigns tend to lower a company's reputation; CSR activities tend to elevate it. Consistent with the online processing model, these effects are not deterministic, but probabilistic. They constitute positive or negative shocks to a company's reputation. Specifically, the interaction between the activist and the firm is modeled as a dynamic stochastic game with three periods $t = 1, 2, 3$. The strength of the firm's reputation is $r \in \mathbb{Z}$, which is the state variable in the model.[14]

Reputational dynamics are determined by the following process:

$$r_t = r_{t-1} + \widetilde{f}_t - \widetilde{a}_t,$$

where $\widetilde{f}_t \in \{0, 1\}$ is a positive shock to the firm's reputation, and $\widetilde{a}_t \in \{0, 1\}$ is a negative shock to the firm's reputation. Let $p = \Pr(\widetilde{f}_t = 1) = P(x_t)$ and $q = \Pr(\widetilde{a}_t = 1) = Q(y_t)$, where $P(0) = 0$, $P'(x) > 0$, $Q(0) = 0$, and $Q'(y) > 0$. Thus, more CSR activities x in a given period increase the probability of a positive impression on the public, while greater campaign intensity y in that period increases the probability of a negative impression. If positive and negative impressions occur in the same period, they offset each other, and the firm's reputation remains unchanged. Because there is a one-to-one relationship between x and p, and y and q, respectively, we can simply refer to p and q as CSR and campaign intensity, respectively.

Letting $h_u(p,q)$, $h_s(p,q)$, and $h_d(p,q)$ denote the probabilities that the firm's reputation increases, stays the same, and decreases from one period to the next, we have $h_u(p,q) = p(1-q)$, $h_d(p,q) = (1-p)q$, and $h_s(p,q) = 1 - h_u(p,q) - h_d(p,q)$.

The impact of reputation on the firm's profitability is given by a reduced-form profit function $\pi(r)$, where $\pi(\cdot)$ is strictly increasing and strictly concave in r. We thus assume that a stronger reputation is valuable to the firm for competitive reasons, but with diminishing returns from increasing reputation. In other words, a single-period profit "hit" from reputational loss is more significant than the single-period profit "bump" from reputational improvement. The company thus experiences decreasing (static) returns from reputation.

The drivers of this value can vary across industries and firms. As discussed above, it may be based on higher demand for the firm's products due to concerned consumers (e.g., Baron 2008; Besley and Ghatak 2007), or reputation may give the firm an edge in recruiting talent, increase employment productivity, or lower the cost of capital, perhaps by attracting a sufficiently large segment of socially conscious investors. The total cost to the firm of private regulation is given by $c(p) = \frac{c}{2}p^2$, where $c > 0$.

CSR activities yield a marginal social benefit of ωp, where $\omega > 0$. This social marginal benefit reflects the real external benefits of CSR activities (e.g., the social benefits of reduced carbon emissions or improved safety standards), as well as the net balance of any changes in surplus among parties external to the firm who are affected by CSR, such as the increase in consumer surplus from a voluntary price cut, or the net change in worker plus supplier surplus due to a code of conduct requiring the firm's upstream suppliers to pay higher wages. Activists may care more passionately about social ills than society at large. This is captured by assuming that the activist values the firm's CSR activities as $\psi \omega p$, where $\psi \geq 1$ measures the activist's "passion." Campaigns are costly, with a cost function of $\frac{\gamma q^2}{2}$, where $\gamma \geq 0$.

Note that the firm's objective is the maximization of the discounted value of its profits; it has no intrinsic preference for engaging in CSR activities. It does so only to improve its reputation or to blunt the effort of the activist. The activist, on the other side, is "pragmatic." It cares only about the level of CSR activities provided by the firm, and it receives no intrinsic utility from harming the firm's reputation. That is, the activist seeks to harm the firm's reputation in order to keep it motivated to engage in more substantial CSR activities.

Not all activists will fall under this description, and some may want to directly hurt the firm's reputation or business operations. In other cases, protest may be largely symbolic or expressive. Still, activists compete in a market for funding and volunteer labor, and need to be pragmatic to some extent if their supporters care about the social ill (Baron 2012). Finally, note that the firm and the activist are assumed to be unable to contract on the provision of CSR activities or the activist's conduct during a campaign. In practice, of course, bargaining between activists and firms sometimes does occur (Baron 2003b), but there are various reasons why bargaining solutions may be infeasible. For legal reasons, US companies are usually unwilling to sign legally binding commitments. Hence, there is no legal mechanism to enforce any agreement. Some activist groups may be unwilling to strike deals with firms lest their volunteers or donors see them as "selling out." Additionally, as discussed above, coming to an agreement with one activist group does not protect a firm from being targeted by a different, perhaps more radical, activist. For these reasons we set bargaining aside and focus on the aspects of the conflict between activists and firms that cannot be solved through negotiations.

The strategic interaction between the activist and the firm is modeled as a dynamic, stochastic game (Doraszelski and Pakes 2007; Mertens and Parthasarathy 1991; Shapley 1953). An equilibrium is described by $\{(p_{rt}, q_{rt}, u_{rt}, v_{rt}) \mid (r, t) \in \mathcal{I} \times \{1, 2, 3\}\}$, where u_{rt} and v_{rt} are the firm's and activist's values in state r, period t. Letting $\beta_F \in (0, 1)$ and $\beta_A \in (0, 1)$ denote the discount factors of the firm and activist, respectively, the values u_{rt} and v_{rt} are given by the Bellman equations:

$$u_{rt} = \max_{p_{rt} \in [0,1]} U_{rt}(p_{rt}, q_{rt}) \equiv \pi_r - \frac{cp_{rt}^2}{2} + \beta_F u_{r,t+1}$$

$$+ \beta_F \{\Delta u_{r,t+1} h_u(p_{rt}, q_{rt}) - \Delta u_{r-1,t+1} h_d(p_{rt}, q_{rt})\}; \qquad (13.2)$$

$$v_{rt} = \max_{q_{rt} \in [0,1]} V_{rt}(p_{rt}, q_{rt}) = \psi \omega p_{rt} - \frac{\gamma q_{rt}^2}{2} + \beta_A v_{r,t+1}$$

$$+ \beta_A \{\Delta v_{r,t+1} h_u(p_{rt}, q_{rt}) - \Delta v_{r-1,t+1} h_d(p_{rt}, q_{rt})\}, \qquad (13.3)$$

where $\Delta u_{rt} \equiv u_{r+1,t} - u_{rt}$ and $\Delta v_{rt} \equiv v_{r+1,t} - v_{rt}$, and it is understood that $u_{r4} = v_{r4} = 0$.

Intuitively, the firm's discounted expected utility consists of the per-period payoff $\pi_r - \frac{cp_{rt}^2}{2}$ plus the discounted expected future payoff from the cases where its reputation stays the same, goes up, or goes down. Similarly, for the activist, its discounted expected utility consists of the per-period payoff $\psi \omega p - \frac{\gamma q_{rt}^2}{2}$ plus the discounted expected payoff from the cases where the company's reputation stays the same, goes up, or goes down. In equilibrium, the firm and the activist choose levels of CSR (for the firm) and campaign activity (for the activist) in each period that are optimal given the choices of the other actor.

We can now consider the case of "offensive" CSR. This corresponds to the CSR activities that the firm would engage in on its own, without an activist. Such activities are usually motivated by competitive strategy, such as the desire to attract socially motivated employees and investors.

We denote this case by the superscript 0. We then have the following result.[15]

Proposition 15 *(Abito, Besanko, and Diermeier 2019). In the absence of an activist the firm chooses the following levels of CSR activities:*

$$p_{r3}^0 = 0,$$

$$p_{r2}^0 = \frac{\beta_F \Delta \pi_r}{c} \in (0, 1),$$

$$p_{r1}^0 = \frac{\beta_F \Delta u_{r2}^0}{c} \in (0, 1).$$

which yields the following per-period payoffs

$$u_{r3}^0 = \pi_r,$$

$$u_{r2}^0 = (1 + \beta_F)\pi_r + \frac{\beta_F^2 (\Delta \pi_r)^2}{2c},$$

$$u_{r1}^0 = \pi_r + \beta_F u_{r2}^0 - \frac{c}{2}(p_{r1}^0)^2 + \beta_F p_{r1}^0 \Delta u_{r2}^0.$$

Note that, in period 3, the firm does not engage in any CSR activity. This is a consequence of assuming a three-period model since current CSR activities influence only future reputational states. The firm does engage in CSR activities in periods 1 and 2 even though no activist is present. However, such activity is decreasing in reputation. That is, we have $p_{r+1,2}^0 < p_{r2}^0$ and $p_{r+1,1}^0 < p_{r1}^0$. Note also that reputation is valuable. That is, the firm's value is strictly increasing in reputation in each period, that is, $\Delta u_{rt}^0 > 0$, $r \in \mathcal{I}, t = 1, 2, 3$, and that increase in value is higher the more patient the firm is, that is, $\frac{\partial \Delta u_{rt}^0}{\partial \beta_F} > 0$, $t = 1, 2$. The firm, however, exhibits diminishing marginal returns to reputation, that is, $\Delta u_{rt}^0 < \Delta u_{r-1,t}^0$, $t = 1, 2$, which leads to decreasing CSR activities in reputation level.

This means that the (assumed) property of diminishing static returns to reputation endogenously "cascades backward" to make the firm's value function concave in reputation in period 2. That is, the firm experiences diminishing *dynamic* returns to reputation: the higher the current reputation, the less likely a firm is to engage in CSR activities.

This is the key insight of the no-activist case: *profit-maximizing firms will tend to coast on their reputation*. It is this feature that creates incentives for activists to engage in campaigning activities. By targeting a firm effectively and thus decreasing the firm's reputation, activists prevent the firm from coasting and force it to continue to invest in CSR activities. To alleviate this effect, firms now have an incentive to invest in *more* CSR activities to prevent or alleviate the negative impact of activist campaigns.

To see this, consider the case with an activist (Abito, Besanko, and Diermeier 2019). First, as in the no-activist case, the firm does not engage in any CSR activities in the last period. Therefore, the activist has no incentive to launch a campaign in period 2 and, a fortiori, in period 3. Hence, the firm's private regulation in period 2 equals the level in the no-activist case, that is, $p_{r2}^* = p_{r2}^0$. The equilibrium values for the firm in periods 2 and 3 correspond to the values in the no-activist benchmark which, as noted above, are strictly increasing in reputation level. The activist's value in period 2, $v_{r2}^* = \psi \omega \frac{\beta_F \Delta \pi_r}{c}$, by contrast, is decreasing in the firm's reputation in period 2. This creates the conflict between the firm and the activist. The activist engages in campaign activities in period 1 because it prefers the firm to be in a lower reputational state in period 2, as a lower-reputation firm undertakes more private regulation in period 2 than a higher-reputation firm. In essence, the activist wants to put the firm in a position where it is "hungry" to improve its reputation between periods 2 and 3. This motivation to prevent the firm from coasting does not emerge from existing static models of activists; it is a direct consequence of the dynamic nature of corporate reputation.

One can now characterize the impact of the activist on private regulation in the first period and on expected private regulation in the second period. This is expressed in the following proposition.[16]

Proposition 16 *(Abito, Besanko, and Diermeier 2019) For any initial reputation level r, the presence of the activist (1) increases private regulation in the first period, that is, $p_{r1}^* > p_{r1}^0$, and (2) increases expected private regulation in the second period, that is, $E_r^*(p_2) > E_r^0(p_2)$.*

Thus, in the presence of an activist, the firm engages in additional CSR activities given by $p_{r1}^* - p_{r1}^0$ and $E_r^*(p_2) - E_r^0(p_2)$. These differences in actual CSR activities in period 1 and expected CSR activities in period 2 are *defensive* in nature. They are not motivated by competitive considerations, for example, to attract conscious consumers, but are driven by the campaign activities of activists. Note that there are two different channels for defensive CSR. The activist increases private regulation *state by state* in period 1, a static effect. In period 2, however, there is no static effect due to the activist since $p_{r2}^* = p_{r2}^0$, that is, second-period private regulation is the same in any given state with or without the activist. The increase in expected private regulation in period 2 arises because the activist campaign (and the associated change in first-period private regulation) changes the *evolution* of reputation between periods 1 and 2. It is purely dynamic in nature.

The risk aversion of the firm with respect to its reputation plays a key role in the proposition. It is what leads to the conflict between the firm and the activist that is the fuel for an activist campaign, and it is what induces the firm to choose a higher level of CSR in period 1 than it would have in the absence of the activist. Indeed, when returns to reputation are increasing, the interests of the firm and the activist are fully aligned; if the activist could somehow help the firm improve its reputation, it would do so.

If the relationship between π_r and r is s-shaped, with an initial region of increasing marginal returns followed by a region of diminishing marginal returns to reputation, the activist would support the firm in the stage of increasing returns to reputation, because as the firm's reputation grows over this range, it would increase its CSR activities. Once the firm crosses the threshold to diminishing returns to reputation, an activist would engage in a corporate campaign. In such cases an activist would appear to "turn" on a firm that it previously supported. Such a pattern would be consistent with changing patterns of activism as a company moves through its life cycle from start-up to mature business.

We can also show that, in the limiting case in which reputational enhancement has no value for a firm with reputation r, we still have $p_{r1}^* > 0$. Thus, the model predicts that a firm would engage in (defensive) CSR activities even if any resulting reputational gains have no impact on the present value of its profits over time. That is, firms would engage in private regulation even if there was no incentive to engage in offensive CSR activities. This extreme case demonstrates a role for activists in stimulating defensive CSR, that is, private regulation that is solely about defending the existing value of a brand rather than making a brand more valuable. For example, Wal-Mart's commitment to refrain from using conflict diamonds is not likely to enhance its competitive position, yet it may lessen the impact of activist campaigns. Note that, in such cases, we would expect companies to communicate their stance to activists and other interested parties but not to advertise it broadly.[17]

The model has various empirical implications. First, firms may use CSR to offset past episodes of social irresponsibility that have damaged their reputations (Kotchen and Moon 2012). This "do good to offset the bad" approach serves as a form of risk mitigation in the face of possible reputation loss (Minor 2015; Minor and Morgan 2011). Second, observed CSR activities can be associated with a reduction in firm value, given the less favorable distribution over future reputational states induced by the campaign (Fisher-Vanden and Thorburn 2011; Jacobs, Singhal, and Subramanian 2010). This is not the case because the firm is failing to maximize shareholder value, but rather because of an event (targeting by an activist) that results in a less favorable reputational trajectory over time. Third, large, well-financed, highly visible firms are more attractive targets for activists and are more vulnerable to crises. Fourth, the activist's campaign intensity and the firm's CSR activities increase in activist passion, patience, and cost efficiency, as well as social marginal benefit. Fifth, the dynamics of corporate reputation and CSR activities can be complex; they may increase or decrease over time. Such patterns do not indicate "success" or "failure" of firm strategies, but are the consequence of the intricate strategic interaction between firms and activists.

The model can be extended to include different activist tactics: rewards versus harm and criticism versus confrontation (Abito, Besanko, and Diermeier 2019). For example, well-financed activists are more likely to rely on confrontation and less likely to rely on criticism. Ultimately, activists that choose both confrontation and criticism are the most effective.

As before, we can also consider settings that involve multiple firms, such as relationships between a supplier and a customer or the impact of market competition. For example, when choosing among targets in a supply chain, activists will prefer to target downstream firms, which sell products to end consumers, as opposed to upstream firms, which sell products to other businesses. In the case of market competition, under most circumstances and holding other characteristics constant, activists will target the market leader more aggressively than the market follower. This phenomenon is accentuated if the market leader's CSR activities have higher social marginal benefit than the follower's, for example, because of scale or a larger supply chain. This is consistent with the stylized facts that McDonald's is a more frequent target of activists than Burger King or Wendy's, and Wal-Mart is more frequently targeted than Target. However, if the industry has extremely weak horizontal product differentiation, for example, in commodities markets, the activist tends to target the follower more aggressively than the leader.

In general, then, there is an interaction between firm-level characteristics and industry-level characteristics when it comes to activist targeting decisions. This can have industrywide consequences. For example, industries in which product differentiation is weak will have fewer CSR activities than industries in which product differentiation is strong. Finally, it is not unusual for activists to target both competitors in an industry simultaneously, especially if activists are well funded. Such industrywide campaigns directed at firms tend to occur in high-profile industries with significant media coverage.

13.6 Appendix

We now solve for the optimal (x_D^*, r^*, h^*) discussed in chapter 13.

To derive x_D^*, r^*, and h^*, note that the activist has an incentive to increase its demands until an accommodating firm is indifferent between conceding and holding out. We can then write

$$-\eta x_D + r \geq -\eta x_0 - h.$$

In fact, the activist's payoff is decreasing in r and h, and increasing in x_D, so this must hold with equality

$$x_D = x_0 + \frac{h+r}{\eta}. \tag{1}$$

Therefore, the optimal campaign must solve (substituting the constraint):

$$max_{(r,h)} U_a^*(r,h) := p\left[\gamma\left(x_0 + \frac{h+r}{\eta}\right) - \alpha r^2\right] + (1-p)[\gamma x_0 - \beta h^2].$$

Necessary conditions for a solution are

$$\frac{\partial U^*}{\partial r} = \frac{p\gamma}{\eta} - 2p\alpha r = 0.$$

Hence,

$$r^* = \frac{\gamma}{2\eta\alpha}. \tag{2}$$

Moreover,

$$\frac{\partial U^*}{\partial h} = \frac{p\gamma}{\eta} - 2(1-p)\beta h = 0.$$

Therefore,

$$h^* = \frac{p\gamma}{2\eta\beta(1-p)}. \tag{3}$$

Substituting (2) and (3) into (1) gives the solution

$$x_D^* = x_0 + \frac{\gamma(p\alpha + (1-p)\beta)}{2\eta^2\alpha\beta(1-p)}.$$

Note that U^* is concave and separable in r and h, so that (2) and (3) are also sufficient conditions.

CHAPTER FOURTEEN

The Strategic Interaction between Activists and Firms

In the introduction we discussed four major forces that have increased reputational risks for companies. These were increased media scrutiny and the rise of social media, higher expectations about corporate conduct along ethical and social dimensions, increasingly complex global supply chains, and more business models based on trust. As we have seen in previous chapters, these factors increase reputational risk for company-originated issues, such as quality and safety concerns or controversies over executive compensation. However, they also lead to higher activist-driven risk, as increased media coverage and the rise of social media lowers the costs of activist campaigns, while higher expectations about corporate conduct lead to more demand for social activism. Moreover, social activism is increasingly global in nature, matching global supply chains and business models.

Activist campaigns are often misunderstood. Only some campaigns directly respond to specific corporate conduct that triggered anger and outrage. Most campaigns are not punitive, but proactive and strategic; they are designed to engender changes in business practices at companies and entire industries. To accomplish these goals, activists use various tactics. Some institute boycotts, while others try to hurt the reputation of the firm. Importantly, reputational harm may be the point of a campaign, not just an unintended by-product, such as the results of a failed negotiation or an ignored threat. Both the possibility and the experience of reputational harm lead companies to invest more in CSR activities than would be warranted purely on competitive grounds. That is, companies engage in CSR activities as a form of reputational insurance against activists or to recover from damaging campaigns. Such CSR activities are thus defensive in nature and can be viewed as a form of reputational risk management. This also explains why CSR investments do not need to be correlated with higher stock returns.

Activists need to think strategically about their campaigns. By targeting the wrong firms or markets, for example, activists may limit their impact. They also need to choose tactics that keep the company motivated to engage in CSR activities. Overly zealous campaigns can lead companies to simply give up or stonewall. Reputational risk due to activism tends to be highest for companies with strong consumer brands that are (in principle) willing to invest in CSR activities in areas that activists care about. There are three different effects which each play a role here. First, such firms are more likely to be targeted. Second, once targeted, activists are likely to emphasize harm rather than rewards. Third, activist demands are higher for such firms.

Companies that find themselves repeatedly targeted by activists even though they engage in CSR activities tend to express surprise, even a sense of being singled out unfairly, but such sentiments reflect a lack of understanding of the strategic nature of activist campaigns. Activist campaigns are forms of competition over a company's reputation with customers and other stakeholders. As such, they are not fundamentally different from competition between firms over customer trust and brand loyalty. While activists have different motivations and goals than competing firms, they need to be taken seriously as sophisticated components of a company's business environment. Companies that are attractive targets need to get used to operating in an activist-rich environment. Moreover, the presence of activists is likely to be permanent unless a company radically changes its business model. For McDonald's, Greenpeace or PETA are as likely to go away as Burger King or KFC. This leads to the need for sophisticated firm strategies.

The study of the interaction between firms and activists is still a young area of research. Theoretical approaches have demonstrated the strategic complexity of corporate campaigns and firm strategies. It is important that empirical studies take these considerations fully into account. If indeed activists select targets strategically and firms engage in defensive CSR, such features need to be incorporated into statistical models to account for possible endogeneity and selection bias. Otherwise, we will draw the wrong inferences about activist campaigns and the CSR activities of firms.

This chapter on stakeholders and activists concludes our analysis of the main factors that shape corporate reputations. In the next part we focus on measurements.

PART V

Beyond Surveys: Measurement and Metrics

CHAPTER FIFTEEN

Surveys and Their Limitations

The empirical research on corporate reputation has predominantly relied on survey-based methodology, taking its cue from the public opinion research tradition and its applications in political science, sociology, and marketing.[1] Much of the progress in understanding the structure and dynamics of public opinion was enabled by the availability of extensive data collection efforts. These include the American National Election Surveys (ANES), which have been conducted over many decades by the University of Michigan, and the World Values Survey (WVS), which started in 1981.[2] The availability of extensive survey data allowed the construction of detailed cross-sectional time series datasets that could then be subjected to careful empirical analysis, an approach which had a profound impact on social science research.

For example, Bartels and Jackman (2014) used decades of ANES data to model generational changes in the US electorate. They develop a mathematical model in which two factors drive change: the political "shocks" (e.g., major political events) experienced in a particular period and "weights" determining how impactful the shocks are for each age group. The authors estimate the parameters of the model using data on the strength of party identification from 1952 to 2008 among a portion of ANES respondents and identify two distinct periods of heightened sensitivity to political events: in childhood (i.e., around age 10) and in middle age (i.e., around age 40). For political scientists, these results are important, as they speak to theories of party identification and the relationship between aging and political attention. Such studies are impossible without the availability of detailed time series data collected over decades.

In addition, survey researchers are also continually developing new methods to obtain more insightful responses from survey respondents. One key example of this approach is found in surveys of "sensitive" issues where respondents may not feel comfortable offering honest answers. In these cases, respondents are likely to lie or fail to respond to a question for fear of being punished for their behavior. Examples include surveys covering illegal activities, workplace misconduct, sexuality, and racial prejudice, among others. In all of these cases, the bias toward more socially desirable answers will result in surveys that drastically misrepresent the issue under study.

To address this concern, researchers have developed a number of survey techniques designed to promote honest answers. Surveys guarantee respondents full anonymity and use implicit measurement techniques, as well as explicit measures such as randomized response designs and list experiments, to obtain information that respondents would normally fail to provide.[3] These methods present respondents with direct questions about the sensitive topic of interest, but couch the questions in a broader context that provides question-level anonymity and prevents the researcher from knowing the exact meaning of the respondent's answer.

For example, in a randomized response design, respondents are presented with two mirrored questions (e.g., "I *have* stolen from my employer," and "I *have never* stolen from my employer"), and are asked to respond to the first question if a (secret) dice roll yields a specific number and the second if the dice does not. Since the dice roll is conducted secretly and is known only to the respondents, the researcher does not know whether the "Yes" they observe is a response to the first or second question. However, the researcher can still use this information to determine the sample proportion of individuals who are answering the first question affirmatively. This is because the responses, while random for each individual, have a known distribution across individuals. That is, since we know the distribution of dice rolls, we can determine how many "Yes" responses are due to the randomization and how many are due to true affirmative answers to the first question (Blair, Imai, and Zhou 2015; Warner 1965; Wu, Wood, and Stevenson 2019).

In the realm of corporate reputation, these types of question formats have significant (and largely untapped) potential, especially in settings where social desirability can dramatically bias the information they receive from both customers and employees. The problem of social desirability means that, rather than reporting their true attitudes, respondents try to "guess" which answers are expected of them. For example, while many customers self-report that they are willing to pay more for a "green" product, research has shown that this claimed willingness rarely translates into observable purchase behavior (Carrigan and Attalla 2001; Devinney, Auger, and Eckhardt 2010). This difference between survey-reported attitudes and observed behavior is easily explained by respondents' desires to provide socially acceptable answers. Taking such responses at face value without controlling for social desirability bias can lead to poor business decisions.

With properly constructed surveys and large, repeatedly collected datasets, mass surveys continue to be a powerful tool for understanding public opinion. In the context of corporate reputations, however, extensive survey data are either extremely limited or proprietary. Also, existing surveys often do not include important measures on value orientation or risk perception that are important drivers of opinion formation. Finally, existing data rely heavily on samples from mass publics. They often are not segmented by relevant constituencies, such as customers (existing or potential), employees, or suppliers. Moreover, certain constituencies, such as investors, regulators, or advocacy groups, are extremely difficult to reach, even by extensive data collection efforts. Some of these concerns could be remedied by extensive data collection efforts at a level commensurate with survey research in political science or sociology. But such efforts are unlikely to occur, even in the private sector, and if they did, the data would in all likelihood not be available to researchers. In sum, whether due to methodological concerns or simply due to practical limitations of data availability and access, an exclusive reliance on mass opinion surveys is problematic.

Therefore, to advance research on corporate reputation, we need to move beyond surveys as the exclusive tool of measurement. In this part we will discuss alternative measurement approaches. The approach we pursue will be heavily centered on the quantitative analysis of media activity, including social media. The idea is to use text as data. For example, individuals directly express their opinions in social media by sending Twitter messages, posting on Facebook, Instagram, or TikTok, or writing blogs. Thus, by analyzing user-generated media directly, we can derive summary measures of opinion and study their properties. This will allow us to identify public sentiment, issue dynamics, value orientations, dominant frames, etc.

This approach has advantages and disadvantages. The main advantage is the tremendous amount of available data. A second advantage is that, in contrast to surveys, members of the public do not respond to questions in a somewhat unfamiliar setting, but express their views in their "natural habitat." Thus, common problems such as question wording, order effects, or a subject's desire to please the interviewer or guess her intent are not present. The downside is the absence of designed measures, control groups, and experimental manipulation.[4] This means, first of all, that user-generated data need to be analyzed with great care. First, the segment of the population that uses social media actively is not a random sample of the population and underrepresents some groups, including older population segments. Second, an expressed opinion such as a tweet is likely to be heavily influenced by other tweets. Indeed, attitude formation through peer-to-peer interaction is a quintessential aspect of social networks. This means it is inappropriate to treat each tweet as an independent observation, and one would have to address all the issues of working with social network data discussed in chapter 8. Moreover, as we saw in chapter 8, during periods of high audience interest, social media can lead to feedback loops that generate "artificial consensus," overstating public support for a given position. Finally, little is known of the psychological processes that shape social media expression. Does it follow the same process as a survey response? If not, what are the differences? That said, with these and other caveats, the mere data volume makes user-generated media a rich source for creating measures and metrics.

A second important data source is traditional media outlets (newspapers, television, radio, and so on). Traditional media content plays two important roles. First, as we have seen throughout the book and especially in chapter 8, the media plays a crucial role in shaping opinions through persuasion, agenda setting, and framing. The media influences what members of the audience are thinking about and how they are thinking about it; media coverage influences considerations and which considerations are top of mind. Much of the research on media effects has been conducted by using laboratory experiments, for example, by providing subjects with fictitious or real media stories and then measuring their changes in attitudes and behavior. But, as we have touched on before, these findings need to be examined by using field data to further evaluate their external validity.

Moreover, once the correlation between media content and opinion formation has been firmly established, we can use media content as an indirect measure of changes in public opinion. That is, rather than measuring the output of the opinion formation process (e.g., through a survey response), we can measure the input (the relevant characteristics of media coverage).[5] For example, recall the discussion in chapter 7 of the shift from individual responsibility to systemic frames during the history of the US tobacco industry. If we were able to measure frames from text, then we could pinpoint when this shift occurred, how quickly it spread, and what accounted for this change in framing. At a practical level, reliable metrics of media coverage can then serve as measures of current opinion as well as early warning systems.

Until recently, researchers had to rely exclusively on manual methods to analyze media coverage, effectively hand-coding thousands of documents (e.g., Jones and Baumgartner 2005). Recent advances in computational linguistics, however, now offer the promise of using text-analytic and machine-learning methods instead of manual coding, allowing researchers to process much larger datasets and reducing their reliance on coder judgment.[6]

We first discuss summary measures of opinions and attitudes. Such summary measures are the equivalent of metrics such as approval ratings, customer satisfaction measures, or net promoter scores generated from survey data. They can be used as operational metrics to assess the current reputational situation of a company or to help gauge whether a strategy is moving the needle. The most widely used approach is *sentiment analysis*. Media sentiment is an aggregate measure derived from the "tone" of a document, that is, whether it is positive or negative with respect to a company or product (Pang and Lee 2008). We will then discuss measures of the emotional content of a text, such as whether it expresses disgust or anger at a company (e.g., Tumasjan et al. 2010), the expression of values and moral attitudes within it (Iliev, Dehghani, and Sagi 2015; Sagi and Dehghani 2014a), and the text's ideological positioning (e.g., Laver, Benoit, and Gary 2003; Slapin and Proksch 2008).

Next, we discuss methods for identifying agenda setting (*what* the public is talking about), and framing (*how* it is talking about it). To study issue agendas, we use an approach known as *topic identification*. Originally developed as a tool for automatic document classification, it can also be used to identify issues in text. By mapping the relative frequency of topic mentions over time, one can measure the relative salience of an issue in the media and how it changes (e.g., Grimmer 2010; Quinn et al. 2010; Takayama, Flournoy, and Kaufmann 1998).

The detection of *frames* is a more difficult problem, as it is very challenging to distinguish a frame, for instance the individual responsibility frame, from the underlying issue like obesity. We discuss two approaches. One is based on lexical cohesion (Klebanov, Diermeier, and Beigman 2008a), while the other uses context vectors (Sagi, Diermeier, and Kaufman 2013). Once frames can be clearly identified and distinguished from the underlying issues, we can understand the origin and dynamics of frames, such as when a frame is emerging and when it becomes dominant.

While these methods have significant promise and allow us to connect the study of corporate reputation with the growing interest in "big data" and "analytics," there are also limitations. We discuss some methodological difficulties of text-analytic approaches and how they can be overcome.

Measuring Opinion

16.1 Sentiment

Our first goal is to develop summary measures of the opinion expressed in a text. A straightforward approach is to categorize a text as positive or negative toward an issue, company, or product. The paradigm here is product reviews as known from yelp.com or tripadvisor.com. But the scope of analysis is considerably wider, including Twitter messages (e.g., Kouloumpis, Wilson, and Moore 2011), blog posts (Dehghani et al. 2014; Hopkins and King 2010), and newspaper editorials or news features (Balahur et al. 2010; Fong et al. 2003; Young and Soroka 2012). This approach is known as *sentiment analysis* (Liu 2010, 2012, 2015; Pang and Lee 2008).

Sentiment analysis tends to operate at the document level, but there are also approaches that operate at the sentence level (e.g., Wiebe, Bruce, and O'Hara 1999) or the aspect level that focus on the sentiment toward a target (e.g., Vo and Zhang 2015). For example, a restaurant review may contain the statement *the food was delicious but the service was slow*. Here the sentiment expressed toward the food is positive, while the one toward the service is negative.

While researchers have applied a multitude of different methods, the approaches generally fall into one of two categories. Some approaches are based on categorizing the content based on the occurrence of particular keywords and dictionaries. Others use machine-learning algorithms to statistically identify specific features that tell one type of text from another.

16.1.1   Dictionary-Based Methods

A straightforward approach is the use of dictionaries (Stone, Dunphy, and Smith 1966). Dictionary-based methods use a list of words with an assigned tone and calculate an overall score to the document by creating a weighted average over word scores. The weights correspond to the relative frequency of a word's occurrence in a document. In principle, such scores can be real numbers or integers. The most common approach is to categorize words as positive ($+1$) or negative (-1). Thus, each word in dictionary w is assigned a positive or negative score by a scoring function $s(w) \in \{+1, -1\}$. Let $f(w, d)$ be the normalized frequency of word w in document d and let W_d denote all the words from the dictionary that occur in document d. Then the sentiment $\sigma(d)$ of document d is simply

$$\sigma(d) = \sum_{w \in W_d} f(w, d)s(w).$$

Here we normalized the sentiment $\sigma(d)$ by the number of words such that $\sigma(d) \in [0, 1]$. This may not be appropriate, for example, if longer documents should receive more weight. Similarly, documents that appear on the front page may receive more weight. Also, one may use metadata such as the circulation or credibility of a media outlet to adjust the weights of documents. Finally, rather than using articles as the unit of analysis, we may use paragraphs or even sentences. This can be important if we have reason to believe that, for example, sentiment expressed in the first paragraph should be weighted more heavily or that we should distinguish between a headline and other sentences used in an article or webposting.

Dictionary-based methods can be used to measure sentiment in mass media sources (e.g., Bösch, Müller, and Schneider 2018; Eshbaugh-Soha 2010; Li et al. 2014; Young and Soroka 2012), but they are also applicable to user-generated messages such as blogs or tweets. For example, Mostafa (2013) used a dictionary collected by Hu and Liu (2004) to measure the overall sentiments for several well-known companies as expressed by Twitter users. Although the sentiments expressed were more positive than negative overall, there were some notable exceptions including *US Bank*, *Pfizer*, and *Comcast*, all of which had decidedly negative mean sentiment scores. In contrast, companies like *Nokia* and *IBM* showed reasonably positive scores, while *Air India* and *Samsung* showed sentiment scores that were fairly neutral.

Some of the major advantages of dictionaries are that they are easy to use, widely available, and require little background in statistics, machine learning, or linguistics. A popular example is SentiWordNet, based on the publicly available WordNet (Baccianella, Esuli, and Sebastiani 2010; Esuli and Sebastiani 2006). It provides (approximately) continuous sentiment scores for a document, but can easily be converted into classifying documents as "positive" or "negative" by defining an appropriate threshold.

Dictionary-based methods, however, also pose problems. The first is *domain-specificity*. Dictionaries are created by researchers for a particular purpose. Applying an off-the-shelf dictionary to a different domain will likely lead to misleading results. For example, terms such as *tax* (as in a *taxing assignment*) or *cost* may convey a negative sentiment in a general document, but may have no such meaning in an earnings report. Indeed, if they occur as *substantial tax savings* or *cost reduction*, then they may be quite positive. While the term *restatement* does not carry negative connotations in everyday discourse, it is likely to be very negative in an audit report, as in *earnings restatement* (Liu 2012; Loughran and McDonald 2011; Wilson, Wiebe, and Hoffmann 2009).

These issues point to the second problem: *lack of validation*. How do we know whether a given dictionary is appropriate for a domain? How do we assess its performance? Dictionaries cannot easily be compared to human coders. Indeed, human subjects do not usually interpret text in consistent ways or as intended by the researchers (Krosnick 1999; Shapiro 1997). More generally, common statistical approaches such as hypothesis testing or statistical significance, as well as other evaluation approaches, cannot easily be applied to dictionaries in a straightforward manner.[1] These issues are better addressed by supervised classification approaches.

16.1.2 Supervised Classification

Supervised classification offers an attractive alternative to dictionary-based approaches. It can be designed for every domain afresh using a common underlying approach, and competing classification methods are subject to comparative evaluation (e.g., Maas et al. 2011; Mullen and Collier 2004). Supervised classification uses machine learning algorithms. This means that algorithms are trained to decide which of several content categories a document should be assigned to. In the case of positive versus negative opinions, two categories are commonly used — one for positive opinions and one for negative ones. However, it is also possible to obtain more granularity by adding additional intermediate buckets (e.g., one for each "star rating" of a customer review). Most of these classification algorithms use a *supervised learning* approach where a preclassified set of documents (the training set) is used to train the algorithm (the classifier), which is then tested on a new corpus. Success of the classifier is measured by its performance on this new test corpus. Good classifiers obtain classification success in the 80–90 percent range. A properly tested classifier can then be used as a measure on a new set of documents. For example, suppose we want to know whether public opinion of Wal-Mart changed after its relief efforts during Hurricane Katrina. We would design a classifier, select a sufficiently large training set, and annotate it by hand into two categories: "positive" (with respect to Wal-Mart) and "negative" (with respect to Wal-Mart). The classifier would then be trained on the training set and evaluated on a different set of documents (the testing set). If the classifier's performance is sufficiently accurate, we could then create a time series with daily proportions of documents coded as positive, and see whether the proportion of positive documents significantly increased after Hurricane Katrina.[2]

Many supervised learning algorithms have been used for text document classification. The algorithms differ in the optimization method they use for this task. Popular methods involve Bayesian inference, maximum entropy, and support vector machines (SVM) (e.g., Liu 2015).[3] For binary (yes or no) classification problems, the two most frequently used evaluation criteria are accuracy and the average of precision and recall. *Accuracy* is defined as the proportion of correct predictions among all predictions. *Precision* and *recall* are the proportion of documents correctly assigned to a category among all the documents assigned to that category and among all the documents that truly belong to that category, respectively. Precision and recall are often used for skewed datasets in which one category has far fewer examples than the other. If the sample is balanced, that is, if there is approximately an equal proportion of positive and negative documents, accuracy is an appropriate measure.

Based on performance in previous classification tasks, Support Vector Machines (SVM) have been identified as one of the most efficient classification methods (Dumais et al. 1998; Joachims 1998; Liu 2015; Pang, Lee, and Vaithyanathan 2002; Sebastiani 2002; Yang and Liu 1999).[4] SVM classification accuracies may vary widely between different classification tasks. They may be over 95 percent for some topic categories in news articles, or as modest as around 75 percent for opinion classification of movie reviews (Pang, Lee, and Vaithyanathan 2002). A classifier is usually considered effective when the accuracy is higher than a baseline method, which can be something as simple as a random guess for balanced datasets or a majority proportion for skewed datasets. That is, if there are 60 percent negative articles, the classifier needs to have better than 60 percent accuracy in identifying documents with negative tonality.

Before a text can be classified, it needs to be represented mathematically. In the case of SVM and many other classification methods, texts are viewed simply as "bags of words" (BOW). That is, the only information used for the analysis is the words of a text and their frequency. The BOW model is insensitive to many potentially informative properties of documents, such as the location of words in the document, word order, grammatical relations, the internal structure of the document at various levels (e.g., paragraph and sentence boundaries), and multiword phrases such as "war on drugs." Some research studies tested more sophisticated document representations which incorporate such information (e.g., word position relation predicates and noun or verb phrases) in a variety of classifiers. In some cases, longer expressions are used, such as *bull_market*, to capture idiosyncratic terms. This is an example of a "bigram," consisting of two words. The general units are *n*-grams. In most applications, however, there is little to no improvement in classification from using more complex linguistic entities as the unit of analysis (Lewis 1992; Manning, Raghavan, and Schütze 2008; Moschitti and Basili 2004; Scott and Matwin 1999).

For our purposes, we will focus on the BOW approach, by far the most common approach. To apply SVM or other classification techniques, documents must be represented in a vector space whose dimensions correspond to the features that are relevant in the classification. Here, the relevant features are words (more precisely, word types), and the vector representing each document is determined by the number of occurrences (or tokens) of each of the words in that document. In the feature space, for a given document a word's value may be Boolean (indicating its presence or absence in the document) or it may be denoted by its frequency in the document (the number of times it occurs), its frequency normalized by document length, or its frequency adjusted by some weighting scheme.

The most common word frequency weighting scheme is a family of measures subsumed under the label $tf * idf$.[5] Here tf and idf stand for "term frequency" (the number of occurrences of the word in the document) and "inverse document frequency" (the inverse number of documents in which the word occurs). The idea is to offset the impact of high-frequency words in the given document by the extent to which they also occur in other documents, based on the assumption that words whose occurrences are dispersed over many documents are less useful in the classification task. Specifically, given a training set of n documents, for a word with term frequency t_f in a document of length l and document frequency d_f, that word's $tf * idf$ value is given by the formula

$$tf * idf := \frac{t_f}{l} \times \log \frac{n}{d_f}.$$

To get from a document to a vector space, a text must be preprocessed. This procedure is also known as "shallow natural language processing." The three main steps are tokenization, stemming, and part-of-speech tagging. A "tokenizer" is an algorithm that splits a document into individual words. It is able to recognize consecutive strings of alphabetical characters as valid words. For example, the sentence

> Mr. President, I express my sincerest sympathies to all families of those who have lost loved ones in the recent accident.

becomes

mr/president/i/express/my/sincerest/sympathies/to/all/families/of/those/who /have/lost/loved/ones/in/the/recent/accident

To reduce the vocabulary size, preprocessing frequently removes words that occur very rarely in the corpus, as well as "stop words," mostly function words such as "the," "a," and "of," which are very common. Stop words are considered useless for classification because they occur frequently in every document. So the words that are both too rare and too frequent are removed. While this process is routine, the exact threshold depends on the application and size of the corpus. "Stemming" reduces the vocabulary size significantly by mapping different forms into the same stem or root. For example, the words "family" and "families" both get reduced to the stem *famil*. Stemming needs to be used with care since it discards some potentially relevant information such as verb tense. While in most applications stemming is unproblematic, sometimes classifying word classes—nouns, verbs, adjectives, and adverbs—in isolation is important. This is accomplished with part-of-speech taggers, which require their own tokenizers. For the sentence above, the taggers would create the following:

president-noun singular sympathies-noun plural families-noun plural, . . .

The data—documents, paragraphs, or sentences—are represented as vectors x_i in an n-dimensional space, with each dimension corresponding to a feature (word) potentially relevant to the classification task. The dimension n here corresponds to the stemmed words that survived elimination of stop words and rare words. For the training phase, the category membership of each data point is known. That is, they are labeled as either "negative" (-1) or "positive" (1). In general, category labels are denoted y_i. In some applications, the ratings are given (e.g., customer reviews that use a star rating system), but in most applications the training set is based on human coding. It is good practice to use more than one coder per data point and to check for intercoder reliability, which varies across applications (e.g., Grimmer 2010; Liu 2015; Pang and Lee 2005). The coded dataset is also known as the "truth dataset" or the "ground truth," as it will be used to train the algorithm. This terminology is somewhat misleading, as human coding can itself be subject to coding error or inconsistency. We will return to this issue below. For now it is important to keep in mind that the usefulness of the algorithm depends on the quality of the training set. Training sets should be representative samples of the underlying corpus, and ideally constitute random samples from the overall corpus. This may become an issue if a preexisting training set is used. Otherwise, random sampling is a good approach. The size of the training set depends on the application. For large datasets a sample of about 500 is a good rule of thumb (Hopkins and King 2010). Formally, a training set of size l is a set of pairs

$$\{(x_1, y_1), \ldots, (x_l, y_l)\}, \quad x_{i=1,\ldots,l} \in \Re^n, \quad y_{i=1,\ldots,l} \in \{+1, -1\}.$$

The SVM model is based on the following idea. If the data points in each of the categories are separable by a hyperplane, then there is a hyperplane that is maximally separating, in that the distance between it and the nearest data point is maximized. This maximally separating hyperplane lies at equal distances between two parallel hyperplanes, each of which is determined by one or more of the data points in one of the two categories.

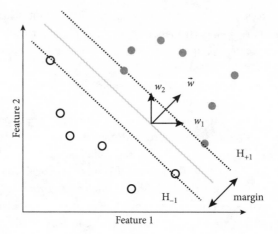

FIGURE 16.1. Example of hyperplanes in a support vector machine model.

These data points on the parallel hyperplanes are called the "support vectors" (SV). The distance between the two parallel hyperplanes is called the "margin." The task of a SVM in the training phase is to find the two separating hyperplanes such that the margin is maximal. Figure 16.1 illustrates the process.

In this example, a document is represented by only two features. So each data point is represented by a pair of coordinates in a two-dimensional space. A hyperplane corresponds to a line in two-dimensional space. In the figure, the maximally separating hyperplane is shown as the light gray line, and the two parallel hyperplanes running through the support vectors are shown as the two dotted lines H_{-1} and H_{+1}.[6]

Note that the vector $\vec{w}$ is perpendicular to the hyperplanes. It provides valuable information about the relative informativeness of each word in determining category membership. The relevant words used for classification are also referred to as "features." In general, since the dimensions of the vector space correspond to the features used in the classification, the components of w can be used as feature-ranking coefficients. Intuitively, feature analysis provides some insight into which words are most responsible for determining whether a particular document is classified as negative or positive. The components of w whose absolute values are highest correspond to the most informative features. This is a common property of all linear classifiers and is closely related to the role played by coefficients in a linear regression model. In movie reviews, for example, adjectives tend to

Document classification process

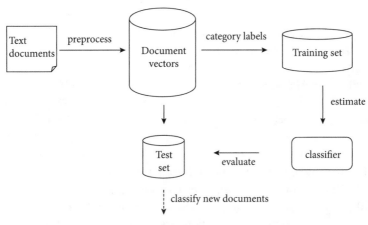

FIGURE 16.2. The work flow of document classification.

be most informative (Narayanan, Arora, and Bhatia 2013; Pang, Lee, and Vaithyanathan 2002).

Next we need to evaluate the accuracy of the classifier. In the context of analyzing customer opinions, classifiers have achieved accuracy levels as high as 88 percent for product reviews (Dave, Lawrence, and Pennock 2003; Haque, Saber, and Shah 2018) and 89 percent for movie reviews (Narayanan, Arora, and Bhatia 2013; Tripathy, Agrawal, and Rath 2016). Importantly, classifiers tend to be highly specific. That is, opinion classifiers trained on movie reviews were not effective in predicting the polarity of restaurant reviews and vice versa (e.g., Finn and Kushmerick 2006). This problem is known as the "domain-dependence phenomenon." It indicates that, at least in the domain of customer reviews, people tend not to use universal opinion descriptors, such as *terrific* or *disappointing*, but rely on domain-specific adjectives, such as *hilarious* or *funny* in the case of movies, and *tasty* or *delicious* in the case of restaurants. Once a classifier has been evaluated and found valid, it can then be used to measure sentiment on a new corpus. This process is summarized in figure 16.2.

Sentiment classification has worked well in consumer reviews and other forms of social media opinions where attitudes are expressed directly and in a straightforward manner ("the food was delicious"). The cases of news sources or policy documents have proven to be much more challenging. They usually require domain knowledge and an understanding of context, and opinions are frequently expressed indirectly, through some form of argument or assessment. The statement "The growth in free cash flow is likely to decline" is usually bad news for a company, while "The growth in SG&A is likely to decline" is usually good news. But this will be missed by any reader who doesn't know the difference between free cash flow and SG&A.

This is especially true of news articles. First, opinion is often expressed indirectly in the context of a specific issue. Second, while editorials may contain some direct expressions of opinion, reports on negative events regarding a company, such as lawsuits, strikes, or decreasing stock prices, will also have an effect on audience attitudes, even though we would not usually consider them expressions of opinion. Similarly, news features may contain references to expert evaluations of the situation, and such third-party assessments may be highly opinionated and may have considerable impact on audience perception (e.g., Kaya, Fidan, and Toroslu 2012; Wilson, Wiebe, and Hoffmann 2009).

This raises a more general issue. Professional journalists draw a clear distinction between expression of opinions (e.g., an editorial) and news coverage. The existing literature on sentiment analysis has followed this distinction and treats opinion and fact as two different categories (Yu and Hatzivassiloglou 2003). Indeed, facts are often discarded in opinion analysis (Hu and Liu 2004). This is perfectly reasonable as an analysis of media coverage, but less reasonable if our goal is to understand public opinion. Here the media is mainly of interest as an input in the opinion formation process. Although facts are neutral in tone, they may easily induce opinions in the minds of the audience. For an investor, a purely factual news story may be interpreted as good news, say, an increasing stock price, or bad news, say, decreasing sales. If we are mainly interested in analyzing the creation of content, that is, the sender side, then discarding facts may be appropriate, but if we are mainly interested in the opinions and attitudes induced in an audience, that is, the receiver side, then including such content can be appropriate.

The indirect expression of opinion and the importance of domain knowledge create specific problems for classification-based approaches, as the construction of the "truth" (training) dataset becomes considerably more challenging. While annotators can reliably classify simpler items like movie reviews (Pang and Lee 2005), performance goes down in business contexts. Yu, Diermeier, and Kaufman (2008) study the annotation of 1,080 randomly selected articles on Wal-Mart during the year

2006. Coders were university undergraduate research assistants. They were provided with an annotation scheme and trained on sample articles. Coding decisions were then discussed. Intercoder agreement was significantly lower than in customer reviews. Coders struggled with distinguishing facts from opinion, as in the following example, taken from an article rated as negative in overall tone:

> Many drive-in sites were sold off to developers. Multiscreen indoor theaters or Wal-Marts sprouted in their place.

They also disagreed on whether an expressed opinion was positive or negative. In some cases the coders appeared to lack background knowledge, as in the following example:

> But a strong, pro-union majority would have an impact. Look at the concrete contract flap stalling the Hoover Dam bypass bridge. And just think of the prospects for Wal-Mart.

Here the annotators had to understand the conflict between unions and Wal-Mart to assess the implications of the paragraph. In other cases, coders' disagreement seemed to reflect value disagreements among the coders. That is, certain coders viewed a particular statement or paragraph more negatively not because they interpreted it differently, but because they disagreed about whether Wal-Mart's actions were problematic. The following sentence is an example of this phenomenon:

> Meanwhile, with the Canadian dollar exchange rate soaring to 90 percent, discussion has started about building a wall along the border to prevent Canadians from hogging all of the Wal-Mart sale items.

The word *hogging* indicates negative tone, but coders who found nothing wrong with Wal-Mart's action coded the sentence as "neutral." The polarized reaction is interesting and could be analyzed on its own terms, say by measuring a coder's underlying value orientation and then creating value-contingent indices, but in a straightforward opinion classification task it presents a problem. Overall, these examples indicate that opinion classification in news data and other "professional texts" such as policy data remains a challenging task. From a practical point of view, commercially created media sentiment indices should be treated with extreme caution, especially when applied to news sources or policy documents. Coders with domain expertise are expensive, as is the use of multiple coders to assess intercoder reliability. Moreover, coder disagreement may not reflect different interpretations of a document, but genuine value disagreement. Yet, even the most sophisticated classification algorithms rely on a well-designed training set based on human coding decisions.

16.1.3 Neural Networks and Deep Learning

One of the most powerful approaches for classification at present is based on recent advances in artificial neural networks that are commonly referenced as "deep learning" (e.g., Devlin et al. 2019; Goldberg 2016, 2017; Moraes, Valiati, and Neto 2013; Tang, Qin, and Liu 2015; Zhang, Wang, and Liu 2018). An artificial neural network is a collection of interconnected nodes, or neurons. Each node uses a mathematical transformation to compute its output based on the inputs it receives. This function is commonly nonlinear, with the sigmoid being the most commonly used function. For a set of N inputs $I_1..I_N$, the neuron computes a weighted sum based on weights $W_1..W_N$, and then applies a sigmoid function to the result to compute the output O:

$$O = \frac{1}{1 + e^{-\sum_{n=1}^{N} W_n I_n}}.$$

The advantage of functions such as the sigmoid is that they nonlinearly transform an arbitrary number of weighted inputs into an output in the range 0..1 with a relatively rapid transition between the two extremes. Frequently, one of the inputs is fixed to a particular value to create a bias as part of the function.

In traditional artificial neural networks, these neurons are divided into several layers. The output of neurons in each layer provides the input to the neurons in the next layer. The first layer is known as the input layer, and the last layer is known as the output layer. Layers in between are referred to as hidden layers because they do not directly interact with the environment. The input layer receives the information to be classified as its input (e.g., the text), and the output layer provides the result of the neural network computation (e.g., the sentiment). The final layer often uses a transformation with desired statistical properties to provide a consistent output, such as the softmax function, which normalizes its inputs into a probability distribution:

$$\sigma\,(X)_i = \frac{e^{x_i}}{\sum_{j=1}^{N} e^{x_j}}.$$

A neural network is useful only after training, which is a process akin to the training of SVMs. For artificial neural networks, backpropagation is a common training technique. The network computes an output for each input in sequence. This output is then compared to the expected output. The resulting error, the difference between the actual output and the expected output, is propagated back through the network, and the weights used by each neuron are slightly modified to reduce this error. This is repeated for the entire training set multiple times (often hundreds), and the output of the network gradually regularizes over this process to match the expected output.

One of the most prominent examples of neural networks applied to text is the Word2Vec algorithm (Mikolov et al. 2013). In this approach the network is provided with part of a small chunk of text with some words missing and is trained to predict the missing words. For example, in the continuous BOW model, a context is provided (e.g., "the president ——— the economy is fine") and the network predicts the target word (e.g., "said").

Deep learning is not substantially different from the process described above, except that multiple hidden networks are used, and the structure of the overall network is more complex, as a single network is often composed of several separate neural networks (e.g., Devlin et al. 2019). In addition, some different network structures and functions are used. Specifically, deep learning often employs convolutional neural networks. In convolutional neural networks, which are modeled after the organization of neurons in the human visual cortex, each layer is only connected to a particular region of the previous layer. While each neuron in the layer receives inputs from a unique region, these regions overlap somewhat. This results in some redundancy in the information represented by the layer and allows for the network to more easily train to identify repeating patterns irrespective of their position in the input. A second stage in such networks often involves subsampling, in which an entire set of neurons in the previous layer is connected to only a few neurons in the current layer.[7]

Importantly, the larger the network is, and especially the more hidden layers a network incorporates, the larger the required training set must be. As this growth is generally exponential in nature, the training set required for deep learning is similarly large, and the computational resources required for training the network likewise increase. The growth in both the availability of large datasets and the available processing power have enabled deep learning to train networks in a way that researchers working with traditional artificial neural networks in the 1990s would have found impossible.

Regardless of the implementation of the network, neural networks can be trained for sentiment analysis (e.g., Moraes, Valiati, and Neto 2013; Tang, Qin, and Liu 2015; see Zhang, Wang, and Liu 2018 for a tutorial). Likewise, the output of neural networks trained to extract features and word meaning from text can be used more generally for document classification and categorization (e.g., Adhikari et al. 2019).[8]

In sum, neural networks and deep learning provide a powerful new approach to sentiment analysis with classification success as high as 94 percent. Whether they are able to address the problems discussed above is an open question. Applications to the study of corporate reputation are still lacking.

16.2   Emotions

An alternative approach to understanding sentiment is to focus on the emotions expressed in a text (e.g., Riloff and Wiebe 2003). This is usually done with dictionary-based approaches. The best-known of these methods is the Linguistic Inquiry and Word Count (LIWC) software package developed by James Pennebaker and his colleagues (Chung and Pennebaker 2011; Pennebaker, Booth, and Francis 2007).[9] LIWC is a dictionary-based approach that is most useful as a simple measure of the emotional content of a text or corpus. It is less successful in identifying whether a particular text (e.g., a product review) represents a positive or negative opinion. At the heart of LIWC is a dictionary in which each word belongs to one or more categories. These categories generally relate to linguistic features (e.g., *pronoun* and *negation*) or psychological variables (e.g., *anger*, *inhibition*). The application of a LIWC dictionary to a text simply entails the counting of how often words from each category appear in the text. For instance, if words from the anger category (e.g., *hate*, *annoy*) appear in the text frequently, then LIWC would judge the text as representing anger. Texts may express more than one emotion, which would be captured by their respective LIWC scores.

LIWC has been successfully applied to many questions in the social sciences, from the political analysis of speeches and tweets (Tumasjan et al. 2010) to the investigation of linguistic markers of suicidal poets (Stirman and Pennebaker 2001) and the emotional makeup of bloggers, such as flares of anger or outrage (Dehghani et al. 2014; Gill, Nowson, and Oberlander 2009).[10]

The emotional content expressed in a text varies by domain. Yu, Kaufman, and Diermeier (2008) describe how movie reviews have the highest emotional content, followed by political speech (floor speeches given in the US Senate) and news items. The same order can be found by investigating positive and negative emotional content separately. In the context of customer reviews, the emotional content is highly correlated with the opinion expressed. That is, if we were to construct a classifier based on LIWC's positive and negative emotional content and compare it to the classification of SVM based on positive versus negative opinion, we would expect the results to be highly correlated. This turns out not to be true for other forms of speech. Yu, Kaufman, and Diermeier (2008), for example, point out that a senator's position on an issue is not well predicted by the emotional content of her speech.

16.3   Values and Ideology

In chapters 3 and 5, we discussed the importance of value orientations in shaping evaluations of an issue as well as beliefs, such as risk assessments. As in the case of sentiment and emotional content, we can also use text-analytic methods to measure value orientations and ideological positioning. This can be used to measure the relative positions of groups including news organizations, NGOs, and activist groups (e.g., Gentzkow and Shapiro 2010), or to assess the distribution of value orientations in different markets and countries. One of the main difficulties in developing techniques to measure value orientations and ideologies is the difficulty of external validation. In some cases, like the classification of NGOs, expert judgments may be appropriate, but this is often not a feasible approach with large user-generated datasets.[11]

However, recent work in political science has developed a variety of methods that, with suitable adjustments, can be applied in our context. The main advantage of working within political domains is that there are well-validated external measures of ideological positioning by politicians and parties. In the context of US politics, roll-call data have been successfully used to reliably locate members of the US Congress on an ideological scale (Clinton, Jackman, and Rivers 2004; Poole and Rosenthal 1997). In the context of European parties, the Manifesto Project provides a reliable measure of the respective ideological positioning of political parties.[12] To estimate value orientations and ideological positions, both dictionary and classification methods can be used. In addition, unsupervised scaling approaches can be useful (Monroe and Maeda 2004; Slapin and Proksch 2008).

The first approach, Wordscore, locates political parties in a unidimensional ideological space (Laver, Benoit, and Gary 2003). The approach works as follows. The first step is to select two reference points on the extremes of the ideological spectrum. In the context of European parties, this may be a communist party on one end and a neofascist party on the other end. In the case of the US, it may be the most liberal and the most conservative senators. Next, select a representative text, such as a party manifesto or a collection of speeches. These reference texts are then used to create a score for each word, that is, the relative frequency with which that word is used in the reference text. For example, words that are rarely used by communists but often used by neofascists are "right-wing" words. We can then use these Wordscores to locate documents such as the manifesto of some other party, P. This is done by first calculating the relative frequency of the words used in party P's manifesto. Then we calculate P's score as the weighted average of its associated Wordscores. If that measure is closer to the score of the fascist party, party P is located on the right of the ideological spectrum. By repeating that process we can line up the parties from right to left. Laver, Benoit, and Gary (2003) show that the Wordscore process can faithfully reproduce the ideological ranking of European parties.

Wordscore is very versatile and easy to use, even in foreign languages. However, the quality of a Wordscore analysis depends heavily on the selection of reference texts. It also potentially conflates stylistic differences with ideological differences (Lowe 2008). Wordscore is essentially a measure of the similarity of texts to the reference texts. In principle, other similarity measures can be used. For example, Huffaker, Swaab, and Diermeier (2011) use file compression metrics as a measure of similarity.[13]

An alternative approach is the use of supervised learning models such as SVM, discussed above in the context of sentiment classification. Diermeier et al. (2012) used SVM to classify US senators along a left-right ideological spectrum. They ranked a sample of 177 senators according to their DW-Nominate scores, a measure based on voting records that locates members of Congress on an ideological spectrum from left to right (Poole and Rosenthal 1997). A major advantage of this approach compared to most classification tasks is that the "truth dataset" used to train the classifiers is not based on human coding, but on nonlinguistic data such as voting behavior or party affiliation. From a subsample of senators, the completed floor speeches of the 25 most liberal and the 25 most conservative senators were used as a training set for the SVM classifier. The trained algorithm then classified the 25 most liberal and 25 most conservative senators in a different subsample. Using a $tf * idf$ representation method, the classifier exhibited accuracy close to 94 percent. This result implies that, out of the 50 most conservative and liberal senators in the sample, 47 were correctly classified solely on the virtue of the words they used in their speeches.

Feature analysis shows that the most separating words used by liberals are from the areas focusing on energy and the environment, corporate interests and lobbying, healthcare, inequality, and education. For conservatives, the key areas are taxation, abortion, stem-cell research, family values, defense, and government administration. This suggests that the two sides talk about different issues. However, even when talking about the same issue, conservatives and liberals use different words, which suggests the use of different frames. For example, among the adjectives of liberal positions was the word *gay*, while for Republicans it was *homosexual. Gay* and *homosexual* thus serve as signal words for a politician's ideological position.

The availability of detailed ideological scores based on voting is very fortuitous. Party labels are not as precise, but can also be used for classification. In this case, classification success is 80 to 81 percent.[14] If such independently derived labels are unavailable, human coding of the training set is a feasible but labor-intensive alternative. If the relevant text is complex and context-dependent, the usual caveats about the use of coders apply, such as lack of understanding and influence of the coder's own ideology.

Finally, value orientations can be directly estimated from political texts (e.g., speeches or press releases) by assuming an underlying low-dimensional ideological space (Monroe and Maeda 2004; Slapin and Proksch 2008). Slapin and Proksch's Wordfish model assumes that a word j from actors i is uttered according to a Poisson distribution with rate λ_{ij}. The rate is modeled as an exponential function of the relative frequency of texts uttered by is, α_i, the relative frequency of word j, ψ_j, and the cross product of two parameters, β_j and θ_i. The parameter β_j measures how well a word discriminates on the underlying ideological space and θ_i is the politician's unobserved position. That is, we have

$$\lambda_{ij} = \exp(\alpha_i + \psi_j + \beta_j \times \theta_i).$$

Parameter θ_i can then be estimated using maximum likelihood estimation. A major advantage of the Wordfish approach is that it does not require external labels or human coding and can be applied to any corpus. Indeed, to create separation along this underlying space, Wordfish organically identifies the keywords that separate actors on one end of the space from those on the other. Note, however, that the algorithm does this by effectively exploiting the *linguistic* variation between actors. Such variation may reflect different value orientations or ideological positions, or it may be due to other causes of variation like stylistic differences. When applied to the ideologically polarized German party system, Wordfish recovers reliable party estimates. It is much less successful when applied to press releases from US senators (Grimmer and Stewart 2013).

As an application of ideology measures to the area of corporate reputations, consider the use of text-analytic methods to assess media slant. The idea here is to use political speech, for example, from members of the US Congress, as a measure of ideological speech and then measure the similarity of the language used in newspapers to political speech (Gentzkow and Shapiro 2010).[15] The goal is to provide a reliable ideological rating of newspapers. The process works as follows. First, use some nonlinguistic measure of political ideology. These can be measures based on roll calls, such as DW-Nominate scores (Poole and Rosenthal 1997) or interest-group ratings of legislators. For example, the organization Americans for Democratic Action (ADA) publishes rankings of members of the US Congress on a left-to-right scale, with 0 being the most conservative score and 100 the most liberal. Both types of rankings have been used extensively in the study of the US Congress. In addition to general rankings, issue-specific rankings are available. The National Farm Bureau, which represents agricultural issues, publishes ratings, as does the National Rifle Association regarding each legislator's stance on gun control. Other issue-specific rankings can be constructed for a specific purpose.

Next, one needs to apply a text-analytic approach to identify speech patterns correlated with the ideological positioning of politicians.[16] This can be done with SVM and feature analysis or Wordscore. Gentzkow and Shapiro (2010) used bigrams such as *death_tax*, a term preferred by Republicans, versus *estate_tax*, the corresponding expression used by Democrats, as well as trigrams such as *credit_card_companies*, popular among Democrats, compared to *embryonic_stem_cells*, widely used by Republicans. Among the most widely used two-word phrases used by the two parties were:[17]

Sample of Two-Word Phrases Preferred by Democrats
middle_class, oil_companies, wildlife_refuge, American_workers, fuel_efficiency

Sample of Two-Word Phrases Preferred by Republicans
stem_cell, natural_gas, death_tax, illegal_aliens, private_property

We can then use these linguistic characteristics as measures of the desired ranking, here newspapers' ideologies. Gentzkow and Shapiro (2010) used a regression approach, but other methods are conceivable, such as Wordscore, classification-based approaches, or compression algorithms.[18] No matter how they are constructed, measures of ideological leanings are very useful. They can be applied to politicians, newspapers, blogs and other social media, interest groups, third-party experts, or any other source or constituency.[19]

However, there are also some shortcomings. Note, for example, that ideological measures conflate differences in *issues* (*what* texts are talking about), with *frames* (*how* they are talking about it). The Republican preference for *death_tax* rather than *estate_tax* reflects a different frame, while the preference for the use of *credit_card_companies* over *embryonic_stem_cells* reflects a difference in issues. Democrats tended to talk more about the regulation of the financial service industries, while Republicans' opposition to stem-cell research was a core element of the party's issue agenda closely related to its antiabortion stance. We understand these differences intuitively by looking at the data, but feature analysis does not distinguish among them. To separate the two dimensions of issues versus framing we need new methods.

CHAPTER SEVENTEEN

Agendas, Topics, and Issues

Suppose we want to the track the agenda of the *New York Times* over time, or compare the news agenda between the US and the UK. At its basic level, that means we are starting with a collection of texts, a corpus, that contains, say, all news articles in the *New York Times* between a beginning and an end date. We may then want to know what the top 10 issues in each year were. To accomplish this we could predefine a list of issues and then classify each article as relating to one of the issues. This is essentially the approach taken by Jones and Baumgartner (2005). Alternatively, we can use tools from text analytics to accomplish the same goal, or at least approximate it.

The trade-off between manual and computational approaches is usually between accuracy and efficiency. Manual coding is typically more accurate than algorithmic approaches, but is much less efficient. Sometimes, however, we may wish to use text-analytic approaches with the explicit purpose of removing human judgment or to uncover novel properties in a corpus.

17.1 Dictionaries, Keywords, and Diagnostic Terms

As in the case of sentiment analysis, we can use dictionaries for the purpose of issue identification. In this setting, the words are not assigned to binary categories that capture sentiment, that is, negative and positive, but to $k \geq 2$ issue domains. Using an analogous approach to the case of sentiment analysis, a document is then assigned an issue score. That is, a given document may be assigned a score of 0.1 for the category *financial performance* and a score of 0.2 for the category *regulatory affairs*. A nice feature of this approach is that a given document or corpus may exhibit multiple issues to varying degrees. A widely used dictionary-based tool for issue classification is Wmatrix (Rayson 2003). It features 23 major categories and 232 subcategories. Example of major categories include *government and the public domain*, *science and technology*, and *emotional actions, states and processes*. The category *emotional actions, states and processes*, for example, can be expanded to sub-categories such as *liking*, *calm/violent/angry*, and *happiness and contentment*. The subcategory *happiness and contentment* can further be subdivided into *happy/sad* and *contentment*. The advantages and drawbacks of dictionary-based methods are the same as those that were discussed in the context of sentiment scoring. Dictionary-based systems are easy to use and widely available, but are often domain-specific or too generic. For example, the term *party* is listed within the *entertainment, sports, and games* category, which creates problems in political science applications. Moreover, the performance of dictionary-based approaches cannot easily be assessed and validated.

The domain-dependence problem can partially be addressed by the use of *keywords*. Keywords are terms that embody the distinct content of a document and differentiate it from other documents. The idea is to examine the distribution of words in a target corpus and compare it to the typical distribution of words in a reference corpus (Scott and Tribble 2006). Keywords that are common throughout a corpus can suggest common themes or issues that exist throughout the corpus. One of the simplest and most efficient means of identifying keywords is through frequency analysis. Words and phrases that are used in a document more frequently than they are generally found in language are likely to be related to its core meaning in one way or another. The best-known implementation of a measure of keywords, "keyness," is through Wordsmith Tools (Scott and Tribble 2006). In the Wordsmith implementation, the relative frequency of a word within a document is compared to its relative frequency in a reference corpus. If that difference is statistically significant (e.g., based on a χ^2 or likelihood ratio test), the word is judged to be a keyword in the text. Importantly, this implementation allows for two distinct types of keywords:

1. *Positive keywords*: These are words that are found in the document more frequently than would be expected based on the reference corpus. They are

therefore likely to be related to the meaning of the text. For example, a text detailing the current state of the aerospace industry might include the terms "airplane," "Boeing," and "Airbus" more frequently than would otherwise be expected. Note that, unless they are filtered out, proper nouns and brand names can be identified as keywords.

2. *Negative keywords*: These are words that are found in the document less frequently than would be expected based on the reference corpus. This could indicate that they are not only unrelated to the content of the document, but in some sense antithetical to it. Because of the low overall frequency of content words in a corpus, negative keywords are relatively infrequent. Most commonly these will be related to the writing style rather than the content, because of the relatively high frequency of function words and connectives. For example, a document written by an author who rarely uses *because* as a connective and prefers *as* or *since* might count *because* as a negative keyword.

When using distributional measures such as keyness, it is important to remember that this measure compares the current document with a reference corpus. That reference corpus provides a baseline for the comparison, and its choice is therefore of critical importance since it affects the identified keywords. In most cases, a neutral corpus such as the British National Corpus is a good choice. However, a more specialized corpus that is more similar to the document in question might yield a smaller and more indicative set of keywords. For example, when examining news articles, using a reference corpus drawn from a newspaper corpus might reduce the occurrence of formulaic news items like *no_comment* as keywords because these terms are infrequent in general usage but are frequent in newspaper articles.

A simple keywords analysis can be surprisingly powerful. For instance, a Wordsmith keyword analysis of Senator McCain's speech in the Senate dated May 12, 1999, reveals the following as the top 10 keywords: *violence, kids, youth, illegally, killing, commit, violent, imprisoned, juvenile,* and *images*. This simple analysis already reveals that the theme of the speech is likely juvenile violence and crime. This is a reasonably accurate description of the text, which describes a proposed amendment regarding the acquisition of weapons by juveniles. Below is the first content paragraph from that speech with the keywords described above emphasized:

This amendment provides that whoever *illegally* purchases a weapon for another individual knowing that the recipient intends to use the weapon to *commit* a *violent* crime may be *imprisoned* for up to 15 years. Further the amendment mandates that whoever *illegally* purchases a weapon for a *juvenile* knowing that the *juvenile* intends to *commit* a *violent* felony with the weapon will receive a mandatory minimum sentence of 10 years and may be *imprisoned* for up to 20 years. Current law provides a maximum prison term of 10 years regardless of the age of the shooter.

This example also indicates some of the limitations of this approach. While the focus on juvenile violence and crime is well captured, there is no mention of "weapon" or "purchase" among the top keywords, which are important themes in McCain's speech.

An alternative approach is the use of *diagnostic terms*. This is often done by using *term frequency–inverse document frequency* or *tf* $*$ *idf*.[1] Intuitively, this captures terms that are particular to some of the documents but not others. In its most simple form, this measure divides the frequency of a term in a document by the logarithm of the proportion of documents in which it appears. For instance, one formula for computing this measure for a particular term c in a document d is

$$tf * idf\,(c, d) = tf\,(c, d) \times \log \frac{|D| + 1}{df\,(c)},$$

where $tf\,(c, d)$ is the term frequency c in the document d, $df\,(c)$ is the number of documents in which c appears, and D is the number of documents in the corpus. This measure is useful because it is highest for frequent terms that appear in few documents, and as such it is similar in utility to a measure of keyness. The words with the highest $tf * idf$ for a particular document are likely to also have a high keyness.

It is possible to generalize this measure and use the overall frequency of the term in the entire corpus rather than its frequency in a particular document. Under this condition, this measure normalizes the frequency of terms by their spread over documents and provides a good indication of whether a particular term is frequent, but appears in only a few documents, or is spread over the entire corpus. A $tf * idf$ analysis of the speech by Senator McCain mentioned above, for example, shows results that are very similar to those obtained by Wordsmith, as shown in table 17.1.

The problem of validation, however, remains unresolved. When we applied keyness to the paragraph from Senator McCain's speech, the top keywords did a decent job of capturing the meaning of the text. In principle, we could use human judgment to assess the success of dictionary-based

TABLE 17.1 **Comparison of keyness and** *tf* ∗ *idf* **measures in Senator McCain's May 12, 1999, speech on the acquisition of weapons by juveniles**

Term	Keyness	*tf* ∗ *idf*
violence	98.16	21.45
kids	59.02	14.00
youth	49.86	12.23
illegally	45.33	11.19
killing	41.97	9.92
commit	38.08	8.98
violent	33.45	9.14
imprisoned	32.32	8.01
juvenile	29.17	8.71
images	29.02	7.47

methods, but doing so would at least partially defeat the purpose of developing a scalable approach to issue identification in text. As in the case of sentiment analysis, supervised learning provides an alternative.

17.2 Supervised Classification

While the underlying algorithms used in a supervised learning approach might vary, the overall structure of these methods is similar. In general, supervised learning approaches apply an optimization algorithm to a search space defined by the provided set of preclassified documents (the training set) to identify a set of diagnostic features, and then use the optimized result to classify new documents, often referred to as the *test set*. These optimization algorithms can be as simple as *least squares approximation*, in which the Euclidean distance between the prediction (i.e., algorithm output) and the expected result (i.e., the provided classification of each document in the test set) is minimized (Suykens and Vandewalle 1999), or *Naïve Bayesian* which relies on an application of Bayes' Rule (Maron and Kuhns 1960). Alternatively, they can be as complex as a *neural network*, in which back propagation is used to gradually adjust the weights of the interneuron connections in the network to properly classify the input (Bishop 1995). As in the case of sentiment analysis, we can also use SVM, the most common supervised learning approach (e.g., Basu, Walters, and Shepherd 2003; Joachims 1998; Suykens and Vandewalle 1999).

In the case of sentiment analysis, we usually restrict ourselves to two categories, *positive* and *negative*. In the case of issue identification, there are now typically more than two categories, one for each issue of interest. The training phase, however, works in the same fashion as in the case of sentiment classification. The analysis would select in advance k issues from a set K and then create a training set where human coders classify documents by hand into the k categories. The training set of l examples then is a set of pairs

$$\{(x_1, y_1), \ldots, (x_l, y_l)\}, \quad x_{i=1,\ldots,l} \in \Re^n, \quad y_{i=1,\ldots,l} \in K.$$

As in the case of sentiment classification, the training sets need to be representative samples of the corpus and of sufficient size. Note also that, in the case of issue classification, developing a solid coding scheme is of supreme importance (Krippendorf 2004). As before, we can evaluate the classification success using accuracy or other measures.[2] A good approach is to use cross-validation, where the corpus is divided into g subgroups. The classifier is then trained on a training set consisting of the $g - 1$ groups and tested on the remaining group. This can be done by using every one of the groups as the "left out" group and averaging over the tests (Hastie, Tibshirani, and Friedman 2001).

Classification approaches offer solutions to the domain-dependence and validation problems. However, they often require manual coding for each new application. The vagaries of human coding are often of greater importance when classification algorithms are applied to issues rather than sentiment, as human coders frequently have more difficulty categorizing a document by issue rather than by sentiment. As a result, classification success can be spotty.

While sentiment analysis usually requires only a binary decision, coding for issues is more complex, as the issues are not all set along one dimension, the boundaries between categories might be vague, and the language used to distinguish between categories might be nuanced (Grimmer and Stewart 2013). Perhaps even more importantly, classification approaches assume that each document belongs to one and only one category. However, that is not always true, especially for longer texts. For example, a speech by a politician may discuss multiple issues, or a newspaper article about Wal-Mart may mention financial performance but also describe difficulties in opening new stores. In these cases, it might be unclear for the coders which of the different categories the text belongs to. As a result of this ambiguity, not only is categorization itself difficult, but different coders might choose different categories for the document. Because the training of the classifier is dependent on the categories chosen by the coders, any inconsistencies in the coding will also be picked up by the classifier. At best, these will result in reduced accuracy in classification. However, any biases in categorization by the coders will be amplified by the trained classifier system. These problems can be avoided by using topic modeling.

17.3 Topic Modeling

The state of the art in identifying issues in a text is *topic modeling* (Blei 2012; Blei, Ng, and Jordan 2003; Boyd-Graber, Hu, and Mimno 2017; Chuang et al. 2015; Grimmer and King 2011; Koreni, Ristov, and Šnajder 2015; Steyvers and Griffiths 2007). At the core of this method is the idea that the distribution of words in a text is a result of the topics discussed within it. Topics are viewed as latent variables to be estimated from a given distribution of words. That is, topic models represent a document as the result of a stochastic process that, given a set of topics, selects which words to include in a text. Formally, a topic is a probability distribution of words capturing the likelihood that a given topic uses a given word. For example, a newspaper article may discuss the topic of accounting problems. Hence, words such as *restatement, audit, earnings*, and so on, occur with high probability. If it captures the topic of labor unrest, words such as *strike, negotiation*, or *union* will be likely.

Topics are not directly observable; they must be estimated from the data. This is done by assuming a stochastic model of how topics determine word frequencies and then estimating the underlying parameters of the model from the data. Topic models usually contain three steps. A topic is defined as a probability distribution over words. For topic j we denote this distribution as π_j, where π_{ji} is the probability that topic j assigns to generating word i. The first step specifies a prior distribution over topics. The widely used latent Dirichlet allocation (LDA) model (Blei, Ng, and Jordan 2003) assumes that each document is characterized by a distribution over topics.[3] That is, a document d is associated with a vector θ_d over the set of topics K. That is, $\theta_d = (\theta_{d1}, \ldots, \theta_{dk})$, where k is the number of topics, $\theta_{dj} \in (0,1)$ for all $j \in K$, and $\sum_{j=1}^{k} \theta_{dj} = 1$. Vectors are assumed to be drawn from a Dirichlet distribution (see Kotz, Balakrishnan, and Johnson 2000 for details) with parameter α, hence the name latent Dirichlet allocation. The process first draws a given topic $\theta_d \sim Dirichlet(\alpha)$. Next, words i are drawn according to the distribution of topics. LDA first selects the topic based on the realized θ_d and then selects the word based on the selected π_{ji}. That is, for each word i a specific topic is realized from a multinomial distribution conditional on θ_d. That is, $\pi_j \sim Multinomial(\theta_d)$. Next, conditional on a realized topic we draw the individual words as $\pi_{ji} \sim Multinomial(j = \theta_d)$.

In sum, a specific topic is drawn from a multinomial distribution conditional on the distribution over topics mixture. Then a word is drawn from a multinomial distribution conditional on the chosen topic. LDA can thus be interpreted as word clusters, where words with a high probability π_{ji} of being selected are representative of a given topic cluster. The number of topics k is fixed in advance. The other parameters are estimated using methods including expectation maximization (Hofmann 1999) and Gibbs sampling (Griffiths and Steyvers 2004; Steyvers and Griffiths 2007). While estimation of the topics for a corpus proceeds in an unsupervised fashion, it is possible to "suggest" specific topics to the model by seeding some of the topic dimensions with keywords, which should be included prior to starting the computation (e.g., Andrzejewski and Zhu 2009). This adds some level of supervision and guidance to the process.

For a given corpus of texts, LDA produces word clusters with statistically distinct patterns of occurrence corresponding to topics (Blei, Ng, and Jordan 2003; Chanen and Patrick 2007). In the context of agenda setting, these topics capture the issues discussed in a text. This means we can then determine the issue composition of a specific collection of texts and see how this issue composition changes over time (AlSumait, Barbará, and Domeniconi 2008; Kim et al. 2013; Mei et al. 2007; Mei and Zhai 2005; Quinn et al. 2010). For example, by considering a large corpus of media texts, we can assess how issue agendas change over time.

Some approaches do not require the researcher to decide on the number of clusters in advance, but estimate them directly (Frey and Dueck 2007; Wallach et al. 2010). However, such estimates heavily depend on the assumed statistical model (Wallach et al. 2010). Other approaches search over various topic models (Grimmer and King 2011).[4]

In contrast to supervised learning models, topic models are more difficult to evaluate. In a sense, they shift the burden from predefining the categories, as in supervised models, to interpreting the topic clusters ex post (Quinn et al. 2010). One approach relies on a comparison with clustering done by humans (e.g., Chanen and Patrick 2007; Grimmer and King 2011). A second approach relates topic clustering to external events

(Grimmer and Stewart 2013). For example, an executive compensation scandal should lead to a significant increase in topics related to executives and corporate governance.

Topic models may also be related to operational measures like customer or stakeholder surveys, or financial measures such as stock prices or bond yields. Kim et al. (2012, 2013) present a novel methodology along these lines for correlating a topic model with time series analysis. The approach requires the availability of two data sources—a corpus where each document is related to a point in time, and a time series measuring some continuous variable that covers that same period of time, such as stock prices. To accomplish the task of correlating the two sources, their method begins by extracting the topics from the corpus without regard for the time series data. The loading for each particular topic for each document then provides a quantitative time series of the development of each topic over time.

The next step involves identifying a relationship between the secondary time series source and each topic. There are various statistical methods that can achieve this result, from simple correlations between the two series at various relative lags to more complex models such as Granger causality (Granger 1969).[5] Kim et al. (2012, 2013) apply the latter to the task of gauging the possibility of a relationship between the time series and each topic. Specifically, Granger causality represents the impact of hypothesized factor x on the dependent variable y at time t and with a maximum lag of p as a regression equation such that

$$y_t = a_0 + a_1 y_{t-1} + a_2 y_{t-2} + \cdots + a_p y_{t-p} + b_0 + b_1 x_{t-1}$$
$$+ b_2 x_{t-2} + \cdots + b_p x_{t-p}.$$

Following the computation of the regression coefficients, a series of F-tests can be used to investigate the possibility that x is Granger causal for y at time t with a particular lag between 1 and p. The coefficients $b_1 \ldots b_p$ are estimates of the impact of x on y_t. To summarize this possible effect for a particular topic, Kim et al. (2012, 2013) use the average coefficient as an overall impact value for each topic on the time series.

Next, topics that are found to be related to the time series are used to construct priors for the next run of the topic model. Within each such topic, words that are found to be positively correlated with the time series are separated from those that are found to be negatively correlated. (Words in a topic that are not found to correlate with the time series are discarded). The data for these word-based time series are constructed based on their frequency of occurrence in the corpus for each day. A new topic prior is constructed separately for each related topic for the positively correlated words and the negatively related words. These priors are then used to seed a new run of topic extraction. The process of generating a set of topics from the corpus and measuring their relatedness to the time series is then repeated iteratively. This iterative process is repeated until some specified termination condition is met (e.g., the topics have stabilized or a specific number of iterations have been computed).[6]

One of the examples in Kim et al. (2013) is especially illuminating with respect to the effect that the time series has on the topic extraction. Using a corpus of *New York Times* articles from July 2000 to December 2001, they extract the set of causal topics using two different time series sources—the stock prices for American Airlines (AAMRQ) and Apple (APPL). Because the 9/11 terrorist attack occurred within the time period encompassed by the corpus, it is expected to affect the results of the analysis for American Airlines (whose stock price was greatly affected by the attack), but less so in the case of Apple. Indeed, this is the result that Kim et al. observe. A topic consisting of the top three words *united*, *trade*, and *terrorism* appears in the analysis of AAMRQ, while there is no mention of terrorism in the first three words of the topics for AAPL. Moreover, the analysis appears to successfully distinguish the two companies, as is evident by the extraction of a topic related to *airlines*, *airport*, and *air* for AAMRQ and a topic on *computer*, *technology*, and *software* for AAPL. However, many of the other dimensions extracted bear very little relation to either the companies' business environment or the terrorist attack. For example, both analyses show a topic that relates to *russia* and *russian*. Nevertheless, the results are encouraging, given that the corpus in question covered a wide range of topics, and given the noisy nature of a time series based on stock prices.

In sum, it is important to understand that there is no perfect approach to issue identification. Each method has its strengths and weaknesses. Dictionary methods are easy to use, but lack measures of validity, while classification models depend on the quality of the test set, and thus often rely on human coders. Unsupervised methods are efficient, but can be difficult to evaluate and tend to heavily depend on the underlying statistical models. Moreover, each method serves a different purpose. If the main goal is to categorize documents into well-established, clear, and mutually exclusive categories, a supervised classification approach is usually best. If the categories are unknown or documents may speak to more than one issue, unsupervised topic models tend to be preferable.

CHAPTER EIGHTEEN

Frames

The identification of frames is one of the more challenging areas of text analytics. One of the difficulties lies in analytically distinguishing what a text is talking about (its issues) from how it talks about them (its frames). Linguists define a frame as "selecting and highlighting some facets of events or issues, and making connections among them so as to promote a particular interpretation, evaluation, and/or solution" (Entman 2003). On the issue of smoking, for example, we have seen the presence of a systemic frame versus an individual responsibility frame in the 1990s. This corresponds to competing frames, and the media may prefer one of these frames over the other or use each equally. Moreover, the prevalence of each frame may change over time, perhaps with one frame becoming more dominant. Which frame is dominant may have important consequences, as they may suggest different policy solutions and different industry targets.

18.1 Metaphors

Consider the following statement about the Paula Deen case, issued after the racial discrimination lawsuit against her was thrown out by a judge (Puente 2013):

> The irony is thicker than her gravy. As I've said all along, you have to play in the court of law and you have to play in the court of public opinion. Like O. J.

Simpson, who won in the court of law but lost in the court of public opinion — Paula's in the same situation. You can't put the toothpaste back in the tube now. It's going to be really challenging for her to piece this together.

This is an example of standard commentary on an issue of current interest. It is easy to understand. Yet, on closer inspection the underlying semantic structure is quite complex. Note, first, that the statement draws from the semantic domain of courts with terms such as *court* and *law*. This, of course, is to be expected since the main issue is a court case. But notice that the statement draws on a variety of analogies and metaphors. They can come from areas such as cooking (*gravy*), where the reference is somewhat tongue-in-cheek, since Paula Dean is a celebrity chef. Or they can come from entirely unrelated areas such as dental care (*toothpaste, tube*). Note also the use of wordplay in the contrast between *court of law* versus *court of public opinion*. Here, court is used once literally (*court of law*) and once metaphorically (*court of public opinion*). This shift from literal to metaphorical is an effective means to express the main point of the statement, that is, that the legal victory will not help Paula Deen much.

The importance of metaphors in the sample statement is no accident. The use of metaphors as an important rhetorical device has long been acknowledged (e.g., Kittay 1987). It makes a particular claim more memorable and vivid. In our example, the toothpaste metaphor fulfills this function. It uses a simple, easy to understand image to convey the view that Paula Deen's situation is beyond fixing. But this assessment could have easily been expressed directly. The toothpaste metaphor is a conventional way to make the same point with stronger emphasis.

More recently, cognitive scientists have argued that metaphors are not merely rhetorical devices but play a crucial role as mental schemes in cognitive processes (Lakoff and Johnson 2003).[1] The basic idea is that metaphors function as devices to understand complex, unfamiliar domains. That is, we use a well-understood domain, the source domain, and superimpose its structure on the target domain. Technically this amounts to a homomorphism, a partial match between the source and target domains. One well-known example is the metaphor that "money is like water." Examples are expressions such as *liquidity, cash flow*, and *the clogged banking system*. The point is that the world of finance is unfamiliar to most and difficult to understand. Using the source domain of water makes it (partially) understandable.

Like any other cognitive scheme, what makes metaphors potent is that, once a scheme is accepted, certain conclusions are plausible, while others become absurd. Consider two views of terrorism. Terrorism is a complex phenomenon that can be understood in different ways. For example, a terrorist attack can be viewed as an act of war or as a crime (Lakoff 2001; Sagi, Diermeier, and Kaufmann 2013). If it is viewed as crime, terrorism needs to be addressed in courts governed by the rule of law. There will be prosecutors, defense attorneys, judges, rules of evidence, and due process. If terrorism is viewed as an act of war, none of these aspects are relevant (other than international law on armed conflicts). Rather, this is the domain of military combat, fighter jets, drone strikes, covert operations, and armed conflict.

More generally, once we accept a conceptual metaphor, certain policies become far more plausible than others. Metaphors are thus a particularly effective form of framing. We can see this in some of the examples discussed in chapter 7. The view that "obesity is an epidemic" has very different policy consequences from "obesity is a genetic disposition" or "obesity is a consequence of lack of willpower." Some of these references are universal, such as those using family relations to conceptualize political structures, as when a leader is called "the father of the nation." Others are highly culture-specific and draw their power from their cultural embeddedness and relevance. For example, British politicians from Churchill to Thatcher frequently used maritime images to elucidate patriotic sentiments triggered by the history of the island nation (Klebanov, Diermeier, and Beigman 2008b; Mautner 2001). In our sample text above, there was a brief reference to O. J. Simpson, easily understandable to anyone familiar with current events in the United States in the 1990s, but mystifying to anyone else. In general, for messages to be persuasive, they need to resonate with the cultural sensitivities of their audience that are most relevant. This is often accomplished by referring to a particular aspect of the cultural common ground shared with the audience.

18.2   Lexical Cohesion

Capturing these phenomena algorithmically is challenging.[2] Topic models provide one option. Methodologically they are based on collocation, which is suitable for identifying the main content of a text but likely to miss cultural references, which can occur throughout a text and are often triggered by a single word. Topic models also require large corpora and are less suitable for analyzing single texts, such as speeches. Overall, topic models are very useful for identifying *what* a text is talking about but much less useful for determining *how* it is talking about it.

Dictionary-based approaches are particularly suitable for uncovering properties related to universal principles, such as emotional content or universal value categories. For example, they are useful for identifying expressed anger in a text or references to harm or purity (Haidt and Graham 2007). However, culturally specific references and metaphorical content are difficult to identify. In principle, it would be possible to construct specific dictionaries for each particular application, but such an approach is too inefficient.

A different approach is to use lexical cohesion. The lexical cohesion approach takes as its point of departure the basic insight that, to be meaningful, a text needs to be *cohesive*, that is, it constitutes a smoothly connected body of ideas that possesses the quality of "hanging together as a whole" (Harman 1976). Apart from grammatical elements, the unifying cohesion of a text is created by the use of words with related meanings, called *lexical cohesion*. The idea is to identify semantic fields related to various content domains. Any speaker of English will see the words *harbor* and *ocean* to be more closely related than *harbor* and *meadow*, but making these connections precise has proven to be challenging.

One such approach is lexical cohesion analysis (LCA) (Klebanov 2006; Klebanov, Diermeier, and Beigman 2008a, 2008b; Klebanov and Shamir 2006). LCA uses a variety of sources of cohesion and combines them using a machine learning decision tree (Quinlan 1993). Specifically, the following sources are used (e.g., Klebanov, Diermeier and Beigman 2008b).

Inverse Frequency. The more frequent the item is in general, the less likely it is to participate in lexical cohesion, that is, cohesive structures tend to rest on the more informative words. This is effectively an application of Shannon's theory of information (Shannon 1948). Various estimations of frequencies are available, such as, Kučera and Francis (1967).

Distance. The further two words are apart in the text, the less likely they are to be detected as a cohesive pair (Klebanov 2007). Distance is measured as the number of intervening words.

Morphological Connection. Words are morphologically connected if they share a stem. This can serve as an important cohesion-creating device (Stotsky 1983). Examples are *economic* and *economy*, but also multistem words such as *airfield* and *aircraft*.

Definition Overlap. Definitions of words are normalized and then assessed for their overlap (Klebanov 2006). The definitions are based on WordNet (Miller et al. 1990).

Co-Occurrences. Kontostathis and Pottenger (2006) showed that latent semantic analysis (LSA) captures the tendency of two terms to co-occur in the same document or with some other group of terms. Corpus co-occurrence scores can then be used as a measure of semantic relatedness.

Free Association. A free association is the first word w that comes to mind when exposed to another word w'. Linguists have argued that free associations capture shared lexical experiences (e.g., Nelson, McEvoy, and Schreiber 2004).[3]

These sources are then used to construct a cohesion detector that is trained on the Klebanov and Shamir (2006) dataset of cohesive pairs. The detector is developed using a decision tree machine-learning algorithm (Quinlan 1993). This works as follows. The decision tree draws on the sources of information, inverse frequency, distance, morphological connection, and so forth. Each stage of the decision tree is a classification decision based on information gain or, equivalently, entropy reduction (Shannon 1948). That is, information gain in a given split is the reduction of entropy achieved by the classification. If we start out with the set T of training examples, the entropy of this set $H(T)$ is the amount of information needed to specify, for every example, which category it belongs to.

$$H(T) = -P(x^+)logP(x^+) - P(x^-)logP(x^-), \qquad (18.4)$$

where $P(x^+)$ is the probability that a pair is *cohesive* and $P(x^-)$ is the probability that a pair is *noncohesive*. Now consider a similar measurement after T has been partitioned in accordance with the n outcomes of a test A. The expected information requirement is the weighted sum of the subsets:

$$H_A(T) = \Sigma_{i=1}^n \frac{|T_i|}{|T|} H(T_i). \qquad (18.5)$$

The gain in information achieved by partitioning T on test A is thus:[4]

$$Gain(A) = H(T) - H_A(T). \qquad (18.6)$$

The application of the decision tree to the set of all possible word pairs in a text results in a set of cohesive word pairs. Klebanov, Diermeier, and Beigman (2008a, 2008b) use these pairs to construct semantic groups based on the *maximum cliques* observed in this set of pairs. A clique is a set of words such that all possible pairwise connections between the words were observed as cohesive in the text. That is, for a group of N words there are $\frac{N(N-1)}{2}$ possible pairwise connections. For that group to be considered a clique, all of these must be observed as cohesive pairs in the output of the decision tree. A maximal clique is a clique such that there are no other words in the set that can be added to the group without violating its status as a clique. In practice, there are often some maximal cliques that show a large degree of overlap, where two cliques share a large proportion of words, but one clique includes some words that are not connected to some of the words in the other clique (and vice versa). To accommodate these cases, the clique requirement can be relaxed and cliques that share more than half of their terms are iteratively merged. The resulting groups of words are considered as representing semantic fields characteristic of the document.

We can see this approach in action by applying it to an example: Margaret Thatcher's 1977 speech to the Conservative Party Conference, the programmatic "Confrontation with Reality" speech, delivered two years before she became Britain's first female prime minister.[5] This also allows us to compare LCA with topic analysis and dictionary-based methods (Klebanov, Diermeier, and Beigman 2008a).

The first approach is topic analysis using LDA (Blei, Ng, and Jordan 2003). Klebanov, Diermeier, and Beigman (2008a) analyze the complete corpus of public statements given by Margaret Thatcher between 1945 and 1990, including speeches, broadcasts, press conferences, interviews, and articles (Collins 1999), and then applied these clusters to the 1977 speech.[6] The four leading topics are:

British Politics (LDA) labour government party conservative election people last policies conservatives said against britain tax manifesto policy years news now section prices country left socialist time inflation next report unemployment campaign majority bbc checked today spending vote end parliament power callaghan nation radio national put office first back programme day record healey

British Political Ideologies (LDA) people party government state society conservative free freedom believe now british own socialism country socialist labour power political way let make public want economic great individual right say like enterprise work wealth well choice years money know nation against british good left private see never back need take social less

Northern Ireland (LDA) ireland northern people prime minister government united kingdom republic irish agreement terrorism security violence political majority ira part ulster

Economy (LDA) tax hon clause bill amendment income case right member time house gentleman new relief people made say act said way land rent secretary macdermot put think year capital point make therefore financial part committee government value get know kind hope give finance small revenue diamond first two thatcher person now

LDA does a good job at identifying the key topics of the speech. Even a casual reading of the speech shows a clearly delineated section where Thatcher states her position on one topic after another, as would be expected in a programmatic speech. Note, however, that we get little information on *how* Thatcher is addressing these issues and what her respective position is. This reinforces the view that the proper role of topic analysis is to identify the issue agenda, but that it is less suited to identifying frames. One revealing example is a cluster that can be referred to as "Home Life"

Home Life (LDA) think just know like people things time get always go women really got minister life woman children prime well yes day something never see work home say quite come now good family house lot sometimes own way look thing going little back right take make job thatcher went course remember

As we will see later, this does not refer to a particular topic, but refers to a key component of Thatcher's rhetoric, although one would be hard pressed to infer this from the topic cluster. Next we consider dictionary-based methods. Klebanov, Diermeier and Beigman (2008a) use the Wmatrix system (Rayson 2003).

The four largest categories are (number of occurrences in parentheses):

Politics (Wmatrix; 130 occurrences) labour(33) conservative(19) election(13) socialist voters tories . . .

Government (Wmatrix) government(41) country(11) nation(7) state parliament council . . .

General Action/Making (Wmatrix) do(10) cut make made task arise making did created doing . . .

Location and Direction (Wmatrix) this(17) there(6) here(4) north where on top of left facing position direction eastern reversed back face inland directed direct stands western end ahead ashore along front . . .

Although Wmatrix correctly identifies the key topics of Politics and Government, the information is less informative than the results of LDA, from which different policy domains such as Economy or Northern Ireland are identified. Note also that two of the largest categories (General Action/Making; Location and Direction) are generic and provide little insight. The reason for these shortcomings is simple. Dictionaries are created by researchers and reflect their interests. Of course, one could create a dictionary suitable for British politics to capture important policy domains, but such an approach would be highly labor intensive. When applied to Thatcher's speech alone, the dictionary approach yields few insights. This is not uncommon for official documents or speeches, which rarely contain direct expressions of emotions or even values. Finally, let us consider LCA. Note first that while LCA and LDA both create groupings, lexical cohesion is not a good alternative to standard topic modeling. While many of the same topics are picked up, they are not as clearly identified. For example, LDA produces the following cluster for the topic of **Northern Ireland**:

Northern Ireland (LDA) ireland northern people prime minister government united kingdom republic irish agreement terrorism security violence political majority ira part ulster

Lexical cohesion analysis produces the following cluster:

Northern Ireland (LCA) britain country ireland nation europe state kingdom land

Now the issue of Northern Ireland appears to connected to the general issue of sovereignty, for example, the reference to Europe. But the original text does *not* exhibit this connection. Here is the most relevant section from Thatcher's speech:

Northern Ireland (Original Text)   If the violence in Britain is deeply disturbing, it is nothing to what has been endured by the people of Northern Ireland for nearly ten years. What happens in Ulster touches us all; it is a part of our country, our United Kingdom. Let the people of Ulster be assured of this the Conservative Party stands rock-firm for the Union of Great Britain and Northern Ireland. Today we express our deep and lasting admiration for Betty Williams and Mairead Corrigan, the Belfast Peace Women who have been awarded the Nobel Peace Prize. Their courage symbolises to us, and to the whole Western world, the yearning of the people of Ulster for peace. And we honour with them the Royal Ulster Constabulary, the Ulster Defence Regiment and our servicemen in Northern Ireland.

The focus here is clearly on security only. The section follows a section on domestic law and order and policing, and is followed by a segment on national defense. Rather than correctly identifying this focus, the strength of LCA lies elsewhere. The second lexically richest group in Thatcher's 1977 speech has to do with fishing, sea, and marine life. Here is the group:

> **Marine Life (LCA)** sea boat port water sailor fishing ashore fish coast navy catch tide bait flag labour terrify land

Thatcher, however, is barely talking about the British fishing industry, and indeed LDA does not identify **fishing** as a separate topic. Rather, items from this domain are predominantly used figuratively, as in "When the tide comes in, all the boats rise," or "They've swallowed the bait and are ripe for the catch." To see this, note the context for the reference to fishing (highlighted in italics):

> **"Following Labour is like swallowing the bait" (Original Text)**   The choice is the classic choice. Labour would do what it has been doing for the last three years, only more so. We shall do what we have said we will do. "Set the people free." The key question I am asked over and over again is, but will a Conservative Government be free? How will you get on with the Trade Unions? And will the Trade Unions allow a Conservative Government to govern? Yes, the word is "allow". People who ask the question are already half way into Labour's trap. *They've swallowed the bait and are ripe for the catch.* Here is the position. The Government dare not fight on its record or on any manifesto that would be acceptable both to its Marxist Left and the people of Britain. So, like an unimaginative parrot, they keep repeating: "The Tories won't be able to work with the Unions."

The context here is the Conservatives' stand toward trade unions, and the reference to fishing is used as a metaphor for "Labour's trap." Similarly, the context for "When the tide comes in, all the boats rise" is a discussion of the benefits of free enterprise. In contrast to the discussion of Northern Ireland, which occurs in a few contiguous paragraphs typical of a topic, references to marine life are scattered throughout the text. This

scattered appearance is characteristic of metaphorical domains. Indeed,
lexically coherent groups that are not topics often function as metaphors.
Note that Thatcher doesn't use just any metaphors, but relies on the content domain of fishing and the sea, a source domain of profound cultural
relevance to Britain's identity as an island nation. A similar concern for cultural relevance can also be seen in the second dominant metaphor, **home
economics**, given by the group:

> **Home Economics (LCA)** pay money rent payment income bill buy obligation
> earn mortgage rate cost store tax

A typical section from the speech is the following (The "4-Budget-a-
Year man" is then Labour Chancellor of the Exchequer, Denis Healey;
italics are added):

> **"Increasing the national debt is like taking out a mortgage" (Original text)**
> Twelve months ago the 4-Budget-a-Year man all but took the country over the
> cliff with him until at the eleventh hour he turned back from Heathrow in a panic
> and headed for home to take out the most massive *mortgage* in our history.

The reference to everyday economic decisions works on various levels. It compares a complex domain (national debt) with a more familiar
domain (mortgages), establishing common ground with ordinary people
who, in Thatcher's view, have been betrayed by Labour and by the unions.
This populist turn requires an emotional connection between the leader
and the people, here based on cultural images of the "island nation" and
a connection with home life.[7] The home-life metaphor also alleviates a
problem specific to Thatcher, the need to establish herself as strong female
leader who came from a modest background—Thatcher was a shopkeeper's daughter, highly unusual given the establishment background of
most British politicians at that time—in male-dominated British politics.
All these strands are nicely integrated in the following section, a combination of the fishing and home-life content domains which are used here to
make a case for limited government:

> **"Governing is like cooking a small fish" (Original text)**   We do not believe that
> if you cut back what Government does, you diminish its authority. On the con-
> trary, a Government that did less, and therefore did it better, would strengthen
> its authority. Our approach was put very simply by a Chinese philosopher

centuries ago. "Govern a great nation," he counseled, "as you would cook a small fish. Don't overdo it."

For a very different use of cultural archetypes, see US President Barack Obama's speech "A More Perfect Union" delivered in Philadelphia in March 2008 (Obama 2008). It was arguably the defining speech of Obama's first presidential campaign, delivered at a pivotal moment when his campaign was under pressure to respond to public attention due to controversial remarks made by the Reverend Jeremiah Wright, Obama's former pastor. Obama's speech has been hailed as a "profile in courage" (*New York Times* 2008) and "hit[ting] the appropriate tone" (Sheppard 2008). When applying LCA to the speech we can identify the following word groups, among others (Klebanov, Kaufer, and Franklin 2010). The four largest groups are:

Religion (LCA) baptist christ christian church god pastor priest rabbi religion religious scripture seminary cross baptize condemnation minister unto pulpit spirit confess reverend flock moses ministry faith sermon sin

Family (LCA) brother cousin daughter family father kid mom mother sister son friend grandchild girl nephew woman marry niece parent grandmother grandfather child uncle

Racial Discrimination (LCA) black discrimination race racial racially racism racist segregated segregation white civil bias slavery affirmative color prejudice inequality brown stereotype hispanic equal

Constitutional Law (LCA) constitution convention declaration father independence liberty philadelphia slavery colony history original document bondage freedom generation struggle founder parchment greatness citizen free civil slave statesman

The groups of racial discrimination and constitutional law are largely topical. The theme of religion, however, on the one hand obliquely refers to the controversial comments by Rev. Wright, but more importantly connects to Martin Luther King's iconic reliance on Christian faith and biblical imagery, especially from the Book of Exodus (notice the mention of Moses) during the civil rights movement. This registry of preaching invokes iconic cultural connections immediately obvious to anyone even vaguely familiar with modern US history. Note that nothing similar was found in Thatcher's speech. There, the reference was to Britain's history as an island nation, while here it is to the civil rights struggle and its connections to biblical themes of liberation from bondage. Both Obama's and Thatcher's invocations of history work well in the their respective contexts. These themes are further emphasized by other semantic groups:

Ocean Journey (LCA) harbor ocean ship vessel foot flag wind incident
Nourishment (LCA) eat jar kitchen sandwich food mustard barbershop table relish hungry

The **journey** metaphor is widely used by political leaders. It has deep cultural roots, for example, to Homer's *Odyssey*, and immediately evokes images of dangers, obstacles, and the ability to overcome them and reach the desired location (Charteris-Black 2005). In the American context, the ocean journey is particularly resonant in its connection with the perilous sea journey by the pilgrims, relating back to the very origin of American history. The domain of **nourishment** is used to underline the urgency of the need for racial reconciliation. This relies on the central metaphor that the "soul is like the body." Both need to be nourished. What food is for the body, the message of race reconciliation is for the soul. Both are vital. A good example is the following statement (highlights in italics added):

Nourishment (Original Text) Throughout the first year of this campaign, against all predictions to the contrary, we saw how *hungry* the American people were for this message of unity.

The connection with hunger highlights the importance of the issue and makes it vivid. Its goal is to persuade his audience that the race issue is important enough for people to base their choice of president on it. With the importance of the theme established, Obama needs to demonstrate that he is the right leader for the task. This is where the **family** group is used to great effect:

Family (Original Text) I am the son of a black man from Kenya and a white woman from Kansas. I was raised with the help of a white grandfather who survived a Depression to serve in Patton's Army during World War II and a white grandmother who worked on a bomber assembly line at Fort Leavenworth while he was overseas. I've gone to some of the best schools in America and lived in one of the world's poorest nations. I am married to a black American who carries within her the blood of slaves and slaveowners—an inheritance we pass on to our two precious daughters. I have brothers, sisters, nieces, nephews, uncles and cousins, of every race and every hue, scattered across three continents, and for as long as I live, I will never forget that in no other country on Earth is my story even possible.

The theme of family is introduced autobiographically. Notice the frequent references to "white" and "black," and other contrasts ("best" and "worst"). Yet these terms are integrated into a family context while never denying its contrasts and tensions. This reference to family does two things. First, it bestows immediate credibility on Obama. It is Obama's biographic integration of the contrasts in modern American life that makes his claim to leadership unique and credible, especially on the topic of race. Second, it applies the metaphor "a nation is like a family" to embrace the complexities of racial relationships in the mitigating context of kinship. In sum, both Margaret Thatcher and Barack Obama faced significant obstacles, often rooted in their personal histories, in their campaigns to lead their countries. In both cases their biographical backgrounds were highly unusual. Thatcher became the first female prime minister in British history, and Obama became the first African American president. Both used their unique biographies (Thatcher's "shopkeeper's daughter" origins, Obama's multiracial origins) to great effect by connecting them to images that are central to the cultural identities of their respective nations. These images are used sparingly; they are neither topics nor themes, but at crucial moments they provide a deeply shared reference with their audience that creates a level of familiarity and community. In their references to both critical historical events and the rules of everyday life, they position the respective campaign issues as both vital and understandable, with ready solutions provided by leaders uniquely qualified to execute them.

In sum, LCA can uncover subtle characteristics of text, including the use of metaphors and images. It is particularly useful for identifying cultural frames. It is advisable to use these approaches in combination. For example, LDA or other topic-identification algorithms can be used to map out the issue landscape. This can then be combined with LCA to identify frames and with dictionary-based approaches (or classification systems such as SVM) to capture emotional content or sentiment. In social science contexts, LCA has largely been used to analyze political speeches or manifestos. As far as we know, there have been no applications to business domains.

18.3   Semantic Space Analysis

As we saw above, LCA is able to identify fairly subtle frames that are only sparsely used throughout a document. But this strength becomes a limitation if we want to compare texts with each other or want to analyze entire corpora. In general, the analysis is computationally demanding, and the results are highly text-specific.

One approach to resolve these problems is semantic space analysis (Sagi, Diermeier, and Kaufman 2013). It is commonly assumed in text analysis and computational linguistics that a word's co-occurrence patterns with other words provide a readily observable approximation of its semantic content; two words are perfect synonyms if they can be exchanged in each context without changing its meaning (Deerwester et al. 1990; Firth 1957; Harris 1954). We have encountered this approach before in the context of topic clustering and LCA (Klebanov, Diermeier, and Beigman 2008b; Kontostathis and Pottenger 2006). Latent semantic analysis (LSA) is a collective term for a family of methods aimed at operationalizing this intuition by deriving a measure of similarity between words from their co-occurrence behavior in a collection of documents.[8] Technically, words are associated with vectors in a high-dimensional space. The vectors represent a word's frequency of co-occurrence with each of a list of "content-bearing" words, a subset of all the words represented in a corpus.[9]

A cell of the matrix $\langle w, c \rangle$ then captures the number of times a content-bearing word c occurred in the context of a word w.[10] A "context" is simply a 15-word window around w. That is, w' occurs in the context of w if w' occurs at most 15 words before w or 15 words after w. This matrix is then reduced using *singular value decomposition* (e.g., Berry 1992; Berry et al. 1993) to a reduced $20,000 \times 100$ matrix. Thus each word is associated with a 100-dimensional context vector. Intuitively, the context vector for a given word is the normalized sum of the word vectors associated with the words surrounding it within a context window. Semantic similarity then corresponds to the closeness of context vectors. That is, if two words (e.g., *obesity* and *overweight*) appear in similar contexts, the vectors representing them will be "close." In contrast, the vectors of two words that tend to appear in very different contexts (e.g., *obesity* and *robbery*) will be "far apart."

The most commonly used measure for closeness between vectors is the cosine between the associated vectors: A large cosine (i.e., low angle) indicates positively correlated co-occurrence profiles, hence, by assumption, it indicates semantic similarity. We can then use this approach to provide a

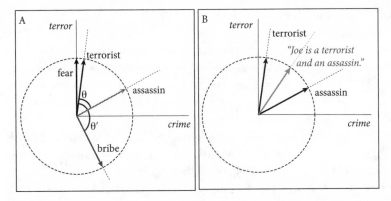

FIGURE 18.1. An illustrative two-dimensional vector space. The horizontal dimension corresponds with the frame "crime" and the vertical dimension corresponds with "terror." Consequently, in (A), the term "fear" is highly aligned with "terror" but not with "crime." The term "terrorist" is more likely to co-occur with the term "assassin" than "bribe," as is illustrated by the angles Θ and Θ', respectively (and their corresponding cosines which are inversely related to the angle). (B) illustrates the computation of a context vector for the context "Joe is a terrorist and an assassin." The context vector is generated by adding together the vectors for the content words "terrorist" and "assassin." Geometrically, this addition is equivalent to concatenating the vectors, with the resulting context vector pointing in the direction of the tip of the final vector. Vector lengths are normalized.

quantitative model of framing. The idea is as follows. Suppose an article blames obesity on the consumption of soft drinks. Then, the terms in the vicinity of the word *obesity* will tend to be associated with words like *sugary*, *fructose*, and *soda*. If it is framed as the fault of the fast food industry, words like *fries*, *trans-fatty acids*, and *fat* are more likely to be prominent.

To see this, consider a very impactful example of framing. Terrorism can be framed as an act of war, but also as a crime. If, as discussed above, *terror* is framed as an act of war, it will tend to appear in contexts that contain words such as *army*, *military*, and *command*. If it is framed as a crime, it will occur in contexts that also mention words such as *jury*, *indictment*, or *trial* (Lakoff 2001). Linguistically this means that if the "terror is war" frame becomes dominant, the word "terror" will become more semantically similar to the word "war." That is, we can view a successful frame as affecting the meaning of a word. Cognitively, this means that if we think of terror we are more likely to think of the military than a jury. Just like the meaning of a term can be gauged by inspection of the text surrounding it, the framing of a concept will be discernible through the terms with which it is used. This is illustrated in figure 18.1.

By observing such patterns across a large body of text, we can track changes in framing over time or across different domains. Since vector similarities are represented as simple scalars, differences in meaning can be explored using standard methods for statistical hypothesis testing. Note that, although the context vectors are associated with concrete words like *obesity* and *robbery*, the similarity measure is quite different from a simple co-occurrence count or some other measure of collocational strength. Rather, we have a relationship between regions in a densely populated vector space. The particular words we choose to represent frames—*obesity* in our example—are merely convenient identifiers for such regions. Consequently, our analysis of the framing of *obesity* yields qualitatively similar results whether the specific word used is *obesity*, *overweight*, or *fat*.

Therefore, we need to focus on the relative distance between vector clusters of contexts. The distance between clusters of vectors is defined as the mean of the distance between all the pairs of individual vectors. That is, for each vector in the first cluster we calculate its distance from all vectors in the second cluster and then average all of these distances, where a distance between vectors is the length of the vector resulting from vector subtraction. One such cluster is based on the uses of the target word (e.g., *obesity*). The other clusters are based on words that characterize possible frames. Changes in these inter-cluster distances indicate changes in semantic distance between the two regions. For example, if the distance between the clusters of uses of *obesity* and *soda* decrease over time, this is taken as an indication of an increase in the use of the soda frame (rather than, say, the fast food frame).

We first discuss two applications as proof of concept. To provide a first example of the method, we explore changes in the perception of the airline industry. To address this issue we use the *New York Times Annotated Corpus (NYT)*, a collection of *New York Times* articles assembled by the Linguistic Data Consortium (2008).[11] The corpus includes all articles published in the *New York Times* from 1987 to 2007. It is composed of over 1.8 million articles totaling over two billion words. The results are portrayed in figure 18.2. The vertical axis captures the semantic distance between two fields, measured as the average distance of the context vectors.

As, expected, the semantic distance between the fields associated with *airline* and *safety* correlates with airline fatalities—with one major exception: 9/11. This indicates that airline crashes are usually covered in the context of airline safety. The year 2001 is a telling anomaly, since the

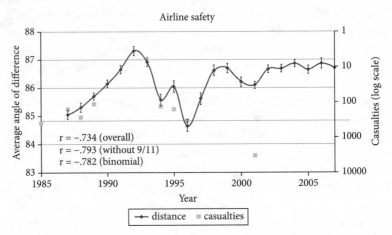

FIGURE 18.2. Distance between semantic fields *airline* and *safety* based on the *New York Times Annotated Corpus* compared to airline fatalities (on log-scale).

discussion focused on terrorism as the cause rather than airline safety. Consequently, we might expect to see the field associated with *security* rather than *safety* show a substantial dip in 2001 as a frame for *airline*. This is indeed the case. The semantic distance between the terms is 88.89 (SD = 0.15) for 2000 and 86.87 (SD = 0.13) for 2001 ($p = 0.0001$).

The second example is how the framing of terror changed after 9/11 (Sagi, Diermeier, and Kaufman 2013). The hypothesis is that we should see a significant decrease in the distance between the semantic fields of *terror* and *war* after 2001. In contrast, we have no such expectation in the case of *terror* and *crime*. Indeed, the distance between the two semantic fields may increase. The analysis is conducted on the corpus of Senate speeches used in Diermeier et al. (2012). The results can be seen in figure 18.3. The vertical axis measures the distance between the vector spaces of *crime* and *war* with respect to *terror*.

As predicted, the distance between the semantic fields for *terror* and *war* is significantly reduced post-2001, while the distance between the vectors for *terror* and *crime* does not show a similar reduction. This analysis provides support for the claim that post-9/11 terror was increasingly framed in terms of war rather than crime.[12]

Next we apply the method to the issue of obesity and its connection to soft drinks versus fast food restaurants in the *New York Times* corpus. The results can be seen in figure 18.4.

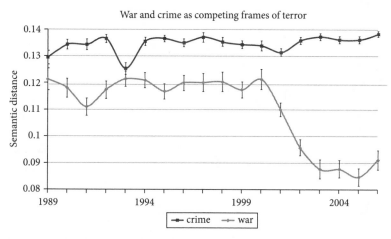

FIGURE 18.3. Distance between semantic fields *terror* (baseline), *crime*, and *war* based on the US Senate Corpus (Diermeier et al. 2012).

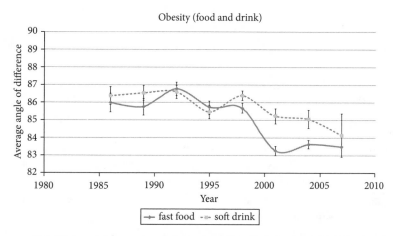

FIGURE 18.4. Distance between semantic fields *obesity* (baseline), *food*, and *drink* based on the *New York Times Annotated Corpus*.

While both seem to be seen as equal contributors in the 1990s, fast food was perceived as contributing more to obesity rates than soft drinks after 2000. Notice that both contributors, soft drinks and fast food, are trending closer to obesity over time, indicating that they are increasingly mentioned together, a worrying development for both industries. As shown in figure 18.5, we can also take a closer look at the reputation of particular

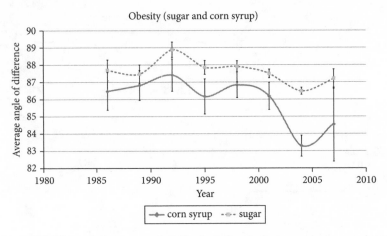

FIGURE 18.5. Distance between semantic fields *obesity* (baseline), *sugar*, and *corn_syrup* based on the *New York Times Annotated Corpus*.

ingredients and see the shift from sugar to high-fructose corn syrup as the main culprit of obesity, at least until 2007.

18.3.1   Industry Frames

We can now use this methodology to study the frames associated with various industries and companies.

BIOTECH. Emerging technologies frequently run into reputational challenges. Some well-known examples discussed in chapter 3 are nuclear power, stem-cell technology, and biotech. As an application of the semantic space approach, we can trace changes in the reputational environment of biotech using changes in the associated frames.[13] Biotech applications for industry fall into two categories.[14] On the one hand, we have what's called "green biotech" — applications to food and agriculture. On the other hand, we have "red biotech" — applications to medicine.

The history of the biotech industry was shaped by a few pivotal events. The first genetically altered product was the Flavr Savr tomato developed by biotech pioneer Calgene. The Flavr Savr tomato contained a modified gene designed to inhibit the release of the polygalacturonase (PG) enzyme — the main cause of tomatoes softening as they ripen. Calgene hoped that, by turning off this enzyme, Flavr Savr tomatoes could be picked vine-ripened. The company envisioned a tomato with improved color and taste that was easier to ship (because it remained firm) and had an extended shelf life in stores. The tomato was first sold in 1994 after Calgene asked for an FDA ruling on the safety of its marker gene.

The next major development was the introduction of Roundup Ready soybeans by Monsanto in 1996. As the name indicates, Roundup Ready seeds are genetically modified to tolerate Monsanto's Roundup agricultural herbicides. This tolerance then allows growers to spray Roundup herbicides on their fields during the growing season to kill weeds while leaving the crops unharmed. By reducing the need for broad herbicide use, Roundup Ready seeds may lead to higher crop yields. Some observers of the history of agricultural biotech have pointed out that, while Calgene successfully managed the public concerns over Flavr Savr, Monsanto failed to do so, leading to severe problems with European regulators and a ban on genetically modified organisms.[15]

Despite these controversies surrounding green biotech, red biotech did not face similar reputational challenges. For example, while Monsanto's entry into Europe led to extensive protests, there were no similar protests against medical applications of biotechnology in Europe or other markets.

We can now use semantic space analysis to assess whether these events correlate with changes in the perception of the industry. To accomplish this task, we use the *New York Times Annotated Corpus* and trace changes in the similarity of the semantic fields associated with *genetic_engineering* to the contexts of *agriculture* versus *medicine*. Suppose that, over time, *genetic_engineering* and closely related terms became more likely to occur in contexts mentioning *agriculture* rather than *medicine*. Then, in the minds of readers, the term *genetic_engineering* will slowly change its meaning toward agricultural applications. For example, when being cued with some biotech reference, audiences will tend to associate "plants" rather than "treatments."

This is indeed what we find in figure 18.6. Here, the vertical axis captures the yearly average distance between the cluster associated with *genetic_engineering* and the clusters associated with *agriculture* and *medicine*, respectively.

Note that the shift occurs after the introduction of Roundup Ready soybeans. There is no such effect for the Flavr Savr tomato.

This difference is even stronger for *genetically_modified*, as in "*genetically_modified_organism* (GMO)." That term came into frequent use only after 1998 and is heavily correlated with agriculture. Indeed, as shown in

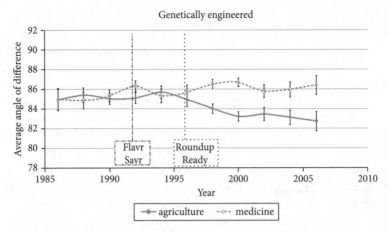

FIGURE 18.6. Distance between semantic fields *genetic_engineering* (baseline), *agriculture*, and *medicine* based on the *New York Times Annotated Corpus*.

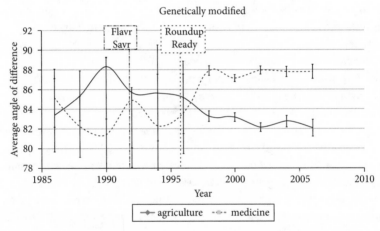

FIGURE 18.7. Distance between semantic fields *genetically_modified* (baseline), *agriculture*, and *medicine* based on the *New York Times Annotated Corpus*.

figure 18.7, the semantic distance to contexts from medicine is sharply increasing. As of today, the term *genetically_modified* is practically synonymous with agricultural biotechnology.

Frames are particularly impactful if they carry positive or negative connotations. We can investigate this by considering the semantic field *genetically_engineered* and then assessing the similarities with other fields from

TABLE 18.1 **Correlations of terms related to genetic engineering**

	Agriculture	Medical
Improvement	−0.20	+0.70
Danger	+0.38	−0.21
Unsafe	+0.33	−0.01

two categories: one the industry context, here agriculture or medicine, the other the semantic fields associated with *unsafe*, *danger*, and *improvement*, respectively. We can then calculate the per-year average distances from the semantic fields associated with *genetically_engineered* and the industry context and, following that, calculate a second set of distances between *genetically_engineered* and the valence fields *unsafe*, *danger*, and *improvement*. Finally, we can calculate the correlations between these distances.

We denote the distance between two fields by *d*. For example, the distance between *genetically_engineered* and *medical* is denoted *d(genetically_engineered, medical)*. The Pearson correlation between *d(genetically_engineered, medical)* and *d(genetically_engineered, improvement)* for the years 1987 to 2007 is $r = 0.70$. Table 18.1 contains the Pearson correlations between industry context distances and valence distances from the field associated with *genetically_engineered*.

As can be seen, the semantic field associated with *improved*, a term that is usually associated with a frame of *progress*, is positively related with medicine and negatively related with agriculture, while the reverse is true for the terms associated with framing in terms of risk and fear (*danger* and *unsafe*). That is, changes in the distance between *genetically_engineered* and *medical* correlate with corresponding changes in the distance between *genetically_engineered* and *improvement*. In contrast, changes in the distance between *genetically_engineered* and *agriculture* are negatively correlated with the corresponding changes in the distance between *genetically_engineered* and *improvement*. The opposite pattern is true of *danger* and *unsafe*. This suggests that for the term *genetically_engineered* medicine is associated with a progress frame, while agriculture is associated with a risk/danger frame.

What we see here is an example of the evolution of frames. Over time the term *genetically_modified* became practically synonymous with agricultural applications. When we hear "genetically modified organisms" we

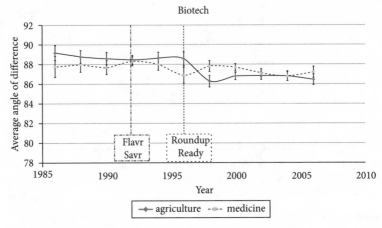

FIGURE 18.8. Distance between semantic fields *biotech* (baseline), *agriculture*, and *medicine* based on the *New York Times Annotated Corpus*.

think of food ingredients, not of bacteria producing a drug. Since agricultural applications tend to be associated with the risk/danger frame, so is the semantic field associated with *genetically_modified*. Thus, "GMO free" becomes a desirable attribute for a food product. The same is true, though to a somewhat lesser extent, for the term *genetically_engineered*. These are examples of frame differentiation, where an originally neutral term starts to carry a valence dimension.

The opposite effect can be seen for the case of *biotech*. As can be seen in figure 18.8, the meaning of *biotech* appears to have been unaffected by the introduction of genetic engineering into agriculture.[16]

The analysis thus predicts that after 1995, when Roundup Ready soybeans were first introduced, we would expect opponents of biotech applications to use the term *genetically_modified* or *GMO* as a framing device to trigger a particular association with a risk/danger frame, while proponents will tend to use more neutral terms such as *biotech*. This is similar to the previously encountered political contexts, where Democrats tend to use the term *gays* while Republicans rely on *homosexuals*.

SUBPRIME MORTGAGES. We can see similar phenomena in other industries. Consider changes in the framing of subprime mortgages. Subprime mortgages featured prominently in the global financial crisis. But a decade earlier, politicians, policy experts, and industry observers regarded subprime mortgages as a desirable vehicle for expanding homeownership

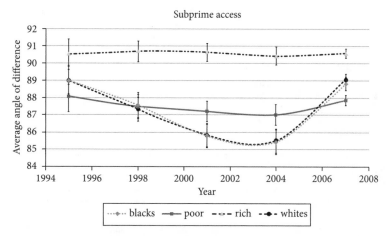

FIGURE 18.9. Distance between semantic fields *subprime* (baseline), *poor, rich, blacks,* and *whites* based on the *New York Times Annotated Corpus.*

to segments of society that had previously lacked access to traditional "prime" loans (Diermeier 2011). Former Countrywide CEO Angelo Mozilo stated that the company's subprime strategy was not solely financially motivated, but also tried to create "multicultural market communities" for borrowers. In 2003 he stated, "The gap between low-income and minority homeownership, and what is classified as white homeownership, remains intolerably too wide" (Bruck 2009). Government-sponsored enterprise Fannie Mae pledged $2 trillion over a decade to expand access to credit to aid "minorities, families headed by women, new immigrants and other under-served consumers" (Diermeier 2011). Note that these statements not only refer to socioeconomic differences (rich versus poor), but introduce themes of minority ownership. This introduces a racial/minority frame. We can then explore variations in the distances between the semantic fields associated with each of the frames and the semantic field associated with subprime mortgages. This is portrayed in figure 18.9.

First, note that the socioeconomic frames (poor/rich) do not vary much over the period investigated. Also, as expected, *poor* is always semantically closer than *rich* to subprime mortgage access. Intuitively, this means that a text on subprime mortgage will naturally tend to talk about poor borrowers without mentioning the rich. The racial/minority frame, however, varies dramatically, becoming closer than the socioeconomic frame but

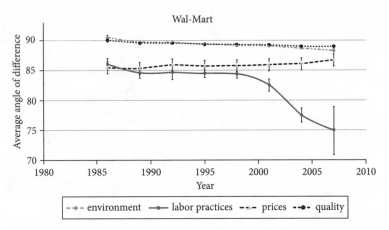

FIGURE 18.10. Distance between semantic fields *Wal-Mart* (baseline), *prices, quality, environment*, and *labor_practices* based on the *New York Times Annotated Corpus*.

then veering away again. This suggests that the minority ownership frame gained traction in the early 2000s, only to lose steam subsequently. Note also that there is no difference between the semantic fields associated with *whites* and *blacks*, a common feature of frames related to race. That is, an article that refers to *blacks* will also tend to refer to *whites*, possibly emphasizing a contrast along racial lines.

WAL-MART.   One can also investigate changes in frames associated with a particular company. Consider Wal-Mart (now called Walmart). During its explosive growth Wal-Mart's business practices had repeatedly attracted criticism. Concerns ranged from the impact on local communities to labor practices, environmental concerns, and sexual discrimination. Here we explore which one of a few selected frames was most closely associated with Wal-Mart over the last two decades. To put any changes in perspective, we use "prices" and "quality" as "control frames," which we expect to not vary much over this period.

As can clearly be seen in figure 18.10, *labor_practices* became significantly more closely associated with Wal-Mart in the news coverage compared to environmental issues, which hardly moved at all. This is a somewhat surprising given Wal-Mart's environmental efforts, especially in the area of energy efficiency. But it indicates that the controversies surrounding Wal-Mart continue to focus on labor issues.

18.3.2   Combining Methods

The various methods can also be combined. For example, the semantic space approach requires us to define the possible frames ex ante. Instead, one can use dictionary-based methods or keyness to identify frames. Sagi and Dehghani (2014a), for example, studied moral frames related to the abortion controversy. Using the US Senate Corpus discussed above, Sagi, Diermeier, and Kaufman (2013) show that the abortion topic is framed differently between Democrats and Republicans in a manner that is consistent with pro-choice and pro-life positions. Sagi and Dehghani (2014a) use terms from the Moral Foundations Dictionary (Graham, Haidt, and Nosek 2009) to denote frames for each of the dimensions of moral foundations theory (Haidt 2007, 2013b): care, fairness, loyalty, authority, and purity. Semantic field analysis was then used to measure the distances between the dictionary terms for each moral foundation dimension and the target topic, here abortion.[17] They found that the most highly engaged moral dimensions are fairness and purity, with Democrats being more concerned with fairness and Republicans more with purity. Indeed, Democrats frame the overall debate in terms of choice (Sagi, Diermeier, and Kaufman 2013). The dimension of harm is less important for both political parties.

CHAPTER NINETEEN

Text-Analytic Methods: Promise and Pitfalls

The use of text-analytic methods to understand perceptions of companies is very promising. It offers the possibility of integrating large-scale data analytics in a field that has suffered from a dearth of data. The use of deep learning and neural networks and the rapid growth of datasets will further accelerate these developments. That said, text-analytic methods need to be used with caution (Grimmer and Stewart 2013). First, as with any other quantitative method, text-analytic methods need to be driven by a clear research question, a solid understanding of the underlying research methodology, domain expertise, and sound judgment both in research design and in the interpretation of the findings. This also frequently requires some in-depth reading of the texts or related materials. Computer algorithms are best understood as amplifiers, not as substitutes for human input (Grimmer and Stewart 2013). This implies that researchers should be wary of blindly applying off-the-shelf methods or commercial software packages, especially if the underlying algorithms are proprietary and opaque.

Second, the proper choice of methods depends on the research question. An analysis of frames requires different tools than an analysis of issue agendas, and an analysis of sentiment requires a different approach than an analysis of values or ideologies. Even within a particular application, various methods have pros and cons. Choosing the number of topics in advance may seem undesirable, but dispensing with this step forces researchers to rely heavily on a particular estimation approach that may lack robustness. Similarly, unsupervised topic modeling may be attractive because it appears to remove the "human element" present in supervised approaches. Yet, the output of such models needs to be interpreted, reintroducing human judgment (Quinn et al. 2010). In general, there is no "best" text-analytic method. Different methods serve different purposes and are characterized by different trade-offs. Indeed, often the various approaches are best used in conjunction, especially if the desired concept is as elusive as corporate reputation.

Third, any method that is used needs to be validated. Ideally, this is done in a statistically rigorous fashion, but even simple comparison with human coders can be very useful. As always, there are trade-offs. Validation for supervised models is easy once initial categories have been chosen, but the construction of the training set depends on human coding, which needs to be carefully evaluated. Unsupervised models do not require this initial step, but are typically more heavily dependent on the statistical properties of the underlying model, and their output is more difficult to validate.

It hardly requires emphasizing that any data created by commercial vendors should be used with extreme caution, especially if the underlying approaches are proprietary and not transparent. Moreover, since human coding is costly, commercial vendors may be tempted to rely on untrained coders who lack domain expertise. Proper coding is expensive and requires care (e.g., Krippendorf 2004; Yu, Diermeier, and Kaufman 2008). This is especially a problem if the corpora contain technical documents, as, for example, in applications in pharma or biotech. At the very least, one should go through a proper evaluation process, for instance by using one's own hand-coded and well-understood dataset and then comparing it to the data supplied by data vendors. Text-analytic models are still models. They are based on a partial and heavily simplified representation of reality. That said, they can be very useful for a well-defined purpose if their reach and limitations are well understood.

We began our discussion with a paradox. Among CEOs and board members, there is broad agreement that a company's reputation ranks at the very top among its most important assets. Yet, by any available measure, trust in corporate leaders has been low in recent years.[1] This tension becomes most visible when viewed in conjunction with the long list of reputational crises filling global headlines. Such crises not only undermine customer trust and destroy value, but can lead to subsequent political and regulatory challenges that can threaten a company's or an entire industry's license to operate. These trends are no accident. At the root of this tension are a few macro trends that have made the management of corporate reputation considerably more challenging: the rapid growth of global media, especially social media; the unintended consequences of globalization, leading to increased supply-chain risk and the rise of global activism; and higher public expectations of companies, from quality and service to expectations of ethical corporate conduct, which are amplified by the rise of trust-based business models that have increased the impact of reputational crises.

Companies' capabilities have not kept pace with these developments. Reputation management is still largely viewed as a PR exercise best relegated to corporate communications. Often it is conflated with business ethics, a sense that all that is required is for a company to "do the right thing." At worst, executives believe that reputation management is nothing else than common sense guided by a moral compass. These views are common but of limited usefulness.

At the root of the problem is a misconception of the source of reputational challenges. Most reputational crises do not happen because of some external event or misfortune; rather, they are the direct consequence of companies' actions or inaction. Decisions are made without consideration for their reputational impact, and decision makers fail to act as the stewards of the company's reputation.

If reputation is indeed a critical asset, it needs to be fostered and protected like other assets. That means it needs to be viewed as an enterprisewide capability, similar to other capabilities such as quality, safety, or customer focus. An effective reputation management system requires the right strategic mindset, supported by processes, values, and culture.

Reputational challenges are essentially public. They put the company on stage and frequently engage highly motivated, often hostile advocates. Such challenges can arise from any area of day-to-day decision making, but executives tend to make decisions without consideration for their reputational impact. The key skill for business leaders to develop is the ability to maintain an external perspective throughout the decision-making processes and to incorporate this perspective into the design of the business decision, such as the launch of a new product and its market-entry strategy. Companies need to understand that their decisions are creating a record today which will serve as the basis for their story tomorrow. Assessing reputational risk requires anticipating what a reputational crisis would look like and then taking proactive steps to prevent it and prepare for it.

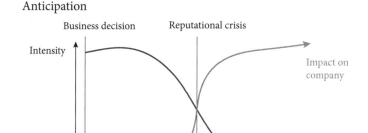

FIGURE 19.1. The relationship between control and crisis severity across time.

Figure 19.1 (Diermeier 2011, p. 182) illustrates this point; it shows the fundamental tension between how control and impact move, which makes reputation management so challenging.

During a reputational crisis, the stakes get higher as the company loses control. Customers and other stakeholders are paying attention, and the company must make decisions under extreme time pressure and with limited access to critical information. It is far better to manage one's reputation well in advance of a crisis while the stakes are still low, the company retains substantial control, and time pressure is limited.

Companies must therefore recognize the reputational impact of any business decision before it is made. In most corporate crises, managers and employees made decisions that had massive reputational consequences. Were these managers aware of these potential consequences? Did they act as guardians of the company's reputation or did they merely focus on their narrow expertise and incentives?

What is needed is not another corporate function, but to develop a reputation management capability. Such a capability needs to be grounded in the company's identity, business model, values, and culture. Having clarity about these business fundamentals is a prerequisite for effective reputation management. Reputations cannot be fostered and protected if it is not clear what needs to be guarded and grown. Such clarity is necessary but not sufficient. To be effective, a reputation management capability requires the proper mindset and processes, and the values and culture that support it. The insights developed in this book can guide its development.

PART VI

Conclusion: Toward a Reputation Management Capability

CHAPTER TWENTY

The Right Mindset: Corporate Reputation as Public Opinion

Effective reputation management begins with the right mindset. A company's reputation is essentially public. Successful reputation management therefore requires the ability to assume external actors' perspectives and viewpoints. Many of these actors (although certainly not all of them) are motivated by moral or ideological concerns that the company or its managers may not share; indeed, they may be openly hostile toward the company's business practices. This often leads to a defensive, reactive posture on the part of business leaders.

The spotlight during a crisis will focus not only on the company's current actions, such as how the CEO answers questions and what the company will do to fix the problem, but also on its past actions. Reporters will ask when the company first knew about the problem, or why management did not do more to fix it. The thought process behind each past decision can be brought out into the public arena and questioned. These past actions and decisions are now part of the record and cannot be changed. Even those actions that looked reasonable at the time may wither under scrutiny from a hostile audience in a crisis context after their negative consequences come to light.

This proactive mindset constitutes the critical switch from a crisis-management to a risk-management mindset. Taking reputational risk seriously does not mean blocking all decisions that carry some reputational downside. Rather, the goal of proactive reputation management is to identify possible risks and mitigate them through current actions to reach an acceptable balance of risk and control. Future reputational risk can be managed today only if it is identified and weighed during the decision-making process.

Once an issue's reputational risk has been identified, the company needs to move to the next step and take appropriate action. The effective mitigation of reputational risk has two critical components: prevention and preparation.

Prevention consists of steps to reduce or eliminate a particular risk. In a quality-management context, it may result in additional quality controls. In a marketing context, it may demand the elimination of problematic sales practices. In a mergers and acquisitions context, it may mean that a company walks away from an acquisition or renegotiates its terms when the target's questionable business practices come to light during due diligence. In general, prevention strategies aim to reduce the likelihood that an adverse event will occur.

But not all risks can be prevented, which brings *preparation* strategies into play. Should an adverse event materialize, these strategies attempt to mitigate its impact. For example, prudent reputational risk management involves a company's awareness that it may lose control over customer perceptions during a reputational crisis. In an activist-rich environment, outreach and collaboration with moderate advocacy groups may create a credible ally, which can prove invaluable during a future confrontation. However, this works only if outreach occurs before the company is targeted. Once the company is assigned the role of the villain, moderate advocates and other credible third parties will likely not be supportive. A preparation strategy therefore involves establishing relationships in advance with trusted third parties, so that the company can call upon them in a crisis. Building such relationships takes time, mutual trust, and, most of all, anticipation; by the time a crisis strikes, it is too late.

These strategies are not necessarily independent, as they can mutually reinforce each other. For example, an insurance company could be concerned about the improper sales practices of its agents, knowing that, even if the agents are independent contractors, the company will take the heat if a problem occurs. Policing each and every agent is impossible. But a prevention strategy, such as a strict compliance program, demonstrates the company's commitment to address the problem. The message is simple: "We have been aware of the problem, and we took the following steps to address it long before it became a media story." Accompanying the policy with audits, secret shopper programs, and similar efforts will further enhance the effectiveness of this approach. This may not solve the issue entirely, but it positions the company as proactive, thoughtful, and concerned about its customers, while reinforcing its operational competence by demonstrating that the problem did not catch the company off guard.

To develop the proper strategic mindset, we need to develop sufficient clarity about the concept of corporate reputation. In this book we have proposed and elaborated the idea that *corporate reputation equals public opinion for companies*. Specifically, this book has two purposes. First, it develops a coherent account of the formation of attitudes toward companies. Second, it introduces a variety of methods that can deepen our understanding of how attitudes toward companies can be identified, measured, and managed.

We first showed that the standard, naïve model of public opinion, what we called the "mental database model" of public opinion, is deeply flawed. When queried, or when they need to make a decision, such as on a product purchase, members of the public do not consult a mental database and retrieve well-formed opinions about companies, products, and services. Rather, opinions are constructed on the spot and exhibit complex cognitive processes which crucially involve coding, storage, and retrieval, governed by a network of associations stored in long-term memory. These networks change over time due to external factors such as personal experience, media coverage, and peer influence.

From the extensive research on the cognitive processes in public perception and attitude formation, we identified six major principles for opinion formation: Repetition (repeated exposure to entities makes it more likely that such entities are encoded in memory), Recency (more recent impressions are more likely to be activated and retrieved from memory), Attention (the greater a person's level of attention is, the more likely he or she is to be aware of an impression, to memorize it, and to recall it), Affect (affect influences the coding, formation, storage, and retrieval of memories and attitudes), Consonance (messages that are consistent with a person's current beliefs or attitudes are more likely to be received, accepted, and stored in memory), and Online Processing (evaluations of entities are based on an online tally, which over time aggregates experienced affect and considerations associated with an entity, while the specific details that originally gave rise to the evaluation are forgotten).

This cognitivist perspective deepens our understanding of the processes of opinion formation, but it also has direct practical consequences. For example, the combination of Online Processing, Affect, Congruence, and

Recency forces us to be very cautious not to overinterpret the reasons given by members of the public for a stated opinion. Often the basic attitude about the company is derived from an online tally which aggregates prior experiences and attitudes, while details are forgotten. Similarly, consistent with the Congruence and Affect principles, respondents will tend to recall specific issues that are congruent with the experienced affect. That is, if a subject expresses a negative opinion, issues that are congruent with the valence of the expressed opinion will more easily come to mind. If an interviewer then asks for a reason for the expressed opinion, subjects will tend to retrieve associations from memory, but these associations may be mere rationalizations of an already existing, affect-laden opinion.

If companies naïvely respond to the expressed concerns, they are missing the deeper reasons for the expressed negative opinion, which is rooted in a network of associations aggregated in an online tally. A better approach is to map out such association networks using experimental methods and then develop strategies that address specific areas of concern.

To better understand these processes, we investigated three domains that are of paramount importance in the context of corporate reputation: moral evaluations, risk perception, and trust. Many of the evaluations of companies are not based on careful deliberation but on affect and emotion. Rather than investigating an issue carefully, members of the public listen to their gut. Our review of the psychological processes that drive evaluations of corporate conduct uncovered a rich set of principles involving value orientations, ideologies, and character assessments, as well as the importance of cultural context and the nature of social relationships. Even beliefs such as risk perception and trust are often influenced by affect and moral judgments. This creates a complex and challenging environment for companies. We discussed these (often subtle) processes in detail and derived implications for corporate strategies. From a practical point of view, fully understanding these processes also provides a methodology for assessing and measuring reputational risk. Which business decisions are most likely to create outrage or fear? How do these risks vary across cultures? What strategies are most effective at alleviating concerns or restoring trust?

The enormous importance of values, attention, and perspectives in shaping opinion naturally leads to questions of what factors shape how networks of associations are formed, and how are they activated. To address these issues, we investigated questions of salience and attention: Which issues do people pay attention to (agenda setting), and how do they view an issue (framing)?

We showed the importance of framing in shaping perception. Frames serve as cognitive mechanisms for interpreting complex issues and simplifying them. Once a frame is accepted, certain policy solutions become plausible, while others seem off the mark. For example, the collapse of a financial institution can be blamed on an incompetent CEO, an ineffective board, or lack of regulatory oversight. Each frame implies different policy solutions (a new CEO; a review of governance processes; reform of the regulatory regime). So, which of the frames will dominate will have significant consequences for the affected business and industry.

We next discussed the importance of the media, both traditional and social, in determining dominant frames and setting the agenda. In this discussion we paid particular attention to some of the severe methodological difficulties in properly assessing media influence. For example, the correlation between the ideological orientation of a news source and its audience is not sufficient evidence for media bias as, in a competitive media market, audiences can select their news sources based on their ideological orientation. We also showed how these difficulties can be overcome by the careful construction of laboratory and field experiments or through the development of sophisticated statistical models that control for self-selection. Finally, we demonstrated how, during times of increased attention, such as a crisis, social influence through mere reporting or social media interaction can generate artificial consensus.

We then discussed the role of stakeholders in shaping corporate reputations, with an emphasis on NGOs and social activists. In recent years we have seen the significant growth of global activism. Activists have learned to play the globalization game and pressure global corporations to change their business practices to drive social change, using the rise in media activity and changing expectations about corporate conduct as levers. Most activist campaigns are highly strategic; they are designed to engender changes in business practices at specific companies and entire industries, often through the threat of inflicting reputational damage on a particular company. Companies need to fully understand these strategies and respond appropriately. In addition to various communication strategies, companies may want to invest in corporate social responsibility (CSR) activities that would not be warranted purely on competitive grounds. The use of CSR as a form of reputational risk management can also explain why CSR investments do not need to be correlated with higher stock returns.

Our last chapters focused on measurement and metrics. In its current state, corporate reputation management is dominated by opinion surveys.

While such surveys can be very useful instruments for gauging public opinion, an exclusive reliance on one method is problematic. Existing datasets are usually proprietary or too limited in scope. Moreover, many surveys used in practice are based on outdated views of how respondents form their opinions about companies. Using the insights about the process of opinion formation can help improve the design and interpretation of opinion surveys.

Next we discussed alternative approaches to measurement. Our focus here was on the use of text-analytic methods, which offer the possibility of integrating large-scale data analytics into the study of corporate reputation. We reviewed various methodologies and approaches, ranging from sentiment analysis and topic identification to the measurement of emotions, values, ideologies, agendas, and frames. Despite the enormous promise of these methods, their application is in its infancy and existing methods need to be used with great caution and carefully validated, especially if they are off-the-shelf proprietary methods provided by commercial vendors that provide no visibility into the actual methodology used. That said, text-analytic methods can be very useful for a well-defined purpose if their reach and limitations are well understood.

CHAPTER TWENTY-ONE

Developing a Reputation Management System

To respond to the multitude of dynamics we have identified, companies need to build effective processes. The tools developed in this book can help with the design and implementation of such systems.

The purpose of a reputation management system is to operational-ize the key principles of the strategic mindset discussed in the previous chapters:

1. Reputation consists of the perceptions of customers and other constituencies.
2. In many cases these perceptions are not derived from actual experience with the company or a deep knowledge of any given issue, but from an ever-changing mixture of opinion and information driven by traditional and social media, and various influencers ranging from experts to advocacy groups.
3. Proactive reputation management requires companies to identify issues early, connect them with their business strategy, develop prevention and preparation strategies, and implement possible changes to the business practices in advance of an issue gaining momentum.

This sequence can break down at various points. Executives may not realize the importance of reputation management for business success, governance structures may be lacking, or incentive structures may reward short-term vision. But companies may also fail to adopt effective strategies because they are simply unaware of the imminent danger. In other words, even perfectly designed governance and decision-making structures will be ineffective if they lack critical intelligence.

Throughout our discussion, we have seen the value of identifying emerging issues early. From a practical point of view, there is significant value in preparing communication or outreach strategies early or changing problematic business practices before they are publicly criticized. Moreover, as discussed in chapter 7, perceptions are often formed early in an issue life cycle and are then reinforced by processes of motivated reasoning. Thus, being able to identify, evaluate, and track emerging issues is an important reputation management capability.

Companies tend to miss emerging issues and underreact. This is often due to insufficient intelligence capabilities. Early in their life cycle, issues do not capture general media attention, but emerge in fringe groups or highly specialized sources, such as scientific publications. Underreaction to emerging issues, however, is not the only problem for companies. So is overreaction. By acting overzealously, a company can trigger the very media interest that had so far eluded the issue. These considerations are particularly important in the case of activists and boycott threats, as discussed in chapter 12. Activists require a media stage to advance their agenda. Often their concerns are more extreme than mainstream opinion or require specialized knowledge not often found in a layperson. This limits audience interest and ultimately engagement. The rise of social media has only partially alleviated this concern. There are still too many issues vying for audience attention. That said, social media can dramatically lower the cost of getting organized once an issue has passed an attention threshold.

To overcome these difficulties, activists often engage in media stunts and provocations like putting up wanted posters, occupying one of the company's properties, or protesting in front of the company headquarters. If well executed, such actions are likely to attract some media attention. Companies then need to assess whether the issue is connected to a core business concern or not. For example, protests over low wages or poor working conditions are less of a concern at Dunkin' than at Starbucks. Dunkin' does not market itself as a socially responsible company, while for Starbucks the benefits policy for its associates is a core component of its brand. Thus, for the same issue, Dunkin' may be well advised to ignore it, while Starbucks would need to address it.

Companies also need to assess whether an issue is likely to gain broad attention. The goal here is not merely to track the attention of an issue through media signal measures and the like, but also to assess which issues are likely to gain attention *before* such attention materializes. The task is to assess the potential risk of an issue rather than actualized attention reflected in the current media coverage. Measures of reach or media signal are not appropriate for this task. Rather, what is required is an assessment of what makes an issue *interesting* and what makes it *important* (Diermeier 2011). Factors that make an issue interesting may be purely accidental and context-dependent, as in the 911 call in the Toyota case, the involvement of a celebrity, or simply the fact that the issue pertains to a well-known consumer brand. Toy safety concerns will garner more attention if they are associated with Mattel, the maker of Barbie dolls, than with some unknown contract manufacturer.

These factors crucially depend on brand and market characteristics and vary by country. What is interesting in China may be of little interest in Colombia. Sometimes external events can make an issue more interesting and raise its level of social importance. For example, the 2006 safety concerns about toys made in China garnered additional interest among the US public since previous news stories had pointed to other instances of quality problems with Chinese contract manufacturers, for example, over contaminated toothpaste (Diermeier 2011). Note that such context factors can change rapidly and are difficult to control. They may be triggered by a competitor's missteps or originate in other industries or nonbusiness contexts such as sports, entertainment, or politics. A famous actress taking up a cause almost always heralds a massive increase in audience interest.

In addition to such context factors, issues can be classified by their intrinsic risk potential, that is, by their likelihood to create negative affect such as fear, undermine trust, and increase risk perception. Part 2 provides a detailed discussion of such factors.

21.1 Issue Management

To address these challenges, early warning systems need to provide three separate capabilities (Diermeier 2011): issue identification, issue evaluation, and issue monitoring.

Issue Identification. The goal of issue identification is to reliably list all issues that may affect a company's reputation or other related risks. This is conceptually a hard problem. The difficulty is that a company may not be aware of problematic issues in the early stages of the issue life cycle.

This is only to be expected, since during such early stages an issue will have little to no impact on a company. But little impact tends to also lead to a lack of awareness. The problem is that during the time when action would be the most effective, a company is least likely to be aware of its existence. Businesses are not the only ones grappling with this problem. It is a pervasive difficulty in areas such as national security, counterterrorism, and financial risk management.

An illustrative example is presented by EntreMed (ENMD), a biotech company with licensing rights to a highly promising drug for cancer treatments. On May 3, 1998, the *New York Times* reported the breakthrough on its front page. As a consequence, EntreMed's stock price rose from $12.06 at the Friday close to open at $85 and close near $52 on Monday. The breakthrough, however, had already been reported in the November 27, 1997, issue of *Nature*, followed by some limited reporting in various news outlets. At that time, however, the stock traded no higher than $15.25. That is, while the material information was already public information, investors were not aware of it (Huberman and Regev 2001). This is not a rare exception. Many issues emerge in fringe groups, obscure websites, research papers, and so forth. In retrospect, such issues could have been identified, but nobody knew where to look, or even that attempting a search would have been a good idea. These were "known unknowns:" investors were generally aware of the importance of new evidence for the efficacy of treatments, but may not have known about the specific evidence reported in the *Nature* article.

Even more problematic are "unknown unknowns," also known as "black swans" or fundamentally unforeseen events (Taleb 2007).[1] Unknown unknowns are not quantifiable risks. In the case of most risks, we do not know which event will occur but we can assign likelihoods to each possible contingency and choose the path of action with the highest expected value. At the very least, this requires that we know what *can* happen; for example, we can make a list of possible contingencies. In the case of an unknown unknown, we do not even know what *may* occur.

It is not possible to resolve these issues in principle, but they can be alleviated in practice. The difficulty is to find the proverbial needle in the haystack without knowing what the needle looks like or where the haystacks are. Under these conditions, information extraction and evaluation are daunting tasks. Some companies have entire teams dedicated to locating emerging issues (Diermeier 2011). Text-analytic methods provide an alternative approach. Topic identification models, in particular, can be fruitfully applied.

Here unsupervised approaches are most appropriate. The goal is not validation but simply identification. Unknown unknowns have the property that we don't know what we are looking for, but once we find it, we know it. Subsequent analysis can then assess whether the identified topic was a false alarm or requires further attention. Approaches that can identify "unusual topics" that differ from the typical issue environment are especially effective. Algorithms, by learning what is regular and typical, can also help identify what is unusual.

That said, existing technologies are not perfect. They generate too many false positives, which need to be screened out, and are best deployed to support human analysts rather than as a stand-alone solution. However, when properly deployed, technology solutions can dramatically enhance the chances of spotting emerging issues.

Issue Evaluation. A good reputation management system needs to be able to identify which issues matter and which do not. It needs to filter out the "false positives" and evaluate the remaining issues in terms of their importance for a particular company. Often such evaluations are done "by hand." That is, domain experts score emerging issues manually, often using a familiar traffic light approach with "red" standing for "serious threat requiring immediate attention," "yellow" for "not a crisis yet, but needs to be monitored and action options developed," and "green" standing for "no (current) worries." There are many reasons why an issue may not require immediate attention. It may be too early in the issue life cycle and may simply fizzle out. Taking action now may only add oil to the fire.

Such approaches are simple and easy to appreciate by senior executives. Yet, a more nuanced approach is often helpful. Issues can be evaluated on various dimensions. First, the issue may be only tangentially related to the core business of the company. Accidentally overpaying suppliers, for example, may raise serious concerns about a company in the payments industry, such as American Express, but it may be a minor headache for a car company such as Mercedes. If an issue is not core, waiting for it to pass is often an appropriate approach (Diermeier 2011). Deciding which issues are core and which are not sounds like a fairly straightforward challenge for companies. In practice, it is anything but, especially if companies feel wrongly accused. During the unintended acceleration crisis, Toyota's leadership focused on the engineering aspect of the problem. But that was only one aspect of the business challenge. The Toyota brand had occupied a dominant position on perceptions of quality and durability. It was the first choice for customers mainly interested in a high-quality car, and resale values were consistently higher than for competitors (Liker and Ogden 2011). By conceptualizing this issue mainly as a (minor) engineering problem, Toyota underestimated its impact on customer perception—eroding trust on key brand attributes. Such evaluations are difficult to automate and often require input from senior executives.

Second, issues need to be evaluated with respect to their intrinsic risk of generating fear, outrage, or perceptions of broken trust. These processes and characteristics are extensively discussed in part 2. Approaches from computational linguistics can automate some of these processes, for example, by scoring the emotional content of documents associated with an issue.

Third, in activist-rich environments, ideological scoring can provide some evidence on the positioning of activists and sources. Such analysis is best done in advance of an emerging crisis as part of a thorough assessment of the company's reputational environment.

Overall, quantitative solutions can provide some additional support in the area of issue evaluation. Yet, given the state of the current technology, human evaluation and assessment continue to be necessary.

Issue Monitoring. A basic question of issue monitoring is whether an issue is gaining traction. This can be examined by tracking the relative frequency of issues over time using topic identification models, discussed in chapter 16. Similarly, issues can be analyzed with respect to their distribution of competitive frames and how that distribution changes over time. Of particular importance is whether a frame is gaining traction or whether a frame is becoming dominant, as in the case of viewing terror as an act of war discussed in chapter 18. This approach can also be used to identify opinion leaders, multipliers, and opinion brokers. Opinion leaders create frames that are likely to gain traction. Opinion multipliers and brokers do not create frames, but increase their popularity and reach.

A related approaches is the use of "memes," effectively n-grams that are frequently used in the conjunction with an issue. For example, an n-gram like *too_big_to_fail* is a good indicator of banking reform. Ideally, such n-grams are properly validated in the context of topic or framing analysis rather than simply based on intuition. The use of n-grams is particularly useful for studying social influence patterns, such as the relationship between user-generated and traditional media (where do issues originate?) or the identification of opinion leaders, multipliers, and opinion brokers (who spreads an issue?). In the context of issue agendas, opinion leaders launch new issues, multipliers increase their reach, and brokers bridge otherwise unconnected communities. For example, a food additive may create concerns within a scientific community. Typically these concerns would be limited to a small community of experts. But sometimes a journalist or advocacy group can pick up on such an issue and serve the role of a broker. A celebrity, such as, a well-known chef, can then serve as a multiplier, leading to widespread attention to the issue. An alternative approach is the use of search behavior, for example, using Google (e.g., Da, Engelberg, and Gao 2011; Yelowitz and Wilson 2015).[2] In addition, the measurement of changes in sentiment, emotional content, or framing can be useful, as they may signal a significant change in public attitudes toward an issue.

Issue monitoring is one of the areas where text-analytic methods are particularly useful. That said, whether they assess sentiment or other features, such measures need to be carefully validated.

21.2 Impact Assessment

The purpose of tracking topic evolution and search behavior is to assess the current issue agenda and public attention, which should guide the development of engagement strategies. Next, we need to know whether such strategies have made an impact. More generally, we would want to develop metrics to assess the current reputation of an industry, company, product, ingredient, and so on. Broadly, there are two approaches companies can pursue. First, there are survey-based metrics. As discussed, properly designed surveys are still a very effective tool for reputation management, but they require significant investment. A second approach is the use of text-analytic metrics which extract tone and other features from text, especially social media sources. One commonly used metric is sentiment indices, which are based on sentiment analysis as discussed in chapter 16. This is a natural operational metric and can be applied broadly. It is particularly useful when used in comparison with product and company benchmarks to measure differential changes.

As an operational metric, sentiment scores can be used in two different ways. First, we can develop direct measures, for example, by analyzing Twitter messages or blogs. User-generated media are particularly fertile sources of such measures, as people tend to express attitudes freely, without interference from laboratory settings, focus groups, or survey questions. But unbiased, direct measures are not always feasible or available. For example, participation in blogs or Twitter is skewed toward computer-literate and younger segments of the population. Moreover, certain segments of interest, such as major investors, board members, and regulators, are unlikely to express their views freely through social media.

In such cases indirect measures are appropriate. For example, as we discuss in part 3, the research on media influence suggests that tone, agenda setting, and issue framing can influence audience opinion. We can then study the prevalent media sentiment among the news sources read by the intended audience. In the case of board members, for example, survey or experimental approaches are often infeasible. Therefore, identifying sentiment in newspapers such as the *Wall Street Journal* or the *Financial Times* can be a good proxy, as these news sources are likely to influence the attitudes of their readers.

When working with media sources, it is important to treat them as inputs into the opinion formation process, not outputs. That is, the goal is to measure public opinion, not media sentiment per se. For example, one should not restrict oneself to explicit expressions of opinions, such as editorials. Rather, news items can have the same or even more impact on audience sentiment, even though, from the point of view of journalists, they are strictly separate from expressions of opinion. Indeed, while the distinction between opinion and news is of crucial significance within the professional ethical code of journalists, from the point of view of assessing corporate reputations, the distinction is unimportant. A quoted opinion by a credible scientist that a certain new technology should be banned can be just as impactful (or more impactful) than the same opinion expressed by a (nonexpert) columnist.

At the most straightforward level, we can aggregate the source sentiment into a time series by calculating simple averages. A first improvement is to also report standard errors, especially if the analyzed news coverage is only a sample of the entire news coverage. Next, if additional metadata about news sources or articles is available, it can help to improve an index, for examples, by controlling for circulation and readership among the target segment. If sentiment classification is done at the article level, the length of an article should increase its relative weight. Front-page articles should be weighted more. If sentiment is classified at the sentence or paragraph level, headlines and first paragraphs should receive higher weights. Duplicates create another problem. An article written by a news agency such as Reuters or the Associated Press may be picked up by multiple sources. Should duplicates be discarded or included? The answer depends on the case. If the various news outlets are unlikely to have overlapping audiences, then duplicates should be included, as the respective sizes of the audiences are additive. If they reach the same audience, it may be better to discard duplicates. In most cases, the right answer is in the middle, where one adds the circulation numbers together and then subtracts the estimated number of common readers.

Finally, we can incorporate psychological principles directly. For example, if we want to incorporate negativity bias (Baumeister et al. 2001), then negative stories should be more heavily weighted than positive ones. A good rule of thumb is to give a negative story four times the weight of a positive one. Other psychological factors can be captured similarly.

The use of sentiment indices is not limited to monitoring changes for companies. They can also be used for products, services, or ingredients. For example, we may want to know how the overall reputation of a company is affected by concerns over a particular product. Rather than relying exclusively on sentiment analysis, we can also track the emotional content of text, both in social media sources and traditional news sources (e.g., Dodds et al. 2011). Finally, we can see how frames and public agendas are shifting, perhaps in response to a communication strategy. Once created, such metrics can be correlated with other metrics, for example, operational metrics such as sales data or employee engagement, or financial metrics.[3]

21.3   Governance and Culture

Who should own reputation management? Our first intuition may be: everyone. That sounds reasonable enough, but if everyone is responsible, no one tends to be accountable. Questions about decision rights, reporting, and accountability still need to be answered. Locating reputation management in the organizational structure of a company can be tricky, even for companies that "get it."

Many board members agree that the ultimate accountability for reputation management processes needs to be located at a level of the organization whose job description is ensuring the long-term success of the company: the board. By setting clear guidelines and emphasizing the need to safeguard the company's reputation, the board can help management avoid shortsighted mistakes.

The optimal location of this responsibility depends on the sources of value and the types of risks. For example, companies with a very active and important stakeholder environment that may spill over into new regulations or legislation might choose to have the policy committee oversee reputation management. For other companies, a good location is the place where enterprise risk management resides, which is typically the audit committee. This location enables better integration with other risk dimensions (that is, financial, brand, and operational risk) and facilitates trade-offs, planning, process evaluation, and strategy reviews. That said, it is very important not to view reputational risk as another item on a growing list of risks. Rather, reputational risk should be viewed as an *amplifier* for other operational, financial, and legal risks. A massive data breach, for example, is not only an operational, financial, and legal risk, but it is also a significant reputational risk, especially for companies where data security and privacy are core competencies, such as a financial service business. For many companies the best option is the executive committee, if it exists, or the entire board, where reputational management can be tightly integrated with strategy. Specific issues can then be delegated to the audit or policy committee.

But the board's role is to oversee and supervise, it is not to manage the company. So where should reputation management reside within a company's decision-making structure? Ultimately, the responsibility for the company's reputation rests with the CEO and senior management, but the day-to-day management of reputational challenges requires careful consideration.

One approach to accomplishing this task has been to create a separate corporate function: a chief reputation officer (CRO) or chief reputational risk officer (CRRO). This approach works only if the position carries weight and if the company can avoid creating yet another corporate officer with little budget and less influence. The danger in this approach is that it could create additional barriers to an integration of reputation management and business strategy, and actually hurt the process rather than help it.

An alternative is the creation of a corporate reputation council (CRC). This is a cross-functional unit composed of senior executives with actual decision-making authority. The composition of the council needs to mirror the organizational structure of the company. In addition, the main corporate functions (marketing, finance, supply chain, human resources, communication, legal, government relations, and so on) need to be represented, as reputational problems are almost always multidimensional.

Whatever the governance function, it is best supported by a tactical team which oversees the reputation management system, providing updates on emerging issues as well as impact assessments to the CRC or its equivalent. The CRC then decides on the overall strategy, which is implemented by the tactical team in partnership with the various business functions.

The final element of a robust reputation management capability is the right culture. Even the most advanced reputation management system is implemented by people. They need to assess the situation, evaluate its risk, and then make the appropriate decision. Getting this right requires not only a strategic mindset, but also the appropriate values and culture to provide useful guidance to individuals. We cannot expect each employee of a company to correctly assess the reputational risk of an issue, but we can expect him or her to raise a red flag when something does not "look right." The structure of values and corporate culture will vary across companies and industries. While some values such as integrity, teamwork, or customer focus will apply to most companies, some, such as a well-developed safety culture, will be more important in certain industries.

A crucial challenge for senior management and boards is to properly assess the state of the company's culture over time and across business segments. Traditional survey approaches are usually ineffective, especially in areas such as safety, diversity, or integrity, where employees may not be comfortable revealing their true attitudes for fear of repercussions by management. Properly designed surveys can alleviate such concerns. Through sophisticated measurement approaches, companies can now better assess the true attitudes of their employees across entire organizations.

Such approaches can provide invaluable insights. For example, business segments can vary dramatically in their safety culture. Identifying such misalignments is particularly important after a merger or acquisition. In other cases business segments are characterized by an inhomogeneous culture. This is often indicative of lack of attention by senior management, which leads to subcultures in various parts of the organization. How should boards and senior management respond to these findings? Remedies include leadership changes and education programs, but also changes in business processes that account for the increased risk due to a lack of cultural alignment.

Many executives mistakenly assume that a good reputation simply follows from having good business practices and doing right by customers, employees, and suppliers. According to this view, a high level of business integrity is believed to be both necessary and sufficient for building and maintaining a stellar reputation, while concrete reputational threats can be delegated to public affairs, legal, or outside advisors.

This view is mistaken. Most reputational crises do not happen because of some external event or misfortune; rather, they are the direct consequence of company actions or inaction. Decisions are made without consideration for their reputational impact. Decision makers fail to act as the stewards of the company's reputation.

While communication plays an important role in the process, active reputation management should be tightly integrated with strategy decisions and coordinated with activities across the enterprise; it requires an enterprisewide capability overseen by the board.

Developing such a capability requires the right mindset integrated with the company's strategy, guided by its culture and values, and supported by carefully designed governance and intelligence processes. We hope that this book will help in creating such a capability.

Acknowledgments

Writing this book has taken a little longer than expected. It was first conceived in the summer of 2013 while I was a professor in the Department of Managerial Economics and Decision Sciences (MEDS) at Northwestern's Kellogg School of Management, and a good portion of the manuscript was finished by early 2014. In the spring of 2014, I decided to leave Northwestern and become Dean of the Harris School of Public Policy at the University of Chicago, followed by my appointment as Provost in July of 2016. Subsequently, I was appointed Chancellor of Vanderbilt University and assumed my role during the COVID-19 pandemic on July 1, 2020. Naturally, this slowed things down a bit.

The book is based on many fruitful collaborations. My greatest debt is to David Baron, who first set me on the path of thinking about companies and their political environment seriously and who has been a great mentor and collaborator over many years. Many of the ideas were discussed with Tim Feddersen, a dear friend for over a quarter of a century and wonderful colleague at Kellogg's MEDS department. Our collaboration in building Kellogg's crisis management curriculum was a key catalyst for many of the concepts developed here. This book is dedicated to him. Much gratitude goes to my collaborators Jose Miguel ("Mike") Abito, Costel Andonie, Eyal Beigman, David Besanko, Adam Galinsky, Jean-Francois Godbout, Justin Heinze, Jennifer Jordan, Stefan Kaufman, Beata Beigman Klebanov, David Pizarro, Tage Rai, Eyal Sagi, David Tannenbaum, Eric

Uhlmann, and Bei Yu. And many thanks to my excellent research assistants Ben Chanzit, Alex Gordon, Kheira Issaoui-Mansouri, Jan Jaro, Daniel Lopez, Mike McMahon, Kym Pram, Agnieszka Roy, Mike Shi, Matthew Sullivan, and Dennis Zhan. I am particularly grateful to Tage Rai, Eyal Sagi, Andrew Wood, and Andrew Menger who read and commented on the entire manuscript.

I am finishing this book during the COVID-19 pandemic, in the fall of 2021, at my new home in Nashville. Many of the crises discussed in this book, while they loomed large at the time, pale in comparison to the current challenges, humanity's greatest global crisis since Word War II. I hope that some of the insights developed in this book will help leaders master current and future crises—we hope of a much smaller magnitude.

Notes

Preface

1. For details on the crisis and Johnson & Johnson's response, see Diermeier (2011) and Greyser (1982).

2. The Johnson & Johnson Credo was written by long-term chairman Robert Wood Johnson in 1943. It can be found at https://www.jnj.com/credo/.

3. Of course, in a given context, figuring out "the right thing to do" is far from trivial.

4. All of these crises are dwarfed by the challenges posed by the 2020–2022 COVID-19 pandemic which caused hundreds of thousands of deaths, shut down much of the global economy, and forced billions to stay at home during extended lockdowns. It affected companies, nonprofits, and government agencies worldwide, and presented the greatest challenge for leaders in a generation. We discuss these challenges throughout the book.

5. A particularly glaring example is the global supply chain disruptions in the fall of 2021, especially for semiconductors.

6. In Chapter 3 we provide an explanation for this observation.

7. Some credit card companies, however, such as Capital One, have used data security as part of their brand.

8. The word "reputation" is of Latin origin from "repeatedly" (*re-*) + "to reckon, consider" (*putare*). Its Greek counterpart is κλέος (*kleos*). Depending on the context, *kleos* can be translated as "glory," "fame," "praise," or "renown," but also "rumor," "report," or "news." But its original meaning is "what is said at a person's funeral; his legacy." For the heroes in the Homeric epics with no hope for rewards in the afterlife, immortality consisted in "renown unperishable" (κλέος αφθιτον). Obtaining everlasting renown was the main motivation of Homeric heroes in their battle for Troy. Dying without renown was the worst of fates. *Kleos* was based in virtuous action but also required a good storyteller, as the *Odyssey* makes abundantly clear.

9. See Eisner LLP (2010) and https://www.eisneramper.com/it-risk-management-0714/.

10. My own effort in this area is Diermeier (2011).

Chapter One

1. While electorates are the primary audience in political applications, politicians and parties also need to connect to donors, volunteers, and interest groups. Given the difficulty in data collection, research in this area has been limited. For examples of work in this area, see Barber, Canes-Wrone, and Thrower (2017), Brown, Powell, and Wilcox (1995), and Francia et al. (2003).

2. For discussions about the persistence and relative importance of party identification, see Achen and Bartels (2016), Ansolabehere, Rodden, and Snyder (2008), Bishop, Oldendick, and Tuchfarber (1978), Converse and Marcus (1979), and Nie, Verba, and Petrocik (1979).

3. Brands are often closely associated with products rather than corporations. They also tend to focus on customer experience. See, however, Kotler, Kartajaya, and Setiawan (2010) for a more expansive concept of brands and marketing. For a recent paper connecting products and partisan orientations, see Bertrand and Kamenica (2018).

Chapter Two

1. There are various definitions of "corporate reputation" (e.g., Argenti and Druckenmiller 2004; Fombrun 1996; Gotsi and Wilson 2001). Many of these definitions point in a similar direction as ours, emphasizing the importance of beliefs by various constituencies. Fombrun (1996, p. 37), for example, defines "corporate reputation as the overall estimation in which a company is held by its constituents." However, in contrast to game-theoretic models of reputation, such as Board and Meyer-Ter-Vehn (2013), such beliefs do not need to constitute a consistent posterior belief about hidden information as in a model of incomplete information.

2. A small segment of the public, however, is very well informed about policy and politics. Converse states this as follows (1990, p. 372): "The two simplest truths I know about the distribution of political information in modern electorates are that the mean is low and the variance high."

3. An excellent overview is given by Kinder (1998b).

4. Ansolabehere, Rodden, and Snyder (2008) argue that using multiple measures of issue positions can reduce instability, suggesting that instability may be the result of measurement error. See also Achen (1975).

5. See also Scheufele and Lewenstein (2005).

6. These phenomena are consistent with the well-known social desirability bias, that is, the tendency of survey respondents to answer questions in a manner that they expect will be viewed favorably by others, such as interviewers (Edwards 1953; Groves and Lyberg 2010; Paulhus 1984; Phillips and Clancy 1972).

7. Research from evolutionary psychology suggests that reciprocity norms are fundamental cognitive models underlying various thought processes (Barkow, Cosmides, and Tooby 1995).

8. The study of these systemic biases is part of the research program on heuristics and biases pioneered by Amos Tversky and Daniel Kahneman in the 1970s (e.g., Tversky and Kahneman 1973, 1974).

9. In recent years, an extensive controversy has arisen over whether many of the effects seen in this and related research programs can be replicated in subsequent, independent studies (Gilbert et al. 2016; Kahneman 2012; Open Science Collaboration 2015; see also Bargh, Chen, and Burrows 1996 versus Doyen et al. 2012 for a direct example). The most severe criticism has been directed at studies where small primes (e.g., showing subjects a flag) lead to large changes in beliefs (e.g., opposition to affirmative action) or changes in behavior (e.g., turnout); see Klein et al. (2014) for examples of such small primes and big effects. Using a larger sample than the original study, for example, Gerber et al. (2016) find no support for the idea that small changes to question wordings can lead to large changes in voter turnout, as argued by Bryan et al. (2011). The word-association tests discussed here, however, are less controversial (e.g., Brader 2006; Lodge and Taber 2013). For instance, in their attempt to replicate 13 proposed relationships from this literature, Klein et al. (2014) find that many of the most widely known effects successfully replicate (e.g., the sunk costs fallacy, differential evaluations of quotes depending on their attribution, variation in implicit attitude toward mathematics).

10. For a critique of this and related work in "implicit egoism" studies on connections between people's names and their locations or occupations, see Simonsohn (2011).

11. See Braun-LaTour et al. (2004) for a discussion on how advertising can influence how customers remember their past. Braun-Latour, Latour, and Loftus (2006) show how a fictitious memory, where subjects are asked to remember a visit to the (fictitious) "Wendy's Playland" can alleviate the impact of a product crisis.

12. See also the work on false memories and food preferences (e.g., Bernstein, Pernat, and Loftus 2011; Laney et al. 2010; Montgomery and Rajagopal 2018).

13. In contrast to semantic memory, which is devoid of context, episodic memory consists of memories of specific, individual events.

14. While the optimal amount of repetition varies based on context, on average, eight to ten exposures to stimuli are required to maximize recall at a later time (Schmidt and Eisend 2015).

15. Forgotten entities, however, can be relearned more quickly compared to new stimuli.

16. See Zaller (1992) for the related concept of receptivity.

17. As we will see later, this also has important consequences for the dynamics of opinion formation.

18. You can try this at home by asking an audience what is the first thing that comes to mind when they hear the name "Exxon."

19. This section is based on Diermeier, Austen-Smith, and Zemel (2011).

20. A recording of the 911 call can be heard at https://www.youtube.com/watch ?v=03m7fmnhO0I.

21. On November 25, 2009, Toyota announced a plan to increase the distance between the floor and gas pedal to address unintended acceleration problems. It also announced plans to install smart gas pedals on certain recalled models and on others where technically feasible. Smart gas pedals shut off when sensors indicate gas and brake pedals are being pressed simultaneously.

22. In late December 2012, Toyota agreed to settle a class-action lawsuit related to the loss of value for Toyota owners for over $1 billion. At that time, personal injury and wrongful death lawsuits against Toyota were still pending (Vlasic 2012).

23. In November 2009, NHTSA received reports of sticky gas pedals in Toyota cars. This led to a recall in January 2010. Toyota claimed that the issue of sticky gas pedals was unrelated to the issues of floor mats. Toyota engineers had previously concluded that the sticky pedals were a customer satisfaction issue, not a safety issue, because they did not affect the ability of drivers to stop their vehicles. This conclusion was supported by the fact that all concerns about sticky pedals were simply reported by dissatisfied customers; no cases were known to have been involved in any accidents. NHTSA urged Toyota to order a recall, and Toyota complied on January 21, 2010. This latest recall covered 2.3 million vehicles (Liker and Ogden 2011).

24. For details on the various reports, see https://one.nhtsa.gov/About-NHTSA /Press-Releases/ci.NHTSA%E2%80%93NASA-Study-of-Unintended-Accelera tion-in-Toyota-Vehicles.print.

25. For example, after winning initial liability trials, Toyota was instructed by a jury in October 2013 to pay compensatory damages and decided to settle before potentially much higher punitive damages could be awarded (Tropp 2013). And in 2014 Toyota settled for $1.2 billion a criminal suit brought by the US Department of Justice, which accused Toyota of having misled US consumers about the extent of sudden acceleration problems (Shepardson 2017).

26. See Diermeier (2011, chap. 2) and Diermeier and Marechal (2003a, 2003b) for details on Mercedes's handling of the Moose Test.

27. A similar strategy was pursued by BP in the aftermath of the Gulf of Mexico oil spill. Following the spill, BP decided to widely publicize its clean-up activities through an extensive advertising campaign, including television ads during the 2013 Super Bowl.

28. For details on Wal-Mart's Katrina response, see Diermeier, Crawford, and Snyder (2011) and Diermeier (2011, chap. 5).

29. The importance of capturing situations with high levels of public attention also has organizational consequences. Companies must develop effective crisis response capabilities that allow managers to react quickly and effectively to unanticipated developments and deliver an impactful and expeditious response while their audiences are still paying attention. Getting things right after the spotlight has moved on will have a far more limited impact as audience receptivity reverts back to its regular, much lower level.

30. Negative affect tends to have stronger impact than positive affect (e.g., Dijksterhuis and Aarts 2003).

31. The potential domain of affective tagging is very large. In an influential experiment, Zajonc (1968, 1980) exposed non-Chinese-speaking subjects to Chinese pictograms (meaningless objects to the subjects) and then asked the subjects to rate them as aesthetically pleasing. The more often subjects were exposed to a given pictogram, the more pleasing it was rated, a finding known as the "mere exposure effect" that has become highly influential in modern advertising. Subjects were not aware of the different exposure frequencies and later could not identify which pictograms were used in the experiments, but their rankings still covaried with exposure time. Affective tagging can explain such findings. Humans are constantly evaluating their environment. Such evaluation triggers brief flashes of affect regarding whether a situation or object is safe or not. Familiar objects, since they do not trigger negative affect, are tagged as safe. Hence, more familiar objects are preferred, even if they are meaningless squiggles on a piece of paper.

32. Affect can also directly impact attitudes, a phenomenon known as "affective transfer" (Lodge and Taber 2013). That is, the evaluation of an object changes if subjects are exposed to an affectively charged stimulus, even if the stimulus is irrelevant to the evaluated entity. For example, priming with a negative word can change evaluations of a political candidate (Lodge and Taber 2013). Advertisers, of course, use this effect all the time.

33. These phenomena belong to the class of processes known as "motivated reasoning," where an individuals' emotions, desires, or goals affect the ways in which they interpret information (Kunda 1990). We discuss motivated reasoning in detail in chapter 7.

34. Early work on consonance found that people use their emerging sense of a conclusion to shift their evaluations of evidence to cohere and move into closer alignment with the conclusion. For example, in an experiment on legal decision making, participants evaluated individual arguments in isolation prior to seeing the case they were part of, and then again after reaching a verdict on the case. It was found that initially ambiguous attitudes toward the evidence shifted toward a more coherent set of attitudes in line with the eventual verdict (Holyoak and Simon 1999). These findings suggest that reasoning is not unidirectional, moving from evidence

to conclusions, but bidirectional, moving from evidence to conclusions and from conclusions to evidence.

35. The effect also occurs if the information is provided after initial opinion formation (Druckman and Bolsen 2011).

36. In settings where subjects are very highly engaged, for example, college students asked about exam policies, subjects do tend to set aside consonance with values or source credibility and respond to the strength of the argument itself (e.g., Petty and Cacioppo 1986). However, such settings require high levels of familiarity with the subject area and substantial levels of involvement. Neither of the conditions is likely to be commonly satisfied in the context of new technologies or other areas related to corporate reputation.

37. To be sure, subjects need to have a minimal level of familiarity or attentiveness to react to cues or make the connection to value orientations. Otherwise they tend to simply adopt the message they receive first (Converse 1964; Zaller 1992).

38. Message flow and content, of course, do not need to be balanced, especially if the media plays a role. We return to this issue in chapter 8.

39. For example, increasing policy knowledge about energy regulations aimed at reducing greenhouse gas emissions leads to higher polarization in support along party lines (Ehret, Van Boven, and Sherman 2018).

40. The importance of cultural credibility does not mean that scientific experts have no impact on public opinion. Bolsen and Druckman (2015) show how scientific expertise can shift or counteract polarization. In this context, *warnings* to dismiss politicized information tend to be more effective than *corrections* that try to reverse a misperception. Lupia (2013) also points to the importance of attention and source credibility.

41. Republicans can be induced to show moderate support for greenhouse gas reduction policies to combat climate change, but only when such policies are promoted by Republican politicians or by both parties (Ehret, Van Boven, and Sherman 2018).

42. Similar results could be found along the individualist-communitarian dimension (Kahan, Slovic, et al. 2008).

43. Results in the conservative prime condition, with a gun rights advocate, a typical conservative position, were in the hypothesized direction, but did not reach conventional significance levels.

44. While online judgments abound, it is true that other, more deliberative assessments of individuals and issues sometimes do take place. These involve the retrieval of facts and experiences from memory to facilitate the formation of an opinion or judgment. Such judgments, however, tend to be rare. See, for example, Hastie and Park (1986), Mackie and Asuncion (1990), and Tormala and Petty (2001).

45. For example, the vividly described 1993 *E. Coli* outbreak happened at Jack in the Box restaurants.

46. For instance, subjects are often asked to describe the color font in which a word is presented when some of the words are, confusingly, the names of colors themselves.

47. For a brief 20-year overview on the implicit bias literature, see Sleek (2018). For a discussion of the impact of even small biases on societal outcomes, see Greenwald, Banaji, and Nosek (2015). Forscher et al. (2019), however, provide a meta-analysis where such societal effects are found to be smaller or less reliable.

48. In many cases, these primes are presented for only a fraction of a second.

49. Note that the IAT and priming tasks differ in the way the stimulus or prime is presented. In classic priming studies, the stimulus precedes the target, while in an IAT they occur simultaneously. Nevertheless, in both cases, the incomparability of the two ideas is what is thought to produce the observed behaviors.

50. See LeBreton, Grimaldi, and Schoen (2020) for an overview of conditional reasoning tests with several examples.

51. Ferguson et al. (2019) point to three properties of new information that shift implicit impressions: diagnosticity (the new information needs to be seen as revealing), believability (the message needs to be believed), and reinterpretation (providing a new context or frame).

52. Note that some of the studies employed interventions aimed at *increasing* a bias. While such strategies are unlikely to be employed in a corporate bias-reduction program, they do provide insight into how these biases can be changed.

53. In a series of papers, Lai et al. (2014, 2016) examine the long-term impact of bias-reduction strategies. Using various intervention techniques and experimental designs, Lai et al. find that only a select few techniques succeed in producing short-term changes in biases and that none of the proposed interventions lead to sustained changes in bias. The combination of these results suggests a potential double difficulty in altering bias: not only do we need to select the right type of intervention, but any effort to permanently change biases must be actively sustained for it to have any meaningful, lasting effect.

These difficulties are further compounded by the lack of clarity over whether induced shifts in these implicitly measured biases will translate to shifts in explicit beliefs and behaviors. Once again, existing evidence suggests that contemporaneous shifts in these concepts may occur with a small, select set of interventions (Forscher et al. 2019) but not for others (Lai et al. 2014). Furthermore, studies that found changes in explicit attitudes from a few specific interventions noted that these changes were smaller than changes in implicit attitudes (Forscher et al. 2019).

54. In their meta-analysis, Forscher et al. (2019) use Hedge's g as a measure of effect size. Hedge's g and the related Cohen's d are used to quantify the size of an effect in relation to the variance in the measured variable. In the psychology literature, values of these measures below 0.35 are considered small (Hyde 2005).

Chapter Three

1. These findings are consistent with an extensive literature that has consistently found that self-interest is surprisingly unimportant in predicting public opinion in politics (e.g., Sears, Hensler, and Spear 1979; Sears et al. 1980). Rather, group effects (especially on matters of race and immigration) and values (such as equality, justice, and individualism) play a much more important role.

2. In one such experiment, infants are presented with puppets: in one case, one puppet is helping another to climb up a hill, while, in another case, it is hindering the climber (Hamlin, Wynn, and Bloom 2007). When presented with these puppet performances, ten-month-old infants will tend to reach for the helping puppet rather than the hinderer.

3. See Rai and Diermeier (2019) for evidence of this pattern, which we discuss in more detail below.

4. This also explains why shareholders usually receive little sympathy in a crisis context, even though they may suffer grave losses, as shareholders tend to be perceived as wealthy, anonymous, and greedy, and thus elicit little sympathy (e.g., Diermeier 2011).

5. For evidence of the positive impact of CSR on product evaluations, see Chernev and Blair (2015).

6. See also Klein and Dawar (2004).

7. The original example is from British philosopher Philippa Foot (1978). See also Jarvis Thomson (1976, 1985). The version here is from Greene and Haidt (2002).

8. Cushman, Young, and Hauser (2006) call this the "action principle."

9. The justification of self-defense is developed in the *Summa Theologiae* (Aquinas [1485] 2006, II-II, q. 64, art. 7). It is an instance of the doctrine of double effect, where an action that causes harm can be justified if it brought about a good outcome, provided that the harm occurred as a side effect and was not intended. It has been particularly important in areas such as abortion, physician-assisted suicide, and self-defense (e.g., Foot 1978; Quinn 1989). The *New Catholic Encyclopedia* (Catholic University of America 2002, p. 880) provides four conditions for the application of the doctrine of double effect:

1. The act itself must be morally good or at least indifferent.
2. The agent may not positively will the bad effect but may merely permit it. If he could attain the good effect without the bad effect he should do so. The bad effect is sometimes said to be indirectly voluntary.
3. The good effect must flow from the action at least as immediately (in the order of causality, though not necessarily in the order of time) as the bad effect. In other words, the good effect must be produced directly by the action, not by the bad effect. Otherwise the agent would be using a bad means to a good end, which is never allowed.

4. The good effect must be sufficiently desirable to compensate for the allowing of the bad effect.

10. Former FDA commissioner's David Kessler's first-person account of these developments is tellingly called "A Question of Intent" (Kessler 2002).

11. Graham et al. (2013) have proposed a sixth principle: liberty/oppression. This principle has been more controversial and plays little role in the context of corporate reputations.

12. Moral attitudes can be measured through the Moral Foundations Questionnaire, a survey tool (Graham et al. 2011), and the Moral Foundations Dictionary, which can be used to analyze texts (Graham, Haidt, and Nosek 2009). For overviews, discussions, and a list of tools, see https://moralfoundations.org.

13. The philosophical literature on the topic is vast, ranging from Plato's *Republic* to Nozick (1974) and Rawls (1971), among many others.

14. Vernon Smith, one of the founders of experimental economics, shared the Nobel Prize in Economics in 2002 with Daniel Kahneman, who introduced the notion of biases and heuristics in his joint work with Amos Tversky. Richard Thaler was awarded the 2018 Nobel Prize in Economics for his foundational work in behavioral economics.

15. For additional evidence on the existence of fairness motives, see Andreoni, Brown, and Vesterlund (2002), Brosnan and de Waal (2003), Cosmides and Tooby (1989), Fehr and Schmidt (1999), Haidt (2003), and Kahneman, Knetsch, and Thaler (1986).

16. Note that the optimal behavior (by both the proposer and the respondent) does not depend on the proposer's disagreement value, unless the value is so high that the proposer prefers his or her disagreement value to any possible proposal. So, for example, suppose that the fairness threshold for a given population of agents is $4, then it should not matter whether the proposer has a disagreement value of $3 or $0.

17. See Baron, Lim, and Liu (2003) for details.

18. Pricing debates are not only limited to developing countries. One of the recurring debates in the United States pertains to the reimportation of drugs from Canada and Mexico due to significant price discounts.

19. Evolutionary psychologists have argued that at the root of concerns over purity and sanctity lies the fear of pathogens, other due to either food poisoning or communicable diseases (Smith et al. 2011).

20. The financial magnitude of such perks can be quite small. For example, in 2009, British Tory MP Sir Peter Viggers was forced to step down after it became known that he had submitted a reimbursement claim of £1,645 for a "floating duck island" in a pond at his country home.

21. For a sense of the importance these tells have to public perceptions, note that a prominent critic of executive compensation packages, Nell Minnow, is using perks as a warning sign of future trouble at a company (Owen 2009).

22. There is, of course, a more complicated economic justification for short sellers that points to their important role in the functioning of financial markets (e.g., Bris, Goetzmann, and Zhu 2007; Diamond and Verrechia 1987), but such arguments are complicated and difficult to communicate.

23. One possible alternative explanation for these results is rarity, as low-probability events can be especially informative. Indeed, in the context of person perception, rare behaviors lead to stronger trait-based attributions (Ditto and Jemmott 1989; Fiske 1980; Jones and Davis 1965; Kelley 1967). However, the act-person dissociation persists even when controlling for perceived rarity. The results can be found whether the same respondents are exposed to both scenarios (intrasubject design) or whether they are split in two subsamples and only observe one randomly assigned scenario (intersubject design). See Tannenbaum, Uhlmann, and Diermeier (2011) for details.

24. Negative rumors also spread more quickly (Donavan, Mowen, and Chakraborty 1999; Kamins, Folkes, and Perner 1997).

25. Animal abuse is a strong predictor of other antisocial and illegal behaviors (Becker et al. 2004; Walton-Moss et al. 2005).

26. The public is unlikely to make the distinction whether the health insurer is a for-profit or a mutual company, especially when also focusing on executive compensation.

27. See Sripada and Konrath (2011) as well as Sripada (2012) for some evidence in support of this argument.

28. Lauer himself was terminated by NBC News in 2017 over allegations of sexual harassment and assault.

29. For an overview on mind perception, see Epley and Waytz (2010).

30. This feature makes Herodotus's description of Xerxes's rage at the Hellespont in book 7 of the *Histories* so memorable. After storms had destroyed the Persian first platoon bridge, Xerxes had the waters whipped 300 times and had shackles thrown into the water as a mark of enslavement.

31. In terms of experience, nonprofits tend to score in the middle between for-profit companies and individuals (Au and Ng 2020).

32. Executives with extensive experience in crisis management tend to guess correctly that the public will have little sympathy with a company (Rai and Diermeier 2015).

33. In this context, notice also the strong desire to identify a guilty party in the COVID-19 pandemic. This may include investigations on the origins of the virus or physical attacks or intimidations of individuals who are perceived as having brought the virus to a country. Subsequently, blame may shift to governmental actors for insufficient planning or an ineffective response, whether such allegations are warranted or not.

34. We discuss the importance of trust in detail in chapter 5.

35. Simply reminding people of money increases perceptions of strength and competence (Vohs, Mead, and Goode 2006).

36. See also Goffman (1961) and, for a more elaborate categorization, Rai and Fiske (2011).

37. This distinction is sometimes obscured by the widely known concept of "gift exchange." Giving and receiving gifts (rather than paying directly) is characteristic of communal relationships and sometimes, as in the case of reciprocating an invitation, giving and receiving is reciprocal. The main difference is that there is no direct expectation of an exchange. A guest who does not immediately offer to reciprocate the invitation may be impolite. A host who asks for a reciprocal invitation will cause consternation. Clark and Mills (1993, p. 687) state this as follows:

> The communal/exchange distinction makes a distinction between the giving and receiving of benefits and the exchange of benefits. The giving and receiving of benefits in communal relationships does not constitute an exchange of benefits, according to the communal/exchange distinction.... Although the term *exchange* has been used broadly in social psychology to refer to mutually rewarding interaction, we do not use the term in that way. Rather, we use it in accord with the dictionary definition of exchange as giving or taking one thing in return for another. For us, an exchange occurs when the parties involved understand that one benefit is given in return for another benefit. (emphasis in original)

38. There are subtle cultural differences in how these relational models are implemented in different cultures. For example, in US culture, when friends go out to dinner at a restaurant it is common to split the bill equally among the diners. This practice emphasizes communal sharing and hence group unity. In Germany, it is common that each diner pays for his or her bill separately, with the server going from person to person, receiving payment and tip. This practice emphasizes proportionality and individual fairness. Needless to say, members of both cultures are often flabbergasted when they are confronted with the other approach.

39. Diermeier (2011, chap. 5) provides a detailed description of Wal-Mart's relief efforts in the aftermath of Hurricane Katrina.

40. These patterns of evaluation are the reverse of those seen in the trolley problem, where attention is now directed toward care rather than harm.

41. The same social relational frames underlying responses to natural disasters may explain other puzzles in how people respond to changes in supply and demand. For example, customers believe it is fair to raise prices in response to an increase in the cost of production. However, they do not believe it is fair to raise prices in response to an increase in demand. For example, people think it is unfair for a hardware store to increase the price of shovels the day after a snowstorm (Kahneman, Knetsch, and Thaler 1986). Similarly, when Coca-Cola considered implementing dynamic pricing in soda machines so that they would charge higher fees on hotter days, consumers felt the practice was highly unfair, and the company abandoned the idea (King and Narayandas 2000). Weather emergencies are a prototypical example of events that trigger community orientations.

42. This approach is also referred to as "relationship regulation" (e.g., Rai and Fiske 2011).

43. Indeed, GE counted on "make-whole" payments to lower its own compensation cost. During the horse race to succeed him, then GE CEO Jack Welch suggested that GE's board offer all potential candidates multimillion-dollar retention bonuses to encourage them to stay at the company and compete for the position. When the board voiced concern at having to pay so many bonuses, Welch assured them that only the selected candidate would stay at GE, and the others would be lured away by a new employer that would pay the promised amount as part of a "make-whole arrangement" (Lorsch and Khurana 2010). Welch's prediction proved accurate.

44. Various studies by financial economists have argued that, in the context of overall increasing market caps, the increase of CEO compensation has not been out of proportion. In their paper "Why Has CEO Pay Increased so Much?" Gabaix and Landier (2008) come to the conclusion that rising CEO compensation—regardless of the ultimate performance in terms of gains in short-term profits—had adequately risen proportional to expanding responsibilities of the position and the rising aggregate market cap of US corporations. The researchers argue that high salaries are necessary for recruitment of top CEOs.

45. Notice the similarity to moral foundations theory (Haidt 2013b). Social relations theory argues that many concerns about purity and loyalty identified by moral foundations theory (Rai and Fiske 2011) are actually variants of the same underlying motive: unity. Similar comments apply, mutatis mutandis, to the fourth principle, authority ranking.

46. The reader will have noticed some overlap between social relations theory, Shweder et al.'s (1997) "big three" of morality, Clark and Mills's (1979, 1993) two orientations, and moral foundations theory (Graham, Haidt, and Nosek 2009; Haidt 2013b; Haidt and Graham 2007; Haidt and Joseph 2004, 2008). The conceptual relationship between these approaches, however, is complex and contested. For example, the concept of "fairness" from moral foundations theory does not have a clear analogue in social relations theory. Rather, according to social relations theory, our fairness intuitions will depend on which social relation is actualized. So, if the relationship is characterized by community sharing, fairness may be about distributing based on needs, as in the case of a natural disaster. If the relationship is based on authority ranking, then fairness may mean allocating more to those in charge. If the relationship is based on equality matching, fairness may mean that everyone is getting the same amount, while if the relationship is structured as a market pricing, allocations may be based on effort or added value.

From a practical point of view, each one of these perspectives provides a different lens on moral judgment, and hence reputational risk. They are best used in conjunction, for example, as filters or dimensions of risk due to outrage that can then be combined into an appropriate measure of risk. In cases of conflict between the different perspectives, deeper analysis is necessary.

47. De Beer's 80-year-long marketing strategy to position diamonds as the symbol of enduring love is perhaps the most successful example of this approach (Bergenstock and Maskulka 2001).

48. When choosing a container to purchase, consumers devote greater effort to searching for higher quality rather than lower price if they believe the container is meant to hold cremated remains rather than a clock (McGraw et al. 2016).

49. As discussed above, we are setting aside the recently proposed sixth principle Liberty/Oppression, as it plays little role in corporate contexts.

Chapter Four

1. For a thorough overview, see Kahneman (2011).

2. A famous example is the "invisible gorilla experiment" (Chabris and Simons 2010; Simons and Chabris 1999). In the experiment, subjects are asked to watch a film where two teams (one wearing white, the other black uniforms) pass a ball back and forth. Their task is to count the number of passes of the white team. This is a demanding task requiring intense focus. Halfway through the film a person wearing a gorilla costume appears, moving about for a few seconds. About half the subjects fail to notice the gorilla; they are too absorbed in their task.

3. There is an ongoing debate within cognitive psychology regarding which system is primary. See, for example, Lai, Hagoort, and Casasanto (2012).

4. For example, human subjects struggle with the logic of if-then statements when such statements are presented in an abstract representation, but do much better when they are presented as social norms of cooperation (Cosmides and Tooby 1992; Wason 1966).

5. In contrast, investors may be thought of as heavily relying on System II processes, but the emerging discipline of behavioral finance has demonstrated the existence of various biases in financial decision making, especially with respect to retail investors (Barberis and Thaler 2003; Shiller 2016; Thaler 1993, 2005). An assessment of modern marketing or behavioral finance is beyond the scope of this book, but it is important to keep in mind that the insights presented here are not restricted to an uninformed and uninterested public but may apply to business constituencies as well.

6. Moral justifications tend to be confirmatory in nature and indeed exhibit aspects of confirmation bias, the tendency to seek out and interpret information to confirm preexisting beliefs and attitudes (Oswald and Grosjean 2004).

7. For an instructive transcript of such an exchange, see Haidt (2013b, p. 46).

8. We investigate the issue of peer-to-peer influence in detail in chapter 9.

Chapter Five

1. This list is only partial. In addition, there is evidence of anchoring effects, confirmations bias, optimism—in other words, people view hazards as more risky for others than themselves, (e.g., Lloyd 2001)—and halo effects, where people first form an overall evaluation and then adjust their attitude toward the components rather than the other way around (e.g., O'Donnell and Schultz 2005), to name just a few. Fischhoff et al. (1978) proposed that risk perception can be reduced to two factors: the degree to which a risk is familiar and the amount of dread evoked by a hazard.

2. This is an instance of one of the most influential framing effects from Tversky and Kahneman (1974). Its discovery led to the development of prospect theory (Kahneman and Tversky 1979).

3. Using loss frames to create successful messaging is another matter. In a series of meta-analyses of gain-loss message framing studies, O'Keefe and Jensen (2006, 2009) found that there was no significant difference between the two frames in terms of average persuasiveness. See also O'Keefe (2012) and O'Keefe and Nan (2012).

4. Pharmacia then spun off its agro-business into a new company, the "new" Monsanto, later acquired by Bayer. Pharmacia was bought by Pfizer. For details on this chain of events, see Monsanto (2018).

5. There is now considerable doubt about the validity of these concerns (Boyle, Dalgleish, and Puzey 2019).

6. There are also potential benefits from the decreased use of chemical insecticides and fertilizers, although the net environmental benefits of GMOs are heavily contested (Brookes and Barfoot 2017; Perry et al. 2016; Tsatsakis et al. 2017).

7. Finucane et al. (2000), for example, showed that the inverse correlation between benefits and risks increased substantially if respondents had to make decisions under time pressure, providing additional support for a System I process.

8. This phenomenon is also referred to as "cultural cognition," that is, the tendency to form beliefs about risks and benefits of an issue or activity based on the fit with a person's cultural orientation (Kahan and Braman 2006; Kahan, Braman, et al. 2008).

9. In some cases, even sensory perception (or at least reports of such perception) can be affected. Hamilton, Lemcke-Stampone, and Grimm (2018) show that conservatives are less likely to say that the winter has been unseasonably warm.

10. In addition to business contexts and business ventures (e.g., MacDuffie 2011; Mayer, Davis, and Schoorman 1995; McAllister 1995; Meqdadi, Johnsen, and Johnsen 2017; Morgan and Hunt 1994; Robson, Katsikeas, and Bellow 2008;

Rousseau et al. 1998; Schoorman, Mayer, and Davis 2007; Svejenova 2006; Wallenburg et al. 2011) trust plays an important role in many social and political interactions, such as governmental institutions (Citrin and Stoker 2018; Hardin 2002; Levi and Stoker 2000; Webster 2018), social networks (Simpson and Willer 2015; Zak, Stanton, and Ahmadi 2007), community organizations (Park, Mosley, and Grogan 2018), and economic development (Dearmon and Grier 2009; Peiró-Palomino and Tortosa-Ausina 2013). See Kramer (1999) and Kramer and Tyler (1995) for overviews.

11. See also Bohnet et al. (2008), Cox (2004), Espín, Exadaktylos, and Neyse (2016), Johnson and Mislin (2011), and Tzieropoulos (2013).

12. Such dispositions are commonly measured using survey questions about respondents' general attitudes toward others, such as their "faith in humanity" (Wang, Ngamsiriudom, and Hsieh 2015), tendency to "count upon other people" (Gefen 2000), or belief that "people are generally reliable" (Kim, Ferrin, and Rao 2008).

13. These first two dimensions are closely related to the dimension of competence and warmth discussed in chapter 3.

14. Such attempts can also backfire if consumers are skeptical of the company's CSR activities (e.g., Ulusoy and Barretta 2016).

15. By the end of August 2013, Netflix had recovered from its crisis. Its number of subscribers totaled 28.6 million, and its stock had rebounded, trading at $288 a share. Many observers credited Netflix's recovery to its willingness to respond to customer feedback, as well as its recent development of original, exclusive TV series like *Arrested Development* and *House of Cards*. Both received multiple Emmy nominations and were praised as examples for the possible future of television. Netflix continued to thrive in subsequent years (CBS/Associated Press 2013).

16. To tease apart the relative contributions of deterrence and retribution, Carlsmith and Sood (2009) had participants evaluate the efficacy of torturing terrorists. The experimenters varied both the potential information that the terrorist had as well as the past crimes that the terrorist had committed. If people endorse torture purely for deterrence, then they should be most willing to support torture when the terrorist holds valuable information. However, if they endorse torture primarily as retribution for wrongdoing, then they should be most willing to endorse torture when the terrorist has committed heinous crimes in the past, regardless of any information the terrorist possesses. The experiments found that retribution is a stronger driver of supporting torture, even though it is often defended on deterrence-based grounds. Once again, stated beliefs do not match actual motives.

17. Priming commitment experimentally can help induce forgiveness (Finkel et al. 2002).

18. An exception may be found in cases where a company is embodied by a charismatic and beloved leader. The adoration bestowed on the late Steve Jobs may have isolated Apple from some missteps that likely would have had a more severe

impact on other companies. For example, in 2010 iPhone 4 users experienced the problem of their device losing signal when held by the lower left corner. Jobs's initial response was to "just avoid holding it in that way," accompanied by an official video that showed customers how to "avoid gripping it in the lower left corner in a way that covers both sides of the black strip in the metal band" (BBC News 2010). Apple eventually provided free cases to solve the problem, but Jobs did not apologize (Helft 2010). Jobs's successor Tim Cook had no such luck. Apple needed to defend itself first against irresponsible labor practices at its main supplier FoxConn, and then found itself under attack for its tax avoidance strategies.

In some cases, supporters may rally around an embattled executive. In the Paula Deen case discussed above, Deen's supporters started a campaign called "Butter for Paula." Supporters were asked to send empty butter wrappers to the companies who had dropped Paula Deen as a form of protest. The slogan of the movement is that "A company without Paula is like a wrapper without butter." By August 2013, the campaign's Facebook page had 600,000 likes (Stump 2013).

19. For example, when presented with legal scenarios, participants made harsher judgments of defendants when presented with negative information about their character, even when that information was completely unrelated to the case (Nadler and McDonnell 2011).

20. CSR activities or a record of good service may provide some evidence for benevolence on behalf of the company.

21. We have seen similar phenomena in the context of the do-no-harm principle and the trolley problem in Chapter 3.

22. Trust can also be restored in game-theoretic experiments (e.g., Bottom et al. 2002).

23. For similar evidence in the context of personal relationships, see John, Barasz, and Norton (2016).

24. There is an exception for integrity-based trust violations. As we will see below, in integrity-based trust violations, most strategies are ineffective. Thus, even creating some doubt through a denial may be better than nothing (Kim et al. 2004).

25. In a jury trial, Shannon Moseley's parents were later awarded $101 million in punitive damages and $4.2 million in compensatory damages (Georgia Trial Lawyers Association 1993).

26. Perhaps the most famous battle between a corporate customer and its supplier is the Ford and Firestone controversy. For details see Pinedo, Seshardri, and Zemel (2000).

27. In interpersonal contexts, effective justifications sometimes point to the role of an altruistic motivation (e.g., Shapiro 1991). This dimension plays little role in the interaction between companies and the public.

28. Focusing on the CEO of a company can moderate this effect. That is, while companies are viewed as lacking feelings, CEOs are viewed as capable of

experience. This makes personal apologies by the CEO more effective than a statement by the company's communications staff (Tang and Gray 2018).

29. Due to their inability to feel, organizations also tend to be seen as less morally motivated (Jago, Kreps, and Laurin 2019).

30. See, for example, Arno (1976) for anthropological evidence and Schweitzer, Hershey, and Bradlow (2006) and Schniter, Sheremeta, and Sznycer (2012) for experimental evidence in Trust Game settings.

31. In a recent study, Halperin et al. (2022) designed a field experiment with Uber customers. Riders who experienced late rides were randomly assigned to various responses from the company, such as an apology or a coupon. Halperin and colleagues then measured the effect of such treatments on future net spending by these customers. They found that coupons, if they were received immediately, increased future demand, while verbal apologies had no effect or, in case of repeated apologies or a particularly bad experience, even backfired. Whether these findings generalize to settings beyond ride-sharing is an open question.

32. The news cycle for bad news is even shorter (Wu et al. 2011).

33. These dynamics mark an important difference between corporate and political crises. "Waiting for things to blow over" often works in political contexts for many reasons, especially during electoral campaigns. During a campaign, the public repeatedly pays attention to politicians. As one story quickly follows another, any particular story is less likely to take firm root in the public's memory. Moreover, voting decisions are driven by many considerations, including expectations about future policies and conduct. In this choice process, even a significant crisis represents only one factor among many, perhaps dimly remembered by voters when casting their ballots. Finally, voters usually have few choices; in the United States frequently only two major competitors split the votes. That means that voters often have to decide "between two evils" and all that matters is who gets the most votes. Suppressing the other side's vote total, for example, through negative advertising, is just as effective as raising one's own total.

Corporate contexts are different. Customers rarely pay the same sustained attention to a company. When they do, however, they do so with heightened focus, so the impact on the company's reputation can be profound and permanent.

34. See Eilert et al. (2017) for the impact of delays in product recall crises.

35. These four dimensions are also known as the "Trust Radar"; see Diermeier (2011, chap. 1) for details.

Chapter Six

1. Respondents also tend to largely neglect the potential social benefits of profits (Bhattacharjee, Dana, and Baron 2017).

2. This is not an isolated case. Laypeople also use folk physics to make sense of the physical world (Ross and Nisbett 1991; Wyer 2004). See also the

related literature on analogies (Gentner 1998) and metaphors (Lakoff and Johnson 1980).

3. Of course, larger or particularly egregious perks can have substantial impacts. See the discussion in chapter 3.

Chapter Seven

1. For a brief history on the US tobacco industry and its political environment, see Diermeier and Thaker (2006). Detailed histories include Brandt (2009), Kessler (2002), Kluger (2010), Milov (2019), and Proctor (2012).

2. The tobacco companies' approach was an instantiation of their general "give an inch, gain a decade" strategy. While the industry vehemently opposed any such labeling requirements, they were particularly concerned (1) that a total ban on advertising would be advocated and (2) that the states could individually push for more extreme restrictions. Weaker labeling and the preemption of tougher regulatory efforts in states such as New York and Massachusetts effectively constituted a "stay of execution" for the industry (Derthick 2002). Subsequent legislation explicitly excluded tobacco from regulation under various statutes such as the Controlled Substances Act, the Consumer Product Safety Act, and the Toxic Substances Act (Nathanson 1999).

3. See Diermeier and Thaker (2006) for details.

4. The exact interpretation and impact of frames continues to be debated. For example, cognitive frames can be made to disappear when subjects receive both competing frames, for example, both a gain and a loss frame (e.g., Druckman 2004). This suggests that once subjects become aware of the logical equivalence the framing effects (at least temporarily) disappear. Additionally, well-informed individuals are less susceptible to cognitive frames.

5. Other terms used are "emphasis frame" or "value frame" (Druckman 2009).

6. This approach can be interpreted as an abstract representation of various approaches in cognitive psychology, such as Goffman's (1974) "frame," Johnson-Lairds's (1983) "mental models," and Lakoff and Johnson's (1980) "metaphors." See also Druckman (2009).

7. For an overview, see Druckman and Lupia (2016) and Busby, Flynn, and Druckman (2018).

8. See Diermeier (2011, chap. 6) for details.

9. In addition to the direct reputational impact of the industry, the issue of intent also had important regulatory implications for the industry. The FDA released a letter in 1994 stating that it could regulate tobacco if there was evidence that the tobacco companies had manipulated tobacco to make it addictive. The tobacco companies challenged the FDA's position in court. In 2000 the US Supreme Court

found, in a 5-4 decision, that the FDA did not have statutory authority to regulate cigarettes. If the agency was to begin regulating tobacco, it would require explicit legislative approval from Congress (Kessler 2002). Such authority, subject to explicit constraints, was granted by Congress in 2009 through the Family Smoking Prevention and Tobacco Control Act.

10. Wigand's story was portrayed in the 1999 Hollywood movie *The Insider*, with Russell Crowe in the role of Jeffrey Wigand.

11. Notice the connection to fairness considerations triggered by the state Medicaid reimbursement lawsuits, that is, the claim that the tobacco companies "do not pay their fair share."

12. The length of the causal chain also matters. Paharia et al. (2009) show that a company is blamed less for a price increase for a lifesaving drug if the price increase is done by a middleman.

13. Some critics argued that FDA oversight did not go far enough. For example, the FDA would be prohibited from banning entire categories of tobacco products. See, for example, US Department of Health and Human Services (2016) and Action on Smoking and Health et al. (2018).

14. See also Nestle (2013) and Oliver (2006).

15. There is no clear equivalent to the issue of secondhand smoking in the context of obesity. Christakis and Fowler (2007) have provided some (heavily criticized) evidence for social contagion effects of obesity, that is, people who have many obese friends, siblings, or spouses are more likely to become obese themselves. But this approach has not gotten much traction in the policy debate on obesity. For a detailed methodological critique of the approach, see Cohen-Cole and Fletcher (2008).

16. Lawrence's (2004) empirical analysis of obesity frames found an increase over time in public-health-related frames. However, this increase largely reflects an increased focus on unhealthy environments rather than a shift of responsibility. Personal choice and lifestyle still remains a powerful frame, which limits the blame put on food companies.

17. One possible explanation is that the frame mentioned arsenic in groundwater. This rather vivid feature of the frame may have triggered a generic fear response that may have swamped the more subtle "green to gold" frame.

Chapter Eight

1. For evidence of the impact of the media coverage on stock market performance, see Dougal et al. (2012), Tetlock (2007, 2015), and Tetlock, Saar-Tsechansky, and Macskassy (2008). For the impact on sales during a product crisis, see Liu and Shankar (2015). For a general discussion of product-harm crises, see Cleeren, Dekimpe, and van Heerde (2017).

2. Freedman, Kearney, and Lederman (2012) also consider the impact on stock prices and find a significant −1.1 percent impact. This result, however, is almost entirely driven by one case, the Thomas the Tank Engine recall from September 2007. For details on the Thomas the Tank Engine recall, see Diermeier (2011, chap. 1).

3. See, however, Lei, Dawar, and Lemmink (2008) and Borah and Tellis (2016).

4. We discuss the separate mechanism of social influence below.

5. For the impact of newspaper op-eds on policy attitudes, see Coppock, Ekins, and Kirby (2018).

6. For detailed studies of the dynamics of public attention, see Jones and Baumgartner (2005).

7. Sorting also occurs in online news environments. Hindman (2009) shows that the readership of online political sites follows a power-law distribution, with the top-10 online sites commanding a majority of the links (Hindman, Tsioutsiouliklis, and Johnson 2003).

8. Such sorting may, of course, have other undesirable effects, such as creating echo chambers that lead to the fragmentation and polarization of the public (Sunstein 2001).

9. See also Puglisi and Snyder (2015). For other definitions of media bias, see Gentzkow, Shapiro, and Stone (2015) and Groeling (2015). Gentzkow, Shapiro, and Stone define media bias in terms of influence on beliefs. We consider these issues below under the rubric of media influence.

10. See also Nyhan (2012). Gans and Leigh (2012) use a similar approach for Australian newspapers. Neither one finds significant evidence of slant.

11. Ho and Quinn (2008) find similar results in the context of judicial decisions.

12. We discuss text-analytic approaches in detail in part 5.

13. Conceptually this approach is similar to Groseclose and Milyo (2005), but it uses far richer news content than just references to think tanks. It also expands the sample from 20 newspapers in the Groseclose-Milyo dataset to 400.

14. A possible source of the close ideological match between newspapers and readership in the Gentzkow and Shapiro analysis is the possibility that the media influences the views of the readership. Gentzkow and Shapiro address this concern by using an instrumental variables approach with religiosity as the instrument, as religiosity is unlikely to be strongly affected by daily news coverage.

15. For research on the impact of advertising, see Blasco and Sobbrio (2012) as well as Ellman and Germano (2009).

16. More generally, this problem can be seen as a form of omitted variable bias since an unobserved variable ("selection" or "sorting") is driving the relationships we observe. Indeed, Heckman's (1979) exposition of this issue makes it clear that this selection bias can be considered and mitigated by treating the underlying problem as a specification error or omitted variable bias. See also Angrist and Pischke (2009).

17. More technically, a good instrument needs to be uncorrelated with *all* confounding variables such that the correlation between the instrument and the error term of the regression is zero. For a more detailed discussion of the specific assumptions required in instrumental variable models, see Angrist and Pischke (2009) and Dougherty (2011).

18. This estimation procedure has two steps: first, estimate the new values of the independent variable using the instrument, and then use those new values to estimate the relationship between the independent and dependent variables. This can be done in separate models or simultaneously using two-stage least squares (2SLS) estimation.

19. See Gentzkow, Shapiro, and Stone (2015), Prat and Strömberg (2013), Groeling (2015), and Snyder and Puglisi (2016) for recent overviews. For models of the impact of media bias on elections, see Bernhard, Krasa, and Polborn (2008), Duggan and Martinelli (2011), Shapiro (2016), and Wolton (2019).

20. DellaVigna et al. (2014) also conducted laboratory experiments which confirm these findings.

21. See also Yanagizawa-Drott (2014) on the impact of radio coverage on the killing of the Tutsi minority in the Rwandan Genocide. Yanagizawa-Drott estimated that more than 50,000, or 10 percent, of the killings can be attributed to the impact of radio coverage.

22. Qin, Strömberg, and Wu (2018) also found that lower-level governments produced less biased content and increased commercial content.

23. A classic account of the importance of agenda setting is Berelson, Lazarsfeld, and McPhee's (1954) account of Truman's 1948 victory due to the shift in attention paid to New Deal issues rather than to foreign policy.

24. For models of the impact of agenda setting, see Mullainathan (2002) and Prat and Strömberg (2013).

25. There is no difference for the coverage of inflation, budget deficit, or trade deficit issues.

26. Sen (1984) has argued that an active media will deal more effectively with catastrophic famines than with widespread hunger and malnutrition, as the former is more newsworthy. That said, Eisensee and Strömberg's (2007) estimates suggest that even famines are likely to be significantly underrepresented in the news. The prevalence of newspapers also matters. Besley and Burgess (2002) studied food distribution and disaster relief efforts in India from 1958 to 1992. They found that the distribution of relief efforts is higher in states with higher newspaper circulation.

27. Eisensee and Strömberg (2007) also discuss the impact of coverage on policy choices, and indeed the connection between public attention and policy choices is a cornerstone of theories of policy making (Jones and Baumgartner 2005; Kingdon 2010). However, in their particular application of disaster relief, such effects may be due to other mechanisms, such as lobbying activity by relief organizations.

For evidence of the impact of coverage on government spending, see Snyder and Strömberg (2010).

28. Mechanical Turk (or MTurk) is an online platform through which "requesters" can remotely "hire" individuals to perform a variety of tasks for them. In the case of social science research, a researcher can use MTurk to recruit subjects into experiments and use the online platform to remotely collect responses from subjects.

29. See Mutz (2011) or Mullinix et al. (2015) for details. Multi-institutional collaboration platforms such as Time Sharing Experiments for the Social Sciences (TESS: https://www.tessexperiments.org) can significantly reduce the costs and infrastructure requirements for running even large-scale survey experiments with representative samples.

30. For overviews of the impact of media coverage on investor behavior, see Dougal et al. (2012) and Klebanov (2006).

31. To capture audience attention in an online setting, articles and headlines are designed to be easily found by search engines, an objective that has given rise to new technologies and services such as search engine optimization. See, e.g., Jacob (2018).

32. Boydstun, Hardy, and Walgrave (2014) provide evidence that while the characteristics hold for typical media coverage, the features of "media storms," or sudden, extensive news coverage that can last for weeks, are different. Once in a media storm, media attention tends to evolve in a more gradual fashion.

33. An example is Gallup's "most important problem" question (Jones and Baumgartner 2005).

34. Jones and Baumgartner (2005) argue that the rate of change of the underlying events can be described by a normal distribution, while the rate of change of news coverage is distributed according to a power law. Boydstun, Walgrave, and Hardy (2014) provide evidence that "media storms" approximate a normal distribution.

35. Despite this rapid short-term change, the overall distribution of issue dimensions is fairly stable, with international affairs, defense, and government operations receiving significantly more coverage than other issues (Boydstun 2013).

36. See Bennet (2003) for a critique of the alarm system approach.

37. Social influence has also been documented in animal experiments. One such example is food choice experiments (e.g., Galef 1996), in which a rat will learn to eat a food item if other rats also consume the item, even if the rat experiences induced nausea when eating the food item or has otherwise learned to avoid it. Other domains where similar phenomena have been observed are tool use, feeding behavior, mate selection, and yawning (e.g., Bandura 1977; Heyes and Galef 1996; Sherry and Galef 1984; Wilson 1975; Zajonc 1965).

38. Henrich (2016) provides a detailed evolutionary explanation of social learning and its astonishing consequences. Human toddlers, for example, dramatically

outperform chimpanzees on social learning, but not on other cognitive tasks. Henrich argues that this ability to learn from others led to cultural innovations that lie at the root of human success. Examples include the ability to create shelter in inhospitable environments, hunting, and food processing techniques including cooking. Henrich then shows that the mastery of such techniques triggered physiological changes due to evolutionary adaptation. For example, the availability of food-processing techniques such as cooking effectively "outsourced" some digestive functions which made the reduction of gut tissue evolutionary efficient.

39. See Bikhchandani, Hirshleifer, and Welch (1998) for an overview of the literature.

40. A more subtle form of social influence involves the concept of "common knowledge" (Aumann 1976). An event is *common knowledge* among a set of agents if every agent knows it, and every agent knows that every agent knows it, and so on (Aumann 1976; Aumann and Brandenburger 1995; Chwe 2001; Morris and Shin 2001a; Rubinstein 1989). In the media coverage setting, the idea is that a citizen who watches the news, for example, about a protest in front of a corporate headquarters, not only learns about the protest, but also recognizes that because the protest is reported on the evening news, other citizens will be aware of the protest as well, and will be aware that others are aware, and so forth. This means that the media creates common knowledge about the event. Common knowledge plays an important role in collective choice situations where coordination matters, such as a consumer boycott, a topic we discuss extensively in chapter 12, but also in financial markets (Morris and Shin 1998, 2001a, 2002).

41. This modeling framework was developed in statistical mechanics. Various versions of the binary opinion model have been proposed over the years, often without reference to each other. We can therefore think about it as a "folk model" of opinion formation. Examples are Galam (2012), Gilbert and Troitzsch (2005), Krapivsky, Redner, and Ben-Naim (2010), and Weidlich and Haag (1983). This version is closest to Diermeier and Andonie (2007).

42. For examples of such models, see Sales-Pardo, Diermeier, and Amaral (2013), and Seaver et al. (2009). For overviews, see Castellano, Fortunato, and Loreto (2009) and Galam (2012).

Chapter Nine

1. For the importance of social media and networks on protest and collective action, see Enikolopov, Makarin, and Petrova (2020), Fergusson and Molina (2019), and Larson et al. (2019). For their impact in product safety crises, see Borah and Tellis (2016). Twitter activity has also been related to stock price returns (Bollen, Mao, and Zeng 2011) and sales data (Asur and Huberman 2010).

2. For overviews of various applications, see Barabási and Bonabeau (2003), Christakis and Fowler (2011), Jackson (2010, 2019), Newman (2010), and Watts (2004).

3. In Manski's typology, these are called "endogenous effects."

4. See also Nickerson (2008) and Sinclair (2012).

5. For the impact on social media sentiment on stock prices, see Bing, Chan, and Ou (2014) and Ranco et al. (2015).

6. The key is to define equivalence classes of configurations that all have the same average opinion. We show this in the chapter's appendix.

7. This is nothing else but the *Hamiltonian*, known from statistical mechanics.

8. This distribution is also known as a *Gibbs distribution*. The proof can be found in this chapter's appendix.

9. This Proposition is based on Georgii (1993) and Liggett (1985). See also Young (1998).

10. There are various ways to add extra complexity to the model. Examples include misperception, a preference for one of the states, or conservatism, a higher threshold to change states. See, for example, Sales-Pardo, Diermeier, and Amaral (2013) and Seaver et al. (2006, 2009). For overviews see Castellano, Fortunato, and Loreto (2009) and Galam (2012).

11. See Guille et al. (2013) for an overview.

12. The core of a network can be calculated through k-core decomposition analysis. See Kitsak et al. (2010) for details.

13. Note that the term $\frac{-2N}{2N-1}$ in $H^\Phi(n)$ is a constant and will cancel out.

Chapter Eleven

1. Private regulation is also referred to as "self regulation" (Maxwell, Lyon, and Hackett 2000) and "civil regulation" (Vogel 2010).

2. See Baron (2005) for a game-theoretic model of the media and their role in boycotts.

3. Chwe (2001) provides a detailed study on how rituals and other dramatic techniques (such as marches) can be used to generate common knowledge to solve coordination problems. Exploring these approaches in the context of corporate campaigns may constitute a fruitful venue for future research.

Chapter Twelve

1. The existing empirical literature on the impact of boycotts and corporate campaigns is more nuanced. Various studies found an decrease in stock price (e.g., Davidson, Worrell, and El-Jelly 1995; Epstein and Schnietz 2002; King and Soule 2007; Pruitt and Friedman 1986; Pruitt, Wei, and White 1988; Vasi and King 2012).

Some found an *increase* (e.g., Koku, Akhigbe, and Springer 1997), and some found no significant effect (e.g., Teoh, Welch, and Wazzan 1999).

However, we need to be cautious in interpreting this evidence. As we have seen, corporate campaigns are not random treatments. They are the consequences of strategic actions taken by activists involving the selection of targets, issues, and tactics, and take into account counterstrategies by companies, such as proactive self-regulation to avoid being targeted in the first place, or protracted intransigence to signal toughness. Moreover, the mere threat of activist campaigns may lead to changes in business practices which may not be observable. Hence, the list of observed boycotts is not a random sample. Not accounting for such selection biases will lead to biased and inconsistent estimates (Heckman 1979).

2. We can focus on concerned Shell customers because Shell customers who do not have any concerns about the Brent Spar issue will simply stay with Shell no matter what Shell does. Customers of Shell's competitors already buy their gasoline elsewhere. Both segments are unaffected by Shell's stand on the Brent Spar.

3. Note this is a social benefit according to the activists and concerned consumers. The actual social welfare implications of onshore disposal are more complex and set aside.

4. Technically, this model represents the complete information version of the game. We will later embed the model in an incomplete information context to capture some of the uncertainty of the decision problem faced by consumers who consider participating in a boycott.

5. Note that Nash equilibria may be inefficient, and games (like the boycott game) may have multiple equilibria. Excellent introductions to game theory as a modeling tool can be found in Myerson (1991) and Osborne and Rubinstein (1994).

6. In addition, there are equilibria where some agents use mixed strategies. These agents must be indifferent between c and their pivot probability, that is, the probability that their participation will lead to the provision of the collective good. Palfrey and Rosenthal (1984) show that as $N \to \infty$, mixed strategy equilibria disappear. That is, in large populations either the collective good is provided for sure or not at all.

7. Technical details can be found in the appendix to this chapter. The argument is based on Ui (2001).

8. See Carlsson and van Damme (1993) or Morris and Shin (2001b) for this so-called global games approach.

9. These models have been popularized as "tipping point" models (Gladwell 2000).

10. Most of the theoretical development of tipping models relies exclusively on numerical examples and simulations (e.g., Granovetter 1978; Oliver 1993).

11. The deeper reason for this result is the fact that the boycott game is a potential game (Monderer and Shapley 1996). See the appendix to this chapter for details.

12. Of course, a higher b can also reflect a higher social benefit, such as a more substantial reduction in pollution. For evidence, see Lenox and Eesley (2009).

13. The original campaign against McDonald's was subsequently transformed into a productive partnership between the Environmental Defense Fund and McDonald's (Livesey 1999).

14. The controversy surrounding Calvin Klein products may indeed make them more appealing to teenage customers attracted by a rebellious image.

15. For a model of targeting, see Baron and Diermeier (2007); for recent empirical evidence on strategic targeting, see Eesley and Lenox (2006), King and McDonnell (2015), and Lenox and Eesley (2009).

16. The emergence of the Environmental, Social, and Governance investor movement (ESG) is likely to further accelerate this trend.

17. In addition to boycotts and strikes, unions also use corporate campaigns similar to the strategies used by activists. Such campaigns also routinely include secondary and tertiary targeting. See Manheim (2000) for details. We discuss corporate campaigns in detail in the next chapter.

18. That is, strikebreakers can be ostracized in the community and excluded from all social contact and cooperation. The more valuable this interaction is for the potential strikebreaker, the more severe the punishment seems. Thus, ceteris paribus, closely knit communities should be more successful in organizing strikes. For a model of such interactions, see Calvert (1995).

19. Unions not only play a role in wage bargaining but also in labor conditions, the administration of workers' grievances, and day-to-day management practices.

20. The actions led to the historic Table Grape Agreement in 1970.

21. About half of all table grape purchases occurred in the 10 major cities (Friedman 1999).

22. In the case of the UFWOC, the National Labor Act had prohibited organizing of farm workers, the result of lobbying by agricultural employers.

23. Some amount of uncertainty is necessary for the result. Interestingly, if consumers' information about participation levels is completely accurate, boycotts/buycotts cannot occur. See Diermeier and Van Mieghem (2008a) for details.

24. See Ui (2001) for details.

Chapter Thirteen

1. Of course, negotiations can and do occur (Baron 2003b).

2. This section is based on Baron and Diermeier (2007).

3. Details of the proof can be found in this chapter's appendix.

4. Lyon and Maxwell (2003) show that voluntary environmental agreements result in exits from the industry.

5. For a model of bargaining between firms and activists, see Baron (2003b).

6. Baron and Diermeier (2007) point out that RAN, for instance, can conduct only three campaigns a year and usually spreads them across different issues.

7. This is reminiscent of Bertrand price competition.

8. Baron and Diermeier (2007) point out that this is an instance of the well-known "hold-up" problem from industrial organization (e.g., Grossman and Hart 1986).

9. See Vogel (2006) for an overview of such arguments.

10. This section is based on Abito, Besanko, and Diermeier (2019).

11. As we discuss later, the benefit of offensive CSR can be arbitrarily small, even converging to zero.

12. We discuss multiple firms below.

13. Importantly, reputations are *not* modeled as rational beliefs in dynamic games with incomplete information as in, for example, Board and Meyer-Ter-Vehn (2013).

14. A three-period model is needed to generate interesting behavior by the activist. The insights of the model generalize to a T-period model.

15. All results require the technical assumption that for all $r \in \mathcal{I}$, $c > \beta_F (1 + \beta_F) \Delta \pi_r$. This assumption says that the marginal cost of private regulation at $p = 1$ exceeds the discounted gain from improving reputation. The impact of the assumption is to eliminate equilibria which involve corner solutions for private regulation ($p = 1$). See Abito, Besanko, and Diermeier (2019) for details.

16. There also exists a corner equilibrium with $p_{r1}^* = p_{r-1,1}^0 = \frac{\beta_F \Delta u_{r-1,2}^0}{c}$ and $q_{r1}^* = 1$. A corner equilibrium exists only if the activist is sufficiently patient, passionate, or cost-efficient, or if the social benefit ω of private regulation is sufficiently large.

17. One reason that companies may not communicate their CSR activities to their customers is that such efforts may be at odds with their value proposition. For example, for customers who are first and foremost interested in low prices, a commitment to fair-trade coffee or conflict-free diamonds may (unintentionally) signal higher prices, which may lead them to shop elsewhere.

Chapter Fifteen

1. Some public opinion scholars have repeatedly expressed concern about too much dependence on this one research tool (e.g., Iyengar and Kinder 1987; Kinder 1998a, 1998b).

2. For more details on these extensively used and highly influential survey programs, visit https://electionstudies.org/ and https://www.worldvaluessurvey.org/.

3. For a discussion of measures of implicit attitudes and beliefs, see chapter 2.

4. The natural experiments by Aral, Muchnik, and Sundararajan (2009) and Fowler and Christakis (2008) discussed in chapter 8 are rare exceptions.

5. This approach has some methodological similarities to measuring "elite opinion" (Jones and Baumgartner 2005; Page, Shapiro, and Dempsey 1987), another area where surveys are typically infeasible.

6. For a discussion of some of the methodological issues in using text as data, see Egami et al. (2018) and Grimmer and Stewart (2013). While public attitudes are influenced by images (e.g., Kinder and Iyengar 1987; Todorov, Baron, and Oosterhof 2008), tone of voice, and other subtle clues, such input cannot yet be processed efficiently. Therefore, we concentrate on input characteristics that can be captured in text. That is, rather than assessing the full impact of a television program or video, we focus only on the data preserved in a transcript.

Chapter Sixteen

1. Young and Soroka (2012) compared the performance of a dictionary to human coders. Weichselbraun, Gindl, and Scharl (2013) propose a method for using Bayesian analysis to add context-based information to improve the performance of general purpose dictionary-based sentiment analysis in various domains.

2. In some applications, it is sufficient to measure overall proportions of a corpus, such as the proportion of documents associated with positive sentiment, rather than the classification of each document. This may lead to improvements in accuracy in large datasets (Hopkins and King 2010).

3. Recently, deep-learning approaches that rely on neural networks have also been applied to sentiment analysis (e.g., Zhang, Wang, and Liu 2018).

4. There are several efficient implementations of the SVM algorithm, such as LIBSVM (Chang and Lin 2001) and SVMlight (Joachims 1999).

5. In practical applications the $tf * idf$ representation should not be used exclusively. Other representations, such as a Boolean approach which indicates only which words are present or absent, provide a robustness check and can sometimes provide additional insights. In an analysis of political debates and blogs, Klebanov, Beigman, and Diermeier (2010) show that a Boolean representation can result in higher accuracy if the goal is classifying a source's perspective, such as an ideological position or support versus opposition of a particular policy proposal, such as partial-birth abortion or the death penalty. On the other hand, using a $tf * idf$ weighting scheme does better in classifying topics. Klebanov, Beigman, and Diermeier (2010) argue that ideological positioning is often indicated by "signal" words. For example, supporters of abortion rights may use the term *fetus*, while opponents prefer

unborn_child. In highly polarized environments, the mere presence or absence of signal words becomes a reliable predictor of ideological positioning.

6. SVMs originally only dealt with linearly separable data, for which at least one hyperplane can be found so that all positive examples are on one side of the hyperplane and all negative examples are on the other side (as shown in figure 16.1). Cortes and Vapnik (1995) extended the method to nonseparable data, which is often the case in real-world classification problems.

7. Devlin et al. (2019) presented a deep-learning neural network that works similarly, called Bidirectional Encoder Representations from Transformers (BERT). BERT uses a similar approach to Word2Vec but applies it continuously across the text using a much bigger and more complex neural network. However, the use of convolutional neural networks instead of the traditional artificial neural network architecture allows BERT to be trained continuously over text in a manner that also recognizes the order in which words appear in the text. Whereas Word2Vec and similar approaches use a BOW approach in which the order of the words does not matter, BERT provides information and predictions that take word order into account.

8. As we discuss below, document classification can be used in the identification of agendas, issues, and frames.

9. Other options are the General Inquirer (Stone, Dunphy, and Smith 1966) and the Dictionary of Affect in Language (Petrone and Whissell 1988).

10. Back, Kufner, and Egloff (2010) used LIWC to trace the emotional content of text messages after 9/11; Graham, Haidt, and Nosek (2009) analyzed church sermons.

11. It is also important to clearly establish the objective of the analysis. In some cases, such as sentiment analysis, the goal is the classification of the text, for instance, a blog post or a speech. In other cases, the goal is the classification of the speaker or source (e.g., a senator or party). Value orientations and ideologies are properties of the speaker and appear to be fairly constant, while sentiment and opinion vary by context (e.g., Diermeier et al. 2012).

12. For details on the Manifesto Project, see https://manifesto-project.wzb.eu/.

13. Compression algorithms such as "zipping" (e.g., PKZip, GZIP, WinZip) compress text files by finding redundancies among the bits found within each file.

14. Dehghani et al. (2014) applied a similar methodology to understanding the ideological differences between conservative and liberal bloggers in the context of the controversy of the so-called Ground Zero mosque. Classification accuracy was as high as 91.8 percent, suggesting a high degree of ideological polarization. Feature analysis revealed that the most distinguishing words are references to the "other side." That is, conservatives are best identified by words such as *socialist, leftists,* or a reference to then Speaker of the US House of Representatives Nancy Pelosi

(D-CA), while liberals tend to use words such as *Republican, right-wing,* or refer to conservative talk show host Glenn Beck.

15. For applications of recent tools from machine learning in measuring ideological positioning, see Gentzkow, Shapiro, and Taddy (2019).

16. Given the computational challenges of working with *n*-grams and data restrictions, Gentzkow and Shapiro (2010) restricted attention to newspaper headlines and the 1000 phrases that were the most successful at separating between the two parties, according to a χ^2-test.

17. Gentzkow and Shapiro (2010) consider only nouns. So, *the_war_on_terror* is treated as the two-word phrase *war_terror*.

18. An alternative approach to capturing similarity is the use of Latent Semantic Analysis (LSA). We discuss LSA below.

19. Sagi and Dehghani (2014a, 2014b) applied a similar approach to study the expression of moral concerns based on moral foundations theory (Haidt and Joseph 2008), using US Senate debates on abortion and Twitter posts related to the federal government shutdown of 2013.

Chapter Seventeen

1. We have encountered *tf* ∗ *idf* representations earlier in the context of supervised classification methods.

2. For an example of a software package for topic classification, see Jurka et al. (2012).

3. LDA is not the only topic identification method. Other options include latent semantic analysis (LSA). For overviews, see Manning, Raghavan, and Schütze (2008). Some topic models require that a text is assigned to a single cluster, unlike the mixed topic models such as LDA.

4. LDA and other topic models can also be applied in studying value orientations. For example, Dehghani et al. (2014) use LDA to identify clusters from conservative and liberal blogs related to the controversy over the so-called Ground Zero mosque. Here LDA is not used for topic analysis, but to identify the main categories associated with moral foundations theory (e.g., Graham, Haidt, and Nosek 2009). Dehghani et al. (2014) find commonality across political orientations on the topic of harm, consistent with the assertion that the avoidance of harm is universally relevant, but they found differences across authority and purity (Graham, Haidt, and Nosek 2009). Differences are particularly pronounced on vices, such as *traitor* or *sin*, rather than virtues such as *honor* or *duty*.

5. For a detailed discussion on some of the statistical issues of using text for causal modeling, see Egami et al. (2018).

6. There are two free parameters that need to be supplied as part of this process. The first is the number of topics used to perform the topic extraction. This is

a standard parameter for this type of analysis, although some newer approaches to topic extraction have suggested algorithms that can be used to do topic extraction without prespecifying it (e.g., Teh and Jordan 2010; Teh et al. 2006). The second parameter, which Kim et al. term μ, determines the strength of the priors constructed based on the statistical analysis. Strong priors (high μ) would mean that the Granger causal information is weighted very heavily by the topic extraction process and might drive the initial Granger causal analysis to dominate the final results, whereas a weak prior might result in the opposite effect—that the topic extraction process dominates the analysis and that the Granger causal information will contribute very little to the final outcome. In practice, Kim et al. (2013) find that larger values of μ are beneficial. They also suggest a method for determining the number of topics automatically by examining how the number of topic priors constructed based on the Granger causal analysis changes—it tends to rise during the first few iterations and then falls off. Kim et al. (2013) suggest that the peak number of topics identified by the Granger causal analysis is the optimum number of topics that should be used for subsequent iterations of the analysis.

Chapter Eighteen

1. For the closely related work on analogies, see Gentner (1998).

2. For overviews, see Shutova (2010) and Veale, Shutova, and Klebanov (2016).

3. Klebanov, Diermeier, and Beigman (2008b) use the the Edinburgh Associative Thesaurus (Kiss et al. 1973) and the University of South Florida free association norms (Nelson, McEvoy, and Schreiber 2004). Only those entries that were produced by at least two subjects were used.

4. The gain criterion has a bias in favor of tests with many outcomes. To correct for this bias generated by a large n, *Gain* is normalized by the information contained in a random split of T into n subsets of the same sizes as the actual test with n outcomes:

$$H_n(A) = -\Sigma_{i=1}^{n} \frac{|T_i|}{|T|} log_2 \frac{|T_i|}{|T|}. \tag{21.7}$$

The final selection criterion is thus:

$$Gain\ Ratio(A) = \frac{Gain(A)}{H_n(A)}. \tag{21.8}$$

5. The speech can be found at https://www.margaretthatcher.org/document/103443.

6. The Thatcher documents are available at http://www.margaretthatcher.org/speeches.

7. This approach has been referred to as "authoritarian populism" (Fairclough 1989).

8. Sagi, Diermeier, and Kaufman (2013) use a particular variant of LSA called Wordspace (Schütze 1996; Takayama, Flournoy, and Kaufman 1998). The specific implementation used was Infomap (Takayama et al. 1999). LSA has been used with great success in areas such as information retrieval (Deerwester et al. 1990).

9. The restriction to such a subset is necessary to make the approach computationally feasible. Sagi, Diermeier, and Kaufman (2013) use the most frequent 20,000 words. There are various approaches to create the list of content-bearing words (Schütze 1996). Sagi, Diermeier, and Kaufman (2013) select as the content-bearing words the 50th through 1,049th most frequently used words.

10. There are various technical subtleties that are omitted here. Stop-words are excluded and raw counts are weighted by a $tf * idf$ measure of the content-bearing word. Finally, the algorithm uses the square root of each cell entry to approximate a normal distribution of counts. See Sagi, Diermeier, and Kaufman (2013) for details.

11. The *New York Times* corpus is available from the Linguistic Data Consortium website: https://catalog.ldc.upenn.edu/LDC2008T19.

12. It is also possible to visualize this space more generally using methods for dimensionality reduction, such as multidimensional scaling. This can be used to dynamically show the changes in semantic fields. The dynamic figure linked below shows how after 9/11, the issue of *terror* is "absorbed" by the frame *war*: https://dx .doi.org/10.1371/journal.pone.0069185.s002.

13. This section is based on unpublished joint work with Eyal Sagi.

14. For details on the reputational environment of biotech, see Diermeier (2011, chap. 6).

15. For details, see Baron (1999), Charles (2002), Diermeier (2011, chap. 6), and Martineau (2001).

16. The term *biotech*, however, did also exhibit meaning changes, though they are not indicated by simply looking at average distances. In 1989, the range of contexts for *biotech* wholly encompassed the range of contexts of the term *medicine*. This is largely a consequence of the lack of agricultural applications of biotech at the time. Thus, *biotech* was used nearly exclusively in a medical context. In time, the range of contexts for *biotech* increased and covered not only medical contexts, but agricultural contexts as well. Over the studied time frame, biotech maintains its balanced position and does not differentiate into specific industry contexts or acquire valence dimensions. For a visualization of these dynamics, see https://figshare.com /articles/media/Biotech_-_Medicine_Agriculture_avi/12291179.

17. Rather than using dictionaries directly, Sagi and Dehghani (2014a) use latent semantic analysis to compute the semantic similarity between moral terms and concepts in the analyzed texts.

Chapter Nineteen

1. Interestingly, during the last two years, trust in CEOs has increased while trust in other institutions, such as media or government, has continued to erode (Edelman 2022). These recent developments may be due to COVID-19, and whether they persist remains to be seen.

Chapter Twenty-One

1. The concept originates from the work of the philosopher of science Sir Karl Popper ([1935] 1959), following in the footsteps of philosopher David Hume ([1758] 1999), who had used it in his analysis of induction.

2. Search behavior needs to be interpreted carefully. In one well-known example, Google provided a service called "Google Flu Trends" that aimed to use search data to predict the prevalence of the seasonal flu. In 2013, however, it wildly overpredicted the number of doctor visits that actually occurred (Lazer et al. 2014). Google has subsequently discontinued this service.

3. For a discussion of some of the statistical modeling issues associated with drawing causal inferences using text data, see Egami et al. (2018). For evidence of the role of the media in finance, see Tetlock (2007, 2015) and Dougal et al. (2012).

Bibliography

Aaker, D. (1991) *Managing Brand Equity*. New York: Free Press.

Aaker, D. (1996) *Building Strong Brands*. New York: Free Press.

Aaker, J., K. Vohs, and C. Mogilner (2010) "Non-Profits Are Seen as Warm and For-Profits as Competent: Firm Stereotypes Matter." *Journal of Consumer Research*, Vol. 37, No. 2, pp. 224–237.

Abito J., D. Besanko, and D. Diermeier (2016) "Corporate Reputational Dynamics and Activist Pressure." In *Strategy beyond Markets*, edited by J. de Figueiredo, M. Lenox, F. Oberholzer-Gee, and R. Vanden Bergh, pp. 235–299. Bingley: Emerald Group.

Abito J., D. Besanko, and D. Diermeier (2019) *Corporate Reputation and Social Activism: Strategic Interaction, Firm Behavior, and Social Welfare*. Oxford: Oxford University Press.

Achen, C. (1975) "Mass Political Attitudes and the Survey Response." *American Political Science Review*, Vol. 69, No. 4, pp. 1218–1231.

Achen, C., and L. Bartels (2016) *Democracy for Realists: Why Elections Do Not Produce Responsive Government*. Princeton, NJ: Princeton University Press.

Action on Smoking and Health, et al. (2018) "Joint Letter to the FDA on a Nicotine Standard Proposed Rule." Available at: https://www.aafp.org/dam/AAFP/documents/advocacy/prevention/tobacco/LT-FDA-NicotineStandardProposed Rule-071618.pdf.

Adam, B. (2000) *The Risk Society and Beyond: Critical Issues for Social Theory*. London: Sage.

Adamic, L., and N. Glance (2005) "The Political Blogosphere and the 2004 U.S. Election: Divided They Blog." In *Proceedings of the 3rd International Workshop on Link Discovery (LinkKDD 05)*, pp. 36–43. New York: ACM.

Adena, M., R. Enikolopov, M. Petrova, V. Santarosa, and E. Zhuravskaya (2015) "Radio and the Rise of the Nazis in Prewar Germany." *Quarterly Journal of Economics*, Vol. 130, No. 4, pp. 1885–1939.

Adhikari, A., A. Ram, R. Tang, and J. Lin (2019) "DocBERT: BERT for Document Classification." *arXiv Preprint*, 1904.08398. Available at: https://arxiv.org/abs/1904.08398.

Agag, G. and A. El-Masry (2016) "Why Do Consumers Trust Online Travel Websites? Drivers and Outcomes of Consumer Trust toward Online Travel Websites." *Journal of Travel Research*, Vol. 56, No. 3, pp. 347–369.

Ahluwalia, R., R. Burnkrant, and H. Unnava (2000) "Consumer Response to Negative Publicity: The Moderating Role of Commitment." *Journal of Marketing Research*, Vol. 37, No. 2, pp. 203–214.

Ajzen, I., and M. Fishbein (1980) *Understanding Attitudes and Predicting Social Behavior.* Englewood Cliffs, NJ: Prentice Hall.

Albert, R., H. Jeong, and A.-L. Barabási (1999) "Diameter of the World-Wide Web." *Nature*, Vol. 401, No. 6749, pp. 130–131.

Alfano, S (2007) "Sen. Byrd: Dogfighting Is Barbaric." *CBS News*, July 20, 2007. Available at: https://www.cbsnews.com/news/sen-byrd-dogfighting-is-barbaric/.

Alhakami, A., and P. Slovic (1994) "A Psychological Study of the Inverse Relationship between Perceived Risk and Perceived Benefit." *Risk Analysis*, Vol. 14, No. 6, pp. 1086–1096.

Alicke, M. D. (1992) "Culpable Causation." *Journal of Personality and Social Psychology*, Vol. 63, No. 3, pp. 368–378.

Alicke, M. D. (2000) "Culpable Control and the Psychology of Blame." *Psychological Bulletin*, Vol. 126, No. 4, pp. 556–574.

Alsop, R. J. (2004a) *The 18 Immutable Laws of Corporate Reputation: Creating, Protecting, & Repairing Your Most Valuable Asset.* New York: Free Press.

Alsop, R. J. (2004b) "Corporate Reputation: Anything but Superficial: The Deep but Fragile Nature of Corporate Reputation." *Journal of Business Strategy*, Vol. 25, No. 6, pp. 21–29.

AlSumait, L., D. Barbará, and C. Domeniconi (2008) "On-line LDA: Adaptive Topic Models for Mining Text Streams with Applications to Topic Detection and Tracking." In *ICDM '08: Proceedings of the 2008 Eighth IEEE International Conference on Data Mining*, pp. 3–12. Washington, DC: IEEE Computer Society.

Althaus, S. L. (2003) *Collective Preferences in Democratic Politics: Opinion Surveys and the Will of the People.* New York: Cambridge University Press.

Anderson, J. (1983) "A Spreading Activation Theory of Memory." *Journal of Verbal Learning and Verbal Behavior*, Vol. 22, No. 3, pp. 261–295.

Anderson, J. (1996) "ACT: A Simple Theory of Complex Cognition." *American Psychologist*, Vol. 51, No. 4, pp. 355–365.

Anderson, L., and C. A. Holt (1996) "Classroom Games: Information Cascades." *Journal of Economic Perspectives*, Vol. 10, No. 4, pp. 187–193.

Anderson, L. and C. A. Holt (1997) "Information Cascades in the Laboratory." *American Economic Review*, Vol. 87, No. 5, pp. 847–862.

Anderson, N. (1965) "Primacy Effects in Personality Impression Formation Using a Generalized Order Effect Paradigm." *Journal of Personality and Social Psychology*, Vol. 2, No. 1, pp. 1–9.

Andreoni, J., P. Brown, and L. Vesterlund (2002) "What Makes an Allocation Fair? Some Experimental Evidence." *Games and Economic Behavior*, Vol. 40, No. 1, pp. 1–24.

Andrzejewski, D. and X. Zhu (2009) "Latent Dirichlet Allocation with Topic-in-Set Knowledge." In *Proceedings of the NAACL HLT 2009 Workshop on Semi-Supervised Learning for Natural Language Processing*, pp. 43–48. Boulder, CO: Association for Computational Linguistics.

Angrist, J., and J.-S. Pischke (2009) *Mostly Harmless Econometrics: An Empiricist's Companion*. Princeton, NJ: Princeton University Press.

Anscombe, G. E. M. (1958) "Modern Moral Philosophy." *Philosophy*, Vol. 33, No. 124, pp. 1–19.

Ansolabehere, S., J. Rodden, and J. M. Snyder (2008) "The Strength of Issues: Using Multiple Measures to Gauge Preference Stability, Ideological Constraint, and Issue Voting." *American Political Science Review*, Vol. 102, No. 2, pp. 215–232.

Aquinas, T. ([1485] 2006). *Summa Theologiae*. Edited by T. Gilby. 60 vols. Cambridge: Cambridge University Press.

Aquino, K., and A. Reed II (2002) "The Self Importance of Moral Identity." *Journal of Personality and Social Psychology*, Vol. 83, No. 6, pp. 1423–1440.

Aral, S., L. Muchnik, and A. Sundararajan (2009) "Distinguishing Influence-Based Contagion from Homophily-Driven Diffusion in Dynamic Networks." *Proceedings of the National Academy of Sciences*, Vol. 106, No. 51, pp. 21544–21549.

Aral, S., and D. Walker (2012) "Identifying Influential and Susceptible Members of Social Networks." *Science*, Vol. 337, No. 6092, pp. 337–341.

Argenti, P. (2004) "Collaborating with Activists: How Starbucks Works with NGOs." *California Management Review*, Vol. 47, No. 1, pp. 91–116.

Argenti, P. (2007) *Corporate Communication*. New York: McGraw-Hill.

Argenti, P. A., and B. Druckenmiller (2004) "Reputation and the Corporate Brand." *Corporate Reputation Review*, Vol. 6, No. 4, pp. 368–374.

Aristotle (2009) *Nicomachean Ethics*. Translated by D. Ross and edited by L. Brown. Oxford: Oxford University Press.

Arno, A. (1976) "Ritual of Reconciliation and Village Conflict Management in Fiji." *Oceania*, Vol. 47, No. 1.

Associated Press (1986) "Migrant Farm Workers End Dispute with Campbell Soup Co." February 22, 1986. Available at: https://www.apnews.com/c3eb40fa19639297e7991c2a14af4cc6.

Asur, S., and B. Huberman (2010) "Predicting the Future with Social Media." In *WI-AT '10: Proceedings of 2010 IEEE/WIC/ACM International Conference on Web Intelligence and Intelligent Agent Technology*, Vol. 1, pp. 492–499. Washington, DC: IEEE Computer Society.

Au, R. H. Y., and G. T. T. Ng, (2020). "Mind Perception and Stereotype Attribution of Corporations and Charities." *British Journal of Social Psychology*, Vol. 60, No. 1, pp. 271–293.

Aumann, R. (1976) "Agreeing to Disagree." *Annals of Statistics*, Vol. 4, No. 6, pp. 1236–1239.

Aumann, R., and A. Brandenburger (1995) "Epistemic Conditions for Nash Equilibrium." *Econometrica*, Vol. 63, No. 5, pp. 1161–1180.

Ba, S., and P. Pavlou (2002) "Evidence of the Effect of Trust Building Technology in Electronic Markets: Price Premiums and Buyer Behavior." *MIS Quarterly*, Vol. 26, No. 3, pp. 243–268.

Baccianella, S., A. Esuli, and F. Sebastiani (2010) "SentiWordNet 3.0: An Enhanced Lexical Resource for Sentiment Analysis and Opinion Mining." In *Proceedings of the Seventh International Conference on Language Resources and Evaluation (LREC'10)*, pp. 2200–2204. Valletta, Malta: European Language Resources Association. Available at: http://lrec-conf.org/proceedings/lrec2010/pdf/769_Paper.pdf.

Back, M., A. Kufner, and B. Egloff (2010) "The Emotional Timeline of September 11, 2001." *Psychological Science*, Vol. 21, No. 10, pp. 1417–1419.

Baddeley, A. D. (1999) *Essentials of Human Memory*. Hove: Psychology Press.

Bakshy, E., B. Karrer, and L. Adamic (2009) "Social Influence and the Diffusion of User-Created Content." In *EC'09: Proceedings of the 10th ACM Conference on Electronic Commerce*, pp. 325–334. New York: ACM.

Bakshy, E., I. Rosenn, C. Marlow, and L. Adamic (2012) "The Role of Social Networks in Information Diffusion." In *Proceedings of the 21st International Conference on World Wide Web*, pp. 519–528. New York: ACM.

Balahur, A., R. Steinberger, M. Kabadjov, V. Zavarella, E. van der Goot, M. Halkia, B. Pouliquen, and J. Belyaeva (2010) "Sentiment Analysis in the News." In *Proceedings of the Seventh International Conference on Language Resources and Evaluation (LREC'10)*, pp. 2216–2220. Available at: http://www.lrec-conf.org/proceedings/lrec2010/pdf/909_Paper.pdf.

Ball, D., P. Simões Coelho, and A. Marchás (2004) "The Role of Communication and Trust in Explaining Customer Loyalty: An Extension to the ESCI Model." *European Journal of Marketing*, Vol. 38, No. 9/10, pp. 1272–1293.

Balter, D. (2008) *The Word of Mouth Manual*. Boston: BZZ.

Banaji, M. A., and A. G. Greenwald (2013) *Blindspot: Hidden Biases of Good People*. New York: Delacorte.

Bandura, A. (1977) *Social Learning Theory*. Englewood Cliffs, NJ: Prentice Hall.

Bandura, A., and R. Walters (1963) *Social Learning and Personality Development*. New York: Holt, Rinehart and Wilson.

Barabas, J., and J. Jerit (2009) "Estimating the Causal Effects of Media Coverage on Policy-Specific Knowledge." *American Journal of Political Science*, Vol. 53, No. 1, pp. 73–89.

Barabási, A.-L., and R. Albert (1999) "Emergence of Scaling in Random Networks." *Science*, Vol. 286, No. 5439, pp. 509–512.

Barabási, A.-L., and E. Bonabeau (2003) "Scale-Free Networks." *Scientific American*, Vol. 288, No.5, pp. 50–59.

Barber, M. J., B. Canes-Wrone, and S. Thrower (2017) "Ideologically Sophisticated Donors: Which Candidates Do Individual Contributors Finance?" *American Journal of Political Science*, Vol. 61, No. 2, pp. 271–288.

Barberis, N., and R. Thaler (2003) "A Survey of Behavioral Finance." In *Handbook of the Economics of Finance*, vol. 1b, *Financial Markets and Asset Pricing*, edited by G. M. Constantinides, M. Harris, and R. M. Stulz, pp. 1053–1128. Dordrecht: Elsevier.

Barela, M. (2003) "United Colors of Benetton: From Sweaters to Success: An Examination of the Triumphs and Controversies of a Multinational Clothing Company." *Journal of International Marketing*, Vol. 11, No. 4, pp. 113–128.

Bargh, J. (1997) "The Automaticity of Everyday Life." In *Advances in Social Cognition*, Vol. 10, edited by R. S. Wyer Jr., pp. 1–61. Mahwah, NJ: Lawrence Erlbaum.

Bargh, J., S. Chaiken, R. Govender, and F. Pratto (1992) "The Generality of the Automatic Attitude Activation Effect." *Journal of Personality and Social Psychology*, Vol. 62, No. 6, pp. 893–912.

Bargh, J., M. Chen, and L. Burrows (1996) "Automaticity of Social Behavior: Direct Effects of Trait Construct and Stereotype Activation on Action." *Journal of Personality and Social Psychology*, Vol. 71, No. 2, pp. 230–244.

Barkow, J., L. Cosmides, and J. Tooby (eds.) (1995) *The Adapted Mind: Evolutionary Psychology and the Generation of Culture*. Oxford: Oxford University Press.

Baron, D. P. (1999) "Integrative Case: Calgene Inc. and Infrastructure Marketing." In *Business and Its Environment*, 3rd ed., pp. 119–126. Upper Saddle River, NJ: Prentice Hall.

Baron, D. P. (2002) "Private Politics and Private Policies: A Theory of Boycotts." Working paper. Stanford University, Stanford, CA.

Baron, D. P. (2003a) *Business and Its Environment*. 4th ed. Upper Saddle River, NJ: Prentice Hall.

Baron, D. P. (2003b) "Private Politics." *Journal of Economics and Management Strategy*, Vol. 12, No. 1, pp. 31–66.

Baron, D. P. (2005) "Competing for the Public through the News Media." *Journal of Economics & Management Strategy*, Vol. 14, No. 2, pp. 339–376.

Baron, D. P. (2006) "Persistent Media Bias." *Journal of Public Economics*, Vol. 90, No. 1–2, pp. 1–36.

Baron, D. P. (2008) "Managerial Contracting and Corporate Social Responsibility." *Journal of Public Economics*, Vol. 92, No. 1–2, pp. 268–288.

Baron, D. P. (2009) "A Positive Theory of Moral Management, Social Pressure, and Corporate Social Performance." *Journal of Economics and Management Strategy*, Vol. 18, No. 1, pp. 7–43.

Baron, D. P. (2012) "The Industrial Organization of Private Politics." *Quarterly Journal of Political Science*, Vol. 7, No. 2, pp. 135–174.

Baron, D. P., and D. Diermeier (2007) "Strategic Activism and Nonmarket Strategy." *Journal of Economics & Management Strategy*, Vol. 16, No. 3, pp. 599–634.

Baron, D. P., S. Lim, and D. Liu (2003) "GlaxoSmithKline and AIDS Drugs Policy." Case Study P39. Stanford, CA: Graduate School of Business.

Baron, D. P., and E. Yurday (2004) "Anatomy of a Corporate Campaign: Rainforest Action Network and Citigroup." Case Study P42A, B, C. Stanford, CA: Graduate School of Business.

Baron, J., R. Gowda, and H. Kunreuther (1993) "Attitudes toward Managing Hazardous Waste: What Should Be Cleaned up and Who Should Pay for It?" *Risk Analysis*, Vol. 13, No. 2, pp. 183–192.

Barrage, L., E. Chyn, and J. Hastings (2020) "Advertising and Environmental Stewardship: Evidence from the BP Oil Spill." *American Economic Journal: Economic Policy*, Vol. 12, No. 1, pp. 33–61.

Bartels, L. (2008) "The Irrational Electorate." *Wilson Quarterly*, Vol. 32, No. 4, pp. 44–50.

Bartels, L. (2010) "The Study of Electoral Behavior." In *The Oxford Handbook of American Elections and Political Behavior*, edited by J. Leighley, pp. 239–261. Oxford: Oxford University Press.

Bartels, L., and S. Jackman (2014) "A Generational Model of Political Learning." *Electoral Studies*, Vol. 33, pp. 7–18.

Basu, A., C. Walters, and M. Shepherd (2003) "Support Vector Machines for Text Categorization." In *Proceedings of The 36th Annual Hawaii International Conference on System Sciences*, pp. 1–7. Washington, DC: IEEE Computer Society.

Batson, C. D. (1987) "Prosocial Motivation: Is It ever Truly Altruistic?" In *Advances in Experimental Social Psychology*, Vol. 20, edited by L. Berkowitz, pp. 65–122. San Diego, CA: Academic Press.

Baumard, N., J. André, and D. Sperber (2013) "A Mutualistic Approach to Morality: The Evolution of Fairness by Partner Choice." *Behavioral Brain Science*, Vol. 36, No. 1, pp. 59–78.

Baumeister, R. F., E. Bratslavsky, C. Finkenauer, and K. D. Vohs (2001) "Bad Is Stronger than Good." *Review of General Psychology*, Vol. 5, No. 4, pp. 323–370.

Baumgartner, F., and B. Jones (2009) *Agendas and Instability in American Politics*. Chicago: University of Chicago Press.

Bazerman, M. H., S. B. White, and G. F. Loewenstein (1995) "Perceptions of Fairness in Interpersonal and Individual Choice Situations." *Current Directions in Psychological Science*, Vol. 4, No. 2, pp. 39–43.

BBC News (2010) "Apple Issues Advice to Avoid iPhone Flaw." June 25, 2010. Available at: http://news.bbc.co.uk/2/hi/technology/8761240.stm.

Becker, J. (2011) "Netflix Introduces New Plans and Announces Price Changes." *Netflix US & Canada Blog*, July 12, 2011. Available at: https://web.archive.org/web/20110713091434/http://blog.netflix.com/2011/07/netflix-introduces-new-plans-and.html.

Becker, K. D., J. Stuewig, V. M. Herrera, and L. A. McCloskey (2004) "Study of Firesetting and Animal Cruelty in Children: Family Influences and Adolescent Outcomes." *Journal of the American Academy of Child & Adolescent Psychiatry*, Vol. 43, No. 7, pp. 905–912.

Belluck, P., J. Preston, and G. Harris (2012) "Cancer Group Backs Down on Cutting Off Planned Parenthood." *New York Times*, February 3, 2012. Available at: https://www.nytimes.com/2012/02/04/health/policy/komen-breast-cancer-cancer-group-reverses-decision-that-cut-off-planned-parenthood.html.

Belson, K. (2016) "Appeals Court Upholds N.F.L.'s Suspension of Adrian Peterson." *New York Times*, August 4, 2016. Available at: https://www.nytimes.com/2016/08/05/sports/football/adrian-peterson-appeals-court-upholds-nfl-suspension.html.

Bendor, J., and P. Swistak (2001) "The Evolution of Norms." *American Journal of Sociology*, Vol. 106, No. 6, pp. 1493–1545.

Bennet, W. L. (2003) "The Burglar Alarm That Just Keeps Ringing: A Response to Zaller." *Political Communication*, Vol. 20, pp. 131–138.

Berelson, B., P. Lazarsfeld, and W. McPhee (1954) *Voting: A Study of Opinion Formation in a Presidential Campaign*. Chicago: University of Chicago Press.

Berg, J., J. Dickhaut, and K. McCabe (1995) "Trust, Reciprocity, and Social History." *Games and Economic Behavior*, Vol. 10, No. 1, pp. 122–142.

Bergenstock, D., and J. Maskulka (2001) "The De Beers Story: Are Diamonds Forever?" *Business Horizons*, Vol. 44, No. 3, pp. 37–44.

Berger, J., and G. Fitzsimons (2008) "Dogs on the Street, Pumas on Your Feet: How Cues in the Environment Influence Product Evaluation and Choice." *Journal of Marketing Research*, Vol. 45, No. 1, pp. 1–14.

Bernhard, D., S. Krasa, and M. Polborn (2008) "Political Polarization and the Electoral Effects of Media Bias." *Journal of Public Economics*, Vol. 92, No. 5–6, pp. 1092–1104.

Bernstein, D., N. Pernat, and E. Loftus (2011) "The False Memory Diet: False Memories Alter Food Preferences." In *Handbook of Behavior, Food and Nutrition*, edited by V. Preedy, R. Watson, and C. Martin, pp. 1645–1663. New York: Springer-Verlag.

Berry, M. W. (1992) "Large-Scale Sparse Singular Value Computations." *International Journal of Supercomputer Applications*, Vol. 6, No. 1, pp. 13–49.

Berry, M. W., T. Do, G. W. Obrien, V. Krishna, and S. Varadhan (1993) "SVD-PACKC: Version 1.0 User's Guide." Knoxville: University of Tennessee.

Bertrand, M., and E. Kamenica (2018) "Coming Apart? Cultural Distances in the United States over Time." *National Bureau of Economic Research*, No. w24771.

Besley, T., and M. Ghatak (2007) "Retailing Public Goods: The Economics of Corporate Social Responsibility." *Journal of Public Economics*, Vol. 91, No. 9, pp. 1645–1663.

Besley, T., and R. Burgess (2002) "The Political Economy of Government Responsiveness: Theory and Evidence from India." *Quarterly Journal of Economics*, Vol. 117, No. 4, pp. 1415–1451.

Bhatnagar, P. (2006) "Defiant Home Depot = Worried Investors: Analysts Bash Home Improvement Retailer's Decision not to Report Crucial Sales Numbers Going forward; Shares See Red on Wall Street." *CNNMoney*, May 16. Available at: https://money.cnn.com/2006/05/16/news/companies/compsales_analysis /index.htm.

Bhattacharjee, A., J. Dana, and J. Baron (2017) "Anti-Profit Beliefs: How People Neglect the Societal Benefits of Profit." *Journal of Personality and Social Psychology*, Vol. 113, No. 5, pp. 671–696.

Bikhchandani, S., D. Hirshleifer, and I. Welch (1992) "A Theory of Fads, Fashion, Custom, and Cultural Change as Informational Cascades." *Journal of Political Economy*, Vol. 100, No. 5, pp. 992–1026.

Bikhchandani, S., D. Hirshleifer, and I. Welch (1998) "Learning from the Behavior of Others: Conformity, Fads, and Informational Cascades." *Journal of Economic Perspectives*, Vol. 12, No. 3, pp. 151–170.

Bing, L., K. Chan, and C. Ou (2014) "Public Sentiment Analysis in Twitter Data for Prediction of a Company's Stock Price Movements." In *ICEBE '14: Proceedings of the 2014 IEEE 11th International Conference on e-Business Engineering*, pp. 232–239. Washington, DC: IEEE Computer Society.

Binmore, K., and L. Samuelson (1994) "An Economist's Perspective on the Evolution of Norms." *Journal of Institutional and Theoretical Economics*, Vol. 150, No. 1, pp. 45–63.

Bishop, C. (1995) *Neural Networks for Pattern Recognition*. New York: Oxford University Press.

Bishop, G., R. Oldendick, and A. Tuchfarber (1978) "Effects of Question Wording and Format on Political Attitude Consistency." *Public Opinion Quarterly*, Vol. 42, No. 1, pp. 81–92.

Bishop, G., A. Tuchfarber, and R. Oldendick (1986) "Opinions on Fictitious Issues: The Pressure to Answer Survey Questions." *Public Opinion Quarterly*, Vol. 50, No. 2, pp. 240–50.

Blackstone, R. (2017) *Obesity: The Medical Practitioner's Essential Guide*. New York: Springer.

Blair, G., K. Imai, and Y.-Y. Zhou (2015) "Design and Analysis of Randomized Response Technique." *Journal of the American Statistical Association*, Vol. 110, No. 511, pp. 1304–1319.

Blasco, A., and F. Sobbrio (2012) "Competition and Commercial Media Bias." *Telecommunications Policy*, Vol. 36, No. 5, pp. 434–447.

Blei, D. (2012) "Probabilistic Topic Models." *Communications of the ACM*, Vol. 55, No. 4, pp. 77–84.

Blei, D., A. Ng, and M. Jordan (2003) "Latent Dirichlet Allocation." *Journal of Machine Learning Research*, Vol. 3, pp. 993–1022.

Blendon, R. J., J. M. Benson, M. Brodie, R. Morin, D. E. Altman, D. Gitterman, M. Brossard, and M. James (1997) "Bridging the Gap between the Public's and Economists' Views of the Economy." *Journal of Economic Perspectives*, Vol. 11, No. 3, pp. 105–118.

Blume, L., and S. Durlauf (2005) "Identifying Social Interactions: A Review." In *Methods in Social Epidemiology*, edited by J. M. Oakes and J. Kaufman. San Francisco: Jossey-Bass.

Board, S., and M. Meyer-Ter-Vehn (2013) "Reputation for Quality." *Econometrica*, Vol. 81, No. 6, pp. 2381–2462.

Bohnet, I. (2016) *What Works: Gender Equality by Design*. Cambridge, MA: Harvard University Press.

Bohnet, I., F. Greig, B. Herrmann, and R. Zeckhauser (2008) "Betrayal Aversion: Evidence from Brazil, China, Oman, Switzerland, Turkey, and the United States." *American Economic Review*, Vol. 98, No. 1, pp. 294–310.

Bollen, J., H. Mao, and X.-J. Zeng (2011) "Twitter Mood Predicts the Stock Market." *Journal of Computational Science*, Vol. 2, No. 1, pp. 1–8.

Bolsen, T., and J. Druckman (2015) "Counteracting the Politicization of Science. " *Journal of Communication*, Vol. 65, No. 5, pp. 745–769.

Bolsen, T., and R. Palm (2021) "Motivated Reasoning and Political Decision Making." In *The Oxford Encyclopedia of Political Decision Making*, edited by D. Redlawsk. New York: Oxford University Press. https://doi.org/10.1093/acrefore/9780190228637.013.923.

Bolton, G. E., and R. Zwick (1995) "Anonymity versus Punishment in Ultimatum Bargaining." *Games and Economic Behavior*, Vol. 10, No. 1, pp. 95–121.

Bolton, L., and J. Alba (2006) "Price Fairness: Good and Service Differences and the Role of Vendor Costs." *Journal of Consumer Research*, Vol. 33, No. 2, pp. 258–265.

Bolton, L., L. Warlop, and J. Alba (2003) "Consumer Perceptions of Price (Un)Fairness." *Journal of Consumer Research*, Vol. 29, No. 4, pp. 474–491.

Bond, R., C. Fariss, J. Jones, A. Kramer, C. Marlow, J. Settle, and J. Fowler (2012) "A 61-Million-Person Experiment in Social Influence and Political Mobilization." *Nature*, Vol. 489, No. 7415, pp. 295–298.

Borah, A., and G. Tellis (2016) "Halo (Spillover) Effects in Social Media: Do Product Recalls of One Brand Hurt or Help Rival Brands?" *Journal of Marketing Research*, Vol. 53, No. 2, pp. 143–160.

Bösch, K., O. Müller, and J. Schneider (2018) "Emotional Contagion through Online Newspapers." In ECIS 2018 Proceedings Research Papers. Available at: https://aisel.aisnet.org/ecis2018_rp/171.

Bottom, W. P., K. Gibson, S. E. Daniels, and J. K. Murnighan (2002) "When Talk Is Not Cheap: Substantive Penance and Expressions of Intent in Rebuilding Cooperation." *Organization Science*, Vol. 13, No. 5, pp. 497–513.

Boyd-Graber, J., Y. Hu, and D. Mimno (2017) "Applications of Topic Models." *Foundations and Trends in Information Retrieval*, Vol. 11, No. 2–3, pp. 143–296.

Boydstun, A. (2013) *Making the News*. Chicago: University of Chicago Press.

Boydstun, A., A. Hardy, and S. Walgrave (2014) "Two Faces of Media Attention: Media Storm versus Non-Storm Coverage." *Political Communication*, Vol. 31, No. 4, pp. 509–531.

Boydstun, A., J. Moody, and H. Thomas III (2010) "Same Day, Different Agenda? A Comparison of News Coverage Across Print, Television, and Online Media Outlets." Paper presented at the Comparative Policy Agendas Conference, June 17–19, Bainbridge Island, WA.

Boydstun, A., and A. Russell (2016) "From Crisis to Stasis: Media Dynamics and Issue Attention in the News." In *Oxford Research Encyclopedia of Politics*, edited by S. Iyengar. New York: Oxford University Press.

Boyle, J., H. Dalgleish, and J. Puzey (2019) "Monarch Butterfly and Milkweed Declines Substantially Predate the Use of Genetically Modified Crops." *Proceedings of the National Academy of Sciences*, Vol. 116, No. 8, pp. 3006–3011.

Brader, T. (2006) *Campaigning for Hearts and Minds*. Chicago: University of Chicago Press.

Brambilla, M., P. Rusconi, S. Sacchi, and P. Cherubini (2011) "Looking for Honesty: The Primary Role of Morality (vs. Sociability and Competence) in Information Gathering." *European Journal of Social Psychology*, Vol. 41, No. 2, pp. 135–143.

Bramoullé, Y., H. Djebbari, and B. Fortin (2009) "Identification of Peer Effects through Social Networks." *Journal of Econometrics*, Vol. 150, No. 1, pp. 41–55.

Brandt, A. (2009) *The Cigarette Century: The Rise, Fall, and Deadly Persistence of the Product That Defined America*. New York: Basic Books.

Brandt, A. (2012) "Inventing Conflicts of Interest: A History of Tobacco Industry Tactics." *American Journal of Public Health*, Vol. 102, No. 1, pp. 63–71.

Bratman, M. (1989) "Intention and Personal Policies." *Philosophical Perspectives*, Vol. 3, pp. 443–469.

Braun-LaTour, K., M. LaTour, J. Pickrell, and E. Loftus (2004) "How and When Advertising Can Influence Memory for Consumer Experience." *Journal of Advertising*, Vol. 33, No. 4, pp. 7–25.

Braun-Latour, K., M. Latour, and E. Loftus (2006) "Is That a Finger in My Chili? Using Affective Advertising for Postcrisis Brand Repair." *Cornell Hotel and Restaurant Administration Quarterly*, Vol. 47, No. 2, pp. 106–120.

Brenan, M. (2020) "Americans Remain Distrustful of Mass Media." Gallup Poll Social Series. Available at: https://news.gallup.com/poll/321116/americans -remain-distrustful-mass-media.aspx.

Brendl, C., A. Chattopadhyay, B. Pelham, and M. Carvallo (2005) "Name Letter Branding: Valence Transfers When Product Specific Needs Are Active." *Journal of Consumer Research*, Vol. 32, No. 3, pp. 405–415.

Bris, A., W. Goetzmann, and N. Zhu (2007) "Efficiency and the Bear: Short Sales and Markets Around the World." *Journal of Finance*, Vol. 62, No. 3, pp. 1029–1079.

Brock, W., and S. Durlauf (2001a) "Discrete Choice with Social Interactions." *Review of Economic Studies*, Vol. 68, No. 2, pp. 235–260.

Brock, W., and S. Durlauf (2001b) "Interactions-Based Models." In *Handbook of Econometrics*, edited by J. Heckman and E. Leamer, pp. 3297–3380. Amsterdam: North-Holland.

Brock, W., and S. Durlauf (2006) "Multinomial Choice with Social Interactions." In *The Economy as an Evolving Complex System, III*, edited by L. Blume and S. Durlauf, pp. 175–206. New York: Oxford University Press.

Broder, J. (2012) "The Electric Car, Unplugged." *New York Times*, March 24, 2012. Available at: http://www.nytimes.com/2012/03/25/sunday-review/the -electric-car-unplugged.html.

Brookes, G., and P. Barfoot (2017) "Environmental Impacts of Genetically Modified (GM) Crop Use 1996–2015: Impacts on Pesticide Use and Carbon Emissions." *GM Crops and Food Biotechnology in Agriculture and the Food Chain*, Vol. 8, No. 2, pp. 117–147.

Brosnan, S. F., and F. B. M. de Waal (2003) "Monkeys Reject Unequal Pay." *Nature*, Vol. 425, No. 6955, pp. 297–299.

Brown, C. W., L. W. Powell, and C. Wilcox (1995) *Serious Money: Fundraising and Contributing in Presidential Nominating Campaigns*. Cambridge: Cambridge University Press.

Brownell, K. D., and K. B. Horgan (2003) *Food Fight: The Inside Story of the Food Industry, America's Obesity Crisis, and What We Can Do about It*. New York: McGraw-Hill.

Bruck, C. (2009) "Angelo's Ashes," *New Yorker*, June 22, 2009. Available at: https:// www.newyorker.com/magazine/2009/06/29/angelos-ashes/.

Bryan, C., G. Walton, T. Rogers, and C. Dweck (2011) "Motivating Voter Turnout by Invoking the Self." *Proceedings of the National Academy of Sciences*, Vol. 108, No. 31, pp. 12653–12656.

Bump, P. (2018) "Half of Republicans Say the News Media Should Be Described as the Enemy of the American People." *Washington Post*, April 26, 2018. Available at: https://www.washingtonpost.com/news/politics/wp/2018/04/26/half-of-republi cans-say-the-news-media-should-be-described-as-the-enemy-of-the-american -people/.

Busby, E., D. Flynn, and J. Druckman (2018) "Studying Framing Effects on Political Preferences: Existing Research and Lingering Questions." In *Doing News Framing Analysis II: Empirical and Theoretical Perspectives*, edited by P. D'Angelo, pp. 27–50. New York: Routledge.

Calvert, R. (1995) "The Rational Choice Theory of Social Institutions: Cooperation, Coordination, and Communication." In *Modern Political Economy: Old Topics, New Directions*, edited by J. Banks and E. Hanushek, pp. 216–268. Cambridge: Cambridge University Press.

Camerer, C. (2003) "Behavioural Studies of Strategic Thinking in Games." *Trends in Cognitive Science*, Vol. 7, No. 5, pp. 225–231.

Cameron, L. A. (1999) "Raising the Stakes in the Ultimatum Game: Experimental Evidence from Indonesia." *Economic Inquiry*, Vol. 37, No. 1, pp. 47–59.

Campbell, A., P. Converse, W. Miller, and D. Stokes (1960) *The American Voter*. New York: John Wiley and Sons.

Caplan, B. (2002) "Systematically Biased Beliefs about Economics: Robust Evidence of Judgmental Anomalies from the Survey of Americans and Economists on the Economy." *Economic Journal*, Vol. 112, No. 479, pp. 433–458.

Carlsmith, K. M. (2006) "The Roles of Retribution and Utility in Determining Punishment." *Journal of Experimental Social Psychology*, Vol. 42, No. 4, pp. 437–451.

Carlsmith, K. M. (2008) "On Justifying Punishment: The Discrepancy between Words and Actions." *Social Justice Research*, Vol. 21, No. 2, pp. 119–137.

Carlsmith, K. M., J. M. Darley, and P. H. Robinson (2002) "Why Do We Punish? Deterrence and Just Deserts as Motives for Punishment." *Journal of Personality and Social Psychology*, Vol. 83, No. 2, pp. 284–299.

Carlsmith, K. M., and A. M. Sood (2009) "The Fine Line between Interrogation and Retribution." *Journal of Experimental Social Psychology*, Vol. 45, No. 1, pp. 191–196.

Carlsson, H. and E. van Damme (1993) "Global Games and Equilibrium Selection." *Econometrica*, Vol. 61, No. 5, pp. 989–1018.

Carrigan, M., and A. Attalla (2001) "The Myth of the Ethical Consumer—Do Ethics Matter in Purchase Behaviour?" *Journal of Consumer Marketing*, Vol. 18, No. 7, pp. 560–578.

Castellano, C., S. Fortunato, and V. Loreto (2009) "Statistical Physics of Social Dynamics." *Review of Modern Physics*, Vol. 81, No. 2, pp. 591.

CBS/Associated Press (2013) "Emmy Nominations 2013: 'House of Cards' Makes History, 'American Horror Story' Leads." *CBS News*, July 28, 2013. Available at: https://www.cbsnews.com/news/emmy-nominations-2013-house-of-cards-makes-history-american-horror-story-leads/.

Catholic University of America (2002) *New Catholic Encyclopedia*. Detroit, MI: Gale.

Centers for Disease Control and Prevention (CDC) (2010) "Adult Obesity." Available at: https://www.cdc.gov/vitalsigns/adultobesity/index.html.

Centers for Disease Control and Prevention (CDC) (2013) "Adult Obesity Facts." Last modified August 16. Available at: http://www.cdc.gov/obesity/data/adult .html.

Centola, D. (2011) "An Experimental Study of Homophily in the Adoption of Health Behavior." *Science*, Vol. 334, No. 6060, pp. 1269–1272.

Chabris, C., and D. Simons (2010) *The Invisible Gorilla: How Our Intuitions Deceive Us*. New York: Broadway.

Chanen, A., and J. Patrick (2007) "Measuring Correlation between Linguists' Judgments and Latent Dirichlet Allocation Topics." In *Proceedings of the Australasian Language Technology Workshop 2007*, edited by N. Colineau and M. Dras.

Chang, C., and C. Lin (2001) "LIBSVM: A Library for Support Vector Machines." *ACM Transactions on Intelligent Systems and Technology*, Vol. 2, No. 3.

Chansanchai, A. (2011) "Is Qwikster Quicksand for Netflix?" *NBC News*, September 19, 2011. Available at: http://www.nbcnews.com/business/qwikster -quicksand-netflix-120744.

Chapman, S., and S. Wutzke (2006) "Not in Our Back Yard: Media Coverage of Community Opposition to Mobile Phone Towers—An Application of Sandman's Outrage Model of Risk Perception." *Australian and New Zealand Journal of Public Health*, Vol. 21, No. 6, pp. 614–620.

Charles, D. (2002) *Lords of the Harvest: Biotech, Big Money, and the Future of Food*. Cambridge: Perseus.

Charteris-Black, J. (2005) *Politicians and Rhetoric: The Persuasive Power of Metaphor*. Houndmills: Palgrave Macmillan.

Chernev, A., and S. Blair (2015) "Doing Well by Doing Good: The Benevolent Halo of Corporate Social Responsibility." *Journal of Consumer Research*, Vol. 41, No. 6, pp. 1412–1425.

Chiang, C.-F., and B. Knight (2011) "Media Bias and Influence: Evidence from Newspaper Endorsements." *Review of Economic Studies*, Vol. 78, No. 3, pp. 795–820.

Chiu, C., Y. Hong, and C. Dweck (1997) "Lay Dispositionism and Implicit Theories of Personality." *Journal of Personal Social Psychology*, Vol. 73, No. 1, pp. 19–30.

Cho, J., and S. Roy (2004) "Impact of Search Engines on Page Popularity." In *WWW '04: Proceedings of the 13th International Conference on World Wide Web*, pp. 20–29. New York: ACM.

Choi, I., and R. Nisbett (1998) "Situational Salience and Cultural Differences in the Correspondence Bias and Actor-Observer Bias." *Personality and Social Psychology Bulletin*, Vol. 24, No. 9, pp. 949–960.

Chong, D. (2000) *Rational Lives: Norms and Values in Politics and Society*. Chicago: University of Chicago Press.

Chong, D., and J. Druckman (2007a) "Framing Public Opinion in Competitive Democracies." *American Political Science Review*, Vol. 101, No. 4, pp. 637–655.

Chong, D., and J. Druckman (2007b) "Framing Theory." *Annual Review of Political Science*, Vol. 10, pp. 103–126.

Chong, D., and J. Druckman (2007c) "A Theory of Framing and Opinion Formation in Competitive Elite Environments." *Journal of Communication*, Vol. 57, No. 1, pp. 99–118.

Chong, D., and J. Druckman (2010) "Dynamic Public Opinion: Communication Effects over Time." *American Political Science Review*, Vol. 104, No. 4, pp. 663–680.

Christakis, N., and J. Fowler (2007) "The Spread of Obesity in a Large Social Network over 32-Years." *New England Journal of Medicine*, Vol. 357, No. 4, pp. 370–379.

Christakis, N., and J. Fowler (2011) *Connected: The Surprising Power of Our Social Networks and How They Shape Our Lives—How Your Friends' Friends' Friends Affect Everything You Feel, Think, and Do*. New York: Little Brown.

Chuang, J., M. E. Roberts, B. M. Stewart, R. Weiss, D. Tingley, J. Grimmer, and J. Heer (2015) "TopicCheck: Interactive Alignment for Assessing Topic Model Stability." In *Proceedings of the 2015 Conference of the North American Chapter of the Association for Computational Linguistics: Human Language Technologies*, pp. 175–184. New York: ACM.

Chung, C., and J. Pennebaker (2011) "Linguistic Inquiry and Word Count (LIWC): Pronounced 'Luke,' and Other Useful Facts." In *Applied Natural Language Processing: Identification, Investigation and Resolution*, edited by P. McCarthy and C. Boonthum-Denecke, pp. 206–229. Hershey, PA: Information Science Reference.

Chwe, M. (2001) *Rational Ritual: Culture, Coordination, and Common Knowledge*. Princeton, NJ: Princeton University Press.

Citrin, J., and L. Stoker (2018) "Political Trust in a Cynical Age." *Annual Review of Political Science*, Vol. 21, No. 1, pp. 49–70.

Clark, M., and J. Mills (1979) "Interpersonal Attraction in Exchange and Communal Relationships." *Journal of Personality and Social Psychology*, Vol. 37, No. 1, pp. 12–24.

Clark, M., and J. Mills (1993) "The Difference between Communal and Exchange Relationships: What It Is and Is Not." *Personality and Social Psychology Bulletin*, Vol. 19, No. 6, pp. 684–691.

Cleeren, K., M. Dekimpe, and K. Helsen (2008) "Weathering Product-Harm Crises." *Journal of the Academy of Marketing Science*, Vol. 36, No. 2, pp. 262–270.

Cleeren, K., M. Dekimpe, and H. J. van Heerde (2017) "Marketing Research on Product-Harm Crises: A Review, Managerial Implications, and an Agenda for

Future Research." *Journal of the Academy of Marketing Science*, Vol. 45, No. 5, pp. 593–615.

Cleeren, K., H. van Heerde, and M. Dekimpe (2013) "Rising from the Ashes: How Brands and Categories Can Overcome Product-Harm Crises." *Journal of Marketing*, Vol. 77, No. 2, pp. 58–77.

Clinton, J., S. Jackman, and D. Rivers (2004) "The Statistical Analysis of Roll Call Data." *American Political Science Review*, Vol. 98, No. 2, pp. 355–370.

Cohen, B. C. (1963) *The Press and Foreign Policy*. Princeton, NJ: Princeton University Press.

Cohen-Cole, E., and J. Fletcher (2008) "Is Obesity Contagious? Social Networks vs. Environmental Factors in the Obesity Epidemic." *Journal of Health Economics*, Vol. 27, No. 5, pp. 1382–1387.

Collins, A., and E. F. Loftus (1975) "A Spreading-Activation Theory of Semantic Processing." *Psychological Review*, Vol. 82, No. 6, pp. 407–428.

Collins, A., and M. R. Quillian (1969) "Retrieval Time from Semantic Memory." *Journal of Verbal Learning and Verbal Behavior*, Vol. 8, No. 2, pp. 240–247.

Collins, M. (1999) "Head-Driven Statistical Models for Natural Language Parsing." *Computational Linguistics*, Vol. 29, No. 4, pp. 589–637.

Converse, J. M. (1987) *Survey Research in the United States*. Berkeley: University of California Press.

Converse, P. E. (1964) "The Nature of Belief Systems in Mass Publics." In *Ideology and Discontent*, edited by D. E. Apter, pp. 206–261. New York: Free Press of Glencoe.

Converse, P. E. (1966) "The Concept of a Normal Vote." In *Elections and the Political Order*, edited by A. Campbell, P. E. Converse, W. E. Miller, and D. E. Stokes, pp. 9–39. New York: John Wiley.

Converse, P. E. (1990) "Popular Representation and the Distribution of Information." In *Information and Democratic Processes*, edited by J. A. Ferejohn and J. H. Kuklinski, pp. 369–388. Urbana: University of Illinois Press.

Converse, P. E., and G. B. Markus (1979) "Plus ça change . . . the New CPS Election Study Panel." *American Political Science Review*, Vol. 73, No. 1, pp. 32–49.

Coombs, W. (2012) *Ongoing Crisis Communication: Planning, Managing, and Responding*. 3rd ed. Thousand Oaks, CA: Sage.

Coombs, W., and S. Holladay (2002) "Helping Crisis Managers Protect Reputational Assets: Initial Tests of the Situational Crisis Communication Theory." *Management Communication Quarterly*, Vol. 16, No. 2, pp. 165–186.

Coombs, W., and S. Holladay (2006) "Unpacking the Halo Effect: Reputation and Crisis Management." *Journal of Communication Management*, Vol. 10, No. 2, pp. 123–137.

Copeland, M. V. (2010) "Reed Hastings: Leader of the pack." *CNNMoney*, November 18. Available at: https://fortune.com/2010/11/18/reed-hastings-leader-of-the -pack/.

Coppock, A., E. Ekins, and D. Kirby (2018) "The Long-Lasting Effects of Newspaper Op-Eds on Public Opinion." *Quarterly Journal of Political Science* Vol. 13, No. 1, pp. 59–87.

Cortes, C., and V. Vapnik (1995) "Support-Vector Networks." *Machine Learning*, Vol. 20, No. 3, pp. 273–297.

Cosmides, L., and J. Tooby (1989) "Evolutionary Psychology and the Generation of Culture, Part II Case Study: A Computational Theory of Social Exchange." *Ethology and Sociobiology*, Vol. 10, pp. 51–97.

Cosmides, L., and J. Tooby (1992) "The Psychological Foundations of Culture." In *The Adapted Mind: Evolutionary Psychology and the Generation of Culture*, edited by J. Barkow, L. Cosmides, and J. Tooby, pp. 163–228. New York: Oxford University Press.

Cowley, S. (2018) "Ex-Equifax Executive Charged with Insider Trading Tied to '17 Breach." *New York Times*, March 14, 2018. Available at: https://www.nytimes .com/2018/03/14/business/equifax-executive-insider-trading.html.

Cowley, S. (2019) "Equifax to Pay at Least $650 Million in Largest-Ever Data Breach Settlement." *New York Times*, July 22, 2019. Available at: https://www .nytimes.com/2019/07/22/business/equifax-settlement.html.

Cox, G., and J. Katz (1999) "The Reapportionment Revolution and Bias in U.S. Congressional Elections." *American Journal of Political Science*, Vol. 43, No. 3, pp. 812–841.

Cox, J. (2004) "How to Identify Trust and Reciprocity." *Games and Economic Behavior*, Vol. 46, No. 2, pp. 260–281.

Craik, F., R. Govoni, M. Naveh-Benjamin, and N. Anderson (1996) "The Effects of Divided Attention on Encoding and Retrieval Processes in Human Memory." *Journal of Experimental Psychology: General*, Vol. 125, No. 2, pp. 159–180.

Crandall, D., D. Cosley, D. Huttenlocher, J. Kleinberg, and S. Suri (2008) "Feedback Effects between Similarity and Social Influence in Online Communities." In *KDD '08: Proceedings of the 14th ACM SIGKDD International Conference on Knowledge Discovery and Data Mining*, pp. 160–168. New York: ACM.

Creswell, J. (2006) "With Links to Board, Chief Saw His Pay Soar." *New York Times*, May 24, 2006. Available at: http://www.nytimes.com/2006/05/24/business /24board.html.

Creswell, J. (2007) "Home Depot Ousts Highly Paid Chief." *New York Times*, Jan 4, 2007. Available at: https://www.nytimes.com/2007/01/04/business/04home .html.

Critcher, C. R., Y. Inbar, and D. Pizarro (2013) "How Quick Decisions Illuminate Moral Character." *Social Psychological and Personality Science*, Vol. 4, No. 3, pp. 308–315.

Crockett, M., Y. Özdemir, and E. Fehr (2014) "The Value of Vengeance and the Demand for Deterrence." *Journal of Experimental Psychology: General*, Vol. 143, No. 6, pp. 2279–2286.

CTS Corporation (2010) "CTS Comments on Accelerator Pedals." January 29, 2010. Available at: https://web.archive.org/web/20100202002612/https://www.ctscorp.com/publications/press_releases/nr100129.htm.

Cuddy, A., S. Fiske, and P. Glick (2007) "The BIAS Map: Behaviors from Intergroup Affect and Stereotypes." *Journal of Personality and Social Psychology*, Vol. 92, No. 4, pp. 631–648.

Cuddy, A., S. Fiske, and P. Glick (2008) "Warmth and Competence as Universal Dimensions of Social Perception: The Stereotype Content Model and the BIAS Map." In *Advances in Experimental Social Psychology*, ed. M. Zanna, pp. 61–149. Burlington, VT: Academic Press.

Cushman, F., and L. Young (2011) "Patterns of Moral Judgment Derive From Non-moral Psychological Representations." *Cognitive Science*, Vol. 35, No. 6, pp. 1052–1075.

Cushman, F., L. Young, and M. Hauser (2006) "The Role of Conscious Reasoning and Intuition in Moral Judgment: Testing Three Principles of Harm." *Psychological Science*, Vol. 17, No. 12, pp. 1082–1089.

Da, Z., J. Engelberg, and P. Gao. (2011) "In Search of Attention." *Journal of Finance*, Vol. 66, No. 5, pp. 1461–1499.

Damasio, A. (1994) *Descartes Error: Emotion, Reason, and the Human Brain*. New York: Avon.

Damasio, A. (2000) *The Feeling of What Happens: Body, Emotion and the Making of Consciousness*. New York: Random House.

Dasgupta, N., and A. Greenwald (2001) "On the Malleability of Automatic Attitudes: Combating Automatic Prejudice with Images of Admired and Disliked Individuals." *Journal of Personality and Social Psychology*, Vol. 81, No. 5, pp. 800–814.

Dash, E. (2007a) "Has the Exit Sign Ever Looked So Good?" *New York Times*, April 8, 2007. Available at: https://www.nytimes.com/2007/04/08/business/yourmoney/08axe.html.

Dash, E. (2007b) "An Ousted Chief's Going-away Pay Is Seen by Many as Typically Excessive." *New York Times*, January 4, 2007. Available at: https://www.nytimes.com/2007/01/04/business/04pay.html.

Dave, K., S. Lawrence, and D. Pennock (2003) "Mining the Peanut Gallery: Opinion Extraction and Semantic Classification of Product Reviews." In *WWW '03: Proceedings of the 12th International Conference on World Wide Web*, pp. 519–528.

Davidson, W., D. Worrell, and A. El-Jelly (1995) "Influencing Managers to Change Unpopular Corporate Behavior through Boycotts and Divestitures: A Stock Market Test." *Business and Society*, Vol. 34, No. 2, pp. 171–196.

Dawar, N., and M. Pillutla (2000) "Impact of Product-Harm Crises on Brand Equity: The Moderating Role of Consumer Expectations." *Journal of Marketing Research*, Vol. 37, No. 2, pp. 215–226.

De Angelis, M., A. Bonezzi, A. Peluso, D. Rucker, and M. Costabile (2012) "On Braggarts and Gossips: A Self-Enhancement Account of Word-of-Mouth Generation and Transmission." *Journal of Marketing Research*, Vol. 49, No. 4, pp. 551–563.

Dearmon, J., and K. Grier (2009) "Trust and Development." *Journal of Economic Behavior & Organization*, Vol. 71, No. 2, pp. 210–220.

Deephouse, D. (2000) "Media Reputation as a Strategic Resource: An Integration of Mass Communication and Resource-Based Theories." *Journal of Management*, Vol. 26, No. 6, pp. 1091–1112.

Deerwester, S., S. Dumais, G. Furnas, T. Landauer, and R. Harshman (1990) "Indexing by Latent Semantic Analysis." *Journal of the American Society for Information Science*, Vol. 41, No. 6, pp. 391–407.

De Figueiredo, J. (2006) "Augusta National Golf Club and the NCWO (A) (B) (C)." Case study. UCLA Andersen School of Management.

Dehghani, M., K. Sagae, S. Sachdeva, and J. Gratch (2014) "Analyzing Political Rhetoric in Conservative and Liberal Weblogs Related to the Construction of the 'Ground Zero Mosque.'" *Journal of Information Technology & Politics*, Vol. 11, No. 1, pp. 1–14.

De Houwer, J., S. Teige-Mocigemba, A. Spruyt, and A. Moors (2009) "Implicit Measures: A Normative Analysis and Review." *Psychological Bulletin*, Vol. 135, No. 3, pp. 347.

DellaVigna, S., R. Enikolopov, V. Mironova, M. Petrova, and E. Zhuravskaya (2014) "Cross-Border Media and Nationalism: Evidence from Serbian Radio in Croatia." *AEJ: Applied Economics*, Vol. 6, No. 3, pp. 103–132.

DellaVigna, S., and E. Kaplan (2007) "The Fox News Effect: Media Bias and Voting." *Quarterly Journal of Economics*, Vol. 122, No. 3, pp. 1187–1234.

Delli Carpini, M. X. D., and S. Keeter (1996). *What Americans Know about Politics and Why It Matters*. New Haven, CT: Yale University Press.

Dempsey, M., and A. Mitchell (2010) "The Influence of Implicit Attitudes on Choice When Consumers Are Confronted with Conflicting Attribute Information." *Journal of Consumer Research*, Vol. 37, No. 4, pp. 614–662.

Dermody, N., M. Jones, and S. Cummin (2013) "The Failure of Imagined Contact in Reducing Explicit and Implicit Out-group Prejudice toward Male Homosexuals." *Current Psychology*, Vol. 32, No. 3, pp. 261–274.

Derthick, M. (2002) *Up in Smoke: From Legislation to Litigation in Tobacco Politics*. Washington, DC: CQ.

DeScioli, P., S. Gilbert, and R. Kurzban (2012) "Indelible Victims and Persistent Punishers in Moral Cognition." *Psychological Inquiry*, Vol. 23, No. 2, pp. 143–149.

DeScioli, P., and R. Kurzban (2009) "Mysteries of Morality." *Cognition*, Vol. 112, No. 2, pp. 281–299.

Deshpandé, R., and Raina, A. (2011) "The Ordinary Heroes of the Taj." *Harvard Business Review*, Vol. 89, No. 12, pp. 119–123.

Deutsch, C. (2001) "A Do-It-Yourselfer Takes on Home Depot." *New York Times*, July 29, 2001. Available at: https://www.nytimes.com/2001/07/29/business/a-do-it-yourselfer-takes-on-home-depot.html.

Devinney, T., P. Auger, and G. Eckhardt (2010) *The Myth of the Ethical Consumer.* Cambridge: Cambridge University Press.

Devlin, J., M.-W. Chang, K. Lee, and K. Toutanova (2019) "BERT: Pre-training of Deep Bidirectional Transformers for Language Understanding." In *Proceedings of NAACL-HLT 2019*, pp. 4171–4186. Stroudsburg, PA: Association for Computational Linguistics.

de Waal, F. (2006) *Primates and Philosophers: How Morality Evolved.* Princeton, NJ: Princeton University Press.

Dezenhall, E., and J. Weber (2007) *Damage Control: Why Everything You Know About Crisis Management Is Wrong.* New York: Portfolio.

Diamond, D., and R. Verrechia (1987) "Constraints on Short-Selling and Asset Price Adjustment to Private Information." *Journal of Financial Economics*, Vol. 18, No. 2, pp. 277–311.

Diermeier, D. (1996) "Shell and Greenpeace (A), (B), and (C)." Case study #P19. Stanford, CA: Stanford University Graduate School of Business. Reprinted in D. Baron, *Management and Its Environment* (2nd–5th eds.), Hoboken, NJ: Prentice Hall (2006).

Diermeier, D. (2007). "Private Politics — A Research Agenda." *Political Economist*, Vol. 14, No. 4, pp. 1–9.

Diermeier, D. (2011) *Reputation Rules: Strategies for Building your Company's Most Valuable Asset.* New York: McGraw-Hill.

Diermeier, D., and C. Andonie (2007) "Spontaneous Coordination." In *Proceedings of the Agent 2007 Workshop on Complex Interaction and Social Emergence*, pp. 329–341. Argonne National Laboratory.

Diermeier, D., D. Austen-Smith, and E. Zemel (2011) "Unintended Acceleration: Toyota's Recall Crisis." Case Study 5–311-504. Evanston, IL: Kellogg School of Management.

Diermeier, D., R. Crawford, and C. Snyder (2011) "Wal-Mart's Katrina Aid." Case Study 5-406-750. Evanston, IL: Kellogg School of Management.

Diermeier, D., and S. Dickinson (2012) "Baxter Dialysis Crisis." Case Study 5-304-507. Evanston, IL: Kellogg School of Management.

Diermeier, D., and S. Gailmard (2003) "Testing Proposer-Pivot Models." Paper presented at the Annual Meeting of the American Political Science Association, Philadelphia, PA.

Diermeier, D., and S. Gailmard (2006) "Self-Interest, Inequality, and Entitlement in Majoritarian Decision-Making." *Quarterly Journal of Political Science*, Vol. 1, No. 4, pp. 327–350.

Diermeier, D., J.-F. Godbout, B. Yu, and S. Kaufmann (2012) "Language and Ideology in Congress." *British Journal of Political Science*, Vol. 42, No. 1, pp. 31–55.

Diermeier D., and A. Marechal (2003a) "Mercedes and the Moose Test (A)." Case Study 5–403-755(A). Evanston, IL: Kellogg School of Management.

Diermeier D., and A. Marechal (2003b) "Mercedes and the Moose Test (B)." Case Study 5–403-755(B). Evanston, IL: Kellogg School of Management.

Diermeier, D., and S. Thaker (2006) "The Politics of Tobacco Control: The U.S. Tobacco Industry in 1996." Case study 5-304-510. Evanston, IL: Kellogg School of Management.

Diermeier, D., and J. Van Mieghem (2008a) "Coordination and Turnout in Large Elections." *Mathematical and Computer Modelling*, Vol. 48, No. 9–10, pp. 1478–1496.

Diermeier, D., and J. Van Mieghem (2008b) "Voting with your Pocketbook: A Stochastic Model of Consumer Boycotts." *Mathematical and Computer Modelling*, Vol. 48, No. 9–10, pp. 1497–1509.

Dijksterhuis, A., and H. Aarts (2003) "On Wildebeests and Humans: The Preferential Detection of Negative Stimuli." *Psychological Science*, Vol 14, No. 1, pp. 14–18.

Dirks, K., P. Kim, C. Cooper, and D. Ferrin (2005) "Understanding the Effects of Substantive Responses on Trust Following a Transgression." *Organizational Behavior and Human Decision Processes*, Vol. 114, No. 2, pp. 87–103.

Ditto, P., and J. Jemmott (1989) "From Rarity to Evaluative Extremity: Effects of Prevalence Information on Evaluations of Positive and Negative Characteristics." *Journal of Personality and Social Psychology*, Vol. 57, No. 1, pp. 16–26.

Dodds, P., K. Harris, I. Kloumann, C. Bliss, and C. Danforth (2011) "Temporal Patterns of Happiness and Information in a Global Social Network: Hedonometrics and Twitter." *PLOS ONE*, Vol. 6, No. 12, e26752.

Donavan, D., J. Mowen, and G. Chakraborty (1999) "Urban Legends: The Word-of-Mouth Communication of Morality Through Negative Story Content." *Marketing Letters*, Vol. 10, No. 1, pp. 23–35.

Doraszelski, U., and A. Pakes (2007) "A Framework for Applied Dynamic Analysis in IO." In *Handbook of Industrial Organization*, Vol. 3, edited by M. Armstrong and R. Porter, pp. 1887–1966. Amsterdam: North-Holland.

Dougal, C., J. Engelberg, D. Garcia, and C. Parsons (2012) "Journalists and the Stock Market." *Review of Financial Studies*, Vol. 25, No. 3, pp. 639–679.

Dougherty, C. (2011) *Introduction to Econometrics*. 4th ed. Oxford: Oxford University Press.

Douglas, M., and A. B. Wildavsky (1982) *Risk and Culture: An Essay on the Selection of Technical and Environmental Dangers*. Berkeley: University of California Press.

Doyen, S., O. Klein, C.-L. Pichon, and A. Cleeremans (2012) "Behavioral Priming: It's All in the Mind, but Whose Mind?" *PLOS ONE*, Vol. 7, No. 1, e29081.

Druckman, J. (2001a) "The Implications of Framing Effects for Citizen Competence." *Political Behavior*, Vol. 23, No. 3, pp. 225–256.

Druckman, J. (2001b) "Using Credible Advice to Overcome Framing Effects." *Journal of Law, Economics, and Organization*, Vol. 17, No. 1, pp. 62–82.

Druckman, J. (2004) "Political Preference Formation: Competition, Deliberation, and the (Ir)relevance of Framing Effects." *American Political Science Review*, Vol. 98, No. 4, pp. 671–686.

Druckman, J. (2009) "Competing Frames in a Political Campaign." In *Winning with Words: The Origins and Impact of Political Framing*, pp. 101–120. Routledge Taylor & Francis.

Druckman, J., and T. Bolsen (2011) "Framing, Motivated Reasoning, and Opinions About Emergent Technologies." *Journal of Communication*, Vol. 61, No. 4, pp. 659–688.

Druckman, J., J. Fein, and T. Leeper (2012) "A Source of Bias in Public Opinion Stability." *American Political Science Review*, Vol. 106, No. 2, pp. 430–454.

Druckman, J., and A. Lupia (2016) "Preference Change in Competitive Political Environments." *Annual Review of Political Science*, Vol. 19, pp. 13–31.

Druckman, J., and K. Nelson (2003) "Framing and Deliberation: How Citizens' Conversations Limit Elite Influence." *American Journal of Political Science*, Vol. 47, No. 4, pp. 729–745.

Dubois, D., D. Rucker, and Z. Tormala (2011) "From Rumors to Facts, and Facts to Rumors: The Role of Certainty Decay in Consumer Communications." *Journal of Marketing Research*, Vol. 48, No. 6, pp. 1020–1032.

Duffy, B., K. Smith, G. Terhanian, and J. Bremer (2005) "Comparing Data from Online and Face-to-Face Surveys." *International Journal of Market Research*, Vol. 47, No. 6, pp. 615–639.

Duggan, J., and C. Martinelli (2011) "A Spatial Theory of Media Slant and Voter Choice." *Review of Economic Studies*, Vol. 78, No. 2, pp. 640–666.

Dumais, S., J. Platt, D. Heckerman, and M. Sahami (1998) "Inductive Learning Algorithms and Representations for Text Categorization." In *CIKM '98: Proceedings of the Seventh International Conference on Information and Knowledge Management*, pp. 148–155. New York: ACM.

Durante, R., and B. Knight (2012) "Partisan Control, Media Bias, and Viewer Responses: Evidence from Berlusconi's Italy." *Journal of the European Economic Association*, Vol. 10, No. 3, pp. 451–481.

Ebbeling, C. B., D. B. Pawlak, and D. S. Ludwig (2002) "Childhood Obesity: Public-Health Crisis, Common Sense Cure." *The Lancet*, Vol. 360, No. 9331, pp. 473–482.

Ebbinghaus, H. ([1885] 2016) *Memory: A Contribution to Experimental Psychology*. Translated by Henry A. Ruger and Clara E. Bussenius. New York: Columbia University Press.

Ebel H., L. Mielsch, and S. Bornholt (2002) "Scale-Free Topology of E-mail Networks." *Physical Review E, Statistical, Nonlinear, and Soft Matter Physics*, Vol. 66, No. 3, pp. 035103.

Edelman (2011) *Edelman Trust Barometer: Global Results*. Available at: https://www.scribd.com/document/47515988/2011-Edelman-Trust-Barometer-Executive-Summary.

Edelman (2019) *Edelman Trust Barometer: Global Report*. Available at: https://www.edelman.com/sites/g/files/aatuss191/files/2019-02/2019_Edelman_Trust_Barometer_Global_Report.pdf.

Edelman (2022). *Edelman Trust Barometer. Global Report*. Available at: https://www.edelman.com/sites/g/files/aatuss191/files/2022-01/2022%20Edelman%20Trust%20Barometer%20FINAL_Jan25.pdf.

Edwards III, G. C. (2003) *On Deaf Ears: The Limits of the Bully Pulpit*. New Haven, CT: Yale University Press.

Edwards, A. L. (1953) "The Relationship Between the Judged Desirability of a Trait and the Probability That the Trait Will Be Endorsed." *Journal of Applied Psychology*, Vol. 37, No. 2, pp. 90–93.

Eesley, C., and M. Lenox (2006) "Firm Responses to Secondary Stakeholder Action." *Strategic Management Journal*, Vol. 27, No. 8, pp. 765–781.

Egami, N., C. J. Fong, J. Grimmer, M. E. Roberts, and B. M. Stewart (2018) "How to Make Causal Inferences Using Texts." *arXiv preprint* arXiv:1802.02163.

Ehret, P. J., L. Van Boven, and D. K. Sherman (2018) "Partisan Barriers to Bipartisanship: Understanding Climate Policy Polarization." *Social Psychological and Personality Science*, Vol. 9, No. 3, pp. 308–318.

Eilert, M., S. Jayachandran, K. Kalaignanam, and T. Swartz (2017) "Does It Pay to Recall Your Product Early? An Empirical Investigation in the Automobile Industry." *Journal of Marketing*, Vol. 81, No. 3, pp. 111–129.

Eisensee, T., and D. Strömberg (2007) "News Droughts, News Floods, and U.S. Disaster Relief." *Quarterly Journal of Economics*, Vol. 122, No. 2, pp. 693–728.

Eisner LLP (2010) "Concerns About Risks Confronting Boards: First Annual Board of Directors Survey." Available at: https://www.finyear.com/attachment/208745/.

Elliott, S. (1995) "Calvin Klein to Withdraw Child Jean Ads." *New York Times*, August 28, 1995. Available at: https://www.nytimes.com/1995/08/28/business/the-media-business-advertising-calvin-klein-to-withdraw-child-jean-ads.html.

Ellison, G. (1993) "Learning, Local Interaction, and Coordination." *Econometrica*, Vol. 61, No. 5, pp. 1047–1071.

Ellman, M., and F. Germano (2009) "What Do the Papers Sell? A Model of Advertising and Media Bias." *Economic Journal*, Vol. 119, No. 537, pp. 680–704.

Enikolopov, R., A. Makarin, and M. Petrova (2020) "Social Media and Protest Participation: Evidence from Russia." *Econometrica*, Vol. 88, No. 4, pp. 1479–1514.

Enikolopov, R., M. Petrova, and E. Zhuravskaya (2011) "Media and Political Persuasion: Evidence from Russia." *American Economic Review*, Vol. 101, No. 7, pp. 3253–3285.

Entman, R. (2003) "Cascading Activation: Contesting the White House's Frame after 9/11." *Political Communication*, Vol. 20, No. 4, pp. 415–432.

Epley, N., and T. Gilovich (2016) "The Mechanics of Motivated Reasoning." *Journal of Economic Perspectives*, Vol. 30, No. 3, pp. 133–140.

Epley, N., and A. Waytz (2010) "Mind Perception." In *Handbook of Social Psychology*, 5th ed., edited by S. Fiske, D. Gilbert, and G. Lindzey, pp. 498–541. Hoboken, NJ: John Wiley.

Epstein, M., and K. Schnietz (2002) "Measuring the Cost of Environmental and Labor Protests to Globalization: An Event Study of the Failed 1999 Seattle WTO Talks." *International Trade Journal*, Vol. 16, No. 2, pp. 129–160.

Epstein, S. (1994) "Integration of the Cognitive and the Psychodynamic Unconscious." *American Psychologist*, Vol. 49, No. 8, pp. 709–724.

Erb, H.-P., A. Bioy, and D. Hilton (2002) "Choice Preferences Without Inferences: Subconscious Priming of Risk Attitudes." *Journal of Behavioral Decision Making*, Vol. 15, No. 3, pp. 251–262.

Eshbaugh-Soha, M. (2010) "The Tone of Local Presidential News Coverage." *Political Communication*, Vol. 27, No. 2, pp. 121–140.

Espín, A., F. Exadaktylos, and L. Neyse (2016) "Heterogeneous Motives in the Trust Game: A Tale of Two Roles." *Frontiers in Psychology*, Vol. 7. DOI: 10.3389/fpsyg.2016.00728.

Esterling, K., D. Lazer, and M. Neblo (2013) "Connecting to Constituents: The Diffusion of Representation Practices among Congressional Websites." *Political Research Quarterly*, Vol. 66, No. 1, pp. 102–114.

Esuli, A., and F. Sebastiani (2006) "SENTIWORDNET: A Publicly Available Lexical Resource for Opinion Mining." In *Proceedings of the 5th International Conference on Language Resources and Evaluation*, pp. 417–422. Genoa: European Language Resources Association.

Fackler, M. (2012) "Japan Power Company Admits Failings on Plant Precautions." *New York Times*, October 12, 2012. Available at: http://www.nytimes.com/2012

/10/13/world/asia/tepco-admits-failure-in-acknowledging-risks-at-nuclear-plant
.html?_r=0.

Fairclough, N. (1989) *Language and Power*. Kiribati: Longman.

Farrell, H., and D. Drezner (2008) "The Power and Politics of Blogs." *Public Choice*,
Vol. 134, No. 1, pp. 15–30.

Fattah, H. (2006) "Caricature of Muhammad Leads to Boycott of Danish Goods."
New York Times, January 31, 2006. Available at: https://www.nytimes.com/2006
/01/31/world/middleeast/caricature-of-muhammad-leads-to-boycott-of-danish-go
ods.html.

Fazio, R., J. R. Jackson, B. C. Dunton, and C. J. Williams (1995) "Variability in Automatic Activation as an Unobtrusive Measure of Racial Attitudes: A Bona Fide
Pipeline?" *Journal of Personality and Social Psychology*, Vol. 69, pp. 1013–1027.

Fazio, R., and M. A. Olson. (2003) "Implicit Measures in Social Cognition
Research: Their Meaning and Use." *Annual Review of Psychology*, Vol. 54, No.
1, pp. 297–327.

Fazio, R., D. Sanbonmatsu, M. Powell, and F. Kardes (1986) "On the Automatic
Activation of Attitudes." *Journal of Personality and Social Psychology*, Vol. 50,
No. 2, pp. 229–238.

Feddersen, T., and T. Gilligan (2001) "Saints and Markets: Activists and the Supply
of Credence Goods." *Journal of Economics & Management Strategy,* Vol. 10, No.
1, pp. 149–171.

Fehr, E., and U. Fischbacher (2004) "Third-Party Punishment and Social Norms."
Evolution and Human Behavior, Vol. 25, No. 2, pp. 63–87.

Fehr, E., U. Fischbacher, and M. Kosfeld (2005) "Neuroeconomic Foundations of
Trust and Social Preferences: Initial Evidence." *American Economic Review*,
Vol. 95, No. 2, pp. 346–351.

Fehr, E., and S. Gächter (2002) "Altruistic Punishment in Humans." *Nature*, Vol.
415, No. 6868, pp. 137–140.

Fehr, E., and K. Schmidt (1999) "A Theory of Fairness, Competition, and Cooperation." *Quarterly Journal of Economics*, Vol. 114, No. 3, pp. 817–868.

Feinberg, M., and R. Willer (2011) "Apocalypse Soon? Dire Messages Reduce
Belief in Global Warming by Contradicting Just-World Beliefs." *Psychological
Science*, Vol. 22, No. 1, pp. 34–38.

Feinberg, M., and R. Willer (2013) "The Moral Roots of Environmental Attitudes."
Psychological Science, Vol. 24, No.1, pp. 56–62.

Feldman, S. (1989) "Measuring Issue Preferences: The Problem of Response Instability." *Political Analysis*, Vol. 1, pp. 25–60.

Feller, W. (1950) *An Introduction to Probability Theory and Its Applications*. Vol.
1. Hoboken, NJ: Wiley.

Ferguson, M., T. Mann, J. Cone, and X. Shen (2019) "When and How Implicit First
Impressions Can Be Updated." *Current Directions in Psychological Science,* Vol.
28, No. 4, pp. 331–336.

Fergusson, L., and C. Molina (2019) "Facebook Causes Protests." *Documento Cede*, No. 41. Available at: https://papers.ssrn.com/sol3/papers.cfm?abstract_id=3553514.

Ferrin, D. L., P. H. Kim, C. D. Cooper, and K. T. Dirks (2007) "Silence Speaks Volumes: The Effectiveness of Reticence in Comparison to Apology and Denial for Responding to Integrity- and Competence-Based Trust Violations." *Journal of Applied Psychology*, Vol. 92, No. 4, pp. 893–908.

Finer, S. E. (1999) *The History of Government from the Earliest Times*. 3 vols. Oxford: Oxford Unviersity Press.

Finkel, E. J., C. E. Rusbult, M. Kumashiro, and P. A. Hannon (2002) "Dealing With Betrayal in Close Relationships: Does Commitment Promote Forgiveness?" *Journal of Personality and Social Psychology*, Vol. 82, No. 6, pp. 956–974.

Finn, A., and N. Kushmerick (2006) "Learning to Classify Documents According to Genre." *Journal of the American Society for Information Science and Technology*, Vol. 57, No. 11, pp. 1506–1518.

Finucane, M., A. Alhakami, P. Slovic, and S. Johnson (2000) "The Affect Heuristic in Judgments of Risks and Benefits." *Journal of Behavioral Decision Making*, Vol. 13, No. 1, pp. 1–17.

Finucane, M., and J. L. Holup (2005) "Psychosocial and Cultural Factors Affecting the Perceived Risk of Genetically Modified Food: An Overview of the Literature." *Social Science and Medicine*, Vol. 60, No. 7, pp. 1603–1612.

Fiorina, M., and S. Abrams (2009) *Disconnect: The Breakdown of Representation in American Politics*. Norman: University of Oklahoma Press.

Firth, J. (1957) *Papers in Linguistics 1934–51*. London: Longmans.

Fischhoff, B., P. Slovic, S. Lichtenstein, S. Read, and B. Combs (1978) "How Safe is Safe Enough? A Psychometric Study of Attitudes towards Technological Risks and Benefits." *Policy Sciences*, Vol. 9, No. 2, pp. 127–152.

Fisher, F. M. (1966) *The Identification Problem in Econometrics*. New York: McGraw-Hill.

Fisher-Vanden, K., and K. Thorburn (2011) "Voluntary Corporate Environmental Initiatives and Shareholder Wealth." *Journal of Environmental Economics and Management*, Vol. 62, No. 3, pp. 430–445.

Fiske, A. P. (1991) *Structures of Social Life: The Four Elementary Forms of Human Relations: Communal Sharing, Authority Ranking, Equality Matching, Market Pricing*. New York: Free Press.

Fiske, A. P., and N. Haslam (2005) "The Four Basic Social Bonds: Structures for Coordinating Interaction." In *Interpersonal Cognition*, edited by M. Baldwin, pp. 267–298. New York: Guilford.

Fiske, A. P., and P. E. Tetlock (1997) "Taboo Trade-offs: Reactions to Transactions That Transgress the Spheres of Justice." *Political Psychology*, Vol. 18, No. 2, pp. 255–297.

Fiske, S. T. (1980) "Attention and Weight in Person Perception: The Impact of Negative and Extreme Behavior." *Journal of Personality and Social Psychology*, Vol. 38, No. 6, pp. 889–906.

Fiske, S. T., A. J. Cuddy, and P. Glick (2007) "Universal Dimensions of Social Cognition: Warmth and Competence." *Trends in Cognitive Sciences*, Vol. 11, No. 2, pp. 77–83.

Fiske, S. T., A. J. C. Cuddy, P. Glick, and J. Xu (2002) "A Model of (Often Mixed) Stereotype Content: Competence and Warmth Respectively Follow From Perceived Status and Competition." *Journal of Personality and Social Psychology*, Vol. 82, No. 6, pp. 878–902.

Fleming, M., and A. O'Connor (2012) "Tracking a Social Media Crisis: Susan G. Komen for the Cure and Planned Parenthood." *Banyan Branch*, February 10, 2012. Available at: https://web.archive.org/web/20120214104835/http://www.banyanbranch.com/social-blog/tracking-a-social-media-crisis-susan-g-komen-for-the-cure-and-planned-parenthood/.

Fombrun, C. J. (1996) *Reputation: Realizing Value from the Corporate Image.* Boston: Harvard Business School Press.

Fombrun, C. J. (1998) "Indices of Corporate Reputation: An Analysis of Media Rankings and Social Monitors' Ratings." *Corporate Reputation Review*, Vol. 1, No. 4, pp. 327–340.

Fombrun, C. J. (2007) "List of Lists: A Compilation of International Corporate Reputation Ratings." *Corporate Reputation Review*, Vol. 10, No. 2, pp. 144–153.

Fong, S., Y. Zhuang, J. Li, and R. Khoury (2003) "Sentiment Analysis of Online News Using MALLET." In *2013 International Symposium on Computational and Business Intelligence*, pp. 301–304. Washington, DC: IEEE Computer Society.

Foot, P. (1978) "The Problem of Abortion and the Doctrine of the Double Effect." In *Virtues and Vices and Other Essays in Moral Philosophy*, edited by P. Foot, pp. 19–32. Berkeley: University of California Press.

Foroni, F., and U. Mayr (2005) "The Power of a Story: New, Automatic Associations from a Single Reading of a Short Scenario." *Psychonomic Bulletin & Review*, Vol. 12, No. 1, pp. 139–144.

Forscher, P., C. Lai, J. Axt, C. Ebersole, M. Herman, P. Devine, and B. Nosek (2019) "A Meta-Analysis of Procedures to Change Implicit Measures." *Journal of Personality and Social Psychology*, Vol. 117, No. 3, pp. 522–559.

Forsythe, R., J. Horowitz, N. Savin, and M. Sefton (1994) "Fairness in Simple Bargaining Experiments." *Games and Economic Behavior*, Vol. 6, No. 3, pp. 347–369.

Fortune (1999) "The FORTUNE Global 5 Hundred Ranked within Industries" *CNNMoney*, August 2, 1999. Available at: https://archive.fortune.com/magazines/fortune/fortune_archive/1999/08/02/263628/index.htm.

Fowler, A., and M. Margolis (2014) "The Political Consequences of Uninformed Voters." *Electoral Studies*, Vol. 34, pp. 100–110.

Fowler, J., and N. Christakis (2008) "Dynamic Spread of Happiness in a Large Social Network: Longitudinal Analysis over 20 Years in the Framingham Heart Study." *BMJ*, Vol. 337. DOI: 10.1136/bmj.a2338.

Francia, P., P. S. Herrnson, J. C. Green, L. W. Powell, and C. Wilcox (2003) *The Financiers of Congressional Elections: Investors, Ideologues, and Intimates*. New York: Columbia University Press.

Frank, R. (1988) *Passions within Reason: The Strategic Role of Emotions*. New York: W. W. Norton.

Freedman, S., M. Kearney, and M. Lederman (2012) "Product Recalls, Imperfect Information, and Spillover Effects: Lessons from the Consumer Response to the 2007 Toy Recalls." *Review of Economics and Statistics*, Vol. 94, No. 2, pp. 499–516.

Frey, B., and D. Dueck (2007) "Clustering by Passing Messages Between Data Points." *Science*, Vol. 315, No. 5814, pp. 972–976.

Friedman, M. (1999) *Consumer Boycotts: Effecting Change Through the Marketplace and the Media*. New York: Routledge.

Friedman, T. (2001) "Foreign Affairs: A Tiger by the Tail." *New York Times*, June 1, 2001. Available at: https://www.nytimes.com/2001/06/01/opinion/foreign-affairs-a-tiger-by-the-tail.html.

Friedson, E. (1953) "The Relation of the Social Situation of Contact to the Media in Mass Communication." *Public Opinion Quarterly*, Vol. 17, No. 2, pp. 230–238.

Fryar, C. D., M. D. Carroll, and C. L. Ogden (2012) "Prevalence of Overweight, Obesity, and Extreme Obesity among Adults: United States, Trends 1960–1962 through 2009–2010." *Centers for Disease Control and Prevention*, September 13, 2012. Available at: http://www.cdc.gov/nchs/data/hestat/obesity_adult_09_10/obesity_adult_09_10.htm.

Fusfeld, D. R. (1980) *The Rise and Repression of Radical Labor in the United States, 1877–1918*. Chicago: Charles H. Kerr.

Gabaix, X., and A. Landier (2008) "Why Has CEO Pay Increased So Much?" *Quarterly Journal of Economics*, Vol. 123, No. 1, pp. 49–100.

Galam, S. (2012) *Sociophysics: A Physicist's Modeling of Psycho-Political Phenomena*. New York: Springer.

Galef, B. (1996) "Food Selection: Problems in Understanding How We Choose Foods to Eat." *Neuroscience and Biobehavioral Reviews*, Vol. 20, No. 1, pp. 67–73.

Gamson, W. A., and A. Modigliani (1987) "The Changing Culture of Affirmative Action." In *Research in Political Sociology*, Vol. 3, edited by R. G. Braungart and M. M. Braungart, pp. 137–177. Greenwich, CT: JAI.

Gans, J., and A. Leigh (2012) "How Partisan Is the Press? Multiple Measures of Media Slant." *Economic Record*, Vol. 88, No. 280, pp. 127–147.

Garcia, S. M., K. Weaver, G. B. Moskowitz, and J. M. Darley (2002) "Crowded Minds: The Implicit Bystander Effect." *Journal of Personality and Social Psychology*, Vol. 83, No. 4, pp. 843–853.

Garrett, L. (2000) *Betrayal of Trust: The Collapse of Global Public Health*. New York: Hyperion.

Gasper, J. (2011) "Shifting Ideologies? Re-examining Media Bias." *Quarterly Journal of Political Science*, Vol. 6, No. 1, pp 85–102.

Gauthier, D. (1986) *Morals by Agreement*. Oxford: Oxford University Press.

Gawronski, B., and G. Bodenhausen (2007) "What Do We Know about Implicit Attitude Measures and What Do We Have to Learn?" In *Implicit Measures of Attitudes*, edited by B. Wittenbrink and N. Schwarz, pp. 265–286. New York: Guilford.

Gayo-Avello, D., P. Metaxas, and E. Mustafaraj (2011) "Limit of Electoral Predictions Using Twitter." In *Proceedings of the Fifth International AAAI Conference on Weblogs and Social Media*, pp. 490–493. Menlo Park, CA: AAAI.

Gefen, D. (2000) "E-Commerce: The Role of Familiarity and Trust." *Omega*, Vol. 28, No. 6, pp. 725–737.

Gefen, D., E. Karahanna, and D. Straub (2003) "Trust and TAM in Online Shopping: An Integrated Model." *MIS Quarterly*, Vol. 27, No. 1, pp. 51–90.

Gefen, D., and D. Straub (2004) "Consumer Trust in B2C e-Commerce and the Importance of Social Presence: Experiments in e-Products and e-Services." *Omega*, Vol. 32, No. 6, pp. 407–424.

Gentner, D. (1998) "Analogy." In *A Companion to Cognitive Science*, edited by W. Becthel and G. Graham, pp. 107–113. Oxford: Blackwell.

Gentzkow, M., E. Glaeser, and C. Goldin (2006) "The Rise of the Fourth Estate: How Newspapers Became Informative and Why It Mattered." In *Corruption and Reform: Lessons from America's Economic History*, edited by E. Glaeser and C. Goldin, pp. 187–230. Chicago: University of Chicago Press.

Gentzkow, M., and J. Shapiro (2006) "Media Bias and Reputation." *Journal of Political Economy*, Vol. 114, No. 2, pp. 280–316.

Gentzkow, M., and J. Shapiro (2010) "What Drives Media Slant? Evidence from U.S. Daily Newspapers." *Econometrica*, Vol. 78, No. 1, pp. 35–71.

Gentzkow, M., J. Shapiro, and M. Sinkinson (2011) "The Effect of Newspaper Entry and Exit on Electoral Politics." *American Economic Review*, Vol. 101, No. 7, pp. 2980–3018.

Gentzkow, M., J. Shapiro, and D. Stone (2015) "Media Bias in the Marketplace: Theory." In *Handbook of Media Economics*, Vol. 2, edited by S. Anderson, D. Strömberg, and J. Waldfogel, pp. 623–646. Amsterdam: Elsevier.

Gentzkow, M., J. Shapiro, and M. Taddy (2019) "Measuring Polarization in High-Dimensional Data: Method and Application to Congressional Speech." *Econometrica*, Vol. 87, No. 4, pp. 1307–1340.

Georgia Trial Lawyers Association (1993) "The Moseley v. GM 'Side-Saddle Fuel Tank' Case." Available at: https://www.gtla.org/index.cfm?pg=SaddleSizeFuel Tank.

Georgii, H.-O. (1993) *Gibbs Measures and Phase Transitions*. Berlin: De Gruyter.

Gerber, A., and D. P. Green (2012) *Field Experiments: Design, Analysis, and Interpretation*. New York: W. W. Norton.

Gerber, A., G. Huber, D. Biggers, and D. Hendry (2016) "A Field Experiment Shows that Subtle Linguistic Cues Might Not Affect Voter Behavior." *Proceedings of the National Academy of Sciences*, Vol. 113, No. 26, pp. 7112–7117.

Gerber, A., G. Huber, D. Doherty, and C. Dowling (2011) "The Big Five Personality Traits in the Political Arena." *Annual Review of Political Science*, Vol. 14, No. 1, pp. 265–287.

Gerber, A., D. Karlan, and D. Bergan (2009) "Does the Media Matter? A Field Experiment Measuring the Effect of Newspapers on Voting Behavior and Political Opinions." *American Economic Journal: Applied Economics*, Vol. 1, No. 2, pp. 35–52.

Germann, F., R. Grewal, W. Ross Jr., and R. Srivastava (2014) "Product Recalls and the Moderating Role of Brand Commitment." *Marketing Letters*, Vol. 25, No. 2, pp. 179–191.

Gigerenzer, G. (2007) *Gut Feelings: The Intelligence of the Unconscious*. New York: Penguin.

Gilbert, D. (1991) "How Mental Systems Believe." *American Psychologist*, Vol. 46, No. 2, pp. 107–119.

Gilbert, D., G. King, S. Pettigrew, and T. Wilson (2016) "Comment on 'Estimating the Reproducibility of Psychological Science.'" *Science*, Vol. 351, No. 6277, pp. 1037.

Gilbert, N., and K. Troitzsch (2005) *Simulation for the Social Scientist*. New York: McGraw-Hill.

Gilens, M. (2001) "Political Ignorance and Collective Policy Preferences." *American Political Science Review*, Vol. 95, No. 2, pp. 379–396.

Gill, A., S. Nowson, and J. Oberlander (2009) "What Are They Blogging About? Personality, Topic and Motivation in Blogs." In *Proceedings of the Third International Conference on Weblogs and Social Media, ICWSM, ICSWM 2009*, edited by E. Adar, M. Hurst, T. Finin, N. Glance, N. Nicolov, and B. Tseng, pp. 18–25. Menlo Park, CA: AAAI.

Gintis, H., J. Henrich, S. Bowles, R. Boyd, and E. Fehr (2008) "Strong Reciprocity and the Roots of Human Morality." *Social Justice Research*, Vol. 21, No. 2, pp. 241–253.

Gladwell, M. (2000) *The Tipping Point: How Little Things Can Make a Big Difference*. New York: Little, Brown.

Gneezy, U., E. A. Keenan, and A. Gneezy (2014) "Avoiding Overhead Aversion in Charity." *Science*, Vol. 346, No. 6209, pp. 632–635.

Gneezy, U., and A. Rustichini (2000) "A Fine Is a Price." *Journal of Legal Studies*, Vol. 29, No. 1, pp. 1–17.

Goffman, E. (1961) *Asylums: Essays on the Social Situation of Mental Patients and Other Inmates*. Garden City, NY: Anchor.

Goffman, E. (1974) *Frame Analysis: An Essay on the Organization of Experience*. Cambridge, MA: Harvard University Press.

Goldberg, B. (2001) *Bias: A CBS Insider Exposes How the Media Distorts the News*. Washington, DC: Regnery.

Goldberg, Y. (2016) "A Primer on Neural Network Models for Natural Language Processing." *Journal of Artificial Intelligence Research*, Vol. 57, pp. 345–420.

Goldberg, Y. (2017). "Neural Network Methods for Natural Language Processing." *Synthesis Lectures on Human Language Technologies*, Vol. 10, No. 1, pp. 1–309.

Goldenberg, J., S. Han, D. R. Lehmann, and J. W. Hong (2009) "The Role of Hubs in the Adoption Process." *Journal of Marketing*, Vol. 73, No. 2, pp. 1–13.

Goldman, D. (2012) "Netflix Starts to Rebound from Qwikster Blunder." *CNNMoney*, January 25, 2012. Available at: https://money.cnn.com/2012/01/25/technology/netflix_earnings/index.html.

Goldsmith, R., B. Lafferty, and S. Newell (2000) "The Impact of Corporate Credibility and Celebrity Credibility on Consumer Reaction to Advertisements and Brands." *Journal of Advertising*, Vol 29, No. 3, pp. 43–54.

Goldsmith-Pinkham, P., and G. Imbens (2013) "Social Networks and Identification of Peer Effects." *Journal of Business & Economic Statistics*, Vol. 31, No. 3, pp. 253–264.

Goode, L. (2013a) "Tesla Owners Hit the Road to Prove Long-Distance Can Be Done." *All Things D*, February 17, 2013. Available at: http://allthingsd.com/20130217/tesla-owners-hit-the-road-to-prove-long-distance-can-be-done/.

Goode, L. (2013b) "Tesla Owners Take Solidarity Road Trip." *Driver's Seat*, February 18, 2013. Available at: http://blogs.wsj.com/drivers-seat/2013/02/18/tesla-owners-take-solidarity-road-trip/.

Goodwin, G. P., J. Piazza, and P. Rozin (2014) "Moral Character Predominates in Person Perception and Evaluation." *Journal of Personality and Social Psychology*, Vol. 106, No. 1, pp. 148.

Goozner, M. (2004) *The $800 Million Pill: The Truth behind the Cost of New Drugs*. Oakland: University of California Press.

Gotsi, M., and A. M. Wilson (2001) "Corporate Reputation: Seeking a Definition." *Corporate Communications: An International Journal*, Vol. 6, No. 1, pp. 24–30.

Graeff, T. R. (2002) "Uninformed Response Bias in Telephone Surveys." *Journal of Business Research*, Vol. 55, No. 3, pp. 251–259.

Graham, J., J. Haidt, S. Koleva, M. Motyl, R. Iyer, S. Wojcik, and P. H. Ditto (2013) "Moral Foundations Theory: The Pragmatic Validity of Moral Pluralism." *Advances in Experimental Social Psychology*, Vol. 47, pp. 55–130.

Graham, J., J. Haidt, and B. Nosek (2009) "Liberals and Conservatives Rely on Different Sets of Moral Foundations." *Journal of Personality and Social Psychology*, Vol. 96, No. 5, pp. 1029–1046.

Graham, J., B. Nosek, J. Haidt, R. Iyer, S. Koleva, and P. Ditto (2011) "Mapping the Moral Domain." *Journal of Personality and Social Psychology*, Vol. 101, No. 2, pp. 366–385.

Grandey, A., G. Fiske, A. Mattila, K. Jansen, and L. Sideman (2005) "Is 'Service with a Smile' Enough? Authenticity of Positive Displays during Service Encounters." *Organizational Behavior and Human Decision Processes*, Vol. 96, No. 1, pp. 38–55.

Granger, C. W. J. (1969) "Investigating Causal Relations by Econometric Models and Cross-Spectral Methods," *Econometrica*, Vol. 37, No. 3, pp. 424–438.

Granovetter, M. (1978) "Threshold Models of Collective Behavior." *American Journal of Sociology*, Vol. 83, No. 6, pp. 1420–1443.

Gray, H., K. Gray, and D. Wegner (2007) "Dimensions of Mind Perception." *Science*, Vol. 315, No. 5812, p. 619.

Gray, K., and D. Wegner (2009) "Moral Typecasting: Divergent Perceptions of Moral Agents and Moral Patients." *Journal of Personality and Social Psychology*, Vol. 96, No. 3, p. 505.

Gray, K., L. Young, and A. Waytz (2012) "Mind Perception is the Essence of Morality." *Psychological Inquiry*, Vol. 23, No. 2, pp. 101–124.

Greene, J., F. Cushman, L. Stewart, K. Lowenberg, L. Nystrom, and J. Cohen (2009) "Pushing Moral Buttons: The Interaction Between Personal Force and Intention in Moral Judgment." *Cognition*, Vol. 111, No. 3, pp. 364–371.

Greene, J., and J. Haidt (2002) "How (and Where) Does Moral Judgment Work?" *Trends in Cognitive Sciences*, Vol. 6, No. 12, pp. 517–523.

Greene, J., R. Sommerville, L. Nystrom, J. Darley, and J. Cohen (2001) "An fMRI Investigation of Emotional Engagement in Moral Judgment." *Science*, Vol. 293, No. 5537, pp. 2105–2108.

Greene, W. (2012) *Econometric Analysis*. New York: Prentice Hall.

Greenfield, R. (2012) "How Apple Fixed Its Foxconn Problem." *The Atlantic*, May 10, 2012. Available at: https://www.theatlantic.com/technology/archive/2012/05/how-apple-fixed-its-foxconn-problem/328307/.

Greenhouse, S. (2013) "Retailers Are Pressed on Safety at Factories." *New York Times*, May 11, 2013. Available at: https://www.nytimes.com/2013/05/11/business/global/clothing-retailers-pressed-on-bangladesh-factory-safety.html.

Greenwald, A. G., and M. R. Banaji (1995) "Implicit Social Cognition: Attitudes, Self-esteem, and Stereotypes." *Psychological Review*, Vol. 102, No. 1, pp. 4–27.

Greenwald, A. G., M. Banaji, and B. Nosek (2015) "Statistically Small Effects of the Implicit Association Test Can Have Societally Large Effects." *Journal of Personality and Social Psychology*, Vol. 108, No. 4, pp. 553–561.

Greenwald, A. G., D. E. McGhee, and J. L. Schwartz (1998) "Measuring Individual Differences in Implicit Cognition: The Implicit Association Test." *Journal of Personality and Social Psychology*, Vol. 74, No. 6, pp. 1464–1480.

Greenwald, A. G., T. A. Poehlman, E. L. Uhlmann, and M. R. Banaji (2009) "Understanding and Using the Implicit Association Test: III. Meta-analysis of Predictive Validity." *Journal of Personality and Social Psychology*, Vol. 97, No. 1, pp. 17–41.

Greyser, S. (1982) "Johnson & Johnson: The Tylenol Tragedy." Case Study 583–043. Cambridge, MA: Harvard Business School.

Griffiths, T., and M. Steyvers (2004) "Finding Scientific Topics." *Proceedings of the National Academy of Sciences*, Vol. 101, No. 1, pp. 5228–5235.

Grimmer, J. (2010) "A Bayesian Hierarchical Topic Model for Political Texts: Measuring Expressed Agendas in Senate Press Releases." *Political Analysis*, Vol. 18, No. 1, pp. 1–35.

Grimmer, J., and G. King (2011) "General Purpose Computer-Assisted Clustering and Conceptualization." *Proceedings of the National Academy of Sciences*, Vol. 108, No. 7, pp. 2643–2650.

Grimmer, J., and B. Stewart (2013) "Text as Data: The Promise and Pitfalls of Automatic Content Analysis Methods for Political Texts." *Political Analysis*, Vol. 21, No. 3, pp. 267–297.

Groeling, T. (2015) "Media Bias by the Numbers: Challenges and Opportunities in the Empirical Study of Partisan News." *Annual Review of Political Science*, Vol. 16, No. 1, pp. 129–151.

Groseclose, T. (2011) *Left Turn*. New York: St. Martin's.

Groseclose, T., and J. Milyo (2005) "A Measure of Media Bias." *Quarterly Journal of Economics*, Vol. 120, No. 4, pp. 1191–1237.

Grossman, S., and O. Hart (1986) "The Costs and Benefits of Ownership: A Theory of Vertical and Lateral Integration." *Journal of Political Economy*, Vol. 94, No. 4, pp. 691–719.

Groves, R. M., and L. Lyberg (2010) "Total Survey Error: Past, Present, and Future." *Public Opinion Quarterly*, Vol. 74, No. 5, pp. 849–79.

Grow, B. (2007) "Out at Home Depot: Behind the Flameout of Controversial CEO Bob Nardelli." *Bloomberg Businessweek*, January 9, 2007. Available at: http://www.nbcnews.com/id/16469224/ns/business-us_business/t/out-home-depot/.

Guille, A., H. Hacid, C. Favre, and D. A. Zighed (2013) "Information Diffusion in Online Social Networks: A Survey." *ACM Sigmod Record*, Vol. 42, No. 2, pp. 17–28.

Güth, W., R. Schmittberger, and B. Schwarze (1982) "An Experimental Analysis of Ultimatum Bargaining." *Journal of Mathematical Psychology*, Vol. 42, No. 4, pp. 227–247.

Hagey, K. (2012) "Komen Flap Spurred by Social Media." *Politico*, February 4, 2012. Available at: https://www.politico.com/story/2012/02/komen-flap-spurred-on-by-social-media-072442.

Haidt, J. (2001) "The Emotional Dog and Its Rational Tail: A Social Intuitionist Approach to Moral Judgment." *Psychological Review*, Vol. 108, No. 4, pp. 814–834.

Haidt, J. (2003) "The Moral Emotions." In *Series in Affective Science: Handbook of Affective Sciences*, edited by R. J. Davidson, K. R. Scherer, and H. H. Goldsmith, pp. 852–870. New York: Oxford University Press.

Haidt, J. (2007) "The New Synthesis in Moral Psychology." *Science*, Vol. 316, No. 5827, pp. 998–1002.

Haidt, J. (2013a) "Moral Psychology for the Twenty-First Century." *Journal of Moral Education*, Vol. 42, No. 3, pp. 281–297.

Haidt, J. (2013b) *The Righteous Mind: Why Good People are Divided by Politics and Religion*. New York: Knopf Doubleday.

Haidt, J., F. Bjorklund, and S. Murphy (2000) "Moral Dumbfounding: When Intuition Finds No Reason." Unpublished manuscript, University of Virginia. Available at: https://polpsy.ca/wp-content/uploads/2019/05/haidt.bjorklund.pdf.

Haidt, J., and J. Graham (2007) "When Morality Opposes Justice: Conservatives Have Moral Intuitions that Liberals May Not Recognize." *Social Justice Research*, Vol. 20, No. 1, pp. 98–116.

Haidt, J., and C. Joseph (2004) "Intuitive Ethics: How Innately Prepared Intuitions Generate Culturally Variable Virtues." *Daedalus*, Vol. 133, No. 4, pp. 55–66.

Haidt, J., and C. Joseph (2008) "The Moral Mind: How Five Sets of Innate Intuitions Guide the Development of Many Culture-Specific Virtues, and Perhaps Even Modules." In *Evolution and Cognition: The Innate Mind*. Vol. 3: *Foundations and the Future,* edited by P. Carruthers, S. Laurence, and S. Stich, pp. 367–391. Oxford: Oxford University Press.

Haidt, J., and S. Kesebir (2010) "Morality." In *Handbook of Social Psychology, 5th Edition*, edited by S. Fiske, D. Gilbert, and G. Lindzey, pp. 797–832. Hoboken, NJ: John Wiley & Sons.

Haidt, J., S. Koller, and M. Dias (1993) "Affect, Culture, and Morality, or Is It Wrong to Eat Your Dog?" *Journal of Personality and Social Psychology*, Vol. 65, No. 4, pp. 613–628.

Hajli, N., J. Sims, A. Zadeh, and M.-O. Richard (2017) "A Social Commerce Investigation of the Role of Trust in a Social Networking Site on Purchase Intentions." *Journal of Business Research*, Vol. 71, pp. 133–141.

Halperin, B., B. Ho, J. List, and I. Muir (2022) "Toward an Understanding of the Economics of Apologies: Evidence from a Large-Scale Natural Field Experiment." *Economic Journal*, Vol. 132, No. 642, pp. 273–298.

Hamilton, L., M. Lemcke-Stampone, and C. Grimm (2018) "Cold Winters Warming? Perceptions of Climate Change in the North Country." *Weather and Climate Society*, Vol. 10, No. 4, pp. 641–652.

Hamlin, J. K., K. Wynn, and P. Bloom (2007) "Social Evaluation by Preverbal Infants." *Nature*, Vol. 450, No. 7169, pp. 557–559.

Haque, T. U., N. N. Saber, and F. M. Shah (2018) "Sentiment Analysis on Large Scale Amazon Product Reviews." In *2018 IEEE International Conference on Innovative Research and Development (ICIRD)*, pp. 1–6. Piscataway, NJ: Institute of Electrical and Electronics Engineers (IEEE).

Hardin, R. (2002) *Trust and Trustworthiness*. New York: Russell Sage Foundation.

Harman, H. (1976) *Modern Factor Analysis*. Chicago: University of Chicago Press.

Harris Insights & Analytics (2016) "Only Nine Percent of U.S. Consumers Believe Pharma and Biotechnology Put Patients over Profits; Only 16 Percent Believe Health Insurers Do." Available at: https://web.archive.org/web/20170121034 239/https://theharrispoll.com/health-and-life/Pharma-Biotech-Patients-Over -Profits.html.

Harris, Z. (1954) "Distributional Structure." *WORD*, Vol. 10, No. 2–3, pp. 146–162.

Haselhuhn, M., M. Schweitzer, and A. Wood. (2010) "How Implicit Beliefs Influence Trust Recovery." *Psychological Science*, Vol. 21, No. 5, pp. 645–648.

Hastie, R., and B. Park (1986) "The Relationship between Memory and Judgment Depends on Whether the Judgment Task Is Memory-Based or On-Line." *Psychological Review*, Vol. 93, No. 3, pp. 258–268.

Hastie, T., R. Tibshirani, and J. Friedman (2001) *The Elements of Statistical Learning*. New York: Springer-Verlag.

Hastings, R. (2011) "An Explanation and Some Reflections." *Netflix US & Canada Blog*, September 18, 2011. Available at: https://web.archive.org/web/20110919151 939/http://blog.netflix.com/2011/09/explanation-and-some-reflections.html.

Heal, G. (2005) "Corporate Social Responsibility? An Economic and Financial Framework." Geneva Papers on Risk and Insurance: Issues and Practice, Vol. 30, No. 3, pp. 387–409.

Hebb, D. O. (1949) *The Organization of Behavior*. New York: Wiley & Sons.

Heckman, J. (1979) "Sample Selection Bias as a Specification Error." *Econometrica*, Vol. 47, No. 1, pp. 153–161.

Heine, S., D. Lehman, E. Ide, C. Leung, S. Kitayama, T. Takata, and H. Matsumoto (2001) "Divergent Consequences of Success and Failure in Japan and North America: An Investigation of Self-Improving Motivations and Malleable Selves." *Journal Personality and Social Psychology*, Vol. 81, No. 4, pp. 599–615.

Heinze, J., E. Uhlmann, and D. Diermeier (2009) "Private Politics—Public Image." Working paper. Evanston, IL: Ford Center for Global Citizenship, Kellogg School of Management.

Heinze, J., E. Uhlmann, and D. Diermeier (2014) "Unlikely Allies: Credibility Transfer during a Corporate Crisis." *Journal of Applied Social Psychology*, Vol. 44, No. 5, pp. 392–397.

Helft, M. (2010) "Apple Goes on the Offensive." *New York Times*, July 17, 2010. Available at: https://www.nytimes.com/2010/07/17/technology/17apple.html.

Hempel, J., and B. Leak (2005) "From Businesses, a Flood of Aid." *Bloomberg BusinessWeek*, September 7, 2005. Available at: https://www.bloomberg.com /news/articles/2005-09-06/from-businesses-a-flood-of-aid.

Hendel, I., S. Lach, and Y. Spiegel (2017) "Consumers' Activism: The Cottage Cheese Boycott." *RAND Journal of Economics*, Vol. 48, No. 4, pp. 972–1003.

Hendry, S., D. Shaffer, and D. Peacock (1989) "On Testifying in One's Own Behalf: Interactive Effects of Evidential Strength and Defendant's Testimonial Demeanor on Mock Jurors' Decisions." *Journal of Applied Psychology*, Vol. 74, No. 4, pp. 539–545.

Henrich, J. (2016). *The Secret of Our Success*. Princeton, NJ: Princeton University Press.

Henrich, J., R. McElreath, A. Barr, J. Ensminger, C. Barrett, A. Bolyanatz, J. Camilo Cardenas, M. Gurven, E. Gwako, N. Henrich, C. Lesorogol, F. Marlowe, D. Tracer, and J. Ziker (2006) "Costly Punishment across Human Societies." *Science*, Vol. 312, No. 5781, pp. 1767–1770.

Heyes, C., and B. Galef Jr. (eds.) (1996) *Social Learning in Animals: The Roots of Culture*. San Diego, CA: Academic Press.

Hibbs Jr., D. A. (1977) "Political Parties and Macroeconomic Policy." *American Political Science Review*, Vol. 71, No. 4, pp. 1467–1487.

Higgins, E., and G. King (1981) "Accessibility of Social Constructs: Information Processing Consequences of Individual and Contextual Variability." In *Personality, Cognition, and Social Interaction*, edited by N. Cantor and J. Kihlstrom, pp. 69–121. Hillsdale, NJ: Erlbaum.

Hill & Knowlton (1953) "To Members of the Planning Committee—Forwarding Memorandum." Available at: http://www.ttlaonline.com/HKWIS/0375.pdf.

Hill, S., J. Lo, L. Vavreck, and J. Zaller (2013). "How Quickly We Forget: The Duration of Persuasion Effects from Mass Communication." *Political Communication*, Vol. 30, No. 4, pp. 521–547.

Hindman, M. (2009) *The Myth of Digital Democracy*. Princeton, NJ: Princeton University Press.

Hindman, M., K. Tsioutsiouliklis, and J. Johnson (2003) "'Googlearchy': How a Few Heavily-Linked Sites Dominate Politics on the Web." Paper presented at the Annual Meeting of the Midwest Political Science Association, Chicago.

Ho, D., and K. Quinn (2008) "Measuring Explicit Political Positions of Media." *Quarterly Journal of Political Science*, Vol. 3, No. 4, pp. 353–377.

Hoffman, E., K. McCabe, K. Shachat, and V. Smith (1994) "Preferences, Property Rights and Anonymity in Bargaining Games." *Games and Economic Behaviour*, Vol. 7, No. 3, pp. 346–380.

Hoffman, E., K. McCabe, and V. Smith (1996) "On Expectations and the Monetary Stakes in Ultimatum Games." *International Journal of Game Theory*, Vol. 25, No. 3, pp. 289–301.

Hoffman, M. (2001) *Empathy and Moral Development: Implications for Caring and Justice*. Cambridge: Cambridge University Press.

Hoffman, M. (2008) "Empathy and Prosocial Behavior." In *Handbook of Emotions*, 3rd ed., edited by M. Lewis, J. M. Haviland-Jones, and L. F. Barrett, pp. 440–455. New York: Guilford.

Hofmann, T. (1999) "Probabilistic Latent Semantic Indexing." In *SIGIR '99: Proceedings of the 22nd Annual International ACM SIGIR Conference on Research and Development in Information Retrieval*, pp. 50–57. New York: ACM.

Holyoak, K. J., and D. Simon (1999) "Bidirectional Reasoning in Decision Making by Constraint Satisfaction." *Journal of Experimental Psychology: General*, Vol. 128, No. 1, pp. 3.

Hong, I. and H. Cho (2011) "The Impact of Consumer Trust on Attitudinal Loyalty and Purchase Intentions in B2C e-Marketplaces: Intermediary Trust vs. Seller Trust." *International Journal of Information Management*, Vol. 31, No. 5, pp. 469–479.

Hopkins, D., and G. King (2010) "A Method of Automated Nonparametric Content Analysis for Social Science." *American Journal of Political Science*, Vol. 54, No. 1, pp. 229–247.

Howard, R. W. (1995) *Learning and Memory: Major Ideas, Principles, Issues and Applications*, Westport: Praeger.

Hsiao, C. (1983) "Identification." In *Handbook of Econometrics*, Vol. 1, edited by Z. Griliches and M. Intriligator, pp. 223–283. Amsterdam: Elsevier.

Hsu, L., and B. Lawrence (2016) "The Role of Social Media and Brand Equity During a Product Recall Crisis: A Shareholder Value Perspective." *International Journal of Research in Marketing*, Vol. 33, No. 1, pp. 59–77.

Hu, M., and B. Liu (2004) "Mining and Summarizing Customer Reviews." In *KDD '04: Proceedings of the Tenth ACM SIGKDD International Conference on Knowledge Discovery and Data Mining*, pp. 168–177. New York: ACM.

Huber, G., S. Hill, and G. Lenz (2012) "Sources of Bias in Retrospective Decision-Making: Experimental Evidence on Voters' Limitations in Controlling Incumbents." *American Political Science Review*, Vol. 106, No. 4, pp. 720–741.

Huberman, G., and T. Regev (2001) "Contagious Speculation and a Cure for Cancer: A Nonevent that Made Stock Prices Soar." *Journal of Finance*, Vol. 56, No. 1, pp. 387–396.

Huffaker, D., R. Swaab, and D. Diermeier (2011) "The Language of Coalition Formation in Online Multiparty Negotiations." *Journal of Language and Social Psychology*, Vol. 30, No. 1, pp. 66–81.

Hull, D. (2013) "Elon Musk vs the *New York Times*: Battle Escalates Thursday with Dueling Blog Posts." *San Jose Mercury News*, February 14, 2013. Available at: https://www.mercurynews.com/2013/02/13/2013-elon-musk-vs-the-new-york -times-battle-escalates-thursday-with-dueling-blog-posts/.

Hume, D. ([1739] 2000) *A Treatise of Human Nature*. Edited by D. Norton and M. Norton. Oxford: Clarendon Press.

Hume, D. ([1758] 1999) *An Enquiry Concerning Human Understanding*. Edited by T. L. Beauchamp. Oxford: Oxford University Press.

Hyde, J. (2005) "The Gender Similarities Hypothesis." *American Psychologist*, Vol. 60, No. 6, pp. 581–592.

Iliev, R., M. Dehghani, and E. Sagi (2015) "Automated Text Analysis in Psychology: Methods, Applications, and Future Developments." *Language and Cognition: An Interdisciplinary Journal of Language and Cognitive Science*, Vol. 7, No. 2, pp. 265–290.

Inbar, Y., D. Pizarro, and F. Cushman (2012) "Benefiting from Misfortune: When Harmless Actions Are Judged to Be Morally Blameworthy." *Personality and Social Psychology Bulletin*, Vol. 38, No. 1, pp. 52–62.

Inglehart, R. (1990) *Culture Shift in Advanced Industrial Society*. Princeton, NJ: Princeton University Press.

Ingram, P., Q. Yue, and H. Rao (2010) "Trouble in Store: Probes, Protests and Store Openings by Wal-Mart, 1998–2007." *American Journal of Sociology*, Vol. 116, No. 1, pp. 53–92.

Iyengar, S., and D. Kinder (1987) *News That Matters: Television and American Opinion*. Chicago: University of Chicago Press.

Jackson, M. (2010) *Social and Economic Networks*. Princeton, NJ: Princeton Unviersity Press.

Jackson, M. (2019) *The Human Network*. New York: Penguin Random House.

Jacob, J. (2018) *Search Engine Optimization Complete Guide: How to Rank on the First Page of Google*. Scotts Valley, CA: CreateSpace.

Jacobs, B., V. Singhal, and R. Subramanian (2010) "An Empirical Investigation of Environmental Performance and the Market Value of the Firm." *Journal of Operations Management*, Vol. 28, No. 5, pp. 430–441.

Jago, A. S., T.A. Kreps, and K. Laurin (2019). "Collectives in Organizations Appear Less Morally Motivated Than Individuals." *Journal of Experimental Psychology: General*, Vol. 148, No. 12, pp. 2229–2244.

James, L. R. (1998) "Measurement of Personality via Conditional Reasoning." *Organizational Research Methods*, Vol. 1, No. 2, pp. 131–163.

James, W. ([1890] 2013). *The Principles of Psychology*. New York: Cosimo.

Jankowski, P. (2013) "Brand Promises Are Very Valuable in the New Heartland." *Forbes*, August 8, 2013. Available at: https://www.forbes.com/sites/paul jankowski/2013/08/08/the-value-of-a-brand-promise-in-the-new-heartland/#371 ca78169ad.

Jenni, K., and G. Loewenstein (1997) "Explaining the Identifiable Victim Effect." *Journal of Risk and Uncertainty*, Vol. 14, No. 3, pp. 235–257.

Joachims, T. (1998) "Text Categorization with Support Vector Machines: Learning with Many Relevant Features." In *European Conference on Machine Learning:*

ECML-98, edited by C. Nédellec and C. Rouveirol, pp. 137–142. Berlin: Springer.

Joachims, T. (1999) "Making Large-Scale Support Vector Machine Learning Practical." In *Advances in Kernel Methods: Support Vector Learning*, edited by B. Schölkopf, C. Burges and A. Smola, pp. 169–184. Cambridge, MA: MIT Press.

John, L. K., K. Barasz, and M. Norton (2016) "Hiding Personal Information Reveals the Worst." *Proceedings of the National Academy of Sciences*, Vol. 113, No. 4, pp. 954–959.

Johnson, N., and A. Mislin (2011) "Trust Games: A Meta-Analysis." *Journal of Economic Psychology*, Vol. 32, No. 5, pp. 865–889.

Johnson-Lairds, P. (1983) *Mental Models: Towards a Cognitive Science of Language, Inference, and Consciousness*. Cambridge, MA: Harvard University Press.

Jones, D., and M. Krantz (2007) "Home Depot Boots CEO Nardelli." *USA TODAY*, January 4, 2007. Available at: https://usatoday30.usatoday.com/print edition/money/20070104/1b_homedepotcov04.art.htm.

Jones, E., and K. Davis (1965) "From Acts to Dispositions: The Attribution Process in Person Perception." In *Advances in Experimental Social Psychology*, Vol. 2, edited by L. Berkowitz, pp. 219–266. New York: Academic Press.

Jones, E., and V. Harris (1967) "The Attribution of Attitudes." *Journal of Experimental Social Psychology*, Vol. 3, No. 1, pp. 1–24.

Jones, E., and R. Nisbett (1971) *The Actor and the Observer: Divergent Perceptions of the Causes of Behavior*. New York: General Learning.

Jones, R. (1997) *Strategic Management in a Hostile Environment: Lessons from the Tobacco Industry*. Westport, CT: Quorum.

Jones, R., and F. Baumgartner (2005) *The Politics of Attention*. Chicago: University of Chicago Press.

Jordan, G. (2001) *Shell, Greenpeace and the Brent Spar*. London: Palgrave Macmillan.

Jordan, J., D. Diermeier, and A. Galinsky (2012) "The Strategic Samaritan: How Effectiveness and Proximity Affect Corporate Responses to External Crises." *Business Ethics Quarterly*, Vol. 22, No. 4, pp. 621–648.

Judd, C., L. James-Hawkins, V. Yzerbyt, and Y. Kashima (2005) "Fundamental Dimensions of Social Judgment: Understanding the Relations between Judgments of Competence and Warmth." *Journal of Personality and Social Psychology*, Vol. 89, No. 6, pp. 899–913.

Jurka, T., L. Collingwood, A. Boydstun, E. Grossman, and W. van Atteveldt (2012) "RTextTools: A Supervised Learning Package for Text Classification." *R Journal*, Vol. 5, No. 1, pp. 6–12.

Kachalia, A., S. R. Kaufman, R. Boothman, S. Anderson, K. Welch, S. Saint, and M. A. Rogers (2010) "Liability Claims and Costs before and after Implementation of a Medical Error Disclosure Program." *Annals of Internal Medicine*, Vol. 153, No. 4, pp. 213–221.

Kaeb, C. (2013) "America's Corporate Shield and Europe's Enterprise Responsibility Following the Rana Plaza Disaster." *Reputation Rules Blog*, August 23, 2013. Available at: https://www.vanderbilt.edu/csdi/events/prvtgov_kaeb.pdf.

Kahan, D. (2009) "Nanotechnology and Society: The Evolution of Risk Perceptions." *Nature Nanotechnology*, Vol. 4, No. 11, pp. 705–706.

Kahan, D., and D. Braman (2006) "Cultural Cognition and Public Policy." *Yale Law & Policy Review*, Vol. 24, No. 1, pp. 149–172.

Kahan, D., D. Braman, P. Slovic, J. Gastil, and G. Cohen (2009) "Cultural Cognition of the Risks and Benefits of Nanotechnology." *Nature Nanotechnology*, Vol. 4, No. 2, pp. 87–90.

Kahan, D., D. Braman, P. Slovic, J. Gastil, G. Cohen, and D. Kysar (2008) "Cultural Cognition and Nanotechnology Risk Perceptions: An Experimental Investigation of Message Framing." *Cultural Cognition Project at Yale Law School*, Yale University.

Kahan, D., P. Slovic, D. Braman, J. Gastil, G. Cohen, and D. Kysar (2008) "Biased Assimilation, Polarization, and Cultural Credibility: An Experimental Study of Nanotechnology Risk Perceptions." *Cultural Cognition Project at Yale Law School*, Yale University.

Kahneman, D. (2011) *Thinking, Fast and Slow*. New York: Farrar, Straus and Giroux.

Kahneman, D. (2012) "A Proposal to Deal with Questions about Priming Effects." *Decision Science News*, September 26, 2012. Available at: http://www.decisionsciencenews.com/?p=3634.

Kahneman, D., J. Knetsch, and R. Thaler (1986) "Fairness as a Constraint on Profit Seeking: Entitlements in the Market." *American Economic Review*, Vol. 76, No. 4, pp. 728–741.

Kahneman, D., and A. Tversky (1979) "Prospect Theory: An Analysis of Decision under Risk." *Econometrica*, Vol. 47, No. 2, pp. 263–292.

Kahneman, D., and A. Tversky (2000) *Choices, Values, and Frames*. Cambridge: Cambridge University Press.

Kamins, M., V. Folkes, and L. Perner (1997) "Consumer Responses to Rumors: Good News, Bad News." *Journal of Consumer Psychology*, Vol. 6, No. 2, pp. 165–187.

Kavilanz, P. (2007) "Nardelli Out at Home Depot: No. 1 Home Improvement Retailer Gives ex-CEO $210 million Package; Vice Chairman Frank Blake Takes the Helm." *CNNMoney*, January 3, 2007. Available at: http://money.cnn.com/2007/01/03/news/companies/home_depot/.

Kaya, M., G. Fidan, and I. H. Toroslu (2012) "Sentiment Analysis of Turkish Political News." In *WI-IAT '12: Proceedings of the 2012 IEEE/WIC/ACM International Joint Conferences on Web Intelligence and Intelligent Agent Technology*, Vol. 1, pp. 174–180. Washington, DC: IEEE Computer Society.

Keim, J. (2018) "Despite Child Abuse Suspension, Adrian Peterson Uses Belt on Son." *ABC News*, November 21, 2018. Available at: https://abcnews.go.com /Sports/child-abuse-suspension-adrian-peterson–son/story?id=59352482.

Keller, E., and B. Libai (2009) "A Holistic Approach to the Measurement of WOM." Paper presented at the ESOMAR Worldwide Media Measurement Conference, Stockholm.

Kelley, H. (1967) "Attribution Theory in Social Psychology." In *Nebraska Symposium on Motivation*, edited by D. Levine and D. E. Berlyne, pp. 192–238. Lincoln: University of Nebraska Press.

Kelley, H. (1973) "The Processes of Causal Attribution." *American Psychologist*, Vol. 28, No. 2, pp. 107–128.

Kepplinger, M. (2007) "Reciprocal Effects: Toward a Theory of Mass Media Effects on Decision Makers." *Harvard International Journal of Press/Politics*, Vol. 12, No. 2, pp. 3–23.

Kervyn, N., S. T. Fiske, and C. Malone (2012) "Brands as Intentional Agents Framework: How Perceived Intentions and Ability Can Map Brand Perception." *Journal of Consumer Psychology*, Vol. 22, No. 2, pp. 166–176.

Kessler, D. (2002) *A Question of Intent: A Great American Battle with a Deadly Industry*. New York: PublicAffairs.

Kessler, D. (2012) *Your Food Is Fooling You: How Your Brain Is Hijacked by Sugar, Fat, and Salt*. New York: Roaring Book.

Key, V. O. (1961) *Public Opinion and American Democracy*. New York: Alfred Knopf.

Kierkegaard, S. (1962) *The Present Age*. Translated by Alexander Dru. New York: Harper and Row.

Kim, D., D. Ferrin, and H. Rao (2008) "A Trust-Based Consumer Decision-Making Model in Electronic Commerce: The Role of Trust, Perceived Risk, and Their Antecedents." *Decision Support Systems*, Vol. 44, No. 2, pp. 544–564.

Kim, H. D., M. Castellanos, M. Hsu, C. Zhai, T. Rietz, and D. Diermeier (2013) "Mining Causal Topics in Text Data: Iterative Topic Modeling with Time Series Feedback." In *CIKM '13: Proceedings of the 22nd ACM International Conference on Information and Knowledge Management*, pp. 885–890. New York: ACM.

Kim, H. D., C. Zhai, T. Rietz, D. Diermeier, M. Hsu, M. Castellanos, and C. Ceja Limon (2012) "InCaToMi: Integrative Causal Topic Miner between Textual and Non-Textual Time Series Data." In *CIKM '12: Proceedings of the 21st ACM International Conference on Information and Knowledge Management*, pp. 2689–2691. New York: ACM.

Kim, P. H., K. Dirks, and C. Cooper (2009) "The Repair of Trust: A Dynamic Bilateral Perspective and Multilevel Conceptualization." *Academy of Management Review*, Vol. 34, No. 3, pp. 401–422.

Kim, P. H., D. Ferrin, C. Cooper, and K. Dirks (2004) "Removing the Shadow of Suspicion: The Effects of Apology Versus Denial for Repairing Competence-Versus Integrity-Based Trust Violations." *Journal of Applied Psychology*, Vol. 89, No. 1, pp. 104–118.

Kinder, D. (1998a) "Communication and Opinion." *Annual Review of Political Science*, Vol. 1, pp. 167–197.

Kinder, D. (1998b) "Opinion and Action in the Realm of Politics." In *Handbook of Social Psychology*, 4th ed., edited by D. T. Gilbert, S. T. Fiske, and G. Lindzey, pp. 778–867. New York: Oxford University Press.

King, B., and M. McDonnell (2015) "Good Firms, Good Targets: The Relationship between Corporate Social Responsibility, Reputation, and Activist Targeting." In *Corporate Social Responsibility in a Globalizing World*, edited by K. Tsutsui and A. Lim, pp. 430–454. New York: Cambridge University Press.

King, B., and N. Pearce (2010) "The Contentiousness of Markets: Politics, Social Movements, and Institutional Change in Markets." *Annual Review of Sociology*, Vol. 36, pp. 249–267.

King, B., and S. Soule (2007) "Social Movements as Extra-Institutional Entrepreneurs: The Effect of Protests on Stock Price Returns." *Administrative Science Quarterly*, Vol. 52, No. 3, pp. 413–442.

King, C., and D. Narayandas (2000) "Coca-Cola's New Vending Machine (A): Pricing to Capture Value, or Not?" Case Study 500-068. Cambridge, MA: Harvard Business School.

Kingdon, J. W. (1984) *Agendas, Alternatives, and Public Policies*. Boston: Little, Brown.

Kiss, G., C. Armstrong, R. Milroy, and J. Piper (1973) "An Associative Thesaurus of English and Its Computer Analysis." In *The Computer and Literary Studies*, edited by A. J. Aitken, R. W. Bailey, and N. Hamilton-Smith, pp. 153–165. Edinburgh: Edinburgh University Press.

Kitsak, B., L. Gallos, S. Havlin, F. Liljeros, L. Muchnik, H. Stanley, and H. Makse (2010) "Identification of Influential Spreaders in Complex Networks." *Nature Physics*, Vol. 6, No. 11, pp. 888–893.

Kittay, E. (1987) *Metaphor: Its Cognitive Force and Linguistic Structure*. Oxford: Clarendon Press.

Klebanov, B. B. (2006) "Measuring Semantic Relatedness Using People and Word-Net." In *Proceedings of the Human Language Technology Conference of the NAACL, Companion Volume: Short Papers*, pp. 13–16. New York: Association for Computational Linguistics.

Klebanov, B. B. (2007) "Experimental and Computational Investigation of Lexical Cohesion in English Texts." PhD diss., Hebrew University of Jerusalem.

Klebanov, B. B., E. Beigman, and D. Diermeier (2010). "Vocabulary Choice as an Indicator of Perspective." In *Proceedings of the 48th Annual Meeting of the*

Association for Computational Linguistics, pp. 253–258. New York: Association for Computational Linguistics.

Klebanov, B. B., D. Diermeier, and E. Beigman (2008a) "Automatic Annotation of Semantic Fields for Political Science Research." *Journal of Information Technology & Politics*, Vol. 5, No. 1, pp. 95–120.

Klebanov, B. B., D. Diermeier, and E. Beigman (2008b) "Lexical Cohesion Analysis of Political Speech." *Political Analysis*, Vol. 16, No. 4, pp. 447–463.

Klebanov, B. B., D. Kaufer, and H. Franklin (2010) "A Figure in a Field: Semantic Field-Based Analysis of Antithesis." *Cognitive Semiotics*, Vol. 6 (Supplement), pp. 121–154.

Klebanov, B. B., and E. Shamir (2006) "On Lexical Cohesive Behavior of Heads of Definite Descriptions: A Case Study." In *Proceedings of the 3rd International Workshop on Natural Language Understanding and Cognitive Science*, pp. 109–119. Lisboa, Portugal: Institute for Systems and Technologies of Information, Control and Communication (INSTICC) Press.

Klein, J., and N. Dawar (2004) "Corporate Social Responsibility and Consumers' Attributions and Brand Evaluations in a Product—Harm Crisis." *International Journal of Research in Marketing*, Vol. 21, No. 3, pp. 203–217.

Klein, N., and N. Epley (2014) "The Topography of Generosity: Asymmetric Evaluations of Prosocial Actions." *Journal of Experimental Psychology: General*, Vol. 143, No. 6, pp. 2366–2379.

Klein, R. A., K. A. Ratliff, M. Vianello, R. B. Adams Jr., S. Bahník, M. J. Bernstein, K. Bocian, M. Brandt, B. Brooks, C. C. Brumbaugh, Z. Cemalcilar, J. Chandler, W. Cheong, W. Davis, T. Devos, M. Eisner, N. Frankowska, D. Furrow, E. Galliani, F. Hasselman, J. A. Hicks, J. Hovermale, S. J. Hunt, J. R. Huntsinger, H. IJzerman, M.-S. John, J. Joy-Gaba, H. Kappes, L. Krueger, J. Kurtz, C. Levitan, R. Mallett, W. Morris, A. Nelson, J. Nier, G. Packard, R. Pilati, A. Rutchick, K. Schmidt, J. Skorinko, R. Smith, T.G. Steiner, J. Storbeck, L. Van Swol, D. Thompson, A. E. van 't Veer, L. A. Vaughn, M. Vranka, A. Wichman, J. Woodzicka, and B. A. Nosek (2014) "Investigating Variation in Replicability: A 'Many Labs' Replication Project." *Social Psychology*, Vol. 45, No. 3, pp. 142–152.

Kluger, R. (2010) *Ashes to Ashes: America's Hundred-Year Cigarette War, the Public Health, and the Unabashed Triumph of Philip Morris*. New York: Random House.

Knobe, J. (2006) "The Concept of Intentional Action: A Case Study in the Uses of Folk Psychology." *Philosophical Studies*, Vol. 130, No. 2, pp. 203–231.

Knobe, J., and J. Prinz (2008) "Intuitions About Consciousness: Experimental Studies." *Phenomenology and the Cognitive Sciences*, Vol. 7, No. 1, pp. 67–83.

Koehler, J., and A. Gershoff (2003) "Betrayal Aversion: When Agents of Protection Become Agents of Harm." *Organizational Behavior and Human Decision Processes*, Vol. 90, No. 2, pp. 244–261.

Kogut, T., and I. Ritov (2005) "The 'Identified Victim' Effect: An Identified Group, or Just a Single Individual?" *Journal of Behavioral Decision Making*, Vol. 18, No. 3, pp. 157–167.

Kohlberg, L. (1958) "The Development of Modes of Thinking and Choices in Years 10 to 16." PhD diss., University of Chicago.

Kohlberg, L. (1969) "Stage and Sequence: The Cognitive Development Approach to Socialization." In *Handbook of Socialization Theory and Research*, edited by D. A. Goslin, pp. 347–480. Chicago: Rand McNally.

Koku, P., A. Akhigbe, and T. Springer (1997) "The Financial Impact of Boycotts and Threats of Boycott." *Journal of Business Research*, Vol. 40, No. 1, pp. 15–20.

Kontostathis, A., and W. Pottenger (2006) "A Framework for Understanding Latent Semantic Indexing (LSI) Performance." *Information Processing and Management*, Vol. 42, No. 1, pp. 56–73.

Koopmans, T. (1949) "Identification Problems in Economic Model Construction." *Econometrica*, Vol. 7, No. 2, pp. 125–144.

Koreni, D., S. Ristov, and J. Šnajder (2015) "Getting the Agenda Right: Measuring Media Agenda Using Topic Models." In *TM '15: Proceedings of the 2015 Workshop on Topic Models: Post-Processing and Applications*, pp. 61–66. New York: ACM.

Kotchen, M. J. (2009) "Voluntary Provision of Public Goods for Bads: A Theory of Environmental Offsets." *Economic Journal*, Vol. 119, No. 537, pp. 883–899.

Kotchen, M., and J. Moon (2012) "Corporate Social Responsibility for Irresponsibility." *B.E. Journal of Economic Analysis and Policy*, Vol. 12, No. 1.

Kotler, P., H. Kartajaya, and I. Setiawan (2010) *Marketing 3.0: From Products to Customers to the Human Spirit*. Hoboken, NJ: John Wiley and Sons.

Kotz, S., N. Balakrishnan, and N. Johnson (2000) *Continuous Multivariate Distributions: Models and Applications*. Vol 1. 2nd ed. New York: John Wiley & Sons.

Kouloumpis, E., T. Wilson, and J. Moore (2011) "Twitter Sentiment Analysis: The Good the Bad and the OMG!" In *Fifth International AAAI Conference on Weblogs and Social Media*, pp. 53–541. Menlo Park, CA: AAAI.

Kramer, R. M. (1999) "Trust and Distrust in Organizations: Emerging Perspectives, Enduring Questions." *Annual Review of Psychology*, Vol. 50, No. 1, pp. 569–598.

Kramer, R. M., and T. R. Tyler (eds.) (1995) *Trust in Organizations: Frontiers of Theory and Research*. London: Sage.

Krapivsky, P. L., S. Redner, and E. Ben-Naim (2010). *A Kinetic View of Statistical Physics*. Cambridge: Cambridge University Press.

Kratz, E. (2005) "For FedEx, It Was Time to Deliver." *Fortune*, October 3, 2005. Available at: https://money.cnn.com/magazines/fortune/fortune_archive/2005/10/03/8356720/index.htm.

Krehbiel, K. (1994) "Like a Rock? General Motors in the Eye of the Media." Case Study No. P9A. Stanford, CA: Graduate School of Business.

Krippendorf, K. (2004) *Content Analysis: An Introduction to Its Methodology*. 2nd ed. Thousand Oaks, CA: Sage.

Krosnick, J. (1999) "Survey Research." *Annual Review of Psychology*, Vol. 50, No. 1, pp. 537–567.

Krosnick, J., N. Malhotra, and U. Mittal (2014) "Public Misunderstanding of Political Facts: How Question Wording Affected Estimates of Partisan Differences in Birtherism." *Public Opinion Quarterly*, Vol. 78, No. 1, pp. 147–165.

Kučera, H., and W. Francis (1967) *Computational Analysis of Present-Day American English*. Providence, RI: Brown University Press.

Kunda, Z. (1990) "The Case for Motivated Reasoning." *Psychological Bulletin*, Vol. 108, No. 3, pp. 480–498.

Kurtz, H. (1993) "NBC Apologizes for Staged Crash, Settles with GM." *Washington Post*, February 2, 1993. Available at: https://www.washingtonpost.com/archive/politics/1993/02/10/nbc-apologizes-for-staged-crash-settles-with-gm/fe1d1da2-9939-4076-a7e2-8e625d7ddede/.

Kwak, H., C. Lee, H. Park, and S. Moon (2010) "What Is Twitter, a Social Network or a News Media?" In *WWW '10: Proceedings of the 19th International Conference on World Wide Web*, pp. 591–600. New York: ACM.

Ladd, J. (2012) *Why Americans Hate the Media and How It Matters*. Princeton, NJ: Princeton University Press.

Lagnado, D. A., and S. Channon (2008) "Judgments of Cause and Blame: The Effects of Intentionality and Foreseeability." *Cognition*, Vol. 108, No. 3, pp. 754–770.

Lagos, M. (2012) "Komen Bay Area Race Hurt by Controversy." *SF Gate*. Available at: https://www.sfgate.com/health/article/Komen-Bay-Area-race-hurt-by-controversy-3851661.php.

Lai, C., M. Marini, S. Lehr, C. Cerruti, J-E. Shin, J. Joy-Gaba, A. Ho, B. Teachman, S. Wojcik, S. Koleva, R. Frazier, L. Heiphetz, E. Chen, R. Turner, J. Haidt, S. Kesebir, C. Hawkins, H. Schaefer, S. Rubichi, G. Sartori, C. Dial, N. Sriram, M. Banaji, and B. Nosek (2014) "Reducing Implicit Racial Preferences: I. A Comparative Investigation of 17 Interventions." *Journal of Experimental Psychology: General*, Vol. 143, No. 4, pp. 1765–1785.

Lai, C., A. Skinner, E. Cooley, S. Murrar, M. Brauer, T. Devos, J. Calanchini, J. Xiao, C. Pedram, C. Marshburn, S. Simon, J. Blanchar, J. Joy-Gaba, J. Conway, L. Redford, R. Klein, G. Roussos, F. Schellhaas, M. Burns, X. Hu, M. McLean, J. Axt, S. Asgari, K. Schmidt, R. Rubinstein, M. Marini, S. Rubichi, J-E. Shin, and B. Nosek (2016) "Reducing Implicit Racial Preferences: II. Intervention Effectiveness Across Time." *Journal of Experimental Psychology: General*, Vol. 145, No. 8, pp. 1001–1016.

Lai, V., P. Hagoort, and D. Casasanto (2012) "Affective Primacy vs. Cognitive Primacy: Dissolving the Debate." *Frontiers in Psychology*, Vol. 3, pp. 243.

Lakoff, G. (2001) "Metaphors of Terror." September 16, 2001. Available at: https://www.press.uchicago.edu/sites/daysafter/911lakoff.html.

Lakoff, G., and M. Johnson (1980). "The Metaphorical Structure of the Human Conceptual System." *Cognitive Science*, Vol. 4, No. 2, pp. 195–208.

Lakoff, G., and M. Johnson (2003) *Metaphors We Live By*. Chicago: University of Chicago Press.

Lammers, J., D. Staple, and A. Galinsky (2010) "Power Increases Hypocrisy: Moralizing in Reasoning, Immorality in Behavior." *Psychological Science*, Vol. 21, No. 5, pp. 737–744.

Laney, C., E. Morris, D. Bernstein, B. Wakefield, and E. Loftus (2010) "Asparagus, a Love Story: Healthier Eating Could Be Just a False Memory Away." *Experimental Psychology*, Vol. 55, No. 5, pp. 291–299.

Langer, E. (1975) "The Illusion of Control." *Journal of Personality and Social Psychology*, Vol. 32, No. 2, pp. 311–328.

Lapsley, D., and B. Lasky (2001) "Protoypic Moral Character." *Identity: An International Journal of Theory and Research*, Vol. 1, No. 4, pp. 345–363.

Larcinese, V., R. Puglisi, and J. Snyder (2011) "Partisan Bias in Economic News: Evidence on the Agenda-Setting Behavior of U.S. Newspapers." *Journal of Public Economics*, Vol. 95, No. 9, pp. 1178–1189.

Larson, J., J. Nagler, J. Ronen, and J. Tucker (2019) "Social Networks and Protest Participation: Evidence from 130 Million Twitter Users." *American Journal of Political Science*, Vol. 63, No. 3, pp. 690–705.

Laver, M., K. Benoit, and J. Gary (2003) "Extracting Policy Positions from Political Texts Using Words as Data." *American Political Science Review*, Vol. 97, No. 2, pp. 311–331.

Lawrence, R. G. (2004) "Framing Obesity: The Evolution of News Discourse on a Public Health Issue." *Harvard International Journal of Press/Politics*, Vol. 9, No. 3, pp. 56–75.

Lazer, D., R. Kennedy, G. King, and A. Vespignani (2014) "The Parable of Google Flu: Traps in Big Data Analysis." *Science*, Vol. 343, No. 6176, pp. 1203–1205.

Lazer, D., A. Pentland, L. Adamic, S. Aral, A.-L. Barabási, D. Brewer, N. Christakis, N. Contractor, J. Fowler, M. Gutmann, T. Jebara, G. King, M. Macy, D. Roy, and M. Van Alstyne (2009) "Computational Social Science." *Science*, Vol. 323, No. 5915, pp. 721–723.

Lazer, D., B. Rubineau, C. Chetkovich, N. Katz, and M. Neblo (2010) "The Coevolution of Networks and Political Attitudes." *Political Communication*, Vol. 27, No. 3, pp. 248–274.

Le Bon, G. (1895) *The Crowd: A Study of the Popular Mind*. New York: MacMillan.

LeBreton, J., E. Grimaldi, and J. Schoen (2020) "Conditional Reasoning: A Review and Suggestions for Future Test Development and Validation." *Organizational Research Methods*, Vol. 23, No. 1, pp. 65–95.

LeDoux, J. (1998) *The Emotional Brain: The Mysterious Underpinnings of Emotional Life*. New York: Simon & Schuster.

LeDoux, J. (2000) "Emotion Circuits in the Brain." *Annual Review of Neuroscience*, Vol. 23, No. 1, pp. 155–184.

Lei, J., N. Dawar, and Z. Gurhan-Canli (2012) "Base-Rate Information in Consumer Attributions of Product-Harm Crises." *Journal of Marketing Research*, Vol. 49, No. 3, pp. 336–348.

Lei, J., N. Dawar, and J. Lemmink (2008) "Negative Spillover in Brand Portfolios: Exploring the Antecedents of Asymmetric Effects." *Journal of Marketing*, Vol. 72, No. 3, pp. 111–123.

Leinwand, P., and C. Mainardi (2011) *The Essential Advantage: How to Win with a Capabilities-Driven Strategy*. Boston: Harvard Business Press.

Lenox M., and C. Eesley (2009) "Private Environmental Activism and the Selection and Response of Firm Targets." *Journal of Economic Management Strategy*, Vol. 18, No. 1, pp. 45–73.

Leonard, D. (2005) "The Only Lifeline was the Wal-Mart." *Fortune*, October 3, 2005. Available at: https://money.cnn.com/magazines/fortune/fortune_archive/2005/10/03/8356743/.

Lerner, M. (1980) *The Belief in a Just World: A Fundamental Delusion*. New York: Springer.

Leskovec, J., L. Backstrom, and J. Kleinberg (2009) "Meme-Tracking and the Dynamics of the News Cycle." In *KDD '09: Proceedings of the 15th ACM SIGKDD International Conference on Knowledge Discovery and Data Mining*, pp. 497–506. New York: ACM.

Leslie, A., J. Knobe, and A. Cohen (2006) "Acting Intentionally and the Side-Effect Effect." *Psychological Science*, Vol. 17, No. 5, pp. 421–427.

Levi, M. and L. Stoker (2000) "Political Trust and Trustworthiness." *Annual Review of Political Science*, Vol. 3, pp. 475–507.

Levs, J. (2009) "Big Three Auto CEOs Flew Private Jets to Ask for Taxpayer Money." *CNN*, November 19, 2009. Available at: http://www.cnn.com/2008/US/11/19/autos.ceo.jets/.

Lewis, M. (1992) "Representation and Learning in Information Retrieval." PhD diss., University of Massachusetts at Amherst. Technical Report 91–93.

Lewis, M. (2010) *The Big Short*. New York: W. W. Norton.

Li, X., H. Xie, L. Chen, J. Wang, and X. Deng (2014) "News Impact on Stock Price Return via Sentiment Analysis." *Knowledge-Based Systems*, Vol. 69, pp. 14–23.

Lichtenstein, S., P. Slovic, B. Fischhoff, M. Layman, and B. Combs (1978) "Judged Frequency of Lethal Events." *Journal of Experimental Psychology: Human Learning and Memory*, Vol. 4, No. 6, pp. 551–578.

Lieberman, M. (2007) "Social Cognitive Neuroscience: A Review of Core Processes." *Annual Review of Psychology*, Vol. 58, pp. 259–289.

Lieberman, M., R. Gaunt, D. Gilbert, and Y. Trope (2002) "Reflection and Reflex-ion: A Social Cognitive Neuroscience Approach to Attributional Inference." In *Advances in Experimental Social Psychology*, Vol. 34, edited by M. P. Zanna, pp. 199–249. San Diego: Academic Press.

Lieberman, M., J. Jarcho, and J. Obayashi (2005) "Attributional Inference Across Cultures: Similar Automatic Attributions and Different Controlled Correc-tions." *Personality and Social Psychology Bulletin*, Vol. 31, No. 7, pp. 889–901.

Liggett, T. (1985) *Interacting Particle Systems*. New York: Springer.

Liker, J., and T. Ogden (2011) *Toyota under Fire: Lessons for Turning Crisis into Opportunity*. New York: McGraw-Hill Education.

Lind, E., and T. Tyler (1988) *The Social Psychology of Procedural Justice: Critical Issues in Social Justice*. New York: Plenum.

Lindenmeier, J., C. Schleer, and D. Pricl (2012) "Consumer Outrage: Emotional Reactions to Unethical Corporate Behavior." *Journal of Business Research*, Vol. 65, No. 9, pp. 1364–1373.

Linguistic Data Consortium (2008) "The New York Times Annotated Corpus." Available at: https://catalog.ldc.upenn.edu/LDC2008T19.

Lippmann, W. ([1922] 1992) *Public Opinion*. New York: Macmillan.

Liu, B. (2010) "Sentiment Analysis and Subjectivity." In *Handbook of Natural Lan-guage Processing*, Vol. 2, edited by N. Indurkhya and F. J. Damerau, pp. 627–666. Boca Raton: CRC.

Liu, B. (2012) *Sentiment Analysis and Opinion Mining*. San Rafael, CA: Morgan & Claypool.

Liu, B. (2015) *Sentiment Analysis: Mining Opinions, Sentiments, and Emotions*. Cambridge: Cambridge University Press.

Liu, Y., and V. Shankar (2015) "The Dynamic Impact of Product-Harm Crises on Brand Preference and Advertising Effectiveness: An Empirical Analysis of the Automobile Industry." *Management Science*, Vol. 61, No. 10, pp. 2514–2535.

Livesey, S. M. (1999) "McDonald's and the Environmental Defense Fund: A Case Study of a Green Alliance." *Journal of Business Communication*, Vol. 36, No. 1, pp. 5–39.

Lloyd, A. (2001) "The Extent of Patients' Understanding of the Risk of Treat-ments." *BMJ Quality and Safety*, Vol. 10, Suppl. 1, pp. i14-i18.

Lodge, M. (1995) "Toward a Procedural Model of Candidate Evaluation." In *Polit-ical Judgment: Structure and Process*, edited by M. Lodge and K. M. McGraw, pp. 111–140. Ann Arbor: University of Michigan Press.

Lodge, M., M. Steenbergen, and S. Brau (1995) "The Responsive Voter: Campaign Information and the Dynamics of Candidate Evaluation." *American Political Science Review*, Vol. 89, No. 2, pp. 309–326.

Lodge, M., and C. Taber (2000) "Three Steps toward a Theory of Motivated Polit-ical Reasoning." In *Elements of Reason: Cognition, Choice, and the Bounds of*

Rationality, edited by A. Lupia, M. McCubbins, and S. Popkin, pp. 183–213. New York: Cambridge University Press.

Lodge, M., and C. Taber (2013) *The Rationalizing Voter*. Cambridge: Cambridge University Press.

Loftus, G. R., and E. F. Loftus. (1976) *Human Memory: The Processing of Information*. Hillsdale, NJ: Lawrence Erlbaum.

Lopatto, E., and D. Armstrong (2012) "Web Fury Spurs Komen Reversal, $3 Million for Planned Parenthood." *Bloomberg News*, February 3, 2012. Available at: https://www.bloomberg.com/news/articles/2012-02-03/web-fury-spurs-komen -reversal-3-million-of-funds-for-planned-parenthood.

Lorenz, J., H. Rauhut, F. Schweitzer, and D. Helbing (2011) "How Social Influence can Undermine the Wisdom of Crowd Effect." *Proceedings of the National Academy of Sciences*, Vol. 108, No. 22, pp. 9020–9025.

Lorsch, J., and R. Khurana (2010) "The Pay Problem: Time for a New Paradigm for Executive Compensation." *Harvard Magazine*, May–June, pp. 30–35.

Losey, J., L. Rayor, and M. Carter (1999) "Transgenic Pollen Harms Monarch Larvae." *Nature*, Vol. 399, No. 6733, p. 214.

Loughran, T., and B. McDonald (2011) "When Is a Liability Not a Liability? Textual Analysis, Dictionaries, and 10-Ks." *Journal of Finance*, Vol. 66, No. 1, pp. 35–65.

Lowe, W. (2008) "Understanding Wordscores." *Political Analysis*, Vol. 16, No. 4, pp. 356–371.

Lupia, A. (2013) "Communicating Science in Politicized Environments." *Proceedings of the National Academy of Sciences*, Vol. 110, No. 3, pp. 14048–14054.

Lynch, R. (2013) "Paula Deen Lawsuit Dismissed, but Not before It Destroyed Career." *Los Angeles Times*, August 23, 2013. Available at: https://www.latimes .com/food/dailydish/la-dd-paula-deen-lawsuit-dismissed-20130823-story.html.

Lyon, T., and J. Maxwell (2003) "Self-Regulation, Taxation and Public Voluntary Environmental Agreements." *Journal of Public Economics*, Vol. 87, No. 7–8, pp. 1453–1486.

Maas, A. L., R. E. Daly, P. T. Pham, D. Huang, A. Y. Ng, and C. Potts (2011) "Learning Word Vectors for Sentiment Analysis." In *Proceedings of the 49th Annual Meeting of the Association for Computational Linguistics: Human Language Technologies*, Vol. 1, pp. 142–150. New York: ACM.

MacDuffie, J. (2011) "Inter-Organizational Trust and the Dynamics of Distrust." *Journal of International Business Studies*. Vol. 42, No. 1, pp. 35–47.

MacIntyre, A. (2007) *After Virtue: A Study in Moral Theory*. 3rd ed. Notre Dame, IN: Notre Dame Press.

Mackie, D., and A. Asuncion (1990) "On-Line and Memory-Based Modification of Attitudes: Determinants of Message Recall-Attitude Change Correspondence." *Journal of Personality and Social Psychology*, Vol. 59, No. 1, pp. 5–16.

Macrae, C., and G. Bodenhausen (2000) "Social Cognition: Thinking Categorically about Others." *Annual Review of Psychology*, Vol. 51, No. 1, pp. 93–120.

MacroTrends.com (2021) "Netflix—Stock Price History NFLX." Available at: https://www.macrotrends.net/stocks/charts/NFLX/netflix/stock-price-history.

Macy, M. (1991) "Chains of Cooperation: Threshold Effects in Collective Action." *American Sociological Review*, Vol. 56, No. 6, pp. 730–747.

Maddux, W., P. Kim, T. Okumura, and J. Brett (2011) "Cultural Differences in the Function and Meaning of Apologies." *International Negotiation*, Vol. 16, No. 3, pp. 405–425.

Maddux, W., P. Kim, T. Okumura, and J. Brett (2012) "Why 'I'm Sorry' Doesn't Always Translate." *Harvard Business Review*. Available at: http://hbr.org/2012/06/why-im-sorry-doesnt-always-translate/ar/1.

Manheim, J. (2000) *The Death of a Thousand Cuts: Corporate Campaigns and the Attack on the Corporation*. New York: Routledge.

Manning, C., P. Raghavan, and H. Schütze (2008) *Introduction to Information Retrieval*. Cambridge: Cambridge University Press.

Manski, C. (1993) "Identification of Endogenous Social Effects: The Reflection Problem." *Review of Economic Studies*, Vol. 60, No. 3, pp. 531–542.

Manski, C. (2000) "Economic Analysis of Social Interactions." *Journal of Economic Perspectives*, Vol. 14, No. 3, pp. 115–136.

Margolis, J., and J. Walsh (2001) *People and Profits?* New York: Psychological Press.

Markus, H., and S. Kitayama (1991) "Culture and the Self: Implications for Cognition, Emotion, and Motivation." *Psychological Review*, Vol. 98, No. 2, pp. 224–253.

Maron, M. E., and J. L. Kuhns (1960) "On Relevance, Probabilistic Indexing and Information Retrieval." *Journal of the ACM*, Vol. 7, No. 3, pp. 216–244.

Martineau, B. (2001) *First Fruit: The Creation of the Flavr Savr Tomato and the Birth of Genetically Engineered Food*. New York: McGraw-Hill.

Mautner, G. (2001) "British National Identity in the European Context." In *Attitudes towards Europe: Language in the Unification Process*, edited by A. Musolff, C. Good, P. Points, and R. Wittlinger, pp. 3–22. Aldershot: Ashgate.

Maxwell, J., T. Lyon, and S. Hackett (2000) "Self-Regulation and Social Welfare: The Political Economy of Corporate Environmentalism." *Journal of Law and Economics*, Vol. 43, No. 2, pp. 583–617.

Mayer, R., J. Davis, and F. D. Schoorman (1995) "An Integrative Model of Organizational Trust." *Academy of Management Review*, Vol. 20, No. 3, pp. 709–734.

McAllister, D. (1995) "Affect- and Cognition-Based Trust as Foundations for Interpersonal Cooperation in Organizations." *Academy of Management Journal*, Vol. 38, No. 1, pp. 24–59.

McClure, J. (1998) "Discounting Causes of Behavior: Are Two Reasons Better than One?" *Journal of Personality and Social Psychology*, Vol. 74, No. 1, pp. 7–20.

McCombs, M., and A. Reynolds (2002) "News Influence on Our Pictures of the World." In *Media Effects: Advances in Theory and Research*, 2nd ed., edited by J. Bryant and D. Zillmann, pp. 1–18. Mahwah, NJ: LEA.

McCombs, M., and D. Shaw (1972) "The Agenda-Setting Function of Mass Media." *Public Opinion Quarterly*, Vol. 36, No. 2, pp. 176–187.

McCombs, M., and D. Shaw (1993) "The Evolution of Agenda-Setting Research: Twenty-Five Years in the Marketplace of Ideas." *Journal of Communication*, Vol. 43, No. 2, pp. 58–67.

McCormick, H., (2016) "The Real Effects of Unconscious Bias in the Workplace." University of North Carolina Chapel Hill Executive Development.

McCrank, J., and A. Saxena (2017) "Equifax Clears Executives Who Sold Shares after Hack." *Reuters*, November 3, 2017. Available at: https://www.reuters.com /article/us-equifax-cyber/equifax-clears-executives-who-sold-shares-after-hack -idUSKBN1D31EK.

McDonnell, M., and B. King (2013). "Keeping Up Appearances: Reputational Threat and Impression Management after Social Movement Boycotts." *Administrative Science Quarterly*, Vol. 58, No. 3, pp. 387–419.

McDonnell, M., B. King, and S. Soule (2015) "A Dynamic Process Model of Private Politics: Activist Targeting and Corporate Receptivity to Social Challenges." *American Sociological Review*, Vol. 80, No. 3, pp. 654–678.

McGraw, A. P., D. Davis, S. Scott, and P. Tetlock (2016) "The Price of not Putting a Price on Love." *Judgment and Decision Making*, Vol. 11, No. 1, pp. 40–47.

McGraw, A. P., J. Schwartz, and P. Tetlock (2011) "From the Commercial to the Communal: Reframing Taboo Trade-Offs in Religious and Pharmaceutical Marketing." *Journal of Consumer Research*, Vol. 39, No. 1, pp. 157–173.

McGraw, A. P., P. Tetlock, and O. Kristel (2003) "The Limits of Fungibility: Relational Schemata and the Value of Things." *Journal of Consumer Research*, Vol. 30, No. 2, pp. 219–229.

McKenzie, C., and L. Mikkelsen (2007) "A Bayesian View of Covariation Assessment." *Cognitive Psychology*, Vol. 54, No. 1, pp. 33–61.

McKnight, D. H., V. Choudhury, and C. Kacmar (2002) "Developing and Validating Trust Measures for E-Commerce: An Integrative Typology." *Information Systems Research*, Vol. 13, No. 3, pp. 334–359.

McPherson, M., L. Smith-Lovin, and J. Cook (2001) "Birds of a Feather: Homophily in Social Networks." *Annual Review of Psychology*, Vol. 27, No. 1, pp. 415–444.

Mei, Q., X. Ling, M. Wondra, H. Su, and C. Zhai (2007) "Topic Sentiment Mixture: Modeling Facets and Opinions in Weblogs." In *WWW '07: Proceedings of the 16th International Conference on World Wide Web*, pp. 171–180. New York: ACM.

Mei, Q., and C. X. Zhai (2005) "Discovering Evolutionary Theme Patterns from Text—An Exploration of Temporal Text Mining." In *KDD '05: Proceedings of the Eleventh ACM SIGKDD International Conference on Knowledge Discovery in Data Mining*, pp. 198–207. New York: ACM.

Meier, B. (1992) "Data Show G.M. Knew for Years of Risk in Pickup Trucks' Design" *New York Times*, November 17, 1992. Available at: https://www.nytimes.com/1992/11/17/us/data-show-gm-knew-for-years-of-risk-in-pickup-trucks-design.html.

Meqdadi, O., T. Johnsen, and R. Johnsen (2017) "The Role of Power and Trust in Spreading Sustainability Initiatives across Supply Networks: A Case Study in the Bio-chemical Industry." *Industrial Marketing Management*, Vol. 62, pp. 61–76.

Mercier, H., and D. Sperber (2011) "Why Do Humans Reason? Arguments for an Argumentative Theory." *Behavioral and Brain Science*, Vol. 34, No. 2, pp. 57–111.

Mertens, J.-F., and T. Parthasarathy (1991) "Nonzero-Sum Stochastic Games." In *Stochastic Games and Related Topics: In Honor of Professor L. S. Shapley*, edited by T. E. S. Raghavan, T. Ferguson, T. Parthasarathy, and O. Vrieze, pp. 145–148, Dordrecht: Kluwer Academic.

Mikhail, J. (2007) "Universal Moral Grammar: Theory, Evidence and the Future." *Trends in Cognitive Sciences*, Vol. 11, No. 4, pp. 143–152.

Mikolov, T., K. Chen, G. Corrado, and J. Dean (2013) "Efficient Estimation of Word Representations in Vector Space." *ArXiv Preprint* ArXiv:1301.3781.

Milgram, S. (1967) "The Small World Problem." *Psychology Today*, Vol. 1, No. 1, pp. 61–67.

Miller, G. (1956) "The Magical Number Seven, Plus or Minus Two." *Psychological Review*, Vol. 63, No. 2, pp. 81–97.

Miller, G. (2007) "Sexual Selection for Moral Virtues." *Quarterly Review of Biology*, Vol. 82, No. 2, pp. 97–125.

Miller, G., R. Beckwith, C. Fellbaum, D. Gross, and K. Miller (1990) "Introduction to WordNet: An On-line Lexical Database." *International Journal of Lexicography*, Vol. 3, No. 4, pp. 235–244.

Miller, N. E., and J. Dollard (1941) *Social Learning and Imitation*. New Haven, CT: Yale University Press.

Mills, J., and M. Clark (1982) "Communal and Exchange Relationships: Controversies and Research." In *Review of Personality and Social Psychology*, edited by L. Wheeler, pp. 121–144. Beverly Hills, CA: Sage.

Milov, S. (2019) *The Cigarette: A Political History*. Cambridge, MA: Harvard University Press.

Minor, D. (2015) "The Value of Corporate Citizenship: Protection." Working Paper 16-021. Cambridge, MA: Harvard Business School.

Minor, D., and J. Morgan (2011) "CSR as Reputation Insurance: Primum Non Nocere." *California Management Review*, Vol. 53, No. 3, pp. 40–59.

Monderer, D., and L. Shapley (1996) "Potential Games." *Games and Economic Behavior*, Vol. 14, No. 1, pp. 124–143.

Money (2013) *Fox Business Network*, February 12, 2013. Available at: https://video.foxbusiness.com/v/2162838842001#sp=show-clips.

Monroe, B., and K. Maeda (2004) "Talk's Cheap: Text-Based Estimation of Rhetorical Ideal-Points." Paper presented at the annual meeting of the Society for Political Methodology, Stanford, CA, July 31, 2004.

Monsanto (2018) "Monsanto History." Available at: https://web.archive.org/web/20180608085541/https://monsanto.com/company/history/.

Montgomery, N. V., and P. Rajagopal (2018) "Motivated Reconstruction: The Effect of Brand Commitment on False Memories." *Journal of Experimental Psychology: Applied*, Vol. 24, No. 2, pp. 159–179.

Moon, Y. (2005) "Online Music Distribution in a Post-Napster World." Case Study No. 9-502-093. Cambridge, MA: Harvard Business School.

Moraes, R., J. F. Valiati, and W. P. G. Neto (2013) "Document-Level Sentiment Classification: An Empirical Comparison between SVM and ANN." *Expert Systems with Applications*, Vol. 40, No. 2, pp. 621–633.

Morales, A., and G. Fitzsimons (2007) "Product Contagion: Changing Consumer Evaluations through Physical Contact with 'Disgusting' Products." *Journal of Marketing Research*, Vol. 44, No. 2, pp. 272–283.

Moraski, L. (2013) "Paula Deen on 'Today': I'm Not a Racist." *CBS News*, June 26, 2013. Available at: https://www.cbsnews.com/news/paula-deen-on-today-im-not-a-racist/.

Morewedge, C., and D. Kahneman (2010) "Associative Processes in Intuitive Judgment." *Trends in Cognitive Sciences*, Vol. 14, No. 10, pp. 435–440.

Morgan, R., and S. Hunt (1994) "The Commitment-Trust Theory of Relationship Marketing." *Journal of Marketing*, Vol. 58, No. 3, pp. 20–38.

Morgenson, G. (2006) "A Year to Suspend Disbelief." *New York Times*, December 31, 2006, p. BU1. Available at: https://www.nytimes.com/2006/12/31/business/yourmoney/31award.html.

Moriuchi, E., and I. Takahashi (2016) "Satisfaction Trust and Loyalty of Repeat Online Consumers within the Japanese Online Supermarket Trade." *Australasian Marketing Journal*, Vol. 24, No. 2, pp. 146–156.

Morris, S. (2000) "Contagion." *Review of Economic Studies*, Vol. 67, No. 1, pp. 57–78.

Morris, S., and H. Shin (1998) "Unique Equilibrium in a Model of Self-Fulfilling Currency Attacks." *American Economic Review*, Vol. 88, No. 3, pp. 587–597.

Morris, S., and H. Shin (2001a) "The CNBC Effect: Welfare Effects of Public Information." *Cowles Foundation Discussion Papers*, No. 1312. New Haven: Yale University.

Morris, S., and H. Shin (2001b) "Global Games: Theory and Applications." Cowles Foundation Discussion Papers No. 1275R. New Haven, CT: Yale University.

Morris, S., and H. Shin (2002) "Social Value of Public Information." *American Economic Review*, Vol. 92, No. 5, pp. 1521–1534.

Moschitti, A., and R. Basili (2004) "Complex Linguistic Features for Text Classification: A Comprehensive Study." In *European Conference on Information Retrieval (ECIR)*, pp. 181–196. Berlin: Springer.

Mostafa, M. (2013) "More than Words: Social Networks' Text Mining for Consumer Brand Sentiments." *Expert Systems with Applications*, Vol. 40, No. 2013, pp. 4241–4251.

Muchnik, L., S. Aral, and S. Taylor (2013) "Social Influence Bias: A Randomized Experiment." *Science*, Vol. 341, No. 6146, pp. 647–651.

Mullainathan, S. (2002) "A Memory-Based Model of Bounded Rationality." *Quarterly Journal of Economics*, Vol. 117, No. 3, pp. 735–774.

Mullainathan, S., and A. Shleifer (2005) "The Market for News." *American Economic Review*, Vol. 95, No. 4, pp. 1031–1053.

Mullen, T., and N. Collier (2004) "Sentiment Analysis Using Support Vector Machines with Diverse Information Sources." In *Proceedings of the 2004 Conference on Empirical Methods in Natural Language Processing*, edited by D. Lin and D. Wu, pp. 412–418. New York: Association for Computational Linguistics.

Müller, F. (1939) "Tabakmissbrauch und Lungencarcinom." *Zeitschrift fur Krebsforsch*, Vol. 49, pp. 57–85.

Mulligan, T., and C. Kraul (1996) "Texaco Settles Race Bias Suit for 176 Million." *Los Angeles Times*, November 16, 1996. https://www.latimes.com/archives/la-xpm-1996-11-16-mn-65290-story.html.

Mullinix, K., T. Leeper, J. Druckman, and J. Freese (2015) "The Generalizability of Survey Experiments." *Journal of Experimental Political Science*, Vol. 2, No. 2, pp. 109–138.

Musk, E. (2013a) "A Most Peculiar Test Drive." *Tesla Blog*, February 13, 2013. Available at: http://www.teslamotors.com/blog/most-peculiar-test-drive.

Musk, E. (2013b) "A Most Peculiar Test Drive—Follow Up." *Tesla Blog*, February 19, 2013. Available at: http://www.teslamotors.com/blog/most-peculiar-test-drive-follow.

Mutz, D. (2011) *Population-Based Survey Experiments*. Princeton, NJ: Princeton University Press.

Myerson, R. (1991) *Game Theory: Analysis of Conflict*. Cambridge, MA: Harvard University Press.

Nadler, J., and M. H. McDonnell (2011) "Moral Character, Motive, and the Psychology of Blame." *Cornell Law Review*, Vol. 97, No. 2, pp. 255–304.

Narayanan, V., I. Arora, and A. Bhatia (2013) "Fast and Accurate Sentiment Classification Using an Enhanced Naive Bayes Model." In *International Conference on Intelligent Data Engineering and Automated Learning*, pp. 194–201. Berlin: Springer.

Nathanson, C. (1999) "Social Movements as Catalysts for Policy Change: The Case of Smoking and Guns." *Journal of Health Politics, Policy, and Law*, Vol. 24, No. 3, pp. 421–488.

National Highway Traffic Safety Administration (NHTSA) (2011) "U.S. Department of Transportation Releases Results from NHTSA-NASA Study of Unintended Acceleration in Toyota Vehicles." Available at: https://one.nhtsa

.gov/About-NHTSA/Press-Releases/2011/U.S.-Department-of-Transportation -Releases-Results-from-NHTSA%E2%80%93NASA-Study-of-Unintended -Acceleration-in-Toyota-Vehicles.

Nebel, J. M. (2015) "Status Quo Bias, Rationality, and Conservatism about Value." *Ethics*, Vol. 125, No. 2, pp. 449–476.

Nelson, D. L., C. L. McEvoy, and T. A. Schreiber (2004) "The University of South Florida Word Association, Rhyme, and Word Fragment Norms." *Behavior Research Methods, Instruments, and Computers*, Vol. 36, No. 3, pp. 402–407.

Nelson, J. (2005) "Finding Useful Questions: On Bayesian Diagnosticity, Probability, Impact, and Information Gain." *Psychological Review*, Vol. 112, No. 4, pp. 979–999.

Nelson, J., C. McKenzie, G. Cottrell, and T. Sejnowski (2010) "Experience Matters: Information Acquisition Optimizes Probability Gain." *Psychological Science*, Vol. 21, No. 7, pp. 960–969.

Nelson, S. (2008) "The Price of Leadership." Available at: https://web.archive .org/web/20100606164545/http://www.landor.com/index.cfm?do=thinking.article &storyid=653&bhcp=1.

Nelson, T., Z. Oxley, and R. Clawson (1997) "Toward a Psychology of Framing Effects." *Political Behavior*, Vol. 19, No. 3, pp. 221–246.

Nemeroff, C., and P. Rozin (1994) "The Contagion Concept in Adult Thinking in the United States: Transmission of Germs and of Interpersonal Influence." *Ethos*, Vol. 22, No. 2, pp. 158–186.

Nestle, M. (2013) *Food Politics: How the Food Industry Influences Nutrition and Health*. Berkeley: University of California Press.

Newcomb, P. (2010) "2010's Top People in Business." *CNNMoney*, November 9, 2010. Available at: https://money.cnn.com/2010/11/19/news/economy/Fortune _businessperson_of_2010_complete_list.fortune/index.htm.

Newman, M. (2002) "Assortative Mixing in Networks." *Physics Review Letters*, Vol. 89, No. 20, pp. 208701-1–208701-4.

Newman, M. (2010) *Networks: An Introduction*. New York: Oxford University Press.

Newman, M., and J. Park (2003) "Why Social Networks Are Different from Other Types of Networks." *Physical Review E*, Vol. 68, No. 3, pp. 036122-1–036122-8.

New York Times (2008) "Mr. Obama's Profile in Courage." *New York Times*, March 19, 2008. Available at: https://www.nytimes.com/2008/03/19/opinion/19wed1. html?_r=1&ref=opinion&oref=slogin.

Nickerson, D. (2008) "Is Voting Contagious? Evidence from Two Field Experiments." *American Political Science Review*, Vol. 102, No. 1, pp. 49–57.

Nie, N., S. Verba, and J. Petrocik (1979) *The Changing American Voter*. Cambridge, MA: Harvard University Press.

Nielsen (2014) "Doing Well by Doing Good." June 3, 2014. Available at: https://web
.archive.org/web/20220404202514/https://www.nielsen.com/wp-content/uploads
/sites/3/2019/04/Nielsen-Global-Corporate-Social-Responsibility-Report-June
-2014.pdf.

Nisbet, M. (2005) "The Competition for Worldviews: Values, Information, and Public Support for Stem Cell Research." *International Journal of Public Opinion Research*, Vol. 17, No. 1, pp. 90–112.

Nisbett, R. E., C. Caputo, P. Legant, and J. Marecek (1973) "Behavior as Seen by the Actor and as Seen by the Observer." *Journal of Personality and Social Psychology*, Vol. 27, No. 2, pp. 154–164.

Nisbett, R. E., K. Peng, I. Choi, and A. Norenzayan (2001) "Culture and Systems of Thought: Holistic versus Analytic Cognition." *Psychological Review*, Vol. 108, No. 2, pp. 291–310.

Nisbett, R. E., and T. D. Wilson (1977) "Telling More Than We Can Know: Verbal Reports on Mental Processes." *Psychological Review*, Vol. 84, No. 3, pp. 231–259.

Nordhaus, W. (1975) "The Political Business Cycle." *Review of Economic Studies*, Vol. 42, No. 2, pp. 169–190.

Normile, D. (2018) "Bucking Global Trends, Japan Again Embraces Coal Power." *Science*, Vol. 360, No. 6388, pp. 476–477.

Nosek, B., C. Hawkins, and R. Frazier (2011) "Implicit Social Cognition: from Measures to Mechanisms." *Trends in Cognitive Sciences*, Vol. 15, No. 4, pp. 152–159.

Nozick, R. (1974) *Anarchy, State, and Utopia*. New York: Basic Books.

Nyhan, B. (2012) "Review: Does the US Media Have a Liberal Bias? A Discussion of Tim Groseclose's 'Left Turn: How Liberal Media Bias Distorts the American Mind.'" *Perspectives on Politics*, Vol, 10, No. 3, pp. 767–785.

Nyhan, B., and J. Reifler (2010) "When Corrections Fail: The Persistence of Political Misperceptions." *Political Behavior*, Vol. 32, No. 2, pp. 303–330.

Obama, B. (2008) "A More Perfect Union." March 18, 2008. Available at: https://www.americanrhetoric.com/speeches/barackobamaperfectunion.htm.

O'Donnell, E., and J. Schultz Jr. (2005) "The Halo Effect in Business Risk Audits: Can Strategic Risk Assessment Bias Auditor Judgment about Accounting Details?" *Accounting Review*, Vol. 80, No. 3, pp. 921–939.

Ohbuchi, K., M. Kameda, and N. Agarie (1989) "Apology as Aggression Control: Its Role in Mediating Appraisal of and Response to Harm." *Journal of Personality and Social Psychology*, Vol. 56, No. 2, pp. 219–227.

Ohtsubo, Y., E. Watanabe, J. Kim, J. Kulas, H. Muluk, G. Nazar, F. Wang, and J. Zhang (2008) "Are Costly Apologies Universally Perceived as Being Sincere? A Test of the Costly Apology-Perceived Sincerity Relationship in Seven Countries." *Evolution, Mind, and Behavior*, Vol. 10, No. 4, pp. 187–204.

O'Keefe, D. (2012) "From Psychological Theory to Message Design: Lessons from the Story of Gain-Framed and Loss-Framed Persuasive Messages." In *Health*

Communication Message Design: Theory and Practice, edited by Hyunyi Cho, pp. 3–20. Thousand Oaks, CA: Sage.

O'Keefe, D., and J. Jensen (2006) "The Advantages of Compliance or the Disadvantages of Noncompliance? A Meta-Analytic Review of the Relative Persuasive Effectiveness of Gain-Framed and Loss-Framed Messages." *Annals of the International Communication Association*, Vol. 30, No. 1, pp. 1–43.

O'Keefe, D., and J. Jensen (2009) "The Relative Persuasiveness of Gain-Framed and Loss-Framed Messages for Encouraging Disease Detection Behaviors: A Meta-Analytic Review." *Journal of Communication*, Vol. 59, No. 2, pp. 296–316.

O'Keefe, D., and X. Nan (2012) "The Relative Persuasiveness of Gain- and Loss-Framed Messages for Promoting Vaccination: A Meta-Analytic Review." *Health Communication*, Vol. 27, No. 8, pp. 776–783.

Oliver, J. E. (2006) *Fat Politics: The Real Story Behind America's Obesity Epidemic*. New York: Oxford University Press.

Oliver, P. (1993) "Formal Models of Collective Action." *Annual Review of Sociology*, Vol. 19, No. 1, pp. 271–300.

Oliver, P., and G. Marwell (1988) "The Paradox of Group Size in Collective Action: A Theory of the Critical Mass. II." *American Sociological Review*, Vol. 53, No. 1, pp. 1–8.

Olson, M. (1965) *The Logic of Collective Action: Public Goods and the Theory of Groups*. Cambridge, MA: Harvard University Press.

Olson, M., and R. Fazio (2006) "Reducing Automatically Activated Racial Prejudice through Implicit Evaluative Conditioning." *Personality and Social Psychology Bulletin*, Vol. 32, No. 4, pp. 421–433.

Onnela, J.-P., J. Saramäki, J. Hyvönen, G. Szabó, D. Lazer, K. Kaski, J. Kertész, and A.-L. Barabási (2007) "Structure and Tie Strengths in Mobile Communication Networks." *Proceedings of the National Academy of Sciences*, Vol. 104, No. 18, pp. 7332–7336.

Open Science Collaboration (2015) "Estimating the Reproducibility of Psychological Science." *Science*, Vol. 349, No. 6251, aac4716.

Osborne, M., and A. Rubinstein (1994) *A Course in Game Theory*. Cambridge, MA: MIT Press.

Oswald, M., and S. Grosjean (2004) "Confirmation Bias." In *Cognitive Illusions: A Handbook on Fallacies and Biases in Thinking, Judgment and Memory*, edited by R. Pohl, pp. 79–96. Hove: Psychology Press.

Owen, D. (2009) "The Pay Problem." *New Yorker*, October 5, 2009. Available at: https://www.newyorker.com/magazine/2009/10/12/the-pay-problem.

Page, B., R. Shapiro, and G. Dempsey (1987) "What Moves Public Opinion?" *American Political Science Review*, Vol. 81, No. 1, pp. 23–43.

Paharia, N., K. Kassam, J. Greene, and M. Bazerman (2009) "Dirty Work, Clean Hands: The Moral Psychology of Indirect Agency." *Organizational Behavior and Human Decision Processes*, Vol. 109, No. 2, pp. 134–141.

Palfrey, T., and H. Rosenthal (1984) "Participation and the Provision of Discrete Public Goods: A Strategic Analysis." *Journal of Public Economics*, Vol. 24, No. 2, pp. 171–193.

Palla, G., A.-L. Barabási, and T. Vicsek (2007) "Quantifying Social Group Evolution." *Nature*, Vol. 446, No. 7136, pp. 664–667.

Pan, B. (2015) "The Power of Search Engine Ranking for Tourist Destinations." *Tourism Management*, Vol. 47, pp. 79–87.

Pang, B., and L. Lee (2004) "A Sentimental Education: Sentiment Analysis Using Subjectivity Summarization Based on Minimum Cuts." In *Proceedings of the 42nd Annual Meeting of the Association for Computational Linguistics*, pp. 271–278. New York: Association for Computational Linguistics.

Pang, B., and L. Lee (2005) "Seeing Stars: Exploiting Class Relationships for Sentiment Categorization with Respect to Rating Scales." In *Proceedings of the 43rd Annual Meeting of the Association for Computational Linguistics*, edited by K. Knight, H. Tou Ng, and K. Oflazer, pp. 115–124. New York: Association for Computational Linguistics.

Pang, B., and L. Lee (2008) "Opinion Mining and Sentiment Analysis." *Foundations and Trends in Information Retrieval*, Vol. 2, No. 1–2, pp. 1–135.

Pang, B., L. Lee, and S. Vaithyanathan (2002) "Thumbs Up? Sentiment Classification Using Machine Learning Techniques." In *Proceedings of the 2002 Conference on Empirical Methods in Natural Language Processing*, pp. 79–86. New York: Association for Computational Linguistics.

Pappas, N. (2016) "Marketing Strategies, Perceived Risks, and Consumer Trust in Online Buying Behaviour." *Journal of Retailing and Consumer Services*, Vol. 29, pp. 92–103.

Park, J., H. Lee, and C. Kim (2014) "Corporate Social Responsibilities, Consumer Trust and Corporate Reputation: South Korean Consumers' Perspectives." *Journal of Business Research*, Vol. 67, No. 3, pp. 295–302.

Park, S., J. Mosley, and C. Grogan (2018) "Do Residents of Low-Income Communities Trust Organizations to Speak on Their Behalf? Differences by Organizational Type." *Urban Affairs Review*, Vol. 54, No. 1, pp. 137–164.

Pattison, P., and S. Wasserman (1999) "Logit Models and Logistic Regressions for Social Networks: II. Multivariate Relations." *British Journal of Mathematical and Statistical Psychology*, Vol. 52, No. 2, pp. 169–193.

Paulhus, D. (1984) "Two-Component Models of Socially Desirable Responding." *Journal of Personality and Social Psychology*, Vol. 46, No. 3, pp. 598–609.

Pavlou, P., and A. Dimoka (2006) "The Nature and Role of Feedback Text Comments in Online Marketplaces: Implications for Trust Building, Price Premiums, and Seller Differentiation." *Information Systems Research*, Vol. 17, No. 4, pp. 392–414.

Pavlou, P., and D. Gefen (2004) "Building Effective Online Marketplaces with Institution-Based Trust." *Information Systems Research*, Vol. 15, No. 1, pp. 37–59.

Pavlou, P., H. Liang, and Y. Xue (2007) "Understanding and Mitigating Uncertainty in Online Exchange Relationships: A Principal-Agent Perspective." *MIS Quarterly*, Vol. 31, No. 1, pp. 105–136.

Peiró-Palomino, J., and E. Tortosa-Ausina (2013) "Can Trust Effects on Development Be Generalized? A Response by Quantile." *European Journal of Political Economy*, Vol. 32, pp. 377–390.

Pelham, B., M. Mirenberg, and J. Jones (2002) "Why Susie Sells Seashells by the Seashore: Implicit Egotism and Major Life Decisions." *Journal of Personality and Social Psychology*, Vol. 82, No. 4, pp. 469–487.

Pennebaker, J., R. Booth, and M. Francis (2007) "Operator's Manual Linguistic Inquiry and Word Count: LIWC2007." Available at: http://www.depts.ttu.edu /psy/lusi/files/LIWCmanual.pdf.

Pennings, J. M. E., B. Wansink, and M. T. G. Meulenberg (2002) "A Note on Modeling the Consumer Reactions to a Crisis: The Case of the Mad Cow Disease." *International Journal of Research in Marketing*, Vol. 19, No. 1, pp. 91–100.

Pepitone, J. (2011) "Netflix Loses 800,000 Subscribers." *CNNMoney*, October 24, 2011. Available at: http://money.cnn.com/2011/10/24/technology/netflix _earnings/index.htm.

Pepitone, J. (2012) "Foxconn Workers Strike over iPhone 5 Demands, Labor Group Says." *CNN Business*, October 7, 2012. Available at: https://money.cnn.com/2012 /10/05/technology/mobile/foxconn-iphone-5-strike/index.html.

Perry, E., F. Ciliberto, D. Hennessy, and G. Moschini (2016) "Genetically Engineered Crops and Pesticide Use in U.S. Maize and Soybeans." *Science Advances*, Vol. 2, No. 8, e1600850.

Peters, E., and P. Slovic (1996) "The Role of Affect and Worldviews as Orienting Dispositions in the Perception and Acceptance of Nuclear Power." *Journal of Applied Social Psychology*, Vol. 26, No. 16, pp. 1427–1453.

Peters, R., V. Covello, and D. McCallum (1997) "The Determinants of Trust and Credibility in Environmental Risk Communication: An Empirical Study." *Risk Analysis*, Vol. 17, No. 1, pp. 43–54.

Peterson, M. (2001) "Lifting the Curtain on the Real Costs of Making AIDS Drugs." *New York Times*, April 24, 2001. Available at: https://www.nytimes.com /2001/04/24/business/lifting-the-curtain-on-the-real-costs-of-making-aids-drugs .html.

Petrone, B., and C. Whissell (1988) "The Dictionary of Affect in Language as a Tool for the Assessment of Affective Tone in a Descriptive Task." *Perceptual and Motor Skills*, Vol. 67, No. 3, pp. 789–790.

Petty, R. E., and J. T. Cacioppo (1986) "The Elaboration Likelihood Model of Persuasion." In *Communication and Persuasion*, edited by R. E. Petty and J. T. Cacioppo, pp. 1–24. New York: Springer.

Pew (2011) "Press Widely Criticized, but Trusted More than Other Information Sources." *Pew Research Center*, September 22, 2011. Available at: https://www.people-press.org/2011/09/22/press-widely-criticized-but-trusted-more-than-other-institutions/.

Phelps, E. (2006) "Emotion and Cognition: Insights from Studies of the Human Amygdala." *Annual Review of Psychology*, Vol. 57, pp. 27–53.

Phillips, D., and K. Clancy (1972) "Some Effects of 'Social Desirability' in Survey Studies." *American Journal of Sociology*, Vol. 77, No. 5, pp. 921–940.

Piazza, J. (2012) "Diabetics Call Paula Deen a Hypocrite for Hiding Disease while Promoting Sugar-Heavy Foods." *Fox News*, January 19, 2012. Available at: https://www.foxnews.com/entertainment/diabetics-call-paula-deen-a-hypocrite-for-hiding-disease-while-promoting-sugar-heavy-foods.

Pillutla, M. M., and J. K. Murnighan (1996) "Unfairness, Anger, and Spite: Emotional Rejections of Ultimatum Offers." *Organizational Behavior and Human Decision Processes*, Vol. 68, No. 3, pp. 208–224.

Pinedo, M., S. Seshadri, and E. Zemel (2000) "The Ford-Firestone Case." New York: Department of Information, Operations, and Management Sciences, Leonard N. Stern School of Business, New York University. Available at: https://www.stern.nyu.edu/om/faculty/zemel/ford_firestone.pdf.

Pizarro, D., C. Laney, E. Morris, and E. Loftus (2006) "Ripple Effects in Memory: Judgments of Moral Blame Can Distort Memory for Events." *Memory and Cognition*, Vol. 34, No. 3, pp. 550–555.

Pizarro, D., and D. Tannenbaum (2011) "Bringing Character Back: How the Motivation to Evaluate Character Influences Judgments of Moral Blame." In *The Social Psychology of Morality: Exploring the Causes of Good and Evil*, edited by M. Mikulincer and P. R. Shaver, pp. 91–108. Washington, DC: American Psychological Association.

Pizzutti dos Santos, C., and K. Basso (2012) "Do Ongoing Relationships Buffer the Effects of Service Recovery on Customers' Trust and Loyalty?" *International Journal of Bank Marketing*, Vol. 30, No. 3, pp. 168–192.

PM Live (2007) "Report Says US Public Think Pharma 'Puts Profits before Patients.'" *PMLive.com*, January 15, 2007. Available at: http://www.pmlive.com/pharma_news/report_says_us_public_think_pharma_puts_profits_before_patients_8517.

Ponte, E. B., E. Carvajal-Trujillo, and T. Escobar-Rodríguez (2015) "Influence of Trust and Perceived Value on the Intention to Purchase Travel Online: Integrating the Effects of Assurance on Trust Antecedents." *Tourism Management*, Vol. 47, pp. 286–302.

Poole, K., and H. Rosenthal (1985) "A Spatial Model for Legislative Roll Call Analysis." *American Journal of Political Science*, Vol. 29, No. 2, pp. 357–384.

Poole, K., and H. Rosenthal (1997) *Congress: A Political-Economic History of Roll Call Voting.* New York: Oxford University Press.

Popper, K. ([1935] 1959) *The Logic of Scientific Discovery.* London: Hutchinson.

Porter, M., and M. Kramer (2006) "Strategy and Society: The Link Between Competitive Advantage and Corporate Social Responsibility." *Harvard Business Review*, Vol. 85, No. 5, pp. 139.

Prat, A., and D. Strömberg (2013) "The Political Economy of Mass Media." In *Advances in Economics and Econometrics: Tenth World Congress.* Vol. 2, *Applied Econometrics*, edited by D. Acemoglu, M. Arellano, and E. Dekel, pp. 135–187. Cambridge: Cambridge University Press.

Prentice, R. A., and J. J. Koehler (2002) "A Normality Bias in Legal Decision Making." *Cornell Law Review*, Vol. 88, pp. 583–650.

Preston, J. (2012) "Komen Split with Planned Parenthood Draws Fire Online." *New York Times*, February 1, 2012. Available at: https://thelede.blogs.nytimes.com /2012/02/01/komen-split-with-planned-parenthood-draws-uproar-online/.

Preston, S., and F. de Waal (2001) "Empathy: Its Ultimate and Proximate Bases." *Behavioral and Brain Sciences*, Vol. 25, No. 1, pp. 1–72.

Price, V., and E.-K. Na (2000) "Citizen Deliberation and Resistance to Framing Effects." Paper presented at the annual meeting of the American Association for Public Opinion Research, Portland, Oregon.

Proctor, R. (2012) *Golden Holocaust: Origins of the Cigarette Catastrophe and the Case for Abolition.* Berkeley: University of California Press.

Pruitt, S., and M. Friedman (1986) "Determining the Effectiveness of Consumer Boycotts: A Stock Price Analysis of Their Impact on Corporate Targets." *Journal of Consumer Policy*, Vol. 9, No. 4, pp. 375–387.

Pruitt, S., K. Wei, and R. White (1988) "The Impact of Union-Sponsored Boycotts on the Stock Prices of Target Firms." *Journal of Labor Research*, Vol. 9, No. 3, pp. 285–289.

Puente, M. (2013) "Experts: Paula Deen Is Done Despite Legal Win." *USA Today*, August 12, 2013. Available at: https://www.usatoday.com/story/life/people/2013 /08/12/paula-deen-legal-woes-diminish-but-career-damage-is-done/2645967/.

Puglisi, R., and J. Snyder Jr. (2011) "Newspaper Coverage of Political Scandals." *Journal of Politics*, Vol. 73, No. 3, pp. 931–950.

Puglisi, R., and J. Snyder Jr. (2015) "The Balanced U.S. Press." *Journal of the European Economic Association*, Vol. 13, No. 2, pp. 240–264.

Qin, B., D. Strömberg, and Y. Wu (2018) "Media Bias in China." *American Economic Review*, Vol. 108, No. 9, pp. 2442–2476.

Quinlan, J. (1993) *C4.5: Programs for Machine Learning.* Burlington, VT: Morgan Kaufmann.

Quinn, K., B. Monroe, M. Colaresi, M. Crespin, and D. Radev (2010) "How to Analyze Political Attention with Minimal Assumptions and Costs." *American Journal of Political Science*, Vol. 54, No. 1, pp. 209–228.

Quinn, W. S. (1989) "Actions, Intentions, and Consequences: The Doctrine of Double Effect." *Philosophy & Public Affairs*, Vol. 18, No. 4, pp. 334–351.

Rai, T., and D. Diermeier (2015) "Corporations are Cyborgs: Organizations Elicit Anger but Not Sympathy When They Can Think but Cannot Feel." *Organizational Behavior and Human Decision Processes*, Vol. 126, pp. 18–26.

Rai, T., and D. Diermeier (2019) "Strategic Consequences of Being Unsympathetic: For-Profit Companies Benefit More than Individuals from Focusing on Responsibility." *Psychology & Marketing*, Vol. 36, No. 2, pp. 150–156.

Rai, T. S., and A. Fiske (2010) "ODD (Observation- and Description-Deprived) Psychological Research." *Behavioral and Brain Sciences*, Vol. 33, No. 2–3, pp. 106–107.

Rai, T. S., and A. Fiske (2011) "Moral Psychology is Relationship Regulation: Moral Motives for Unity, Hierarchy, Equality, and Proportionality." *Psychological Review*, Vol. 118, No. 1, pp. 57–75.

Ranco, G., D. Aleksovski, G. Caldarelli, M. Grar, and I. Mozeti (2015) "The Effects of Twitter Sentiment on Stock Price Returns." *PLOS ONE*, Vol. 10, No. 9, e0138441.

Rand, D. G., J. D. Greene, and M. A. Nowak (2012) "Spontaneous Giving and Calculated Greed." *Nature*, Vol. 489, No. 7416, pp. 427–430.

Rawls, J. (1971) *A Theory of Justice*. Cambridge, MA: Belknap Press of Harvard University Press.

Rayson, P. (2003) "Matrix: A Statistical Method and Software Tool for Linguistic Analysis through Corpus Comparison." PhD diss., Lancaster University.

Redlawsk, D. (2002) "Hot Cognition or Cool Consideration? Testing the Effects of Motivated Reasoning on Political Decision Making." *Journal of Politics*, Vol. 64, No. 4, pp. 1021–1044.

Reeder, G., and M. Brewer (1979) "A Schematic Model of Dispositional Attribution in Interpersonal Perception." *Psychological Review*, Vol. 86, No. 1, pp. 61–79.

Reichheld, F. (1996) *The Loyalty Effect*. Brighton: Harvard Business School Press.

Reinhardt, A. (1998) "Steve Jobs: There's Sanity Returning." *Bloomberg News*, May 25, 1998. Available at: https://www.bloomberg.com/news/articles/1998-05-25/steve-jobs-theres-sanity-returning.

Riccio, M., S. Cole, and E. Balcetis (2013) "Seeing the Expected, the Desired, and the Feared: Influences on Perceptual Interpretation and Directed Attention." *Social and Personality Psychology Compass*, Vol. 7, No. 6, pp. 401–414.

Riek, B., E. Mania, and S. Gaertner (2006) "Intergroup Threat and Outgroup Attitudes: A Meta-Analytic Review." *Personality and Social Psychology Review*, Vol. 10, No. 4, pp. 336–353.

Riloff, E., and J. Wiebe (2003) "Learning Extraction Patterns for Subjective Expressions." In *Proceedings of the 2003 Conference on Empirical Methods in Natural Language Processing*, pp. 105–112. Stroudburg, PA: Association for Computational Linguistics.

Rimmer, M. (2022) "The People's Vaccine: Intellectual Property, Access to Essential Medicines, and the Coronavirus COVID-19." *Journal of Intellectual Property Studies*, Vol. 5, No. 1, pp. 1–71.

Rindova, V., I. Williamson, A. Petkova, and J. Sever (2005) "Being Good or Being Known: An Empirical Examination of the Dimensions, Antecedents and Consequences of Organizational Reputation." *Academy of Management Journal*, Vol. 48, No. 6, pp. 1033–1049.

Roberts, P., and G. Dowling (2002) "Corporate Reputation and Sustained Superior Financial Performance." *Strategic Management Journal*, Vol. 23, No. 12, pp. 1077–1093.

Robson, M., C. Katsikeas, and D. Bello (2008) "Drivers and Performance Outcomes of Trust in International Strategic Alliances: The Role of Organizational Complexity." *Organization Science*, Vol. 19, No. 4, pp. 647–665.

Roehm, M., and A. Tybout (2006) "When Will a Brand Scandal Spill Over, and How Should Competitors Respond?" *Journal of Marketing Research*, Vol. 43, No. 3, pp. 366–373.

Roehm, M., and A. Tybout (2008) "Managing the Unthinkable: What to Do When a Scandal Hits Your Brand." In *Kellogg on Advertising and Media*, edited by B. J. Calder, pp. 159–177. Hoboken, NJ: Wiley.

Rorschach, H. (1927) *Rorschach Test Psychodiagnostic Plates*. Cambridge, MA: Hogrefe.

Ross, D., S. Ceci, D. Dunning, and M. Toglia (1994) "Unconscious Transference and Mistaken Identity When a Witness Misidentifies a Familiar but Innocent Person." *Journal of Applied Psychology*, Vol. 79, No. 6, pp. 918–930.

Ross, L., and R. Nisbett (1991) *The Person and the Situation: Perspectives of Social Psychology*. New York: McGraw-Hill.

Rottenstreich, Y., and C. Hsee (2001) "Money, Kisses and Electric Shocks: On the Affective Psychology of Risk." *Psychological Science*, Vol. 12, No. 3, pp. 185–190.

Rousseau, D., S. Sitkin, R. Burt, and C. Camerer (1998) "Not So Different after All: A Cross-Discipline View of Trust." *Academy of Management Review*, Vol. 23, No. 3, pp. 393–404.

Royzman, E., and J. Baron (2002) "The Preference for Indirect Harm." *Social Justice Research*, Vol. 15, No. 2, pp. 165–184.

Rozin, P., and E. Royzman (2001) "Negativity Bias, Negativity Dominance, and Contagion." *Personality and Social Psychology Review*, Vol. 5, No. 4, 296–320.

Róycka-Tran, J., P. Boski, and B. Wojciszke (2015) "Belief in a Zero-Sum Game as a Social Axiom: A 37-Nation Study." *Journal of Cross-Cultural Psychology*, Vol. 46, No. 4, pp. 525–548.

Rubel, O., P. A. Naik, and S. Srinivasan (2011) "Optimal Advertising When Envisioning a Product-Harm Crisis." *Marketing Science*, Vol. 30, No. 6, pp. 1048–1065.

Rubinstein, A. (1989) "The Electronic Mail Game: Strategic Behavior Under 'Almost Common Knowledge.'" *American Economic Review*, Vol. 79, No. 3, pp. 385–391.

Sabin, J., B. Nosek, A. Greenwald, and F. Rivara (2009) "Physicians' Implicit and Explicit Attitudes About Race by MD Race, Ethnicity, and Gender." *Journal of Health Care for the Poor and Underserved*, Vol. 20, No. 3 pp. 896–913.

Sagi, E., and M. Dehghani (2014a) "Measuring Moral Rhetoric in Text." *Social Science Computer Review*, Vol. 32, No. 2, pp. 132–144.

Sagi, E., and M. Dehghani (2014b) "Moral Rhetoric in Twitter: A Case Study of the US Federal Shutdown of 2013." In *Proceedings of the 36th Annual Conference of the Cognitive Science Society*, edited by P. Bello, M. Guarini, M. McShane, and B. Scassellati, pp. 1347–1352. Red Hook, NY: Curran.

Sagi, E., D. Diermeier, and S. Kaufman (2013) "Identifying Issue Frames in Text." *PLOS ONE*, Vol. 8, No. 7, e69185.

Sales-Pardo, M., D. Diermeier, and L. A. N. Amaral (2013) "The Impact of Individual Biases on Consensus Formation." *PLOS ONE* Vol. 8, No. 5, e58989.

Salganik, M., P. Dodds, and D. Watts (2006) "Experimental Study of Inequality and Unpredictability in an Artificial Cultural Market." *Science*, Vol. 311, No. 5762, pp. 854–856.

Sandman, P. (1989) "Hazard versus Outrage in the Public Perception of Risk." In *Effective Risk Communication*, edited by V. Covello, D. McCallum, and M. Pavlova, pp. 45–49. New York: Plenum.

Sanfey, A., J. Rilling, J. Aronson, L. Nystrom, and J. Cohen (2003) "The Neural Basis of Economic Decision-Making in the Ultimatum Game." *Science*, Vol. 300, No. 5626, pp. 1755–1758.

Savadori, L., S. Savio, E. Nicotra, R. Rumiati, M. Finucane, and P. Slovic (2004) "Expert and Public Perception of Risk from Biotechnology." *Risk Analysis*, Vol. 24, No. 5, pp. 1289–1299.

Schein, C., and K. Gray (2015) "The Unifying Moral Dyad: Liberals and Conservatives Share the Same Harm-Based Moral Template." *Personality and Social Psychology Bulletin*, Vol. 41, No. 8, pp. 1147–1163.

Schelling, T. (1960) *The Strategy of Conflict.* Cambridge, MA: Harvard University Press.

Scheufele, D., and B. Lewenstein (2005) "The Public and Nanotechnology: How Citizens Make Sense of Emerging Technologies." *Journal of Nanoparticle Research*, Vol. 7, No. 6, pp. 659–667.

Schlenker, B., and B. Darby (1981) "The Use of Apologies in Social Predicaments." *Social Psychology Quarterly*, Vol. 44, No. 3, pp. 271–278.

Schlesinger, M., S. Mitchell, and B. Gray (2004) "Restoring Public Legitimacy to the Nonprofit Sector: A Survey Experiment Using Descriptions of Nonprofit Ownership." *Nonprofit and Voluntary Sector Quarterly*, Vol. 33, No. 4, pp. 673–710.

Schlosser, E. (2002) *Fast Food Nation: The Dark Side of the All-American Meal.* New York: Perennial.

Schmidt, S., and M. Eisend (2015) "Advertising Repetition: A Meta-Analysis on Effective Frequency in Advertising." *Journal of Advertising,* Vol. 44, No. 4, pp. 415–428.

Schniter, E., R. Sheremeta, and D. Sznycer (2012) "Building and Rebuilding Trust with Promises and Apologies." *Journal of Economic Behavior & Organization,* Vol. 94, pp. 242–254.

Schoorman, F. D., R. Mayer, and J. Davis (2007) "An Integrative Model of Organizational Trust: Past, Present, and Future." *Academy of Management,* Vol. 32, 344–354.

Schuldt, J. P., S. H. Konrath, and N. Schwarz (2011) "Global Warming or Climate Change? Whether the Planet is Warming Depends on Question Wording." *Public Opinion Quarterly,* Vol. 75, No. 1, pp. 115–124.

Schultz, M., J. Mouritsen, and G. Gabrielsen (2001) "Sticky Reputation: Analyzing a Ranking System." *Corporate Reputation Review,* Vol. 4, No. 1, pp. 24–41.

Schuman, H., and S. Presser (1981) *Questions and Answers in Attitude Surveys.* New York: Academic Press.

Schütze, C. (1996) *The Empirical Base of Linguistics: Grammaticality Judgments and Linguistic Methodology.* Chicago: University of Chicago Press.

Schwartz, G. S., T. R. Kane, J. M. Joseph, and J. T. Tedeschi (1978) "The Effects of Post-Transgression Remorse on Perceived Aggression, Attributions of Intent, and Level of Punishment." *British Journal of Social and Clinical Psychology,* Vol. 17, No. 4, pp. 293–297.

Schweinsberg, M., N. Madan, M. Vianello, S. A. Sommer, J. Jordan, W. Tierney, E. Awtrey, L. Zhu, D. Diermeier, J. Heinze, M. Srinivasan, D. Tannenbaum, E. Bivolaru, J. Dana, C. Davis-Stober, C. Du Plessis, Q. Gronau, A. Hafenbrack, E. Liao, et al. (2016) "The Pipeline Project: Pre-publication Independent Replications of a Single Laboratory's Research Pipeline." *Journal of Experimental Social Psychology,* Vol. 66, pp. 55–67.

Schweitzer, M., J. Hershey, and E. Bradlow (2006) "Promises and Lies: Restoring Violated Trust." *Organizational Behavior and Human Decision Processes,* Vol. 101, No. 1, pp. 1–19.

Scott, M., and C. Tribble (2006) *Textual Patterns: Keyword and Corpus Analysis in Language Education.* Amsterdam: Benjamins.

Scott, S. and S. Matwin (1999) "Feature Engineering for Text Classification." In *ICML '99: Proceedings of the Sixteenth International Conference on Machine Learning,* pp. 379–388. San Francisco: Morgan Kaufmann.

Sears, D., C. Hensler, and L. Speer (1979) "Whites' Opposition to 'Busing': Self-Interest or Symbolic Politics?" *American Political Science Review,* Vol. 73, No. 2, pp. 369–384.

Sears, D., R. Lau, T. Tyler, and H. Allen Jr. (1980) "Self-Interest vs. Symbolic Politics in Policy Attitudes and Presidential Voting." *American Political Science Review*, Vol. 74, No. 3, pp. 670–684.

Seaver, S. M. D., D. Diermeier, R. Malmgren, A. Moreira, M. Sales-Pardo, and L. A. N. Amaral (2009) "Micro-Bias and Macro-Performance." *European Physical Journal B*, Vol. 67, No. 3, pp. 367–375.

Seaver, S. M. D., R. D. Malmgren, A. A. Moreira, M. Sales-Pardo, D. Diermeier, and L. A. N. Amaral (2006) "Social Cognition in Complex Team Networks." In *Proceedings of the 2005 Workshop on Social Agents*. Argonne, IL: Argonne National Laboratory.

Sebastiani, F. (2002) "Machine Learning in Automated Text Categorization." *ACM Computing Surveys*, Vol. 34, No. 1, pp. 1–47.

Sen, A. (1984) *Resources, Values and Development*. Oxford: Basil Blackwell.

Shannon, C. (1948) "A Mathematical Theory of Communication." *Bell System Technical Journal*, Vol. 27, No. 3, pp. 379–423.

Shapiro, D. (1991) "The Effects of Explanations on Negative Reactions to Deceit." *Administrative Science Quarterly*, Vol. 36, No. 4, pp. 614–630.

Shapiro, G. (1997). "The Future of Coders: Human Judgments in a World of Sophisticated Software." In *Text Analysis for the Social Sciences: Methods for Drawing Statistical Inferences from Texts and Manuscripts*, edited by C. W. Roberts, pp. 225–238. New York: Routledge.

Shapiro, J. (2016) "Special Interests and the Media: Theory and an Application to Climate Change." *Journal of Public Economics*, Vol. 144, pp. 91–108.

Shapley, L. S. (1953) "Stochastic Games." *Proceedings of the National Academy of Sciences*, Vol. 39, No. 10, pp. 1095–1100.

Shaw, R. (1996) *The Activist's Handbook: A Primer*. Berkeley: University of California Press.

Shen, F. and H. Edwards (2005) "Economic Individualism, Humanitarianism, and Welfare Reform: A Value Based Account of Framing Effects." *Journal of Communication*, Vol. 55, No. 4, pp. 795–809.

Shepardson, D. (2017) "U.S. Judge Dismisses Criminal Charge in Toyota Sudden Acceleration Case." *Reuters*, October 5, 2017. Available at: https://www.reuters.com/article/us-usa-toyota/u-s-judge-dismisses-criminal-charge-in-toyota-sudden-acceleration-case-idUSKBN1CA2R2.

Sheppard, K. (2008) "The Racial Stalemate." *American Prospect*, March 18, 2008. Available at: https://prospect.org/article/racial-stalemate/.

Sherman, S. (2013) "False Recall and Recognition of Brand Names Increases over Time." *Memory*, Vol. 21, No. 2, pp. 219–229.

Sherry, D. F., and B. G. Galef (1984) "Cultural Transmission without Imitation: Milk Bottle Opening by Birds." *Animal Behaviour*, Vol. 32, No. 3, pp. 937–938.

Shiller, R. (2016) *Irrational Exuberance*. Princeton, NJ: Princeton University Press.

Shutova, E. (2010) "Models of Metaphor in NLP." In *ACL '10: Proceedings of the 48th Annual Meeting of the Association for Computational Linguistics*, edited by J. Hajič, S. Carberry, S. Clark, and J. Nivre, pp. 688–697.

Shweder, R., N. Much, M. Mahapatra, and L. Park (1997) "The 'Big Three' of Morality (Autonomy, Community, Divinity) and the 'Big Three' Explanations of Suffering." In *Morality and Health*, edited by A. Brandt and P. Rozin, pp. 119–169. New York: Routledge.

Siegel, M. (2013) "Law Spoils Tobacco's Taste, Australians Say." *New York Times*, July 10, 2013. Available at: https://www.nytimes.com/2013/07/11/business/global/law-spoils-tobaccos-taste-australians-say.html.

Simons, D. J., and C. F. Chabris (1999) "Gorillas in our Midst: Sustained Inattentional Blindness for Dynamic Events." *Perception*, Vol. 28, No. 9, pp. 1059–1074.

Simonsohn, U. (2011). "Spurious? Name Similarity Effects (Implicit Egotism) in Marriage, Job, and Moving Decisions." *Journal of Personality and Social Psychology*, Vol. 101, No. 1, pp. 1–24.

Simpson, B., and R. Willer (2015) "Beyond Altruism: Sociological Foundations of Cooperation and Prosocial Behavior." *Annual Review of Sociology*, Vol. 41, pp. 43–63. New York: Association for Computational Linguistics.

Sinclair, B. (2012) *The Social Citizen*. Chicago: University of Chicago Press.

Singer, N. (2012) "With Support off as Events Begin, Komen Works to Revive Its Image." *New York Times*, 28 April, 2012. Available at: https://www.nytimes.com/2012/04/28/us/with-komen-image-hurt-support-for-affiliates-lags.html.

Sirdeshmukh, D., J. Singh, and B. Sabol (2002) "Consumer Trust, Value, and Loyalty in Relational Exchanges." *Journal of Marketing*, Vol. 66, No. 1, pp. 15–37.

Sjöberg, L. (2000) "Factors in Risk Perception." *Risk Analysis*, Vol. 20, No. 1, pp. 1–11.

Skaczkowski, G., S. Durkin, Y. Kashima, and M. Wakefield (2018) "Influence of Premium vs Masked Cigarette Brand Names on the Experienced Taste of a Cigarette after Tobacco Plain Packaging in Australia: An Experimental Study." *BMC Public Health*, Vol. 18, Article No. 295.

Skowronski, J., and D. Carlston (1987) "Social Judgment and Social Memory: The Role of Cue Diagnosticity in Negativity, Positivity, and Extremity Biases." *Journal of Personality and Social Psychology*, Vol. 52, No. 4, pp. 689–699.

Skowronski, J., and D. Carlston (1989) "Negativity and Extremity Biases in Impression Formation: A Review of Explanations." *Psychological Bulletin*, Vol. 105, No. 1, pp. 131–142.

Slapin, J., and S. Proksch (2008) "A Scaling Model for Estimating Time Series Party Positions from Texts." *American Journal of Political Science*, Vol. 52, No. 3, pp. 705–722.

Sleek, S. (2018) "The Bias Beneath: Two Decades of Measuring Implicit Associations." *Association for Psychological Science*, January 31, 2018. Available at: https://www.psychologicalscience.org/observer/the-bias-beneath-two-decades-of-measuring-implicit-associations.

Slovic, P. (1987) "Perception of Risk." *Science*, Vol. 236, No. 4799, pp. 280–285.

Slovic, P. (1992) "Perception of Risk: Reflections on the Psychometric Paradigm." In *Social Theories of Risk*, edited by S. Krimsky and D. Golding, pp. 117–152, Santa Barbara, CA: Praeger.

Slovic, P. (2000) *The Perception of Risk*. London: Earthscan.

Slovic, P. (2010) *The Feeling of Risk: New Perspectives on Risk Perception*. London: Earthscan.

Slovic, P., B. Fischhoff, and S. Lichtenstein (1982) "Why Study Risk Perception?" *Risk Analysis*, Vol. 2, No. 2, pp. 83–93.

Slovic, P., M. Finucane, E. Peters, and D. MacGregor (2002) "The Affect Heuristic." In *Heuristics and Biases: The Psychology of Intuitive Judgment*, edited by T. Gilovich, D. Griffin, and D. Kahneman, pp. 397–420. New York: Cambridge University Press.

Slovic, P., M. Finucane, E. Peters, and D. MacGregor (2004) "Risk as Analysis and Risk as Feelings: Some Thoughts about Affect, Reason, Risk, and Rationality." *Risk Analysis*, Vol. 24, No. 2, pp. 311–322.

Slovic, P., and E. Peters (2006) "Risk Perception and Affect." *Current Directions in Psychological Science*, Vol. 15, No. 6, pp. 322–325.

Small, D., and G. Loewenstein (2003) "Helping a Victim or Helping the Victim: Altruism and Identifiability." *Journal of Risk and Uncertainty*, Vol. 26, No. 1, pp. 5–16.

Small, D., and G. Loewenstein (2005) "The Devil You Know: The Effects of Identifiability on Punishment." *Journal of Behavioral Decision Making*, Vol. 18, No. 5, pp. 311–318.

Small, D., G. Loewenstein, and P. Slovic (2007) "Sympathy and Callousness: The Impact of Deliberative Thought on Donations to Identifiable and Statistical Victims." *Organizational Behavior and Human Decision Processes*, Vol. 102, No. 2, pp. 143–153.

Smith, K. B., D. Oxley, M. V. Hibbing, J. R. Alford, and J. R. Hibbing (2011) "Disgust Sensitivity and the Neurophysiology of Left-Right Political Orientations." *PLOS ONE*, Vol. 6, No. 10, e25552.

Smith, N. C. (1990) *Morality and the Market: Consumer Pressure for Corporate Accountability*. London: Routledge.

Sniderman, P., and S. Theriault (2004) "The Structure of Political Argument and the Logic of Issue Framing." In *Studies in Public Opinion: Attitudes, Nonattitudes, Measurement Error, and Change*, edited by W. Saris and P. Sniderman, pp. 133–165. Princeton, NJ: Princeton University Press.

Snyder, C. R., and R. L. Higgins (1988) "Excuses: Their Effective Role in the Negotiation of Reality." *Psychological Bulletin*, Vol. 104, No. 1, pp. 23–35.

Snyder, J., and R. Puglisi (2016) "Empirical Studies of Media Bias." In *Handbook of Media Economics*, Vol. 2, edited by S. Anderson, J. Waldfogel, and D. Strömberg, pp. 648–667. Amsterdam: Elsevier.

Snyder, J., and D. Strömberg (2010) "Press Coverage and Political Accountability." *Journal of Political Economy*, Vol. 118, No. 2, pp. 355–408.

Soderstrom, S., B. Uzzi, D. Rucker, J. Fowler, and D. Diermeier (2016) "Timing Matters: How Social Influence Affects Adoption Pre- and Post-Product Release." *Sociological Science*, Vol. 3, pp. 915–939.

Soetevent, A. (2006) "Empirics of the Identification of Social Interactions; An Evaluation of the Approaches and Their Results." *Journal of Economics Surveys*, Vol. 20, No. 2, pp. 193–228.

Solnit, R. (2010) *A Paradise Built in Hell: The Extraordinary Communities that Arise in Disaster*. New York: Penguin.

Spranca, M., E. Minsk, and J. Baron (1991) "Omission and Commission in Judgment and Choice." *Journal of Experimental Social Psychology*, Vol. 27, No. 1, pp. 76–105.

Sripada, C. (2012) "What Makes a Manipulated Agent Unfree?" *Philosophy and Phenomenological Research*, Vol. 85, No. 3, pp. 563–593.

Sripada, C., and S. Konrath (2011) "Telling More than We Can Know About Intentional Action." *Mind and Language*, Vol. 26, No. 3, pp. 353–380.

Srivastava, R., T. McInish, R. Wood, and A. Capraro (1997) "Part IV: How Do Reputations Affect Corporate Performance? The Value of Corporate Reputation: Evidence from the Equity Markets." *Corporate Reputation Review*, Vol. 1, No. 1, pp. 61–68.

Staats, C. (2015) "Understanding Implicit Bias: What Educators Should Know." *American Educator*, Winter 2015–2016, Available at: https://www.aft.org/ae/winter2015-2016/staats.

Steiner, I. (1954) "Primary Group Influences on Public Opinion." *American Sociological Review*, Vol. 19, No. 3, pp. 260–267.

Stewart, M. (1993) "The Effect on Tobacco Consumption of Advertising Bans in OECD Countries." *International Journal of Advertising*, Vol. 12, No. 2, pp. 155–180.

Steyvers, M., and T. Griffiths (2007) "Probabilistic Topic Models." In *Handbook of Latent Semantic Analysis*, edited by T. K. Landauer, D. S. McNamara, S. Dennis, and W. Kintsch, pp. 427–448. Mahwah, NJ: Lawrence Erlbaum.

Stirman, S., and J. Pennebaker (2001) "Word Use in the Poetry of Suicidal and Nonsuicidal Poets." *Psychosomatic Medicine*, Vol. 63, No. 4, pp. 517–522.

Stone, D. (1997) *Policy Paradox: The Art of Political Decision Making*. New York: W. W. Norton.

Stone, P., D. Dunphy, and M. Smith (1966) *The General Inquirer: A Computer Approach to Content Analysis*. Cambridge, MA: MIT Press.

Stotsky, S. (1983) "Types of Lexical Cohesion in Expository Writing: Implications for Developing the Vocabulary of Academic Discourse." *College Composition and Communication,* Vol. 34, No. 4, pp. 430–446.

Strauss, D. (2012) "Komen Founder Nancy Brinker Stepping down in Leadership Shake-up." *The Hill*, August 9, 2012. Available at: https://thehill.com/policy /healthcare/122109-komen-founder-nancy-brinker-stepping-down-in-leadership -shake-up/.

Strom, S. (2013) "U.S. Standards for School Snacks Move beyond Cafeteria to Fight Obesity." *New York Times*, June 27, 2013. Available at: https://www.nytimes .com/2013/06/28/business/us-takes-aim-on-snacks-offered-for-sale-in-schools .html.

Stroop, J. R. (1935) "Studies of Interference in Serial Verbal Reactions." *Journal of Experimental Psychology*, Vol. 18, No. 6, pp. 643–662.

Stump, S. (2013) "Paula Deen Fans Mail Butter Wrappers to Retailers in Protest." *Today*, July 18, 2013. Available at: https://www.today.com/food/paula-deen-fans -mail-butter-wrappers-retailers-protest-6C10674057.

Sullivan, M. (2013) "Problems with Precision and Judgment, but Not Integrity, in Tesla Test." *Public Editor's Journal*, February 18, 2013. Available at: http: //publiceditor.blogs.nytimes.com/2013/02/18/problems-with-precision-and-judg ment-but-not-integrity-in-tesla-test/.

Sun, L., and S. Kliff (2012) "Susan G. Komen Foundation Takes Steps to Rebuild Trust after PR Fiasco." *Washington Post*, February 4, 2012. Available at: https://www.washingtonpost.com/national/health-science/2012/02/04/gIQAdljR qQ_story.html.

Sunstein, C. (2001). *Republic.com*. Princeton, NJ: Princeton University Press.

Sunstein, C. (2005) "Moral Heuristics." *Behavioral and Brain Sciences*, Vol. 28, No. 4, pp. 531–573.

Susan G. Komen for the Cure (2013) "2010–2011 Annual Report." Available at: https://ww5.komen.org/uploadedFiles/Content/AboutUs/Financial/FY11%20re port%20FINAL%20100812.pdf.

Suykens, J. A., and J. Vandewalle (1999) "Least Squares Support Vector Machine Classifiers." *Neural Processing Letters*, Vol. 9, No. 3, pp. 293–300.

Svejenova, S. (2006) "How Much Does Trust Really Matter? Some Reflections on the Significance and Implications of Madhok's Trust-Based Approach." *Journal of International Business Studies*, Vol. 37, No. 1, pp. 12–20.

Tabuchi, H. (2012) "Japanese Prime Minister Says Government Shares Blame for Nuclear Disaster." *New York Times*, March 3, 2012. Available at: https://www .nytimes.com/2012/03/04/world/asia/japans-premier-says-government-shares -blame-for-fukushima-disaster.html.

Taibbi, M. (2009) "The Great American Bubble Machine." *Rolling Stone*, July 9–23, 2009. Available at: https://www.rollingstone.com/politics/politics-news/the -great-american-bubble-machine-195229/.

Takayama, Y., R. Flournoy, and S. Kaufmann (1998) *Information Mapping: Concept-based Information Retrieval Based on Word Associations.* Stanford, CA: CSLI.

Takayama, Y., R. Flournoy, S. Kaufmann, and S. Peters (1999) "Information Retrieval Based on Domain-Specific Word Associations." In *Proceedings of the Pacific Association for Computational Linguistics (PACLING'99)*, edited by N. Cercone and K. Naruedomkul, pp. 155–161. Waterloo, ON: Department of Computer Science, University of Waterloo.

Taleb, N. N. (2007) *The Black Swan.* New York: Random House.

Tang, D., B. Qin, and T. Liu (2015) "Document Modeling with Gated Recurrent Neural Network for Sentiment Classification." In *Proceedings of the 2015 Conference on Empirical Methods in Natural Language Processing*, edited by L. Màrquez, C. Callison-Burch, and J. Su, pp. 1422–1432. Lisbon: Association for Computational Linguistics.

Tang, S., and K. Gray (2018). "CEOs Imbue Organizations with Feelings, Increasing Punishment Satisfaction and Apology Effectiveness." *Journal of Experimental Social Psychology*, Vol. 79, pp. 115–125.

Tannenbaum, D., E. Uhlmann, and D. Diermeier (2011) "Moral Signals, Public Outrage, and Immaterial Harms." *Journal of Experimental Social Psychology*, Vol. 47, No. 6, pp. 1249–1254.

Taylor, S., and S. Fiske (1978) "Salience, Attention, and Attribution: Top of the Head Phenomena." *Advances in Experimental Social Psychology*, Vol. 11, pp. 249–288.

Teh, Y., and M. Jordan (2010) "Hierarchical Bayesian Nonparametric Models with Applications." In *Bayesian Nonparametrics*, edited by N. Hjort, C. Holmes, P. Mueller, and S. Walker, pp. 158–207. Cambridge: Cambridge University Press.

Teh, Y., M. Jordan, M. Beal, and D. Blei (2006) "Hierarchical Dirichlet Processes." *Journal of the American Statistical Association*, Vol. 101, No. 476, pp. 1566–1581.

Teoh, S., I. Welch, and C. Wazzan (1999) "The Effect of Socially Activist Investment Policies on the Financial Markets: Evidence from the South African Boycott." *Journal of Business*, Vol. 72, No. 1, pp. 35–89.

Terhune, C., and J. Lublin (2006) "At Home Depot, CEO 'Pay Rage' Boils Over in Vote." *Wall Street Journal*, June 2, 2006. Available at: http://online.wsj.com /article/SB114920597819569285.html.

Tesh, S. (1988) *Hidden Arguments: Political Ideology and Disease Prevention Policy.* New Brunswick, NJ: Rutgers University Press.

Tetlock, P. (2002) "Social Functionalist Frameworks for Judgment and Choice: Intuitive Politicians, Theologians, and Prosecutors." *Psychological Review*, Vol. 109, No. 3, pp. 451–471.

Tetlock, P. (2007) "Giving Content to Investor Sentiment: The Role of Media in the Stock Market." *Journal of Finance*, Vol. 62, No. 3, pp. 1139–1168.

Tetlock, P. (2015) "The Role of Media in Finance." In *Handbook of Media Economics*, Vol. 1, edited by S. Anderson, J. Waldfogel, and D. Strömberg, pp. 701–721. Amsterdam: North-Holland.

Tetlock, P., O. Kristel, S. Elson, M. Green, and J. Lerner (2000) "The Psychology of the Unthinkable: Taboo Trade-Offs, Forbidden Base Rates, and Heretical Counterfactuals." *Journal of Personality and Social Psychology*, Vol. 78, No. 5, pp. 853–870.

Tetlock, P., M. Saar-Tsechansky, and S. Macskassy (2008) "More than Words: Quantifying Language to Measure Firms' Fundamentals." *Journal of Finance*, Vol. 63, No. 3, pp. 1437–1467.

Tetlock, P., P. Visser, R. Singh, M. Polifroni, A. Scott, S. Elson, P. Mazzocco, and P. Rescober (2007) "People as Intuitive Prosecutors: The Impact of Social-Control Goals on Attributions of Responsibility." *Journal of Experimental Social Psychology*, Vol. 43, No. 2, pp. 195–209.

Thaler, R. H. (1988) "Anomalies: The Ultimatum Game." *Journal of Economic Perspectives*, Vol. 2, No. 4, pp. 195–206.

Thaler, R. H. (ed.) (1993) *Advances in Behavioral Finance*. New York: Russell Sage Foundation.

Thaler, R. H. (ed.) (2005) *Advances in Behavioral Finance*. Vol. 2. Princeton, NJ: Princeton University Press.

Thomson, J. (1976) "Killing, Letting Die, and the Trolley Problem." *The Monist*, Vol. 59, No. 2, pp. 204–217.

Thomson, J. (1985) "The Trolley Problem." *Yale Law Journal*, Vol. 94, No. 6, pp. 1395–1415.

Tinic, S. (1997) "United Colors and Untied Meanings: Benetton and the Commodification of Social Issues." *Journal of Communication*, Vol. 47, No. 3, pp. 3–25.

Tobacco Tactics (2020) "Tobacco Industry Research Committee." Available at: https://tobaccotactics.org/wiki/tobacco-industry-research-committee/.

Todd, A. R., G. V. Bodenhausen, J. A. Richeson, and A. D. Galinsky (2011) "Perspective Taking Combats Automatic Expressions of Racial Bias." *Journal of Personality and Social Psychology*, Vol. 100, No. 6, pp. 1027–1042.

Todorov, A., S. G. Baron, and N. N. Oosterhof (2008) "Evaluating Face Trustworthiness: A Model Based Approach." *Social Cognitive and Affective Neuroscience*, Vol. 3, No. 2, pp. 119–127.

Tolchin, M. (1993) "G. M. Pickup Case Is Taken Over by the Secretary of Transportation." *New York Times*, November 19, 1993. Available at: https://www.nytimes.com/1993/11/19/us/gm-pickup-case-is-taken-over-by-the-secretary-of-transportation.html.

Tomlinson, E., B. Dineen, and R. Lewicki (2004) "The Road to Reconciliation: Antecedents of Victim Willingness to Reconcile Following a Broken Promise." *Journal of Management*, Vol. 30, No. 2, pp. 165–187.

Tomlinson, E., and R. Mayer (2009) "The Role of Causal Attribution Dimensions in Trust Repair." *Academy of Management Review*, Vol. 34, No. 1, pp. 85–104.

Tormala, Z., and R. Petty (2001) "On-Line versus Memory-Based Processing: The Role of 'Need to Evaluate' in Person Perception." *Personality and Social Psychology Bulletin*, Vol. 27, No. 12, pp. 1599–1612.

Treisman, R. (2021) "From 'Jolene' to Vaccine: Dolly Parton Gets COVID-19 Shot She Helped Fund." *National Public Radio*, March 3, 2021. Available at https://www.npr.org/sections/coronavirus-live-updates/2021/03/03/973240792/from-jolene-to-vaccine-dolly-parton-gets-covid-19-shot-she-helped-fund.

Tripathy, A., A. Agrawal, and S. K. Rath (2016) "Classification of Sentiment Reviews Using n-Gram Machine Learning Approach." *Expert Systems with Applications*, Vol. 57, pp. 117–126.

Trivers, R. (1971) "The Evolution of Reciprocal Altruism." *Quarterly Review of Biology*, Vol. 46, No. 1, pp. 35–57.

Tropp, J. (2013) "Toyota Agrees to Settlement in Fatal Acceleration Crash." *New York Times*, October 26, 2013. Available at: https://www.nytimes.com/2013/10/26/business/toyota-agrees-to-settlement-in-fatal-acceleration-crash.html.

Tsatsakis, A., M. Nawaz, V. Tutelyan, K. Golokhvast, O.-I. Kalantzi, D. Chung, S. Kang, M. Coleman, N. Tyshko, S. Yang, and G. Chung (2017) "Impact on Environment, Ecosystem, Diversity and Health from Culturing and Using GMOs as Feed and Food." *Food and Chemical Toxicology*, Vol. 107, No. A, pp. 108–121.

Tumasjan, A., T. Sprenger, P. Sandner, and I. Welp (2010) "Predicting Elections with Twitter: What 140 Characters Reveal about Political Sentiment." In *Proceedings of the Fourth International AAAI Conference on Weblogs and Social Media*, Vol. 4, No. 1, pp. 178–185. Menlo Park, CA: AAAI Press.

Turban, D., and D. Greening (1997) "Corporate Social Performance and Organizational Attractiveness to Prospective Employees." *Academy of Management Journal*, Vol. 40, No. 3, pp. 658–672.

Turiel, E. (1983) *The Development of Social Knowledge: Morality and Convention.* Cambridge: Cambridge University Press.

Tversky, A., and D. Kahneman (1973) "Availability: A Heuristic for Judging Frequency and Probability." *Cognitive Psychology*, Vol. 5, No. 2, pp. 207–232.

Tversky, A., and D. Kahneman (1974) "Judgment under Uncertainty: Heuristics and Biases." *Science*, Vol. 185, No. 4157, pp. 1124–1131.

Tversky, A., and D. Kahneman (1982) "Judgments of and by Representativeness." In *Judgment under Uncertainty: Heuristics and Biases*, edited by D. Kahneman, P. Slovic, and A. Tversky, pp. 84–100. New York: Cambridge University Press.

Tybout, A. M., B. J. Calder, and B. Sternthal. (1981) "Using Information Processing Theory to Design Marketing Strategies." *Journal of Marketing Research*, Vol. 18, No. 1, pp. 73–79.

Tzieropoulos, H. (2013) "The Trust Game in Neuroscience: A Short Review." *Social Neuroscience*, Vol. 8, No. 5, pp. 407–416.

Uhlmann, E. L., K. Leavitt, J. I. Menges, J. Koopman, M. Howe, and R. E. Johnson (2012) "Getting Explicit About the Implicit: A Taxonomy of Implicit Measures and Guide for Their Use in Organizational Research." *Organizational Research Methods*, Vol. 15, No. 4, pp. 553–601.

Uhlmann, E. L., G. Newman, V. L. Brescoll, L. Zhu, A. Galinsky, and D. Diermeier (2010) "Poisoning the Well: The Contagious Effects of Corporate Crises on Product Evaluations and Consumption." Working paper. Evanston, IL: Ford Center for Global Citizenship, Kellogg School of Management.

Uhlmann, E., D. Pizarro, and D. Diermeier (2015) "A Person-Centered Approach to Moral Judgment." *Perspectives on Psychological Science*, Vol. 10, No. 1, pp. 72–81.

Uhlmann, E., D. Tannenbaum, M. Srinivasan, and D. Diermeier (2009). "No Good Deed Goes Unpunished? Negative Consequences of Positive Acts." Working paper. Evanston, IL: Ford Center for Global Citizenship, Kellogg School of Management.

Uhlmann, E. L., and L. Zhu (2014) "Acts, Persons, and Intuitions: Person-Centered Cues and Gut Reactions to Harmless Transgressions." *Social Psychological and Personality Science*, Vol. 5, No. 3, pp. 279–285.

Uhlmann, E., L. Zhu, and D. Diermeier (2014) "When Actions Speak Volumes: The Role of Inferences about Moral Character in Outrage over Racial Bigotry." *European Journal of Social Psychology*, Vol. 44, No. 1, pp. 23–29.

Uhlmann, E., L. Zhu, and D. Tannenbaum (2013) "When It Takes a Bad Person to Do the Right Thing." *Cognition*, Vol. 126, No. 2, pp. 326–334.

Ui, T. (2001) "Robust Equilibria of Potential Games." *Econometrica*, Vol. 69, No. 5, pp. 1373–1380.

Uleman, J., A. Saribay, and C. Gonzalez (2008) "Spontaneous Inferences, Implicit Impressions, and Implicit Theories." *Annual Review of Psychology*, Vol. 59, pp. 329–360.

Ulusoy, E., and P. Barretta (2016) "How Green Are You, Really? Consumers' Skepticism toward Brands with Green Claims." *Journal of Global Responsibility*, Vol. 7, No. 1, pp. 72–83.

US Department of Health and Human Services (2016) "Deeming Tobacco Products to be Subject to the Food, Drug, and Cosmetic Act, as Amended by the Family Smoking Prevention and Tobacco Control Act; Regulations Restricting the Sale and Distribution of Tobacco Products and Required Warning Statements for Tobacco Product Packages and Advertisements." Available at: https://www.fda.gov/media/97875/download.

US Department of Health and Human Services, Office of the Surgeon General (1994) "Preventing Tobacco Use among Young People." *Morbidity and Mortality Weekly Report*, Vol. 43, No. RR-4. Available at: https://www.cdc.gov/mmwr /PDF/rr/rr4304.pdf.

US Department of Health and Human Services, Office of the Surgeon General (2006) "The Health Consequences of Involuntary Exposure to Tobacco Smoke: A Report of the Surgeon General." Available at: https://www.ncbi.nlm.nih.gov /books/NBK44324/pdf/Bookshelf_NBK44324.pdf.

US Department of Health and Human Services, Office of the Surgeon General (2010) "The Surgeon General's Vision for a Healthy and Fit Nation." Available at: https://www.ncbi.nlm.nih.gov/books/NBK44660/.

US Securities and Exchange Commission (2000) "Employment Agreement between Robert L. Nardelli and the Home Depot, Inc." Available at: https://cor porate.findlaw.com/contracts/compensation/employment-agreement-the-home -depot-inc-and-robert-l-nardelli.html.

Valdes-Dapena, P. (2013) "What We Learned from Our Tesla Model S Drive." *CNNMoney*, February 16, 2013. Available at: http://money.cnn.com/2013/02/15 /autos/tesla-model-s-lessons/index.html.

Van Bavel, J., and T. West (2017) "Seven Steps to Reduce Bias in Hiring." *Wall Street Journal*, February 20, 2017. Available at: https://www.wsj.com/articles /seven-steps-to-reduce-bias-in-hiring-1487646840.

Vandenbergh, M. (2013) "Private Environmental Governance." *Cornell Law Review*, Vol. 99, No. 1, pp. 129–200.

van Heerde, H. J., K. Helsen, and M. G. Dekimpe (2007) "The Impact of a Product-Harm Crisis on Marketing Effectiveness." *Marketing Science,* Vol. 26, No. 2, pp. 230–245.

van Leeuwen, F., and J. Park (2011) "Moral Virtues and Political Orientation: Assessing Priorities under Constraint." University of Bristol: Working paper.

Vasi, I., and B. King (2012) "Social Movements, Risk Perceptions, and Economic Outcomes: The Effect of Primary and Secondary Stakeholder Activism on Firms' Perceived Environmental Risk and Financial Performance." *American Sociological Review*, Vol. 77, No. 4, pp. 573–596.

Veale, T., E. Shutova, and B. Klebanov (2016) "Metaphor: A Computational Perspective." *Synthesis Lectures on Human Language Technologies*, Vol. 9, No. 1, pp. 1–160.

Verhulst, B., and M. Lodge (2013) "Reaction Time Measures in Implicit Attitudes Research." In *Political Science Research Methods in Action*, eds. Bruter et al., pp. 64–92.

Verplaetse, J., S. Vanneste, and J. Braeckman (2007) "You Can Judge a Book by Its Cover: The Sequel. A Kernel of Truth in Predictive Cheating Detection." *Evolution and Human Behavior*, Vol. 28, No. 4, pp. 260–271.

Vidal, J. (1997) *McLibel: Burger Culture on Trial*. London: Macmillan.

Vlachos, P., A. Tsamakos, A. Vrechopoulos, and P. Avramidid (2009) "Corporate Social Responsibility: Attributions, Loyalty, and the Mediating Role of Trust." *Journal of the Academy of Marketing Science*, Vol 37, No. 2, pp. 170–180.

Vlasic, B. (2012) "Toyota Agrees to Settle Lawsuit Tied to Accelerations." *New York Times*, December 27, 2012. Available at: https://www.nytimes.com/2012/12/27/business/toyota-settles-lawsuit-over-accelerator-recalls-impact.html.

Vo, D.-T., and Y. Zhang (2015) "Target-Dependent Twitter Sentiment Classification with Rich Automatic Features." In *IJCAI'15: Proceedings of the 24th International Conference on Artificial Intelligence*, pp. 1347–1353.

Vogel, D. (2006) *The Market for Virtue: The Potential and Limits of Corporate Social Responsibility*. Washington, DC: Brookings Institution Press.

Vogel, D. (2010) "The Private Regulation of Global Corporate Conduct: Achievements and Limitations." *Business & Society*, Vol. 49, No. 1, pp. 68–87.

Vohs, K., N. Mead, and M. Goode (2006) "The Psychological Consequences of Money." *Science*, Vol. 314, No. 5802, pp. 1154–1156.

Wakefield, M., L. Hayes, S. Durkin, and R. Borland (2013) "Introduction Effects of the Australian Plain Packaging Policy on Adult Smokers: A Cross-Sectional Study." *BMJ Open*, Vol. 3, No. 7, e003175.

Waldfogel, J. (1993) "The Deadweight Loss of Christmas." *American Economic Review*, Vol. 83, No. 5, pp. 1328–1336.

Walker, K. (2010) "A Systematic Review of the Corporate Reputation Literature: Definition, Measurement, and Theory." *Corporate Reputation Review*, Vol. 12, No. 4, pp. 357–387.

Walker, L., and K. Hennig (2004) "Differing Conceptions of Moral Exemplarity: Just, Brave, and Caring." *Journal of Personality and Social Psychology*, Vol. 86, No. 4, pp. 629–647.

Walker, L., and R. Pitts (1998) "Naturalistic Conceptions of Moral Maturity." *Developmental Psychology*, Vol. 34, No. 3, pp. 403–419.

Wallach, H., L. Dicker, S. Jensen, and K. Heller (2010) "An Alternative Prior Process for Nonparametric Bayesian Clustering." In *Proceedings of the 13th International Conference on Artificial Intelligence and Statistics*, pp. 892–899. Cambridge, MA: Proceedings of Machine Learning Research.

Wallenburg, C., D. Cahill, A. Michael Knemeyer, and T. Goldsby (2011) "Commitment and Trust as Drivers of Loyalty in Logistics Outsourcing Relationships: Cultural Differences Between the United States and Germany." *Journal of Business Logistics*, Vol. 32, No. 1, pp. 83–98.

Walton-Moss, B., J. Mangello, V. Frye, and J. Campbell (2005) "Risk Factors for Intimate Partner Violence and Associated Injury Among Urban Women." *Journal of Community Health*, Vol. 30, No. 5, pp. 377–389.

Wang, S., W. Ngamsiriudom, and C.-H. Hsieh (2015) "Trust Disposition, Trust Antecedents, Trust, and Behavioral Intention." *Service Industries Journal*, Vol. 35, No. 10, pp. 555–572.

Wang, W., and I. Benbasat (2005) "Trust in and Adoption of Online Recommendation Agents." *Journal of the Association for Information Systems*, Vol. 6, No. 3, pp. 72–101.

Warner, S. L. (1965) "Randomized Response: A Survey Technique for Eliminating Evasive Answer Bias." *Journal of the American Statistical Association*, Vol. 60, No. 309, pp. 63–69.

Washington Post, Kaiser Family Foundation, and Harvard University (1996) "Survey of Americans and Economists on the Economy." Available at: https://www.kff.org/wp-content/uploads/2019/05/1199-T.pdf.

Wason, P. C. (1966) "Reasoning." In *New Horizons in Psychology*, edited by B. M. Foss, pp. 135–151. Harmondsworth: Penguin.

Wasserman, S., and P. Pattison (1996) "Logit Models and Logistic Regressions for Social Networks: I. An Introduction to Markov Graphs and p*." *Psychometrika*, Vol. 61, No. 3, pp. 401–425.

Watts, D. (2004) "The 'New' Science of Networks." *Annual Review of Sociology*, Vol 30, pp. 243–270.

Watts, D., and S. Strogatz (1998) "Collective Dynamics of 'Small-World' Networks." *Nature*, Vol. 393, No. 6684, pp. 440–442.

Webster, S. (2018) "Anger and Declining Trust in Government in the American Electorate." *Political Behavior*, Vol. 40, No. 4, pp. 933–964.

Weichselbraun, A., S. Gindl, and A. Scharl (2013) "Extracting and Grounding Context-Aware Sentiment Lexicons." *IEEE Intelligent Systems*, Vol. 28, No. 2, pp. 39–46.

Weidlich, W., and G. Haag (1983) *Concepts and Models of a Quantitative Sociology*. Berlin: Springer Verlag.

Weiner, B. (1985) "An Attributional Theory of Achievement Motivation and Emotion." *Psychological Review*, Vol. 92, No. 4, pp. 548.

Weiner, B., J. Amirkhan, V. S. Folkes, and J. A. Verette (1987) "An Attributional Analysis of Excuse Giving: Studies of a Naive Theory of Emotion." *Journal of Personality and Social Psychology*, Vol. 52, No. 2, pp. 316–324.

Weiser, B. (1993) "Does TV News Go Too Far? A Look Behind the Scenes at NBC's Truck Crash Test." *Washington Post*, February 28, 1993. Available at: https://www.washingtonpost.com/archive/politics/1993/02/28/does-tv-news-go-too-far-a-look-behind-the-scenes-at-nbcs-truck-crash-test/c7e6e79b-ed2b-4cbb-9347-ada724bd34f4/.

Wennekers, A., L. Vanderberg, K. Zoon, and E. van Reijmersdal (2015) "Distinguishing Implicit from Explicit Brand Attitudes in Brand Placement Research." In *Advances in Advertising Research, Vol. 6, The Digital, the Classic, the Subtle, and the Alternative*, edited by P. Verlegh, H. Voorveld, and M. Eisend, pp. 253–267. Dordrecht: Springer.

White, J. (2009) "Misconceptions about High-Fructose Corn Syrup: Is It Uniquely Responsible for Obesity, Reactive Dicarbonyl Compounds, and Advanced Glycation Endproducts?" *Journal of Nutrition*, Vol 139, No. 6, pp. 1219–1227.

White, M. (1997) "Toy Rover Sales Soar into Orbit: Mars Landing Puts Gold Shine Back into Space Items." *Arizona Republic*, July 12, 1997, p. E1.

Wiebe, J., R. Bruce, and T. O'Hara (1999) "Development and Use of a Gold Standard Data Set for Subjectivity Classifications." In *ACL '99: Proceedings of the 37th Annual Meeting of the Association for Computational Linguistics*, pp. 246–253. Stroudsburg, PA: Association for Computational Linguistics.

Willis, J., and A. Todorov (2006) "First Impressions: Making Up Your Mind after a 100-ms Exposure to a Face." *Psychological Science*, Vol. 17, No. 7, pp. 592–298.

Wilson, E. O. (1975) *Sociobiology: The New Synthesis*. Cambridge, MA: Belknap Press of Harvard University Press.

Wilson, T., and S. Hodges (1992) "Attitudes as Temporary Constructions." In *The Construction of Social Judgments*, edited by L. Martin and A. Tesser, pp. 37–65, Hillsdale, NJ: Erlbaum.

Wilson, T., J. Wiebe, and P. Hoffmann (2009) "Recognizing Contextual Polarity: An Exploration of Features for Phrase-Level Sentiment Analysis." *Computational Linguistics*, Vol. 35, No. 3, pp. 399–433.

Wingfield, N. (2011) "Netflix Market Value Shrivels." *New York Times Bits Blog*, October 25, 2011. Available at: http://bits.blogs.nytimes.com/2011/10/25/netflix-market-value-shrivels/.

Wittenbrink, B., C. Judd, and B. Park (1997) "Evidence for Racial Prejudice at the Implicit Level and Its Relationship with Questionnaire Measures." *Journal of Personal and Social Psychology*, Vol. 72, No. 2, pp. 262–274.

Wojciszke, B., M. Dowhyluk, and M. Jaworski (1998) "Moral Competence-Related Traits: How Do They Differ?" *Polish Psychological Bulletin*, Vol. 29, No. 4, pp. 283–294.

Wolfers, J., and E. Zitzewitz (2004) "Prediction Markets." *Journal of Economic Perspectives*, Vol. 18, No. 2, pp. 107–126.

Wolman, L. (1914) *The Boycott in American Trade Unions*. Baltimore, MD: Johns Hopkins University Press.

Wolton, S. (2019) "Are Biased Media Bad for Democracy?" *American Journal of Political Science*, Vol. 63, No. 3, pp. 548–562.

Woolner, A., and F. Gillette (2013) "For Paula Deen, Management Mess Leads to Career Meltdown." *Bloomberg Businessweek*, July 3, 2013. Available at: https://www.bloomberg.com/news/articles/2013-07-03/for-paula-deen-management-mess-leads-to-career-meltdown.

Wright, S., A. Aron, T. McLaughlin-Volpe, and S. Ropp (1997) "The Extended Contact Effect: Knowledge of Cross-Group Friendships and Prejudice." *Journal of Personality and Social Psychology*, Vol. 73, No. 1, pp. 73–90.

Wu, A., A. Wood, and R. Stevenson (2019) "A Validation Study of Individual-Level Survey Methodologies for Sensitive Questions." Paper presented at PolMeth XXXVI: 2019 Conference of the Society for Political Methodology.

Wu, S., C. Tan, J. Kleinberg, and M. W. Macy (2011) "Does Bad News Go Away Faster?" Paper presented at the Fifth International AAAI Conference on Weblogs and Social Media.

Wundt, E. (1927) "Wilhelm Wundts Werke. Ein Verzeichnis seiner sämtlichen Schriften" [Wilhelm Wundt's works: An index of all his writings]. Munich: C. H. Beck.

Wyer Jr., R. S. (2004) "A Personalized Theory of Theory Construction." *Personality and Social Psychology Review*, Vol. 8, No. 2, pp. 201–209.

Wyer Jr., R. S., and T. K. Srull (1989) *Memory and Cognition in Its Social Context.* Hillsdale, NJ: Lawrence Erlbaum.

Xu, K., and W. Li (2013) "An Ethical Stakeholder Approach to Crisis Communication: A Case Study of Foxconn's 2010 Employee Suicide Crisis." *Journal of Business Ethics*, Vol. 117, No. 2, pp. 371–386.

Yanagizawa-Drott, D. (2014) "Propaganda and Conflict: Evidence from the Rwandan Genocide." *Quarterly Journal of Economics*, Vol. 129, No. 4, pp. 1947–1994.

Yang, L., F. Tjiptono, and W. Poon (2018) "Will You Fly with This Airline in the Future? An Empirical Study of Airline Avoidance after Accidents." *Journal of Travel and Tourism Marketing*, Vol. 35, No. 9, pp. 1145–1159.

Yang, Y., and X. Liu (1999) "A Re-examination of Text Categorization Methods." In SIGIR '99: *Proceedings of the 22nd Annual International ACM SIGIR Conference on Research and Development in Information Retrieval*, pp. 42–49. New York: ACM.

Ybarra, O. (2002) "Naive Causal Understanding of Valenced Behaviors and Its Implications for Social Information Processing." *Psychological Bulletin*, Vol. 128, No. 3, pp. 421–441.

Yelowitz, A., and M. Wilson (2015) "Characteristics of Bitcoin Users: An Analysis of Google Search Data." *Applied Economics Letters*, Vol. 22, No. 13, pp. 1030–1036.

Yoon, Y., Z. Gürhan-Canli, and N. Schwarz (2006). "The Effect of Corporate Social Responsibility (CSR) Activities on Companies with Bad Reputations." *Journal of Consumer Psychology*, Vol. 16, No. 4, pp. 377–390.

Young, H. (1998) *Individual Strategy and Social Structure: An Evolutionary Theory of Institutions*, Princeton, NJ: Princeton University Press.

Young, L., and S. Soroka (2012) "Affective News: The Automated Coding of Sentiment in Political Texts." *Political Communication*, Vol. 29, No. 2, pp. 205–231.

Yu, B., D. Diermeier, and S. Kaufman (2008) "The Wal-Mart Corpus: A Multi-Granularity Corporate Opinion Corpus for Opinion Retrieval, Classification and Aggregation." Working paper. Evanston, IL: Ford Center for Global Citizenship, Kellogg School of Management.

Yu, B., S. Kaufmann, and D. Diermeier (2008) "Classifying Party Affiliation from Political Speech." *Journal of Information Technology & Politics*, Vol. 5, No. 1, pp. 33–48.

Yu, H., and V. Hatzivassiloglou (2003) "Towards Answering Opinion Questions: Separating Facts from Opinions and Identifying the Polarity of Opinion Sentences." In *EMNLP '03: Proceedings of the 2003 Conference on Empirical Methods in Natural Language Processing*, pp. 129–136. Stroudsburg, PA: Association for Computational Linguistics.

Zajonc, R. (1965) "Social Facilitation." *Science*, Vol. 149, No. 3681, pp. 269–274.

Zajonc, R. (1968) "Attitudinal Effects of Mere Exposure." *Journal of Personality and Social Psychology*, Vol. 9, No. 2, pp. 1–27.

Zajonc, R. (1980) "Feeling and Thinking: Preferences Need No Inferences." *American Psychologist*, Vol. 35, No. 2, pp. 151–175.

Zajonc, R. (2000) "Feeling and Thinking: Closing the Debate over the Independence of Affect." In *Feeling and Thinking: The Role of Affect in Social Cognition. Studies in Emotion and Social Interaction*, edited by J. P. Forgas, pp. 31–58. New York: Cambridge University Press.

Zak, P., A. Stanton, and S. Ahmadi (2007) "Oxytocin Increases Generosity in Humans." *PLOS ONE*, Vol. 2, No. 11, e1128.

Zaller, J. (1992) *The Nature and Origins of Mass Opinion*. New York: Cambridge University Press.

Zaller, J. (2003) "A New Standard of News Quality: Burglar Alarms for the Monitorial Citizen." *Political Communication*, Vol. 20, No. 2, pp. 109–130.

Zaller, J., and S. Feldman (1992) "A Simple Theory of the Survey Response: Answering Questions versus Revealing Preferences." *American Journal of Political Science*, Vol. 36, No. 3, pp. 579–616.

Zhang, L., S. Wang, and B. Liu (2018) "Deep Learning for Sentiment Analysis: A Survey." *Wiley Interdisciplinary Reviews: Data Mining and Knowledge Discovery*, Vol. 8, No. 4, e1253.

Zhu, L., E. L. Uhlmann, and D. Diermeier (2014) "Moral Evaluations of Bigots and Misanthropes." Working paper. Available at: https://osf.io/a4uxn.

Index

Page numbers followed by "f" or "t" refer to figures or tables, respectively.